Western Civilizations

Their History & Their Culture

Joshua Cole

Carol Symes

Western
Civilizations

Their History & Their Culture

EIGHTEENTH EDITION

VOLUME B

W. W. NORTON & COMPANY ▪ NEW YORK ▪ LONDON

Copyright © 2014, 2011, 2008, 2005, 2002, 1998, 1993, 1988, 1984, 1980, 1973, 1968, 1963, 1958, 1954, 1949, 1947, 1941 by W. W. Norton & Company, Inc.

Editor: Jon Durbin
Associate editor: Justin Cahill
Editorial assistant: Penelope Lin
Project editor: Melissa Atkin
Managing editor, College: Marian Johnson
Copyeditor: Jude Grant
E-media editors: Steve Hoge, Tacy Quinn
Ancillary editor: Lorraine Klimowich
Assistant editor, E-media: Stefani Wallace
Photo editor: Evan Luberger
Photo research: Rona Tucillo
Marketing manager, History: Sarah England
Production manager, College: Sean Mintus
Design director: Rubina Yeh
Book designer: Judith Abbate / Abbate Design
Composition: Jouve
Cartographers: Mapping Specialists
Manufacturing: Transcontinental

Library of Congress has catalogued the one-volume edition as follows:

Cole, Joshua, 1961–
    Western civilizations : their history & their culture / Joshua Cole and Carol Symes. —Eighteenth edition.
        pages cm
    Includes bibliographical references and index.

ISBN 978-0-393-92213-4 (hardcover)
    1. Civilization, Western—Textbooks.   2. Europe—Civilization—Textbooks.   I. Symes, Carol.   II. Title.
    CB245.C56 2013
    909'.09821—dc23

                                                        2013029952

This edition:
ISBN: 978-0-393-92217-2 (pbk.)

W. W. Norton & Company, Inc., 500 Fifth Avenue, New York, N. Y. 10110
wwnorton.com

W. W. Norton & Company Ltd., Castle House, 75/76 Wells Street, London W1T 3QT

1 2 3 4 5 6 7 8 9 0

To our families:

Kate Tremel, Lucas and Ruby Cole
Tom, Erin, and Connor Wilson

with love and gratitude for their support.
And to all our students, who have also been
our teachers.

JOSHUA COLE (Ph.D., University of California, Berkeley) is Associate Professor of History at the University of Michigan, Ann Arbor. His publications include work on gender and the history of the population sciences, colonial violence, and the politics of memory in nineteenth- and twentieth-century France, Germany, and Algeria. His first book was *The Power of Large Numbers: Population, Politics, and Gender in Nineteenth-Century France* (Ithaca, NY: Cornell University Press, 2000).

CAROL SYMES (Ph.D., Harvard University) is Associate Professor of History and Director of Undergraduate Studies in the history department at the University of Illinois, Urbana-Champaign, where she has won the top teaching award in the College of Liberal Arts and Sciences. Her main areas of study include medieval Europe, the history of information media and communication technologies, and the history of theater. Her first book was *A Common Stage: Theater and Public Life in Medieval Arras* (Ithaca: Cornell University Press, 2007).

Brief Contents

Contents

Chapter 18 ▪ THE FRENCH REVOLUTION   581

Maps

Primary Sources

This new edition of *Western Civilizations* sharpens and expands the set of tools we have developed to empower students—our own and yours—to engage effectively with the themes, sources, and challenges of history. It presents a clear and vigorous narrative, supplemented by a compelling selection of primary sources and striking images. At the same time, as the authors of this book's previous edition, we have worked to develop a unified program of pedagogical elements that guide students toward a more thorough understanding of the past, and of the ways that historians reconstruct that past. This framework helps students to analyze and interpret historical evidence on their own, encouraging them to become active participants in the learning process.

Moreover, the wide chronological scope of this book offers an unusual opportunity to trace central human developments (population movements, intellectual currents, economic trends, the formation of political institutions, the power of religious belief, the role of the arts and of technologies) in a region of the world whose cultural diversity has been constantly invigorated and renewed by its interactions with peoples living in other places. Students today have a wide selection of introductory history courses to choose from, thanks to the welcome availability of introductory surveys in Latin American, African, and Asian history, alongside both traditional and innovative offerings in the history of the United States and Europe. Global history has also come into its own in recent years. But our increasing awareness that no region's history can be isolated from global processes and connections has merely heightened the need for a richly contextualized and broad-based history such as that represented in *Western Civilizations*.

As in previous editions, we have attempted to balance the coverage of political, social, economic, and cultural phenomena with extensive treatment of material culture, daily life, gender, sexuality, art, science, and popular culture. And following the path laid out by the book's previous authors, Judith Coffin and Robert Stacey, we have insisted that the history of European peoples must be understood through their interactions with peoples in other parts of the world. Our treatment of this history is accordingly both deep and dynamic, attentive to the latest developments in historical scholarship.

Given the importance of placing human history in a global context, those of us who study the histories of ancient, medieval, and modern Europe are actively changing the ways that we teach this history. For good reasons reflected in the title of this book, few historians today would uphold a monolithic vision of a single and enduring "Western civilization" whose inevitable march to domination can be traced chapter by chapter through time. This older paradigm, strongly associated with the curriculum of early twentieth-century American colleges and universities, no longer conforms to what we know about the human past. Neither the "West" nor "Europe" can be seen as distinct, unified entities in space or time; the meanings attributed to these geographical expressions have changed in significant ways. Moreover, historians now agree that a linear notion of any civilization persisting unchanged over the centuries was made coherent only by leaving out the intense conflicts, extraordinary ruptures, and dynamic changes that took place at the heart of the societies we call "Western." Smoothing out the rough edges of the past does students no favors; even an introductory text such as this one should present the past as it appears to the historians who study it—that is, as complex panorama of human effort, filled with possibility and achievement but also fraught with discord, uncertainty, accident, and tragedy.

We know that current and future users of our text will be enthusiastic to see the efforts made in this new edition to update and reorganize the Late Medieval and Early Modern periods in order to place them in a larger Atlantic World context. The major highlight of this reorganization is a brand new chapter, entitled "Europe in the Atlantic World, 1550–1650." It places the newly integrated space of the Atlantic at the center of the story, exploring the ways, that religious warfare, economic developments, population movements, and cultural trends shaped—and were shaped by—historical actors on this dynamic frontier. Another significant result of the reorganization of these two periods is to provide a clearer chronological framework for the narrative, so that the students can better see how major topics and events emerge from their historical contexts. This, of course, was part of a larger effort begun across the entire text in the previous edition. These revisions demonstrate our dual commitment to keep the book current and up-to-date, while striving to integrate strong pedagogical features that help students build their study and history skills.

New and Revised Pedagogical Features

In our ongoing effort to shape students' engagement with history, this book is designed to reinforce your course objectives by helping students to master core content while challenging them to think critically about the past. In order to achieve these aims, our previous edition augmented the traditional strengths of *Western Civilizations* by introducing several exciting new features. These have since been refined and revised in accordance with feedback from student readers and teachers of the book. The most important and revolutionary feature is the pedagogical structure that supports each chapter. As we know from long experience, many students in introductory survey courses find the sheer quantity of information overwhelming, and so we have provided guidance to help them navigate through the material and to read in meaningful ways.

At the outset of each chapter, the **Before You Read This Chapter** feature offers three preliminary windows onto the material to be covered: *Story Lines*, *Chronology*, and *Core Objectives*. *Story Lines* allow the student to become familiar with the primary narrative threads that tie the chapter's elements together, and the *Chronology* grounds these *Story Lines* in the period under study. *Core Objectives* provide a checklist to ensure that the student is aware of the primary teaching points in the chapter. The student is then reminded of these teaching points upon completing the chapter, in the **After You Read This Chapter** section, which prompts the student to revisit the chapter in three ways. The first, *Reviewing the Core Objectives*, asks the reader to reconsider core objectives by answering a pointed question about each one. The second, *People, Ideas, and Events in Context*, summarizes some of the particulars that students should retain from their reading, through questions that allow them to relate individual terms to the major objectives and story

lines. Finally, *Thinking about Connections*, new to this edition, allow for more open-ended reflection on the significance of the chapter's material, drawing students' attention to issues that connect it to previous chapters and giving them insight into what comes next. As a package, the pedagogical features at the beginning and end of each chapter work together to enhance the student's learning experience, by breaking down the process of reading and analysis into manageable tasks.

A second package of pedagogical features is designed to capture students' interest and to compel them to think about what is at stake in the construction and use of historical narratives. Each chapter opens with a vignette that showcases a particular person or event representative of the era as a whole. Within each chapter, an expanded program of illustrations and maps has been enhanced by the addition of **Guiding Questions** (following these illustrations' and maps' captions) that urge the reader to explore the historical contexts and significance of these features in a more analytical way. The historical value of images, artifacts, and material culture is further emphasized in another feature we introduced in our previous edition, **Interpreting Visual Evidence**. This section provides discussion leaders with a provocative departure point for conversations about the key issues raised by visual sources, which students often find more approachable than texts. Once this conversation has begun, students can further develop their skills by **Analyzing Primary Sources**, through close readings of primary texts accompanied by cogent interpretive questions. The dynamism and diversity of Western civilizations are also illuminated through a look at **Competing Viewpoints** in each chapter, in which specific debates are presented through paired primary-source texts. The bibliographical **Further Readings**, located at the end of the book, has also been edited and brought up-to-date.

In addition to these features, which have proven successful, we are delighted to introduce an entirely new segment with this eighteenth edition. The new **Past and Present** features in the main text prompt students to connect events unfolding in the past with the breaking news of our own time, by taking one episode from each chapter and comparing it with a phenomenon that resonates more immediately with our students. To bring this new feature to life for students, we have also created a new series of **Author Videos**, in which we describe and analyze these connections across time and place. There are a number of illuminating discussions, including, "Spectator Sports," which compares the Roman gladiatorial games with NFL Football; "The Reputation of Richard III," which shows how modern forensics like those we see used on numerous TV shows were recently used to identify the remains of Richard III;

"The Persistence of Monarchies in a Democratic Age," which explains the origins and evolution of our ongoing fascination with royals like Louis XIV and Princess Diana; and "The Internet and the Enlightenment Public Sphere," which compares the kinds of public networks that helped spread Enlightenment ideas to the way the Internet can be used today to spread political ideas in movements such as the Arab Spring and Occupy Wall Street. Through this new feature, not only do we want to encourage students to recognize the continuing relevance of seemingly distant historical moments, but also we want to encourage historically-minded habits that will be useful for a lifetime. If students learn to see the connections among their world and the past, they will be more apt to place unfolding developments and debates in a more informed and complex historical context.

A Tour of New Chapters and Revisions

Our previous edition of *Western Civilizations* featured significant changes to each of the book's first five chapters, and this process of revision has continued in the present edition. In Chapter 1, the challenge of locating and interpreting historical evidence drawn from nontextual sources (archaeological, environmental, anthropological, mythic) is a special focus. Chapter 2 further underscores the degree to which recent archeological discoveries and new historical techniques have revolutionized our understanding of ancient history, and have also corroborated ancient peoples' own understandings of their past. Chapter 3 offers expanded coverage of the diverse polities that emerged in ancient Greece, and of Athens' closely related political, documentary, artistic, and intellectual achievements. Chapter 4's exploration of the Hellenistic world includes an unusually wide-ranging discussion of the scientific revolution powered by this first cosmopolitan civilization. Chapter 5 emphasizes the ways that the unique values and institutions of the Roman Republic are transformed through imperial expansion under the Principate.

With Chapter 6, a more extensive series of revisions has resulted in some significant reshaping and reorganization, so that the book's narrative reflects recent scholarship. The story of Rome's transformative encounter with early Christianity has been rewritten to ensure clarity and also to emphasize the fundamental ways that Christianity itself changed through the Roman Empire and in contact with peoples from northwestern Europe. Chapter 7, which examines Rome's three distinctive successor civilizations, now offers more extensive coverage of the reign of Justinian

and emergence of Islam. Balanced attention to the interlocking histories of Byzantium, the Muslim caliphates, and western Europe has carried forward in subsequent chapters. Chapters 8 contains an entirely new section, "A Tour of Europe around the Year 1000," with coverage of the Viking diaspora, the formation of Scandinavian kingdoms and the empire of Cnute, early medieval Rus' and eastern Europe, and the relationship among Mediterranean microcosms. It also features greatly expanded coverage of economy, trade, and the events leading up to the First Crusade. Chapter 9, which now covers the period 1000–1250, features a new segment on the Crusader States and crusading movements within Europe.

Chapter 10's treatment of the medieval world between 1250 and 1350 is almost wholly new, reflecting cutting-edge scholarship on this era. It includes a fresh look at the consolidation of the Mongol Khanates, new images and maps, some new sources, and a new *Interpreting Visual Evidence* segment on seals and their users. Chapters 11 and 12 have been thoroughly reorganized and rewritten to ensure that the narrative of medieval Europeans' colonial ventures (from the western Mediterranean to the eastern Atlantic and Africa, and beyond) is integrated with the story of the Black Death's effects on the medieval world and the impetus for the intellectual and artistic innovations of the Renaissance. In previous editions of the book, these concurrent phenomena were treated as separate, as though they took place in three separate periods (the later Middle Ages, the Renaissance, and the Age of Exploration). This made the connections among them almost impossible to explain or appreciate. In this eighteenth edition, therefore, the voyages of Columbus are firmly rooted in their historical contexts while the religious, social, and cultural upheavals of the Reformation (Chapter 13) are more clearly placed against a backdrop of political and economic competition in Europe and the Americas.

This program of revisions sets the stage for the most significant new chapter in the book: Chapter 14, "Europe in the Atlantic World, 1550–1650." This chapter, the hinge between the book's first and second halves, resulted from a close collaboration between us. It is designed to function either as the satisfying culmination of a course that surveys the history of Western civilizations up to the middle of the seventeenth century (like that taught by Carol Symes) or to provide a foundation for a course on the history of the modern West (like that taught by Joshua Cole). The chapter illuminates the changing nature of Europe as it becomes fully integrated into the larger Atlantic world that dramatically impacts all of its internal political, social, cultural, and economic development. In addition to greatly enhanced treatment of the transatlantic slave trade and the Columbian

Exchange, it also features new sections on the different models of colonial settlement in the Caribbean and the Americas, as well as expanded coverage of the Thirty Years' War.

The new emphasis on the emergence of the Atlantic world carries over to Chapter 15, which covers the emergence of powerful absolutist regimes on the continent and the evolution of wealthy European trading empires in the Americas, Africa, and Asia. This material has now been reorganized to clarify developments over time, as the early successes of the Spanish empire are gradually eclipsed by the successes of the Dutch, the French, and the British empires. A new document on the Streltsy rebellion, meanwhile, allows students to better understand the contested nature of power under the Russian tsars during the absolutist period. We have retained the emphasis on intellectual and cultural history in Chapter 16, on the Scientific Revolution, and in Chapter 17, on the Enlightenment. In Chapter 16 we have enhanced our treatment of the relationship between Christian faith and the new sciences of observation with a new primary-source document by Pierre Gassendi. In Chapter 17, meanwhile, we have sought to set the Enlightenment more clearly in its social and political context, connecting it more explicitly to the theme of European expansion into the Americas and the Pacific. This helps, for example, in connecting a document like the American Declaration of Independence with the ideas of European Enlightenment thinkers.

Chapters 18–19 cover the political and economic revolutions of the late eighteenth and early nineteenth centuries. Chapter 18 covers the French Revolution and the Napoleonic empires in depth, while also drawing attention to the way that these central episodes were rooted in a larger pattern of revolutionary political change that engulfed the Atlantic world. Chapter 19 emphasizes both the economic growth and the technological innovations that were a part of the Industrial Revolution, while also exploring the social and cultural consequences of industrialization for men and women in Europe's new industrial societies. The *Interpreting Visual Evidence* feature in Chapter 19 allows students to explore the ways that industrialization created new perceptions of the global economy in Europe, changing the way people thought of their place in the world.

Chapters 20–21 explore the successive struggles between conservative reaction and radicals in Europe, as the dynamic forces of nationalism unleashed by the French Revolution redrew the map of Europe and threatened the dynastic regimes that had ruled for centuries. Here, however, we have sought to clarify the periodization of the post-Napoleonic decades by focusing Chapter 20 more clearly on the conservative reaction in Europe after 1815, and the ideologies of conservatism, liberalism, republicanism, socialism,

and nationalism. By setting the 1848 revolutions entirely in Chapter 21 (rather than split between the two chapters as in previous editions) instructors should be able to demonstrate more easily the connection between these political movements and the history of national unification in Germany and Italy in subsequent decades. While making these changes in the organization of the chapters, we have retained our treatment of the important cultural movements of the first half of the nineteenth century, especially Romanticism.

Chapter 22 takes on the history of nineteenth-century colonialism, exploring both its political and economic origins and its consequences for the peoples of Africa and Asia. The chapter gives new emphasis to the significance of colonial conquest for European culture, as colonial power became increasingly associated with national greatness, both in conservative monarchies and in more democratic regimes. Meanwhile, Chapter 23 brings the narrative back to the heart of Europe, covering the long-term consequences of industrialization and the consolidation of a conservative form of nationalism in many European nations even as the electorate was being expanded. The chapter emphasizes the varied nature of the new forms of political dissent, from the feminists who claimed the right to vote to the newly organized socialist movements that proved so enduring in many European countries.

Chapters 24 and 25 bring new vividness to the history of the First World War and the intense conflicts of the interwar period, while Chapter 26 uses the history of the Second World War as a hinge for understanding European and global developments in the second half of the twentieth century. The *Interpreting Visual Evidence* feature in Chapter 24 allows for a special focus on the role of propaganda among the belligerent nations in 1914–1918; and the chapter's section on the diplomatic crisis that preceded the First World War has been streamlined to allow students to more easily comprehend the essential issues at the heart of the conflict. In Chapter 25 the *Interpreting Visual Evidence* feature continues to explore the theme touched on in earlier chapters, political representations of "the people," this time in the context of fascist spectacles in Germany and Italy in the 1930s. These visual sources help students to understand the vulnerability of Europe's democratic regimes during these years as they faced the dual assault from fascists on the right and Bolsheviks on the left.

Chapters 27–29 bring the volumes to a close in a thorough exploration of the Cold War, decolonization, the collapse of the Soviet Union and the Eastern Bloc in 1989–1991, and the roots of the multifaceted global conflicts that beset the world in the first decade of the twenty-first century. Chapter 27 juxtaposes the Cold War with decolonization, showing how this combination sharply diminished the ability of European nations to control events in the international arena, even as they succeeded in rebuilding their economies at home. Chapter 28 explores the vibrancy of European culture in the crucial period of the 1960s to the early 1990s, bringing new attention to the significance of 1989 as a turning point in European history. Finally, extensive revisions to Chapter 29, add to the issues covered in our treatment of Europe's place in the contemporary globalized world. The chapter now includes a new section on efforts to deal with climate change, as well as expanded discussion of the impact of global terrorism, and recent developments in the Arab-Israeli conflict. The discussion on the financial crisis of 2008 and the presidency of Barack Obama has been brought up to date, and two new sections have been added to allow students to think about the Arab Spring of 2011 and the European debt crisis of recent years in connection with the broader history of European democracy, nation-building, and colonialism in the modern period.

Media Resources for Instructors and Students

LMS COURSEPACKS WITH STRONG ASSESSMENT AND LECTURE TOOLS

- **Dynamic Author Videos (55 total)** in which the authors discuss two of the main topics or themes in each chapter. New to this edition, illustrations, maps, and other types of media are integrated into the interviews to make them richer and more dynamic. These segments can serve as lecture launchers or as a preview tool for students before and after they read a chapter. (Available in PowerPoint and on Norton StudySpace.)
- **NEW *Past and Present* Author Videos (29 total)** that connect topics across time and place and show why history is relevant to understanding our world today (see further explanation above). Examples include "Spectator Sports," "Medieval Plots and Modern Movies," "Global Pandemics," and "The Atlantic Revolutions and Human Rights" (Available in PowerPoint and on Norton StudySpace.)
- **NEW Guided Reading Exercises** by Scott Corbett (Ventura College) are designed to help students learn how to effectively read a textbook. The reading exercises, which are keyed to each chapter's *People, Ideas, and Events in Context*

questions, instill a three-step Note-Summarize-Assess pedagogy. Exercises are based on actual passages from the textbook (three exercises per chapter). Feedback will provide model responses with direct page references. (Available only in the Norton Coursepack.)
- **NEW 36 Map Exercises** can be assigned for assessment. These activities ask students a series of questions about historical events that must be answered by clicking on the map to record the answer. (Available only in the Norton Coursepack.)
- **NEW Chrono-Quiz** improving on the ever-popular Chrono-Sequencer, the Chrono-Quiz is now available as an assessment activity that will report to the school's native LMS. (Available only in the Norton Coursepack.)
- **NEW *StoryMaps*** break complex maps into a sequence of four to five annotated screens that focus on the *story* behind the *geography*. There are ten StoryMaps that include such topics as The Silk Road, The Spread of the Black Death, and Nineteenth-Century Imperialism. (Available only on wwnorton .com/web/westernciv18/instructors.)

INSTRUCTOR'S MANUAL

Bob Brennan (Cape Fear Community College)
Bruce Delfini (Rockland Community College)
Christopher Laney (Berkshire Community College)
Alice Roberti (Santa Rosa Community College)

The Instructor's Manual for *Western Civilizations*, Eighteenth edition, is designed to help instructors prepare lectures and exams. The Instructor's Manual contains detailed chapter outlines, general discussion questions, document discussion questions, lecture objectives, interdisciplinary discussion topics, and recommended reading and film lists. **This edition has been revised to include sample answers to all of the student-facing comprehension questions in the text.**

TEST BANK

Geoffrey Clark (SUNY Potsdam)
Donna Trembinski (St. Francis Xavier University)

The Test Bank contains over 2,000 multiple-choice, true/false, and essay questions. This edition of the Test Bank has been completely revised for content and accuracy. All test questions are now aligned to Bloom's Taxonomy for greater ease and effectiveness of assessment.

FOR STUDENTS

wwnorton.com/web/westernciv18
Free and open to all students, Norton StudySpace includes

- **Author Videos (over 80 in all)** for every chapter, including the new *Past and Present* segments that connect topics. Examples include
  - "Medieval Plots and Modern Movies"
  - "Controlling Consumption" (the legalization of controlled substances, from sixteenth-century regulations to contemporary marijuana policy)
  - "The Internet and the Enlightenment Public Sphere"
- **Chapter Outlines and Quizzes.** Quiz feedback is aligned to student learning outcomes and core objectives, along with page references.
- **World History Tours,** powered by Google Earth™, now operate from within the browser, eliminating the need to download third-party applications or files.
- **iMaps** allow students to view layers of information on each map.
- **Map Worksheets** provide each map without labels for offline re-labeling and quizzing.
- **Flashcards** align key terms and events with brief descriptions and definitions.
- Over **400 primary-source documents and images**
- **Ebook links** tie the online text to all study and review materials.

A FEW WORDS OF THANKS

Our first edition as members of *Western Civilizations'* authorial team was a challenging and rewarding one. Our second edition has been equally rewarding in that we have been able to implement a number of useful and engaging changes in the content and structure of the book, which we hope will make it even more student- and classroom-friendly. We are very grateful for the expert assistance and support of the Norton team, especially that of our editor, Jon Durbin. Melissa Atkin, our fabulous project editor, has driven the book beautifully through the manuscript process. Justin Cahill has provided good critiques of the illustrations and the new *Past and Present* features in addition to all the other parts of the project he has handled so skillfully. Evan Luberger and Rona Tucillo did an excellent job finding many of the exact images we specified. Lorraine Klimowich did an expert job developing the print ancillaries. Sean Mintus has efficiently marched

us through the production process. Steve Hoge has done a great job developing the book's fantastic emedia, particularly the new *Past and Present* Author Videos, the new Guided Reading Exercises, and the new StoryMaps. Jude Grant and John Gould were terrific in skillfully guiding the manuscript through the copyediting and proofreading stages. Finally, we want to thank Sarah England for spearheading the marketing campaign for the new edition. We are also indebted to the numerous expert readers who commented on various chapters and who thereby strengthened the book as a whole. We are thankful to our families, for their patience and advice, and to our students, whose questions and comments over the years have been essential to the framing of this book. And we extend a special thanks to, and hope to hear from, all the teachers and students we might never meet—their engagement with this book will frame new understandings of our shared past and its bearing on our future.

REVIEWERS

17th Edition Consultants
Paul Freedman, Yale University
Sheryl Kroen, University of Florida
Michael Kulikowski, Pennsylvania State University
Harry Liebersohn, University of Illinois,
    Urbana-Champaign
Helmut Smith, Vanderbilt University

17th Edition Reviewers
Donna Allen, Glendale Community College
Ken Bartlett, University of Toronto
Volker Benkert, Arizona State University
Dean Bennett, Schenectady City Community College
Patrick Brennan, Gulf Coast Community College
Neil Brooks, Community College of Baltimore County,
    Essex
James Brophy, University of Delaware
Kevin Caldwell, Blue Ridge Community College
Keith Chu, Bergen Community College
Alex D'Erizans, Borough of Manhattan Community
    College, CUNY
Hilary Earl, Nipissing University
Kirk Ford, Mississippi College
Michael Gattis, Gulf Coast Community College
David M. Gallo, College of Mount Saint Vincent
Jamie Gruring, Arizona State University
Tim Hack, Salem Community College
Bernard Hagerty, University of Pittsburg
Paul T. Hietter, Mesa Community College

Paul Hughes, Sussex County Community College
Kyle Irvin, Jefferson State Community College
Llana Krug, York College of Pennsylvania
Guy Lalande, St. Francis Xavier University
Chris Laney, Berkshire Community College
Charles Levine, Mesa Community College
Michael McKeown, Daytona State University
Dan Puckett, Troy State University
Dan Robinson, Troy State University
Craig Saucier, Southeastern Louisiana University
Aletia Seaborn, Southern Union State College
Victoria Thompson, Arizona State University
Donna Trembinski, St. Francis Xavier University
Pamela West, Jefferson State Community College
Julianna Wilson, Pima Community College

18th Edition Reviewers
Matthew Barlow, John Abbott College
Ken Bartlett, University of Toronto
Bob Brennan, Cape Fear Community College
Jim Brophy, University of Delaware
Keith Chu, Bergen Community College

Geoffrey Clark, SUNY Potsdam
Bill Donovan, Loyola University Maryland
Jeff Ewen, Sussex County Community College
Peter Goddard, University of Guelph
Paul Hughes, Sussex County Community College
Michael Kulikowski, Penn State University
Chris Laney, Berkshire Community College
James Martin, Campbell University
Derrick McKisick, Fairfield University
Dan Puckett, Troy University
Major Ben Richards, US Military Academy
Bo Riley, Columbus State Community College
Kimlisa Salazar, Pima Community College
Sara Scalenghe, Loyola University Maryland
Suzanne Smith, Cape Fear Community College
Bobbi Sutherland, Dordt College
David Tengwall, Anne Arundel Community College
Pam West, Jefferson State Community College
Julianna Wilson, Pima Community College
Margarita Youngo, Pima Community College

Western Civilizations

Their History & Their Culture

STORY LINES

- The Mongol Empire widened channels of communication, commerce, and cultural exchange between Europe and the Far East. At the same time, Europeans were extending their reach into the Atlantic Ocean.

- Western civilizations' integration with this wider medieval world led to new ways of mapping, measuring, and describing that world.

- Despite these broadening horizons, most Europeans' lives were bounded by their communities and focused on the parish church.

- Meanwhile, the growing strength of the kings of France and England drew them into terminal disputes that led to the Hundred Years' War.

- As global climate change affected the ecosystems of Europe and caused years of famine, the integrated networks of the medieval world facilitated the rapid transmission of the Black Death.

CHRONOLOGY

1206–1260	Rapid expansion of the Mongol Empire under Genghis Khan and his heirs
1240	Kievan Rus' is taken by the Mongols; Khanate of the Golden Horde established
1260–1294	Reign of Kublai Khan, Great Khan and emperor of China
1271–1295	Travels of Marco Polo
1309	"Babylonian Captivity" of the papacy in Avignon begins
1315–1322	The Great Famine in Europe
1320	The Declaration of Arbroath proclaims Scotland's independence from England
1326–1354	The travels of Ibn Battuta
1337	Beginning of the Hundred Years' War
1347–1353	Spread of the Black Death
1352	Mandeville's *Book of Marvels* is in circulation

Before You Read This Chapter

The Medieval World, 1250–1350

W hen Christopher Columbus set out to find a new trade route to the East, he carried with him two influential travel narratives written centuries before his voyage. One was *The Book of Marvels*, composed around 1350 and attributed to John de Mandeville, an English adventurer (writing in French) who claimed to have reached the far horizons of the globe. The other was Marco Polo's *Description of the World*, an account of that Venetian merchant's journey through the vast Eurasian realm of the Mongol Empire to the court of the Great Khan in China. He had dictated it to an author of popular romances around 1298, when both men (Marco Polo and his ghostwriter) were in prison—in Columbus's own city of Genoa, coincidentally. Both of these books were the product of an extraordinary era of unprecedented interactions among the peoples of Europe, Asia, and the interconnected Mediterranean world. And both became extraordinarily influential, inspiring generations of mercantile adventurers, ambitious pilgrims, and armchair travelers. Eventually, they would fuel the imaginations of those future mariners who launched a further age of discovery (see Chapter 12).

In many ways, these narratives were as fantastical as they were factual. That makes them problematic sources for historians to use, but it also makes them representative of an era that seemed wide open to every sort of influence. This was a time when ease of communication and commercial exchange made Western civilizations part of an interlocking network that potentially spanned the globe. Although this network would prove fragile in the face of a large-scale demographic crisis, the Black Death, it created a lasting impression of infinite possibilities. Indeed, it was only *because* of this network's connective channels that the Black Death was able to wreak such devastation in the years around 1350. Looking back, we can see the century leading up to this near-global crisis as the beginning of a new global age.

Europeans' integration with this widening world not only put them into contact with unfamiliar cultures and commodities, it opened up new ways of looking at the world they already knew. New artistic and intellectual responses are discernible in this era, as are a host of new inventions and technologies. At the same time, involvement in this wider world placed new pressures on long-term developments within Europe: notably the growing tensions among large territorial monarchies, and between these secular powers and the authority of the papacy. By the early fourteenth century, the papal court would literally be held hostage by the king of France. A few decades later, the king of England would openly declare his own claim to the French throne. The ensuing struggles for sovereignty would have a profound impact on the balance of power in Europe, and further complicate Europeans' relationships with one another and with their far-flung neighbors.

THE MONGOL EMPIRE AND THE REORIENTATION OF THE WEST

In our long-term survey of Western civilizations, we have frequently noted the existence of strong links between the Mediterranean world and the Far East. Trade along the network of trails known as the Silk Road can be traced far back into antiquity, and we have seen that such overland networks were extended by Europe's waterways and by the sea. But it was not until the late thirteenth century that Europeans were able to establish direct connections with India, China, and the so-called Spice Islands of the Indonesian archipelago. For Europeans, these connections would prove profoundly important, as much for their impact on the European imagination as for their economic significance. For the peoples of Asia, however, the more frequent appearance of Europeans was less consequential than the events that made these journeys possible: the rise of a new empire that encompassed the entire continent.

The Expansion of the Mongol Empire

The Mongols were one of many nomadic peoples inhabiting the vast steppes of Central Asia. Although closely connected with the Turkish populations with whom they frequently intermarried, the Mongols spoke their own distinctive language and had their own homeland, located to the north of the Gobi Desert in what is now known as Mongolia. Essentially, the Mongols were herdsmen whose daily lives and wealth depended on the sheep that provided shelter (sheepskin tents), woolen clothing, milk, and meat. But the Mongols were also highly accomplished horsemen and raiders. Indeed, it was to curtail their raiding ventures that the Chinese had fortified their Great Wall, many centuries before. Primarily, though, China defended itself from the Mongols by attempting to ensure that they remained internally divided, with their energies turned against each other.

In the late twelfth century, however, a Mongol chief named Temujin (c. 1162–1227) began to unite the various tribes under his rule. He did so by incorporating the warriors of each defeated tribe into his own army, gradually building up a large and terrifyingly effective military force. In 1206, his supremacy over all these tribes was reflected in his new title: Genghis Khan, from the Mongol words meaning "universal ruler." This new name also revealed wider ambitions, and in 1209 Genghis Khan began to direct his enormous army against the Mongols' neighbors. Taking advantage of the fact that China was then divided into three warring states, he launched an attack on the Chin Empire of the north, managing to penetrate deep into its interior by 1211. These initial attacks were probably looting expeditions rather than deliberate attempts at conquest, but the Mongols' aims were soon sharpened under Genghis Khan's successors. Shortly after his death in 1227, a full-scale invasion of both northern and western China was under way. In 1234, these regions also fell to the Mongols. By 1279, one of Genghis Khan's numerous grandsons, Kublai Khan, would complete the conquest by adding southern China to this empire.

For the first time in centuries, China was reunited, and under Mongol rule. It was also connected to western and central Asia in ways unprecedented in its long history, since Genghis Khan had brought crucial commercial cities and Silk Road trading posts (Tashkent, Samarkand, and Bukhara) into his empire. One of his sons, Ögedei (*EHRG-*

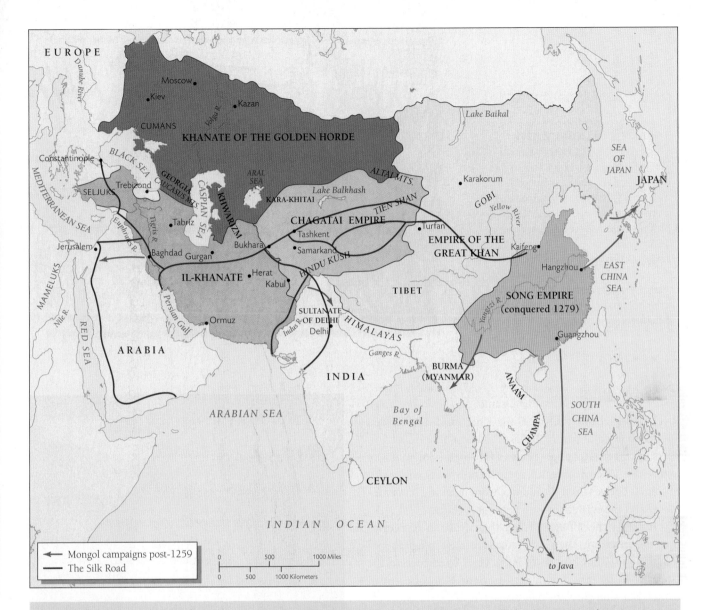

THE STATES OF THE MONGOL EMPIRE. Like Alexander's, Genghis Khan's empire was swiftly assembled and encompassed vast portions of Europe and Asia. ▪ *How many different Mongol khanates were there after 1260, when Kublai Khan came to power, and were these domains mapped onto older divisions within Western civilizations?* ▪ *How might the Mongol occupation of the Muslim world have aided the expansion of European trade?* ▪ *At the same time, why would it have complicated the efforts of crusader armies in the Holy Land?*

uh-day), building on these achievements, laid plans for an even more far-reaching expansion of Mongol influence. Between 1237 and 1240, the Mongols under his command conquered the Russian capital at Kiev and then launched a two-pronged assault directed at the rich lands of the eastern European frontier. The smaller of the two Mongol armies swept through Poland toward Germany; the larger army went southwest toward Hungary. In April of 1241, the smaller Mongol force met a hastily assembled army of Germans and Poles at the battle of Liegnitz, where the two sides fought to a bloody standstill. Two days later, the larger Mongol army annihilated the Hungarian army at the river

Sajo. It could have moved even deeper into Europe after this important victory, but it withdrew when Ögedei Khan died in December of that same year.

Muscovy and the Mongol Khanate

As we have seen in previous chapters, the Russian capital at Kiev had fostered crucial diplomatic and trading relations with both western Europe and Byzantium, and with the Islamic Caliphate at Baghdad. That dynamic changed with the arrival of the Mongols, who shifted the locus of

THE BATTLE OF LIEGNITZ, 1241. This image from a fourteenth-century chronicle shows heavily armored knights from Poland and Germany (at right) confronting the swift-moving mounted archers of the Mongol cavalry. Mongol warriors often had the advantage over Europeans because their smaller, faster horses carried lighter loads and because the warriors themselves could shoot down their opponents at long range. ▪ *Which army appears to be gaining the upper hand here?*

power from Kiev to their own camp on the lower Volga River. This became known as the Khanate of the Golden Horde, an integral part of the larger Mongol Empire for 150 years. Its magnificent name evokes the impression made by tents that shone with wealth, some literally hung with cloth of gold. It derives from the Mongol word meaning "encampment" and the related Turkish word *ordu* ("army").

Initially, the Mongols ruled their Russian territories directly, installing their own administrative officials and requiring Russian princes to show their obedience to the Great Khan by traveling in person to the Mongol court in China. But after Kublai Khan's death in 1294, the Mongols began to tolerate the existence of several semi-independent principalities from which they demanded regular tribute. Kiev never recovered its dominant position, but one of these newer principalities would eventually form the core of a Russian state called Muscovy, centered on the duchy of Moscow. As the tribute-collecting center for the Mongol Khanate, Moscow received some protection against attack. Its dukes were even encouraged to absorb neighboring territories in this region, in order to increase Moscow's security. But this also meant that the Muscovite dukes could extend their powers even further without attracting too much attention from their Mongol overlords, whose power base was far away.

Compared to Kiev, Moscow's location was less advantageous for forging commercial contacts with the Baltic and Black Sea regions. Its direct ties with western Europe were also less developed, but this had little to do with geography. The Moscovites were staunchly loyal to the Orthodox

A MONGOL ROBE IN CLOTH OF GOLD. The majestic term *Khanate of the Golden Horde* captures both the power and the splendor of the Mongol warriors who conquered Rus' and many other lands. The robe depicted here dates from the late thirteenth or early fourteenth century and was made from cloth of gold: silk woven with gold (and sometimes silver) thread, a precious but surprisingly durable material that was also used for banners and even tents. A robe similar to this one was sold at auction in 2011, for nearly a quarter of a million dollars.

Church of Byzantium and had watched relations between the Latin West and the Greek East deteriorate drastically during the Crusades. They became openly hostile to western Europeans after Constantinople was captured and sacked by crusaders in 1204 (see Chapter 9), an event that led Moscovites to see themselves as the last remaining protectors of the Orthodox Roman Church. Eventually, as we shall see in Chapter 12, they would claim to be the rightful heirs of Roman imperial power.

The Making of the Mongol Ilkhanate

As Ögedei Khan moved into the lands of Rus' and eastern Europe, Mongol armies were also sent to subdue the vast territory that had been encompassed by the former Persian Empire, then by the empires of Alexander and Rome. Indeed, the strongest state in this region was known as the sultanate of Rûm, the Arabic word for "Rome." This was a Sunni Muslim sultanate that had been founded by the Seljuq Turks in 1077, just prior to the launching of the First Crusade, and which consisted of Anatolian provinces formerly belonging to the eastern Roman Empire. It had

successfully withstood waves of crusading aggression from Latin Christendom while capitalizing on the further misfortunes of Byzantium, taking over several key ports on the Mediterranean and the Black Sea while cultivating a flourishing overland trade as well. But in 1243, the Seljuqs of Rûm were forced to surrender to the Mongols, who had already succeeded in occupying what is now Iraq, Iran, portions of Pakistan and Afghanistan, and the Christian kingdoms of Georgia and Armenia.

Thereafter, the Mongols easily found their way into regions weakened by centuries of Muslim infighting and Christian crusading movements. Byzantium, as we noted in Chapter 9, had been fatally weakened by the Fourth Crusade: Constantinople was now controlled by the Venetians, and Byzantine successor states centered on Nicaea (in Anatolia) and Epirus (in northern Greece) were hanging on by their fingertips. The capitulation of Rûm left

THE MONGOL RULER OF MUSLIM PERSIA, HIS CHRISTIAN QUEEN, AND HIS JEWISH HISTORIAN. The *Compendium of Chronicles* by the Jewish-born Muslim polymath Rashid al-Din (1247–1318) exemplifies the pluralistic culture encouraged by Mongol rule: written in Persian (and often translated into Arabic), it celebrates the achievements of Hulagu Khan (1217–1265), a grandson of Genghis and brother of Kublai, who consolidated Persia and its neighboring regions into the Ilkhanate. But it also embeds those achievements within the long history of Islam. This image depicts Hulagu with his wife, Dokuz Khatun, who was a Turkic princess and a Christian. ▪ *Why would Rashid al-Din have wanted to place the new Mongol dynasty in this historical context?*

remaining Byzantine possessions in Anatolia without a buffer, and most of these were absorbed by the Mongols. In 1261, the emperor Michael VIII Peleologus (r. 1259–82) managed to regain control of Constantinople and its immediate hinterland, but the depleted empire he ruled was ringed about by hostile neighbors. The crusader principality of Antioch, which had been founded in 1098, finally succumbed to the Mongols in 1268. The Mongols themselves were only halted in their drive toward Palestine by the Mamluk Sultanate of Egypt, established in 1250 and ruled by a powerful military caste of non-Arab Muslims.

All of these disparate territories came to be called the Ilkhanate, the "subordinate khanate," meaning that its Mongol rulers paid deference to the Great Khan. The first Ilkhan was Hulagu, brother of China's Kublai Khan. His descendants would rule this realm for another eighty years, eventually converting to Islam but remaining hostile toward the Mamluk Muslims, who remained their chief rivals.

The Pax Mongolica *and Its Price*

Although the Mongols' expansion of power into Europe had been checked in 1241, their combined conquests made them masters of territories that stretched from the Black Sea to the Pacific Ocean: one-fifth of the earth's surface, the largest land empire in history. Within this domain, no single Mongol ruler's power was absolute. Kublai Khan (1260–1294), who took the additional title *khagan*, or "Great Khan," never claimed to rule all Mongol khanates directly. In his own domain of China and Mongolia, his power was highly centralized and built on the intricate (and ancient) imperial bureaucracy of China; but elsewhere, Mongol governance was directed at securing a steady payment of tribute from subject peoples, which meant that local rulers could retain much of their power.

This distribution of authority made Mongol rule flexible and adaptable to local conditions—in this, it resembled the Persian Empire (see Chapter 3) and could also be regarded as building on Hellenistic and Roman examples. But if their empire resembled those of antiquity in some respects, the Mongol khans differed from most contemporary Western rulers in being highly tolerant of all religious beliefs. This was an advantage in governing peoples who observed an array of Buddhist, Christian, and Muslim practices, not to mention Hindus, Jews, and the many itinerant groups and individuals whose languages and beliefs reflect a melding of many cultures.

This acceptance of cultural and religious difference, alongside the Mongols' encouragement of trade and love of

rich things, created ideal conditions for some merchants and artists. Hence, the term *Pax Mongolica* ("Mongol Peace") is often used to describe the century from 1250 to 1350, a period in many ways analogous to that fostered by the Roman Empire at its greatest extent (see Chapter 5). No such term should be taken at face value, however: this peace was bought at a great price. Indeed, the artists whose varied talents created the gorgeous textiles, utensils, and illuminated books prized by the Mongols were not all willing participants in a peaceful process. Many were captives or slaves subject to ruthless relocation. During more settled years, the Mongols would often transfer entire families and communities of craftsmen from one part of the empire to another, encouraging a fantastic blend of artistic techniques, materials, and motifs. The result was an intensive period of cultural exchange that might combine Chinese, Persian, Venetian, and Russian influences (among many others) in a single work of art. These objects encapsulate the many conflicting legacies of the Mongols' empire.

The Mongol Peace was also achieved at the expense of many flourishing Muslim cities that had preserved the heritage of even older civilizations and that were devastated or crippled during the bloody process of Mongol expansion. The city of Heràt, situated in one of Afghanistan's few fertile valleys and described by the Persian poet Rumi as "the pearl in the oyster," was entirely destroyed by Genghis Khan in 1221 and did not fully recover for centuries. Baghdad, the splendid capital of the Abbasid Caliphate and a haven for artists and intellectuals since the eighth century (Chapter 8), was savagely besieged and sacked by the Mongols in 1258. Amid many other atrocities, the capture of the city resulted in the destruction of the House of Wisdom, a library and research center where Muslim scientists, philosophers, and translators preserved classical knowledge (including the works of Plato and Aristotle) and advanced cutting-edge scholarship in such fields as mathematics, engineering, and medicine. Baghdad's destruction is held to mark the end of Islam's golden age, since the establishment of the Mongol Ilkhanate in Persia eradicated a continuous zone of Muslim influence that had blended cultures stretching from southern Spain and North Africa to India.

Bridging East and West

To facilitate the movement of people and goods within their empire, the Mongols began to control the caravan routes that led from the Mediterranean and the Black Sea through Central Asia and into China, policing bandits and making conditions safer for travelers. They also encouraged and streamlined trade by funneling many exchanges through the Persian city of Tabriz, on which both land and sea routes from China converged. These measures accelerated and intensified the contacts possible between the Far East and the West. Prior to Mongol control, such commercial networks had been inaccessible to most European merchants. The Silk Road was not so much a highway as a tangle of trails and trading posts, and there were few outsiders who understood its workings. Now travelers at both ends of the route found their way smoothed.

Among the first travelers from the West were Franciscan missionaries whose journeys were bankrolled by European rulers. In 1253, William of Rubruck was sent by King Louis IX of France as his ambassador to the Mongol court, with letters of introduction and instructions to make a full report of his findings. Merchants quickly followed. The most famous of these are three Venetians: the brothers Niccolò and Matteo Polo, and Niccolò's son, Marco (1254–1324). Marco Polo's account of his travels (which began when he was sev-

enteen) includes a report of his twenty-year sojourn in the service of Kublai Khan and the story of his journey home through the Spice Islands, India, and Persia. As we noted above, this book had an enormous effect on the European imagination; Christopher Columbus's copy still survives.

Even more impressive in scope than Marco's travels are those of the Muslim adventurer Ibn Battuta (1304–1368), who left his native Morocco in 1326 to go on the sacred pilgrimage to Mecca—but then kept going. By the time he returned home in 1354, he had been to China and sub-Saharan Africa as well as to the ends of both the Muslim and Mongolian worlds: a journey of over 75,000 miles.

Yet the window of opportunity that made such journeys possible was relatively narrow. By the middle of the fourteenth century, hostilities among and within various components of the Mongol Empire were making travel along the Silk Road perilous. The Mongols of the Ilkhanate, who dominated the ancient trade routes that ran through

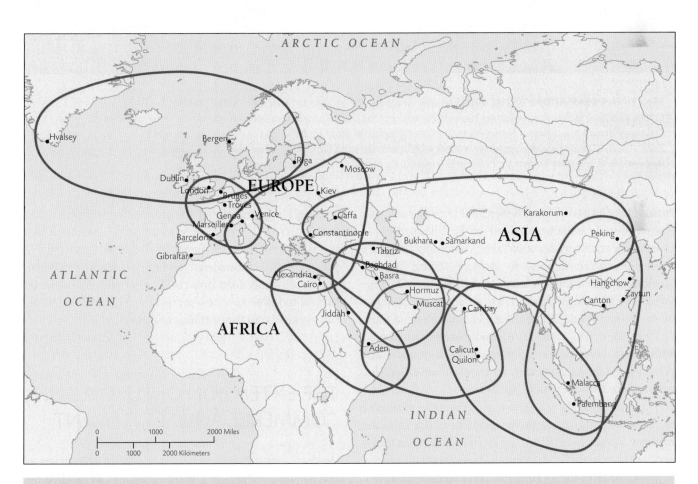

THE MEDIEVAL WORLD SYSTEM, c. 1300. At the turn of the fourteenth century, Western civilizations were more closely connected to one another and to the rest of the world than ever before: waterways and overland routes stretched from Greenland to the Pacific coast of Southeast Asia. ▪ *How has Europe's relationship with its neighbors changed as a result of its integration into this wider world?* ▪ *How might we need to see seemingly marginal territories (like Rus' or Hungary, Scotland or Norway) as central to one or more interlocking components of this system?*

VENETIAN AMBASSADORS TO THE GREAT KHAN. Around 1270, the Venetian merchants Niccolò and Matteo Polo returned to Europe after their first prolonged journey through the empire of the Great Khan, bearing with them an official letter to the Roman pope. This image, from a manuscript of Marco Polo's *Description of the World*, shows his father and uncle at the moment of their arrival in the Great Khan's court, to which they have seemingly brought a Christian cross and a Bible. ▪ *Based on what you've learned about the Mongols and the medieval world, is it plausible that the Polo brothers would have carried these items with them?*

Persia, came into conflict with merchants from Genoa who controlled trade at the western ends of the Silk Road, especially in the transport depot of Tabriz. Mounting pressures finally forced the Genoese to abandon Tabriz, thereby breaking one of the major links in the commercial chain forged by the Mongol Peace. Then, in 1346, the Mongols of the Golden Horde besieged the Genoese colony at Caffa on the Black Sea. This event simultaneously disrupted trade while serving as a conduit for the Black Death, which passed from the Mongol army to the Genoese defenders, who returned with it to Italy (see below).

Over the next few decades, the European economy would struggle to overcome the devastating effects of the massive depopulation caused by plague, which made recovery from these setbacks slower and harder. In the meantime, in 1368, the last Mongol rulers of China were overthrown. Most Westerners were now denied access to its borders, while the remaining Mongol warriors were restricted to cavalry service in the imperial armies of the new Ming dynasty. The conditions that had fostered an integrated trans-Eurasian cultural and commercial network were

no longer sustainable. Yet the view of the world that had been fostered by Mongol rule continued to exercise a lasting influence. European memories of the Far East would be preserved and embroidered, and the dream of reestablishing close connections between Europe and China would survive to influence a new round of commercial and imperial expansion in the centuries to come.

THE EXTENSION OF EUROPEAN COMMERCE AND SETTLEMENT

Western civilizations' increased access to the riches of the Far East during the period of the Pax Mongolica ran parallel to a number of ventures that were extending Europeans' presence in the Mediterranean and beyond it. These endeavors were both mercantile and colonial, and in many cases resulted in the control of strategic trade routes or islands by representatives of a single adventurous state.

The language of crusading, with which we have become familiar, now came to be applied to these economic and political initiatives, whose often violent methods could be justified on the grounds that they were supporting papally sanctioned Christian causes. To take one prominent example, the strategic goal of the Crusades that targeted North Africa in this era was to cut the economic lifelines that supported Muslim settlements in the Holy Land. Yet the only people who stood to gain from this were the merchants who dreamed of controlling the commercial routes that ran through Egypt, not only those that connected North Africa to the Silk Road but the conduits of the sub-Saharan gold trade.

The Quest for African Gold

The European trade in African gold was not new. It had been going on for centuries, facilitated by Muslim middlemen whose caravans brought a steady supply from the Niger River to the North African ports of Algiers and Tunis. In the early thirteenth century, rival bands of merchants from Catalonia and Genoa had established trading colonies in Tunis to expedite this process, exchanging woolen cloth from northern Europe for both North African grain and sub-Saharan gold.

But the medieval demand for gold accelerated during the late thirteenth and fourteenth centuries and could not be satisfied by these established trading relationships. The luxuries coveted by Europeans were now too costly to be bought solely with bulk goods, which were in any case a cumbersome medium of exchange. Although precious textiles (usually silk) were a form of wealth valued by the Mongols, the burgeoning economy of the medieval world demanded a reliable and abundant supply of more portable currency. Silver production, which had enabled the circulation of coinage in Europe, fell markedly during the 1340s as Europeans reached the limits of their technological capacity to extract silver ore from deep mines. This shortfall would lead to a serious cash-flow problem, since more European silver was moving east than could now be replenished from extant sources.

Gold therefore represented an obvious alternative currency for large transactions, and in the thirteenth century some European rulers began minting gold coins. But Europe itself had few natural gold reserves. To maintain and expand these currencies, new sources of gold were needed. The most obvious source was Africa, especially Mali and Ghana—which was called "the Land of Gold" by Muslim geographers.

Models of Mediterranean Colonization: Catalonia, Genoa, and Venice

The heightened European interest in the African gold trade, which engaged the seafaring merchants of Genoa and Catalonia in particular, coincided with these merchants' creation of entrepreneurial empires in the western Mediterranean. During the thirteenth century, Catalan adventurers conquered and colonized a series of western Mediterranean islands, including Majorca, Ibiza, Minorca, Sardinia, and Sicily. Except in Sicily, which already had a large and diverse population that included many Christians (see Chapter 8), the pattern of Catalan conquest was largely the same on all these islands: expulsion or extermination of the existing population, usually Muslim; the extension of economic concessions to attract new settlers; and a heavy reliance on slave labor to produce foodstuffs and raw materials for export.

These Catalan colonial efforts were mainly carried out by private individuals or companies operating under royal charters; they were not actively sponsored by the state. They therefore contrast strongly with the established colonial practices of the Venetian maritime empire, whose strategic ventures were focused mainly on the eastern Mediterranean, where the Venetians dominated the trade in spices and silks. Venetian colonies were administered directly by the city's rulers or their appointed colonial governors. These colonies included long-settled civilizations like Greece, Cyprus, and the cities of the Dalmatian coast, meaning that Venetian administration laid just another layer on top of many other economic, cultural, and political structures.

The Genoese, to take yet another case, also had extensive interests in the western Mediterranean, where they traded bulk goods such as cloth, hides, grain, timber, and sugar. They too established trading colonies, but these tended to consist of family networks that were closely integrated with the peoples among whom they lived, whether in North Africa, Spain, or the shores of the Black Sea.

From the Mediterranean to the Atlantic

For centuries, European maritime commerce had been divided between this Mediterranean world and a very different northeastern Atlantic world, which encompassed northern France, the Low Countries, the British Isles, and Scandinavia. Starting around 1270, however, Italian merchants began to sail through the Straits of Gibraltar and

Competing Viewpoints

Two Travel Accounts

> Two of the books that influenced Columbus and his contemporaries were travel narratives describing the exotic worlds that lay beyond Europe: worlds that may or may not have existed as they are described. The first excerpt below is taken from the account dictated by Marco Polo of Venice in 1298. The young Marco had traveled overland from Constantinople to the court of Kublai Khan in the early 1270s, together with his father and uncle. He became a gifted linguist, and remained at the Mongol court until the early 1290s, when he returned to Europe after a journey through Southeast Asia, Indonesia, and the Indian Ocean. The second excerpt is from the Book of Marvels attributed to John de Mandeville. This is an almost entirely fictional account of wonders that also became a source for European ideas about Southeast Asia. This particular passage concerns a legendary Christian figure called Prester ("Priest") John, who is alleged to have traveled to the East and become a great ruler.

Marco Polo's Description of Java

Departing from Ziamba, and steering between south and south-east, fifteen hundred miles, you reach an island of very great size, named Java. According to the reports of some well-informed navigators, it is the greatest in the world, and has a compass above three thousand miles. It is under the dominion of one king only, nor do the inhabitants pay tribute to any other power. They are worshipers of idols.

The country abounds with rich commodities. Pepper, nutmegs, spikenard, galangal, cubebs, cloves and all the other valuable spices and drugs, are the produce of the island; which occasion it to be visited by many ships laden with merchandise, that yields to the owners considerable profit.

The quantity of gold collected there exceeds all calculation and belief. From thence it is that . . . merchants . . . have imported, and to this day import, that metal to a great amount, and from thence also is obtained the greatest part of the spices that are distributed throughout the world. That the Great Khan [Kublai] has not brought the island under subjection to him, must be attributed to the length of the voyage and the dangers of the navigation.

Source: *The Travels of Marco Polo*, trans. William Marsden, rev. and ed. Manuel Komroff (New York: 1926), pp. 267–68.

John de Mandeville's Description of Prester John

This emperor Prester John has great lands and has many noble cities and good towns in his realm and many great, large islands. For all the country of India is separated into islands by the great floods that come from Paradise, that divide the land into many parts. And also in the sea he has many islands. . . .

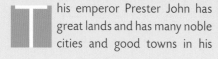

on up to the wool-producing regions of England and the Low Countries. This was a step toward the extension of Mediterranean patterns of commerce and colonization into the Atlantic Ocean. Another step was the discovery (or possibly the rediscovery) of the Atlantic island chains known as the Canaries and the Azores, which Genoese sailors reached in the fourteenth century.

Efforts to colonize the Canary Islands, and to convert and enslave their inhabitants, began almost immediately. Eventually, the Canaries would become the focus of a new wave of colonial settlement sponsored by the Portuguese, and the base for Portuguese voyages down the west coast of Africa. They would also be the jumping-off point from which Christopher Columbus would sail

This Prester John has under him many kings and many islands and many varied people of various conditions. And this land is full good and rich, but not so rich as is the land of the Great Khan. For the merchants do not come there so commonly to buy merchandise as they do in the land of the Great Khan, for it is too far to travel to....

[Mandeville then goes on to describe the difficulties of reaching Prester John's lands by sea.]

This emperor Prester John always takes as his wife the daughter of the Great Khan, and the Great Khan in the same way takes to wife the daughter of Prester John. For these two are the greatest lords under the heavens.

In the land of Prester John there are many diverse things, and many precious stones so great and so large that men make them into vessels such as platters, dishes, and cups. And there are many other marvels there that it would be too cumbrous and too long to put into the writing of books. But of the principal islands and of his estate and of his law I shall tell you some part.

This emperor Prester John is Christian and a great part of his country is Christian also, although they do not hold to all the articles of our faith as we do....

And he has under him 72 provinces, and in every province there is a king. And these kings have kings under them, and all are tributaries to Prester John.

And he has in his lordships many great marvels. For in his country is the sea that men call the Gravelly Sea, that is all gravel and sand without any drop of water. And it ebbs and flows in great waves as other seas do, and it is never still. . . . And a three-day journey from that sea there are great mountains out of which flows a great flood that comes out of Paradise. And it is full of precious stones without any drop of water....

He dwells usually in the city of Susa [in Persia]. And there is his principal palace, which is so rich and so noble that no one will believe the report unless he has seen it. And above the chief tower of the palace there are two round pommels of gold and in each of them are two great, large rubies that shine full brightly upon the night. And the principal gates of his palace are of a precious stone that men call sardonyxes [a type of onyx], and the frames and the bars are made of ivory.

And the windows of the halls and chambers are of crystal. And the tables upon which men eat, some are made of emeralds, some of amethyst, and some of gold full of precious stones. And the legs that hold up the tables are made of the same precious stones....

Source: *Mandeville's Travels*, ed. M. C. Seymour (Oxford: 1967), pp. 195–99 (language modernized from Middle English by R. C. Stacey).

Questions for Analysis

1. What does Marco Polo want his readers to know about Java, and why? What does this suggest about the interests of these intended readers?

2. What does Mandeville want his readers to know about Prester John and his domains? Why are these details so important?

3. Which of these accounts seems more trustworthy, and why? Even if we cannot accept one or both at face value, what insight do they give us into the expectations of Columbus and the other European adventurers who relied on these accounts?

westward across the Atlantic Ocean in the hope of reaching Asia (see Chapter 12).

There was also a significant European colonial presence in the northern Atlantic, and had been for centuries. Viking settlers had begun to colonize Greenland in the late tenth century, and around 1000 had established a settlement in a place they called Vinland: the coast of Newfoundland in present-day Canada. According to the sagas that tell the story of these explorations, written down in the late twelfth and thirteenth centuries, a band of adventurers led by Leif Eiriksson had intended to set up a permanent colony there. Numerous expeditions resulted in the construction of houses, a fortification, and even attempts to domesticate livestock transported from Scandinavia. Yet North America

THE CHURCH AT HVALSEY, GREENLAND. Located on the southern tip of Greenland, Hvalsey was originally a farmstead established in the late tenth century by the uncle of Eirik the Red, father of the explorer Leif. The church at Hvalsey, pictured here, was built in the twelfth century and would have been roofed with turf. It was the site of the last documented event in the history of Norse settlement on the island, a wedding that took place in 1408. By that time, the population had largely died out due to starvation and disease.

did not become home to a permanent European population at this time; the sagas report that relations with indigenous peoples were fraught, and there may have been other factors hindering settlement.

However, Norse settlers did build a viable community on Greenland, which eventually formed part of the kingdom of Norway. This was facilitated by the warming of the earth's climate between 800 and 1300—the same phenomenon that partly enabled the agricultural revolution discussed in Chapter 8. For several centuries, these favorable climatic conditions made it possible to sustain some farming activities on the southern coastline of that huge island, supplemented by fishing, hunting, and foraging. But with the gradual cooling of the climate in the fourteenth century, which caused famines even in the rich farmlands of Europe, this fragile ecosystem was gradually eroded and the Greenlanders died out.

WAYS OF KNOWING AND DESCRIBING THE WORLD

The success of European commercial and colonial expansion in this era both drove and depended on significant innovations in measuring and mapping. It also coincided with intellectual, literary, and artistic initiatives that aimed to capture and describe the workings of this wider world, and to imagine its celestial (or infernal) counterparts.

Economic Tools: Balance Sheets, Banks, Charts, and Clocks

The economic boom that resulted from the integration of European and Asian commerce called for the refinement of existing business models and accounting techniques. New forms of partnership and the development of insurance contracts helped to minimize the risks associated with long-distance trading. Double-entry bookkeeping, widely used in Italy by the mid-fourteenth century, gave merchants a much clearer picture of their profits and losses by ensuring that both credits and debits were clearly laid out in parallel columns, a practice that facilitated the balancing of accounts. The Medici family of Florence established branches of their bank in each of the major cities of Europe and were careful that the failure of one would not bankrupt the entire firm, as earlier branch-banking arrangements had done. Banks also experimented with advanced credit techniques borrowed from Muslim and Jewish financiers,

DEVIL WITH EYEGLASSES. Spectacles were most commonly worn by those who made a living by reading and writing, notably bureaucrats and lawyers. In this conceptualization of hell, the devil charged with keeping track of human sin wears eyeglasses.
■ *What might this image reveal about popular attitudes toward record-keeping and the growing legal and administrative bureaucracies of the later Middle Ages?*

allowing their clients to transfer funds without any real money changing hands—and without endangering their capital by carrying it with them. Such transfers were carried out by written receipts: the direct ancestors of the check, the money order, and the currency transfer.

Other late medieval technologies kept pace in different ways with the demands for increased efficiency and accuracy. Eyeglasses, first invented in the 1280s, were perfected in the fourteenth century, extending the careers of those who made a living by reading, writing, and accounting. The use of the magnetic compass helped ships sail farther away from land, making longer-distance Atlantic voyages possible for the first time. And as more and more mariners began to sail waters less familiar to them, pilots began to make and use special charts that mapped the locations of ports. Called *portolani*, these charts also took note of prevailing winds, potential routes, good harbors, and known perils.

Among the many implements of modern daily life invented in this era, the most familiar are clocks. Mechanical clocks came into use shortly before 1300 and proliferated immediately thereafter. They were too large and expensive for private purchase, but towns vied with one another to install them in prominent public buildings, thus advertising municipal wealth and good governance. Mechanical timekeeping had two profound effects. One was the further stimulation of interest in complex machinery of all sorts, an interest already awakened by the widespread use of mills in the eleventh and twelfth centuries (see Chapter 8).

More significant was the way that clocks regulated daily life. Until the advent of clocks, time was flexible. Although days had been *theoretically* divided into hours, minutes, and seconds since the time of the Sumerians (see Chapter 1),

PORTOLAN CHART. Accurate mapping was essential to the success of maritime colonial ventures in the thirteenth and fourteenth centuries. The chart shown here is the oldest surviving example of a map used by mariners to navigate between Mediterranean ports. (The word *portolan* is used to describe such charts.) It dates from the end of the thirteenth century, and its shape clearly indicates that it was made from an animal hide. Although parchment was extremely durable, it would have slowly worn away owing to prolonged exposure to salt water and other elements—hence the rarity of this early example.

there had never been a way of mapping these temporal measurements onto an actual day. Now, clocks relentlessly divided time into exact units, giving rise to new expectations about labor and productivity. People were expected to start and end work "on time," to make the most of the time spent at work, and even to equate time with money. Like the improvements in bookkeeping, timekeeping made some kinds of work more efficient, but it also created new tensions and obsessions.

Knowledge of the World and of God

In the mid-thirteenth century, Thomas Aquinas had constructed a theological view of the world as rational, organized, and comprehensible to the inquiring human mind (see Chapter 9). Confidence in this picture began to wane in the fourteenth century, even before the Black Death posed a new challenge to it. Philosophers such as William of Ockham (d.c. 1348), an English member of the Franciscan order, denied that human reason could prove fundamental theological truths such as the existence of God. He argued that human knowledge of God, and hence salvation, depends entirely on what God himself has chosen to reveal through scripture. Instead, Ockham urged humans to investigate the natural world and to better understand its laws—without positing any necessary connection between the observable properties of nature and the unknowable essence of divinity.

This philosophical position, known as nominalism, had its roots in the philosophy of Plato (see Chapter 4) and has had an enormous impact on modern thought. The nominalists' distinction between the rational comprehensibility of the real world and the spiritual incomprehensibility of God encourages investigation of nature without reference to supernatural explanations: one of the most important foundations of the modern scientific method (see Chapter 16). Nominalism also encourages empirical observation, since it posits that knowledge of the world should rest on sensory experience rather than abstract theories. The philosophical principles laid down by these observers of the medieval world are thus fundamental to modern science.

Creating God's World in Art

Just as a fascination with the natural world informed developments in medieval science, the artists of this era were paying close attention to the way plants, animals, and human beings really looked. Carvings of leaves and flowers were increasingly made from direct observation and are clearly recognizable to modern botanists as distinct

Vikings Encounter the Natives of North America

Although Norse voyagers had explored and settled the coast of Newfoundland around the year 1000, written accounts of these exploits were not made or widely circulated until the thirteenth century. The excerpt below comes from one of these narrative histories, the Grænlendinga Saga *("Greenlanders' Saga"). Its hero is Thorfinn Karlsefni, a Norwegian adventurer who arrives in Greenland and marries Gudrid, the twice-widowed sister-in-law of the explorer Leif Eiriksson. Leif had established the original colony of Vinland, but had since returned to Greenland.*

here was still the same talk about Vinland voyages as before, and everyone, including [his wife] Gudrid, kept urging Karlsefni to make the voyage. In the end he decided to sail and gathered a company of sixty men and five women. He made an agreement with his crew that everyone should share equally in whatever profits the expedition might yield. The took livestock of all kinds, for they intended to make a permanent settlement there if possible.

Karlsefni asked Leif if he could have the houses in Vinland; Leif said that he was willing to lend them, but not to give them away.

They put to sea and arrived safe and sound at Leif's Houses and carried their hammocks ashore. Soon they had plenty of good supplies, for a fine big rorqual* was driven ashore; they went down and cut it up, and so there was no shortage of food.

The livestock were put out to grass, and soon the male beasts became very frisky and difficult to manage. They had brought a bull with them.

Karlsefni ordered timber to be felled and cut into lengths for a cargo for the ship, and it was left out on a rock to season. They made use of all the natural resources of the country that were available, grapes and game of all kinds and other produce.

The first winter passed into summer, and then they had their first encounter with Skrælings,[†] when a great number of them came out of the wood one day. The cattle were grazing near by and the bull began to bellow and roar with great vehemence. This terrified the Skrælings and they fled, carrying their packs which contained furs and sables and pelts of all kinds. They made for Karlsefni's houses and tried to get inside, but Karlsefni had the doors barred against them. Neither side could understand the other's language.

Then the Skrælings put down their packs and opened them up and offered their contents, preferably in exchange for weapons; but Karlsefni forbade his men to sell arms. Then he hit on the idea of telling the women to carry milk out to the Skrælings, and when the Skrælings saw the milk they wanted to buy nothing else. And so the outcome of their trading expedition was that the Skrælings carried their purchases away in their bellies, and left their packs and furs with Karlsefni and his men.

After that, Karlsefni ordered a strong wooden palisade to be erected round the houses, and they settled in.

---

species. Statues of humans also became more realistic in their portrayals of facial expressions and bodily proportions. According to a story in circulation around 1290, a sculptor working on a likeness of the German emperor allegedly made a hurried return trip to study his subject's face a second time, because he'd heard that a new wrinkle had appeared on the emperor's brow.

This trend toward naturalism extended to manuscript illumination and painting. The latter was, to a large extent, a new art. As we saw in Chapter 1, wall paintings are among the oldest forms of artistic expression in human history, and throughout antiquity and the Middle Ages artists had decorated the walls of public and private buildings with frescoes (paintings executed on "fresh"—wet—plaster). But in addition to frescoes, Italian artists in the thirteenth century began to adapt the techniques used by icon painters in Byzantium, making freestanding pictures on pieces of wood or canvas using tempera (pigments mixed with water and natural gums). Because these altarpieces, devotional images, and portraits were portable, they were also more commercial. As long as artists could afford the necessary materials, they did not have to wait for specific commissions. This meant that they had more freedom to choose their subject matter and to put an individual stamp on their

About this time Karlsefni's wife, Gudrid, gave birth to a son, and he was named Snorri.

Early next winter the Skrælings returned, in much greater numbers this time, bringing with them the same kind of wares as before. Karlsefni told the women, 'You must carry out to them the same produce that was most in demand last time, and nothing else.' . . .

[B]ut a Skræling was killed by one of Karlsefni's men for trying to steal some weapons. The Skrælings fled as fast as they could, leaving their clothing and wares behind . . .

'Now we must devise a plan,' said Karlsefni, 'for I expect they will pay us a third visit, and this time with hostility and in greater numbers. This is what we must do: ten men are to go out on the headland here and make themselves conspicuous, and the rest of us are to go into the wood and make a clearing there, where we can keep our cattle when the Skrælings come out of the forest. We shall take our bull and keep him to the fore.'

The place where they intended to have their encounter with the Skrælings had the lake on one side and the woods on the other.

Karlsefni's plan was put into effect, and the Skrælings came right to the place that Karlsefni had chosen for the battle. The fighting began, and many of the Skrælings were killed. There was one tall and handsome man among the Skrælings and Karlsefni reckoned that he must be their leader. One of the Skrælings had picked up an axe, and after examining it for a moment he swung it at a man standing beside him, who fell dead at once. The tall man then took hold of the axe, looked at it for a moment, and then threw it as far as he could out into the water. Then the Skrælings fled into the forest as fast as they could, and that was the end of the encounter.

Karlsefni and his men spent the whole winter there, but in the spring he announced that he had no wish to stay there any longer and wanted to return to Greenland. They made ready for the voyage and took with them much valuable produce, vines and grapes and pelts. They put to sea and reached Eiriksfjord safely and spent the winter there.

*A kind of whale, the largest species of which is a blue whale.

†A Norse word meaning "savages," applied to the different indigenous peoples of Greenland and of North America.

Questions for Analysis

1. What policies do the Norse settlers adopt toward the native peoples they encounter on the coast of Newfoundland? How effective are they?

2. Given their extensive preparations for colonization and the success of their early efforts, why do you think that Karlsefni and his companions abandoned their settlement in North America? Are there clues discernible in the text?

3. Compare this encounter to the sources describing other interactions between Europeans and the indigenous inhabitants of the New World after 1492 (see Chapters 12 and 14). How do you account for any similarities? What are some key differences?

work—one of the reasons why we know the names of many more artists from this era.

One of these, Giotto di Bondone of Florence (c. 1267–1337), painted both walls and portable wooden panels. Like some of his contemporaries, Giotto (*gee-OHT-toh*) was preeminently an imitator of nature. Not only do his human beings and animals look lifelike, they seem to do natural things. When Christ enters Jerusalem on Palm Sunday, boys climb trees to get a better view; when Saint Francis is laid out in death, someone checks to see whether he has really received the *stigmata*, the marks of Christ's wounds; and when the Virgin's parents, Joachim and Anna, meet after a long separation, they embrace and kiss one another tenderly. Although many of the artists who came after Giotto moved away from naturalism, this style would become the norm by 1400. It is for this reason that Giotto is often regarded as the first painter of the Renaissance (see Chapter 11).

A Vision of the World We Cannot See

One of Giotto's exact contemporaries had a different way of capturing the spiritual world in a naturalistic way, and he worked in a different medium. Dante Alighieri (1265–1321)

Interpreting Visual Evidence

Seals: Signs of Identity and Authority

For much of human history, applying a seal to a document was the way to certify its legality and to identify the people who had ratified it. During antiquity and the early Middle Ages, this meant only powerful men—kings, bishops, heads of monasteries—and occasionally powerful women. But as participation in documentary practices became more and more common, corporations (like universities and crusading orders), towns, and many individual people also came to use seals. The devices (images) and legends (writing) on these seals were carefully chosen to capture central attributes of their owners' personality or status. Seals were made by pressing a deeply incised lead matrix onto hot wax or resin, which would quickly dry to form a durable impression. The images reproduced here are later engravings that make the features of the original seals easier to see.

A. Seal of the town of Dover, 1281. Dover has long been one of the busiest and most important port cities of England because of its strategic proximity to France; indeed, the Dover Strait that separates this town from Calais, just across the English Channel, is only twenty-one miles wide. In 1281, when this seal was used, ferries and other ships like the one depicted here (in a later engraving) would have made this crossing several times a day. The legend around the edges of the seal reads (in Latin): "Seal of the commune of barons of Dover." It reflects the extraordinary status accorded to the freemen of Dover by the English crown: because of their crucial role in the economy and defense of the kingdom, they were considered a corporate body and entitled to representation in Parliament alongside individual barons.

B. Personal seal of Charles II, king of Naples and Sicily, 1289. Charles II (b. 1254, r. 1285–1309) was the son and heir of Charles of Anjou, who became King Charles I of Sicily in 1266 and died in 1285. This means that Charles II had succeeded his father and had reigned as king for four years before he used this seal to ratify an agreement to his own daughter's marriage in 1289. Yet the seal in image B was clearly made for him when he was a young man—probably when he was first knighted. It depicts him as count of Anjou (see the heraldic fleur-de-lys) and gives him his other princely titles, including "Son of King Charles of Sicily." Although he was thirty-five-years old, a king in his own right, and a father, he was still using this older seal!

Questions for Analysis

1. Medieval towns represented themselves in a variety of ways on their seals: sometimes showing a group portrait of town councilors, sometimes a local saint, sometimes a heraldic beast, sometimes distinctive architectural features. Why would Dover choose this image? What messages does this seal convey?

2. Think carefully about the mystery of Charles II's seal. Usually, an important agreement like a marriage contract (with the son of the French king, no less!) would have carried a king's official, royal seal. What are all the possible reasons why Charles would still have been using this outdated seal? What are the possible ramifications of this choice? In your role as historian-detective, how would you go about solving this mystery?

3. The seals of medieval women were almost always shaped like almonds (pointed ovals— the technical term is *vesica-shaped*). Yet Ingeborg's seal is round, like the seals of men and corporations. Why might that be the case?

4. In general, what are the value of seals for the study of history? What are the various ways in which they function as sources?

C. Seal of Ingeborg Håkansdotter, duchess of Sweden, 1321. Ingeborg (1301–1361) was the daughter of King Håkon V of Norway and was betrothed to a Swedish duke, Erick Magnusson, when she was only eleven years old. After a dramatic series of events that left her a young widow, she became the regent for her son, Magnus was elected king of both Norway and Sweden in 1319. Ingeborg herself was barely eighteen at the time. The legend on her seal (image C) reads "Ingeborg by the Grace of God Duchess of Norway"—her official title.

eral fates: this is his ingenious way of commenting on current events and passing judgment on his enemies. In many ways, this monumental poem represents the fusion of classical and Christian cultures, Latin learning and vernacular artistry.

PAPAL POWER AND POPULAR PIETY

Dante's *Comedy* responded creatively to the political turmoil that engulfed Italy during his lifetime, a situation that was transforming the papacy in ways that he condemned. Indeed, many of the men whom Dante imaginatively placed in Hell were popes or men who had held high office in the Church, or foreign rulers who sought to subjugate Italian territories (like the Holy Roman Emperor), or rapacious Italian princes and factional leaders who fought among themselves, creating a state of permanent warfare among and within cities (like Dante's native Florence). But despite the weakening authority of the papal office, which caused violent divisions within the Church, popular piety arguably achieved its strongest expressions during this era.

The Legacy of Innocent III

As we saw in Chapter 9, Innocent III's reign marked the height of papal power, but it also sowed seeds of disaster. The popes of the thirteenth century continued to centralize the government of the Church, as Innocent had done, but they simultaneously became involved in protracted political struggles that compromised the papacy's credibility.

For example, because the Papal States bordered on the kingdom of Sicily—which comprised the important city of Naples and southern Italy, too—subsequent popes came into conflict with its ruler, the emperor Frederick II, who proved a fierce opponent. And instead of excommunicating him and calling for his deposition, as Innocent might have done, the reigning pope called a crusade against him—a cynical admission of crusading's overtly political motives. To implement this crusade, the papacy became preoccupied with finding a military champion to advance their cause. They found him in Charles of Anjou, the youngest brother of the French king Louis IX (see below). But Charles made matters worse by antagonizing his own subjects, who offered their allegiance to the king of Aragon. The pope then made Aragon the target of another crusade, which resulted in the death of the new French king, Philip III (r. 1270–85). In the wake of this debacle, Philip's son, Philip IV, resolved to punish the papacy for misusing its powers.

THE MEETING OF JOACHIM AND ANNA BY GIOTTO.
According to legend, Anna and Joachim were an aged and infertile couple who were able to conceive their only child, Mary, through divine intervention. Hence, this painting may portray the moment of her conception—but it also portrays the affection of husband and wife. ▪ *What human characteristics and values does it convey to the viewer?*

of Florence pioneered what he called a "sweet new style" of poetry in his native tongue, which was now so different from the Latin of Roman Italy that it had become a language in its own right. Yet as a scholar and devotee of classical Latin verse, Dante also strove to make this Italian vernacular an instrument for serious political and social critique. His great work, known in his own day as the *Comedy* (called by later admirers the *Divine Comedy*) was composed during the years he spent in exile from his beloved city, after the political party he supported was ousted from power in 1301.

The *Comedy* describes the poet's imaginary journey through hell, purgatory, and paradise, a journey beginning in a "dark wood": a metaphor for the personal and political crises that threatened Dante's faith and livelihood. In the poem, the narrator is led out of this forest and through the first two realms (hell and purgatory) by the Roman poet Virgil (see Chapter 5), who represents the best of classical culture. But he can only be guided toward knowledge of the divine in paradise by his deceased beloved, Beatrice, who symbolizes Christian wisdom. In the course of this visionary pilgrimage, Dante's narrator meets the souls of many historical personages and contemporaries, questioning them closely and inviting them to explain why they met their sev-

The Limits of Papal Propaganda

In 1300, Pope Boniface VIII (r. 1294–1303) celebrated a papal jubilee in Rome and offered a full crusader's indulgence to every pilgrim: the promise of absolution from all sins. It was a tacit recognition that Rome, not Jerusalem, was now the center of the Christian world—and also a tacit admission that the Crusades of the past two centuries had failed.

But just nine years after this confident assertion of Rome's unassailable status, Rome had become obsolete. The new capital of Christendom was in France, because King Philip IV had challenged Boniface to a political duel and won. The pretext was unimpressive: Boniface had protested against Philip's plan to bring a French bishop to trial on a charge of treason—thus violating the bishop's ecclesiastical immunity. Philip, who had probably anticipated this objection, accused Boniface of heresy and sent a troop of knights to arrest him. At the papal residence of Anagni in 1303, Boniface (then in his seventies) was so mistreated by Philip's thugs that he died a month later. Philip then pressed his advantage. He forced the new pope, Clement V, to thank him publically for his zealous defense of the faith and then, in 1309, moved the entire papal court from Rome to Avignon (*AH-vee-nyon*), a city near the southeastern border of his own realm.

The papacy's capitulation to French royal power illustrates the enormous gap that had opened up between rhetoric and reality in the centuries since the Investiture Conflict (see Chapter 8). Although Boniface was merely repeating an old claim, that kings ruled only by divine approval as recognized by the Church, the fact was that the Church now exercised its authority only by bowing to the superior power of a particular king.

The Babylonian Captivity of the Papacy

The papacy would remain in Avignon for nearly seventy years, until 1378 (see Chapter 11). This period is often called the "Babylonian Captivity" of the papacy, recalling the Jews' exile in Babylon during the sixth century B.C.E. (see Chapter 2). Even though the move was probably supposed to be temporary, it was not reversed after Philip IV's death in 1314, perhaps because many found that doing business in Avignon was easier than doing business in Rome. Not only was it closer to the major centers of power in northwestern Europe, it was now far removed from the tumultuous politics of Italy and was safe from the aggressive attentions of the German emperors.

All of these considerations were important for a succession of popes closely allied with the aims of the French monarchy. In time, Avignon began to feel like home; in fact it *was* home for all of the popes elected there, who were natives of the region, as were nearly all the cardinals whom they appointed. This further cemented their loyalty to the French king. And the longer the papacy stayed, the larger its bureaucracy grew and the harder it was to contemplate moving it.

Although the papacy never abandoned its claims to the overlordship of Rome and the Papal States, making good on these claims required decades of diplomacy and a great deal of money. The Avignon popes accordingly imposed new taxes and obligations on the wealthy dioceses of France, England, Germany, and Spain. Judicial cases from ecclesiastical courts also brought large revenues into the papal coffers. Most controversially, the Avignon popes

THE PAPAL PALACE AT AVIGNON. This great fortified palace was begun in 1339 and symbolizes the apparent permanence of the papal residence in Avignon. ▪ *Why would it have been constructed as a fortress as well as a palace?*

claimed the right to appoint bishops and priests to vacant offices anywhere in Christendom, directly, therefore bypassing the rights of individual dioceses and allowing the papacy to collect huge fees from successful appointees.

By these and other measures, the Avignon popes further strengthened administrative control over the Church. But they also further weakened the papacy's moral authority. Stories of the court's unseemly luxury circulated widely, especially during the reign of the notoriously corrupt Clement VI (r. 1342–52), who openly sold spiritual benefits for money (boasting that he would appoint a jackass to a bishopric if he thought it would turn a profit) and insisted that his sexual transgressions were therapeutic. His reign coincided with the Black Death, whose terrifying and demoralizing effects were not alleviated by the quality of his leadership.

Uniting the Faithful: The Power of Sacraments

Despite the centralizing power of the papacy, which came to fruition under Innocent III, most medieval Christians accessed the Church at a local level, within their communities. Somewhat paradoxically, this was another of Innocent III's legacies: because he had insisted that all people should have direct access to religious instruction, nearly all of Europe was covered by a network of parish churches by the end of the thirteenth century. In these churches, parish priests not only taught the elements of Christian doctrine, they administered the sacraments ("holy rites") that conveyed the grace of God to individual Christians, marking significant moments in the life cycle of every person and significant times in the Christian calendar.

Medieval piety came to revolve around these seven sacraments: baptism, confirmation, confession (or penance), communion, marriage, extreme unction (last rites for the dying), and ordination (of priests). Baptism, a ceremony of initiation administered in the early centuries of Christianity to adults (see Chapter 6), had become a sacrament administered to infants as soon as possible after birth, to safeguard their souls in case of an early death. The confirmation of adolescents reaffirmed the promises made on a child's behalf at baptism by parents and godparents. Periodic confession of sins to a priest guaranteed forgiveness by God; for if a sinner did not perform appropriate acts of penance, atonement for sins would have to be completed in purgatory—that netherworld between heaven and hell explored by Dante, whose existence was made a matter of Church doctrine

for the first time in 1274 (though its existence had been posited by Pope Gregory the Great centuries earlier—see Chapter 7).

Marriage was a relatively new sacrament, increasingly emphasized but very seldom practiced as a ceremony; in reality, marriage in this period required only the exchange of solemn promises and was often formed simply by an act of sexual intercourse or the fact of cohabitation. Extreme unction refers to the holy oil with which the priest anointed the forehead of a dying person, signifying the final absolution of all sins and thus offering a final assurance of salvation. Like baptism, this rite could, in an emergency, be administered by any Christian believer. The other sacraments, however, could be administered only by a properly ordained priest— or, in the case of confirmation and ordination, by a bishop. Ordination was therefore the only sacrament reserved for the small percentage of Christians who became priests, and it conveyed to the priest the special authority to share God's grace through the sacraments: a power that could never be lost, even by a priest who led an immoral life.

This sacramental system was the foundation on which the practices of medieval popular piety rested. Pilgrimages, for example, were a form of penance and could lessen one's time in purgatory. Crusading was a kind of extreme pilgrimage that promised the complete fulfillment of all penances the crusader might owe for all the sins of his (or her) life. Many other pious acts—saying the prayers of the rosary, for example, or giving alms to the poor—could also serve as penance for one's sins while constituting good works that would help the believer in his or her journey toward salvation.

The Miracle of the Eucharist

Of these sacraments, the one was most central to the religious lives of medieval Christians was the communion ceremony of the Mass, also known as the Eucharist. As we noted in Chapter 9, the ritual power of the Mass was greatly enhanced in the twelfth century, when the Church began promoting the doctrine of transubstantiation. Christians attending Mass were taught that when the priest spoke the ritual words "This is my body" and "This is my blood," the substances of bread and wine on the altar were miraculously transformed into the body and blood of Jesus Christ. To consume one or both of these substances was to ingest holiness; and so powerful was this idea that most Christians received the sacramental bread just once a year, at Easter. Some holy women, however, attempted to sustain themselves by consuming only the single morsel of bread consecrated at daily Mass.

"THIS IS MY BODY": THE ELEVATION OF THE HOST.
This fresco from a chapel in Assisi was painted by Simone Martini in the 1320s. It shows the moment in the Mass when the priest raises the eucharistic host so that it can be seen by the faithful. The Latin phrase spoken at this moment, *Hoc est corpus meum* ("This is my body"), came to be regarded as a magical formula because it could transform one substance into another: *hocus pocus*. ■ *Since medieval Christians believed that the sight of the host was just as powerful as ingesting it, how would they have responded to this life-size image of the elevation?* ■ *What does the appearance of angels (above the altar) signify?*

The Pursuit of Holiness

The fundamental theme of preachers in this era, that salvation lay open to any Christian who strove for it, helps to explain the central place of the Mass and other sacraments in daily life. It also led many to seek out new paths that could lead to God. As we noted in Chapter 9, some believers who sought to achieve a mystical union with God (through rigorous prayer, penance, and personal sacrifice) were ultimately condemned for heresy because they did not subordinate themselves to the authority of the Church. But even less radical figures might find themselves treading on dangerous ground, especially if they published their ideas. For example, the German preacher Master Eckhart (c. 1260–1327), a Dominican friar, taught that there is a "spark" deep within every human soul and that God lives in this spark. Through prayer and self-renunciation, any person could therefore retreat into the inner recesses of her being and access divinity. This conveyed the message that a layperson might attain salvation through her own efforts, without the intervention of a priest or any of the sacraments he alone could perform. As a result, many of Eckhart's teachings were condemned. But views like these would find support in the teachings of popular preachers after the Black Death, when close-knit communities revolving around the parish church were broken up or weakened (see Chapter 11).

STRUGGLES FOR SOVEREIGNTY

When the French king Philip IV transplanted the papal court from Rome to Avignon, he was not just responding to previous popes' abuse of power: he was bolstering his own. By the middle of the thirteenth century, the growth of strong territorial monarchies, combined with the increasing sophistication of royal justice, taxation, and propaganda, had given some secular rulers a higher degree of power than any western European ruler had wielded since the time of Charlemagne (see Chapter 7).

Meanwhile, monarchs' willingness to support the Church's crusading efforts not only yielded distinct economic and political advantages, it also allowed them to assert their commitment to the moral and spiritual improvement of their realms. Although a king still needed to be anointed with holy oil at the time of his coronation in order to claim that he ruled "by the grace of God"—a rite that required a bishop and, by extension, papal support—a king's authority in his own realm rested on the acquiescence of the aristocracy and on popular perceptions of his reputation for justice, piety, and regard for his subjects' prosperity. On the wider stage of the

Yet, to share in the miracle of the Eucharist, one did not have to consume it. One had only to witness the elevation of the host, the wafer of bread raised up by the priest, which "hosted" the real presence of Jesus Christ. Daily attendance at Mass simply to view the consecration of the host was therefore a common form of devotion, and this was facilitated by the practice of displaying a consecrated wafer in a special reliquary called a monstrance ("showcase"), which could be set up on an altar or carried through the streets. Believers sometimes attributed astonishing properties to the eucharistic host, feeding it to sick animals or rushing from church to church to see the consecrated bread as many times as possible in a day. Some of these practices were criticized as superstitious. But, by and large, these expressions of popular piety were encouraged and fervently practiced by many.

medieval world, it also rested on his successful assertion of his kingdom's sovereignty.

The Problem of Sovereignty

Sovereignty can be defined as inviolable authority over a defined territory. In Chapter 9, we noted that Philip Augustus was the first monarch to call himself "king of France" and not "king of the French." In other words, he was defining his kingship in geographical terms, claiming that there was an entity called France and that he was king within that area.

But what was France? Was it the tiny "island" (Île-de-France) around Paris, which had been his father's domain? If so, then France was very small—and very vulnerable, which would make it hard to maintain a claim to sovereignty. Was it, rather, any region whose lord was willing to do homage to the French king, like Champagne or Normandy? In that case, the king would need to enforce these rights of lordship constantly and, if necessary, exert his rule directly—as Philip did when he took Normandy away from England's King John in 1214.

But what if some of France's neighboring lords ruled in their own right, as did the independent counts of Flanders, thus threatening the security of France's borders? In that case, the king would either need to forge an alliance with these borderlands or negate their independence. He would need to assert his sovereignty by absorbing these regions into an ever-growing kingdom.

This is the problem: a claim to sovereignty is only credible if it can be backed up with real power, and a state's or ruler's power must never seem stagnant or passive. The problem of sovereignty, then, is a zero-sum game: one state's sovereignty is won and maintained by diminishing that of other states. Although many French citizens today would assert that France has, in some mystical way, always existed in its present form, the fact is that France and every other modern European state was being cobbled together in the medieval period through a process of annexation and colonization—just as the United States was assembled at the expense of the empires that had colonized North America (the British, French, and Spanish), not to mention the killing or displacement of autonomous native peoples.

The process of achieving sovereignty is thus an aggressive and often violent one, affecting not only the rulers of territories but their peoples, too. In Spain, the "Reconquest" of Muslim lands, which had accelerated in the twelfth century, continued apace in the thirteenth and fourteenth, to the detriment of these regions' Muslim and Jewish inhabitants. German princes continued to push northward into the Baltic, where native peoples'

resistance to colonizing efforts was met with brutal force. Meanwhile, the Scandinavian kingdoms that had been forming in the eleventh and twelfth centuries were warring among themselves and their neighbors for the control of contested regions and resources. Italy and the Mediterranean became a constant battleground, as we have observed. Among all these emerging states, the two most strident and successful in their assertion of sovereignty were France and England.

The Prestige of France: The Saintly Kingship of Louis IX

After the death of Philip Augustus in 1223, the heirs to the French throne continued to pursue an expansionist policy, pushing the boundaries of their influence out to the east and south. There were significant pockets of resistance, though, notably from the southwestern lands that the kings of England had inherited from Eleanor of Aquitaine (see Chapter 9) and from the independent towns of Flanders that had escaped conquest under Philip Augustus. In 1302, citizen militias from several of these towns, fighting on foot with farming implements and other unconventional weapons, even managed to defeat a heavily armed French cavalry. This victory at the Battle of Courtrai (Kortrijk) is still celebrated as a national holiday in Belgium (although, ironically, its ultimate meaning is currently at the center of a divisive controversy between French- and Flemish-speaking Belgians).

This defeat was a setback for Philip IV of France, but we have already observed that Philip had other ways of asserting the power of French sovereignty. Much of that power derived from his grandfather, Louis IX (r. 1226–70), who would probably have been horrified by the ways his grandson used it. Louis was famous for his piety and for his conscientious exercise of his kingly duties. Unlike most of his fellow princes, he not only pledged to go on crusade—he actually went. And while both of his campaigns were notorious failures (he died on the second, in 1270) they cemented Louis's saintly reputation and political clout.

First, Louis's willingness to risk his life (and that of his brothers) in the service of the Church would give him tremendous influence in papal affairs—a key factor in making his youngest brother, Charles of Anjou, the king of Naples and Sicily. Second, the necessity of ensuring the good governance of his kingdom during his years of absence prompted Louis to reform or invent many key aspects of royal governance, which made France the bureaucratic rival of England for the first time. Third, Louis's first crusading venture was

A CONTAINER FOR THE CROWN OF THORNS. The Sainte-Chapelle, built by Louis IX, was a giant reliquary for the display of this potent artifact and symbol that Christ's divine majesty, which increased the prestige of king of France.

seen as confirmation that the king of France had inherited the mantle of Charlemagne as the protector of the Church and the representative of Christ on earth. Although it was a military fiasco, this crusade found lasting artistic expression in the Sainte-Chapelle (Holy Chapel), a gorgeous jewel box of a church that Louis built in Paris for his collection of Passion relics—that is, artifacts thought to have been used for the torture and crucifixion of Christ. The most important of these was the Crown of Thorns, intended by Pilate as a mocking reference to "the king of the Jews" (see Chapter 6). Now that this holy crown belonged to Louis and was housed in Paris, it could be taken as a sign that Paris was the new Jerusalem.

Widely regarded as a saint in his lifetime, Louis was formally canonized in 1297—by the same Pope Boniface VIII brought down by Philip IV. Indeed, Boniface partly intended this gesture as a rebuke to the saint's grandson. Philip himself, however, turned it to his advantage. He even used his grandfather's pious reputation as a cloak for his frankly rapacious treatment of the Knights Templar, whose military order he suppressed in 1314 so that he could confiscate its extensive property and dissolve his own debts to the order. He had expelled the Jews from his realm in 1306 for similar reasons.

Castles and Control: Edward I and the Expansion of English Rule

The expulsion of Jews who depended on a king's personal protection had actually been a precedent set by Philip's contemporary and kinsman, Edward I of England

(r. 1272–1307). Unlike Philip, Edward had to build up the sovereignty of his state almost from scratch. His father, Henry III (1216–1272), had a long but troubled reign. Inheriting the throne as a young boy, shortly after his father John's loss of Normandy and capitulation to Magna Carta (see Chapter 9), Henry had to contend with factions among his regents and, later, the restive barons of his realm who rose against him on several occasions. His son Edward even sided with the rebels at one point, but later worked alongside his father to suppress them. When Edward himself became king in 1272, he took steps toward ensuring that there would be no further revolts on his watch, tightening his control on the aristocracy and their lands, diffusing their power by strengthening that of Parliament, reforming the administration of the realm, and clarifying its laws.

Having seen to the internal affairs of England, Edward looked to its borders. Since Welsh chieftains had been major backers of the barons who had rebelled against his father, Edward was determined to clean up the border region and bring "wild Wales" within the orbit of English sovereignty. He initially attempted to do this by making treaties with various Welsh princes, but none of these arrangements were stable or gave Edward the type of control he wanted. He accordingly embarked on an ambitious and ruthless campaign of castle-building, ringing the hilly country with enormous fortifications on a scale not seen in most of Europe; they were more

CAERNARVON CASTLE. One of many massive fortifications built by Edward I, this castle was the birthplace of the first English "Prince of Wales" and the site where the current Prince of Wales, Charles, was formally invested with that title in 1969. ▪ *Castles of this size and strength had been constructed in the Crusader States and on the disputed frontiers of Muslim and Christian Spain but never before in Britain (see the photos on pages 292 and 295 of Chapter 9).* ▪ *What does their construction reveal about Edward's attitude toward the Welsh?*

Analyzing Primary Sources

A Declaration of Scottish Independence

In April of 1320, a group of powerful Scottish lords gathered at the abbey of Arbroath to draft a letter to Pope John XII in Avignon. The resulting "Declaration of Arbroath" petitioned the exiled pope (a Frenchman loyal to the French king) to recognize the Scots as a sovereign nation and to support their right to an independent kingdom that would be free from encroachment by the English. The Scots' elected king, Robert the Bruce, had been excommunicated by a previous pope, who had also upheld English claims to lordship in Scotland. The letter therefore makes a number of different arguments for the recognition of the Scots' right to self-governance.

 e know, most holy father and lord, and have gathered from the deeds and books about men in the past, that . . . the nation of the Scots has been outstanding for its many distinctions. It journeyed from the lands of Greece and Egypt by the Tyrrhenian Sea and the Pillars of Hercules, . . . but could not be subdued anywhere by any peoples however barbaric. . . . It took possession of the settlements in the west which it now desires, after first driving out the Britons and totally destroying the Picts, and although often attacked by the Norwegians, Danes and English. Many were its victories and innumerable its efforts. It has held these places always free of all servitude, as the old histories testify.

One hundred and thirteen kings of their royal lineage have reigned in their kingdom, with no intrusion by a foreigner.

If the noble qualities and merits of these men were not obvious for other reasons, they shine forth clearly enough in that they were almost the first to be called to his most holy faith by the King of Kings and Lord of Lords, our Lord Jesus Christ, after his Passion and Resurrection, even though they were settled on the most distant boundaries of the earth. . . .

Thus our people lived until now in freedom and peace . . . , until that mighty prince Edward [I] king of England (the father of the present king) in the guise of a friend and ally attacked our kingdom in hostile fashion, when it had no head and the people were not harbouring any evil treachery, nor were they accustomed to

wars or attacks. His unjust acts, killings, acts of violence, pillagings, burnings, imprisonments of prelates, burnings of monasteries, robbings and killings of regular clergy, and also innumerable other outrages, which he committed against the said people, sparing none on account of age or sex, religion or order—no one could write about them or fully comprehend them who had not been instructed by experience.

From these countless ills we have been set free, with the help of Him who follows up wounds with healing and cures, by our most energetic prince, king and lord Sir Robert [the Bruce, r. 1306–29]. . . . By divine providence his succession to his right according to our laws and customs which we intend to maintain to the death, together with the due consent

like crusader castles, and Edward certainly treated the Welsh (who were actually his fellow Christians) as infidels. Indeed, he treated conquered Wales like a crusader state, making it a settler colony and subjecting the Welsh to the overlordship of his own men. When his son, the future Edward II, was born in 1284 at the great castle he had built at Caernarvon, he gave the infant the title "Prince of Wales," a title usually borne by a Welsh chieftain.

Edward then turned to Scotland, England's final frontier. Until now, control of Scotland had not been an English concern: the Scottish border had been peaceful for many years, and the Scottish kings did homage to the English king for some of their lands. In 1290, however, the succession to the Scottish throne was disputed among many rival

claimants, none of whom had enough backing to secure election. Edward intervened, pressing his own claim to the kingdom and seemingly prepared to take Scotland by conquest. To avoid this, the Scots forged an alliance with the French, but this did not prevent Edward's army from fighting its way through to Scone Abbey in 1296.

Scone was a symbolic target: the site of the Stone of Destiny on which Scottish kings were traditionally enthroned. So Edward seized this potent symbol, brought it back to Westminster Abbey in London, and embedded it in the coronation chair of his namesake, Edward the Confessor, the last Anglo-Saxon king of England (see Chapter 8). Save for a brief hiatus in 1950 (when the stone was stolen from the abbey by Scottish nationalists, students and assent of us all, have made him our prince and king. . . . But if he should give up what he has begun, seeking to subject us or our kingdom to the king of the English, . . . we would immediately strive to expel him as our enemy and a subverter of his right and ours, and we would make someone else our king, who is capable of seeing to our defence. For as long as a hundred of us remain alive, we intend never to be subjected to the lordship of the English, in any way. For it is not for glory in war, riches or honours that we fight, but only for the laws of our fathers and for freedom, which no good man loses except along with his life.

Therefore, most holy father and lord, we implore your holiness with all vehemence in our prayers that you . . . look with paternal eyes on the troubles and difficulties brought upon us and the church of God by the English. And that you deign to admonish and exhort the king of the English, who ought to be satisfied with what he has (since England was formerly enough for seven kings or more), to leave us Scots in peace, living as we do in the poor country of Scotland beyond which there is no dwelling place, and desiring nothing but our own. . . .

It is important for you, holy father, to do this, since you see the savagery of the heathen raging against Christians (as the sins of Christians require), and the frontiers of Christendom are being curtailed day by day, and you have seen how much it detracts from your holiness's reputation if (God forbid!) the church suffers eclipse or scandal in any part of it during your time. Let it then rouse the Christian princes who are covering up their true motivation when they pretend that they cannot go to the assistance of the Holy Land on account of wars with their neighbours. The real reason that holds them back is that in warring with their smaller neighbours they anticipate greater advantage to themselves and weaker resistance. . . .

But if your Holiness too credulously trusts the tales of the English fully, or does not leave off favouring the English to our confusion, then we believe that the Most High will blame you for the slaughter of bodies. . . . Dated at our monastery at Arbroath in Scotland 6 April 1320 in the fifteenth year of our said king's reign.

Questions for Analysis

1. On what grounds does this letter justify the political independence of the Scots? What different arguments does it make? Which, in your view, is the most compelling one?

2. Why does this letter mention crusading? What are the Scottish lords implying about the relationship between Europe's internal conflicts and the ongoing wars with external adversaries?

3. Imagine that you are an adviser to the pope. Based on your knowledge of the papacy's situation at this time, would you advise him to do as this letter asks? Why or why not?

---

at the University of Glasgow) it would remain there until 1996, as a sign that the sovereignty of Scotland had yielded to that of England. (It will be temporarily returned to London when the next English monarch is crowned.)

Edward considered the subjugation of Scotland to be England's manifest destiny: he called himself "the Hammer of the Scots," and when he died he charged his son Edward II (r. 1307–1327) with the completion of his task. But Edward, unlike his father, was not a ruthless and efficient advocate of English expansion. And he had to contend with a rebellion led by his own queen, Isabella of France, who also engineered his abdication and murder. Their son, Edward III (r. 1327–1377), would eventually renew his grandfather's expansionist policies—but his main target would be France,

not Scotland. He would thus launch Europe's two strongest monarchies into a war that lasted over a hundred years.

The Outbreak of the Hundred Years' War

The Hundred Years' War was the largest, longest, and most wide-ranging military conflict since Rome's wars with Carthage in the third and second centuries B.C.E. (see Chapter 5). Although England and France were its principal antagonists, almost all of the major European powers became involved in it at some stage. Active hostilities began in 1337 and lasted until 1453, interrupted by truces of varying lengths.

The most fundamental source of conflict, and the most difficult to resolve, was the fact that the kings of England held the duchy of Gascony as vassals of the French king; this had been part of Eleanor of Aquitaine's domain, added to the Anglo-Norman Empire in 1154 (see Chapter 9). In the twelfth and thirteenth centuries, when the French kings had not yet absorbed this region into their domain, this fact had seemed less of an anomaly. But as Europe's territorial monarchies began to claim sovereignty based on the free exercise of power within the "natural" boundaries of their domains, the English presence in "French" Gascony became more and more problematic. That England also had close commercial links, through the wool trade, with Flanders—which consistently resisted French imperialism—added fuel to the fire. So did the French alliance with the Scots, who continued to resist English imperialism.

Complicating this volatile situation was the disputed succession of the French crown. In 1328, the last of Philip IV's three sons died without leaving a son to succeed him: the Capetian dynasty, founded by the Frankish warlord Hugh Capet in 987 (see Chapter 8), had finally exhausted itself. A new dynasty, the Valois, came to the throne—but only by insisting that women could neither inherit royal power nor pass it on. For otherwise, the heir to France was Edward III of England, whose ambitious mother, Isabella, was Philip IV's only daughter. When his claim was initially passed over, Edward was only fifteen and in no position to protest. In 1337, however, when the disputes over Gascony and Scotland erupted into war, Edward raised the stakes by claiming to be the rightful king of France, a claim that subsequent English kings would maintain until the eighteenth century.

Although France was richer and more populous than England by a factor of at least three to one, the English crown was more effective in mobilizing the entire population, for reasons that we discussed in Chapter 9. Edward III was therefore able to levy and maintain a professional army of seasoned and well-disciplined soldiers, cavalry, and archers. The huge but virtually leaderless armies assembled by the French proved no match for the tactical superiority of these smaller English forces. English armies pillaged the French countryside at will, while civil wars broke out between embattled French lords. A decade after the declaration of war, French knights were defeated in two humiliating battles, at Crécy (1346) and Calais (1347). The English seemed invincible. Yet they were no match for an adversary approaching from the Far East.

FROM THE GREAT FAMINE TO THE BLACK DEATH

By 1300, Europe was connected to Asia and the lands in between by an intricate network that fostered commerce, communication, and connections of all kinds. Yet Europe was also reaching its own ecological limits. Between 1000 and 1300, the population had tripled, and a sea of grain

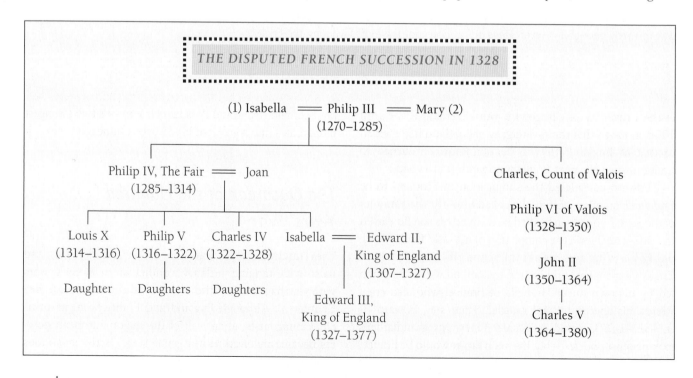

THE DISPUTED FRENCH SUCCESSION IN 1328

(1) Isabella ══ Philip III ══ Mary (2)
(1270–1285)

Philip IV, The Fair ══ Joan
(1285–1314)

Charles, Count of Valois

Philip VI of Valois
(1328–1350)

Louis X   Philip V   Charles IV   Isabella ══ Edward II,
(1314–1316)   (1316–1322)   (1322–1328)   King of England
                                                              (1307–1327)

John II
(1350–1364)

Daughter   Daughters   Daughters

Edward III,
King of England
(1327–1377)

Charles V
(1364–1380)

Past and Present

Global Pandemics

 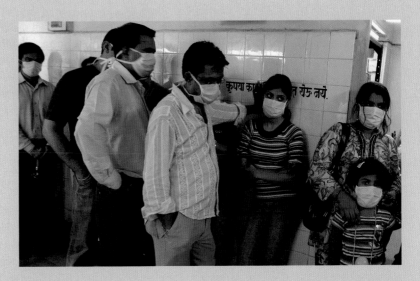

Although advances in medical science have made the causes of disease less mysterious, the rapid spread of new viruses is still terrifying and the variety of human responses to the possibility of sudden infection have changed little over time. The image on the left shows monks receiving the blessings of a priest at a special service in honor of St. Sebastian, who was regarded as a healer to those stricken with plague. On the right, citizens of Mumbai wear masks as they wait to receive testing for the swine flu virus.

 Watch related author interview on StudySpace
wwnorton.com/web/westernciv18

fields stretched, almost unbroken, from Ireland to the Ukraine. Forests had been cleared, marshes drained, and pastureland reduced by generations of peasants performing lifetimes of backbreaking labor. But still, Europe was barely able to feed its people. At the same time, the warming trend that had begun in the late eighth century reversed itself. Even a reduction of one or two degrees centigrade is enough to cause substantial changes in rainfall patterns, shorten growing seasons, and lessen agricultural productivity. So it did in Europe, with disastrous consequences.

Evil Times: The Seven Years' Famine

Between the years 1315 to 1322, the cooling climate caused nearly continuous adverse weather conditions in northern Europe. Winters were extraordinarily severe: in 1316, the Baltic Sea froze over and ships were trapped in the ice. Rains prevented planting in spring or summer, and when a crop did manage to struggle through it would be dashed by rain and hail in autumn. In the midst of these natural calamities, dynastic warfare continued in the sodden wheatfields, as the princes of Scandinavia and the Holy Roman Empire fought for supremacy and succession. In the once-fertile fields of Flanders, French armies slogged through mud in continued efforts to subdue the Flemish population. On the Scottish and Welsh borders, uprisings were ruthlessly suppressed and the paltry storehouses of the natives were pillaged to feed the English raiders.

The result was human suffering more devastating than that caused by any famine affecting Europe since that time: hence the acceptance of the name "Great Famine" to describe this terrible crisis. Weakened by years of malnutrition and relentless efforts to counteract the climactic effects on the landscape, between 10 and 15 percent of the population of northern Europe perished. Many starved, and others

The Code of Chivalry: Putting Honor before Plunder

The Hundred Years' War between England and France pitted these two countries' warrior aristocracies against one another. Yet these knights had a great deal in common: they all spoke French, many were closely related, and they were supposed to share a common set of values. The following excerpt is taken from The Book of Chivalry *written in French by Geoffroi de Charny, a French nobleman and veteran of this war's first major battles who ultimately died in combat at Poitiers in 1356. Because the war was fought almost entirely on French soil, Geoffroi was keenly aware of the toll it took on the land and its people. In the following passage, he addresses the problem of how a knight can sustain his honor when he is driven to acquire booty for himself through the theft of others' property.*

Those Who Are Brave but Too Eager for Plunder

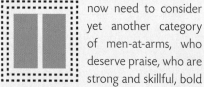 now need to consider yet another category of men-at-arms, who deserve praise, who are strong and skillful, bold and sparing no effort, some of whom always want to be at the forefront, riding as foragers to win booty or prisoners or other profit from the enemies of those on whose side they fight. And they know well how to do it skillfully and cleverly; and because they are so intent on plunder, it often happens that on the entry into a town won by force, those who are so greedy for plunder dash hither and thither and find themselves separated from those of their companions who have no thought for gain but only for completing their military undertaking. And it often happens that such men, those who ride after and hunt for great booty, are killed in the process—frequently it is not known how, sometimes by their enemies, sometimes through quarrels in which greed for plunder sets one man against another. It often occurs that through lack of those who chase after plunder before the battle is over, that which is thought to be already won can be lost again and lives or reputations as well. It can also happen in relation to such people who are very eager for booty that when there is action on the battlefield, there are a number of men who pay more attention to taking prisoners and other profit, and when they have seized them and other winnings, they are more anxious to safeguard their captives and their booty than to help to bring the battle to a good conclusion. And it may well be that a battle can be lost in this way. And one ought instead to be wary of the booty which results in the loss of honor, life, and possessions. In this vocation one should therefore set one's heart and mind on winning honor, which endures for ever, rather than on winning profit and booty, which one can lose within one single hour. And yet one should praise and value those men-at-arms who are able to make war on, inflict damage on, and win profit from their enemies, for they cannot do it without strenuous effort and great courage. But again I shall repeat: he who does best is most worthy.

Questions for Analysis

1. How does Geoffroi justify the act of plundering? What insights into contemporary military tactics does this passage provide?

2. Given that Geoffroi would have seen Englishmen pillaging French lands, do you find his justification of this activity surprising? Why or why not?

fell victim to epidemic diseases that affected both animals and people. In southern Europe, around the shores of the Mediterranean, the effects of climate change were more muted, and there were also different channels through which food could be distributed. Nonetheless, the overall health of this region suffered from the disruption of trade and the shortage of some staple goods, as well as from the highly unstable political situation we have already discussed.

As food grew scarcer, prices climbed unpredictably. Plans for future crops, which kept hope alive, would be dashed when spring arrived and flooded fields prevented seeds from germinating. Cold summers and autumns were spent foraging for food. Hunting was restricted to the nobility, but even those who risked the death penalty for poaching found little game. Wages did not keep pace with rising costs, and so those who lived in towns

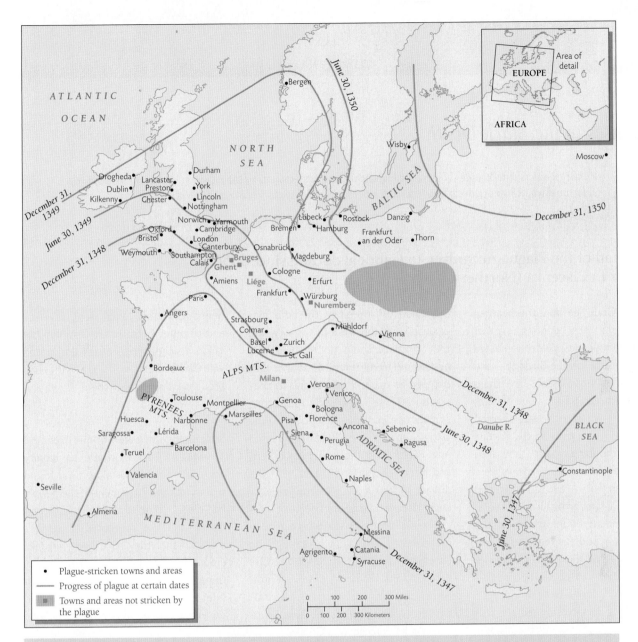

THE PROGRESS OF THE BLACK DEATH, FOURTEENTH CENTURY. ▪ *What trajectories did the Black Death follow once it was introduced into Europe?* ▪ *How might the growth of towns, trade, and travel have contributed to the spread of the Black Death?* ▪ *Would such a rapid advance have been likely during the early Middle Ages or even in the ancient world?*

and depended on markets had less to spend on scarce provisions. Only a year after the famine began, townspeople were dying of ailments that would not have been fatal in good years.

The effects of the famine were especially devastating for children, since even those who survived would be highly susceptible to disease, owing to the severe impairment of their immune systems. It may have been the Great Famine, then, that paved the way for the more transient (if more horrific) destruction of the Black Death.

A Crisis of Connectivity: Tracking the Black Death

The Black Death is the name given to a deadly pandemic that spread from China to Mongolia, northern India, and the Middle East during the 1330s and 1340s. By 1346, the plague had reached the Black Sea, where it was transmitted to the Genoese colonists at Caffa (as we noted above). From there, in 1347, Genoese ships inadvertently

Competing Viewpoints

Responses to the Black Death

> *Many chroniclers, intellectuals, and private individuals have left accounts of the plague in which they attempt to understand why it had occurred, how it spread, and how communities should respond to it.*

The Spread of the Plague According to Gabriele de' Mussi (d. 1356), a Lawyer in Piacenza (Northern Italy)

Oh God! See how the heathen Tartar races, pouring together from all sides, suddenly infested the city of Caffa [on the Black Sea] and besieged the trapped Christians there for almost three years.... But behold, [in 1346] the whole army was affected by a disease which overran the Tartars and killed thousands upon thousands every day. It was as though arrows were raining down from heaven to strike and crush the Tartars' arrogance. All medical advice and attention was useless; the Tartars died as soon as the signs of disease appeared on their bodies: swellings in the armpit or groin caused by coagulating humours, followed by a putrid fever.

The dying Tartars, stunned and stupefied by the immensity of the disaster brought about by the disease, and realising that they had no hope of escape, lost interest in the siege. But they ordered corpses to be placed in catapults and lobbed into the city in the hope that the intolerable stench would kill everyone inside. What seemed like mountains of dead were thrown into the city, and the Christians could not hide or flee or escape from them, although they dumped as many of the bodies as they could in the sea. And soon the rotting corpses tainted the air and poisoned the water supply.... Moreover one infected man could carry the poison to others, and infect people and places with the disease by look alone. No one knew, or could discover, a means of defence.

Thus almost everyone who had been in the East... fell victim... through the bitter events of 1346 to 1348—the Chinese, Indians, Persians, Medes, Kurds, Armenians, Cilicians, Georgians, Mesopotamians, Nubians, Ethiopians, Turks, Egyptians, Arabs, Saracens and Greeks....

* * *

As it happened, among those who escaped from Caffa by boat were a few sailors who had been infected with the poisonous disease. Some boats were bound for Genoa, others went to Venice and to other Christian areas. When the sailors reached these places and mixed with the people there, it was as if they had brought evil spirits with them....

* * *

Scarcely one in seven of the Genoese survived. In Venice, where an inquiry was held into the mortality, it was found that more than 70 percent of the people had died.... The rest of Italy, Sicily and Apulia and the neighbouring regions maintain that they have been virtually emptied of inhabitants.... The Roman Curia at Avignon, the provinces on both sides of the Rhône, Spain, France, and the Empire cry up their griefs....

* * *

Everyone has a responsibility to keep some record of the disease and the deaths, and because I am myself from Piacenza I have been urged to write more about what happened there in 1348....

brought it to Sicily and northern Italy. From Italy, it spread westward along trade routes, first striking seaports, then turning inland with the travelers who carried it. It moved with astonishing rapidity, advancing about two miles per day, summer or winter. By 1350, it had reached Scandinavia and northern Russia, then spread southward again until it linked up with the original waves of infection that had brought it from Central Asia to the Black Sea. It continued to erupt in local epidemics for the next 300 years; some localities could expect a renewed outbreak every decade. The last Europe-wide instance occurred between 1661 and 1669, although there were

I don't know where to begin. Cries and laments arise on all sides. Day after day one sees the Cross and the Host being carried about the city, and countless dead being buried.... The living made preparations for their [own] burial, and because there was not enough room for individual graves, pits had to be dug in colonnades and piazzas, where nobody had ever been buried before. It often happened that man and wife, father and son, mother and daughter, and soon the whole household and many neighbours, were buried together in one place....

A Letter from the Town Council of Cologne to the Town Council of Strasbourg (Germany), 12 January 1349

Very dear friends, all sorts of rumours are now flying about against Judaism and the Jews prompted by this unexpected and unparalleled mortality of Christians.... Throughout our city, as in yours, many-winged Fame clamours that this mortality was initially caused, and is still being spread, by the poisoning of springs and wells, and that the Jews must have dropped poisonous substances into them. When it came to our knowledge that serious charges had been made against the Jews in several small towns and villages on the basis of this mortality, we sent numerous letters to you and to other cities and towns to uncover the truth behind these rumours, and set a thorough investigation in train....

If a massacre of the Jews were to be allowed in the major cities (something which we are determined to prevent in our city, if we can, as long as the Jews are found to be innocent of these or similar actions) it could lead to the sort of outrages and disturbances which would whip up a popular revolt among the common people—and such revolts have in the past brought cities to misery and desolation. In any case we are still of the opinion that this mortality and its attendant circumstances are caused by divine vengeance and nothing else. Accordingly we intend to forbid any harassment of the Jews in our city because of these flying rumours, but to defend them faithfully and keep them safe, as our predecessors did—and we are convinced that you ought to do the same....

Source: From Rosemary Horrox, ed. and trans., *The Black Death* (Manchester: 1994), pp. 16–21, 219–20.

Questions for Analysis

1. How does Gabriele de' Mussi initially explain the causes of the plague? How does his understanding of it change as he traces its movements from East to West—and closer to Italy?

2. Why does the Council of Cologne wish to quell violence against the Jews? How does this reasoning complement or challenge what we have learned so far about the treatment of Jews in medieval Europe?

3. In your view, do these two perspectives display a rational approach to the horrors of the Black Death? Why or why not?

sporadic outbreaks in Poland and Russia until the end of the eighteenth century.

What caused the Black Death? In 2011, scientists were able to confirm that it can be traced to the deadly microbe *Yersinia pestis*, and that it did indeed originate in China. *Y. pestis* actually causes three different kinds of contagion: bubonic plague and its even deadlier cousins, septicemic plague and pneumonic plague. In its bubonic form, this microbe is carried by fleas that travel on the backs of rats; humans catch it only if they are bitten by an infected flea or rat. Bubonic plague attacks the lymphatic system, producing enormous swellings (buboes) of the lymph nodes in the groin, neck, and armpits. Septicemic plague occurs when an infected flea introduces the microbe directly into the human bloodstream, causing death within hours, often before any symptoms of the disease can manifest themselves. Pneumonic plague, perhaps the most frightening variation, results when *Y. pestis* infects the lungs, allowing the contagion to spread silently and invisibly, in the same ways as the common cold.

One of the things that made the Black Death so terrifying, therefore, was that it manifested itself in several different ways. Those afflicted by the hideous bubonic plague might actually recover, while others—seemingly untouched— might die suddenly, mysteriously. Immediate reactions understandably ranged from panic to resignation. Observers quickly realized that the plague was contagious, but precisely how it spread remained enigmatic. Some believed that it was caused by breathing "bad air" and so urged people to flee from stricken areas, which caused the disease to spread even faster.

Others looked for scapegoats and revived old conspiracy theories that implicated Jews in the poisoning of wells. Scores of Jewish communities were attacked and thousands of their inhabitants massacred in the Rhineland, southern France, and Christian Spain. (No such attacks are known to have occurred in Muslim areas of Spain or elsewhere in the Muslim world.) The papacy and some local authorities tried to halt these attacks, but these admonitions came too late. Another response to the plague was the flagellant movement, so called because of the whips (*flagella*) with which traveling bands of penitents lashed themselves in order to appease the wrath of God. But the unruly and sometimes hysterical mobs that gathered around the flagellants aroused the concern of both ecclesiastical and secular authorities, and the movement was suppressed by papal order.

CONCLUSION

The century between 1250 and 1350 was a time of significant change within all Western civilizations. The growing power of some monarchies led to encroachments on territories and cities that had once been independent, and that fueled resistance to these internal acts of colonization. The papacy, whose power had seemed so secure at the turn

After You Read This Chapter

Visit StudySpace for quizzes, additional review materials, and multimedia documents. **wwnorton.com/web/westernciv18**

REVIEWING THE OBJECTIVES

- The conquests of the Mongols had a significant impact on Europe. How?
- The expansion of commerce and communication between Eastern and Western civilizations created a new world system. What were some key characteristics of this system? What kinds of exchange did it enable?
- What were the short- and longer-term causes for the papacy's loss of prestige? Why was the papal court moved to Avignon?
- What is sovereignty? What were the effects of competition for sovereign among European rulers?
- What caused the Black Death? In what sense can it be seen as a product of the new world system that began with the Mongol conquests?

of the thirteenth century, would itself become a pawn in the keeping of the French king by the beginning of the fourteenth. Rome thereby lost its last source of authority while the New Rome, Constantinople, struggled to rebuild its prestige in the face of Mongol expansion. Yet for the Mongol khans and the merchants they favored, for seafaring civilizations like Venice and Genoa, for ambitious students at the universities, and for men on the make, the opportunities for advancement and mobility were great.

And there were still other factors at play during this era. Even in good times, Europe's population had outgrown its capacity to produce food, and when the climate grew cooler, years of cold summers and heavy rainfall took an enormous toll. Those regions most closely tied to the new global networks were also densely settled and urban, which made the shortage of food and the spread of disease more acute there. In short, the benefits and drawbacks of increased globalization were already beginning to manifest themselves in the early fourteenth century—700 years ago. The Black Death can be understood as the ultimate example of medieval connectivity and also as a modern phenomenon.

The scale of mortality caused by this pandemic is almost unimaginable, to us as to those who survived it. At least a third, and probably half, of Europe's people died between 1347 and 1353. In the countryside, entire villages disappeared. Cities and towns, overcrowded and unsanitary, were particularly vulnerable to plague and, thereafter, to outbreaks of violence. The immediate social consequences were profound, and so were the economic ones. Crops rotted in the fields, manufacturing ceased, and trade came to a standstill in affected areas. Basic commodities became scarcer and prices rose, prompting ineffectual efforts to control prices and to force the remaining able-bodied laborers to work.

These were the short-term effects. How did the Black Death matter to those who survived it—including ourselves? According to Ibn Khaldun (1332–1406), a Muslim historian who is considered one of the founders of modern historical methods, it marked the end of the old world and the beginning of a new one, which would require new systems of government, bodies of knowledge, and forms of art. Was he right? We will begin to answer that question in Chapter 11.

PEOPLE, IDEAS, AND EVENTS IN CONTEXT

- What accounts for the success of **GENGHIS KHAN** and his successors? What circumstances enabled **MARCO POLO**'s travels to China? To what extent does the term *PAX MONGOLICA* describe this era in history?

- How did seafaring communities like that of **GENOA** rise to prominence in this era? Why were new navigational aids like **PORTOLAN CHARTS** necessary?

- How do the paintings of **GIOTTO** capture contemporary attitudes toward the world? How does **DANTE**'s artistry respond to the religious and political trends of his day?

- What was at stake in the controversy between **BONIFACE VIII** and **PHILIP IV**? Why is the papacy's residency at **AVIGNON** called the **BABYLONIAN CAPTIVITY**? What is a **SACRAMENT**, and why were these rites so important?

- In what different ways did **LOUIS IX** of France and **EDWARD I** of England contribute to the sovereignty of their respective kingdoms? What was the relationship between claims to sovereignty and the causes of the **HUNDRED YEARS' WAR**?

- How did climate change contribute to the outbreak of the **GREAT FAMINE?**

- What were the long-term and short-term causes of the **BLACK DEATH?**

THINKING ABOUT CONNECTIONS

- If the Mongol khan Ögedei had not died in 1241, the Mongols could conceivably have continued their westward movement into Europe. Given what you have learned about Mongol rule, how might this have changed the history of the world?

- How do the patterns of conquest and colonization discussed in this chapter compare to those of earlier periods, particularly those of antiquity? How many of these developments were new in 1250–1350?

- We live in a world in which the global circulation of people, information, goods, and bacteria is rapid. How does the medieval system compare to ours? What features seem familiar?

STORY LINES

- The Black Death altered Europe in profound ways. The opportunities and challenges of this era are dynamically reflected in an array of developments.

- Some of these developments are associated with a new artistic and cultural movement known as the Renaissance, which began in Italy.

- Here, renewed appreciation of the classics and of Greek was facilitated by the flight of Greek-speaking intellectuals from Byzantium, as the Ottoman Turks absorbed the remaining lands of the eastern Roman Empire.

- Meanwhile, the competing territorial claims of Europe's sovereign powers led to large-scale warfare.

- Even after the papacy's return to Rome from Avignon, the failure of internal reform efforts led to the decline of papal credibility. Consequently, a number of influential religious leaders sought more radical reforms.

CHRONOLOGY

Before
You
Read
This
Chapter

Rebirth and Unrest, 1350–1453

n June 1381, thousands of laborers from the English countryside rose up in rebellion against local authorities. Most were peasants or village craftsmen who were dismissed as ignorant by contemporary chroniclers. Yet the revolt was carefully coordinated: Plans were spread in coded messages circulated by word of mouth and by the followers of a renegade Oxford professor, John Wycliffe, who had called for the redistribution of Church property and taught that common people should be able to read the Bible in their own language. The rebellion's immediate catalyst had been a series of exorbitant taxes levied by Parliament for the support of the ongoing war with France. But its more fundamental cause was an epidemic that had occurred thirty years earlier. The Black Death had reduced the entire population of Europe by 30 to 50 percent and had drastically altered the world of those who survived it. In this new world, workers were valuable and could stand up to those who paid them poorly or treated them like slaves. In that fateful summer of 1381, the workers of England even vowed to kill representatives of both the Church and the government—to kill (as they put it) all the lawyers—and to destroy all the documents that had been used to keep them in subjection. It was

357

a revolution, and it partly succeeded. Although the leaders were eventually captured and executed, the rebellion had made the strength of the common people known to all.

The fourteenth century is often seen as a time of crisis in the history of Western civilizations. Famine and plague cut fearful swaths through the population; war was a brutally recurrent fact of life; and the papacy spent seventy years in continuous exile from Italy, only to see its prestige decline further after its return to Rome. But this was also a time of extraordinary opportunity and achievement. The exhausted land of Europe recovered from centuries of overfarming, while workers gained the economic edge; eventually, some even gained social and political power. Meanwhile, popular and intellectual movements sought to reform the Church. A host of intellectual, artistic, and scientific innovations contributed to all of these phenomena.

This era of rebirth and unrest has been called by two different names: the later Middle Ages and the Renaissance. The latter refers to an intellectual and artistic movement that began in northern Italy, where the citizens of warring city-states desperately sought new models of governance and cultural cohesion by looking back to the older civilizations of Greece and Rome. But these are not two separate historical periods; rather they reflect two different ways of looking back at an era that is considered to be the immediate precursor of modernity. To understand it, we need to study it holistically. And we need to begin with a survey of Western civilizations after the Black Death.

THE PLAGUE CLAIMS A VICTIM. A priest gives last rites to a bedridden plague victim as a smiling devil pierces the dying man with a spear and as Christ looks mercifully down from heaven.
▪ *What are the possible meanings of this image?* ▪ *What does it reveal about contemporary attitudes toward death by plague?*

LIFE AFTER THE BLACK DEATH

By 1353, when the bubonic plague began to loosen its death grip on Europe, the Continent had lost nearly half of its population. This happened suddenly, within a half century, owing to a combination of famine and disease (see Chapter 10). In the following century, recurring outbreaks of the plague and frequent warfare in some regions would result in further drastic reductions. In Germany, some 400,000 villages disappeared. Around Paris, more than half of the farmland formerly under cultivation became pastureland. Elsewhere, abandoned fields returned to woodland, increasing the forested areas of Europe by about a third.

Life after the Black Death would therefore be radically different for those who survived it, because this massive depopulation would affect every aspect of existence, from nutrition to social mobility to spirituality.

First and foremost, it meant a relative abundance of food. The price of grain fell, which made it more affordable.

At the same time, the scarcity of workers made peasant labor more valuable: wages rose and work became easily obtainable. With wages high and food prices low, ordinary people could now afford more bread and could also spend their surplus cash on dairy products, meat, fish, fruits, and wine. As a result, the people of Europe were better nourished than they had ever been—better than many are today. A recent study of fifteenth-century rubbish dumps has concluded that the people of Glasgow (Scotland) ate a healthier diet in 1405 than they did in 2005.

The Rural Impact

In the countryside, a healthier ecological balance was almost immediately reestablished in the wake of the plague. And gradually, with the lessened demand for fuel and building materials, forests that had almost disappeared began to recover and expand. Meanwhile, the declining demand for grain allowed many farmers to expand their livestock herds. By turning arable land into pastureland, farmers reduced the need to hire so many workers and they also improved the fertility of the soil through manuring. Some farmers were even able to enlarge their holdings, because so much land had been abandoned.

Most of these innovations were made by small farmers because many great lords—individuals as well as monasteries—were slower to adjust to the changing circumstances. But some large landholders were quick to seize the advantage, responding to the shortage of workers and the rising cost of wages by forcing their tenants to perform additional unpaid labor. In parts of eastern Europe, many free peasants became serfs for the first time as a result. In Castile, Poland, and Germany, too, lords succeeded in imposing new forms of servitude.

In France and the Low Countries, by contrast, peasants remained relatively free, although many were forced to pay a variety of new fees and taxes to their lords or to the king. In England, where peasant bondage had been more common than in France, serfdom eventually disappeared altogether. Although the Peasants' Revolt of 1381 was ultimately unsuccessful, increased economic opportunity allowed English serfs to vote with their feet, either by moving to town or to the lands of a lord who offered more favorable terms: lower rents, more animals, fewer work requirements, and greater personal freedoms. Geographical mobility and social mobility are, as we have often noted, intertwined.

The Urban Impact

Mortality rates were high in the crowded cities and towns of Europe, but not all cities were equally affected by the plague and many recovered quickly. In London and Paris, for example, large-scale immigration from the countryside reversed the short-term declines caused by the plague. Many of these newcomers were women, whose economic opportunities (usually very limited) were greatly enhanced by urban labor shortages. Other urban areas suffered more from internal violence or warfare than from disease. In Florence, for example, the population rebounded quickly after the Black Death but was eventually depleted by civil unrest: by 1427, it had dropped from around 300,000 to about 100,000. In Toulouse (southwestern France), the population remained fairly stable until 1430, when it was reduced by a staggering 75 percent as a result of the ravages of the Hundred Years' War.

So while the overall population of Europe declined drastically because of the plague, it is noteworthy that a far larger percentage of all people were living in towns by 1500: approximately 20 percent as opposed to 10 or 15 percent prior to the Black Death. Fueling this urban growth was the increasing specialization of the late-medieval economy. With farmers under less pressure to produce grain in bulk, land could be devoted to livestock, dairy farming, and the production of a more diverse array of fruits and vegetables; and these could now be exchanged more efficiently on the open market.

Towns with links to extant trading networks benefited accordingly. In northern Germany, a group of entrepreneurial cities formed a coalition to build an entirely new mercantile corporation, the Hanseatic League, whose members came to control commerce from Britain and Scandinavia to the Baltic. In northern Italy, the increased demand for luxury goods—which even some peasants and urban laborers could now afford—brought renewed wealth to the spice- and silk-trading city of Venice and also to the fine-cloth manufacturers of Milan and the jewelers of Florence. Milan's armaments industry also prospered, supplying its warring neighbors and the armies of Europe.

Of course, not all urban areas flourished. The Franco-Flemish cities that had played such a large role in economic and cultural life since the eleventh century suffered a serious economic depression, exacerbated by incessant wars in the region. But, on the whole, surviving Europeans profited from the plague. A century afterward, they were poised to extend their commercial networks farther into Africa, Asia, and (ultimately) the Americas (see Chapter 12).

Popular Revolts and Rebellions

Although the consequences of the Black Death were ultimately beneficial for many, Europeans did not adjust easily to this new world; established elites, in particular, resisted the demands of newly powerful workers. When these demands were not met, violence erupted. Between 1350 and 1425, hundreds of popular rebellions challenged the status quo in many regions of Europe. In 1358, peasants in northeastern France rose up violently against their lords, destroying property, burning buildings and crops, and even murdering targeted individuals. This incident is known as the Jacquerie Rebellion, because all French peasants were caricatured by the aristocracy as "Jacques" ("Jack").

In England, as we have already noted, a very different uprising occurred in June of 1381, far more organized and involving a much wider segment of society. Thousands of people marched on London, targeting the bureaucracies of the royal government and the Church, capturing and killing the archbishop of Canterbury, and meeting personally with the fourteen-year-old king, Richard II, to demand an end to serfdom and taxation and to call for the redistribution of property. It ended with the arrest and execution of the ringleaders. In Florence, workers in the cloth industry—known as the Ciompi (*chee-OHM-pee*)—protested high unemployment and mistreatment by the manufacturers who also ran the Florentine government. They seized control of the city, demanding relief from taxes, full employment, and political representation. They maintained power for a remarkable six weeks before their reforms were revoked.

The local circumstances that lay behind each of these revolts were unique, but all of them exhibit certain common features. First of all, they were not bread riots spurred by destitution: those who took part in them were not protesting starvation wages, they were empowered by the new economic conditions and wanted to leverage their position in order to enact even larger changes. Some rebellions, like the English Peasants' Revolt, were touched off by resistance to new and higher taxes. Others, like the Jacquerie and the revolt of the Ciompi, took place at moments when unpopular governments were weakened by factionalism and military defeat. The English revolt was also fueled by the widespread perception of corruption within the Church and the royal administration.

Behind this social and political unrest, therefore, lies not poverty and hunger but the growing prosperity and self-confidence of village communities and urban laborers who were taking advantage of the changed economic circumstances that arose from the plague. For the most part, the rebels' hopes that they could fundamentally alter the conditions of their lives were frustrated. Kings, aristocrats, and urban oligarchs sometimes lost their nerve in the middle of an uprising, but they were almost always successful, after a time, in reasserting dominance. Yet this tradition of popular rebellion would remain an important feature of Western civilizations. It would eventually fuel the American War of Independence and the French Revolution (see Chapter 18), and it continues to this day.

Aristocratic Life in the Wake of the Plague

Although the urban elites and rural aristocracies of Europe did not adapt easily to "the world turned upside down" by the plague, this was hardly a period of crisis for those in power. Quite the contrary: many great families became far wealthier than their ancestors had ever been. Nor did the plague undermine the dominant position they had established. It did, however, make their situations substantially more complex and uncertain, at a time when the costs of maintaining a fashionable lifestyle were escalating rapidly.

Across Europe, most noble families continued to derive much of their revenue from vast land holdings. Many also tried to increase their sources of income through investment in trading ventures. In Catalonia, Italy, Germany, and England, this became common practice. In France and Castile, however, direct involvement in commerce was regarded as socially demeaning and was, therefore, avoided by established families. Commerce could still be a route to ennoblement in these kingdoms; but once aristocratic rank was achieved, one was expected to abandon these employments and adopt an appropriate way of life: living in a rural

A HUNTING PARTY. This fifteenth-century illustration shows an elaborately dressed group of noblemen and noblewomen setting out with falcons, accompanied by their servants and their dogs. Hunting, an activity restricted to the aristocracy, was an occasion for conspicuous consumption and display.

castle or urban palace surrounded by a lavish household, embracing the values and conventions of chivalry (engaging in the hunt, commissioning a family coat of arms), and serving the ruler at court and in war.

What it meant to be "noble" became, as a result, even more difficult to define than it had been during the twelfth and thirteenth centuries. In countries where noble rank entailed clearly defined legal privileges—such as the right to be tried only in special courts—proven descent from noble ancestors might be sufficient to qualify a family as noble in the eyes of the law. Legal nobility of this sort was, however, a somewhat less exclusive distinction than one might expect. In fifteenth-century Castile and Navarre, 10 to 15 percent of the total population had claims to be recognized as noble on these terms. In Poland, Hungary, and Scotland, the legally privileged nobility was closer to 5 percent, whereas in England and France fewer than 2 percent could plausibly claim the legal privileges of noble status.

Fundamentally, however, nobility was expressed and epitomized by an individual's lifestyle. Hereditary land ownership, political influence, deference from social inferiors, courtly manners, and the ostentatious display of wealth— these combined to constitute a family's honor and hence to mark it as noble. This means that, in practice, the social distinctions between noble and non-noble families were very hard to discern. And even on the battlefield, where the mark of nobility was to fight on horseback, the supremacy of the mounted knight was being threatened by the growing importance of professional soldiers, archers, crossbowmen, and artillery experts. There were even hints of a more radical critique of the aristocracy's claims to innate superiority. As the English rebels put it in 1381: "When Adam dug and Eve spun, Who then was a gentleman?" In other words, all social distinctions are entirely artificial.

Precisely because nobility was contested, those who claimed it took elaborate measures to assert their exclusive right to this status through conspicuous consumption. This accounts, in part, for the extraordinary number, variety, and richness of the artifacts and artworks that survive from this period. Aristocrats— or those who wanted to be classed as such—vied with one another in hosting lavish banquets, which required numerous costly utensils, specially decorated dining chambers, legions of servants, and the most exotic foods attainable. They dressed in rich and extravagant clothing: close-fitting doublets and hose with long pointed shoes for men, multilayered silk dresses with ornately festooned headdresses for women. They maintained enormous households: in France, around 1400, the Duke of Berry had 400 matched pairs of hunting dogs and 1,000 servants. They took part in elaborately ritualized tournaments and pageants, in which the participants pretended to be the heroes of chivalric romances. Aristocrats also emphasized their tastes and refinement by supporting authors and artists and some-

A NOBLE BANQUET. Uncle of the mad king Charles VI, the Duke of Berry left politics to his brothers, the Duke of Burgundy and the Duke of Anjou. In return, he received enormous subsidies from the royal government, which he spent on sumptuous buildings, festivals, and artworks, including the famous Book of Hours (prayer book), which includes this image. Here, the duke (seated at right, in blue) gives a New Year's Day banquet for his household, who exchange gifts while his hunting dogs dine on scraps from the table. In the background, knights confront one another in a tournament.

times by becoming accomplished artists themselves. Nobility existed only if it was recognized, and to be recognized noble status had to be constantly reasserted and displayed.

Rulers contributed to this process; indeed, they were among its principal supporters and patrons. Kings and princes across Europe competed in founding chivalric orders such as the Knights of the Garter in England and the Order of the Star in France. These orders honored men who had demonstrated the idealized virtues of knighthood, virtues celebrated as characteristic of the nobility as a whole. By exalting the nobility as a class, then, chivalric orders helped cement the links that bound the nobility to their kings and princes. These bonds were further strengthened by the gifts, pensions, offices, and marriage prospects that kings and princes could bestow on their noble followers.

Given the decline in the agricultural revenues of many noble estates, such rewards of princely service were critically important to maintaining noble fortunes. Indeed, the alliance that was forged in the fifteenth century between kings and their noble supporters would become one of the most characteristic features of Europe's ruling class. In France, this "Old Regime" (*ancien régime*) alliance lasted until the French Revolution of 1789. In Germany, Austria, and Russia, it would last until the outbreak of World War I. In England, it persisted in some respects until World War II.

Capturing Reality in Writing

The writings of literary artists who survived the Black Death, or who grew up in the decades immediately following it, are characterized by intense observations of the real world—and by appeals to a far larger and more diverse audience than their predecessors. We have noted that vernacular languages were becoming powerful vehicles for poetry and narrative in the twelfth century (see Chapter 9). Now they were being used to express some of the most innovative and critical perspectives on changing social mores, political developments, and philosophical outlooks. Behind this phenomenon lie three interrelated developments: the growing identification between vernacular language and the community of a realm, the still-increasing accessibility of education, and the emergence of a substantial reading public for literature in these languages. We can see these influences at work in three of the major authors who flourished during this period: Giovanni Boccaccio, Geoffrey Chaucer, and Christine de Pisan.

Boccaccio (*bohk-KAHT-chee-oh*, 1313–1375) is best known for *The Decameron*, a collection of prose tales about sex, adventure, and trickery. He presents these stories as being told over a period of ten days (hence the title of the book, which means "work of ten days"), by and for a sophisticated party of young women and men who have taken up residence in a country villa outside Florence in order to escape the ravages of the Black Death. Boccaccio borrowed the outlines of many of these tales from earlier sources, especially the fabliaux discussed in Chapter 9, but he couched them in a freely colloquial Italian. Whereas Dante had used the same Florentine dialect to evoke the awesome landscape of sacred history in the exquisite verse of his *Divine Comedy* (Chapter 10), Boccaccio used it to capture the foibles of human beings and their often graphic sexual exploits in plainspoken prose.

The English poet Geoffrey Chaucer (c. 1340–1400) is similar in many ways to Boccaccio, whose influence on him was profound. Chaucer was among the first generation of English authors whose compositions can be understood by modern readers of that language with relatively little effort. By the late fourteenth century, the Anglo-Saxon (Old English) tongue of England's preconquest inhabitants had mixed with the French dialect spoken by their Norman conquerors, to create the language which is the ancestor of our own: Middle English.

Chaucer's masterpiece is *The Canterbury Tales*. Like *The Decameron*, this is a collection of stories held together by a framing narrative. In this case, the stories are told by an array of people traveling together on a pilgrimage from London to the shrine of Saint Thomas Becket at Canterbury. But there are also significant differences between *The Decameron* and *The Canterbury Tales*. Chaucer's stories are in verse, for the most part, and they are recounted by people of all different classes—from a high-minded knight to a poor university student to a lusty widow. Each character tells a story that is particularly illustrative of his or her own occupation and outlook on the world, forming a kaleidoscopic human comedy.

This period, a generation or so after the Black Death, also saw the emergence of professional authors who made their living through the patronage of the aristocracy and the publication of their works. One of the first was a woman, Christine de Pisan (c. 1365–c. 1434). Although born in northern Italy, Christine spent her adult life in France, where her husband was a member of the king's household. When he died, the widowed Christine wrote to support herself and her children. She mastered a wide variety of literary genres, including treatises on chivalry and warfare, which she dedicated to King Charles VI of France. She also wrote for a larger and more popular audience. For example, her imaginative *Book of the City of Ladies* is an extended defense of the character, capacities, and history of women, designed to help female readers refute their male detractors. Christine also took part in a vigorous pamphlet campaign that condemned the misogynistic claims made by influential (male) authors like Boccaccio. This debate was ongoing for several hundred years and became so famous that it was given a name: the *querelle des femmes*, "the debate over women." Remarkably, Christine also wrote a song in praise of Joan of Arc. Sadly, she probably lived long enough to learn that this other extraordinary woman had been put to death for behaving in a way that was considered dangerously unwomanly (see below).

Visualizing Reality

Just as the desire to capture real experiences and convey real emotions was a dominant trait of the literature produced after the Black Death, so it was in the visual arts. This is evident both in the older arts of manuscript illumination and also in the new kinds of sculpture we discussed in Chapter 10. A further innovation in the fifteenth century was the technique of painting in oils, a medium pioneered in Flanders, where artists found a ready market for their works among the nobility and wealthy merchants.

CHRISTINE DE PISAN. One of the most prolific authors of the Middle Ages, Pisan used her influence to uphold the dignity of women and to celebrate their history and achievements. Here she is seen describing the prowess of an Amazon warrior who could defeat men effortlessly in armed combat.

Oil paints were a revolutionary development: because they do not dry as quickly as water-based pigments, a painter can work more slowly and carefully, taking time with more difficult aspects of the work and making corrections as needed. Masterful practitioners of this technique include Rogier van der Weyden (c. 1400–1464), who excelled at communicating both deep spiritual messages and the minute details of everyday life (see **Interpreting Visual Evidence** on page 366). Just as contemporary saints saw divinity in material objects, so too an artist could portray the Virgin and Child against a background vista of ordinary life, with people going about their business or a man urinating against a wall. This was not blasphemous. To the contrary, it conveyed the message that the events of the Bible are constantly present, here and now: Christ is our companion, such artworks suggest, not some distant figure whose life and outlook are irrelevant to us.

The same immediacy is also evident in medieval drama. Plays were often devotional exercises that involved the efforts of an entire community, but they also celebrated that community. In the English city of York, for example, an annual series of pageants reenacted the entire history of human salvation from the Creation to the Last Judgment in a single summer day, beginning at dawn and ending late at night. Each pageant was produced by a particular craft guild and showcased that guild's special talents: "The Last Supper" was performed by the bakers, whose bread was a key element in their reenactment of the first Eucharist, while "The Crucifixion" was performed by the nail makers and painters, whose wares were thereby put on prominent display in the depiction of Christ's bloody death on the cross. In Italy, confraternities competed with one another to honor the saints with songs and processions. In Catalonia and many regions of Spain, there were elaborate dramas celebrating the life and miracles of the Virgin, one of which is still performed every year in the Basque town of Elche: it is the oldest European play in continuous production. In northern France, the Low Countries, and German-speaking lands, civic spectacles were performed over a period of several days, celebrating local history or the place of the community in the sacred history of the Bible. But not all plays were pious. Some honored visiting kings and princes. Others celebrated the flouting of social conventions, featuring cross-dressing and the reversal of hierarchies. They were further expressions of the topsy-turvy world created by the Black Death.

Why a Woman Can Write about Warfare

Christine de Pisan (c. 1365–c. 1434) was one of the West's first professional writers, best known today for her Book of the City of Ladies *and* The Treasure of the City of Ladies, *works that aimed to provide women with an honorable and rich history and to combat generations of institutionalized misogyny. But in her own time, Christine was probably best known for the work excerpted here,* The Book of the Deeds of Arms and of Chivalry, *a manual of military strategy and conduct written at the height of the Hundred Years' War, in 1410.*

As boldness is essential for great undertakings, and without it nothing should be risked, I think it is proper in this present work to set forth my unworthiness to treat such exalted matter. I should not have dared even to think about it, but although boldness is blameworthy when it is foolhardy, I should state that I have not been inspired by arrogance or foolish presumption, but rather by true affection and a genuine desire for the welfare of noble men engaging in the profession of arms. I am encouraged, in the light of my other writings, to undertake to speak in this book of the most honorable office of arms and chivalry. . . . So to this end I have gathered together facts and subject matter from various books to produce this present volume. But inasmuch as it is fitting for this matter to be discussed factually, diligently, and sensibly . . . and also in consideration of the fact that military and lay experts in the aforesaid art of chivalry are not usually clerks or writers who are expert in

language, I intend to treat the matter in the plainest possible language. . . .

As this is unusual for women, who generally are occupied in weaving, spinning, and household duties, I humbly invoke . . . the wise lady Minerva [Athena], born in the land of Greece, whom the ancients esteemed highly for her great wisdom. Likewise the poet Boccaccio praises her in his *Book of Famous Women,* as do other writers praise her art and manner of making trappings of iron and steel, so let it not be held against me if I, as a woman, take it upon myself to treat of military matters. . . .

O Minerva! goddess of arms and of chivalry, who, by understanding beyond that of other women, did find and initiate among the other noble arts and sciences the custom of forging iron and steel armaments and harness both proper and suitable for covering and protecting men's bodies against arrows slung in battle—helmets, shields, and protective covering having come first from you—you instituted and gave directions for drawing up a battle order, how to begin an assault

and to engage in proper combat. . . . In the aforementioned country of Greece, you provided the usage of this office, and insofar as it may please you to be favorably disposed, and I in no way appear to be against the nation from which you came, the country beyond the Alps that is now called Apulia and Calabria in Italy, where you were born, let me say that like you I am an Italian woman.

Source: From *The Book of the Deeds of Arms and of Chivalry,* ed. Charity Cannon Willard and trans. Sumner Willard (University Park, PA: 1999), pp. 11–13.

Questions for Analysis

1. Christine very cleverly deflects potential criticism for her "boldness" in writing about warfare. What tactics does she use?

2. The Greco-Roman goddess Athena (Minerva) was the goddess of wisdom, weaving, and warfare. Why does Christine invoke her aid? What parallels does she draw between her own attributes and those of Minerva's?

THE BEGINNINGS OF THE RENAISSANCE IN ITALY

Rummaging through some old books in a cathedral library, an Italian bureaucrat attached to the papal court at Avignon was surprised to find a manuscript of Cicero's letters—letters that no living person had known to exist. They had probably been copied in the time of Charlemagne, but had then been forgotten for hundreds of years. How many other works of this great Roman orator had been lost to posterity? Clearly, thought Francesco Petrarca (1304–1374), he was living in an age of ignorance. A great gulf seemed to open up between his own time and

PETRARCH'S COPY OF VIRGIL. Petrarch's devotion to the classics of Roman literature prompted him to commission this new frontispiece for his treasured volume of Virgil's poetry. It was painted by the Sienese artist Simone Martini, who (like Petrarch) was attached to the papal court at Avignon. It is an allegorical depiction of Virgil (top right) and his poetic creations: the hero Aeneas (top left, wearing armor) and the farmer and shepherd whose humble labors are celebrated in Virgil's lesser-known works. The figure next to Aeneas is the fourth-century scholar Servius, who wrote a famous commentary on Virgil. He is shown drawing aside a curtain to reveal the poet in a creative trance. The two scrolls proclaim (in Latin) that Italy was the country that nourished famous poets and that Virgil helped it to achieve the glories of classical Greece. ■ *How does this image encapsulate and express Petrarch's devotion to the classical past?*

that of the ancients: a middle age that separated him from those well-loved models.

For centuries, Christian intellectuals had regarded "the dark ages" as the time between Adam's expulsion from Eden and the birth of Christ. But now, Petrarch (the name by which English-speakers call Petrarca) redefined that concept and applied it to his own era. According to him, the Middle Ages was not the pagan past but the time that separated him from direct communion with the classics. Yet this did not stop him from trying to bridge the gap. "I would

have written to you long ago," he said in a Latin letter to the Greek poet Homer (dead for over 2,000 years), "had it not been for the fact that we lack a common language."

Petrarch was famous in his own day as an Italian poet, a Latin stylist, and a tireless advocate for the resuscitation of the classical past. The values that he and his followers began to espouse would give rise to a new intellectual and artistic movement in Italy, a movement strongly critical of the present and admiring of a past that had disappeared with the fragmentation of Rome's empire and the end of Italy's greatness. We know this movement as the Renaissance, from the French word for "rebirth" that was applied to it in the eighteenth century and popularized in the nineteenth, when the term *medieval* was also invented. It has since become shorthand for the epoch *following* the Middle Ages—but it was really part of that same era.

Renaissance Classicism

Talking about "the Renaissance," then, is a way of talking about some significant changes in education and artistic outlook that transformed the culture of northern Italy from the late fourteenth to the early sixteenth centuries and that eventually influenced the rest of Europe in important ways. The term has often been taken literally, as though the cultural accomplishments of antiquity had ceased to be appreciated and therefore needed to be "reborn." Yet we have been tracing the enduring influence of classical civilization for many chapters, and we have constantly noted the reverence accorded to the heritage of antiquity, not to mention the persistence of Roman law and Roman institutions.

That said, one can certainly find distinguishing traits that make the concept of "renaissance" newly meaningful in this era. For example, there was a significant quantitative difference between the ancient texts available to scholars in the first thousand years after Rome's fragmentation and those that became accessible in the fourteenth and fifteenth centuries. The discovery of "new" works by Livy, Tacitus, and Lucretius expanded the classical canon considerably, supplementing the well-studied works of Virgil, Ovid, and Cicero. More important was the expanded access to ancient Greek literature in western Europe. In the twelfth and thirteenth centuries, as we have seen in Chapters 8 and 9, Greek scientific and philosophical works became available to western Europeans thanks to increased contact with Islam, via Latin translations of Arabic translations of the original Greek.

Still, no Greek poems or plays were yet available in Latin translations, and neither were the major dialogues of Plato. Moreover, only a handful of western Europeans could

Interpreting Visual Evidence

Realizing Devotion

These two paintings by the Flemish artist Rogier van der Weyden (*FAN-der-VIE-den*, c. 1400–1464) capture some of the most compelling characteristics of late medieval art, particularly the trend toward realistic representations of holy figures and sacred stories. On the left (image A), the artist depicts himself as the evangelist Luke, regarded in Christian tradition as a painter of portraits; he sketches the Virgin nursing the infant Jesus in a town house overlooking a Flemish city. On the right (image B), van der Weyden imagines the entombment of the dead Christ by his followers, including the Virgin (left), Mary Magdalene (kneeling), and the disciple John (right). Here, he makes use of a motif that became increasingly prominent in the later Middle Ages: Christ as the Man of Sorrows, displaying his wounds and inviting the viewer to share in his suffering. In both paintings, van der Weyden emphasizes the humanity of his subjects rather than their iconic status (see Chapter 7), and he places them in the urban and rural landscapes of his own world.

Questions for Analysis

1. How are these paintings different from the sacred images of the earlier Middle Ages (see, for example, pages 214 and 217)? What messages does the artist convey by setting these events in his own immediate present?

2. In what ways do these paintings reflect broad changes in popular piety and medieval devotional practices? Why, for example, would the artist display the dead and wounded body of Christ—rather than depicting him as resurrected and triumphant, or as an all-seeing creator and judge?

3. In general, how would you use these images as evidence of the worldview of the fifteenth century? What do they tell us about people's attitudes, emotions, and values?

A. Saint Luke drawing the portrait of the Virgin.

B. The Deposition.

read the language of classical Greece. But as the Mongols and, after them, the Ottoman Turks put increasing pressure on the shrinking borders of Byzantium (see below), more and more Greek-speaking intellectuals fled to Italy, bringing their books and their knowledge with them.

Thanks to these developments, some Italian intellectuals not only had increased access to more classical texts, they also used these texts in new ways. For centuries, Christian scholars had worked to bring ancient writings and values into line with their own beliefs (see Chapter 6). By contrast, the new reading methods pioneered by Petrarch and others fostered an increased awareness of the conceptual gap that separated the contemporary world from that of antiquity. This awakened a determination to recapture truly ancient worldviews and value systems, and it would eventually be expressed in visual terms, too. In the second half of the fifteenth century, especially, classical models contributed strikingly to the distinctive artistic style that is most strongly associated with the Renaissance (something we will address in Chapter 12).

Another distinguishing feature of this new perspective on the classical past was the way that it became overtly materialistic and commercialized. The competition among and within Italian city-states fostered a culture of display that used the symbols and artifacts of ancient Rome as pawns in an endless power game. Meanwhile, the relative weakness of the Church contributed to the growth of claims to power based on classical models—even by Italian bishops and Church-sponsored universities. When the papacy was eventually restored to Rome, it too had to compete in this Renaissance arena, by patronizing the artists and intellectuals who espoused these aesthetic and political ideals.

Renaissance Humanism

The most basic feature of this new intellectual and political agenda is summarized in the term *humanism*. This was a program of study that aimed to replace the scholastic emphasis on logic and theology—which would continue to be central to the curriculum of medieval universities like Paris and Oxford—with the study of ancient literature, rhetoric, history, and ethics. That is, the goal of a humanist education was the understanding of the human experience as viewed through the lenses of the classical past, and devoted to the fulfillment of human potential in the present. By contrast, a scholastic education filtered human experience through the teachings of scripture and the Church fathers, with human salvation as the ultimate goal.

Moreover, some intellectuals like Petrarch believed that the university curriculum concentrated too much on abstract speculation, rather than the achievement of virtue and ethical conduct in the here-and-now. He felt that the true Christian thinker must cultivate literary eloquence and so inspire others to do good through the pursuit of beauty and truth. And according to him, the best models of eloquence were to be found in the classics of Latin literature, which were also filled with ethical wisdom. Petrarch dedicated himself, therefore, to rediscovering such texts and to writing his own poems and moral treatises in a Latin style modeled on classical authors.

Humanists accordingly preferred ancient writings to those of more recent authors, including their own contemporaries. And although some humanists wrote in Italian as well as Latin, most regarded vernacular literature as a lesser diversion suitable only for the uneducated; serious scholarship and praiseworthy poetry could be written only in Latin or Greek. Proper Latin, moreover, had to be the classical Latin of Cicero and Virgil (Chapter 5), not the evolving language common to universities, international diplomacy, the law, and the Church. Renaissance humanists therefore condemned the living Latin of their day as a barbarous departure from classical (and therefore "correct") standards of Latin style. And ironically, their determination to revive this older language actually killed the lively Latin that had continued to flourish in Europe. By insisting on outmoded standards of grammar, syntax, and diction, they turned Latin into a fossilized discourse that ceased to have any direct relevance to daily life. They thus contributed, unwittingly, to the ultimate triumph of the various European vernaculars they despised, as well as to the demise of Latin as a common medium of communication.

Because humanism was an educational program designed to produce virtuous citizens and able public officials, it largely excluded women because women were largely excluded from Italian political life. Here again there is a paradox: as more and more Italian city-states fell into the hands of autocratic rulers, the humanist educational curriculum lost its immediate connection to the republican ideals of ancient Rome. Nevertheless, humanists never lost their conviction that the study of the "humanities" (as the humanist curriculum came to be known) was the best way to produce political leaders.

Why Italy?

These new attitudes toward education and the ancient past were fostered in a northern Italy for historically specific reasons. After the Black Death, this region was the most densely populated part of Europe; other urban areas, notably northeastern France and Flanders, had been decimated by the Great Famine as well as the plague. This region also differed from the rest of urbanized Europe because aristocratic families customarily lived in cities rather than in rural castles and consequently became more fully involved in public affairs than their counterparts north of the Alps. Moreover, many town-dwelling aristocrats were engaged in banking or mercantile enterprises, while many rich mercantile families imitated the manners of the aristocracy. The Florentine ruling family, the Medici, originally made their fortune in banking and commerce and yet were able to assimilate into the nobility.

These developments help to explain the emergence of the humanist ideals described above. Newly wealthy families were not content to have their sons learn only the skills necessary to becoming successful businessmen; they sought teachers who would impart the knowledge and finesse that would enable them to cut a figure in society, mix with their noble neighbors, and speak with authority on public affairs. Consequently, Italy produced and attracted a large number of independent intellectuals who were not affiliated with monasteries, cathedral schools, or universities—many of whom served as schoolmasters for wealthy young men while acting as cultural consultants and secretaries for their families. These intellectuals advertised their learning by producing political and ethical treatises and works of literature that would attract the attention of wealthy patrons or reflect well on the patrons they already had. As a result, Italian schools and private tutors turned out the best-educated laymen in all of Europe, men who constituted a new generation of wealthy, knowledgeable patrons ready to invest in the cultivation of new ideas and new forms of literary and artistic expression.

A second reason why late-medieval Italy was the birthplace of the Renaissance movement has to do with its vexed political situation. Unlike France and England, or the kingdoms of Spain, Scandinavia, and eastern Europe, Italy had no unifying political institutions. Italians therefore looked to the classical past for their time of glory, dreaming of a day when Rome would be, again, the center of the world. They boasted that ancient Roman monuments were omnipresent in their landscape and that classical Latin literature referred to cities and sites they recognized as their own.

Italians were particularly intent on reappropriating their classical heritage because they were seeking to establish an independent cultural identity that could help them oppose the intellectual and political supremacy of France. The removal of the papacy to Avignon had heightened antagonism between the city-states of Italy and the burgeoning nation-state beyond the Alps. This also explains the Italians' rejection of the scholasticism taught in northern Europe's universities and their embrace of intellectual alternatives. As Roman literature and learning took hold in the imaginations of Italy's intellectuals, so too did Roman art and architecture, for Roman models could help Italians create an artistic alternative to the dominant French school of Gothic architecture, just as Roman learning offered an intellectual alternative to the scholasticism of Paris.

Finally, this Italian Renaissance could not have occurred without the underpinning of Italian wealth gained through the commercial ventures described in Chapter 10. This wealth meant that talented men seeking employment and patronage were more likely to stay at home, fueling the artistic and intellectual competition that arose from the intensification of urban pride and the concentration of individual and family wealth in urban areas. Cities themselves became the primary patrons of art and learning in the fourteenth century.

The Renaissance of Civic Ideals

Petrarch's personal goal was a solitary life of contemplation and asceticism. But subsequent Italian intellectuals, especially those of Florence, developed a different vision of life's true purpose. For them, the goal of classical education was civic enrichment. Humanists such as Leonardo Bruni (c. 1370–1444) and Leon Battista Alberti (1404–1472) agreed with Petrarch on the importance of eloquence and the value of classical literature, but they also taught that man's nature equips him for action, for usefulness to his family and society, and for serving the state—ideally a city-state after the Florentine model. In their view, ambition and the quest for glory are noble impulses that ought to be encouraged and channeled toward these ends. They also refused to condemn the accumulation of material possessions, arguing that the history of human progress is inseparable from the human dominion of the earth and its resources.

Many of the humanists' civic ideals are expressed in Alberti's treatise *On the Family* (1443), in which the nuclear family is presented as the fundamental unit of the city-state and, as such, to be governed in such a way as to further the city-state's political and economic goals. Alberti accordingly argued that the family should mirror the city-state's organization. He therefore consigned women—who, in reality, governed the household—to childbearing, child rearing, and subservience to men even within this domestic realm. He asserted, furthermore, that women should play no role whatsoever in the public sphere. Although such dismissals of women's abilities were fiercely resisted by actual women, the humanism of the Renaissance was characterized by a pervasive denigration of them—a

Analyzing Primary Sources

A Renaissance Attitude toward Women

Italian society in the fourteenth and fifteenth centuries was characterized by marriage patterns in which men in their late twenties or thirties customarily married women in their mid- to late teens. This demographic fact probably contributed to the widely shared belief that wives were essentially children, who could not be trusted with important matters and who were best trained by being beaten. Renaissance humanism did little to change such attitudes. In some cases, it even reinforced them.

fter my wife had been settled in my house a few days, and after her first pangs of longing for her mother and family had begun to fade, I took her by the hand and showed her around the whole house. I explained that the loft was the place for grain and that the stores of wine and wood were kept in the cellar. I showed her where things needed for the table were kept, and so on, through the whole house. At the end there were no household goods of which my wife had not learned both the place and the purpose. . . .

Only my books and records and those of my ancestors did I determine to keep well sealed. . . . These my wife not only could not read, she could not even lay hands on them. I kept my records at all times . . . locked up and arranged in order in my study, almost like sacred and religious objects. I never gave my wife permission to enter that place, with me or alone. . . .

[Husbands] who take counsel with their wives . . . are madmen if they think true prudence or good counsel lies in the female brain. . . . For this very reason I have always tried carefully not to let any secret of mine be known to a woman. I did not doubt that my wife was most loving, and more discreet and modest in her ways than any, but I still considered it safer to have her unable, and not merely unwilling, to harm me. . . . Furthermore, I made it a rule never to speak with her of anything but household matters or questions of conduct, or of the children.

Source: Leon Battista Alberti, "On the Family," in *The Family in Renaissance Florence*, ed. and trans. Renée N. Watkins (Columbia, SC: 1969), pp. 208–13, as abridged in Julie O'Faolain and Lauro Martines, eds., *Not in God's Image: Women in History from the Greeks to the Victorians* (New York: 1973), pp. 187–88.

Questions for Analysis

1. For what reasons did Alberti argue that a wife should have no access to books or records?

2. Would you have expected humanism to make attitudes to women more liberal and "modern"? How do views like Alberti's challenge such assumptions?

3. Compare Alberti's view of women to that of Christine de Pisan (page 364). How do you think Christine would have responded to this passage?

---

denigration often mirrored in the works of classical literature that these humanists so much admired.

The Emergence of Textual Criticism

The humanists of Florence eventually surpassed Petrarch in their knowledge of classical literature and philosophy, especially that of ancient Greece. In this, they were aided by a number of Byzantine scholars who had migrated to Italy in the first half of the fifteenth century and who gave instruction in the ancient form of their own native language. Wealthy, well-connected Florentines increasingly aspired to acquire Greek masterpieces for themselves, which often involved journeys back to Constantinople. In 1423, one adventurous bibliophile managed to bring back 238 manuscript books, among them rare works of Sophocles, Euripides, and Thucydides. These were quickly paraphrased in Latin and thus made accessible to western Europeans for the first time.

This influx of new classical texts spurred a new interest in textual criticism. A pioneer in this activity was Lorenzo Valla (1407–1457). Born in Rome and active primarily as a secretary to the king of Naples and Sicily, Valla had no allegiance to the republican ideals of the Florentine humanists. Instead, he turned his skills to the painstaking analysis of Greek and Latin writings in order to show how the historical study of language could discredit old assumptions and even unmask some texts as forgeries. For example, some papal propagandists argued that the papacy's claim to secular power in Europe derived from rights granted to the bishop of Rome by the emperor Constantine in the fourth century, enshrined in a document known as "The Donation of Constantine." By analyzing the language of this spurious text, Valla proved that it could not have been written in the time of Constantine because it contained more recent Latin usages and vocabulary.

This demonstration not only discredited more traditional scholarly methods, it made the concept of anachronism central to all subsequent textual study and historical thought. Indeed, Valla even applied his expert knowledge of Greek to elucidating the meaning of Saint Paul's letters, which he believed had been obscured by Jerome's Latin translation (see Chapter 6). This work was to prove an important link between Italian Renaissance scholarship and the subsequent Christian humanism of the north, which in turn fed into the Reformation (see Chapter 13).

THE END OF THE EASTERN ROMAN EMPIRE

The Greek-speaking refugees who arrived in Italy after the Black Death were self-appointed exiles. They were responding to the succession of calamities that had reduced the once-proud eastern Roman Empire to a scattering of embattled provinces. As we've noted, when Constantinople fell to western crusaders in 1204, the surrounding territories of Byzantium were severed from the capital that had held them together as constituent parts of that empire (see Chapter 9). When the Latin presence in Constantinople was finally expelled in 1261, imperial power had been so weakened that it extended only into the immediate hinterlands of the city and to parts of the Greek Peloponnese. The rest of the empire had become a collection of small principalities that existed in precarious alliance with the Mongols and indeed depended on the Pax Mongolica for survival (see Chapter 10). Then, with the coming of the Black Death, the imperial capital suffered the loss of half of its inhabitants and

shrunk still further. Meanwhile, the disintegration of the Mongol Empire laid the larger region of Anatolia open to a new set of invaders.

The Rise of the Ottoman Turks

Like the Mongols, the Turks were originally a nomadic people whose economy depended on raiding. When the Mongols arrived in northwestern Anatolia, the Turks were already established there and were being converted to Islam by the resident Muslim powers of the region: the Seljuq Sultanate of Rûm and the Abbasid Caliphate of Baghdad. But when the Mongols toppled these older powers, they eliminated the two traditional authorities that had kept Turkish border chieftains in check. Now they were free to raid, unhindered, along the soft frontiers of Byzantium. At the same time, they remained far enough from the centers of Mongol authority to avoid being destroyed themselves. One of their chieftains, Osman Gazi (1258–1326), established his own independent kingdom. Eventually, his name would characterize the Turkish dynasty that controlled the most ancient lands of Western civilizations for six centuries: the Ottomans.

By the mid-fourteenth century, Osman's successors had solidified their preeminence by capturing a number of important cities. These successes brought the Ottomans to the attention of the Byzantine emperor, who hired a contingent of them as mercenaries in 1345. They were extraordinarily successful—so much so that the eastern Roman Empire could not control their movements. They struck out on their own and began to extend their control westward. By 1370, their holdings stretched all the way to the Danube. In 1389, they defeated a powerful coalition of Serbian forces at the battle of Kosovo, which enabled them to begin subduing Bulgaria, the Balkans, and eventually Greece. In 1396, the Ottoman army even attacked Constantinople itself, although it withdrew to repel an ineffectual crusading force that had been hastily sent by the papacy.

In 1402, another attack on Constantinople was deflected—this time, by a more potent foe who had ambitions to match those of the Ottomans. Timur the Lame (Tamerlane, as he was called by European admirers) was born to a family of small landholders in the Mongol Khanate of Chagatai (named for its first ruler, the second son of Genghis Khan). Although Timur may have been a Turk himself, he acted as the spiritual heir of the Mongol Empire. While still a young man, he rose to prominence as a military leader and gained a reputation for tactical genius. He was no politician, though, and never officially assumed the title of khan in any of the territories he dominated. Instead, he moved ceaselessly from conquest to conquest, becoming the master of lands stretching

THE HEAD OF TIMUR THE LAME. This bust of the Mongol leader known in the West as Tamerlane is based on a forensic reconstruction of his exhumed skull.

from the Caspian Sea to the Volga River, as well as most of Persia. For a time, it looked briefly as if the Mongol Empire might be reunited under his reign. But Timur died in 1405, on his way to invade China, and his various conquests fell into the hands of local rulers. Mongol influence continued in the Mughal Empire of India, whose rulers claimed descent from the followers of Genghis Khan. But in Anatolia, the Ottoman Turks were once again on the rise.

The Fall of Constantinople

After the death of Timur, Ottoman pressure on Constantinople resumed and escalated. During the 1420s and 1430s, monasteries and schools that had been established since the fourth century found themselves in the path of an advancing army, and a steady stream of fleeing scholars strove to salvage a millennium's worth of Byzantine books—many of them preserving the heritage of ancient Greece and the Hellenistic

world. Then, in 1451, the Ottoman sultan Mehmet II turned his full attention to the conquest of the imperial city. In 1453, after a brilliantly executed siege, his army succeeded in breaching its walls. The Byzantine emperor was killed in the assault, the city itself was plundered, and its remaining population was sold into slavery. The Ottomans then settled down to rule their new capital in a style reminiscent of their Byzantine predecessors.

The Ottoman conquest of Constantinople administered an enormous shock to European rulers and intellectuals—and, indeed, the latter would profit mightily from this event. Yet its actual political and economic impact was minor. Ottoman control may have reduced European access to the Black Sea, but the bulk of the Far Eastern luxury trade with Europe had never passed through Black Sea ports in the first place. Europeans got most of their spices and silks through Venice, which imported them from Alexandria and Beirut, and these two cities did not fall to the Ottomans until the 1520s. Moreover, as we saw in Chapter 10, Europeans already had colonial ambitions and significant trading interests in Africa and the Atlantic that connected them to far-reaching networks.

But if the practical effects of the Ottoman conquest were modest where western Europe was concerned, the effects on the Turks themselves were transformative. Vast new wealth poured into Anatolia, which the Ottomans increased by carefully tending to the industrial and commercial interests of their new capital city, Constantinople, which they also called Istanbul—the Turkish pronunciation of the Greek phrase *eis tan polin* "in (or to) the city." Trade routes were redirected to feed the capital, and the Ottomans became a naval power in the eastern Mediterranean as well as in the Black Sea. As a result, Constantinople's population grew rapidly, from fewer than 100,000 in 1453 to more than 500,000. By 1600, it was the largest city in the world outside of China.

Slavery and Social Advancement in the Ottoman Empire

Despite the Ottomans' careful attention to commerce, their empire continued to rest on the spoils of conquest. To manage its continual expansion, the size of the Ottoman army and administration grew exponentially, drawing more and more manpower from conquered territories. And because both army and bureaucracy were largely composed of slaves, the demand for more soldiers and administrators could best be met through further conquests that would capture yet more slaves. Those conquests, however, required a still larger army and an even more extensive bureaucracy—and so the cycle continued. It mirrors, in many respects, the

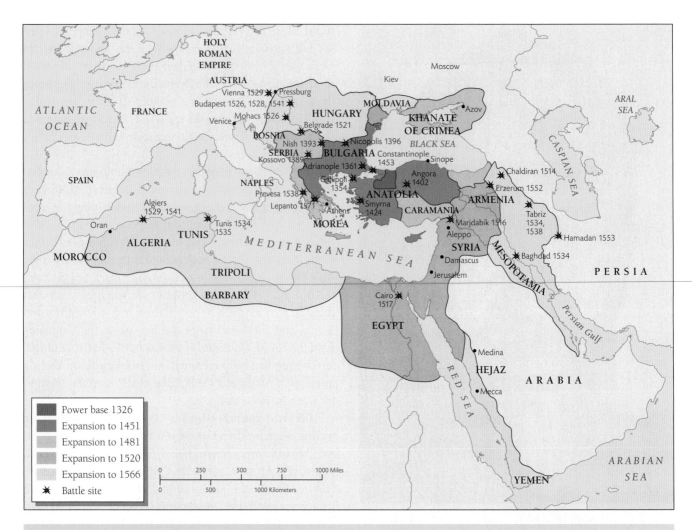

Legend:
- Power base 1326
- Expansion to 1451
- Expansion to 1481
- Expansion to 1520
- Expansion to 1566
- ✳ Battle site

Scale: 0, 250, 500, 750, 1000 Miles / 0, 500, 1000 Kilometers

THE GROWTH OF THE OTTOMAN EMPIRE. Consider the patterns of Ottoman expansion revealed in this map. ▪ *Where is Constantinople, and how might the capture of Constantinople in 1453 have facilitated further conquests?* ▪ *Compare the extent of the Ottoman Empire in 1566 with that of the Byzantine Empire under Justinian (see the map on page 212). How would you account for their similarities?*

dilemma of the Roman Empire in the centuries of its rapid expansion beyond Italy (see Chapter 5), which created an insatiable demand for slaves.

Not only were slaves the backbone of Ottoman government, they were also critical to the lives of the Turkish upper class. One of the important measures of status in Ottoman society was the number of slaves in one's household. After the capture of Constantinople, new wealth would permit some elites to maintain households in the thousands. By the sixteenth century, the sultan alone possessed more than 20,000 slave attendants, not including his bodyguard and elite infantry units, both of which also comprised slaves.

Where did all of these slaves come from? Many were captured in war. Many others were taken on raiding forays into Poland and Ukraine and sold to Crimean slave merchants, who shipped their captives to the slave markets of Constantinople. But slaves were also recruited (some willingly, some by coercion) from rural areas of the Otto-

man Empire itself. Because the vast majority of slaves were household servants and administrators rather than laborers, some men willingly accepted enslavement, believing that they would be better off as slaves in Constantinople than as impoverished peasants in the countryside. In the Balkans especially, many people were enslaved as children, handed over by their families to pay the "child tax" the Ottomans imposed on rural areas too poor to pay a monetary tribute. Although an excruciating experience for families, this practice did open up opportunities for social advancement. Special academies were created at Constantinople to train the most able of the enslaved male children to act as administrators and soldiers, some of whom rose to become powerful figures in the Ottoman Empire.

For this reason, slavery carried relatively little social stigma. Even the sultan himself was most often the son of an enslaved woman. And because Muslims were not permitted to enslave other Muslims, the vast majority of Ottoman

SULTAN MEHMET II, "THE CONQUEROR" (r. 1451–81). This portrait, executed by the Ottoman artist Siblizade Ahmed, exhibits features characteristic of both Central Asia and Europe. The sultan's pose—his aesthetic appreciation of the rose, his elegant handkerchief—are indicative of the former, as is the fact that he wears the white turban of a scholar and the thumb ring of an archer. But the subdued coloring and three-quarter profile may reflect the influence of Italian portraits. ▪ *What did the artist achieve through this blending of styles and symbols?* ▪ *What messages does this portrait convey?*

welcome refuge from the persecutions and expulsions that had characterized Jewish life in late-medieval Europe. After their expulsion from Spain in 1492 (see Chapter 12), more than 100,000 Spanish (Sephardic) Jews ultimately immigrated to the territories of the Ottoman Empire.

Because the Ottoman sultans were Sunni Muslims, they often dealt harshly with other Muslim sects. But they were extremely tolerant of non-Muslims. They organized the major religious groups of their empire into legally recognized units and permitted them considerable rights of self-government. They were especially careful to protect and promote the authority of the Greek Orthodox patriarch of Constantinople over the Orthodox Christians of their empire. As a result, the Ottomans enjoyed staunch support from their Orthodox Christian subjects during their wars with the Christians of western Europe.

Russia: "The Third Rome"

The Orthodox Church also received staunch support from the Russian people, whose own Church had been founded by Byzantine missionaries in the tenth century (see Chapter 8) and whose written language was based on the Greek alphabet and Greek grammar. Indeed, the emerging duchy of Muscovy (see Chapter 10) saw itself as the natural protector and ally of the eastern Roman Empire, and its alienation from western Europe increased as Byzantium grew weaker and the responsibility for defending Orthodox Christianity devolved onto the Russian Church.

But when the patriarch of Constantinople agreed to submit to the authority of Rome in 1438, in the desperate hope that the papacy would rally military support for the besieged city, Russian clergy refused to follow suit. After Constantinople fell to the Turks—predictably, without any help from Latin Christendom—the Russian Church emerged as the only surviving proponent of Orthodox Christianity.

Its sense of isolation was increased by developments on its western borders. In the thirteenth century, the small kingdom of Poland had struggled to defend itself from absorption by German princes. But when the Holy Roman Empire's strength waned after the death of Frederick the Great (see Chapter 9), Poland's situation grew more secure. In 1386, its reigning queen, Jadwiga, subsequently enabled its dramatic expansion when she married Jagiello, the duke of neighboring Lithuania, thus doubling the size of her kingdom. Lithuania had begun to carve out an extensive territory stretching from the Baltic to modern-day Belarus and Ukraine, and this expansionist momentum increased after its union with Poland. In 1410, a combined Polish and Lithuanian force defeated the Teutonic Knights at the Battle of Tannenberg,

slaves were Christian—although many eventually converted to Islam. And because so many of the elite positions within Ottoman government were held by these slaves, the paradoxical result was that Muslims, including the Turks themselves, were effectively excluded from the main avenues of social and political influence in the Ottoman Empire. Avenues to power were therefore remarkably open to men of ability and talent, most of them non-Muslim slaves.

Nor was this power limited to the government and the army. Commerce and business also remained largely in the hands of non-Muslims, most frequently Greeks, Syrians, and Jews. Jews in particular found in the Ottoman Empire a crushing the military order that controlled a crucial region lying between the allied kingdoms. Thereafter, Poland-Lithuania began to push eastward toward Muscovy.

Although many of Lithuania's aristocratic families were Orthodox Christians, the established church in Poland was loyal to Rome. Thus, when the inhabitants of Muscovy started to feel threatened by Poland-Lithuania, one way of constructing a shared Muscovite identity was to direct hostility toward Latin Christendom. Another was to take up the imperial mantle that had been abandoned when Constantinople fell, and to declare the Muscovite state the divinely appointed successor to Rome. To drive the point home, Muscovite dukes began to take the title of tsar, "caesar." "Two Romes have fallen," said a Muscovite chronicler, "the third is still standing, and a fourth there shall not be."

WARFARE AND NATION-BUILDING IN EUROPE

War has always been an engine for the development of new technologies. This is something we have noted since Chapter 1, but in the era after the Black Death the pace and scale of warfare was escalated to an unprecedented degree—and so was the deployment of new weapons. Although explosives had been invented in China, and originally used in displays of fireworks, they were first put to devastating and destructive effect in Europe. In fact, the earliest cannons were as dangerous to those who fired them as to those who were targeted. But by the middle of the fifteenth century, they were reliable enough to revolutionize the nature of warfare. In 1453, heavy artillery played a leading role in the outcomes of two crucial conflicts: the Ottoman Turks breached the ancient defenses of Constantinople with cannon fire and the French captured the English-held city of Bordeaux, bringing an end to the attenuated conflict known as the Hundred Years' War.

Thereafter, cannons made it more difficult for rebellious aristocrats to hole up in their stone castles and so consequently aided in the consolidation of national monarchies. Cannons placed aboard ships made Europe's developing navies more effective. A handheld firearm, the pistol, was also invented in the fourteenth century, and around 1500 the musket ended forever the military dominance of heavily armored cavalry, giving the advantage to foot soldiers recruited from the ranks of average citizens.

This suggests that there is a symbiotic relationship between warfare and nation-building as well as between warfare and technology. Because Europeans were almost constantly at war from the fourteenth century to the middle of the twentieth, governments claimed new powers to tax their subjects and to control their subjects' lives. Armies became larger, military technology deadlier. Wars became more destructive, society more militarized. As a result of these developments, the most successful European states were aggressively expansionist and aggressively engaged in creating an idea of national identity that would bind people together against a common enemy.

The Hundred Years' War Resumes

The hostilities that make up the Hundred Years' War can be divided into three main phases (see the maps on page 000). The first phase dates from the initial declaration of war in 1337 (see Chapter 10), after which the English won a series of startling military victories before the Black Death put a temporary halt to the hostilities. The war then resumed in 1356, with another English victory at Poitiers. Four years later, in 1360, Edward III decided to leverage his strong position: he renounced his larger claim to the French throne, and in return he was to be guaranteed full sovereignty over a greatly enlarged duchy of Gascony and the promise of a huge ransom for the king of France, whom he held captive.

But the terms of the treaty were never honored, nor did it resolve the underlying issues that had led to the war itself, namely the problem of making good on any claim to sovereignty in contested territory and the question of the English king's place in the French royal succession. The French king continued to treat the English king as his vassal, while Edward and his heirs quickly renewed their claim to the throne of France.

Although there were no pitched battles in France itself for two decades after this, a destabilizing proxy war developed during the 1360s and 1370s, which spread violence to neighboring regions. Both the English troops (posted in Gascony) and the French troops (eager to avenge their losses) were reluctant to settle down. Many organized into "Free Companies" of mercenaries and hired themselves out in the service of hostile factions in Castile and competing city-states in northern Italy. By 1376, when the conflict between England and France was reignited, the Hundred Years' War had become a Europe-wide phenomenon.

England's Disputed Throne and the Brief Victory of Henry V

In this second phase of the war, the tide quickly shifted in favor of France. The new king, Charles V (r. 1364–80), imposed a series of taxes to fund the raising of an army,

A FIFTEENTH-CENTURY SIEGE WITH CANNONS. Cannons were an essential element in siege warfare during the Hundred Years' War.

restored order by disbanding the Free Companies, and hired the leader of one of these bands as the commander of his army. He thereby created a professional military that could match the English in discipline and tactics. By 1380, English territories in France had been reduced to a core area around the southwestern city of Bordeaux and the port of Calais in the extreme northeast.

Meanwhile, the aging Edward III has been succeeded by his nine-year-old grandson, Richard II (r. 1377–99), who was too young to prosecute a claim to the French crown. This was problematic, because the war had been extremely popular in England. Indeed, its mismanagement by Richard's advisers was one of the issues that triggered the Peasants' Revolt in 1381. And when Richard came of age and showed no signs of martial ambition, many of his own aristocratic relatives turned against him. Richard retaliated against the ringleader of this faction, his cousin Henry of Lancaster, by sending him into exile and confiscating his property. Henry's supporters used this as pretext for rebellion. In 1399, Richard was deposed by Henry and eventually murdered.

As a usurper whose legitimacy was always in doubt, Henry IV (r. 1399–1413) struggled to maintain his authority in the face of retaliatory rebellions and other challenges to his kingship. The best way to unite the country would have been to renew the war against France, but Henry was

frequently ill and in no position to lead an army into combat. But when his son Henry V succeeded him in 1413, the new king immediately began to prepare for an invasion. His timing was excellent: the French royal government was foundering owing to the insanity of the reigning king, Charles VI (r. 1380–1422). A brilliant diplomat as well as a capable soldier, Henry V sealed an alliance with the powerful Duke of Burgundy, who was allegedly loyal to France but stood to gain from its defeat at the hands of the English. Henry also made a treaty with the German emperor, who agreed not to come to France's aid.

When he crossed the Channel in the autumn of 1415, Henry V's troops thus faced a much-depleted French army that could not rely on reinforcements. Although it was still vastly larger and boasted hundreds of mounted knights, it was undisciplined. It was also severely hampered by bad weather and deep mud when the two armies clashed at Agincourt on October 25 of that year—conditions that favored the lighter English infantry. Henry's men managed to win a crushing victory.

Then, over the next five years, Henry conquered most of northern France. In 1420, the ailing Charles VI was forced to recognize him as heir to the throne of France, thereby disinheriting his own son. (This prince bore the ceremonial title of *dauphin*, "the dolphin," from the heraldic device of the borderland province he inherited.) Henry sealed the deal by

marrying the French princess, Catherine, and fathering an heir to the joint kingdom of England and France.

Joan of Arc's Betrayal and Legacy

Unlike his great-grandfather Edward III, who used his claim to the French throne largely as a bargaining chip to secure sovereignty over Gascony (see Chapter 10), Henry V honestly believed himself to be the rightful king of France. And his astonishing success in capturing the kingdom seemed to put the stamp of divine approval on that claim. But Henry's successes in France also transformed the nature of the war, turning it from a profitable war of conquest and plunder into an extended and expensive military occupation. It might have been sustainable had Henry been as long-lived as many of his predecessors. But he died early in 1422, just short of his thirty-sixth birthday. King Charles VI died only a few months later.

The new king of England and France, Henry VI (r. 1422–61), was only an infant, and yet the English armies under the command of his regents continued to press southward into territories held by the dauphin. Although it seemed unlikely that English forces would ever succeed

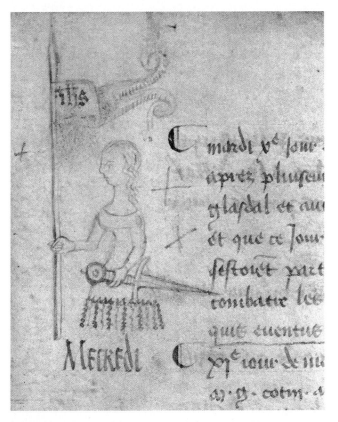

JOAN OF ARC. A contemporary sketch of Joan was drawn in the margin of this register documenting official proceedings at the Parlement of Paris in 1429.

in dislodging him, confidence in the dauphin's right to the throne had been shattered by his own mother's declaration that he was illegitimate. It might have happened that England would once again rule an empire comprising much of northern France, as it had for a century and a half after the Norman conquest.

But this scenario fails to reckon with Joan of Arc. In 1429, a peasant girl from Lorraine (a territory only nominally part of France) made her way to the dauphin's court and announced that an angel had told her that he, Charles, was the rightful king, and that she, Joan, should drive the English out of France. The fact that she even got a hearing underscores the hopelessness of the dauphin's position, as does the extraordinary fact that he gave her a contingent of troops. With this force, Joan liberated the strategic city of Orléans, then under siege by the English, after which a series of victories culminated in Charles's coronation in the cathedral of Reims, the traditional site for the crowning of French kings.

But, despite her miraculous success, Joan was an embarrassment whose very charisma made her dangerous: a peasant leading aristocrats, a woman leading men, and a commoner who claimed to have been commissioned by God. When, a few months later, the Burgundians captured her in battle and handed her over to the English, the king she had helped to crown did nothing to save her. Accused of witchcraft, condemned by the theologians of Paris, and tried for heresy by an English ecclesiastical court, Joan was burned to death in the market square at Rouen in 1431. She was nineteen years old.

The French forces whom Joan had inspired, however, continued on the offensive. In 1435, the duke of Burgundy withdrew from his alliance with England, and when the young English king, Henry VI, proved first incompetent and then insane, a series of French military victories brought hostilities to an end with the capture of Bordeaux in 1453. English kings would threaten to renew the war for another century, and Anglo-French hostility would last until the defeat of Napoleon in 1815. But after 1453, English control over French territory would be limited to the port of Calais, which eventually fell in 1558.

The Long Shadow of the Hundred Years' War

The Hundred Years' War challenged the very existence of France. The disintegration of that kingdom, first during the 1350s and 1360s, and again between 1415 and 1435, glaringly revealed the fragility of the bonds that tied the king to the nobility, and the royal capital Paris to the kingdom's

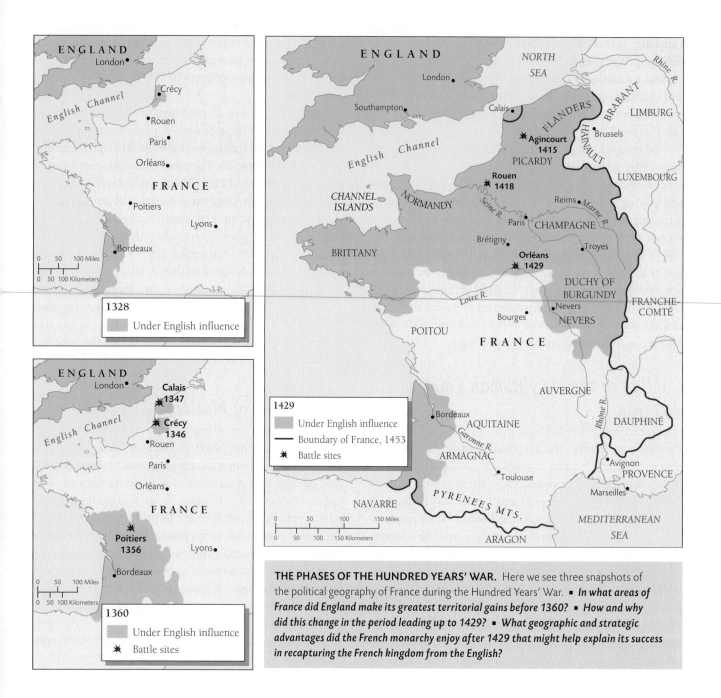

THE PHASES OF THE HUNDRED YEARS' WAR. Here we see three snapshots of the political geography of France during the Hundred Years' War. ▪ *In what areas of France did England make its greatest territorial gains before 1360?* ▪ *How and why did this change in the period leading up to 1429?* ▪ *What geographic and strategic advantages did the French monarchy enjoy after 1429 that might help explain its success in recapturing the French kingdom from the English?*

outlying regions. Nonetheless, the king's power was actually increased by the war's end, laying the foundations on which the power of early modern France would be built.

The Hundred Years' War also had dramatic effects on the English monarchy. When English armies in France were successful, the king rode a wave of popularity that fueled an emerging sense of English identity. When the war turned against the English, however, defeats abroad undermined support for the monarch at home. Of the nine English kings who ruled England between 1307 and 1485, five were deposed and murdered by factions.

This was a consequence of England's peculiar form of kingship, whose strength depended on the king's ability to mobilize popular support through Parliament while maintaining the support of his nobility through successful wars. Failure to maintain this balance was even more destabilizing in England than it would have been elsewhere, precisely because royal power was so centralized. In France, the nobility could endure the insanity of Charles VI because his government was not powerful enough to threaten them. In England, neither the nobility nor the nation could afford the weak kingship of Henry VI. The result was an aristocratic rebellion against the king that led to a full-blown civil war: the Wars of the Roses, so called—by the novelist Sir Walter Scott (1771–1832)—because of the floral emblems, red and white, adopted by the two competing noble families

Lancaster and York. It ended only when a Lancastrian claimant, Henry Tudor (r. 1485–1509), resolved the dynastic feud by marrying Elizabeth of York, ruling as Henry VII and establishing a new Tudor dynasty whose symbol was a rose with both white and red petals. His son was Henry VIII (see Chapter 13).

So, despite England's ultimate defeat, the Hundred Years' War strengthened English identity in several ways. First, it equated national identity with the power of the state and its king. Second, it fomented a strong anti-French sentiment that led to the triumph of the English vernacular over French for the first time since the Norman conquest over 300 years earlier: the first English court to speak English was that of Richard II, a patron of Geoffrey Chaucer. And having lost its continental possessions, England became, for the first time, a self-contained island nation that looked to the sea for defense and opportunity—not to the Continent. This would later prove to be an advantage in many ways.

Conflict in the Holy Roman Empire and Italy

Elsewhere in Europe, the perpetual warfare that began to characterize the history of Western civilizations in this period was even more destructive than it proved to be in the struggle between England and France. In the lands of the Holy Roman Empire, armed conflict among territorial princes, and between these princes and the German emperor, weakened all combatants significantly. Periodically, a powerful emperor would emerge to play a major role, but the dominant trend was toward the continuing dissolution of power, with German princes dividing their territories among their heirs while free cities and local lords strove to shake off the princes' rule. Between 1350 and 1450, near anarchy prevailed in many regions. Only in the eastern regions of the empire were the rulers of Bavaria, Austria, and Brandenburg-Prussia able to strengthen their authority, mostly by supporting the efforts of the nobility to subject their peasants to serfdom and by conquering and colonizing new territories on their eastern frontiers.

In northern and central Italy, the last half of the fourteenth century was also marked by incessant conflict. With the papacy based in Avignon, the Papal States collapsed and Rome itself was riven by factional violence. Warfare among northern city-states added to the violence caused by urban rebellions in the wake of the plague. But around 1400, Venice, Milan, and Florence had succeeded in stabilizing their differing forms of government. Venice was now ruled by an oligarchy of merchants; Milan by a family of despots; and Florence was ruled as a republic but dominated by the influence of a few wealthy clans, especially the Medici banking family. Having settled their internal problems, these three cities then began to expand their influence by subordinating other cities to their rule.

Eventually, almost all the towns of northern Italy were allied with one of these powers. An exception was Genoa, which had its own trading empire in the Mediterranean and Atlantic (see Chapter 10). The papacy, meanwhile, reasserted its control over central Italy when it was restored to Rome in 1377. The southern kingdom of Naples and Sicily persisted as a separate entity but a constantly unstable one, riven by local warfare and poor government. After 1453, when the Hundred Years' War had ended and Ottoman expansion had been checked at Constantinople, an uneasy peace was achieved in Italy. But diplomacy and frequently shifting alliances did little to check the ambitions of any one state for further expansion, and it could not change the fact that none of these small-scale states could oppose the powerful national monarchies or empires that surrounded Italy.

The Growth of National Monarchies

In France and England, then, as well as in smaller kingdoms like Scotland and Portugal, the later Middle Ages saw the emergence of European states more cohesive than any that had existed before. (In Chapter 12, we will see how powerful this cohesion made the new united kingdom of Spain.) The basic political patterns established in the formative twelfth and thirteenth centuries had made this possible, yet the active construction of a sense of national identity in these territories, and the fusion of that identity with kingship, were new phenomena. Forged by war and fueled by the growing cultural importance of vernacular languages, this fusion produced a new type of political organization: the national monarchy.

The advantages of these national monarchies when compared to older forms of political organization—such as the empire, the principality, or the city-state—would become very evident. When the armies of France or Spain invaded the Italian peninsula at the end of the fifteenth century, neither the militias of the city-states nor the far-flung resources of Venice were a match for them. Germany and the Low Countries would suffer similar invasions only a few generations later and, along with Italy, would remain battlegrounds for competing armies until the middle of the nineteenth century. But the new national monarchies brought significant disadvantages, too. They guaranteed the prevalence of warfare in Europe as they continued their struggle for sovereignty and territory, and they would eventually transport their rivalry to every corner of the globe in the late nineteenth and early twentieth centuries.

The Condemnation of Joan of Arc by the University of Paris, 1431

After Joan's capture by the Burgundians, she was handed over to the English and tried for heresy at an ecclesiastical court set up in Rouen. It was on this occasion that the theology faculty of Paris pronounced the following verdict on her actions.

 ou, Joan, have said that, since the age of thirteen, you have experienced revelations and the appearance of angels, of St. Catherine and St. Margaret, and that you have very often seen them with your bodily eyes, and that they have spoken to you. As for the first point, the clerks of the University of Paris have considered the manner of the said revelations and appearances . . . Having considered all . . . they have declared that all the things mentioned above are lies, falsenesses, misleading and pernicious things and that such revelations are superstitions, proceeding from wicked and diabolical spirits.

Item: You have said that your king had a sign by which he knew that you were sent by God, for St. Michael, accompanied by several angels, some of which having wings, the others crowns, with St. Catherine and St. Margaret, came to you at the chateau of Chinon. All the company ascended through the floors of the castle until they came to the room of your king, before whom the angel bearing the crown bowed. . . .

As for this matter, the clerks say that it is not in the least probable, but it is rather a presumptuous lie, misleading and pernicious, a false statement, derogatory of the dignity of the Church and of the angels. . . .

Item: you have said that, at God's command, you have continually worn men's clothes, and that you have put on a short robe, doublet, shoes attached by points, also that you have had short hair, cut around above the ears, without retaining anything on your person which shows that you are a woman, and that several times you have received the body of Our Lord dressed in this fashion, despite having been admonished to give it up several times, the which you would not do. You have said that you would rather die than abandon the said clothing, if it were not at God's command, and that if you were wearing those clothes and were with the king, and those of your party, it would be one of the greatest benefits for the kingdom of France. You have also said that not for anything would you swear an oath not to wear the said clothing and carry arms any longer. And all these things you say you

have done for the good and at the command of God. As for these things, the clerics say that you blaspheme God and hold him in contempt in his sacraments; you transgress Divine Law, Holy Scripture, and canon law. You err in the faith. You boast in vanity. You are suspected of idolatry and you have condemned yourself in not wishing to wear clothing suitable to your sex, but you follow the custom of Gentiles and Saracens.

Source: Carolyne Larrington, ed. and trans., *Women and Writing in Medieval Europe* (New York: 1995), pp. 183–84.

Questions for Analysis

1. Paris was in the hands of the English when this condemnation was issued. Is there any evidence that its authors were coerced into making this pronouncement?

2. On what grounds was Joan condemned for heresy?

3. In what ways does Joan's behavior highlight larger trends in late medieval spirituality and popular piety?

THE TRIALS OF THE ROMAN CHURCH

Although the century after the Black Death would witness the papacy's return to Rome, it would also witness changes in the Church that would have far-reaching consequences in the centuries to come. Like other large landowners, the monasteries of Europe suffered from the economic changes brought about by the new world order, as did the Church's bishops, who confronted the same dilemmas as the secular nobility. But no ecclesiastical institution suffered more severe trials than the papacy, which endured almost seventy years of exile from Rome followed by a debilitating forty-year schism. It then faced a protracted battle with reformers who sought to reduce the pope's role

in Church governance. Even though the papacy won this battle in the short term, the renewed abuse of papal power would, in the long run, bring about the permanent schism caused by the Reformation of the sixteenth century (see Chapter 13).

The Great Western Schism

In the decades that were transforming European society in so many other ways, calls for the papacy's return to Rome grew more insistent. It was eventually brought about by the letter-writing campaign of the nun and mystic Catherine of Siena (1347–1380), whose teasing but pious missives to Gregory XI (r. 1370–78) alternately shamed and coerced him. In 1377, he was persuaded to make the move.

But the papacy's restoration was short lived. A year after Gregory's return to Rome, he died. His cardinals—many of them Frenchmen—struggled to interpret the wishes of the volatile Romans, whose habit of expressing themselves through violence was unsettling to outsiders. Later, the cardinals would claim to have capitulated to the Roman mob when they elected an Italian candidate, Urban VI. When Urban fell out with them soon afterward, the cardinals fled the city and, from a safe distance, declared his selection invalid because it had been made under duress. They then elected a new pope, a Frenchman who took the name Clement VII. Urban retaliated by naming a new and entirely Italian College of Cardinals and by refusing Clement access to the city. The French pope and his cardinals withdrew ignominiously to the papal palace in Avignon, while the Italian pope remained in Rome.

The resulting rift is known as the Great Schism, or the Great Western Schism (to distinguish it from the Great East–West Schism between the Latin and Orthodox Churches). Between 1378 and 1417, the Roman Church was divided between two (and, ultimately, three) competing papacies, each claiming to be legitimate and each denouncing the heresy of the others.

Not surprisingly, Europe's religious allegiances fractured along the political lines drawn by the ongoing Hundred Years' War: France and her allies Scotland, Castile, Aragon, and Naples recognized the pope in Avignon; whereas England, Germany, northern Italy, Scandinavia, Bohemia, Poland, and Hungary recognized the Roman pope. Nor was there any obvious way to end this embarrassing state of affairs. The two rival Colleges of Cardinals continued to elect successors every time a pope died, perpetuating the problem. Finally, in 1409, some cardinals from both camps met at Pisa, where they ceremoniously declared the deposition of both popes and named a new one from among their number. But neither of the popes reigning in Rome and Avignon accepted that decision, so there were now three rival popes excommunicating one another instead of only two.

The Council of Constance and the Failure of the Conciliar Movement

This debacle was ultimately addressed between 1414 and 1418 at the Council of Constance, the largest and longest ecclesiastical gathering since the Council of Nicea, over a thousand years before (see Chapter 6). Its chief mission was to remove all rival claimants for papal office before agreeing on the election of a new pope: an Italian who took the name Martin V. But many of the council's delegates had even more far-reaching plans for the reform of the Church, ambitions that stemmed from the legal doctrine that gave the council power to depose and elect popes in the first place.

This doctrine, known as conciliarism, holds that supreme authority within the Church rests not with the pope but with a representative general council—and not just the council convened at Constance but any future council. The delegates at Constance thus decreed that general councils should meet regularly to oversee the governance of the Church, and to act as a check on the unbridled use of papal power.

Had conciliarism triumphed, the Reformation of the following century might not have occurred. But, predictably, Martin V and his successors did everything they could to undermine this doctrine, precisely because it limited their power. When the next general council met at Siena in 1423, Pope Martin duly sent representatives—who then turned around and went back to Rome. (The Council of Constance had specified that councils must meet frequently but had not specified how long those meetings should last.) The following year, the delegates to a general council at Basel took steps to ensure that the pope could not dismiss it, after which a lengthy struggle for power ensued between the advocates of papal monarchy and the conciliarists. Twenty-five years later, in 1449, the Council of Basel dissolved itself, bringing to an end a radical experiment in conciliar government—and dashing the hopes of those who thought it would lead to an internal reformation thorough enough to keep the Roman Church intact.

Spiritual Challenges

We have noted that the spiritual and social lives of medieval Christians were inextricably intertwined; indeed, any distinction between the two would have made little sense to

Past and Present

Replacing "Retired" Popes

When Benedict XVI decided to retire from papal office in February 2013, pundits and theologians alike struggled to find a precedent for this extraordinary decision. Most reached back to the year 1417, when Pope Martin V was elected at the Council of Constance (left) to replace the "retired" Gregory XII. But in this case, the retirement was not voluntary—and it was accompanied by the enforced resignation of an additional rival pope and the excommunication of yet another. The installation mass of Pope Francis in March 2013 (right) was much more universally celebrated and much more public than that of his medieval predecessor.

Watch related author interview on StudySpace
wwnorton.com/web/westernciv18

---

the people of this era. The parish church stood literally at the center of their lives. Churchyards were communal meeting places, sometimes even the sites of markets, and church buildings were a refuge from attack and a gathering place for parish business. The church's holidays marked the passage of the year, and the church's bells marked the hours of the day. The church was holy, but it was also essential to daily life.

Yet, in the wake of the Black Death, when many parishes ceased to exist and many communities were decimated, an increasing number of medieval Christians were not satisfied with these conventional practices and developed forms of piety that were distinctly controversial. Many are regarded today as saints, but this was not necessarily the case in their lifetimes. Indeed, the distinction between the superhuman powers of a saint and those of a witch could be difficult to discern. As Joan of Arc's predicament reveals, medieval women found it particularly challenging to find outlets for their piety that would not earn

them the condemnation of the Church. (Executed as heretic, Joan would be officially exonerated a generation later, but she would not be canonized as a saint until 1920, when belief in her intercession during World War I gained wide support and was considered a decisive factor in the victory of France and its allies.)

Many women therefore internalized their devotional practices or confined them to the domestic sphere—sometimes to the inconvenience of their families and communities. For example, the young Catherine of Siena (who later convinced the papacy to return to Rome) refused to help with the housework or to support her working-class family; instead, she took over one of the house's two rooms for her own private prayers, confining her parents and a dozen siblings to the remaining room. Julianne of Norwich (1342–1416) withdrew from the world into a small cell built next to her local church, where she spent the rest of her life in prayer and contemplation. Her

Council or Pope?

> The Great Schism spurred a fundamental and far-reaching debate about the nature of authority within the Church. Arguments for papal supremacy rested on traditional claims that the popes were the successors of Saint Peter, to whom Jesus Christ had delegated his own authority. Arguments for the supremacy of a general council had been advanced by many intellectuals throughout the fourteenth century, but it was only in the circumstances of the schism that these arguments found a wide audience. The following documents trace the history of the controversy, from the declaration of conciliar supremacy at the Council of Constance (Haec Sancta), to the council's efforts to guarantee regular meetings of general councils thereafter (Frequens), to the papal condemnation of appeals to the authority of general councils issued in 1460 (Execrabilis).

Haec Sancta Synodus (1415)

This holy synod of Constance . . . declares that being lawfully assembled in the Holy Spirit, constituting a general council and representing the Catholic Church Militant, it has its power directly from Christ, and that all persons of whatever rank or dignity, even a Pope, are bound to obey it in matters relating to faith and the end of the Schism and the general reformation of the church of God in head and members.

Further, it declares that any person of whatever position, rank, or dignity, even a Pope, who contumaciously refuses to obey the mandates, statutes, ordinances, or regulations enacted or to be enacted by this holy synod, or by any other general council lawfully assembled, relating to the matters aforesaid or to other matters involved with them, shall, unless he repents, be . . . duly punished. . . .

Source: R. L. Loomis, ed. and trans., *The Council of Constance* (New York: 1961), p. 229.

Frequens (1417)

The frequent holding of general councils is the best method of cultivating the field of the Lord, for they root out the briars, thorns, and thistles of heresies, errors, and schisms, correct abuses, make crooked things straight, and prepare the Lord's vineyard for fruitfulness and rich fertility. Neglect of general councils sows the seeds of these evils and encourages their growth. This truth is borne in upon us as we recall times past and survey the present.

Therefore by perpetual edict we . . . ordain that henceforth general councils shall be held as follows: the first within the five years immediately following the end of the present council, the second within seven years from the end of the council next after this, and subsequently

younger contemporary, the housewife Margery Kempe (c. 1372–c. 1439), resented the fact that she had a husband, several children, and a household to support, and thus could not take such a step. In later life, she renounced her wifely duties and devoted her life to performing acts of histrionic piety, which alienated many of those who came into contact with her. For example, she was so moved by the contemplation of Jesus's sufferings on the cross that she would cry hysterically for hours, disrupting the Mass. When on pilgrimage in Rome, she cried at the sight of babies that reminded her of the infant Jesus, or young men whom she thought resembled him.

The extraordinary piety of such individuals could be inspiring, but it could also threaten the Church's control over religious life and the links that bound individuals to their communities. It could, therefore, be dangerous. More safely orthodox was the practical mysticism preached by Thomas à Kempis, whose *Imitation of Christ* (c. 1427) taught readers how to appreciate aspects of the divine in their everyday lives. Originally written in Latin, *The Imitation* was quickly

every ten years forever.... Thus there will always be a certain continuity. Either a council will be in session or one will be expected at the end of a fixed period. . . .

Source: R. L. Loomis, ed. and trans., *The Council of Constance* (New York: 1961), pp. 246–47.

Execrabilis (1460)

An execrable abuse, unheard of in earlier times, has sprung up in our period. Some men, imbued with a spirit of rebellion and moved not by a desire for sound decisions but rather by a desire to escape the punishment for sin, suppose that they can appeal from the Pope, Vicar of Jesus Christ—from the Pope, to whom in the person of blessed Peter it was said, "Feed my sheep" and "whatever you bind on earth will be bound in heaven"—from this Pope to a future council. How harmful this is to the Christian republic, as well as how contrary to canon law, anyone who is not ignorant of the law can understand. For . . . who would not consider it ridiculous to appeal to something which does not now exist anywhere nor does anyone know when it will exist? The poor are heavily oppressed by the powerful, offenses remain unpunished, rebellion against the Holy See is encouraged, license for sin is granted, and all ecclesiastical discipline and hierarchical ranking of the Church are turned upside down.

Wishing therefore to expel this deadly poison from the Church of Christ, and concerned with the salvation of the sheep committed to us . . . with the counsel and assent of our venerable brothers, the Cardinals of the Holy Roman Church, together with the counsel and assent of all those prelates who have been trained in canon and civil law who follow our Court, and with our own certain knowledge, we condemn appeals of this kind, reject them as erroneous and abominable, and declare them to be completely null and void. And we lay down that from now on, no one should dare . . . to make such an appeal from our decisions, be they legal or theological, or from any commands at all from us or our successors. . . .

Source: Reprinted by permission of the publisher from Gabriel Biel, *Defensorium Obedientiae Apostolicae et Alia Documenta*, ed. and trans. Heiko A. Oberman, Daniel E. Zerfoss, and William J. Courtenay (Cambridge, MA: 1968), pp. 224–27. Copyright © 1968 by the President and Fellows of Harvard College.

Questions for Analysis

1. On what grounds does *Haec Sancta* establish the authority of a council? Why would this be considered a threat to papal power?

2. Why was it considered necessary for councils to meet regularly (*Frequens*)? What might have been the logical consequences of such regular meetings?

3. On what grounds does *Execrabilis* condemn the appeals to future councils that have no specified meeting date? Why would it not have condemned the conciliar movement altogether?

---

translated into many vernacular languages and is now more widely read than any other Christian book except the Bible.

Popular Reform Movements

For the most part, the threat of heretical movements was less dangerous to the Church than the corruption of the papacy. But in the kingdoms of England and Bohemia (the modern Czech Republic), some popular movements did pose serious challenges. The key figure in both cases was John Wycliffe (c. 1330–1384), an Oxford theologian and powerful critic of the Church. A survivor of the Black Death, Wycliffe lived at a time when the authority and integrity of the papacy were at a particularly low ebb. Indeed, he concluded that the empty sacraments of a corrupt Church could not save anyone. He therefore urged the English king to confiscate ecclesiastical wealth and to replace corrupt priests and bishops with men who would live according to apostolic standards of poverty and piety.

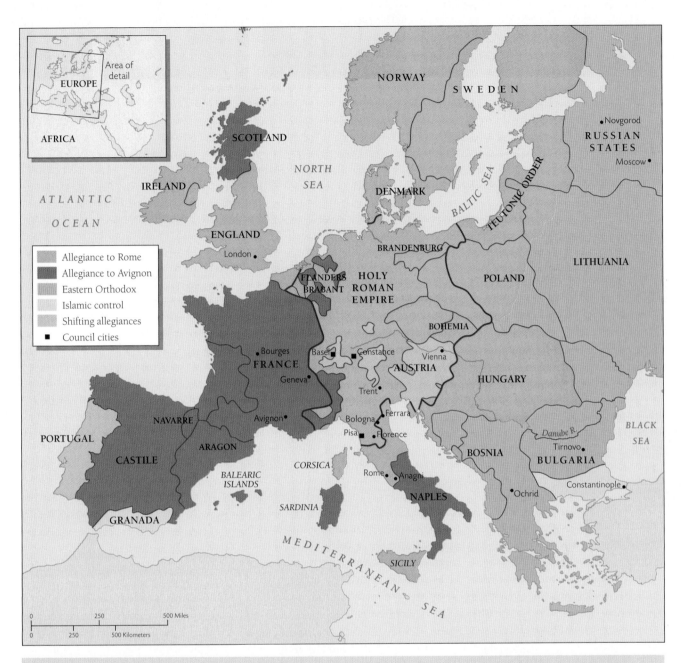

THE GREAT SCHISM, 1378–1417. During the Great Western Schism, the various territories of Europe were divided in their allegiances.
▪ *According to the map key, who were they choosing between?* ▪ *What common interests would have united the supporters of the Avignon pope or of the Roman pope?* ▪ *Why would areas like Portugal and Austria waver in their support?*

Some of Wycliffe's followers, known to their detractors as Lollards (from a word meaning "mumblers" or "beggars"), went even further, dismissing the sacraments as fraudulent attempts to extort money from the faithful. Lollard preachers also advocated for direct access to the scriptures and promoted an English translation of the Bible sponsored by Wycliffe himself.

Wycliffe's teachings played an important role in the Peasants' Revolt of 1381, and Lollardy gained numerous adherents in the decades after his death. The movement

was even supported by a number of aristocratic families; certainly the idea of dissolving the Church's wealth would have been attractive to many of those who stood to gain from it. But, after a failed Lollard uprising in 1414, both the movement and its supporters went underground in England.

In Bohemia and eastern Europe, however, Wycliffe's ideas lived on and struck even deeper roots. They were adopted by Jan Hus (c. 1373–1415), a charismatic teacher at the royal university in Prague. In contrast to the Lollards,

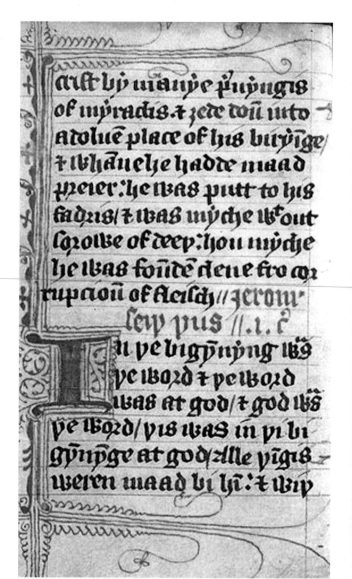

who had scornfully dismissed the Mass and thereby lost much popular support, Hus emphasized the centrality of the Eucharist to Christian piety. Indeed, he demanded that the laity be allowed to receive not only the conse- crated bread but also the consecrated wine, which was usually reserved solely for priests. This demand became a rallying cry for the Hussite movement. Influential nobles also supported Hus, partly in the hope that the reforms he demanded might restore revenues they had lost to the Church over the previous century.

Accordingly, most of Bohemia was behind him when Hus traveled to the Council of Constance to publish his views and to urge the assembled delegates to undertake sweeping reforms. But rather than giving him a hearing, the other delegates to the council convicted Hus of heresy and

had him burned at the stake. Back home, Hus's supporters raised the banner of open revolt, and the aristocracy took advantage of the situation to seize Church property. Between 1420 and 1424, armed bands of fervent Hussites resoundingly defeated several armies, as priests, artisans, and peasants rallied to pursue Hus's goals of religious reform and social justice.

These victories increased popular fervor, but they also made radical reformers increasingly volatile. In 1434, accordingly, a more conservative arm of the Hussite movement was able to negotiate a settlement with the Bohemian church. By the terms of this settlement, Bohemians could receive both the bread and wine of the Mass, which thus placed them beyond the pale of Latin orthodoxy and effectively separated the Bohemian national church from the Church of Rome.

Lollardy and Hussitism exhibit a number of striking similarities. Both began in the university and then spread to the countryside. Both called for the clergy to live in simplicity and poverty, and both attracted noble support, especially in their early days. Both movements were also strongly nationalistic, employing their own vernacular languages (English and Czech) and identifying themselves with the English or Czech people in opposition to a "foreign" Church. They also relied on vernacular preaching and social activism. In all these respects, they established patterns that would emerge again in the vastly larger currents of the Protestant Reformation (see Chapter 13).

CONCLUSION

The century after the Black Death was a period of tremendous creativity and revolutionary change. The effects of the plague were catastrophic, but the resulting food surpluses, opportunities for expansion, and labor shortages encouraged experimentation and opened up broad avenues for enrichment. Europe's economy diversified and expanded, and increasing wealth and access to education produced new forms of art and new ways of looking at the world. Hundreds and perhaps thousands of new schools were

After You Read This Chapter

Visit StudySpace for quizzes, additional review materials, and multimedia documents. **wwnorton.com/web/westernciv18**

REVIEWING THE OBJECTIVES

- The Black Death had short-term and long-term effects on the economy and societies of Europe. What were some of the most important changes?
- The later "Middle Ages" and "the Renaissance" are often perceived to be two different periods, but the latter was actually part of the former. Explain why.
- What were some of the intellectual, cultural, and artistic innovations of this era in Italy and elsewhere in Europe?
- How were some European kingdoms becoming stronger and more centralized during this period? What are some examples of national monarchies?
- The conciliar movement sought to limit the power of the papacy. How? Why was this movement unsuccessful?

established, and scores of new universities would emerge as a result. Women were still excluded from formal schooling but nevertheless became active—and in many cases dominant—participants in literary endeavors, cultural life, and religious movements. Average men and women not only became more active in cultivating their own worldly goals, they also took control of their spiritual destinies at a time when the institutional Church provided little inspiring leadership.

Meanwhile, some states were growing stronger and more competitive while other regions remained deeply divided. The rise of the Ottoman Empire eventually absorbed many of the oldest territories of Western civilizations, including the venerable Muslim caliphate at Baghdad, the Near Eastern portions of the former Mongolian Empire, the Christian Balkans and Greece, and—above all—the surviving core of the eastern Roman Empire at Constantinople. Greek-speaking refugees streamed into Italy, many bringing with them classics of Greek philosophy and literature hitherto unknown in Europe. Fueled by new ideas and a fervid nostalgia for the ancient past, Italians began to experiment with new ways of reading ancient texts, advo-

cating a return to classical models while at the same time trying to counter the political and artistic authority of the more powerful kingdoms north of the Alps.

In contrast to Italy, these emerging national monarchies cultivated group identity through the promotion of a shared vernacular language and allegiance to a strong, more centralized state. These tactics would allow smaller kingdoms like Poland and Scotland to increase their territories and their influence and would lead France and England into an epic battle for sovereignty and hegemony. The result, in all cases, was the escalation of armed conflict as incessant warfare drove more powerful governments to harvest a larger percentage of their subjects' wealth through taxation, which they proceeded to invest in ships, guns, and the standing armies made possible by new technologies and more effective administration.

In short, the generations who survived the calamities of famine, plague, and warfare seized the opportunities their new world presented to them. In the latter half of the fifteenth century, they stood on the verge of an extraordinary period of expansion and conquest that enabled them to dominate the globe.

PEOPLE, IDEAS, AND EVENTS IN CONTEXT

- Compare and contrast the **BLACK DEATH**'s effects on rural and urban areas.
- In what ways do rebellions like the **ENGLISH PEASANTS' REVOLT** reflect the changes brought about by the plague? How do the works of **GIOVANNI BOCCACCIO, GEOFFREY CHAUCER**, and **CHRISTINE DE PISAN** exemplify the culture of this era?
- What was **HUMANISM**? How was it related to the artistic and intellectual movement known as the **RENAISSANCE**?
- How did the **OTTOMAN EMPIRE** come to power? What were some consequences of its rise?
- On what grounds did **MUSCOVY** claim to be "the third Rome"? What is the significance of the title **TSAR**?
- What new military technologies were in use during the **HUNDRED YEARS' WAR**? How did this conflict affect other parts of Europe, beyond England and France? What role did **JOAN OF ARC** play?
- How did the **COUNCIL OF CONSTANCE** respond to the crisis of the **GREAT SCHISM**?
- Why did **CONCILIARISM** fail? How did **JOHN WYCLIFFE** and **JAN HUS** seek to reform the Church?

THINKING ABOUT CONNECTIONS

- In the year 2000, a group of historians was asked to identify the most significant historical figure of the past millennium. Rather than selecting a person (e.g., Martin Luther, Shakespeare, Napoleon, Adolf Hitler), they chose the microbe *Yersinia pestis*, which had caused the Black Death. Do you agree with this assessment? Why or why not?
- In your view, which was more crucial to the formation of the modern state: the political and legal developments we surveyed in Chapter 9 or the emergence of national identities we discussed in this chapter? Why?
- Was the conciliar movement doomed to failure, given what we have learned about the history of the Roman Church? How far back does one need to go, in order to trace the development of disputes over ecclesiastical governance?

Before You Read This Chapter

STORY LINES

- The invention of the printing press enabled the dissemination of information, including reports on the riches of the New World.

- Competition for power in Italy led to increased violence and to the increase of artistic patronage, providing opportunities to a new breed of Renaissance men.

- The humanist approach to education that had developed in Italy spread to other parts of Europe, influencing new approaches to biblical scholarship and political philosophies.

- Spain, the newest and most powerful European state, completed its "reconquest" of the Iberian Peninsula in 1492 and then looked to counter the successful colonial ventures of the Portuguese, which led, in turn, to the early beginnings of a Spanish empire in the Americas.

CHRONOLOGY

1454–1455	Gutenberg's printed Bible completed
1488	Bartolomeu Dias rounds the Cape of Good Hope (Africa)
1492	Christopher Columbus embarks
1494	The Treaty of Tordesillas divides the New World
1498	Vasco da Gama reaches India
1511	Portuguese ventures to Indonesia
1512	Michelangelo completes his painting of the Sistine Chapel's ceiling
1513	Niccolò Machiavelli's *The Prince* completed
	Vasco Núñez de Balboa reaches the Pacific Ocean
1516	Thomas More publishes *Utopia*
1519–1522	Magellan's fleet circumnavigates the globe
1533	Aztec wars enable Cortés's conquest of Mexico
	Pizarro's conquest of the Inca Empire

Innovation and Exploration, 1453–1533

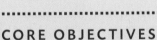
What if exact copies of an idea could circulate quickly, all over the world? What if the same could be done for the latest news, the oldest beliefs, the most beautiful poems, the most exciting—and deadly—discoveries? It would be doing for knowledge what the invention of coinage did for wealth: making it portable, easier to use and disseminate. Indeed, it's no accident that the man who developed such a technology, Johannes Gutenberg of Mainz (c. 1398–1468), was the son of a goldsmith who made coins for the bishop of that German city. Both crafts were based on the same principle and used the same basic tools. Coins are metal disks that have each been stamped with identical words and images, impressed on them with a reusable matrix. The pages of the first printed books—and later newspapers, leaflets, and pamphlets—were stamped with ink spread on rows of movable type (lead or cast-iron letter forms and punctuation marks) slotted into frames to form lines of words. Once a set of pages was ready, a press could make hundreds of copies in a matter of hours, many hundreds of times faster than the same page could be copied by hand. Afterward, the type could be reused.

A major stimulus for this invention was the more widespread availability of paper, a trend that had begun in the late thirteenth century. Parchment, northern Europe's chief writing material since the advent of the codex (see Chapter 6), was extremely expensive to manufacture and required special training on the part of those who used it—one reason why writing remained a specialized skill for much of the Middle Ages, while the ability to read was common. Paper, made from rags turned into pulp by mills, was both cheaper and far easier to use; accordingly, books became cheaper and written communication became easier and more widespread. Growing levels of literacy led to a growing demand for books, which in turn led to experimentation with different methods of book production—and to Gutenberg's breakthrough of the 1450s. By 1455, his workshop had printed multiple copies of the Latin Bible, of which forty-eight complete or partial volumes survive. Although printing never entirely replaced traditional modes of publication via manuscript, it made the cost of books affordable and revolutionized the spread of information.

In fact, the printing press played a crucial role in many of the developments that we will study in this chapter. The artistic and intellectual experiments that contributed to an Italian Renaissance were rapidly exported to other parts of Europe, and specifications for innovative weapons would be printed on the same presses that churned out humanist biographies. News of Columbus's first voyage and the subsequent conquests of the Americas would spread via the same media as critiques of European imperialism there. Printing not only increased the volume and rapidity of communication, it made it more difficult for those in power to censor dissenting opinions.

But at the same time as it created new forms of agency, the printing press also become an indispensable tool of more traditional powers, making it possible for rulers to govern growing empires abroad and increasingly centralized states at home. The "reconquest" of Spain and the extension of Spanish imperialism to the New World were both facilitated by the circulation of printed propaganda. The widespread availability of reading materials even helped to standardize national languages, by enabling governments to promote one official printed dialect over others. Hence the "king's English," the variety of the language spoken around London, was imposed as the only acceptable literary and bureaucratic language throughout the English realm, contributing to the growth of a common linguistic identity among readers. For these reasons, among others, many historians consider the advent of print to be both the defining event and the driving engine of modernity, and

it coincided with another essentially modern development: the discovery of a "New World."

RENAISSANCE IDEALS— AND REALITIES

The intellectual and artistic movement that had begun in Italy during the fourteenth century was, as we noted in Chapter 11, characterized by an intense interest in the classical past and by a new type of educational program known as humanism. These Renaissance ideals—and the realities that both undergirded and complicated them—would be extended and diversified in the later fifteenth century through the medium of the printing press. By the time the Ottoman conquest of Constantinople was complete, just a year before Gutenberg's workshop began to produce pages of the Bible, decades of uncertainty and warfare had propelled hundreds of refugees from the eastern Roman Empire into Italy. Many carried with them precious manuscripts of Greek texts that had long been unavailable in western Europe: the epics of Homer, the major surviving works of Athenian dramatists, the dialogues of Plato. Prior to the invention of print, such manuscripts could be owned and studied by only a very few, very privileged men. Now printers in Venice and other European cities rushed to produce cheap editions of these texts as well as Greek grammars and glossaries that could facilitate reading them.

Within a few decades, so many men were engaged in the study of Plato that an informal "Platonic Academy" had formed in Florence. There, the work of intellectuals like Marsilio Ficino (1433–1499) and Giovanni Pico della Mirandola (1463–1494) was fostered by the patronage of the wealthy Cosimo de' Medici. Based on his reading of Plato, Ficino's philosophy moved away from the focus on ethics and civic life that had been such a feature of earlier humanist thought. He taught instead that the individual should look primarily to the salvation of his immortal soul, to free it from its "always miserable" mortal body: a very Platonic idea that was also compatible with much late-medieval Christian piety. His disciple Pico likewise rejected the everyday world of public affairs but took a more exalted view of man's intellectual and artistic capacities, arguing that man (but not woman) can aspire to union with God through the exercise of his unique talents. Ficino's great achievement was his translation of Plato's works into Latin, which made them widely accessible in Europe for the first time—again, thanks to the medium of print.

THE SPREAD OF PRINTING

| Up until 1470 | 1471–1500 |

THE SPREAD OF PRINTING. This map shows how quickly the technology of printing spread throughout Europe between 1470 and 1500.

- *In what regions were printing presses most heavily concentrated?* • *What factors would have led to their proliferation in the Low Countries, northern Italy, and Germany—as compared to France, Spain, and England?* • *Why would so many have been located along waterways?*

Printing, Patriotism, and the Past

> The printing press helped to create new communities of readers by standardizing national languages and even promoting patriotism. And while it enabled authors of new works to reach larger audiences, it also allowed printers to popularize older writings that had previously circulated in manuscript. The two sources presented here exemplify two aspects of this trend. The first is the preface to a version of the legend of King Arthur, which was originally written by an English soldier called Sir Thomas Malory, who completed it in 1470. It was printed for the first time in 1485, when it quickly became a best seller. The author of this preface was also the printer, William Caxton of London, who specialized in publishing books that glorified England's history and heritage. The second excerpt is from the concluding chapter of Machiavelli's treatise The Prince. Like the book itself, these remarks were originally addressed to Lorenzo de' Medici, head of Florence's most powerful family. But when The Prince was printed in 1532, five years after Machiavelli's death, the author's passionate denunciation of foreign "barbarians" and lament for Italy's lost glory would have resonated with a wider Italian-speaking public.

William Caxton's preface to Thomas Malory's Le Morte d'Arthur ("The Death of Arthur"), 1485

AFTER I had accomplished and finished diverse histories, both of contemplation and of other historical and worldly acts of great conquerors and princes, . . . many noble and diverse gentlemen of this realm of England came and demanded why I had not made and imprinted the noble history of the Holy Grail, and of the most renowned Christian king and worthy, King Arthur, which ought most to be remembered among us Englishmen before all other Christian kings. . . . The said noble gentlemen instantly required me to imprint the history of the said noble king and conqueror King Arthur, and of his knights, with the history of the Holy Grail . . . considering that he was a man born within this realm, and king and emperor of the same: and that there be, in French, diverse and many noble volumes of his acts, and also of his knights. To whom I answered that diverse men hold opinion that there was no such Arthur, and that all such books as have been made of him be feigned and fables, because some chronicles make of him no mention. . . . Whereto

they answered, and one in special said, that in him that should say or think that there was never such a king called Arthur might well be accounted great folly and blindness. . . . For in all places, Christian and heathen, he is reputed and taken for one of the Nine Worthies, and the first of the three Christian men. And also, he is more spoken of beyond the sea, and there are more books made of his noble acts than there be in England, as well in Dutch, Italian, Spanish, and Greek, as in French. . . . Wherefore it is a marvel why he is no more renowned in his own country. . . .

Then all these things aforesaid alleged, I could not well deny but that there was such a noble king named Arthur, reputed one of the Nine Worthies, and first and chief of the Christian men. And many noble volumes be made of him and of his noble knights in French, which I have seen and read beyond the sea, which be not had in our maternal tongue. . . . Wherefore, among all such [manuscript] books as have late been drawn out briefly into English I have . . . undertaken to imprint a book of the noble histories of the said

King Arthur, and of certain of his knights, after a copy unto me delivered—which copy Sir Thomas Malory did take out of certain books of French, and reduced it into English. And I, according to my copy, have done set it in print, to the intent that noble men may see and learn the noble acts of chivalry, the gentle and virtuous deeds that some knights used in those days, by which they came to honor, and how they that were vicious were punished and oft put to shame and rebuke; humbly beseeching all noble lords and ladies (with all other estates of what estate or degree they be) that shall see and read in this said book and work, that they take the good and honest acts to their remembrance, and follow the same. . . . For herein may be seen noble chivalry, courtesy, humanity, friendliness, hardiness, love, friendship, cowardice, murder, hate, virtue, and sin. Do after the good and leave the evil, and it shall bring you to good fame and renown.

Source: Sir Thomas Malory, *Le Morte d'Arthur* (London: 1485), (text and spelling slightly modernized).

From the conclusion of Niccolò Machiavelli's *The Prince* (completed 1513, printed 1533)

Reflecting in the matters set forth above and considering within myself where the times were propitious in Italy at present to honor a new prince and whether there is at hand the matter suitable for a prudent and virtuous leader to mold in a new form, giving honor to himself and benefit to the citizens of the country, I have arrived at the opinion that all circumstances now favor such a prince, and I cannot think of a time more propitious for him than the present. If, as I said, it was necessary in order to make apparent the virtue of Moses, that the people of Israel should be enslaved in Egypt, and that the Persians should be oppressed by the Medes to provide an opportunity to illustrate the greatness and the spirit of Cyrus, and that the Athenians should be scattered in order to show the excellence of Theseus, thus at the present time, in order to reveal the valor of an Italian spirit, it was essential that Italy should fall to her present low estate, more enslaved than the Hebrews, more servile than the Persians, more disunited than the Athenians, leaderless and lawless, beaten, despoiled, lacerated, overrun and crushed under every kind of misfortune.... So Italy now, left almost lifeless, awaits the coming of one who will heal her wounds, putting an end to the sacking and looting in Lombardy and the spoliation and extortions in the Realm of Naples and Tuscany, and cleanse her sores that have been so long festering. Behold how she prays God to send her some one to redeem her from the cruelty and insolence of the barbarians. See how she is ready and willing to follow any banner so long as there be someone to take it up. Nor has she at present any hope of finding her redeemer save only in your illustrious house [the Medici] which has been so highly exalted both by its own merits and by fortune and which has been favored by God and the church, of which it is now ruler....

This opportunity, therefore, should not be allowed to pass, and Italy, after such a long wait, must be allowed to behold her redeemer. I cannot describe the joy with which he will be received in all these provinces which have suffered so much from the foreign deluge, nor with what thirst for vengeance, nor with what firm devotion, what solemn delight, what tears! What gates could be closed to him, what people could deny him obedience, what envy could withstand him, what Italian could withhold allegiance from him? THIS BARBARIAN OCCUPATION STINKS IN THE NOSTRILS OF ALL OF US. Let your illustrious house then take up this cause with the spirit and the hope with which one undertakes a truly just enterprise....

Source: Niccolò Machiavelli, *The Prince,* ed. and trans. Thomas G. Bergin (Arlington Heights, IL: 1947), pp. 75–76, 78.

Questions for Analysis

1. What do these two sources reveal about the relationship between patriotism and the awareness of a nation's past? Why do you think that Caxton looks back to a legendary medieval king, whereas Machiavelli's references are all to ancient examples? What do both excerpts reveal about the value placed on history in the popular imagination?

2. How does Caxton describe the process of printing a book? What larger conclusions can we draw from this about the market for printed books in general?

3. Why might Machiavelli's treatise have been made available in a printed version, nearly twenty years after its original appearance in manuscript? How might his new audience have responded to its message?

The Politics of Italy and the Philosophy of Machiavelli

But not all Florentines were galvanized by Platonic ideals. Indeed, the most influential philosopher of this era—and one of the most widely read authors of all time—was a thoroughgoing realist who spent more time studying Roman history than Greek philosophy: Niccolò Machiavelli (1469–1527). Machiavelli's political writings reflect the unstable political situation of his home city as well as his wider aspirations for a unified Italy that could revive the glory of ancient Rome. We have observed that Italy had been in political disarray for centuries, a situation exacerbated by the "Babylonian Captivity" of the papacy and the controversies raging after its return to Rome (see Chapters 10 and 11). Now Italy was becoming the arena in which bloody international struggles were being played out. The kings of France and Spain both had imperial ambitions, and both claimed to be the rightful champions of the papacy. Accordingly, both sent invading armies into the peninsula while they busily competed for the allegiance of the various city-states, which in turn were torn by internal dissension.

In 1498, Machiavelli became a prominent official in the government of a new Florentine republic, set up four years earlier when a French invasion of the region had led to the expulsion of the ruling Medici family. His duties largely involved diplomatic missions to other Italian city-states. While in Rome, he became fascinated with the attempt of Cesare Borgia, son of Pope Alexander VI, to create his own principality in central Italy. He noted with approval Cesare's ruthlessness and his complete subordination of personal ethics to political ends. He remembered this example in 1512, when the Medici returned to overthrow the Florentine republic and Machiavelli was deprived of his position, imprisoned, tortured, and exiled. He now devoted his energies to the articulation of a political philosophy suited to the times and to the tastes of the family that had ousted him from his job.

On the surface, Machiavelli's two great works of political analysis appear to contradict each other. In his *Discourses on Livy*, which drew on the works of that Roman historian (see Chapter 5), he praised the ancient Roman Republic as a model for his own contemporaries, lauding constitutional government, equality among citizens, and the subordination of religion to the service of the state. There is little doubt, in fact, that Machiavelli was a committed believer in the free city-state as the ideal form of human government. But Machiavelli also wrote *The Prince*, "a handbook for tyrants" in the eyes of his critics, and he dedicated this work to Lorenzo, son of Piero de' Medici, whose family had overthrown the Florentine republic that Machiavelli had served.

THE STATES OF ITALY, c. 1494. This map shows the divisions of Italy on the eve of the French invasion in 1494. Contemporary observers often described Italy as being divided among five great powers: Milan, Venice, Florence, the Papal States, and the united Kingdoms of Naples and Sicily. ▪ *Which of these powers would have been most capable of expanding their territories?* ▪ *Which neighboring states would have been most threatened by such attempts at expansion?* ▪ *Why would Florence and the Papal States so often find themselves in conflict with each other?*

Because *The Prince* has been so much more widely read than *Discourses*, it has often been interpreted as an endorsement of power for its own sake. Machiavelli's real position was quite different. In the political chaos of early-sixteenth-century Italy, he saw the likes of Cesare Borgia as the only hope for revitalizing the spirit of independence among his contemporaries, and so making Italy fit, eventually, for self-governance. However dark his vision of human nature, Machiavelli never ceased to hope that his contemporaries would rise up, expel French and Spanish occupying forces, and restore ancient traditions of liberty and equality. He regarded a period of despotism as a necessary step toward that end, not as a permanently desirable form of government.

Machiavelli continues to be a controversial figure. Some modern scholars, like many of his own contemporaries, represent him as disdainful of conventional morality, interested solely in the acquisition and exercise of power. Others see him as an Italian patriot. Still others see him as a realist influenced by Saint Augustine (see Chapter 6), who understood that, in a fallen world populated by sinful people, a ruler's good intentions do not guarantee that his policies will have good results. Accordingly, Machiavelli insisted that a prince's actions must be judged by their consequences and not by their intrinsic moral quality. He argued that "the necessity of preserving the state will often compel a prince to take actions which are opposed to loyalty, charity, humanity, and religion." As we shall see in later chapters, many subsequent political philosophers would go even further than Machiavelli in arguing that the preservation of the state—and the avoidance of political chaos—does indeed warrant the exercise of absolute power on the part of the ruler (see Chapters 14 and 15).

The Ideal of the Courtier

Machiavelli's political theories were informed by years of diplomatic service in the courts of Italy, and so was his engaging literary style. Indeed, he never abandoned his interest in the literary arts of the court and continued to write poems, plays, and adaptations of classical comedies. In this he resembled another poet-courtier, Ludovico Ariosto (1474–1533), who undertook diplomatic missions for the Duke of Ferrara and some of Rome's most powerful prelates. His lengthy verse narrative, *Orlando Furioso* (The Madness of Roland), was a retelling of the heroic exploits celebrated in the French *Song of Roland* (see Chapter 8)—but without the heroism. Although very different in form and tone from *The Prince*, it shared that work's skepticism of political or chivalric ideals. Instead, it emphasized the comedy of its lovers' passionate exploits and sought to charm an audience who sought consolation in pleasure and beauty.

Thus a new Renaissance ideal was born, one that promoted the arts of pleasing the powerful secular and ecclesiastical princes who were in a position to employ clever men like Machiavelli and Ariosto: the ideal of the courtier. The components of this ideal were embodied by their contemporary, the diplomat and nobleman Baldassare Castiglione (1478–1529), who would later write a manual for those who aspired to acquire these skills. If *The Prince* was a forerunner of modern self-help books, *The Book of the Courtier* was an early handbook of etiquette; and both stand in sharp contrast to the treatises on public virtue composed in the previous century. Whereas Bruni and Alberti (see Chapter 11) had taught the sober virtues of strenuous service on behalf of the city-state, Castiglione taught how to attain the elegant and seemingly effortless skills necessary for advancement in princely courts.

More than anyone else, Castiglione articulated and popularized the set of talents still associated with the "Renaissance man": one accomplished in many different pursuits, witty, cultured, and stylish. And in many ways, this new ideal actually represents a *rejection* of the older ideals associated with the Renaissance as a rebirth of classical education for public men. Castiglione even rejected the misogyny of the humanists by stressing the ways in which court ladies could rise to influence and prominence through the graceful exercise of their womanly powers. Widely read throughout Western civilizations, his *Courtier* set the standard for polite behavior until the First World War.

The Dilemma of the Artist

Without question, the most enduring legacy of the Italian Renaissance has been the contributions of its artists, particularly those who embraced new media and new attitudes toward the human body. We have already noted (see Chapter 11) the creative and economic opportunities afforded by painting on canvas or wood, which freed artists from having to work on site and entirely on commission: such paintings are portable—unlike wall paintings—and can be displayed in different settings, reach different markets, and be more widely distributed. We also saw that the use of oil paints, pioneered in Flanders, further revolutionized painting styles. To these benefits, the artists of Italy added an important technical ingredient: mastery of a vanishing (one-point) perspective that gave to painting an illusion of three-dimensional space. They also experimented with effects of light and shade, and studied intently the anatomy and proportions of the human body. These techniques also influenced the sculptors of this age.

THE IMPACT OF PERSPECTIVE. Masaccio's painting *The Trinity with the Virgin* illustrates the startling sense of depth made possible by observing the rules of one-point perspective.

Behind all of the beautiful artworks created in this era, which led to the glorification of the artist as a new type of hero, lie the harsh political and economic realities within which these artists worked. Increasing private wealth and the growth of lay patronage opened up new markets and created a huge demand for buildings and objects that could increase those grappling for prestige. Portraiture was a direct result of this trend, since princes and merchants alike sought to glorify themselves and their families and to compete with their neighbors and rivals. An artist therefore had to study the techniques of the courtier as well as the new artistic techniques in order to succeed in winning a patron. He also had to be ready to perform other services for which he had to cultivate other talents: overseeing the building and decoration of palaces; designing tableware, furniture, fanciful liveries for servants and soldiers; and even decorating guns. Some artists, like Leonardo da Vinci, were prized as much for their capacity to invent deadly weapons as for their paintings and sculptures.

New Illusions and the Career of Leonardo

For much of the fifteenth century, the majority of the great painters were Florentines who followed in the footsteps of the precocious Masaccio (1401–1428), who had died prematurely at the age of twenty-seven. His lasting legacy was the pioneering use of one-point perspective and dramatic lighting effects. Both are evident in his painting of the Trinity, where the body of the crucified Christ appears to be thrust forward by the impassive figure of God the Father, while the Virgin's gaze directly engages the viewer. Masaccio's most obvious successor was Sandro Botticelli (1445–1510), who excelled in depicting graceful motion and the sensuous pleasures of nature. He is most famous today for paintings that evoke classical mythology and that seem to be devoid of any Christian frame of reference.

The most adventurous and versatile artist of this period was Leonardo da Vinci (1452–1519). Leonardo personifies the Renaissance ideal: he was a painter, architect, musician, mathematician, engineer, and inventor. The illegitimate son of a notary, he set up an artist's shop in Florence by the time he was twenty-five and gained the patronage of the Medici ruler, Lorenzo the Magnificent. Yet Leonardo had a weakness: he worked slowly, and he had difficulty finishing anything. This naturally displeased Lorenzo and other Florentine patrons, who regarded artists as craftsmen who worked on specific projects, and on their patrons' time—not their own. Leonardo, however, strongly objected to this view; he considered himself to be an inspired, independent innovator. He therefore left Florence in 1482 and went to work for the of Sforza dictators Milan, whose favor he courted by emphasizing his skills as a maker of bombs, heavy ordinance, and siege engines. He remained there until the French invasion of 1499; he then wandered about, finally accepting the patronage of the French king, under whose auspices he lived and worked until his death.

Paradoxically, considering his skill in fashioning deadly weapons, Leonardo was convinced of the essential divinity of all living things. He was a vegetarian—unusual at the time—and when he went to the marketplace to buy caged birds he released them to their native habitat when he had finished observing them. His approach to painting was that it should be the most accurate possible imitation of nature. He made careful studies: blades of grass, cloud formations, a waterfall. He obtained human corpses for dissection and reconstructed in drawing the minutest features of anatomy, carrying this knowledge over to his paintings. *The Virgin of the Rocks* typifies not only his technical skill but also his passion for science and his belief in the universe as a well-ordered place.

THE BIRTH OF VENUS. This painting was executed by Sandro Botticelli in Florence, and represents the artist's imaginative treatment of stories from ancient mythology. Here, he depicts the moment when Aphrodite, goddess of love, was spontaneously engendered from the foam of the sea by Chronos, the god of time.

THE VIRGIN OF THE ROCKS. This painting reveals Leonardo's interest in the variety of human faces and facial expressions and in natural settings.

The figures are arranged geometrically, with every stone and plant depicted in accurate detail. In *The Last Supper*, painted on the refectory walls of a monastery in Milan (and now in an advanced state of decay), he displayed his equally keen studies of human psychology. In this image, a serene Christ has just announced to his disciples that one of them will betray him. The artist succeeds in portraying the mingled emotions of surprise, horror, and guilt on the faces of the disciples as they gradually perceive the meaning of their master's statement. He also implicates the painting's viewers in this dramatic scene, since they too dine alongside Christ, in the very same room.

Renaissance Arts in Venice and Rome

The innovations of Florentine artists were widely imitated. By the end of the fifteenth century, they had influenced a group of painters active in the wealthy city of Venice, among them Tiziano Vecellio, better known as Titian (c. 1490–1576). Many of Titian's paintings evoke the luxurious, pleasure-loving life of this thriving commercial center; for although they copied Florentine techniques,

Analyzing Primary Sources

Leonardo da Vinci Applies for a Job

Few sources illuminate the tensions between Renaissance ideals and realities better than the résumé of accomplishments submitted by Leonardo da Vinci to a prospective employer, Ludovico Sforza of Milan. In the following letter, Leonardo explains why he deserves to be appointed chief architect and military engineer in the duke's household administration. He got the job and moved to Milan in 1481.

1. I have the kind of bridges that are extremely light and strong, made to be carried with great ease, and with them you may pursue, and, at any time, flee from the enemy; . . . and also methods of burning and destroying those of the enemy.

2. I know how, when a place is under attack, to eliminate the water from the trenches, and make endless variety of bridges . . . and other machines. . . .

3. . . . I have methods for destroying every rock or other fortress, even if it were built on rock, etc.

4. I also have other kinds of mortars [bombs] that are most convenient and easy to carry. . . .

5. And if it should be a sea battle, I have many kinds of machines that are most efficient for offense and defense. . . .

6. I also have means that are noiseless to reach a designated area by secret and tortuous mines. . . .

7. I will make covered chariots, safe and unattackable, which can penetrate the enemy with their artillery. . . .

8. In case of need I will make big guns, mortars, and light ordnance of fine and useful forms that are out of the ordinary.

9. If the operation of bombardment should fail, I would contrive catapults, mangonels, trabocchi [trebuchets], and other machines of marvelous efficacy and unusualness. In short, I can, according to each case in question, contrive various and endless means of offense and defense.

10. In time of peace I believe I can give perfect satisfaction that is equal to any other in the field of architecture and the construction of buildings. . . . I can execute sculpture in marble, bronze, or clay, and also in painting I do the best that can be done, and as well as any other, whoever he may be.

Having now, most illustrious Lord, sufficiently seen the specimens of all those who consider themselves master craftsmen of instruments of war, and that the invention and operation of such instruments are no different from those in common use, I shall now endeavor . . . to explain myself to your Excellency by revealing to your Lordship my secrets. . . .

Source: Excerpted from Leonardo da Vinci, *The Notebooks*, in *The Italian Renaissance Reader*, eds. Julia Conaway and Mark Mosa (Harmondsworth, UK: 1987), pp. 195–96.

Questions for Analysis

1. Based on the qualifications highlighted by Leonardo in this letter, what can you conclude about the political situation in Milan and the priorities of its duke? What can you conclude about the state of military technologies in this period and the conduct of warfare?

2. What do you make of the fact that Leonardo mentions his artistic endeavors only at the end of the letter? Does this fact alter your opinion or impression of him? Why or why not?

---

most Venetian painters showed little of that city's concerns for philosophical or religious allegory. Their aim was to appeal to the senses by painting idyllic landscapes and sumptuous portraits of the rich and powerful. In the subordination of form and meaning to color and elegance, they may have mirrored the tastes of the men for whom they worked.

Rome, too, became a major artistic center in this era and a place where the Florentine school exerted a more potent influence. Among its eminent painters was Raffaello Sanzio (1483–1520), or Raphael. Although influenced by Leonardo, Raphael cultivated a more spiritual and philosophical approach to his subjects. As we noted in Chapter 4, his fresco *The School of Athens* depicts both the harmony

THE LAST SUPPER. This fresco on the refectory wall of the monastery of Santa Maria delle Grazie in Milan is a testament to both the powers and limitations of Leonardo's artistry. It skillfully employs the techniques of one-point perspective to create the illusion that Jesus and his disciples are actually dining at the monastery's head table, but because Leonardo had not mastered the techniques of fresco painting, he applied tempera pigments to a dry wall that had been coated with a sealing agent. As a result, the painting's colors began to fade just years after its completion. By the middle of the sixteenth century, it had seriously deteriorated. Large portions of it are now invisible.

and the differences of Platonic and Aristotelian thought (see page 117). It also includes a number of Raphael's contemporaries as models. The image of Plato is actually a portrait of Leonardo, while the architect Donato Bramante (c. 1444–1514) stands in for the geometer Euclid, and Michelangelo for the philosopher Heraclitus.

Michelangelo Buonarroti (1475–1564), who spent many decades in Rome in the service of a papacy, was another native of Florence. Like Leonardo, he was a polymath: painter, sculptor, architect, poet—and he expressed himself in all these forms with a similar power. But if Leonardo was a naturalist, Michelangelo was an idealist—despite the harsh political and material realities of the conditions in which he worked. At the center of all of his work, as at the center of Renaissance humanism, is the male figure: the embodied masculine mind.

Michelangelo's greatest achievements in painting appear in a single location, the Sistine Chapel of the Vatican palace, yet they are products of two different periods in the artist's life and consequently exemplify two different artistic styles and outlooks on the human condition. More famous are the extraordinary frescoes painted on the ceiling from 1508 to 1512, depicting scenes from the book of Genesis. All the panels in this series, including *The Creation of Adam*, exemplify the young artist's commitment to classical artistic principles. Correspondingly, all affirm the sublimity of the Creation and the heroic qualities of humankind. But a quarter of a century later, when Michelangelo returned to work in the Sistine Chapel, both his style and mood had changed dramatically. In the enormous *Last Judgment*, a fresco completed on the chapel's altar wall in 1536, Michelangelo repudiated classical restraint and substituted a style that emphasized tension and distortion, a humanity wracked with fear, guilt, and frailty. He included himself in it—painting a grotesque self-portrait on the flayed skin of Saint Bartholomew, who was allegedly martyred by being skinned alive. One wonders whether Michelangelo intended this as a metaphor for the challenges of working in the service of the papal court.

Michelangelo and the Renaissance of Sculpture

Although sculpture was not a new medium for artists, as oil painting was, it became an important area of Renaissance innovation. For the first time since late antiquity, monumental

SELF-PORTRAIT OF THE ARTIST AS A YOUNG MAN: DETAIL FROM *THE SCHOOL OF ATHENS.* We have already analyzed aspects of Raphael's famous group portrait of the Greek philosophers, with Plato and Aristotle at their center (see page 118). In addition to featuring his own contemporaries as models—including the artists Leonardo and Michelangelo and the architect Bramante—Raphael put himself in the picture, too. ▪ *What messages does this choice convey?*

statues became figures "in the round" rather than sculptural elements incorporated into buildings or featured as effigies on tombs. By freeing sculpture from its bondage to architecture, the Renaissance reestablished it as a separate art form.

The first great master of Renaissance sculpture was Donatello (c. 1386–1466). His bronze statue of David, triumphant over the head of the slain Goliath, is the first freestanding nude of the period. Yet this *David* is clearly an agile adolescent rather than a muscular Greek athlete like that of Michelangelo's *David*, executed in 1501, as a public expression of Florentine civic life: not merely graceful but heroic. Michelangelo regarded sculpture as the most exalted of the arts because it allowed the artist to imitate God most fully in re-creating human forms. Furthermore, in Michelangelo's view,

THE POWER AND VULNERABILITY OF THE MALE BODY. Donatello's *David* (left) was the first freestanding nude executed since antiquity. It shows the Hebrew leader as an adolescent youth and is a little over five feet tall. The *David* by Michelangelo (center) stands thirteen feet high and was placed prominently in front of Florence's city hall to proclaim the city's power and humanistic values. Michelangelo's *Descent from the Cross* (right), which shows Christ's broken body in the arms of the elderly Nicodemus, was made by the sculptor for his own tomb. (The Gospels describe Nicodemus as a Pharisee who became a follower of Jesus and who was present at his death.) ▪ *Why would Michelangelo choose this figure to represent himself?* ▪ *How does his representation of David—and the context in which this figure was displayed—compare to that of Donatello?*

the most God-like sculptor disdained slavish naturalism; anyone could make a plaster cast of a human figure, but only an inspired creative genius could endow his sculpted figures with a sense of life. Accordingly, Michelangelo's sculpture subordinated reality to the force of his imagination and sought to express his ideals in ever more astonishing forms. He also insisted on working in marble—the "noblest" sculptural material—and by creating figures twice as large as life. By sculpting a serenely confident young man at the peak of physical fitness, Michelangelo celebrated the Florentine republic's own determination in resisting tyrants and upholding ideals of civic justice.

Yet the serenity seen in *David* is no longer prominent in the works of Michelangelo's later life when, as in his painting, he began to explore the use of anatomical distortion to create effects of emotional intensity. While his statues remained awesome in scale, they also communicate rage, depression, and sorrow. The culmination of this trend is his unfinished but intensely moving *Descent from the Cross*, a depiction of an old man (the sculptor himself) grieving over the distorted, slumping body of the dead Christ.

Renaissance Architecture

To a much greater extent than either sculpture or painting, Renaissance architecture had its roots in the classical past. The Gothic style pioneered in northern France (see Chapter 9) had not found a welcome reception in Italy; most of the buildings constructed there were Romanesque in style, and the great architects influenced by the Renaissance movement generally adopted their building plans from these structures—some of which they believed (mistakenly) to be ancient. They also copied decorative devices from the authentic ruins of ancient Rome. But above all, they derived their influence from the writings of Vitruvius (fl. c. 60–15 B.C.E.), a Roman architect and engineer whose multivolume *On Architecture* was among the humanists' rediscovered ancient texts. The governing principles laid out by Vitruvius were popularized by Leon Battista Alberti in his own book, *On the Art of Building*, which began to circulate in manuscript around 1450.

In keeping with these classical models, Renaissance buildings emphasize geometrical proportion. These aesthetic values were also reinforced by the interest in Pla-

ST. PETER'S BASILICA, ROME. This eighteenth-century painting shows the massive interior of the Renaissance building. But were it not for the perspective provided by the tiny human figures, the human eye would be fooled into thinking this a much smaller space.

tonic philosophy, which taught that certain mathematical ratios reflect the harmony of the universe. For example, the proportions of the human body serve as the basis for the proportions of the quintessential Renaissance building: St. Peter's Basilica in Rome. Designed by some of the most celebrated architects of the time, including Bramante and Michelangelo, it is still one of the largest buildings in the world. Yet it seems smaller than a Gothic cathedral because it is built to human scale. The same artful proportions are evident in smaller-scale buildings too, as in the aristocratic country houses later designed by the northern Italian architect Andrea Palladio (1508–1580), who created secular miniatures of ancient temples (such as the Roman Pantheon) to glorify the aristocrats who dwelled within them.

THE RENAISSANCE NORTH OF THE ALPS

Despite Italian resentment of the political encroachment of foreign monarchs, contacts between Italy and northern Europe were close throughout this period. Italian merchants and financiers were familiar figures at northern courts; students from all over Europe studied at Italian universities such as Bologna or Padua; northern poets (including Geoffrey Chaucer; see Chapter 11) and their works traveled to

and from Italy; and northern soldiers were frequent; combattants in Italian wars. Yet only at the very end of the fifteenth century did the innovative artistry and learning of Italy begin to be exported across the Alps into northern Europe and across the eastern Mediterranean into Spain.

A variety of explanations have been offered for this delay. Northern European intellectual life in the later Middle Ages was dominated by universities such as those of Paris, Oxford, and Prague, whose curricula focused on the study of philosophical logic, Christian theology, and (to a lesser extent) medicine. These rigorous courses of study left little room for the study of classical literature. In Italy, by contrast, universities were more often professional schools specializing in law and medicine and were more integrally tied to the nonacademic intellectual lives of the cities in which they were situated. As a result, a more secular, urban-oriented educational tradition took shape in Italy, as we saw in our previous discussion of humanism. In northern Europe, by contrast, those scholars who *were* influenced by Italian ideas usually worked outside the university system under the private patronage of kings and princes.

Before the turn of the sixteenth century, northern rulers were also less committed to patronizing artists and intellectuals than were the city-states and princes of Italy. In Italy, as we may have seen, such patronage was an important arena for competition between political rivals. In northern Europe, however, political units were larger and political rivals were fewer. It was therefore less necessary to use art for political purposes in a kingdom than it was in a city-state—a major exception being the independent duchy of Burgundy, which surpassed even the French court in its magnificence. A statue erected in a central square of Florence would be seen by all the city's residents. In Paris, such a statue would be seen by only a tiny minority of the French king's subjects. But as royal courts became more firmly established in royal capitals and so became showcases for royal power, kings needed to impress townspeople, courtiers, and visitors—and they consequently relied more and more on artists and intellectuals to advertise their wealth and taste.

Christian Humanism and the Career of Erasmus

In general, then, the Renaissance movement of northern Europe differed from that of Italy because it grafted certain Italian ideals onto preexisting traditions, rather than sweeping away older forms of knowledge. This can be seen very clearly in the case of the intellectual development known as Christian humanism. Although Christian humanists shared the Italian humanists' scorn for scholasticism's limitations, northern humanists were more committed to seeking ethical guidance from biblical and religious precepts, as well as from Cicero or Virgil. Like their Italian counterparts, they embraced the wisdom of antiquity, but the antiquity they favored was Christian as well as classical—the antiquity of the New Testament and the early Church. Similarly, northern artists were inspired by the accomplishments of Italian masters and copied their techniques, but they depicted classical subjects less frequently and almost never portrayed completely nude human figures.

Any discussion of Christian humanism must begin with the career of Desiderius Erasmus (c. 1469–1536). The illegitimate son of a priest, Erasmus was born near Rotterdam in the Netherlands. Later, as a result of his wide travels, he became a virtual citizen of all Europe. Forced into a monastery against his will when he was a teenager, the young Erasmus found little formal instruction there—but plenty of freedom to read what he liked. He devoured all the classics he could get his hands on, alongside the writings of the church fathers (see Chapter 6). When he

***ERASMUS* BY HANS HOLBEIN THE YOUNGER.** This is generally regarded as the most evocative portrait of the preeminent Christian humanist.

Past and Present

The Reputation of Richard III

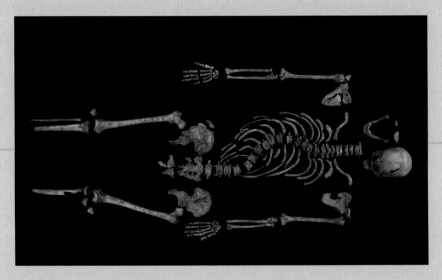

England's King Richard III (r. 1483–1485) has been a byword for villainy since the time of his death, when Sir Thomas More and other propagandists working for his successor, Henry VII, alleged that his physically deformed body was matched by the depravity of his actions. For centuries, historians have debated the truth of both claims. Was Richard really a hunchback—and a murderer, too? In 2012, the stunning discovery of Richard's body (under a parking lot near the medieval battlefield where he died) confirmed that he had indeed suffered from severe scoliosis. The other claim has yet to be proven.

 Watch related author interview on StudySpace
wwnorton.com/web/westernciv18

was about thirty years old, he obtained permission to leave the monastery and enroll in the University of Paris, where he completed the requirements for a bachelor's degree in divinity.

But Erasmus subsequently rebelled against what he considered the arid learning of Parisian academe. Nor did he ever serve actively as a priest. Instead, he made his living from teaching, writing, and the proceeds of various ecclesiastical offices that required no pastoral duties. Ever on the lookout for new patrons, he traveled often to England, stayed for three years in Italy, and resided in several different cities in Germany and the Low Countries before settling finally, toward the end of his life, in Basel (Switzerland). By means of a voluminous correspondence with learned friends, Erasmus became the leader of a humanist coterie. And through the popularity of his numerous publications, he also became the arbiter of northern European cultural tastes during his lifetime.

Erasmus's many-sided intellectual activity may be assessed from two different points of view: the literary and the doctrinal. As a Latin prose stylist, Erasmus was unequaled since the days of Cicero. Extraordinarily eloquent and witty, he reveled in tailoring his mode of discourse to fit his subject, creating dazzling verbal effects and coining puns that took on added meaning if the reader knew Greek as well as Latin. Above all, Erasmus excelled in the deft use of irony, poking fun at everything, including himself. For example, in his *Colloquies* (Discussions) he has a fictional character lament the evils of the times: "Kings make war, priests strive to line their pockets, theologians invent syllogisms, monks roam outside their cloisters, the commons riot, and Erasmus writes colloquies."

But although Erasmus's urbane Latin style and humor earned him a wide audience on those grounds alone, he intended everything he wrote to promote what he called the "philosophy of Christ." Erasmus believed that the society of

his day had lost sight of the Gospels' teachings. Accordingly, he offered his contemporaries three different kinds of writings: clever satires in which people could recognize their own foibles, serious moral treatises meant to offer guidance toward proper Christian behavior, and scholarly editions of basic Christian texts.

In the first category belong the works of Erasmus that are still widely read today: *The Praise of Folly* (1509), in which he ridiculed pedantry and dogmatism, ignorance and gullibility—even within the Church; and the *Colloquies* (1518), in which he held up contemporary religious practices for examination, couching a serious message in the ironic tone we just noted. In these books, Erasmus let fictional characters do the talking so his own views on any given topic can only be determined by inference. But in his second mode, Erasmus spoke clearly in his own voice. In the *Handbook of the Christian Knight* (1503), he used the popular language of chivalry as a means to encourage a life of inward piety; in the *Complaint of Peace* (1517), he argued movingly for Christian pacifism. Erasmus's pacifism was one of his most deeply held values, and he returned to it again and again in his published works.

Despite the success of these writings, Erasmus considered textual scholarship his greatest achievement. Revering the authority of the earliest church fathers, he brought out reliable printed editions of works by Saints Augustine, Jerome, and Ambrose. He also used his extraordinary command of Latin and Greek to produce a more accurate edition of the New Testament. For after reading Lorenzo Valla's *Notes on the New Testament* in 1504, Erasmus became convinced that nothing was more imperative than divesting the Christian scriptures of myriad errors in transcription and translation that had piled up over the course of preceding centuries. He therefore spent ten years comparing all the early Greek biblical manuscripts he could find in order to establish an authoritative text. When it finally appeared in 1516, Erasmus's Greek New Testament, published together with explanatory notes and his own new Latin translation, became one of the most important scholarly landmarks of all time. In the hands of Martin Luther, it would play a critical role in the early stages of the Reformation (see Chapter 13).

The Influence of Erasmus

One of Erasmus's closest friends, and a close second to him in distinction among Christian humanists, was the Englishman Sir Thomas More (1478–1535). In later life, following a successful career as a lawyer and speaker of the House of Commons, More was appointed lord chancellor of England in 1529. He was not long in this position, however, before he opposed King Henry VIII's plan to establish a national church under royal control that would deny the supremacy of the pope (see Chapter 13). (He was eventually executed and is now revered as a Catholic martyr.) Much earlier, however, in 1516, More published his most famous book, *Utopia* (No Place).

Purporting to describe an ideal community on an imaginary island, the book is really an Erasmian critique of contemporary culture: disparities between poverty and wealth, drastic punishments, religious persecution, and the senseless slaughter of war. In contrast to Europeans, the inhabitants of the fictional Utopia hold all their goods in common, work only six hours a day (so that all may have leisure for intellectual pursuits), and practice the natural virtues of wisdom, moderation, fortitude, and justice. Although More advanced no explicit arguments here in favor of Christianity, he might have meant to imply that if the Utopians could manage their society so well without the benefit of Christian revelation, Europeans who knew the Gospels ought to be able to do even better.

Erasmus and More head a long list of energetic and eloquent northern humanists who made signal contributions to the collective enterprise of revolutionizing the

***SIR THOMAS MORE* BY HANS HOLBEIN THE YOUNGER.** Holbein's skill in rendering the gravity and interiority of his subject is matched by his masterful representation of the sumptuous chain of office, furred mantle, and velvet sleeves that indicate the political and professional status of Henry VIII's lord chancellor.

study of early Christianity, and their achievements had a direct influence on Protestant reformers—as we shall see in the next chapter. Yet very few of them were willing to join Luther and other Protestant leaders in rejecting the fundamental principles on which the power of the Roman Church was based. Most tried to remain within its fold while still espousing an ideal of inward piety and scholarly inquiry. But as the leaders of the Church grew less and less tolerant of dissent, even mild criticism came to seem like heresy. Erasmus himself died early enough to escape persecution, but several of his less fortunate followers did not.

The Literature of the Northern Renaissance

Although Christian humanism would be severely challenged by the Reformation, the artistic Renaissance in the North would flourish. Poets in France and England vied with one another to adapt the elegant lyric forms pioneered by Petrarch (Chapter 11) and popularized by many subsequent poets, including Michelangelo. The sonnet was particularly influential and would become one of the verse forms embraced by William Shakespeare (1554–1616; see chapter 14). Another English poet, Edmund Spenser (c. 1552–1599), drew on the literary innovation of Ariosto's *Orlando Furioso*: his *Faerie Queene* is a similarly long chivalric romance that revels in sensuous imagery. Meanwhile, the more satirical side of Renaissance humanism was embraced by the French writer François Rabelais (*RA-beh-lay*, c. 1494–1553).

Like Erasmus, whom he greatly admired, Rabelais began his career in the Church; but he soon left the cloister to study medicine. A practicing physician, Rabelais interspersed his professional activities with literary endeavors, the most enduring of these are the twin books *Gargantua* and *Pantagruel*, a series of "chronicles" describing the lives and times of giants whose fabulous size and gross appetites serve as vehicles for much lusty humor. Also like Erasmus, Rabelais also satirized religious hypocrisy, scholasticism, superstition, and bigotry. But unlike Erasmus, who wrote in a highly cultivated classical Latin style comprehensible only to learned readers, Rabelais chose to address a different audience by writing in extremely crude French and by glorifying every human appetite as natural and healthy.

Northern Architecture and Art

Although many architects in northern Europe continued to build in the flamboyant Gothic style of the later Middle Ages, the classical values of Italian architects can be seen in some of the splendid new castles constructed in France's Loire valley—châteaux too elegant to be defensible—and in the royal palace (now museum) of the Louvre in Paris, which replaced an old twelfth-century fortress. The influence of Renaissance ideals are also visible in the work of the German artist Albrecht Dürer (*DIRR-er*, 1471–1528). Dürer was the first northerner to master the techniques of proportion and perspective, and he shared with contemporary Italians a fascination with nature and the human body. He also took advantage of the printing press to circulate his work to a wide audience, making his delicate pencil drawings into engravings that could be mass produced.

But Dürer never really embraced classical subject, drawing inspiration instead from more traditional Christian legends and from the Christian humanism of Erasmus. For example, Dürer's serenely radiant engraving of Saint Jerome seems to express the scholarly absorption that Erasmus would have enjoyed while working quietly in his study. Indeed, Dürer aspired to immortalize Erasmus himself in a major portrait, but the paths of the two men crossed only once. Instead, the accomplishment of capturing Erasmus's pensive spirit in oils was left to another northern artist, the German Hans Holbein the Younger (1497–1543). Holbein also painted an acute portrait of Erasmus's friend and kindred spirit, Sir Thomas More. These two portraits, in themselves, exemplify a Renaissance emphasis on the making of naturalistic likenesses that express human individuality.

Tradition and Innovation in Music

Like the visual arts, the gorgeous music produced during this era was nourished by patrons' desire to surround themselves with beauty. Yet unlike painting and sculpture, musical practice did not reach back to classical antiquity but drew instead on well-established medieval conventions. Even before the Black Death, a musical movement called *ars nova* ("new art") was already flourishing in France, and it had spread to Italy during the lifetime of Petrarch. Its outstanding composers had been Guillaume de Machaut (c. 1300–1377) and Francesco Landini (c. 1325–1397).

The madrigals (part-songs) and ballads composed by these musicians and their successors expanded on earlier genres of secular music, but their greatest achievement was a highly complicated yet delicate contrapuntal style adapted for the liturgy of the Church. Machaut was the first-known composer to provide a polyphonic (harmonized) version of the major sections of the Mass. In the fifteenth century, the dissemination of this new musical aesthetic combined with a host of French, Flemish, and Italian elements in the multicultural courts of Europe, particularly that of Burgundy.

SAINT JEROME IN HIS STUDY BY DÜRER. Jerome, the biblical translator of the fourth century (see Chapter 6), was a hero to both Dürer and Erasmus: the paragon of inspired Christian scholarship. Note how the scene exudes contentment, even down to the sleeping lion, which seems more like an overgrown tabby cat than a symbol of Christ.

By the beginning of the sixteenth century, Franco-Flemish composers came to dominate many important courts and cathedrals, creating a variety of new forms and styles that bear a close affinity to Renaissance art and poetry.

Throughout Europe, the general level of musical proficiency in this era was very high. The singing of part-songs was a popular pastime in homes and at informal social gatherings, and the ability to read a part at sight was expected of the educated elite. Aristocratic women, in particular, were expected to display mastery of the new musical instruments that had been developed to add nuance and texture to existing musical forms, including the lute, the viol, the violin, and a variety of woodwind and keyboard instruments like the harpsichord.

Although most composers of this period were men trained in the service of the Church, they rarely made sharp distinctions between sacred and secular music. Like sculpture, music was coming into its own as a serious independent art. As such, it would become an important medium for the expression of both Catholic and Protestant ideals during the Reformation and also one of the few art forms equally acceptable to all.

THE POLITICS OF CHRISTIAN EUROPE

We have already observed how the intellectual and artistic activity of the Renaissance movement was both fueled and hindered by the political developments of the later fifteenth century—within Italy, and throughout Europe. In 1453, France had emerged victorious in the Hundred Years' War, while England plunged into a further three decades of bloody civil conflict that touched every corner of that kingdom. The French monarchy was therefore able to rebuild its power and prestige while at the same time extending its control over regions that had long been controlled by the English crown and that were now part of an enlarged kingdom of France.

In 1494, the French king Charles VIII acted on a plan to expand his reach even further, into Italy. Leading an army of 30,000 well-trained troops across the Alps, he intended to press ancestral claims to the duchy of Milan and the kingdom of Naples. This effort yielded only a tenuous hold on Naples by the time Charles left a year later, and it solidified Italian opposition to French occupation, as we noted above; in our discussion of Machiavelli.

The rulers of Spain, whose territorial claims on Sicily also extended to Naples, were spurred by this to forge an uneasy alliance among the Papal States, some principalities of the Holy Roman Empire, Milan, and Venice. But the respite was brief. Charles's successor, Louis XII, launched a second invasion in 1499. For over a generation, until 1529, warfare in Italy was virtually uninterrupted. Alliances and counteralliances among city-states became further catalysts for violence and made Italy a magnet for mercenaries who could barely be kept in check by the generals who employed them.

Meanwhile, northern Italian city-states' virtual monopoly of trade with Asia, which had been one of the chief economic underpinnings of artistic and intellectual patronage, was being gradually eroded by the shifting of trade routes from the Mediterranean to the Atlantic (Chapters 10 and 11). It was also hampered by the increasing power of the Ottoman Empire, and even by the imperial pretensions of a new Russian ruler.

The Imperial Power of Ivan the Great

In previous chapters, we noted that the Russian duchy of Muscovy had become the champion of the Greek Orthodox Church and, as such, considered itself a true heir of Rome. After the fall of Constantinople to the Ottomans, the Muscovite grand duke even assumed the imperial title *tsar* (caesar)

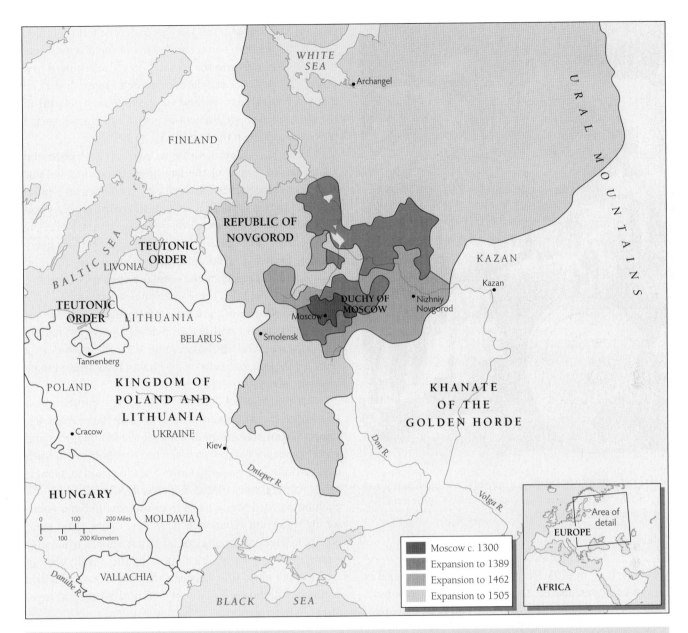

THE EXPANSION OF MUSCOVITE RUSSIA TO 1505. The grand duchy of Moscow was the heart of what would soon become the Russian Empire. ■ *With what other empires and polities did the Muscovites have to compete during this period of expansion?* ■ *How did the relative isolation of Moscow, compared with early Kiev, allow for the growth of Muscovite power, on the one hand, and Moscow's distinctively non-Western culture, on the other?* ■ *How might the natural direction of the expansion of Muscovite power until 1505 help to encourage attitudes often at odds with those of western European civilization?*

and borrowed the Byzantine ideology of the ruler's divine election. These claims would eventually undergird the sacred position later ascribed to the tsars. But ideology alone could not have built the Russian Empire. Behind its growth lay the steadily growing power of its rulers, especially that of Grand Duke Ivan III (1462–1505), known as Ivan the Great, the first to lay down a distinctive imperial agenda.

Ivan launched a series of conquests that annexed all the independent principalities lying between Moscow and

the border of Poland-Lithuania. After invading Lithuania in 1492 and 1501, Ivan even succeeded in bringing parts of that domain (portions of modern Belarus and Ukraine) under his control. Meanwhile, he married the niece of the last Byzantine emperor, giving real substance to the claim that Muscovy was New Rome. He also rebuilt his fortified Moscow residence, known as the Kremlin, in magnificent Italianate style. He would later adopt, as his imperial insignia, the double-headed eagle of Rome and its legions. By the

IVAN THE GREAT. This modern tribute to Ivan III prominently displays the two-headed eagle of imperial Rome. ▪ *What is the significance of this symbolic choice?*

that were emerging in this era. For under the terms of these concordats, kings now received many of the revenues that had previously gone to the papacy. They also acquired new powers to appoint candidates to church offices. It was, in many ways, a drastic reversal of the hard-won reforms of the eleventh and twelfth centuries that had created such a powerful papacy in the first place.

Having given away so many sources of revenue and authority, the popes of the late fifteenth century became even more dependent on their own territories in central Italy. But to tighten their hold on the Papal States, they had to rule like other Italian princes: leading armies, jockeying for alliances, and undermining their opponents by every possible means—including covert operations, murder, and assassination. Judged by the secular standards of the day, these efforts paid off: the Papal States became one of the better-governed and wealthier principalities in Italy. But such methods did nothing to increase the popes' reputation for piety, and disillusionment with the papacy as a force for the advancement of spirituality became even more widespread.

With both papal authority and Rome's spiritual prestige in decline, kings and princes became the primary figures to whom both clergy and laity looked for religious and moral guidance. Many secular rulers responded to such expectations aggressively, closing scandal-ridden monasteries, suppressing alleged heretics, regulating vice, and prohibiting the lower classes from dressing like the nobility. By these and other such measures, rulers could present themselves as champions of moral reform while also strengthening their political power. The result was an increasingly close link between national monarchies and national churches, a link that would become even stronger after the Reformation.

time of his death in 1505, Muscovy was firmly established as a dominant power. Indeed, the power of the tsar was more absolute in this period than that of any European monarch.

The Growth of National Churches

Meanwhile, as Muscovy laid claim to the mantle of Roman imperial power, the papacy was pouring resources into the glorification of the original Rome and the aggrandizement of the papal office. But neither the city nor its rulers could keep pace with their political and religious rivals. Following the Council of Constance (see Chapter 11), the papacy's victory over the conciliarists was a costly one. To win the support of Europe's kings and princes, various popes negotiated a series of religious treaties known as "concordats," which granted these rulers extensive authority over churches within their domains. The papacy thus secured its theoretical supremacy at the expense of its real power. Reigning popes also strengthened the national monarchies

The Triumph of the "Reconquista"

The kingdoms of the Iberian Peninsula were also in constant conflict during this period. In Castile, civil war and incompetent governance allowed the Castilian nobility to gain greater control over the peasantry and greater independence from the monarchy. In Aragon, royal government benefited from the extended commercial influence of Catalonia, which was under Aragonese authority. But after 1458, Aragon too became enmeshed in a civil war, a war in which both France and Castile became involved.

A solution to the disputed succession that had caused the war in Aragon would ultimately lie in the blending of powerful royal families. In 1469, Prince Ferdinand of Aragon was recognized as the undisputed heir to that throne

FERDINAND AND ISABELLA HONORING THE VIRGIN. In this contemporary Spanish painting, the royal couple are shown with two of their children and two household chaplains and in the company of the Blessed Virgin, the Christ Child, and saints from the Dominican order (the Dominicans were instrumental in conducting the affairs of the Spanish Inquisition). ▪ *How clear is the distinction between these holy figures and the royal family?* ▪ *What message is conveyed by their proximity?*

and, in the same year, secured this position by marrying Isabella, the heiress to Castile. Isabella became a queen in 1474, Ferdinand a king in 1479; and although Castile and Aragon continued to be ruled as separate kingdoms until 1714—there are tensions between the two former kingdoms even now—the marriage of Ferdinand and Isabella enabled the pursuit of several ambitious policies. In particular, their union allowed them to spend their combined resources on the creation of Europe's most powerful army, which was initially employed to conquer the last remaining principality of what had been al-Andalus: Muslim Spain. That principality, Granada, fell in 1492.

The End of the Convivencia and the Expulsion of the Jews

For more than seven relatively centuries, Spain's Jewish communities had enjoyed the many privileges extended by their Muslim rulers, who were also relatively tolerant of their Christian subjects. Indeed, scholars often refer to this period of Spain's history as a time of *convivencia,* a word that means "living together" or "harmonious coexistence." While relations among various religious and ethnic groups were not always uniformly peaceful or positive, the policies of Muslim rulers in al-Andalus had enabled an extraordinary hybrid culture to flourish there.

The aims of the Spanish Reconquista were diametrically opposed to those of "living together." The crusading ideology of "reconquest" sought instead to forge a single, homogenous community, based on the fiction that Spain had once been entirely Christian and should be restored to its former purity. The year 1492 therefore marks not only the end of Muslim rule in medieval Spain but also the culmination of a process of Jewish exclusion that had accelerated in the late thirteenth century (see Chapter 9). Within this history, the Spanish expulsion of the Jews stands out for the staggering scope of the displacements and destruction it entailed: at least 100,000 and possibly as many as 200,000 men, women, and children were deprived of their homes and livelihoods.

The Christian monarchs' motives for ordering this expulsion are still debated. Tens of thousands of Spanish Jews had converted to Christianity between 1391 and 1420, many as a result of coercion but some from sincere religious conviction. And for a generation or so, it seemed possible that these converts, known as *conversos,* might successfully assimilate into Christian society. But the same civil wars that led to the union of Ferdinand and Isabella made the *conversos* targets of discriminatory legislation. Conflict may also have fueled popular suspicions that these converts remained Jews in secret. To make "proper" Christians out of the *conversos,* the "Most Catholic" monarchs—as they were now called—may have concluded that they needed to remove any potentially seditious influences that might stem from the continuing presence of a Jewish community in Spain.

What became of the Spanish Jews? Some traveled north, to the Rhineland towns of Germany or to eastern Europe, but most settled in Muslim regions of the Mediterranean and Middle East. Many found a haven in the Ottoman Empire. As we already noted, there were many opportunities for advancement in the Ottoman imperial bureaucracy, while the Ottoman economy benefited from the highly skilled labor of Jewish artisans and the vast trading networks of Jewish merchants. In time, new forms and expressions of Jewish culture would emerge, and new communities would form. And although the extraordinary opportunities afforded by the *Convivencia* could never be revived, the descendants of these Spanish Jews—known as

Sephardi Jews, or Sephardim—still treasure the traditions and customs formed in Spain over a thousand years ago.

The Extension of the Reconquista

Although the Christian kingdoms of Iberia had been devoted, for centuries, to the reconquest of territory, the victory over the Muslims of Granada and the expulsion of the Jews in 1492 were watershed events. They mark the beginning of a sweeping initiative to construct a new basis for the precariously united kingdoms of Aragon and Castile, one that could transcend rival regional identities. Like other contemporary monarchs, Ferdinand and Isabella sought to strengthen their emerging nation-state by constructing an exclusively Christian identity for its people and by attaching that new identity to the crown and promoting a single national language, Castilian Spanish. They also succeeded in capturing and redirecting another language: the rhetoric of crusade.

The problem with the crusading ethos, as we have seen, is that it always seeks new outlets. Having created a new exclusively Christian Spanish kingdom through the defeat of all external enemies and internal threats, where were the energies harnessed by the Reconquista to be directed? The answer came from an unexpected quarter and had very unexpected consequences. Just a few months after Ferdinand and Isabella marched victoriously into Granada, the queen granted three ships to a Genoese adventurer who promised to reach India by sailing westward across the Atlantic Ocean, claiming any new lands he found for Spain. Columbus never reached India, but he did help to extend the tradition of reconquest to the New World—with far-reaching consequences.

NEW TARGETS AND TECHNOLOGIES OF CONQUEST

The Spanish monarchs' decision to underwrite a voyage of exploration was spurred by their desire to counter the successful Portuguese ventures of the past half century. For it was becoming clear that a tiny kingdom on the northwestern tip of the Iberian Peninsula would soon dominate the sea-lanes if rival entrepreneurs did not attempt to find alternate routes and establish equally lucrative colonies. This competition with Portugal was another reason why Isabella turned to a Genoese sea captain when she sought to expand Spain's wealth and global influence—not to a Portuguese one.

Prince Henry the Navigator and Portuguese Colonial Initiatives

Although Portugal had been an independent Christian kingdom since the twelfth century (see Chapter 9), it was never able to compete effectively with its more powerful neighbors (Muslim or Christian) on land. But when the focus of European economic expansion began to shift toward the Atlantic (see Chapter 10), Portuguese mariners were well placed to take advantage of the trend. A central figure in the history of Portuguese maritime imperialism is Prince Henry, later called "the Navigator" (1394–1460), a son of King João I of Portugal and his English queen, Philippa of Lancaster (sister of England's Henry IV).

Prince Henry was fascinated by the sciences of cartography and navigation, and he helped to ensure that Portuguese sailors had access to the latest charts and navigational instruments. He was also inspired by the stories told by John de Mandeville and Marco Polo—particularly the legend of Prester John, a mythical Christian king dwelling somewhere at the end of the earth, whom Europeans believed would be their ally against the Muslims if only they could locate him. More concretely, Prince Henry had ambitions to extend Portuguese control into the Atlantic, to tap into the burgeoning market for slaves in the Ottoman Empire and to establish direct links with the sources of African gold.

Prince Henry played an important part in organizing the Portuguese colonization of Madeira, the Canary Islands, and the Azores—and in the process he pioneered the Portuguese slave trade, which almost entirely eradicated the population of the Canaries before targeting Africa. By the 1440s, Portuguese explorers had reached the Cape Verde Islands. In 1444, they landed on the African mainland in the area that became known as the Gold Coast, where they began to collect cargoes of gold and slaves for export back to Portugal. Prince Henry personally directed eight of the thirty-five Portuguese voyages to Africa that occurred during his lifetime. And in order to outflank the cross-Saharan gold trade, largely controlled by the Muslims of North Africa and mediated by the Genoese, he decided to intercept this trade at its source by building a series of forts along the African coastline. This was also his main reason for colonizing the Canary

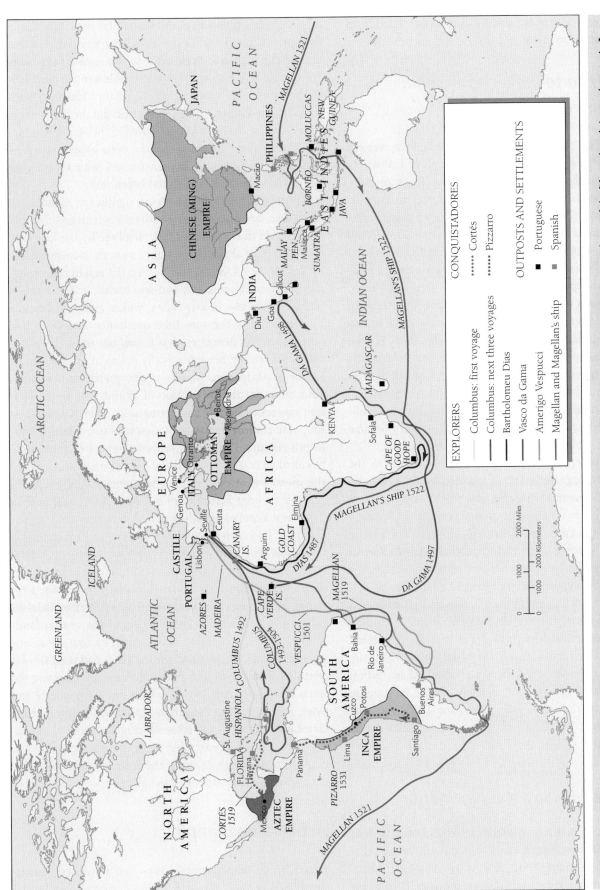

OVERSEAS EXPLORATION IN THE FIFTEENTH AND SIXTEENTH CENTURIES. ▪ *What were the major routes taken by European explorers of the fifteenth and sixteenth centuries?* ▪ *What appear to be the explorers' main goals?* ▪ *How might the establishment of outposts in Africa, America, and the East Indies have radically altered the balance of power in the Old World, and why?*

Islands, which he saw as a staging ground for expeditions into the African interior.

From Africa to India and Beyond: An Empire of Spices

By the 1470s, Portuguese sailors had rounded the western coast of Africa and were exploring the Gulf of Guinea. In 1483, they reached the mouth of the Congo River. In 1488, the Portuguese captain Bartholomeu Dias was accidentally blown around the southern tip of Africa by a gale, after which he named the point "Cape of Storms." But King João II (r. 1481–95) took a more optimistic view of Dias's achievement: he renamed it the Cape of Good Hope and began planning a naval expedition to India. In 1497–98, accordingly, Vasco da Gama rounded the cape, and then, with the help of a Muslim navigator named Ibn Majid, crossed the Indian Ocean to Calicut, on the southwestern coast of India. For the first time, this opened a viable sea route between Europe and the Far Eastern spice trade. Although Gama lost half his fleet and one-third of his men on his two-year voyage, his cargo of spices was so valuable that his losses were deemed insignificant. His heroism became legendary, and his story became the basis for the Portuguese national epic, the *Lusiads*.

Now masters of the quickest route to riches in the world, the Portuguese swiftly capitalized on their decades of accomplishment. Not only did their trading fleets sail regularly to India, there were Portuguese efforts to monopolize the entire spice trade: in 1509, the Portuguese defeated an Ottoman fleet and then blockaded the mouth of the Red Sea, attempting to cut off one of the traditional routes by which spices had traveled to Alexandria and Beirut. By 1510, Portuguese military forces had established a series of forts along the western Indian coastline, including their headquarters at Goa. In 1511, Portuguese ships seized Malacca, a center of the spice trade on the Malay Peninsula. By 1515, they had reached the Spice Islands (East Indies) and the coast of China. So completely did the Portuguese now dominate the spice trade that by the 1520s even the Venetians were forced to buy their pepper in the Portuguese capital of Lisbon.

Naval Technology and Navigation

The Portuguese caravel—the workhorse ship of those first voyages to Africa—was based on ship and sail designs that had been in use among Portuguese fishermen since the thirteenth century. Starting in the 1440s, however, Portuguese shipwrights began building larger caravels of about 50 tons

displacement equipped with two masts, each carrying a triangular (lateen) sail. Columbus's *Niña* was a ship of this design, although it was refitted with two square sails in the Portuguese-held Canary Islands to enable it to sail more efficiently before the wind during the Atlantic crossing. Such ships required much smaller crews than did the multi-oared galleys that were still commonly used in the Mediterranean. By the end of the fifteenth century, even larger caravels of around 200 tons were being constructed, with a third mast and a combination of square and lateen sails.

Europeans were also making significant advances in navigation during this era. Quadrants, which could calculate latitude in the Northern Hemisphere by the height of the North Star above the horizon, were in widespread use by the 1450s. As sailors approached the equator, however, the quadrant became less and less useful, and navigators instead made use of astrolabes, which reckoned latitude by the height of the sun. Like quadrants, astrolabes had been in use for centuries. But it was not until the 1480s that the astrolabe became a really practical instrument for seaborne navigation, thanks to the preparation of standard tables for the calculation of latitude whose preparation was sponsored by the Portuguese crown. Compasses, too, were coming into more widespread use during the fifteenth century. Longitude, however, remained impossible to calculate accurately until the eighteenth century, when the invention of the marine chronometer finally made it possible to keep accurate time at sea. In this prior age of discovery, Europeans sailing east or west across the oceans generally had to rely on their skill at dead reckoning to determine where they were.

European sailors also benefited from a new interest in maps and navigational charts. Especially important were books known as *rutters* or *routiers*. These contained detailed sailing instructions and descriptions of the coastal landmarks a pilot could expect to encounter en route to a variety of destinations. Mediterranean sailors had used similar portolan charts since the thirteenth century, mapping the ports along the coastlines, tracking prevailing winds and tides, and indicating dangerous reefs and shallow harbors (see Chapter 10). In the fifteenth century, these mapmaking techniques were extended to the Atlantic Ocean; by the end of the sixteenth century, the accumulated knowledge contained in rutters spanned the globe.

Artillery and Empire

Larger, more maneuverable ships and improved navigational aids made it possible for the Portuguese and other European mariners to reach Africa, Asia, and—eventually—

SPANISH GALLEON. The larger, full-bottomed ships that came into use during the fifteenth century would become engines of imperial conquest and the vessels that brought the riches of those conquests back to Europe. This wooden model was made for the Museo Storico Navale di Venezia (Naval History Museum) in Venice, Italy.

the Americas. But fundamentally, these European commercial empires were military achievements that capitalized on what Europeans had learned in their wars against each other. Perhaps the most critical military advance was the increasing sophistication of artillery, a development made possible not only by gunpowder but also by improved metallurgical techniques for casting cannon barrels. By the middle of the fifteenth century, as we observed in Chapter 11, the use of artillery pieces had rendered the stone walls of medieval castles and towns obsolete, a fact brought home in 1453 by the successful French siege of Bordeaux (which ended the Hundred Years' War), and by the Ottoman siege of Constantinople (which ended the Byzantine Empire).

Indeed, the new ship designs (first caravels, and then the heavier galleons) were important in part because their larger size made it possible to mount more effective artillery pieces on them. European vessels were now conceived as floating artillery platforms, with scores of guns mounted in fixed positions along their sides and swivel guns mounted fore and aft. These guns were vastly expensive, as were the ships that carried them, but for those rulers who could afford them, such ships made it possible to back mercantile ventures with military power. As we already noted, Vasco da Gama had been able to sail into the Indian Ocean in 1498, but the Portuguese did not gain control of that ocean until 1509, when they defeated combined Ottoman and Indian naval forces. Portuguese trading outposts in Africa and Asia were essentially fortifications, built not so much to guard against the attacks of native peoples as to ward off assaults from other Europeans. Without this essential military component, the European maritime empires that were emerging in this period could not have existed.

Atlantic Colonization and a New Kind of Slavery

Although slavery had effectively disappeared in much of northwestern Europe by the early twelfth century, it continued in parts of the Mediterranean world and had been introduced into some regions of eastern Europe after the Black Death. But this slavery existed on a very small scale. There were no slave-powered factories or large-scale agricultural systems in this period. The only major slave markets and slave economies were in the Ottoman Empire, and there slaves ran the vast Ottoman bureaucracy and staffed the army. And in all these cases, as in antiquity, no aspect of slavery was racially based. In Italy and elsewhere in the medieval Mediterranean world, slaves were often captives from an array of locales. In eastern Europe, they were functionally serfs. Most Ottoman slaves were European Christians, predominantly Poles, Ukrainians, Greeks, and Bulgarians. In the early Middle Ages, Germanic and Celtic peoples had been widely enslaved. Under the Roman Empire, slaves had come from every part of the known (and unknown) world.

What was new about the slavery of the late fifteenth century was its increasing racialization—an aspect of modern slavery that has made an indelible impact on our own society. To Europeans, African slaves were visible in ways that other slaves were not, and it became convenient for those who dealt in them to justify the mass deportation of entire populations by claiming their racial inferiority and their "natural" fitness for a life of bondage. This nefarious practice, too, has had long-lasting and tragic consequences that still afflict the civilizations of our own world.

In Lisbon, which became a significant market for enslaved Africans during Prince Henry's lifetime, something on the order of 15,000 to 20,000 African captives were sold within a twenty-year period. In the following half century, by about 1505, the numbers amounted to 150,000. For the most part, the purchasers of these slaves regarded them as

The Ottomans' Army of Slaves

Although the growing African slave trade was creating a newly racialized idea of slavery in the Caribbean and the Americas, slavery in Europe was not tied to race. Indeed, slavery could be a path to upward mobility in the Ottoman Empire. The following account is from a memoir written by Konstantin Mihailovic, a Serbian Christian who was captured as a youth by the army of Sultan Mehmet II. For eight years, he served in the Ottoman janissary ("gate-keeper") corps. In 1463, the fortress he was defending for the sultan was captured by the Hungarians, after which he recorded his experiences for a Christian audience.

Whenever the Turks invade foreign lands and capture their people, an imperial scribe follows immediately behind them, and whatever boys there are, he takes them all into the janissaries and gives five gold pieces for each one and sends them across the sea [to Anatolia]. There are about two thousand of these boys. If, however, the number of them from enemy peoples does not suffice, then he takes from the Christians in every village in his land who have boys, having established what is the most every village can give so that the quota will always be full. And the boys whom he takes in his own land are called *cilik*. Each one of them can leave his property to whomever he wants after his death. And those whom he takes among the enemies are called *pendik*. These latter after their deaths can leave nothing; rather, it goes to the emperor, except that if someone comports himself well and is so deserving that he be freed, he may leave it to whomever he wants. And on the boys who are across the sea the emperor spends nothing; rather, those to whom they are entrusted must maintain them and send them where he orders. Then they take those who are suited for it on ships and there they study and train to skirmish in battle. There the emperor already provides for them and gives them a wage. From there he chooses for his own court those who are trained and then raises their wages.

Source: Konstantin Mihailovic, *Memoirs of a Janissary* (Michigan Slavic Translations 3), trans. Benjamin Stolz (Ann Arbor, MI: 1975), pp. 157–59.

Questions for Analysis

1. Why might the Ottoman emperor have established this system for "recruiting" and training janissaries? What are its strengths and weaknesses?

2. Based on your knowledge of Western civilizations, how unusual would you deem this method of raising troops? How does it compare to the strategies of other rulers we have studied?

status symbols; it became fashionable to have African footmen, page boys, and ladies' maids. In the Atlantic colonies—Madeira, the Canaries, and the Azores—land was still worked mainly by European settlers and sharecroppers. Slave labor, if it was employed at all, was generally used only in sugar mills. On Madeira and the Canaries, where sugar became the predominant cash crop during the last quarter of the fifteenth century, some slaves were introduced as agricultural laborers. But even sugar production did not lead to the widespread introduction of slavery on these islands.

However, a new kind of slave-based sugar plantation began to emerge in Portugal's eastern Atlantic colonies in the 1460s, starting on the Cape Verde Islands and then extending southward into the Gulf of Guinea. These islands were not populated when the Portuguese began to settle them, and their climate generally discouraged most Europeans from living there. They were ideally located, however, along the routes of slave traders venturing outward from the nearby West African coast. It was this plantation model that would be exported to Brazil by the Portuguese and to the Caribbean islands of the Americas by their Spanish conquerors, with incalculable consequences for the peoples of Africa, the Americas, and Europe (see Chapter 14).

EUROPEANS IN A NEW WORLD

Like his contemporaries, Christopher Columbus (1451–1506) understood that the world was a sphere. But like them, he also thought it was much smaller than it actually is. (As we saw in Chapter 4, the accurate calculation of the globe's circumference made in ancient Alexandria had been suppressed centuries later by Roman geographers.) Furthermore, it had long been accepted that there were only three continents, Europe, Asia, and Africa—hence Columbus's decision to reach Asia by sailing west, a plan that seemed even more plausible after the discovery and colonization of the Canary Islands and the Azores. The existence of these islands reinforced a new hypothesis that the Atlantic was dotted with similar lands all the way to Japan. This emboldened Columbus's royal patrons, who became convinced that the Genoese mariner could reach China in about a month, after a stop for provisions on the Canaries. This turned out to be a kind of self-fulfilling prophecy, for when Columbus reached the Bahamas and the island of Hispaniola after only a month's sailing, he reported that he had reached the outer islands of Asia.

The Shock of Discovery

Of course, Columbus was not the first European to set foot on the American continents. As we have already learned, Viking sailors briefly settled present-day Newfoundland, Labrador, and perhaps even portions of New England around the year 1000 (see Chapter 8). But knowledge of these Viking landings had been forgotten or ignored outside of Iceland for hundreds of years. It wasn't until the 1960s that the stories of these expeditions were corroborated by archaeological evidence. Moreover, the tiny Norwegian colony on Greenland—technically part of the North American landmass—had been abandoned in the fifteenth century, when the cooling of the climate (see Chapter 10) destroyed the fragile ecosystems that had barely sustained the lives of Norse settlers there.

Although Columbus brought back no spices to prove that he had found an alternate route to Asia, he did return with some small samples of gold and a few indigenous people—whose existence gave promise of entire tribes that might be "saved" by conversion to Christianity and whose lands could provide homes for Spanish settlers seeking new frontiers after the Reconquista. This provided sufficient incentive for the "Most Catholic" monarchs to finance three further expeditions by Columbus, and many more by other adventurers, missionaries, and colonists.

Meanwhile, the Portuguese, who had already obtained a papal bull granting them (hypothetical) ownership of all lands south of the Canaries, rushed to establish their own claims. After two years of wrangling and conflicting papal pronouncements, the Treaty of Tordesillas (1494) sought to demarcate Spanish and Portuguese possession of as-yet-undiscovered lands. The Spanish would ultimately emerge as the big winners in this gambling match. Within a decade, the coasts of two hitherto unknown continents were identified, as were clusters of new islands, most on the Spanish side of the (still disputed) meridian.

Gradually, Europeans reached the conclusion that the voyages of Columbus and his immediate successors had revealed an entirely "New World." And—shockingly—this world had not been foretold either by the teachings of Christianity or the wisdom of the ancients. Among the first to champion the fact of two new continents' existence was the Italian explorer and geographer Amerigo Vespucci (1454–1512), whose name was soon adopted as a descriptor for them. Eventually, those who came to accept this fact were forced to question the reliability of the key sources of knowledge on which Western civilizations had hitherto hinged (see Chapter 14).

At first, the realization that the Americas (as they were now called) were not an outpost of Asia came as a disappointment to the Spanish: two major land masses and two vast oceans disrupted their plans to beat the Portuguese to the Spice Islands. But new possibilities gradually became clear. In 1513, the Spanish explorer Vasco Núñez de Balboa first viewed the Pacific Ocean from the Isthmus of Panama, and news of the narrow divide between two vast oceans prompted Ferdinand and Isabella's grandson to renew their dream. This young monarch, Charles V (1500–1556), ruled not only Spain but the huge patchwork of territories encompassed by the Holy Roman Empire. In 1519, he accepted Ferdinand Magellan's proposal to see whether a route to Asia could be found by sailing around South America.

But Magellan's voyage demonstrated beyond question that the world was simply too large for any such plan to be feasible at that time. Of the five ships that left Spain under his command, only one returned, three years later, having been forced to circumnavigate the globe. Out of a crew of 265 sailors, only 18 survived. Most had died of scurvy or starvation; Magellan himself had been killed in a skirmish with native peoples in the Philippines.

This fiasco ended all hope of discovering an easy southwest passage to Asia—although the deadly dream

Interpreting Visual Evidence

America as an Object of Desire

Under the influence of popular travel narratives that had circulated in Europe for centuries, Columbus and his fellow voyagers were prepared to find the New World full of cannibals. They also assumed that the indigenous peoples' custom of wearing little or no clothing—not to mention their "savagery"—would render their women sexually available. In a letter sent back home in 1495, one of Columbus's men recounted a notable encounter with a "cannibal girl" whom he had taken captive in his tent and whose naked body aroused his desire. He was surprised to find that she resisted his advances so fiercely that he had to tie her up—which of course made it easier for him to "subdue" her. In the end, he cheerfully reports, the girl's sexual performance was so satisfying that she might have been trained, as he put it, in a "school for whores."

The Flemish artist Jan van der Straet (1523–1605) would have heard many such reports of the encounters between (mostly male) Europeans and the peoples of the New World. This engraving, based on one of his drawings, is among the thousands of mass-produced images that circulated widely in Europe, thanks to the invention of printing. It imagines the first encounter between a male "Americus" (like Columbus or Amerigo Vespucci himself) and the New World, "America," depicted as a voluptuous, available woman. The Latin caption reads: "America rises to meet Americus; and whenever he calls her, she will always be aroused."

Americen Americus retexit, & ... AMERICA. Semel vocauit inde semper excitam ... .

Ioan Stradanus invent.
Theodor. Galle sculp.

Questions for Analysis

1. Study the details of this image carefully. What does each symbolize, and how do they work together as an allegory of conquest and colonization?

2. On what stereotypes of indigenous peoples does this image draw? Notice, for example, the cannibalistic campfire of the group in the background or the posture of "America."

3. The New World itself—America—is imagined as female in this image. Why is this? What messages might this—and the suggestive caption—have conveyed to a European viewer?

of a northwest passage survived and motivated many European explorers of North America into the twentieth century. It has been revived today: in our age of global warming, the retreat of Arctic pack ice has led to the opening of new shipping lanes, and in 2008 the first commercial voyage successfully traversed the Arctic Ocean.

The Dream of Gold and the Downfall of Empires

Although the unforeseen size of the globe made a westward passage to Asia untenable, given the technologies then available, Europeans were quick to capitalize on the sources of wealth that the New World itself could offer. What chiefly fired the imagination were those small samples of gold that Columbus had initially brought back to Spain. While rather paltry in themselves, they nurtured hopes that gold might lie piled in ingots somewhere in these vast new lands, ready to enrich any adventurer who discovered them. Rumor fed rumor, until a few freelance Spanish soldiers really did strike it rich beyond their most avaricious imaginings.

Their success, though, had little to do with their own efforts. Within a generation after the landing of the first ships under Columbus's command, European diseases had spread rapidly among the indigenous peoples of the Caribbean and the coastlines of the Americas. These diseases—especially measles and smallpox—were not fatal to those who carried them, because Europeans had developed immunities over many generations. But to the peoples of this New World, they were deadly in the extreme. For example, there were probably 250,000 people living on Hispaniola when Columbus arrived; within thirty years—a single generation—70 percent had perished from disease.

Moreover, the new waves of *conquistadores* (conquerors) were assisted by the complex political, economic, and military rivalries that already existed among the highly sophisticated societies they encountered. The Aztec Empire of Mexico rivaled any European state in its power, culture, and wealth—and like any successful empire it had subsumed many neighboring territories in the course of its own conquests. Its capital, Tenochtitlán (*ten-och-tit-LAN*, now Mexico City), amazed its European assailants, who had never seen anything like the height and grandeur of its buildings or the splendor of its public works. This splendor was itself evidence of the Aztecs' imperial might, which was resisted by many of the peoples from whom they demanded tribute.

The Aztecs' eventual conqueror, Hernán Cortés (1485–1547), had arrived in Hispaniola as a young man, in the wake of Columbus's initial landing. He had received a land grant from the Spanish crown and acted as magistrate of one of the first towns established there. In 1519, he headed an expedition to the mainland, which had been the target of some earlier exploratory missions that had not resulted in any permanent settlements—owing largely to the tight control of the Aztecs, whose imperial domain extended far beyond Tenochtitlán.

When Cortés arrived on the coast of the Aztec realm, he formed an intimate relationship with a native woman known as La Malinche. She became his consort and interpreter in the Nahua language, which was a lingua franca among the many different ethnic groups within the empire. With her help, he discovered that some peoples subjugated by the Aztecs were rebellious, and so he began to form stra-

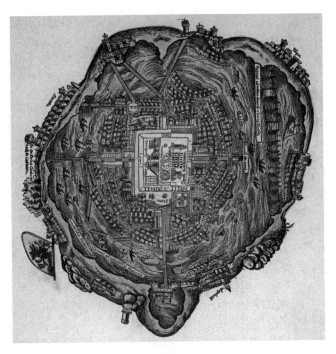

THE AZTEC CITY OF TENOCHTITLÁN. The Spanish conquistador Bernal Díaz del Castillo (1492–1585) took part in the conquest of the Aztec Empire and later wrote a historical account of his adventures. His admiring description of the Aztec capital at Tenochtitlán records that the Spaniards were amazed to see such a huge city built in the midst of a vast lake, with gigantic buildings arranged in a meticulous urban plan around a central square and broad causeways linking the city to the mainland. This hand-colored woodcut was included in an early edition of Hernán Cortés's letters to Emperor Charles V, printed at Nuremberg (Germany) in 1524.

tegic alliances with their leaders. Cortés himself could only muster a force of a few hundred men, but his native allies numbered in the thousands.

These strategic alliances were crucial: although Cortés and his men had potentially superior weapons—guns and horses—these were more effective for their novelty than their utility. In fact, the rifles were of inferior quality, while gunpowder dampened by the humid climate had a tendency to misfire or fail to ignite altogether. So Cortés adopted the tactics and weaponry of his native allies in his dealings with the Aztec king, Montezuma II (r. 1502–1520), and in his final assaults upon the fortification of Tenochtitlán. In the end, though, it was European bacteria (not European technology or cunning) that led to his victory: the Aztecs were devastated by an outbreak of the plague virus that had arrived along with Cortés and his men. In 1521, their empire fell.

In 1533, another lucky conquistador, Francisco Pizarro, would manage to topple the highly centralized empire of the Incas, based in what is now Peru, by similar voluntary and involuntary means. In this case, he took advantage of an ongoing civil war that had weakened the reigning dynasty. He was also assisted by an epidemic of smallpox. Like Cortés, Pizarro promised his native allies liberation from an oppressive regime. Those formerly subject to the Aztecs and Incas would soon be able to judge how partial these promises were.

The Price of Conquest

The astonishing conquests of Mexico and Peru gave the conquistadors access to hoards of gold and silver that had been accumulated for centuries by Aztec and Inca rulers. Almost immediately, however, a search for the sources of these precious metals was launched by agents of the Spanish crown. The first gold deposits were discovered in Hispaniola, where surface mines were speedily established using native laborers, who were already dying in appalling numbers from disease and were now further decimated by brutality and overwork. The population dwindled further, to a mere 10 percent of its Pre-Columbian strength.

The loss of so many workers made the mines of Hispaniola uneconomical to operate, so European colonists turned instead to cattle raising and sugar production. Modeling their sugarcane plantations on those of the Cape Verde Islands and St. Thomas (São Tomé) in the Gulf of Guinea, colonists began to import thousands of African slaves to labor in the new industry. Sugar production was, by its nature, a capital-intensive undertaking. The need to import slave labor added further to its costs, guaranteeing that control over the new industry would fall into the hands of a few extremely wealthy planters and financiers.

Despite the establishment of sugar production in the Caribbean and cattle ranching on the Mexican mainland—whose devastating effects on the fragile ecosystem of Central America will be discussed in Chapter 14—it was mining that would shape the Spanish colonies most fundamentally in this period. If gold was the lure that had initially inspired the conquest, silver became its most lucrative export. Even before the discovery of vast silver deposits, the Spanish crown had taken steps to assume direct control over all colonial exports. It was therefore to the Spanish crown that the profits of empire were channeled. Europe's silver

SPANISH CONQUISTADORS IN MEXICO. This sixteenth-century drawing of conquistadors slaughtering the Aztec aristocracy emphasizes the advantages that plate armor and steel swords gave to the Spanish soldiers.

A Spanish Critique of New World Conquest

Not all Europeans approved of European imperialism or its "civilizing" effects on the peoples of the New World. One of the most influential contemporary critics was Bartolomé de las Casas (1484–1566). In 1502, when Bartolomé was eighteen years old, he and his father joined an expedition to Hispaniola. In 1510, he became the first ordained priest in the Americas and eventually became bishop of Chiapas (Mexico). Although he was a product of his times—he owned many slaves—he was also prescient in discerning the devastating effects of European settlement in the West Indies and Central America, and he particularly deplored the exploitation and extermination of indigenous populations. The following excerpt is from one of the many eloquent manifestos he published in an attempt to gain the sympathies of the Spanish crown and to reach a wide readership. It was printed in 1542 but draws on the impressions and opinions he had formed since his arrival in New Spain as a young man.

od made all the peoples of this area, many and varied as they are, as open and as innocent as can be imagined. The simplest people in the world—unassuming, long-suffering, unassertive, and submissive—they are without malice or guile, and are utterly faithful and obedient both to their own native lords and to the Spaniards in whose service they now find themselves.... They are innocent and pure in mind and have a lively intelligence, all of which makes them particularly receptive to learning and understanding the truths of our Catholic faith and to being instructed in virtue; indeed, God has invested them with fewer impediments in this regard than any other people on earth....

It was upon these gentle lambs ... that from the very first day they clapped eyes on them the Spanish fell like ravening wolves upon the fold, or like tigers and savage lions who have not eaten meat for days. The pattern established at the outset has remained unchanged to this day, and the Spaniards still do nothing save tear the natives to shreds, murder them and inflict upon them untold misery, suffering and distress, tormenting, harrying and persecuting them mercilessly....

When the Spanish first journeyed there, the indigenous population of the island of Hispaniola stood at some three million; today only two hundred survive. The island of Cuba, which extends for a distance almost as great as that separating Valladolid from Rome, is now to all intents and purposes uninhabited; and two other large, beautiful and fertile islands, Puerto Rico and Jamaica, have been similarly devastated. Not a living soul remains today on any of the islands of the Bahamas ... even though every single one of the sixty or so islands in the group ... is more fertile and more beautiful than the Royal Gardens in Seville and the climate is as healthy as anywhere on earth. The native population, which once numbered some five hundred thousand, was wiped out by forcible expatriation to the island of Hispaniola, a policy adopted by the Spaniards in an endeavour to make up losses among the indigenous population of that island....

At a conservative estimate, the despotic and diabolical behaviour of the Christians has, over the last forty years, led to the unjust and totally unwarranted deaths of more than twelve million souls, women and children among them....

The reason the Christians have murdered on such a vast scale and killed anyone and everyone in their way is purely and simply greed.... The Spaniards have shown not the slightest consideration for these people, treating them (and I speak from first-hand experience, having been there from the outset) not as brute animals—indeed, I would to God they had done and had shown them the consideration they afford their animals—so much as piles of dung in the middle of the road. They have had as little concern for their souls as for their bodies, all the millions that have perished having gone to their deaths with no knowledge of God and without the benefit of the Sacraments. One fact in all this is widely known and beyond dispute, for even the tyrannical murderers themselves acknowledge the truth of it: the indigenous peoples never did the Europeans any harm whatever....

Source: Bartolomé de las Casas, *A Short Account of the Destruction of the Indies,* trans. Nigel Griffin (Harmondsworth, UK: 1992), pp. 9–12.

Questions for Analysis

1. Given his perspective on the behavior of his countrymen, how might Bartolomé de las Casas have justified his own presence in New Spain (Mexico)? What do you think he may have hoped to achieve by publishing this account?

2. What comparisons does the author make between New Spain (Mexico) and the Old, and between indigenous peoples and Europeans? What is he trying to convey?

3. Compare this account with the contemporary engraving on page 000. What new light does this excerpt throw on that visual allegory? How might a reader-viewer of the time have reconciled these two very different pictures of European imperialism?

shortage, which had been acute for centuries, therefore came to an end.

Yet this massive infusion of silver into the European economy created more problems than it solved, because it accelerated an inflation that had already begun in the late fifteenth century. Initially, inflation had been driven by the renewed growth of the European population, an expanding colonial economy, and a relatively fixed supply of food. Thereafter, thanks to the influx of New World silver, inflation was driven by the hugely increased supply of coinage. As we shall see, this abundance of coinage led to the doubling and quadrupling of prices in the course of the sixteenth century and the collapse of this inflated economy—paradoxically driving a wave of impoverished Europeans to settle in the New World in ever greater numbers.

CONCLUSION

The expansion of the Mediterranean world into the Atlantic, which had been ongoing since the thirteenth century, was the essential preliminary to Columbus's voyages and to the rise of European empires in Africa, India, the Caribbean, and the Americas. Other events and innovations that we have surveyed in this chapter played a key role, too: the relatively rapid communications facilitated by the printing press; the tussle for power in Italy that led to the development of ever deadlier weapons; the navigational and colonial initiatives of the Portuguese; and the success of the Spanish Reconquista, which displaced Spain's venerable Jewish community and enabled Spanish rulers and adventurers to seek their fortunes overseas.

After You Read This Chapter

Visit StudySpace for quizzes, additional review materials, and multimedia documents. **wwnorton.com/web/westernciv18**

REVIEWING THE OBJECTIVES

- The artists of Italy were closely tied to those with political and military power. How did this relationship affect the kinds of work these artists produced?
- What aspects of Renaissance artistry and learning were adopted in northern Europe?
- What was the Reconquista, and how did it lead to a new way of thinking about Spanish identity?
- Europeans, especially the Portuguese, were developing new technologies and techniques that enabled exploration and colonial ventures in this period. What were they?
- The "discovery" of the New World had profound effects on the indigenous peoples and environment of the Americas. Describe some of these effects.

For the indigenous peoples and empires of the Americas, the results were cataclysmic. Within a century of Europeans' arrival, between 50 and 90 percent of some native populations had perished from disease, massacre, and enslavement. Moreover, Europeans' capacity to further their imperial ambitions wherever ships could sail and guns could penetrate profoundly destabilized Europe and its neighbors, sharpening the divisions among competing kingdoms and empires.

The ideals of the humanists and the artistry associated with the Renaissance often stand in sharp contrast to the harsh realities alongside which they coexisted and in which they were rooted. Artists could thrive in the atmosphere of competition and one-upmanship that characterized this period, but they could also find themselves reduced to the status of servants in the households of the wealthy and powerful—or forced to subordinate their artistry to the demands of warfare and espionage. Meanwhile, intellectuals and statesmen looked for inspiration to the precedents and glories of the past. But to which aspects of the past? Some humanists may have wanted to revive the principles of the Roman Republic, but many of them worked for ambitious despots who modeled themselves on Rome's dictators. The theories that undergirded European politics and colonial expansion were being used to legitimize many different kinds of power, including that of the papacy. All of these trends would be carried forward in the sixteenth century and would have a role to play in the upheaval that shattered Europe's fragile religious unity. It is to this upheaval, the Reformation, that we turn in Chapter 13.

PEOPLE, IDEAS, AND EVENTS IN CONTEXT

- Why was **GUTENBERG**'s invention of the **PRINTING PRESS** such a significant development?
- How did **NICCOLÒ MACHIAVELLI** respond to Italy's political situation within Europe? In what ways do artists like **LEONARDO DA VINCI** and **MICHELANGELO BUONARROTI** exemplify the ideals and realities of the Renaissance?
- How did northern European scholars like **DESIDERIUS ERASMUS** and **THOMAS MORE** apply humanist ideas to Christianity? How were these ideas expressed in art?
- What is significant about **IVAN THE GREAT**'s use of the title **TSAR**? In what other ways did the Russian emperor claim to be the heir of Rome?
- How did **ISABELLA OF CASTILE** and **FERDINAND OF ARAGON** succeed in creating a unified Spain through the **RECONQUISTA**?
- How does **PRINCE HENRY THE NAVIGATOR** exemplify the motives for pursuing overseas expansion? Why were the Portuguese so successful in establishing colonies in this period?
- What were the expectations that launched **COLUMBUS**'s voyage? What enabled the Spanish **CONQUISTADORS** to subjugate the peoples of the **AMERICAS**?

THINKING ABOUT CONNECTIONS

- Phrases like "Renaissance man" and "a Renaissance education" are still part of our common vocabulary. Given what you have learned in this chapter, how has your understanding of such phrases changed? How would you explain their true meaning to others?
- How do the patterns of conquest and colonization discussed in this chapter compare to those of earlier periods, for example the era of the Crusades or the empires of antiquity? How many of these developments were new?
- Although the growth of the African slave trade would result in a new racialization of slavery in the Atlantic world, the justifications for slavery had very old roots. How might Europeans have used Greek and Roman precedents in defense of these new ventures? (See Chapters 4 and 5.)

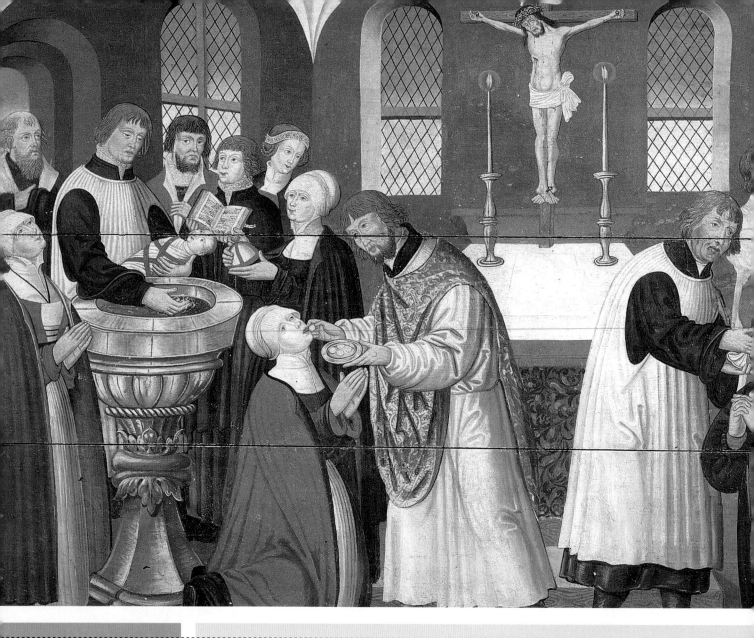

STORY LINES

- The movement catalyzed by Martin Luther's challenge to the Church grew out of much earlier attempts at reform, but it was also a response to more recent religious and political developments.

- Within a decade after Luther's break with Rome, religious dissent was widespread and a number of different Protestant faiths were taking hold in various regions of Europe.

- Protestantism transformed not only the political landscape of Europe but also basic structures of the family and the attitudes toward marriage and sexuality which still shape our lives today.

- These changes also affected the structures and doctrine of the Roman Catholic ("universal") Church, which reemerged as an institution different in many ways from the medieval Church and more similar to that of today.

Before You Read This Chapter

CHRONOLOGY

1517	Luther posts the Ninety-five Theses
1520s	Lutheranism becomes the official religion of Scandinavian countries
1521	Luther is excommunicated at the Diet of Worms
1525	Swabian peasants' revolt
1529	Luther breaks with Zwingli
1534	Henry VIII establishes the Church of England
1534	Ignatius Loyola founds the Society of Jesus (the Jesuits)
1541	Geneva adopts a theocratic government based on Calvinism
1545–1563	Council of Trent is convened
1555	Peace of Augsburg
1553–1558	Mary Tudor attempts to restore the Catholic faith in England
1559	Elizabeth reestablishes Protestantism in England
1564	Index of prohibited books is published for the first time

The Age of Dissent and Division, 1500–1564

CORE OBJECTIVES

- **DEFINE** the main premises of Lutheranism.

- **EXPLAIN** why Switzerland emerged as an important Protestant center.

- **IDENTIFY** the ways in which family structures and values changed during the Reformation.

- **UNDERSTAND** the reasons behind England's unusual brand of Protestantism.

- **DESCRIBE** the Catholic Church's response to the challenge of Protestantism.

n 1517, on the night before the Feast of All Saints—All Hallows' Eve, or Halloween—a professor of theology at a small university in northern Germany published a series of debating points on the door of Wittenberg's All Saints' Church, which served as the university's chapel. (It was also known as "Castle church," because it formed part of the princely palace recently built for the local ruler, the elector of Saxony.) This was not a prank; it was the usual method of announcing a scholarly disputation, and the door of the church had been used for this purpose since the university's founding in 1502. Yet there was something peculiarly appropriate in Martin Luther's choice of an evening traditionally associated with mischief-making. Although he cannot have anticipated the magnitude of mischief it would cause, the posting of ninety-five theses was a subversive act. For one thing, the sheer number of propositions that Dr. Luther offered to debate was unusual. But what really caught the attention of his fellow scholars was their unifying theme—the corruption of the Church and, in particular, the office of the pope—and the rational yet passionate manner in which that theme was expounded. It was a topic very much in vogue at the time, but it had seldom been dissected so clearly by a licensed theologian who was also a monk, an ordained priest, a charismatic teacher, and a man of strong convictions.

Thanks to Luther's well-placed correspondents, this document and the debate it stimulated soon found audiences well beyond Wittenberg. By the time the papacy formally retaliated, in 1520, dissent was widespread—and not only among academics. Many of Europe's kings and princes saw the political advantages of either defying or defending the pope, and they chose sides accordingly. Luther's own lord, Frederick III of Saxony, would spend the rest of his life shielding the man who had first expounded those theses in his own Castle church.

Luther had grown up in a largely peaceful Europe. After two centuries of economic, social, and political turmoil, its economy was expanding, its cities were growing, and its major monarchies were secure. Indeed, governments at every level were extending and deepening their control over people's lives, and the population itself was increasing. Europeans had also embarked on a new period of colonial expansion. Meanwhile, the Church had weathered the storms of the Avignon captivity and the Great Schism. Heresies had been suppressed or contained. In the struggle over conciliarism, the papacy had won the support of all major European rulers, which effectively relegated the conciliarists to academic isolation at the University of Paris. At the local level, the devotion of ordinary Christians was strong and the parish a crucial site of community identity. To be sure, there were some problems. The educational standards of parish clergy were higher than they had ever been, but reformers noted that too many priests were ignorant or neglectful of their spiritual duties. Monasticism, by and large, seemed to have lost its spiritual fire. Religious enthusiasm sometimes led to superstition. Yet, on the whole, these problems were manageable.

No one could have predicted that Europe's religious and political coherence would be irreparably shattered in the course of a generation, or that the next century would witness an appallingly destructive series of wars. Nor could anyone have foreseen that the catalyst for these extraordinary events would be a university professor. The debate ignited by Martin Luther (1483–1546) would set off the chain reaction we know as the Reformation. Initially intended as a call for another phase in the Church's long history of internal reforms, Luther's teachings instead launched a religious revolution that would splinter western Christendom into a variety of Protestant ("dissenting") faiths, while prompting the Roman Church to reaffirm its status as the only true Catholic ("universal") faith through a parallel revolution. At the same time, these movements deepened existing divisions among peoples, rulers, and

states. The result was a profound transformation of the religious, social, and political landscape that affected the lives of everyone in Europe—and everyone in the new European colonies, then and now.

MARTIN LUTHER'S CHALLENGE

To explain the impact of Martin Luther's ideas, we must answer three central questions:

1. Why did Luther's theology lead him to break with Rome?
2. Why did large numbers of people rally to his cause?
3. Why did so many German princes and towns impose the new Protestant religion within their territories?

As we shall see, those who followed Luther found his message appealing for different reasons. Many peasants hoped that the new religion would free them from the exactions of their lords; towns and princes thought it would allow them to consolidate their political independence; national-

MARTIN LUTHER. This late portrait is by Lucas Cranach the Elder (1472–1553), court painter to the electors of Brandenburg and a friend of Luther.

ists thought it would liberate Germany from the demands of foreign popes bent on feathering their own nests in central Italy.

But what Luther's followers shared was a conviction that their new understanding of Christianity would lead to spiritual salvation, whereas the traditional religion of Rome would not. For this reason, *reformation* is a misleading term for the movement they initiated. Although Luther himself began as a reformer seeking to change the Church from within, he quickly developed into an uncompromising opponent of its principles and practices. Many of his followers were even more radical. The movement that began with Luther therefore went beyond "reformation." It was a frontal assault on religious, political, and social institutions that had been in place for a thousand years.

Luther's Quest for Justice

Although Martin Luther became an inspiration to millions, he was a terrible disappointment to his father. The elder Luther was a Thuringian peasant who had prospered through some in business ventures. Eager to see his clever son rise still further, he sent young Luther to the University of Erfurt to study law. In 1505, however, Martin shattered his hopes by becoming a monk of the Augustinian order. In some sense, though, Luther was a chip off the old block. Throughout his life, he lived simply and expressed himself in the vigorous, earthy vernacular of the German peasantry.

Luther arrived at his personal understanding of religious truth through a dramatic conversion experience. As a monk, he zealously pursued all the traditional means for achieving holiness. Not only did he fast and pray continuously, but also he reportedly confessed his sins so often that his exhausted confessor would sometimes jokingly suggest that he should do something really bad if he wanted to do penance. Yet, try as he might, Luther could find no spiritual peace; he feared that he could never perform enough good deeds to deserve so great a gift as salvation. But an insight then led to a new understanding of God's justice.

For years, Luther had worried that it seemed unfair for God to issue commandments that he knew humans could not observe—and then to punish them with eternal damnation. But after becoming a professor of theology at the University of Wittenberg, Luther's further study of the Bible suggested to him that God's justice lay not in his power to punish but rather in his mercy. As Luther later wrote, "I began to understand the justice of God as that by which God makes *us* just, in his mercy and through faith . . . and at this I felt as though I had been born again, and had gone through open gates into paradise." Since this realization came to Luther in the tower room of his monastery, it is often termed his "tower experience."

Lecturing at Wittenberg in the years immediately following this incident, which occurred around 1515, Luther pondered a passage in Saint Paul's Letter to the Romans—"[T]he just shall live by faith" (1:17)—until he reached his central doctrine of "justification by faith alone." Luther

LUTHER'S TRANSLATION OF THE BIBLE. The printing press was instrumental to the rapid dissemination of Luther's messages, as well as those of his supporters and challengers. Also essential was the fact that Luther addressed his audience in plain language, in their native German, and that pamphlets and vernacular Bibles like this one could be rapidly and cheaply mass produced.

concluded that God's justice does not demand endless good works and religious rituals for salvation, because humans can never be saved by their own weak efforts. Rather, humans are saved by God's grace alone, which God offers as an utterly undeserved gift to those whom he has predestined for salvation. Because this grace comes to humans through the gift of faith, men and women are "justified" (i.e., made worthy of salvation) by faith alone. Those whom God has justified through faith will manifest that fact by performing works of piety and charity; but such works are not what saves them. Piety and charity are merely visible signs of each believer's invisible spiritual state, which is known to God alone.

SAINT PETER'S BASILICA, ROME. The construction of a new papal palace and monumental church was begun in 1506. This enormous complex replaced a modest, dilapidated Romanesque basilica that had replaced an even older church built on the site of the apostle Peter's tomb. ■ *How might this building project have been interpreted in different ways, depending on one's attitude toward the papacy?*

The essence of this doctrine was not original to Luther. It had been central to the thought of Augustine (see Chapter 6), the patron saint of Luther's own monastic order. During the twelfth and thirteenth centuries, however, theologians such as Peter Lombard and Thomas Aquinas (see Chapter 9) had developed a very different understanding of salvation. They emphasized the role that the Church itself (through its sacraments) and the individual believer (through acts of piety and charity) could play in the process of salvation. None of these theologians claimed that a human being could earn his or her way to heaven by good works alone, but the late medieval Church had encouraged this misunderstanding by presenting the process of salvation in increasingly quantitative terms—declaring, for example, that by performing a specific action (such as a pilgrimage or a pious donation), a believer could reduce the penance she or he owed to God by a specific number of days.

Since the fourteenth century, popes had claimed to dispense such special grace from the so-called Treasury of Merits, a storehouse of surplus good works piled up by Christ and the saints in heaven. By the late fifteenth century, when Luther was a child, the papacy began to claim that the dead could receive this grace, too, and so speed their way through purgatory. In both cases, grace was withdrawn from this "Treasury" through indulgences: special remissions of penitential obligations. When indulgences were first conceived in the eleventh and twelfth centuries, they could be earned only by demanding spiritual exercises, such as joining a crusade. By the end of the fifteenth century, however, indulgences were for sale.

To many, this looked like heresy, specifically simony: the sin of exchanging God's grace for cash. It had been a practice loudly condemned by Wyclif and his followers (see Chapter 11), and it was even more widely criticized by reformers like Erasmus (see Chapter 12). But Luther's objections to indulgences had much more radical consequences, because they rested on a set of theological premises that, taken to their logical conclusion, resulted in dismantling much of contemporary religious practice, not to mention the authority and sanctity of the Church. Luther himself does not appear to have realized this at first. But as the implications of his ideas became clear, he did not withdraw them. Instead, he pressed on.

The Scandal of Indulgences

Luther developed his ideas in an academic setting, but in 1517 he was provoked by a local abuse of spiritual power into attacking actual practice. The worldly bishop

POPE LEO X. Raphael's portrait shows the pope with his nephews: Giulio de' Medici (who would succeed him as pope in 1523) and Cardinal de Rossi.

Albert of Hohenzollern, youngest brother of the elector of Brandenburg, had sunk into debt and paid a large sum for papal permission to hold the lucrative bishoprics of Magdeburg and Halberstadt concurrently—even though, at twenty-three, he was not old enough to be a bishop at all. Moreover, when the prestigious archbishopric of Mainz fell vacant in the next year, Albert bought that, too. Obtaining the necessary funds by taking out loans from a German banking firm, he then struck a bargain with Pope Leo X (r. 1513–21): Leo would authorize the sale of indulgences in Albert's ecclesiastical territories—where Luther lived—with the understanding that half of the income would go to Rome for the building of St. Peter's Basilica, the other half to Albert.

Luther did not know the sordid details of Albert's bargain, but he did know that a Dominican friar named Tetzel was soon hawking indulgences throughout much of the region and that Tetzel was deliberately giving people the impression that an indulgence was an automatic ticket to heaven for oneself or one's loved ones in purgatory. For Luther, this was doubly offensive: not only was Tetzel violating Luther's conviction that people are saved by God's grace, not the purchase of papal favors; he was also misleading people into thinking that if they purchased an indulgence, they no longer needed to confess their sins to a priest. Tetzel was thus putting innocent souls at risk. So Luther's ninety-five theses were focused on dismantling the doctrine of indulgences.

Luther wrote up these points for debate in Latin, not German, but they were soon translated and published even more widely, and the hitherto obscure academic suddenly gained widespread notoriety. Tetzel and his allies demanded that Luther withdraw his theses. Rather than backing down, however, Luther became even bolder in his attacks. In 1519, at a public disputation held in Leipzig and attended by throngs of people, Luther defiantly maintained that the pope and all clerics were merely fallible men and that the highest authority for an individual's conscience was the truth of scripture.

Luther's year of greatest activity came in 1520, when he composed a series of pamphlets setting forth his three primary premises: justification by faith, the authority of scripture, and "the priesthood of all believers." We have already examined the meaning of the first premise. By the second, he meant that the reading of scripture took precedence over Church traditions—including the teachings of all theologians—and that beliefs (such as purgatory) or practices (such as prayers to the saints) not explicitly grounded in scripture should be rejected as human inventions. Luther also declared that Christian believers were spiritually equal before God, which meant denying that priests, monks, and nuns had any special qualities by virtue of their vocations: hence "the priesthood of all believers."

From these premises, a host of practical consequences logically followed. Because works could not lead to salvation, Luther declared fasts, pilgrimages, and the veneration of relics to be spiritually valueless. He also called for the dissolution of all monasteries and convents. He advocated a demystification of religious rites, proposing the substitution of German and other vernaculars for Latin and calling for a reduction in the number of sacraments from seven to two. In his view, the only true sacraments were baptism and the Eucharist, both of which had been instituted by Christ. (Later, he included penance.) Although Luther continued to believe that Christ was really present in the consecrated bread and wine of the Lord's Supper, he insisted that it was only through the faith of each individual believer that this sacrament could lead anyone to God; it was not a magical act performed by a priest.

To further emphasize that those who served the Church had no supernatural authority, Luther insisted on calling them "ministers" or "pastors" rather than priests. He also

Interpreting Visual Evidence

Decoding Printed Propaganda

The printing press has been credited with helping to spread the teachings of Martin Luther, and so securing the success of the Protestant Reformation. But even before Luther's critiques were published, reformers were using the new technology to disseminate images that attacked the corruption of the Church.

After Luther rose to prominence, both his supporters and detractors vied with one another in disseminating propaganda that appealed, visually, to a lay audience and that could be understood even by those who were unable to read.

The first pair of images below is really a single printed artifact datable to around 1500: an early example of a "pop-up" card. It shows Pope Alexander VI (r. 1492–

1503) as stately pontiff (image A) whose true identity is concealed by a flap. When the flap is raised (image B), he is revealed as a devil. The Latin texts read: "Alexander VI, *pontifex maximus*" (image A) and "I am the pope" (image B).

The other two examples represent two sides of the debate as it had developed by 1530, and both do so with reference to the same image: the seven-headed

A. Alexander as pontiff.

B. Alexander as a devil.

beast mentioned in the Bible's Book of Revelation. On the left (image C), a Lutheran engraving shows the papacy as the beast, with seven heads representing seven orders of Catholic clergy. The sign on the cross (referring to the sign hung over the head of the crucified Christ) reads, in German: "For money, a sack full of indulgences." The Latin words on either side say "Reign of the Devil." On the right (image D), a Catholic engraving produced in Germany shows Luther as Revelation's beast, with its seven heads labeled: "Doctor–Martin–Luther–Heretic–Hypocrite–Fanatic–Barabbas," the last alluding to the thief who should have been executed instead of Jesus, according to the Gospels.

Questions for Analysis

1. Given that this attack on Pope Alexander VI precedes Martin Luther's critique of the Church by nearly two decades, what can you conclude about its intended audience? To what extent can it be read as a barometer of popular disapproval? What might have been the reason(s) for the use of the concealing flap?

2. What do you make of the fact that both Catholic and Protestant propagandists were using the same imagery? What do you make of key differences: for example, the fact that the seven-headed beast representing the papacy sprouts out of an altar in which a Eucharistic chalice is displayed, while the seven-headed Martin Luther is reading a book?

3. All of these printed images also make use of words. Would the message of each image be clear without the use of texts? Why or why not?

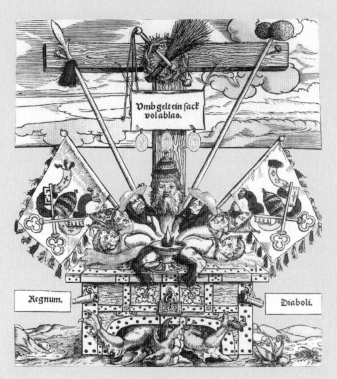

C. The seven-headed papal beast.

D. The seven-headed Martin Luther.

proposed to abolish the entire ecclesiastical hierarchy from popes to bishops on down. Finally, on the principle that no spiritual distinction existed between clergy and laity, Luther argued that ministers could and should marry. In 1525, he himself took a wife, Katharina von Bora, one of a dozen nuns he had helped escape from a Cistercian convent.

The Break with Rome

Widely disseminated by means of the printing press, Luther's polemical pamphlets of 1520 electrified much of Germany, gaining him passionate popular support and touching off a national religious revolt against the papacy. In highly colloquial German, Luther declared that "if the pope's court were reduced ninety-nine percent it would still be large enough to give decisions on matters of faith"; that "the cardinals have sucked Italy dry and now turn to Germany"; and that, given Rome's corruption, "the reign of Antichrist could not be worse." As word of Luther's defiance spread, his pamphlets became a publishing sensation. Whereas the average press run of a printed book before 1520 had been 1,000 copies, the first run of *To the Christian Nobility* (1520) was 4,000—and it sold out in a few days. Many thousands of copies quickly followed. Even more popular were woodcut illustrations mocking the papacy and exalting Luther. These sold in the tens of thousands and could be readily understood even by those who could not read. (See **Interpreting Visual Evidence** on pages 428–29.)

Luther's denunciations reflected widespread public dissatisfaction with the conduct and corruption of the papacy. Pope Alexander VI (r. 1492–1503) had bribed cardinals to gain his office and had then used the money raised from the papal jubilee of 1500 to support the military campaigns of his illegitimate son. Julius II (r. 1503–13) devoted his reign to enlarging the Papal States in a series of wars; a contemporary remarked that he would have deserved the glory he won— if only he had been a secular prince. Leo X (r. 1513–21), Luther's opponent, was a member of the Medici family of Florence. Although an able administrator, he was also a self-indulgent aesthete. In *The Praise of Folly*, first published in 1511 and frequently reprinted (see Chapter 12), Erasmus had declared that if the popes of his day were ever forced to lead Christlike lives, as their office surely required, they would be incapable of it. In *Julius Excluded*, published anonymously in 1517, he went even further, imagining a conversation at the gates of heaven between Saint Peter and Julius II, in which Peter refuses to admit the pope because he cannot believe that this armored, vainglorious figure could possibly be his own earthly representative.

In Germany, resentment of the papacy ran especially high because there were no special agreements (concordats) limiting papal authority in its principalities, as there were in Spain, France, and England (see Chapter 12). As a result, German princes complained that papal taxes were so high that the country was drained of its wealth. And yet Germans had almost no influence over papal policy. Frenchmen, Spaniards, and Italians dominated the College of Cardinals and the papal bureaucracy, and the popes were almost invariably Italian—as they would continue to be until 1978 and the election of Pope John Paul II. As a result, graduates from the rapidly growing German universities almost never found employment in Rome. Instead, many joined the throngs of Luther's supporters to become leaders of the new religious movement.

Emperor Charles V and the Condemnation at Worms

In the year 1520, Pope Leo X issued a papal edict condemning Luther's publications as heretical and threatening him with excommunication if he did not recant. This edict was of the most solemn kind, known as a *bulla,* or "bull," from the lead seal it bore. Luther's reponse was flagrantly defiant: rather than acquiescing to the pope's demand, he staged a public burning of the document. Thereafter, his heresy confirmed, he was formally given over for punishment to his lay overlord, Frederick III "the Wise" of Saxony. Frederick, however, proved a supporter of Luther and a critic of the papacy. Rather than burning Luther at the stake for heresy, Frederick declared that Luther had not yet received a fair hearing. Early in 1521, he therefore brought him to the city of Worms to be examined by a select representative assembly known as a "diet."

At Worms, the diet's presiding officer was the newly elected Holy Roman Emperor, Charles V. As a member of the Habsburg family, he had been born and bred in his ancestral holding of Flanders, then part of the Netherlands. By 1521, however, through the unpredictable workings of dynastic inheritance, marriage, election, and luck, he had become not only the ruler of the Netherlands but also king of Germany and Holy Roman emperor, duke of Austria, duke of Milan, and ruler of the Franche-Comté. And as the grandson of Ferdinand and Isabella on his mother's side, he was also king of Spain; king of Naples, Sicily, and Sardinia; and ruler of all the Spanish possessions in the New World. Governing such an extraordinary combination

THE EUROPEAN EMPIRE OF CHARLES V, c. 1526. Charles V ruled a vast variety of widely dispersed territories in Europe and the New World, and as Holy Roman emperor he was also the titular ruler of Germany. ▪ *What were the main countries and kingdoms under his control?* ▪ *Which regions would have been most threatened by Charles's extraordinary power, and where might the rulers of these regions turn for allies?* ▪ *How might the expansion of the Ottoman Empire have complicated political and religious struggles within Christian Europe?*

of territories posed enormous challenges. Charles's empire had no capital and no centralized administrative institutions; it shared no common language, no common culture, and no geographically contiguous borders. It thus stood completely apart from the growing nationalism that was shaping late medieval states.

Charles recognized the diversity of his empire and tried wherever possible to rule it through local officials and institutions. But he could not tolerate threats to the two fundamental forces that held his empire together: himself as emperor and Catholicism—as the religion of Rome was coming to be called. Beyond such political calculations,

THE WARTBURG, EISENACH (GERMANY). This medieval stronghold became the refuge of Martin Luther after his condemnation at the Diet of Worms in 1520. His room in the castle has since been preserved.

THE EMPEROR CHARLES V. This portrait by the Venetian painter Titian depicts Europe's most powerful ruler sitting quietly in a chair, dressed in simple clothing of the kind worn by judges or bureaucrats. ▪ *Why might Charles have chosen to represent himself in this way—rather than in the regalia of his many royal, imperial, and princely offices?*

however, Charles was also a faithful and committed servant of the Church, and he was deeply disturbed by the prospect of heresy within his empire. There was therefore little doubt that the Diet of Worms would condemn Martin Luther for heresy. And when Luther refused to back down, thereby endangering his life, his lord Frederick the Wise once more intervened, this time arranging for Luther to be "kidnapped" and hidden for a year at the elector's castle of the Wartburg, where he was kept out of harm's way.

Thereafter, Luther was never again in mortal danger. Although the Diet of Worms proclaimed him an outlaw, this edict was never enforced. Instead, Charles V left Germany in order to conduct a war with France, and in 1522 Luther returned in triumph to Wittenberg, to find that the changes he had called for had already been put into practice by his university supporters. When several German princes formally converted to Lutheranism, they brought their territories with them. In a little over a decade, a new form of Christianity had been established.

The German Princes and the Lutheran Church

At this point, the last of our three major questions must be addressed: Why did some German princes, secure in their own powers, nonetheless establish Lutheran religious practices within their territories? This is a crucial development, because popular support for Luther would not have been enough to ensure the success of his teachings had they not been embraced by a number of powerful rulers and free cities. Indeed, it was only in those territories where Lutheranism was formally established that the new religion prevailed. Elsewhere in Germany, Luther's sympathizers were forced to flee, face death, or conform to Catholicism.

The power of individual rulers to control the practice of religion in their own territories reflects developments we have noted in previous chapters. Rulers had long sought to control appointments to Church offices in their own realms, to restrict the flow of money to Rome and to limit the independence of ecclesiastical courts. The monarchs of Europe—primarily the kings of France and Spain—had already taken advantage of the continuing struggles between the papacy and the conciliarists to extract many concessions from the embattled popes during the fifteenth century (see Chapters 11 and 12). But in Germany, as noted above, neither the emperor nor the princes were strong enough to secure special treatment.

This changed as a result of Luther's initiatives. As early as 1520, the papacy's fiery challenger had recognized

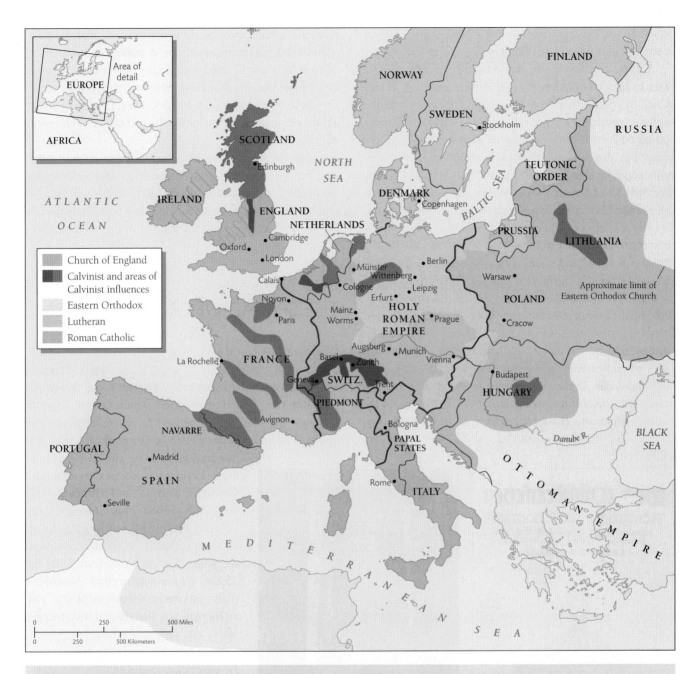

CONFESSIONAL DIFFERENCES, c. 1560. The religious affiliations (confessions) of Europe's territories had become very complicated by the year 1560, roughly a generation after the adoption of Lutheranism in some areas. ▪ *What major countries and kingdoms had embraced Protestantism by 1560?* ▪ *To what extent do these divisions conform to political boundaries, and to what extent would they have complicated the political situation?* ▪ *Why might Lutheranism have spread north into Scandinavia but not south into Bavaria or west across the Rhine?*

that he could never hope to institute new religious practices without the strong arms of princes, so he explicitly encouraged them to confiscate the wealth of the Church as an incentive. At first the princes bided their time, but when they realized that Luther had enormous public support and that Charles V could not act swiftly enough, several moved to introduce Lutheranism into their territories. Personal piety surely played a role in individual cases, but political and economic considerations were generally more decisive. Protestant princes could consolidate authority by naming their own religious officials, cutting off fees to Rome, and curtailing the jurisdiction of Church courts. They could also guarantee that the political and religious boundaries of their territories would now coincide. No longer would a rival ecclesiastical prince (such as a bishop or archbishop) be able to use his spiritual position to undermine a neighboring secular prince's sovereignty.

Similar considerations also moved a number of free cities to adopt Lutheranism. Acting independently of any prince, town councils could establish themselves as the supreme governing authorities within their jurisdictions, cutting out local bishops or powerful monasteries. Given the added fact that under Lutheranism monasteries and convents could be shut down and their lands appropriated by the newly sovereign secular authorities, the practical advantages of the new faith were overwhelming.

Once safely ensconced in Wittenberg under princely protection, Luther began to express ever more vehemently his own political and social views, which tended toward the strong support of the new political order. In a treatise of 1523, *On Temporal Authority*, he insisted that "godly" (Protestant) rulers must be obeyed in all things and that even "ungodly" ones should never be targets of dissent because tyranny "is not to be resisted but endured." In 1525, when peasants throughout Germany rebelled against their landlords, Luther therefore responded with intense hostility. In his vituperative pamphlet of 1525, *Against the Thievish, Murderous Hordes of Peasants*, he urged readers to

hunt the rebels down as though they were mad dogs: to "strike, strangle, stab secretly or in public, and remember that nothing can be more poisonous than a man in rebellion." After the ruthless suppression of this revolt, which may have cost as many as 100,000 lives, the firm alliance of Lutheranism with state power helped preserve and sanction the existing social order.

In his later years, Luther concentrated on debating with younger, more radical religious reformers who challenged his political conservatism, while offering spiritual counsel to all who sought it. Never tiring in his amazingly prolific literary activity, he wrote an average of one treatise every two weeks for twenty-five years.

THE SPREAD OF PROTESTANTISM

Originating as a term applied to Lutherans who "protested" the Catholic authority of Charles V, the word *Protestant* was soon applied to a much wider range of dissenting Christianities. Lutheranism itself struck lasting roots in northern Germany and Scandinavia, where it became the state religion of Denmark, Norway, and Sweden as soon as the 1520s. Other early Lutheran successes in southern Germany, Poland, and Hungary were eventually rolled back. Elsewhere in Europe, meanwhile, competing forms of Protestantism soon emerged from the seeds that Luther had sown. By the 1550s, Protestantism had become a truly international movement and also an increasingly diverse and divisive one.

Protestantism in Switzerland

In the early sixteenth century, Switzerland was ruled neither by kings nor by territorial princes; instead, prosperous Swiss cities were either independent or on the verge of becoming so. Hence, when the leading citizens of a Swiss municipality decided to adopt Protestant reforms, no one could stop them. Although religious arrangements varied from city to city, three main forms

THE ANABAPTISTS' CAGES, THEN AND NOW. After the three Anabaptist leaders of Münster were executed in 1535, their corpses were prominently displayed in cages hung from a tower of the marketplace church. As can be seen from the photo on the right, the bones are gone but the iron cages remain. ▪ *What would be the purpose of keeping these cages on display? What different meanings might this sight convey?*

of Protestantism emerged in Switzerland between 1520 to 1550: Zwinglianism, Anabaptism, and Calvinism.

Zwinglianism, founded by Ulrich Zwingli (*TSVING-lee*, 1484–1531) in Zürich, was the most theologically moderate form of the three. Zwingli had just begun his career as a Catholic priest when his humanist-inspired study of the Bible convinced him that Catholic theology and practice conflicted with the Gospels. His biblical studies eventually led him to condemn religious images and hierarchical authority within the Church. Yet he did not speak out publicly until Luther set a precedent. In 1522, accordingly, Zwingli began attacking the authority of the Catholic Church in Zürich. Soon much of northern Switzerland had accepted his religious leadership.

Although Zwingli's reforms closely resembled those of the Lutherans in Germany, Zwingli differed from Luther as to the theology of the Eucharist. Whereas Luther believed in the real presence of Christ's body in the sacrament, for Zwingli the Eucharist conferred no grace at all; it was simply a reminder and celebration of Christ's historical sacrifice on the cross. This fundamental disagreement prevented Lutherans and Zwinglians from uniting in a common Protestant front. When Zwingli died in battle against Catholic forces in 1531, his movement was absorbed by the more systematic Protestantism of John Calvin (see below).

Before Calvinism prevailed, however, an even more radical form of Protestantism arose in Switzerland and parts of Germany. The first Anabaptists were members of Zwingli's circle in Zürich, but they broke with him around 1525 on the issue of infant baptism. Because Anabaptists were convinced that the sacrament of baptism was only effective if administered to willing adults who understood its significance, they required followers who had been baptized as infants to be baptized again as adults (the term *Anabaptism* means "rebaptism"). This doctrine reflected the Anabaptists' fundamental belief that the true church was a small community of believers whose members had to make a deliberate, inspired decision to join it.

No other Protestant groups were prepared to go so far in rejecting the medieval Christian view of the Church as a single vast body to which all members of society belonged from birth. And in an age when almost everyone assumed that religious and secular authority were inextricably connected, Anabaptism was bound to be anathema to all established powers, both Protestant and Catholic. It was a movement that appealed to sincere religious piety in calling for pacifism, strict personal morality, and extreme simplicity of worship.

This changed when a group of Anabaptist extremists managed to gain control of the German city of Münster in 1534. These zealots were driven by millenarianism, the belief that God intends to institute a completely new order of justice and spirituality throughout the world before the end of time. Determined to help God bring about this goal, the extremists attempted to turn Münster into a new Jerusalem. A former tailor named John of Leyden assumed the title "king of the New Temple" and proclaimed himself the successor of the Hebrew king David. Under his leadership, Anabaptist religious practices were made obligatory, private property was abolished, and even polygamy was permitted on the grounds of Old Testament precedents. Such practices were deeply shocking to Protestants and Catholics alike. Accordingly, Münster was besieged and captured by Catholic forces little more than a year after the Anabaptist takeover. The new "David," together with two of his lieutenants, was put to death by torture, and the three bodies were displayed in iron cases in the town square.

Thereafter, Anabaptists throughout Europe were ruthlessly persecuted on all sides. The few who survived banded together in the Mennonite sect, named for its founder, the Dutchman Menno Simons (c. 1496–1561). This sect, dedicated to pacifism and the simple "religion of the heart" of original Anabaptism, is still particularly strong in the central United States.

John Calvin's Reformed Theology

A year after the events in Münster, a twenty-six-year-old Frenchman named John Calvin (1509–1564), published the first version of his *Institutes of the Christian Religion*, the most influential formulation of Protestant theology ever written. Born in Noyon, in northern France, Calvin had originally trained for the law; but by 1533, he was studying the Greek and Latin classics while living off the income from a priestly benefice. As he later wrote, he was "obstinately devoted to the superstitions of popery" until he experienced a miraculous conversion. He became a Protestant theologian and propagandist, eventually fleeing the Swiss city of Basel to escape persecution.

Although some aspects of Calvin's early career resemble those of Luther's, the two men were very different. Luther was an emotionally volatile personality and a lover of controversy. He responded to theological problems as they arose or as the impulse struck him; he never attempted to systematize his beliefs. Calvin, however, was a coolly analytical legalist, who resolved in his *Institutes* to set forth all the principles of Protestantism comprehensively, logically, and systematically. As a result, after several revisions and enlargements (the definitive edition appeared in 1559), Calvin's *Institutes* became the Protestant equivalent of Thomas Aquinas's *Summa Theologiae* (see Chapter 9).

JOHN CALVIN. This recently discovered portrait by an anonymous artist shows the young Protestant reformer as a serene and authoritative figure. It places the grotesque caricature of Calvin (right) in perspective.

CALVIN AS SEEN BY HIS ENEMIES. In this image, which circulated among Calvin's Catholic detractors, the reformer's facial features are a disturbing composite of fish, toad, and chicken.

Calvin's austere and stoical theology started with the omnipotence of God. For Calvin, the entire universe depends utterly on the will of the Almighty, who created all things for his greater glory and who knows all things present and to come. Because of man's original fall from grace, all human beings are sinners by nature, bound to an evil inheritance they cannot escape. Yet God (for reasons of his own) has predestined some for eternal salvation and damned all the rest to the torments of hell. Nothing that individual humans may do can alter fate; all souls are stamped with God's blessing or curse before they are born. Nevertheless, Christians cannot be indifferent to their conduct on earth. If they are among the elect, God will implant in them the desire to live according to his laws. Upright conduct is thus a sign, though not an infallible one, that an individual has been chosen to sit at the throne of glory. Membership in the Reformed Church (as Calvinist churches are more properly known) is another presumptive sign of election to salvation. But most of all, Calvin urged Christians to conceive of themselves as chosen instruments of God, charged to work actively to fulfill God's purposes on earth. Because sin offends God, Christians should do all they can to prevent it, not because their actions will lead to anyone's salvation (they will not), but simply because God's glory is diminished if sin is allowed to flourish unchecked by the efforts of those whom he has chosen for salvation.

Calvin always acknowledged a great theological debt to Luther, but his religious teachings diverged from those of the Wittenberg reformer in several essentials. First of all, Luther's attitude toward proper Christian conduct in the world was much more passive than Calvin's. For Luther, a Christian should endure the trials of this life through suffering, whereas for Calvin the world was to be mastered in unceasing labor for God's sake. Calvin's religion was also more controlling than Luther's. Luther, for example, insisted that his followers attend church on Sunday, but he did not demand that during the remainder of the day they refrain from all pleasure or work. Calvin, however, issued stern strictures against worldliness of any sort on the Sabbath and forbade all sorts of minor self-indulgences, even on non-Sabbath days.

The two men also differed on fundamental matters of church governance and worship. Although Luther broke with the Catholic system of hierarchical church government, Lutheran district superintendents exercised some of the same powers as bishops, including supervision of parish clergy. Luther also retained many features of traditional Christian worship, including altars, music, and ritual. Calvin, however, rejected everything that smacked to him of "popery." He argued for the elimination of all traces of hierarchy within any church. Instead, each congregation should elect its own ministers, and assemblies of ministers and "elders" (laymen responsible for maintaining proper religious conduct among the faithful) were to govern the Reformed Church as a whole. Calvin also insisted on the utmost simplicity in worship, prohibiting (among much else) vestments, processions, instrumental music, and religious images of any sort, including stained-glass windows. He also dispensed with all remaining vestiges of Catholic sacramental theology by making the sermon, rather than the Eucharist, the centerpiece of reformed worship.

Calvinism in Geneva

Consistent with his theological convictions, Calvin was intent on putting his religious teachings into practice. Sensing an opportunity in the French-speaking Swiss city of Geneva—then in the throes of political and religious upheaval—he moved there late in 1536 and immediately began preaching and organizing. In 1538, his activities caused him to be expelled by the city council, but in 1541 he returned and brought the city under his sway.

With Calvin's guidance, Geneva's government became a theocracy. Supreme authority was vested in a "consistory" composed of twelve lay elders and between ten and twenty pastors, whose weekly meetings Calvin dominated. In addition to passing legislation proposed by a congregation of ministers, the consistory's main function was to supervise morality, both public and private. To this end, Geneva was divided into districts, and a committee of the consistory visited every household, without prior warning, to check on the behavior of its members. Dancing, card playing, attending the theater, and working or playing on the Sabbath: all were outlawed as works of the devil. Innkeepers were forbidden to allow anyone to consume food or drink without first saying grace, or to permit any patron to stay up after nine o'clock. Adultery, witchcraft, blasphemy, and heresy all became capital crimes. Even penalties for lesser crimes were severe. During the first four years after Calvin gained control in Geneva, there were no fewer than fifty-eight executions in this city with a total population of only 16,000.

As rigid as such a regime may seem today, Calvin's Geneva was a beacon of light to thousands of Protestants throughout Europe in the mid-sixteenth century. Calvin's disciple John Knox (c. 1514–1572), who brought the reformed religion to Scotland, declared Geneva "the most perfect school of Christ that ever was on earth since the days of the Apostles." Converts such as Knox flocked to Geneva for refuge or instruction and then returned home to become ardent proselytizers for the new religion. Geneva thus became the center of an international movement dedicated to spreading reformed religion to France and the rest of Europe through organized missionary activity and propaganda.

These efforts were remarkably successful. By the end of the sixteenth century, Calvinists were a majority in Scotland (where they were known as Presbyterians) and Holland (where they founded the Dutch Reformed Church). They were also influential in England, although the Church of England adopted reformed theology but not reformed worship (Calvinists who sought further reforms in worship were known as Puritans). There were also substantial Calvinist minorities in France (where they were called Huguenots), Germany, Hungary, Lithuania, and Poland. By the end of the sixteenth century, Calvinism would spread to the New World.

The Beginnings of Religious Warfare

Less than a generation after Luther's challenge to the Church, wars between Catholic and Protestant rulers began. In Germany, Charles V attempted to establish Catholic unity by launching a military campaign against several German princes who had instituted Lutheran worship in their territories. But despite several notable victories, his efforts to defeat the Protestant princes failed. In part, this was because Charles was also involved in wars against France; but primarily, it was because the Catholic princes of Germany worked against him, fearing that any suppression of Protestant princes might also diminish their own independence. As a result, the Catholic princes' support for the foreign-born Charles was only lukewarm; at times, they even joined with Protestants in battle against him.

This regional warfare sputtered on and off until a compromise settlement was reached via the Peace of Augsburg in 1555. Its governing principle was *cuius regio, eius religio*, "as the ruler, so the religion." This meant that in those principalities where Lutherans ruled, Lutheranism would be the sole state religion; but where Catholic princes ruled, the people of their territories would also be Catholic. For better and for worse, the Peace of Augsburg was a historical milestone. For the first time since Luther had been excommunicated, Catholic rulers were forced to acknowledge the legality of Protestantism. Yet the peace also set a dangerous precedent because it established the principle that no sovereign state can tolerate religious diversity. Moreover, it excluded Calvinism entirely and thus spurred German Calvinists to become aggressive opponents of the status quo. As a result, Europe would be riven by religious warfare for another century and would export sectarian violence to the New World (see Chapter 14).

THE DOMESTICATION OF REFORM

Within two decades, Protestantism had become a diverse revolutionary movement whose radical claims for the spiritual equality of all Christians had the potential to undermine the political, social, and even gender hierarchies on which European society rested. Luther himself did not anticipate that his ideas might have such implications, and he was genuinely shocked when the rebellious German peasants and the radical Anabaptists at Münster interpreted his teachings in this way. And Luther was by no means the only staunchly conservative Protestant. None of the prominent early Protestants were social or political radicals; most depended on the support of existing elites: territorial princes, of course, but also the ruling elites of towns. As a result, the Reformation movement was speedily "domesticated" in two senses. Its revolutionary potential was muffled—Luther himself rarely spoke about "the priesthood of all believers" after 1525—and there was an increasing emphasis on the patriarchal family as the central institution of reformed life.

Reform and Discipline

As we have seen, injunctions to lead a more disciplined and godly life had been a frequent message of religious reform movements since the Black Death (see Chapter 11). Many of these efforts were actively promoted by princes and town councils, most famously perhaps in Florence, where the Dominican preacher Girolamo Savonarola led the city on an extraordinary but short-lived campaign of puritanism and moral reform between 1494 and 1498. And there are numerous other examples of rulers legislating against sin. When Desiderius Erasmus called on secular authorities to think of themselves as abbots and of their territories as giant monasteries, he was sounding an already-familiar theme.

Protestant rulers, however, took the need to enforce godly discipline with particular seriousness, because the depravity of human nature was a fundamental tenet of Protestant belief. Like Saint Augustine at the end of the fourth century (see Chapter 6), Protestants believed that people would inevitably turn out bad unless they were compelled to be good. It was therefore the responsibility of secular and religious leaders to control and punish the behavior of their people, because otherwise their evil deeds would anger God and destroy human society.

Protestant godliness began with the discipline of children. Luther himself wrote two catechisms (instructional tracts) designed to teach children the tenets of their faith and the obligations—toward parents, masters, and rulers—that God imposed on them. Luther also insisted that all children, boys and girls alike, be taught to read the Bible in their own languages. Schooling thus became a characteristically Protestant preoccupation and rallying cry. Even the Protestant family was designated a "school of godliness," in which fathers were expected to instruct and discipline their wives, their children, and their household servants.

But family life in the early sixteenth century still left much to be desired in the eyes of Protestant reformers. Drunkenness, domestic violence, illicit sexual relations, lewd dancing, and the blasphemous swearing of oaths were frequent topics of reforming discourse. Various methods of discipline were attempted, including private counseling, public confessions of wrongdoing, public penances and shamings, exclusion from church services, and even imprisonment. All these efforts met with varying, but generally modest, success. Creating godly Protestant families, and enforcing godly discipline on entire communities, was going to require the active cooperation of godly authorities.

Protestantism, Government, and the Family

The domestication of the Reformation in this sense took place principally in the free towns of Germany, Switzerland, and the Netherlands—and from there spread westward to North America. Protestant attacks on monasticism and clerical celibacy found a receptive audience among townsmen who resented the immunity of monastic houses from taxation and regarded clerical celibacy as a subterfuge for the seduction of their own wives and daughters. Protestant emphasis on the depravity of the human will and the consequent need for that will to be disciplined by authority also resonated powerfully with guilds and town governments, which were anxious to maintain and increase the control exercised by urban elites (mainly merchants and master craftsmen) over the apprentices and journeymen who made up the majority of the male population. By eliminating the competing jurisdictional authority of the Catholic Church, Protestantism allowed town governments to consolidate all authority within the city into their own hands.

Competing Viewpoints

Marriage and Celibacy: Two Views

These two selections illustrate the strongly contrasting views on the spiritual value of marriage versus celibacy that came to be embraced by Protestant and Catholic religious authorities. The first selection is part of Martin Luther's more general attack on monasticism, which emphasizes his contention that marriage is the natural and divinely intended state for all human beings. The second selection, from the decrees of the Council of Trent (1545–63), restates traditional Catholic teaching on the holiness of marriage but also emphasizes the spiritual superiority of virginity to marriage as well as the necessity of clerical celibacy.

Luther's Views on Celibacy (1535)

Listen! In all my days I have not heard the confession of a nun, but in the light of Scripture I shall hit upon how matters fare with her and know I shall not be lying. If a girl is not sustained by great and exceptional grace, she can live without a man as little as she can without eating, drinking, sleeping, and other natural necessities.

Nor, on the other hand, can a man dispense with a wife. The reason for this is that procreating children is an urge planted as deeply in human nature as eating and drinking. That is why God has given and put into the body the organs, arteries, fluxes, and everything that serves it. Therefore what is he doing who would check this process and keep nature from running its desired and intended course? He is attempting to keep nature from being nature, fire from burning, water from wetting, and a man from eating, drinking, and sleeping.

Source: E. M. Plass, ed., *What Luther Says*, vol. 2 (St. Louis, MO: 1959), pp. 888–89.

Canons on the Sacrament of Matrimony (1563)

Canon 1. If anyone says that matrimony is not truly and properly one of the seven sacraments . . . instituted by Christ the Lord, but has been devised by men in the Church and does not confer grace, let him be anathema [cursed].

Canon 9. If anyone says that clerics constituted in sacred orders or regulars [monks and nuns] who have made solemn profession of chastity can contract marriage . . . and that all who feel that they have not the gift of chastity, even though they have made such a vow, can contract marriage, let him be anathema, since God does not refuse that gift to those who ask for it rightly, neither does *he suffer us to be tempted above that which we are able.*

Canon 10: If anyone says that the married state excels the state of virginity or celibacy, and that it is better and happier to be united in matrimony than to remain in virginity or celibacy, let him be anathema.

Source: H. J. Schroeder, *Canons and Decrees of the Council of Trent* (St. Louis, MO: 1941), pp. 181–82.

Questions for Analysis

1. On what grounds does Luther attack the practice of celibacy? Do you agree with his basic premise?

2. How do the later canons of the Catholic Church respond to Protestant views like Luther's? What appears to be at stake in this defense of marriage and celibacy?

Meanwhile, Protestantism reinforced the control of individual men over their own households by emphasizing the family as the basic unit of religious education. In place of a priest, an all-powerful father figure was expected to assume responsibility for instructing and disciplining his household according to the precepts of reformed religion. At the same time, Protestantism introduced a new religious ideal for women. No longer was the original nun the exemplar of female holiness; in her place now stood the married and obedient Protestant "goodwife." As one Lutheran prince wrote in 1527: "Those who bear children please God better than all the monks and nuns singing and praying." To this extent, Protestantism resolved the tensions between piety and sexuality that had long characterized Christian teachings, by declaring the holiness of marital sex.

But this did not promote a new view of women's spiritual potential, nor did it elevate their social and political status. Quite the contrary: Luther regarded women as more sexually driven than men and less capable of controlling their sexual desires—reflecting the fact that Luther confessed himself incapable of celibacy. His opposition to convents allegedly rested on his belief that it was impossible for women to remain chaste, so sequestering them simply made illicit behavior inevitable. To prevent sin, it was necessary that all women should be married, preferably at a young age, and so placed under the governance of a godly husband.

For the most part, Protestant town governments were happy to cooperate in shutting down female monasteries. The convent's property went to the town, after all. But conflicts did arise between Protestant reformers and town fathers over marriage and sexuality, especially over the reformers' insistence that both men and women should marry young as a restraint on lust. In many towns, men were traditionally expected to delay marriage until they had achieved the status of master craftsman—a requirement that had become increasingly difficult to enforce as guilds sought to restrict the number of journeymen permitted to become masters. In theory, then, apprentices and journeymen were not supposed to marry. Instead, they were expected to frequent brothels and taverns, a legally sanctioned outlet for extramarital sexuality long viewed as necessary to men's physical well-being, but that Protestant reformers now deemed morally abhorrent.

Towns responded in a variety of ways to these opposing pressures. Some instituted special committees to police public morals, of the sort we have noted in Calvin's Geneva. Some abandoned Protestantism altogether. Others, like the German town of Augsburg, alternated between Protestantism and Catholicism for several decades. Yet regardless of a town's final choice of religious allegiance, by the end of the sixteenth century a revolution had taken place with respect to governments' attitudes toward public morality. In their competition with each other, neither Catholics nor Protestants wished to be seen as soft on sin. The result was the widespread abolition of publicly licensed brothels, the outlawing of prostitution, and far stricter governmental supervision of many other aspects of private life than had ever been the case in any Western civilization.

The Control of Marriage

Protestantism also increased parents' control over their children's choice of marital partners. The medieval Church had defined marriage as a sacrament that did not require the involvement of a priest. The mutual free consent of two individuals, even if given without witnesses or parental approval, was enough to constitute a legally valid marriage in the eyes of the Church. Opposition to this doctrine came from many quarters, especially from families who stood to lose from this liberal doctrine. Because marriage involved rights of inheritance to property, it was regarded as too important a matter to be left to the choice of adolescents. Instead, parents wanted the power to prevent unsuitable matches and, in some cases, to force their children to accept the marriage arrangements their families might negotiate on their behalf. Protestantism offered an opportunity to achieve such control. Luther had declared marriage to be a purely secular matter, not a sacrament at all, and one that could be regulated however the governing authorities thought best. Calvin largely followed suit, although Calvinist theocracy drew less of a distinction than did Lutheranism between the powers of church and state.

Even the Catholic Church was eventually forced to give way. Although it never abandoned its insistence that both members of a couple must freely consent to their marriage, by the end of the sixteenth century the Church's new doctrine required formal public notice of intent to marry and insisted on the presence of a priest at the actual wedding ceremony. Both were efforts to prevent elopements, allowing families time to intervene before an unsuitable marriage was concluded. Individual Catholic countries sometimes went even further in trying to assert parental control over their children's choice of marital partners. In France, for example, although couples might still marry without parental consent, those who did so now forfeited all of their rights to inherit their families' property. In somewhat different ways, both Protestantism and Catholicism thus moved to strengthen the control that parents could exercise over their children—and, in the case of Protestantism, that husbands could exercise over their wives.

THE REFORMATION OF ENGLAND

In England, the Reformation took a rather different course than it did in continental Europe. Although a long tradition of popular reform survived into the sixteenth century, the number of dissidents was too small and their influence too limited to play a significant role there. Nor was England particularly oppressed by the papal exactions and abuses that roiled Germany. When the sixteenth century began, English monarchs already exercised close control over Church appointments within the kingdom; they also received the lion's share of the papal taxation collected from England. Nor did ecclesiastical courts inspire any particular resentments. On the contrary, these courts would continue to function in Protestant England until the eighteenth century. Why, then, did sixteenth-century England become a Protestant country at all?

"The King's Great Matter"

In 1527, King Henry VIII of England had been married to Ferdinand and Isabella's daughter, Catherine of Aragon, for eighteen years. Yet all the offspring of this union had died

HENRY VIII OF ENGLAND. Hans Holbein the Younger executed several portraits of the English king. This one represents him in middle age, confident of his powers.

in infancy, with the exception of a daughter, Mary. Because Henry needed a male heir to preserve the peaceful succession to the throne and because Catherine was now past childbearing age, Henry had political reasons to propose a change of wife. He also had more personal motives, having become infatuated with a lady-in-waiting named Anne Boleyn.

Henry therefore appealed to Rome to annul his marriage to Catherine, arguing that because she had previously been married to his older brother Arthur (who had died in adolescence), Henry's marriage to Catherine had been invalid from the beginning. As Henry's representatives pointed out, the Bible pronounced it "an unclean thing" for a man to take his brother's wife and cursed such a marriage with childlessness (Leviticus 20:31). Even a papal dispensation, which Henry and Catherine had long before obtained for their marriage, could not exempt them from such a clear prohibition—as the marriage's childlessness proved.

Henry's petition put Pope Clement VII (r. 1523–34) in an awkward position. Both Henry and Clement knew that popes in the past had granted annulments to reigning monarchs on far weaker grounds than the ones Henry was alleging. If, however, the pope granted Henry's annulment, he would cast doubt on the validity of all papal dispensations. More seriously, he would provoke the wrath of the emperor Charles V, Catherine of Aragon's nephew, whose armies were in firm command of Rome and who at that moment held the pope himself in captivity. Clement was trapped; all he could do was procrastinate and hope that the matter would resolve itself. For two years, he allowed Henry's case to proceed in England without ever reaching a verdict. Then, suddenly, he transferred the case to Rome, where the legal process began all over again.

Exasperated by these delays, Henry began to increase the pressure on the pope. In 1531, he compelled an assembly of English clergy to declare him "protector and only supreme head" of the Church in England. In 1532, he encouraged Parliament to produce an inflammatory list of grievances against the English clergy and used this threat to force them to concede his right, as king, to approve or deny all Church legislation. In January 1533, Henry married Anne Boleyn (already pregnant) even though his marriage to Queen Catherine had still not been annulled. The new archbishop of Canterbury, Thomas Cranmer, later provided the required annulment in May, acting on his own authority.

In September, Princess Elizabeth was born; her father, disappointed again in his hopes for a son, refused to attend her christening. Nevertheless, Parliament settled the succession to the throne on the children of Henry and Anne,

The Six Articles of the English Church

Although Henry VIII withdrew the Church of England from obedience to the papacy, he continued to reject most Protestant theology. Some of his advisers, most notably Thomas Cromwell, were committed Protestants; and the king allowed his son and heir, Edward VI, to be raised as a Protestant. But even after several years of rapid (and mostly Protestant) change in the English Church, Henry reasserted a set of traditional Catholic doctrines in the Six Articles of 1539. These would remain binding on the Church of England until the king's death in 1547.

 irst, that in the most blessed sacrament of the altar, by the strength and efficacy of Christ's mighty word, it being spoken by the priest, is present really, under the form of bread and wine, the natural body and blood of our Savior Jesus Christ, conceived of the Virgin Mary, and that after the consecration there remains no substance of bread or wine, nor any other substance but the substance of Christ, God and man;

Secondly, that communion in both kinds is not necessary for salvation, by the law of God, to all persons, and that it is to be believed and not doubted . . . that in the flesh, under the form of bread, is the very blood, and with the blood, under the form of wine, is the very flesh, as well apart as though they were both together;

Thirdly, that priests, after the order of priesthood received as afore, may not marry by the law of God;

Fourthly, that vows of chastity or widowhood by man or woman made to God advisedly ought to be observed by the law of God. . . .

Fifthly, that it is right and necessary that private masses be continued and admitted in this the king's English Church and congregation . . . whereby good Christian people . . . do receive both godly and goodly consolations and benefits; and it is agreeable also to God's law;

Sixthly, that oral, private confession is expedient and necessary to be retained and continued, used and frequented in the church of God.

Source: *Statutes of the Realm*, vol. 3 (London: 1810–28), p. 739 (modernized).

Questions for Analysis

1. Three of these six articles focus on the sacrament of the Eucharist (the Mass). Given what you have learned in this chapter, why would Henry have been so concerned about this sacrament? What does this reveal about his values and those of his contemporaries?

2. Given Henry's insistence on these articles, why might he have allowed his son to be raised a Protestant? What does this suggest about the political situation in England?

redirected all papal revenues from England into the king's hands, prohibited appeals to the papal court, and formally declared "the King's highness to be Supreme Head of the Church of England." In 1536, Henry executed his former tutor and chancellor Sir Thomas More (see Chapter 12) for his refusal to endorse this declaration of supremacy, and took the first steps toward dissolving England's many monasteries. By the end of 1539, the monasteries and convents were gone and their lands and wealth confiscated by the king, who distributed them to his supporters.

These measures, largely masterminded and engineered by Henry's Protestant adviser, Thomas Cromwell (c. 1485–1540), broke the bonds that linked the English Church to Rome. But they did not make England a Protestant country.

Although certain traditional practices (such as pilgrimages and the veneration of relics) were prohibited, the English Church remained overwhelmingly Catholic in organization, doctrine, ritual, and language. The Six Articles promulgated by Parliament in 1539 at Henry VIII's behest left no room for doubt as to official orthodoxy: oral confession to priests, masses for the dead, and clerical celibacy were all confirmed; the Latin Mass continued; and Catholic Eucharistic doctrine was not only confirmed but its denial made punishable by death. To most English people, only the disappearance of the monasteries and the king's own continuing matrimonial adventures (he married six wives in all) were evidence that their Church was no longer in communion with Rome.

The Reign of Edward VI

For truly committed Protestants, and especially those who had visited Calvin's Geneva, the changes Henry VIII enforced on the English Church did not go nearly far enough. In 1547, the accession of the nine-year-old king Edward VI (Henry's son by his third wife, Jane Seymour) gave them the opportunity to finish the task of reform. Encouraged by the apparent sympathies of the young king, Edward's government moved quickly to reform the doctrine and ceremonies of the English Church. Priests were permitted to marry; English services replaced Latin ones; the veneration of images was discouraged, and the images themselves were defaced or destroyed; prayers for the dead were declared useless, and endowments for such prayers were confiscated; and new articles of belief were drawn up, repudiating all sacraments except baptism and communion and affirming the Protestant creed of justification by faith alone. Most important, *The Book of Common Prayer*, authored by Archbishop Cranmer and considered one of the great landmarks of English literature, was published to define precisely how the new English-language services of the church were to be conducted. Much remained unsettled with respect to both doctrine and worship; but by 1553, when the youthful Edward died, the English Church appeared to have become a distinctly Protestant institution.

Mary Tudor and the Restoration of Catholicism

Edward's successor, however, was his pious and much older half sister Mary (r. 1553–58), granddaughter of "the most Catholic monarchs" of Spain, Ferdinand and Isabella (see Chapter 11). Mary speedily reversed her half brother's religious policies, restoring the Latin Mass and requiring married priests to give up their wives. She even prevailed on Parliament to vote a return to papal allegiance. Hundreds of Protestant leaders fled abroad, many to Geneva; others, including Archbishop Thomas Cranmer, were burned at the stake for refusing to abjure their Protestantism. News of the martyrdoms spread like wildfire through Protestant Europe. In England, however, Mary's policies sparked relatively little resistance. After two decades of religious upheaval, most English men and women were probably

QUEEN MARY AND QUEEN ELIZABETH. The two daughters of Henry VIII were the first two queens regnant of England: the first women to rule in their own right. Despite the similar challenges they faced, they had strikingly different fates and have been treated very differently in popular histories. ■ *How do these two portraits suggest differences in their personalities and their self-representation as rulers?*

hoping that Mary's reign would bring some stability to their lives.

This, however, Mary could not do. The executions she ordered were insufficient to wipe out religious resistance—instead, Protestant propaganda about "Bloody Mary" caused widespread unease, even among those who welcomed the return of traditional religious forms. Nor could Mary do anything to restore monasticism: too many leading families had profited from Henry VIII's dissolution of the monasteries for this to be reversed. Mary's marriage to her cousin Philip, Charles V's son and heir to the Spanish throne, was another miscalculation. Although the marriage treaty stipulated that Philip could not succeed her in the event of her death, her English subjects never trusted him. When the queen allowed herself to be drawn by Philip into a war with France on Spain's behalf—in which England lost Calais, its last foothold on the European continent—many people became highly disaffected. Ultimately, however, what doomed Mary's policies was simply the accident of biology: Mary was unable to conceive an heir. When she died after only five years of rule, her throne passed to her Protestant sister, Elizabeth.

The Elizabethan Compromise

The daughter of Henry VIII and Anne Boleyn, Elizabeth (r. 1558–1603) was predisposed in favor of Protestantism by the circumstances of her parents' marriage as well as by her upbringing. But Elizabeth was no zealot and wisely recognized that supporting radical Protestantism in England might provoke bitter sectarian strife. Accordingly, she presided over what is often known as "the Elizabethan settlement." By a new Act of Supremacy (1559), Elizabeth repealed Mary's Catholic legislation, prohibiting foreign religious powers (i.e., the pope) from exercising any authority within England and declaring herself "supreme governor" of the English church—a more Protestant title than Henry VIII's "supreme head," since most Protestants believed that Christ alone was the head of the Church. She also adopted many of the Protestant liturgical reforms instituted by her half-brother, Edward, including Cranmer's revised version of *The Book of Common Prayer*. But she retained vestiges of Catholic practice, too, including bishops, church courts, and vestments for the clergy. On most doctrinal matters, including predestination and free will, Elizabeth's Thirty-nine Articles of Faith (approved in 1562) struck a decidedly Protestant, even Calvinist, tone. But the prayer book was more moderate and, on the critical issue of the Eucharist, deliberately ambiguous. By combining Catholic and Protestant interpretations ("This is my body. . . . Do this in remembrance of me") into a single declaration, the prayer book permitted an enormous latitude for competing interpretations of the service by priests and parishioners alike.

Yet religious tensions persisted in Elizabethan England, not only between Protestants and Catholics but also between moderate and more extreme Protestants. The queen's artful fudging of these competing Christianities was by no means a recipe for success. Rather, what preserved "the Elizabethan settlement" and ultimately made England a Protestant country was the extraordinary length of Queen Elizabeth's reign, combined with the fact that for much of that time Protestant England was at war with Catholic Spain. Under Elizabeth, Protestantism and English nationalism gradually fused together into a potent conviction that God himself had chosen England for greatness. After 1588, when English naval forces won an improbable victory over a Spanish Armada (see Chapter 14), Protestantism and Englishness became nearly indistinguishable to most of Queen Elizabeth's subjects. Laws against Catholic practices became increasingly severe, and although an English Catholic tradition did survive, its adherents were a persecuted minority. Significant, too, was the situation in Ireland, where the vast majority of the population remained Catholic despite the government's efforts to impose Protestantism on them. As a result, Irishness would be as firmly identified with Catholicism as was Englishness with Protestantism; but it was the Protestants who were in power in both countries.

THE REBIRTH OF THE CATHOLIC CHURCH

So far, our emphasis on the spread of Protestantism has cast the spotlight on dissident reformers such as Luther and Calvin. But there was also a powerful internal reform movement within the Church in these same decades, which resulted in the birth (or rebirth) of a Catholic ("universal") faith. For some, this movement is the "Catholic Reformation"; for others, it is the "Counter-Reformation." Those who prefer the former term emphasize that the Church was continuing significant reforming movements that can be traced back to the eleventh century (see Chapter 8) and which gained new momentum in the wake of the Great Schism (see Chapter 11). Others insist that most Catholic reformers of this period were reactionary, inspired primarily by the urgent need to resist Protestantism and to strengthen the power of the Roman Church in opposition to it.

Past and Present

Controlling Consumption

Although laws regulating the conspicuous consumption of expensive commodities—especially status-conscious clothing—were common during the later Middle Ages, it was not until after the Reformation that both Protestant and Catholic leaders began to criminalize formerly acceptable bodily practices and substances. New theories of sensory perception, the availability of new products like coffee and tobacco, and a new concern to internalize reform led some authorities to outlaw prostitution (hitherto legal) and to ban normal social practices like drinking and dancing. The image on the left shows the militant Catholic League founded in sixteenth-century France, which combatted Protestantism and promoted strict religious observance. The image on the right shows Czech protesters calling for the decriminalization of marijuana.

 Watch related author interview on StudySpace
wwnorton.com/web/westernciv18

Catholic Reforms

Even before Luther's challenge to the Church, as we have seen, there was a movement for moral and institutional reform within some religious orders. And while these efforts received strong support from several secular rulers, the papacy showed little interest in them. In Spain, for example, reforming activities directed by Cardinal Francisco Ximenes de Cisneros (1436–1517) led to the imposition of strict rules of behavior and the elimination of abuses prevalent among the clergy. Ximenes (*he-MEN-ez*) also helped to regenerate the spiritual life of the Spanish Church. In Italy, meanwhile, earnest clerics labored to make the Italian Church more worthy of its prominent position. Reforming existing monastic orders was a difficult task, not least because the papal court set such a poor example; but Italian reformers did manage to

establish several new orders dedicated to high ideals of piety and social service. In northern Europe, Christian humanists such as Erasmus and Thomas More also played a role in this Catholic reform movement, not only by criticizing abuses and editing sacred texts but also by encouraging the laity to lead lives of sincere religious piety (see Chapter 12).

As a response to the challenges posed by Protestantism, however, these internal reforms proved entirely inadequate. Starting in the 1530s, therefore, a more aggressive phase of reform began to gather momentum under a new style of vigorous papal leadership. The leading Counter-Reformation popes—Paul III (r. 1534–49), Paul IV (r. 1555–59), Pius V (r. 1566–72), and Sixtus V (r. 1585–90)—were the most zealous reformers of the Church since the eleventh century. All led upright lives; some, indeed, were so grimly ascetic that contemporaries longed for the bad old days. As a Spanish councilor wrote of Pius V in 1567, "We should like

THE COUNCIL OF TRENT. This fresco depicts the General Council of the Catholic Church, which met at intervals for nearly twenty years between 1545 and 1563 in the city of Trent (in modern-day Italy) in order to enact significant internal reforms.

***THE INSPIRATION OF SAINT JEROME* BY GUIDO RENI (1635).** The Council of Trent declared Saint Jerome's Latin translation of the Bible, the Vulgate, to be the official version of the Catholic Church. Since biblical scholars had known since the early sixteenth century that Saint Jerome's translation contained numerous mistakes, Catholic defenders of the Vulgate insisted that even his mistakes had been divinely inspired. ▪ *How does Guido Reni's painting attempt to make this point?*

it even better if the present Holy Father were no longer with us, however great, inexpressible, unparalleled, and extraordinary His Holiness may be." In confronting Protestantism, however, an excessively holy pope was vastly preferable to a self-indulgent one. And these Counter-Reformation popes were not merely holy men. They were also accomplished administrators who reorganized papal finances and filled ecclesiastical offices with bishops and abbots no less renowned for austerity and holiness than were the popes themselves.

Papal reform efforts intensified at the Council of Trent, a general council of the entire Church convoked by Paul III in 1545, which met at intervals thereafter until 1563. The decisions taken at Trent (a provincial capital of the Holy Roman Empire, located in modern-day Italy) provided the foundations on which a new Catholic Church would be erected. Although the council began by debating some form of compromise with Protestantism, it ended by reaffirming all of the Catholic tenets challenged by Protestant critics. "Good works" were affirmed as necessary for salvation, and all seven sacraments were declared indispensable means of grace, without which salvation was impossible. Transubstantiation, purgatory, the invocation of saints, and the rule of celibacy

for the clergy were all confirmed as dogmas—essential elements—of the Catholic faith. The Bible, in its imperfect Vulgate form, and the traditions of apostolic teaching were held to be of equal authority as sources of Christian truth. Papal supremacy over every bishop and priest was expressly maintained, and the supremacy of the pope over any Church council was taken for granted outright, signaling a final defeat of the still-active conciliar movement. The Council of Trent even reaffirmed the doctrine of indulgences that had touched off the Lutheran revolt, although it condemned the worst abuses connected with their sale.

The legislation of Trent was not confined to matters of doctrine. To improve pastoral care of the laity, bishops and priests were forbidden to hold more than one spiritual office. To address the problem of an ignorant priesthood,

The Demands of Obedience

The necessity of obedience in the spiritual formation of monks and nuns can be traced back to the Rule *of Saint Benedict in the early sixth century, and beyond. In keeping with the mission of its founder, Ignatius of Loyola (1491–1556), the Society of Jesus brought a new militancy to this old ideal.*

Rules for Thinking with the Church

1. Always to be ready to obey with mind and heart, setting aside all judgment of one's own, the true spouse of Jesus Christ, our holy mother, our infallible and orthodox mistress, the Catholic Church, whose authority is exercised over us by the hierarchy.

2. To commend the confession of sins to a priest as it is practised in the Church; the reception of the Holy Eucharist once a year, or better still every week, or at least every month, with the necessary preparation. . . .

4. To have a great esteem for the religious orders, and to give the preference to celibacy or virginity over the married state. . . .

6. To praise relics, the veneration and invocation of Saints: also the stations, and pious pilgrimages, indulgences, jubilees, the custom of lighting candles in the churches, and other such aids to piety and devotion. . . .

9. To uphold especially all the precepts of the Church, and not censure them in any manner; but, on the contrary, to defend them promptly, with reasons drawn from all sources, against those who criticize them.

10. To be eager to commend the decrees, mandates, traditions, rites, and customs of the Fathers in the Faith or our superiors. . . .

11. That we may be altogether of the same mind and in conformity with the Church herself, if she shall have defined anything to be black which to our eyes appears to be white, we ought in like manner to pronounce it to be black. For we must undoubtingly believe, that the Spirit of our Lord Jesus Christ, and the Spirit of the Orthodox Church His Spouse, by which Spirit we are governed and directed to salvation, is the same. . . .

From the Constitutions of the Jesuit Order

Let us with the utmost pains strain every nerve of our strength to exhibit this virtue of obedience, firstly to the Highest Pontiff, then to the Superiors of the Society; so that in all things . . . we may be most ready to obey his voice, just as if it issued from Christ our Lord . . . leaving any work, even a letter, that we have begun and have not yet finished; by directing to this goal all our strength and intention in the Lord, that holy obedience may be made perfect in us in every respect, in performance, in will, in intellect; by submitting to whatever may be enjoined on us with great readiness, with spiritual joy and perseverance; by persuading ourselves that all things [commanded] are just; by rejecting with a kind of blind obedience all opposing opinion or judgment of our own. . . .

Source: Henry Bettenson, ed., *Documents of the Christian Church,* 2nd ed. (Oxford: 1967), pp. 259–61.

Questions for Analysis

1. How might Loyola's career as a soldier have inspired the language used in his "Rules for Thinking with the Church"?

2. In what ways do these Jesuit principles respond directly to the challenges of Protestant reformers?

a theological seminary was to be established in every diocese. The council also suppressed a variety of local religious practices and saints' cults, replacing them with new cults authorized and approved by Rome. To prevent heretical ideas from corrupting the faithful, the council further decided to censor or suppress dangerous books. In 1564, a specially appointed commission published the first *Index of Prohibited Books,* an official list of writings forbidden to faithful Catholics. Ironically, all of Erasmus's works were immediately placed on the *Index,* even though he had been a chosen champion of the Church against Martin Luther only forty years before. A permanent agency known as the

Congregation of the Index was later set up to revise the list, which was maintained until 1966, when it was abolished after the Second Vatican Council (1962–1965). For centuries, it was to become symbolic of the doctrinal intolerance that characterized sixteenth-century Christianity, both in its Catholic and Protestant varieties.

Ignatius Loyola and the Society of Jesus

In addition to the concerted activities of popes and the legislation of the Council of Trent, a third main force propelling the Counter-Reformation was the foundation of the Society of Jesus (commonly known as the Jesuits) by Ignatius Loyola (1491–1556). In the midst of a career as a mercenary, this young Spanish nobleman was wounded in battle in 1521, the same year in which Luther defied authority at the Diet of Worms. While recuperating, he turned from the reading of chivalric romances to a romantic vernacular retelling of the life of Jesus—and the impact of this experience convinced him to become a spiritual soldier of Christ.

For ten months, Ignatius lived as a hermit in a cave near the town of Manresa, where he experienced ecstatic visions and worked out the principles of his subsequent guidebook, the *Spiritual Exercises*. This manual, completed in 1535 and first published in 1541, offered practical advice on how to master one's will and serve God through a systematic program of meditations on sin and the life of Christ. It eventually became the basic handbook for all Jesuits and has been widely studied by Catholic laypeople as well. Indeed, Loyola's *Spiritual Exercises* ranks alongside Calvin's *Institutes* as the most influential religious text of the sixteenth century.

The Jesuit order originated as a small group of six disciples who gathered around Loyola during his belated career as a student in Paris. They vowed to serve God in poverty, chastity, and missionary work and were formally constituted by Pope Paul III in 1540. By the time of Loyola's death, the Society of Jesus already numbered some 1,500 members. It was by far the most militant of the religious orders fostered by the Catholic reform movements of the sixteenth century—not merely a monastic society but a company of soldiers sworn to defend the faith. Their weapons were not bullets and swords but eloquence, persuasion, and instruction in correct doctrines; yet the Society also became accomplished in more worldly methods of exerting influence. Its organization was patterned after that of a military unit, whose commander-in-chief enforced the iron discipline of all members. Individuality was suppressed, and a stoical obedience was required from the rank and file. Indeed, the Jesuit general, sometimes known as the "black pope" (from the color of the order's habit), was elected for life and answered only to the pope in Rome, to whom all senior Jesuits took a special vow of strict obedience. As a result of this vow, all Jesuits were held to be at the pope's disposal at all times.

The activities of the Jesuits consisted primarily of proselytizing and establishing schools. This meant they were ideal missionaries. Accordingly, Jesuits were soon dispatched to preach to non-Christians in India, China, and Spanish America. One of Loyola's closest associates, Francis Xavier (ZAY-vyer, 1506–1552), baptized thousands of people and traveled thousands of miles in South and East Asia. Although Loyola had not at first conceived of his society as a battalion of "shock troops" in the fight against Protestantism, that is what it primarily became. Through preaching and diplomacy—sometimes at the risk of their lives—Jesuits in the second half of the sixteenth century helped to colonize the world. In many places, they were instrumental in keeping rulers and their subjects loyal to Catholicism; in others, they met martyrdom; and in some others, notably Poland and parts of Germany and France, they succeeded in regaining territory previously lost to followers of Luther and Calvin. Wherever they were allowed to settle, they set up schools and colleges, on the grounds that only a vigorous Catholicism nurtured by widespread literacy and education could combat Protestantism.

A New Catholic Christianity

The greatest achievement of these reform movements was the revitalization of the Church. Had it not been for such determined efforts, Catholicism would not have swept over the globe during the seventeenth and eighteenth centuries—or reemerged in Europe as a vigorous spiritual force. There were some other consequences as well. One was the rapid advancement of lay literacy in Catholic countries. Another was the growth of intense concern for acts of charity; because Catholicism continued to emphasize good works as well as faith, charitable activities took on an extremely important role.

There was also a renewed emphasis on the role of religious women. Reformed Catholicism did not exalt marriage as a route to holiness to the same degree as did Protestantism, but it did encourage the piety of a female religious elite. For example, it embraced the mysticism of Saint Teresa of Avila (1515–1582) and established new orders of nuns, such as the Ursulines and the Sisters of Charity. Both Protestants

TERESA OF AVILA. Teresa of Avila (1515–1582) was one of many female religious figures who played an important role in the reformed Catholic Church. She was canonized in 1622. This image is dated 1576. The Latin wording on the scroll unfurled above Teresa's head reads: "I will sing forever of the mercy of the Holy Lord."

and Catholics continued to exclude women from the priesthood or ministry, but Catholic women could pursue religious lives with at least some degree of independence, and the convent continued to be a route toward spiritual and even political advancement in Catholic countries.

The reformed Catholic Church did not, however, perpetuate the tolerant Christianity of Erasmus. Instead, Christian humanists lost favor with the papacy, and even scientists such as Galileo were regarded with suspicion (see Chapter 16). Yet contemporary Protestantism was just as intolerant, and even more hostile to the cause of rational thought. Indeed, because Catholic theologians turned for guidance to the scholasticism of Thomas Aquinas, they tended to be much more committed to the dignity of human reason than were their Protestant counterparts, who emphasized the literal interpretation of the Bible and the importance of unquestioning faith. It is no coincidence that René Descartes, one of the pioneers of rational philosophy ("I think, therefore I am"), was educated by Jesuits.

It would be wrong, therefore, to claim that the Protestantism of this era was more forward-looking or progressive than Catholicism. Both were, in fact, products of the same troubled time. Each variety of Protestantism responded

to specific historical conditions and the needs of specific peoples in specific places, while carrying forward certain aspects of the Christian tradition considered valuable by those communities. The Catholic Church also responded to new spiritual, political, and social realities—to such an extent that it must be regarded as distinct from either the early Church of the later Roman Empire or even the oft-reformed Church of the Middle Ages. That is why the phrase "Roman Catholic Church" has not been used in this book prior to this chapter, because the Roman Catholic Church as we know it emerged for the first time in the sixteenth century. Like Protestantism, it is a more modern phenomenon.

CONCLUSION

The Reformation grew out of complex historical processes that we have been tracing in the last few chapters. Foremost among these was the increasing power of Europe's sovereign states. As we have seen, those German princes who embraced Protestantism were moved to do so by the desire for sovereignty. The kings of Denmark, Sweden, and England followed suit for many of the same reasons. Since Protestant leaders preached absolute obedience to godly rulers, and since the state in Protestant countries assumed direct control of its churches, Protestantism bolstered state power. Yet the power of the state had been growing for a long time prior to this, especially in such countries as France and Spain, where Catholic kings already exercised most of the same rights that were seized by Lutheran authorities and by Henry VIII of England in the course of their own reformations. Those rulers who aligned themselves with Catholicism, then, had the same need to bolster their sovereignty and power.

Ideas of national identity, too, were already influential and thus available for manipulation by Protestants and Catholics alike. These religions, in turn, became new sources of both identity and disunity. Prior to the Reformation, peoples in the different regions of Germany spoke such different dialects that they had difficulty understanding each other. But Luther's Bible gained such currency that it eventually became the linguistic standard for all these disparate regions, which eventually began to conceive of themselves as part of a single nation. Yet religion alone could not achieve the political unification of Germany, which did not occur for another 300 years (see Chapter 21); indeed, it contributed to existing divisions by cementing the opposition of Catholic princes and peoples. Elsewhere in Europe—as in the Netherlands, where Protestants fought successfully against a foreign, Catholic overlord—religion created a shared identity where politics could not. In England, where it is arguable that a sense of nationalism had already been fostered before the Reformation, membership in the Church of England became a new, but not uncontested, attribute of "Englishness."

Ideals characteristic of the Renaissance also contributed something to the Reformation and the Catholic responses to it. The criticisms of Christian humanists helped to prepare Europe for the challenges of Lutheranism, and close textual study of the Bible led to the publication of the newer, more accurate editions used by Protestant reformers. For example, Erasmus's improved edition of the Latin New Testament enabled Luther to reach some crucial conclusions concerning the meaning of penance and became the foundation for Luther's own translation of the Bible. However, Erasmus was no supporter of Lutheran principles and most other Christian humanists followed suit, shunning Protestantism

After You Read
This Chapter

Ⓢ Visit StudySpace for quizzes, additional review materials, and multimedia documents. **wwnorton.com/web/westernciv18**

REVIEWING THE OBJECTIVES

- The main premises of Luther's theology had religious, political, and social implications. What were they?
- Switzerland fostered a number of different Protestant movements. Why was this the case?
- The Reformation had a profound effect on the basic structures of family life and on attitudes toward marriage and morality. Describe these changes.
- The Church of England was established in response to a specific political situation. What was this?
- How did the Catholic Church respond to the challenge of Protestantism?

as soon as it became clear to them what Luther was actually teaching. Indeed, in certain basic respects, Protestant doctrine was completely at odds with the principles, politics, and beliefs of most humanists, who became staunch supporters of the Catholic Church.

In the New World and Asia, both Protestantism and Catholicism became forces of imperialism and new catalysts for competition. The race to secure colonies and resources now became a race for converts, too, as missionaries of both faiths fanned out over the globe. In the process, the confessional divisions of Europe were mapped onto these regions, often with violent results. Over the course of the ensuing century, newly sovereign nation-states would struggle for hegemony at home and abroad, setting off a series of religious wars that would cause as much destruction as any plague. Meanwhile, western civilizations' extension into the Atlantic would create new kinds of ecosystems, forms of wealth, and types of bondage.

PEOPLE, IDEAS, AND EVENTS IN CONTEXT

- How did **MARTIN LUTHER**'s attack on **INDULGENCES** tap into more widespread criticism of the papacy? What role did the printing press and the German vernacular play in the dissemination of his ideas?
- Why did many German principalities and cities rally to Luther's cause? Why did his condemnation at the **DIET OF WORMS** not lead to his execution on charges of heresy?
- How did the Protestant teachings of **ULRICH ZWINGLI**, **JOHN CALVIN**, and the **ANABAPTISTS** differ from one another and from those of Luther?
- What factors made some of Europe's territories more receptive to **PROTESTANTISM** than others? What was the meaning of the principle **CUIUS REGIO, EIUS REGIO**, established by the Peace of Augsburg?
- How did the **REFORMATION** alter the status and lives of women in Europe? Why did it strengthen male authority in the family?
- Why did **HENRY VIII** break with Rome? How did the **CHURCH OF ENGLAND** differ from other Protestant churches in Europe?
- What decisions were made at the **COUNCIL OF TRENT**? What were the founding principles of **IGNATIUS LOYOLA**'s **SOCIETY OF JESUS**, and what was its role in the **COUNTER-REFORMATION** of the **CATHOLIC CHURCH**?

THINKING ABOUT CONNECTIONS

- Our study of Western civilizations has shown that reforming movements are nothing new: Christianity has been continuously reformed throughout its long history. What made this Reformation so different?
- Was a Protestant break with the Catholic Church inevitable? Why or why not?
- The political, social, and religious structures put in place during this era continue to shape our lives in such profound ways that we scarcely notice them—or we assume them to be inevitable and natural. In your view, what is the most far-reaching consequence of this age of dissent and division, and why? In what ways has it formed your own values and assumptions?

Before
You
Read
This
Chapter

Europe in the Atlantic World, 1550–1660

CORE OBJECTIVES

- **TRACE** the new linkages between Western civilizations and the Atlantic world, and describe their consequences.

- **DESCRIBE** the different forms of unfree labor that developed in European colonies during this period.

- **IDENTIFY** the monarchies that dominated Europe and the Atlantic world and the newer powers whose influence was expanding.

- **EXPLAIN** the reasons for Europe's religious and political instability and its consequences for Europe's monarchies and the Atlantic world.

- **UNDERSTAND** how artists and intellectuals responded to the crises and uncertainties of this era.

The Atlantic Ocean thrashes the western shores of Europe and Africa with wind-driven waves that have traveled thousands of miles from the American coasts. Its immense area links continents shaped by a wide variety of climates, including the arid desert of the Sahara, the more temperate zones of Europe and North America, the tropical islands of the Gulf of Mexico and the Caribbean, and the rain forests of the Amazon basin in South America. This ecological diversity, and the hitherto infrequent and limited movement of peoples on opposite sides of the ocean, meant that each of these regions nurtured its own forms of plant and animal life, its own unique microbes and pathogens.

In the sixteenth century, the emergence of the Atlantic world as an arena of cultural and economic exchange broke down the isolation of these ecosystems. Transatlantic commerce and migration now eclipsed the importance of trade and movement in the Mediterranean, which had been the crucial connector of Western civilizations since the Bronze Age (see Chapter 2). Populations—humans, animals, and plants—on once-remote shores came into frequent and intense contact. On the one hand, Europeans brought diseases that devastated the peoples of the Americas, along with

453

gunpowder and a hotly divided Christianity. On the other, the huge influx of silver from South America transformed (and eventually exploded) the cash-starved European economy while the arrival of American stimulants such as tobacco, sugar, and chocolate fostered new consumer appetites that could only be satisfied by new regimes of unfree labor.

Eventually, the need for slaves to power the plantations that supplied these consumer products fostered a vast industry of human trafficking, which led to the forcible removal of nearly 11 million people from Africa over the course of three centuries. Colonial settlement in North and South America also created new social hierarchies and new forms of inequality, which unsettled even long-established structures in Europe. The peoples of the Americas were forced to deal with the presence of newly

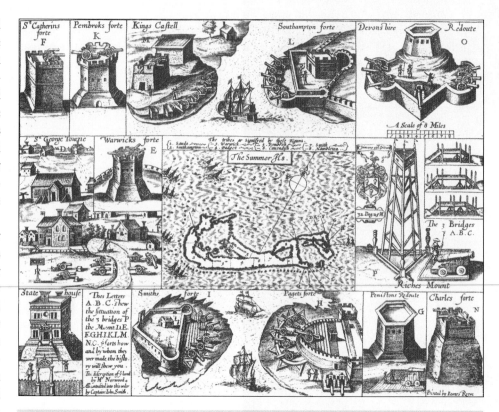

THE ISLAND OF BERMUDA. This map of "The Summer Isle" and the accompanying images of its major fortifications and sites, was drawn by Captain John Smith and published in *The Generall Historie of Virginia, New-England, and the Summer Isles* (1624). ■ *Why would such features be of interest to readers of this pamphlet?*

arrived settlers, and settlers in turn confronted both indigenous peoples and the meddling interference of distant imperial bureaucracies.

Meanwhile, these European states were riven by internal dissent and engaged in deadly competitions among themselves—and these, too, were exported to the Atlantic world. Galvanized by the crisis of the Reformation (see Chapter 13), the Roman Catholic Church sought to redress the loss of religious dominance in Europe by spreading its influence to the Americas and Asia through the work of new missionary orders. The Spanish crown, which controlled the most developed colonial empire of the time, was also the most zealous defender of the Catholic faith—which meant that wars within Spain's Protestant Dutch provinces and with Protestant England affected colonial politics, too. Similar attempts by the Catholic Habsburg monarchy to enforce religious uniformity among the varied territories of central Europe led to the Thirty Years' War, one of the longest and bloodiest conflicts in history. In both direct and indirect ways, these deadly disputes stimulated the migration of persecuted minorities (Catholic and Protestant) across the Atlantic, replanting and propagating these rivalries.

But religion was not the only cause of conflict within Europe. Another was the growing tension between powerful monarchs and landowning elites, who disputed the right of the crown and its administrators to raise revenues through increased taxation. Supporting colonial expansion in the Atlantic world and fighting wars within Europe were expensive projects, and they placed strain on traditional alliances and ideas of kingship. Political and moral philosophers accordingly struggled to redefine the role of government in a world of religious pluralism and to articulate new political ideologies that did not necessitate violence among people of different faiths. Intellectuals and artists also strove to reassess Europeans' place in this expanding Atlantic world, to process the flood of new information and commodities, and to make sense of the profound changes in daily life.

THE EMERGENCE OF THE ATLANTIC WORLD

With the few exceptions that we have noted in previous chapters, even the most skilled of Europe's sailors were limited to coastal cruising along the Atlantic's eastern shores until the fifteenth century. But after the Portuguese and Spanish established settlements on the Canary Islands, this archipelago off the northwestern coast of Africa became a permanent base of operations for successive exploratory ventures. From here, generations of Portuguese sailors learned to navigate the West African coast, after which they successfully rounded the Cape of Good Hope and began to establish trading colonies in the Indian Ocean (see Chapter 12). During these years, Portuguese sailors also launched the first kidnapping raids for slaves along the Atlantic coast of Senegal. When they found that some African chieftains were willing to facilitate the capture of people from rival tribes, the Portuguese began to set up coastal outposts where they could trade livestock, foodstuffs, cotton, copper, and iron for ivory, gold, finished textiles, and human beings.

Competing Colonial Ventures

At the same time, Spanish successes in Mexico soon encouraged other European kingdoms to attempt imperial ventures of their own. Finding that Spanish and Portuguese holds on the Caribbean and South America were firm in practice as well as in theory—Protestant rulers were obviously not bound by the Treaty of Tordesillas (1494) and all subsequent papal pronouncements that favored Catholic colonial ventures—northern European explorers targeted the North American coast. Although the Englishman John Cabot had explored the mouth of the St. Lawrence River in 1497–98, it was nearly a century before Walter Raleigh's attempt to start an English colony just north of Spanish Florida in 1585. The settlement at Roanoke Island (present-day North Carolina) was intended to solidify English claims to the territory of Virginia, named for England's "Virgin Queen" Elizabeth and originally encompassing the North American seaboard from South Carolina to Maine, including Bermuda.

This ill-conceived experiment ended with the disappearance of the first colonists, but it was followed by Christopher Newport's expedition to the Chesapeake Bay in 1606, a voyage funded by a private London firm called the Virginia Company. Newport and his followers did not conceive of themselves as empire builders. They were not being sponsored by the English king, and they probably did not intend to settle permanently in the New World. They were "gentleman planters" whose goal was to provide agricultural goods for the European market and so to make their fortunes before returning home. Nevertheless, with the Spanish model much in mind, Newport's band reserved the right to "conquer" any peoples who proved uncooperative. So when Native Americans of the Powhatan tribe killed one-third of the settlers during a raid in 1622, the colonists responded by crushing the Powhatans and seizing their lands.

For decades thereafter, the native populations of North America remained capable of both threatening and fostering the survival of fragile settlements that had gained a toehold on the continent. Bitter conflicts and occasional cooperation between newcomers and indigenous peoples are part of a larger history of intermittent struggle and coexistence that began the moment Columbus first landed on Hispaniola. Especially in the early years of colonization, when the number of European immigrants was small, some Native American peoples sought to take advantage of these new contacts, to trade for goods otherwise unavailable to them. European settlers, for their part, often exhibited a combination of paternalism and contempt for the peoples they encountered. Some hoped to convert Americans to Christianity, others sought to use them as labor for their economic enterprises. Ultimately, however, the balance was tipped by larger environmental, biological, and demographic factors that lay outside the control of individuals.

The Columbian Exchange

The accelerating rate of global connections in the sixteenth century precipitated an extraordinary movement of peoples, plants, animals, goods, cultures, and diseases. This is known as the "Columbian exchange," a term coined by the historian Alfred Crosby in 1972, with reference to Columbus's voyage. Yet this exchange soon came to encompass lands that still lay far beyond the purview of Columbus and his contemporaries: not just the African and Eurasian landmass and the vast terrain of the Americas but Australia and the Pacific Islands, too.

Because of its profound consequences for human populations and for the environment, the Columbian exchange is considered a fundamental turning point in both human history and the history of the earth's ecology. The exchange put new agricultural products into circulation, introduced new domesticated species of animals, and accidentally encouraged the spread of deadly diseases and the devastating takeovers of invasive plants and animals. Both natural ecosystems and human immune systems around the world were destroyed or transformed. For example, the introduction of pigs and dogs on islands in the Atlantic and Pacific resulted in the extinction of indigenous animals and birds. The landscapes of Central America and southwestern North America were denuded of vegetation after Spanish settlers turned to large-scale herding and ranching operations. Honeybees displaced native insect populations and encouraged the propagation of harmful plant species.

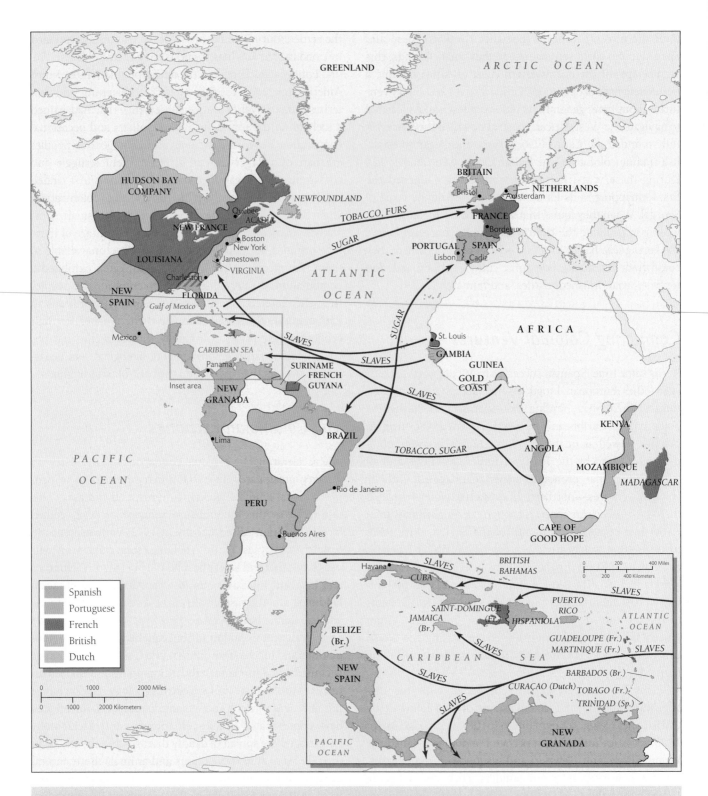

THE ATLANTIC WORLD. ▪ *Trace the routes of the triangular trade. What products did French and British colonies in North America provide to the European market?* ▪ *Which colonies were most dependent on slave labor?* ▪ *What products did they produce, and how did these enter into the triangle?*

Then there were the unintended exchanges: gray squirrels and raccoons from North America found their way to Britain and the European continent. Brown rats and even some species of earthworms were accidentally transported to the Americas. Insects from all over the world traveled to new environments and spread unfamiliar forms of bacteria and pollen.

Obviously, the transfer of human populations in the form of settlers, soldiers, merchants, sailors, indentured servants, and slaves accelerated the process of change. Some groups were wiped out through violence, forced resettlement, and bacteria. As much as 90 percent of the pre-Columbian population of the Americas died from communicable diseases such as smallpox, cholera, influenza, typhoid, measles, malaria, and bubonic plague—all brought from Europe. Syphilis, by contrast, appears to have been brought to Europe from the Americas; some scholars have even asserted that it was Columbus's own sailors who transmitted the disease across the Atlantic.

Meanwhile, the importation of foodstuffs from one part of the world to another, and their cultivation in new habitats, revolutionized the diets of local populations. The American potato (which could be grown in substandard soil and stored for long periods) eventually became the staple diet of the European poor. Tomatoes, although not widely consumed in Europe until the nineteenth century, are now an essential ingredient in many regional Italian dishes. Indeed, the foods and flavors that characterize today's iconic cuisines are, to an extraordinary degree, the result of the Columbian exchange—suggesting that many new, exotic foods quickly become fashionable and then habitual. Who can imagine an English meal without potatoes? Switzerland or Belgium without chocolate? Thai food without chili peppers? Or, on the other side of the Atlantic, Hawaii without pineapples? Florida without oranges? Colombia without coffee? Of the components that make up the quintessential American hamburger—ground-beef patties on a bun with lettuce, tomato, pickles, onion, and (if you like) cheese—only one of these ingredients is indigenous to America. Everything else is Old World: the beef, the wheat for the bun, the cucumber for the pickle, the onion, the lettuce. Even the name is European, a reference to the town of Hamburg in Germany.

THE COLUMBIAN EXCHANGE

The following list names just a few of the commodities and contagions that moved between the Old and New Worlds in this era.

Old World → New World	New World → Old World
• Wheat	• Corn
• Sugar	• Potatoes
• Bananas	• Beans
• Rice	• Squash
• Wine vines	• Pumpkins
• Horses	• Tomatoes
• Pigs	• Avocados
• Chickens	• Chili peppers
• Sheep	• Pineapples
• Cattle	• Cocoa
• *Smallpox*	• Tobacco
• *Measles*	• *Syphilis*
• *Typhus*	

Colonial Populations Compared

In contrast to the more than 7 million slaves who were taken from Africa to labor and die on plantations across the Atlantic, only about 1.5 million Europeans immigrated to the Americas in the two centuries after Columbus's first voyage. The total number who initially emigrated from Spain is estimated at 200,000 to 250,000; most of these were men. By 1570, given the high mortality of migrants and some returns to Europe, the population had been reduced to about 150,000. The Spanish crown did what it could to encourage a new wave of settlement, but even in a period of demographic growth the number of those who chose to seek their fortunes abroad remained relatively small. Transatlantic travel was expensive and uncertain, and the demand for a European labor force remained low as long as Native Americans could be conscripted and enslaved.

The population of the Spanish Americans thus remained largely urban during this period, with most colonists living in the military and administrative centers of the empire. Even the owners of large plantations lived in cities, corresponding from afar with the foremen who managed their estates. Only those who had been granted *encomiendas* tended to live on the lands entrusted to them by the Spanish crown (the Spanish verb *encomendar* means "to trust"). The *encomienda* system reminds us that Spanish conquests in the New World were an extension of the earlier Reconquista (see Chapter 12) of Spain itself. Originally set up to manage

Muslim populations in territories captured by Christian crusaders, this arrangement as carried forward in the new colonies of South America made *encomenderos* agents of the crown. Technically, the lands they oversaw were still owned by native peoples. But in practice, many *encomenderos* were able to exploit the land for their own profit, treating native workers like serfs. Some were descendants of the first conquistadors, others were drawn from Aztec and Inca elites. Many were women: the daughters of the Aztec emperor Montezuma had been given extensive lands to hold in trust after their father's capitulation to Cortés.

In North America, by contrast, English colonies in New England and the Chesapeake Bay were small and rural. But they also grew more quickly, with settlers numbering about 250,000 by 1700. Part of the reason for this was the greater impetus for emigration caused by overpopulation in the British Isles. The persecution of various Protestant groups also played an important role in driving immigration, especially to the New England colonies, where the relocation of entire families and even communities was common. The colonies in Virginia offered further incentives by granting 100 acres to each settler.

But these factors did not swell the numbers of migrants so much as the encouragement of indentured servitude, a practice that brought thousands of "free" European laborers across the Atlantic to work under terms that made them little different from slaves. Perhaps 75 to 80 percent of the people who arrived in the Chesapeake colony in the 1600s were indentured servants, and nearly a quarter of these were women. The successful use of indentured servants to grow tobacco in North America led some landowners to try the same system on plantations in the Caribbean islands. Ultimately, however, the plantation system rendered its greatest profits through the use of African slaves.

New Social Hierarchies in New Spain

After the conquests of the Aztec and Inca Empires (see Chapter 12), the Spanish established colonial governments in Peru and Mexico, controlled from a central bureaucracy in Madrid. This centralization was facilitated by the highly organized structure of Aztec society in Mexico and that of the Incas in Peru. Native peoples already lived, for the most part, in large, well-regulated villages and towns. The Spanish government could therefore work closely with local elites to maintain order. Indeed, the *encomienda* system was initially so effective because it was built on these existing structures and did not attempt to uproot or eliminate existing native cultures. Instead, it focused on controlling and exploiting native labor, especially in extracting mineral resources. Although farming

and ranching were encouraged in Central and South America, and later in Florida and California, the Spanish colonial economy was dominated by mining for a century and a half.

While the Spanish collected tribute from all the communities of their empire and worked assiduously to convert native peoples to Catholicism, they did not attempt to change basic patterns of life. The result was widespread cultural assimilation by the relatively small numbers of (usually male) settlers, which was also assisted by the normalcy of intermarriage between (male) colonizers and (female) colonial subjects. This pattern gave rise to a complex and distinctive caste system in New Spain, with a few "pure-blooded" Spanish immigrants at the top, a very large number of Creoles (peoples of mixed descent) in the middle, and Native Americans at the bottom.

In theory, these racial categories corresponded to class distinctions, but in practice race and class did not always coincide. Racial concepts and practices were extremely flexible, and prosperous individuals or families of mixed descent often found ways to establish their "pure" Spanish ancestry by adopting the social practices of the new Spanish colonial elites. The lingering effects of this complicated stratification are still evident in Latin America today.

Sugar, Slaves, and the Transatlantic Triangle

The Europeans who settled in the Americas faced a major problem: labor. Mining and plantation agriculture required many workers, and the indigenous labor supply of the Americas was limited; as we have seen, the introduction of new diseases resulted in the deaths of millions of Native Americans in the space of only a few decades. Meanwhile, the return of the bubonic plague to Europe in the seventeenth century, along with the slowing population growth that accompanied the wars of religion, meant that colonists could not look to Europe to satisfy their labor needs. Colonial agents thus began to import slaves from Africa to bolster the labor force and to produce the wealth they so avidly sought. And overwhelmingly, that wealth was derived not from gold or silver but from a new commodity for which there was an insatiable appetite in Europe: sugar.

Sugar was also at the center of the "Triangular Trade" that linked markets for goods in Africa, the Americas, and Europe—all of which were driven by slave labor. For example, slave ships that transported African slaves to the Caribbean might trade their human cargo for molasses made on the sugar plantations of the islands. These ships would then proceed to New England where the molasses

Enslaved Native Laborers at Potosí

Since the Spanish crown received one-fifth of all revenues from the mines of New S___ over the mercury used to refine the silver ore into silver, it had an important stake in e___ this end, the crown granted colonial mine owners the right to conscript native peoples and ___ when it came to the treatment of the workers. This account, dated to about 1620, describes t___ these native laborers at Potosí (also discussed in Chapter 12).

According to His Majesty's warrant, the mine owners on this massive range [at Potosí] have a right to the conscripted labor of 13,300 Indians in the working and exploitation of the mines, both those [mines] which have been discovered, those now discovered, and those which shall be discovered. It is the duty of the *Corregidor* [municipal governor] of Potosí to have them rounded up and to see that they come in from all the provinces between Cuzco . . . and as far as the frontiers of Tarija and Tomina. . . .

The conscripted Indians go up every Monday morning to the . . . foot of the range; the *Corregidor* arrives with all the provincial captains or chiefs who have charge of the Indians assigned him for his miner or smelter; that keeps him busy till 1 P.M., by which time the Indians are already turned over to these mine and smelter owners.

After each has eaten his ration, they climb up the hill, each to his mine, and go in, staying there from that hour until Saturday evening without coming out of the mine; their wives bring them food, but they stay constantly underground, excavating and carrying out the ore from which they get the silver. They all have tallow candles, lighted day and night; that is the light they work with, for as they are underground, they have need for it all the time. . . .

These Indians have different functions in the handling of the silver ore; some break it up with bar or pick, and dig down in, following the vein in the mine; others bring it up; others up above keep separating the good and the poor in piles; others are occupied in taking it down from the range to the mills on

herds of llamas; every da___ more than 8,000 of these na___ of burden for this task. These tea___ who carry the metal are not conscript___ but are hired.

Source: Antonio Vázquez de Espinosa, *Compendium and Description of the West Indies*, trans. Charles Upson Clark (Washington, DC: 1968), p. 62.

Questions for Analysis

1. From the tone of this account, what do you think was the narrator's purpose in writing? Who is his intended audience?

2. Reconstruct the conditions in which these laborers worked. What would you estimate to be the human costs of this week's labor? Why, for example, would a fresh workforce be needed every Monday?

would be traded to distillers who used the sugary syrup to make rum. Loaded up with a consignment of rum, the slaver would return to the African coast to repeat the process. An alternative triangle might see cheap manufactured goods move from England to Africa, where they would be traded for slaves. Those slaves would then be shipped to Virginia and exchanged for tobacco, which would be shipped back to England to be processed and distributed.

Although the transatlantic slave trade was theoretically controlled by the governments of European colonial powers—Britain officially entered this trade in 1564, the year of William Shakespeare's birth—private entrepre-

neurs and working-class laborers were active at every stage of the supply chain: in the ports of West Africa, where captured slaves cast their eyes on their homelands for the last time; on the ships where these captives were imprisoned; and in the slave markets of the Americas, as agents for the landowners and merchants who bid against one another to purchase the human chattel that had survived the terrible voyage.

Many other branches of the economy in Europe and the Americas were also linked to the slave trade: from the investors in Amsterdam, London, Lisbon, and Bordeaux who financed the slave trader's journey, to the insurance

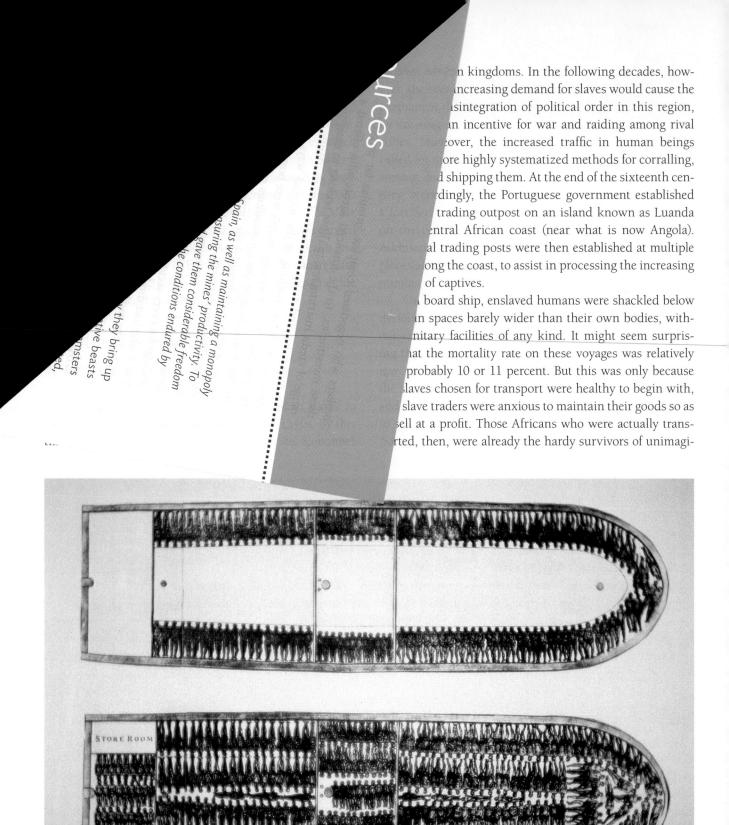

...n kingdoms. In the following decades, how-
...increasing demand for slaves would cause the
...sintegration of political order in this region,
...an incentive for war and raiding among rival
...over, the increased traffic in human beings
...ore highly systematized methods for corralling,
...d shipping them. At the end of the sixteenth cen-
...dingly, the Portuguese government established
...trading outpost on an island known as Luanda
...entral African coast (near what is now Angola).
...al trading posts were then established at multiple
...ong the coast, to assist in processing the increasing
...of captives.

...board ship, enslaved humans were shackled below
...n spaces barely wider than their own bodies, with-
...nitary facilities of any kind. It might seem surpris-
...at the mortality rate on these voyages was relatively
...probably 10 or 11 percent. But this was only because
...slaves chosen for transport were healthy to begin with,
...slave traders were anxious to maintain their goods so as
...ell at a profit. Those Africans who were actually trans-
...rted, then, were already the hardy survivors of unimagi-

HOW SLAVES WERE STOWED ABOARD SHIP DURING THE MIDDLE PASSAGE. Men were "housed" on the right, women on the left, children in the middle. The human cargo was jammed onto platforms six feet wide without sufficient headroom to permit an adult to sit up. This diagram is from evidence gathered by English abolitionists and depicts conditions on the Liverpool slave ship *Brookes*.

nable hardships. For in order to place the above statistic in a larger context, we need to consider how many would have died before the ships were ready to transport them. One historian has estimated that 36 out of 100 people captured in the African interior would perish in the six-month-long forced march to the coast of Angola. Another dozen or so would die in the prisons there. Eventually, perhaps 57 of the original 100 captives would be taken on board a slave ship. Some 51 would survive the journey and be sold into slavery on arrival. If the destination was Brazil's sugar plantations, only 40 would still be alive after two years. In other words, the actual mortality rate of these new slaves was something more like 60 percent—and this doesn't begin to account for their life expectancy.

The people consigned to this fate struggled against it, and their initiatives helped to shape the emerging Atlantic world. When the opportunity presented itself, slaves banded together in revolt—a perpetual possibility that haunted slave owners and led to draconian regimes of violence and punishment (as in ancient Rome; see Chapter 5). When revolt was impossible, there were other forms of resistance, among them suicide and infanticide. Above all, slaves sought to escape. Almost as soon as the slave trade escalated, there were communities of escaped slaves throughout the Americas. Many of these independent settlements were large enough to assert and defend their autonomy. One such community, founded in 1603 in the hinterlands of Brazil's Pernambuco Province, persisted for over a century and had as many as 20,000 inhabitants. Most others were much smaller and more ephemeral, but their existence testifies to the limits of imperial authority at the fringes of the new American colonies.

CONFLICT AND COMPETITION IN EUROPE AND THE ATLANTIC WORLD

Most of Europe had enjoyed steady economic growth since the middle of the fifteenth century. The colonization of the Americas seemed to promise prosperity for the decades to come, while providing an outlet for European expansion and aggression. But in the second half of the sixteenth century, prolonged political, religious, and economic crises destabilized Europe. These crises were, in essential ways, the product of long-term developments within and between Europe's most powerful states, but they were exacerbated by these same states' imperial ambitions. Inevitably, then, European conflicts spread to European colonial holdings. Eventually,

the outcome of these conflicts would determine which European powers were best positioned to enlarge their presence in the Atlantic world—and beyond.

New World Silver and Old World Economies

In the latter half of the sixteenth century, an unprecedented inflation in prices profoundly destabilized the European economy. And because nothing on this scale had ever happened before, even during the Roman Empire's turbulent third century (see Chapter 6), it caused widespread panic. Although the twentieth century would see more dizzying inflations than this, skyrocketing prices were a terrifying novelty in this era, causing what some historians have termed a "price revolution."

Two developments in particular underlay this phenomenon. The first was demographic. After the plague-induced decline of the fourteenth century (see Chapter 11), Europe's population grew from roughly 50 million people

PEASANTS HARVESTING WHEAT, SIXTEENTH CENTURY.
The inflation that swept through Europe in the late sixteenth century affected poorer workers most acutely as the abundant labor supply dampened wages while at the same time the cost of food rose because of poor harvests.

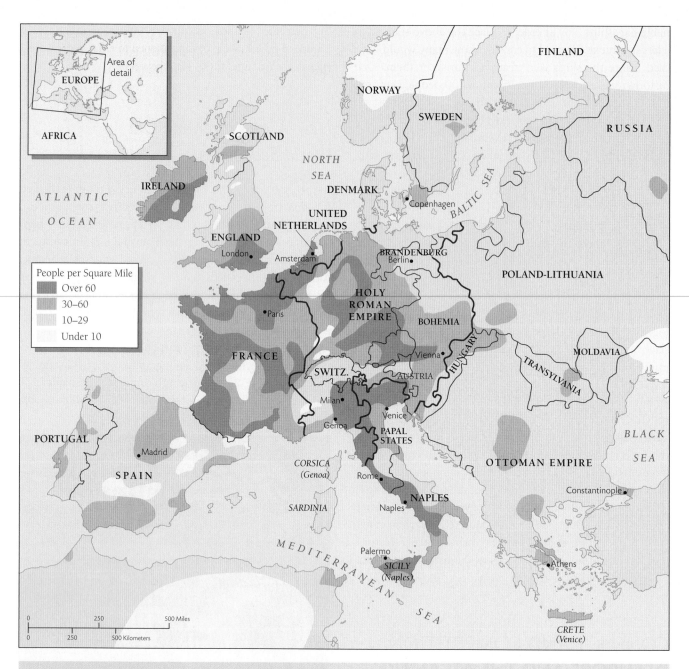

POPULATION GROWTH c. 1600. ▪ *In what regions did the population grow more rapidly?* ▪ *Why were the largest gains in population on the coasts?* ▪ *How would urbanization affect patterns of life and trade?*

in 1450 to 90 million in 1600: that is, it increased by nearly 80 percent in a relatively short span of time. Yet Europe's food supply remained nearly constant, meaning that food prices were driven sharply higher by the greater demand for basic commodities. Meanwhile, the enormous influx of silver and gold from Spanish America flooded Europe's previously cash-poor economy (see Chapter 12). This sudden availability of ready coin drove prices higher still.

How? In just four years, from 1556 to 1560, about 10 million ducats' worth of silver passed through the Spanish

port of Seville: that is roughly equivalent to 10 billion U.S. dollars in today's currency. (A single gold ducat, the standard unit of monetary exchange for long-distance trade, would be worth nearly a thousand dollars.) Consequently, the market was flooded with coins whose worth quickly became debased because there were so many of them. And still silver poured in, cheapening the coinage even more: between 1576 and 1580, the amount of imported silver had doubled, becoming 20 million ducats; and between 1591 and 1595 it more than quadrupled. Because most of this money was used by the Spanish crown to pay its armies and the many creditors who had financed its imperial ventures, a huge volume of coinage was put quickly into circulation through European banks, making the problem of inflation even more widespread. Since some people suddenly had more money to pay for goods and services, those who supplied these commodities could charge higher and higher prices. "I learned a proverb here," said a French traveler in Spain in 1603: "Everything costs a lot, except silver."

The New European Poor

In this climate, aggressive entrepreneurs profited from financial speculation, landholders from the rising prices of agricultural produce, and merchants from increasing demand for luxury goods. But laborers were caught in a vice. Prices were rising steeply, but wages were not keeping pace owing to the population boom that kept labor relatively cheap. As the cost of food staples rose, poor people had to spend an ever-greater percentage of their paltry incomes on necessities. In Flanders, for example, the cost of wheat tripled between 1550 and 1600; grain prices in Paris quadrupled; and the overall cost of living in England more than doubled in Shakespeare's lifetime. When disasters such as wars or bad harvests drove grain prices out of their reach, as they frequently did, the poor starved to death.

The price revolution also placed new pressures on the sovereign states of Europe. Inflation depressed the real value of money, so fixed incomes derived from taxes and rents yielded less and less actual wealth. Governments were therefore forced to raise taxes merely to keep their revenues constant. Yet most states needed even more revenue than before, because they were engaging in more wars and warfare was becoming increasingly expensive. The only recourse, then, was to raise taxes precipitously. Hence, governments faced continuous threats of defiance and even armed resistance from their citizens, who could not afford to foot these bills.

Although prices rose less rapidly after 1600, as both population growth and the flood of silver began to slow, the ensuing decades were a time of economic stagnation. A few areas—notably the Netherlands (see below)—bucked the trend, and the rich were usually able to hold their own, but the laboring poor made no advances. Wages continued to rise far more slowly than prices. Indeed, the lot of the poor in many places deteriorated further, as helpless civilians were plundered by rapacious tax collectors, looting soldiers, or sometimes both. In England, peasants who had been dispossessed of property or driven off once-common lands were branded as vagrants, and vagrancy itself became a criminal offense. It was this population of newly impoverished Europeans who became the indentured servants or deported criminals of the American colonies.

The Legacy of the Reformation: The French Wars of Religion

Compounding these economic problems were the wars that erupted within many European states. As we began to observe in Chapter 9, most medieval kingdoms were created through the colonization of smaller, traditionally autonomous territories—either by conquest or through marriage alliances with ruling families. Now these enlarged monarchies began to make ever-greater financial claims on their citizens while at the same time demanding religious uniformity among them. The result was regional and civil conflict, as local populations and even elites rebelled against the centralizing demands of monarchs who often embraced a different religion than that of their subjects. Although the Peace of Augsburg (1555) had established that each territory would follow the religion of its ruler, in an effort to end civil strife (see Chapter 13), it was based on the premise that no state can tolerate religious diversity. This was a dangerous precedent, considering the rapid spread of new religious ideas throughout Europe and their export to the New World.

France was the first of these monarchies to be enflamed by religious warfare. Calvinist missionaries from Geneva had made significant headway there (Calvin himself was French), assisted by the conversion of many aristocratic Frenchwomen, who in turn converted their husbands. By the 1560s, French Calvinists—known as Huguenots (HEW-guh-nohz)—made up between 10 and 20 percent of the population. But there was no open warfare until dynastic politics led factions within the government to break down along religious lines, pitting the (mostly southern) Huguenots against the (mostly northern) Catholic aristocracy. In some places, mobs incited by members of the clergy on both sides used this opportunity to settle local scores.

While the Huguenots were not strong enough to win any major scuffle, there were too many to be ignored, and in 1572 the two sides almost brokered a truce: the presumptive heir to the throne, Prince Henry of Navarre—who had become a Protestant—was to marry the Catholic sister of the reigning king, Henry III. But the compromise was undone by the Queen Mother, Catherine de Medici, whose Catholic faction plotted to kill all the Huguenot leaders while they were assembled in Paris for her daughter's wedding. In the early morning of St. Bartholomew's Day (August 24), most of these Protestant aristocrats were

HENRY IV OF FRANCE. The rule of Henry of Navarre (r. 1589–1610) initiated the Bourbon dynasty that would rule France until 1792 and ended the bitter civil war between Catholic and Huguenot factions.

France had a regional component, the edict also reinforced a tradition of regional autonomy in southwestern France, in spite of the monarchy's centralized power. The success of this effort can be measured by the fact that peace was maintained in France even after Henry IV was assassinated by a Catholic in 1610.

The wars of religion may be one reason that France did not enter the competition for Atlantic wealth until the seventeenth century, despite their early involvement in North American explorations. It was not until 1608 that French colonial settlements received much royal support, after which Catholic (but not Huguenot) immigration to "New France" was encouraged. Meanwhile, there were three failed attempts to establish French outposts in Portuguese Brazil, the last of which (in 1612–15) resulted only in the export of six Amazonian villagers to France, where they aroused great curiosity in an organized tour of French towns. The Brazilians' Catholic hosts even arranged for them to be publicly baptized as part of an attempt to bolster support for the Catholic cause: an episode that further illustrates the strong connection between the expansion of European influence abroad and the politics of religion at home.

The Revolt of the Netherlands and the Dutch Trading Empire

Warfare between Catholics and Protestants also broke out in the Netherlands during this period. Controlled for almost a century by the same Habsburg family that ruled Spain and its overseas empire, the Netherlands had prospered through intense involvement with trade in the Atlantic world. Their inhabitants had the greatest per capita wealth in all Europe, and the metropolis of Antwerp was northern Europe's leading commercial and financial center. So when the Spanish king and emperor Philip II (r. 1556–98) attempted to tighten his hold there in the 1560s, the fiercely independent Dutch cities resented this imperial intrusion and were ready to fight it.

This conflict took on a religious dynamic because Calvinism had spread into the Netherlands from France. Philip, an ardent defender of the Catholic faith, could not tolerate this combination of political and religious disobedience. When crowds began ransacking and desecrating Catholic churches throughout the country, Philip dispatched an army of 10,000 Spanish soldiers to wipe out Protestantism in his Dutch territories. A reign of terror ensued: some 12,000 people were rounded up on charges of heresy or sedition, thousands of whom were convicted and executed for treason.

murdered in their beds, and thousands of humble Protestants were slaughtered in the streets or drowned in the Seine. When word of the Parisian massacre spread to the provinces, local massacres proliferated.

Henry of Navarre escaped, along with his bride, but the war continued for more than two decades. Finally, Catherine's death in 1589 was followed by that of her son, Henry III, who had produced no heir to supplant Henry of Navarre. He became Henry IV, renouncing his Protestant faith in order to placate France's Catholic majority. Then, in 1598, Henry made a landmark effort to end conflict by issuing the Edict of Nantes, which recognized Catholicism as the official religion of the realm but enabled Protestants to practice their religion in specified places. This was an important step toward a policy of religious tolerance: for the first time, French Protestants were allowed to hold public office and to enroll in universities and work in hospitals, and they were even allowed to fortify some towns for their own military defense. And because the religious divide in

PROTESTANTS RANSACKING A CATHOLIC CHURCH IN THE NETHERLANDS.
Protestant destruction of religious images provoked a stern response from Philip II.
▪ *Why would Protestants have smashed statuary and other devotional artifacts?*

with Japan and maintained military and trading outposts in China and India, too.

In the Atlantic world itself, the Dutch did not have much of a significant presence. However, they did establish an outpost in North America, the colony known as New Amsterdam—until it was surrendered to the English in 1667, when it was renamed New York. Their remaining territorial holdings in the Atlantic were Dutch Guyana (present-day Surinam) on the coast of South America, and the islands of Curaçao and Tobago in the Caribbean. But if the Dutch did not match the Spanish or the English in their accumulation of land, the establishment of a second merchant enterprise, the Dutch West India Company, allowed them to dominate the Atlantic slave trade with Africa after 1621.

In constructing this new transoceanic trading empire in slaves and spices, the Dutch pioneered a new financial mechanism for investing in colonial enterprises: the joint-stock company. The Dutch East and West India Companies were early examples, raising cash by selling shares to individual investors whose liability was limited to the sum of their investment. These investors were not part of the company's management, but they were entitled to a share in the profits. Originally, the Dutch East India Company intended to pay off its investors within ten years, but when the period was up, they convinced investors who wanted to realize their profits immediately to sell their shares on the open market. The creation of a market in shares—we now call it a stock market—was an innovation that spread quickly. Arguably, stock markets now control the world's economy.

The Struggle of England and Spain

Religious strife could spark civil war, as in France, or political rebellion, as in the Netherlands. But it could also provoke warfare between sovereign states, as in the struggle between England and Spain. In this case, religious conflict was entangled with both dynastic claims and economic competition in the Atlantic world.

The dynastic competition came from the English royal family's division along confessional lines. The Catholic queen Mary (r. 1553–58), eldest daughter of Henry VIII and granddaughter of Ferdinand and Isabella of Spain (see Chapter 13), had married her cousin Philip II of Spain in 1554 and ruled at a time of great strife between Catholics and Protestants

These events catalyzed the Protestant opposition. A Dutch aristocrat, William of Orange, emerged as the anti-Spanish leader and sought help from religious allies in France, Germany, and England. Organized bands of Protestant privateers (that is, privately owned ships) began harassing the Spanish navy in the waters of the North Atlantic. In 1572, William's Protestant army seized control of the Netherlands' northern provinces. Although William was assassinated in 1584, his efforts were instrumental in forcing the Spanish crown to recognize the independence of a northern Dutch Republic in 1609. Once united, these seven northern provinces became wholly Calvinist; the southern region, still largely Catholic, remained under Spanish rule.

After gaining its independence, the new Dutch Republic emerged as the most prosperous European commercial empire of the seventeenth century. Indeed, its reach extended well beyond the Atlantic world, targeting the Indian Ocean and East Asia as well. In general, the Dutch colonial project owed more to the strategic "fort and factory" model of expansion favored by the Portuguese than to the Spanish technique of territorial conquest and settlement. For example, the Dutch established a colony on the Cape of Good Hope at the southern tip of Africa, which facilitated the eastward spread of their influence. Many of its early initiatives were spurred by the establishment of the Dutch East India Company, a private mercantile corporation that came to control Sumatra, Borneo, and the Moluccas (the so-called Spice Islands). This meant that the Dutch had a lucrative monopoly on the European trade in pepper, cinnamon, nutmeg, mace, and cloves. The company also secured an exclusive right to trade

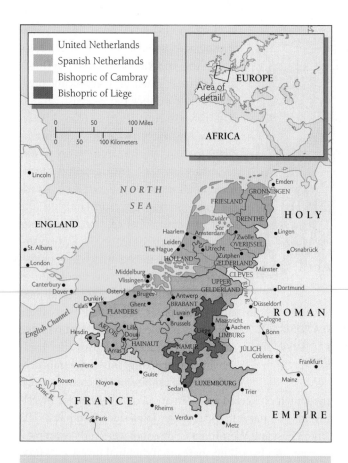

NORTH SEA

ENGLAND

HOLY

ROMAN

EMPIRE

FRANCE

THE NETHERLANDS AFTER 1609. ▪ *What were the two main divisions of the Netherlands?* ▪ *Which was Protestant, and which was Catholic?* ▪ *How could William of Orange and his allies use the geography of the northern Netherlands against the Spanish?*

on the high seas. In a particularly dramatic exploit lasting from 1577 to 1580, prevailing winds and a lust for booty propelled Drake all the way around the world, to return with stolen Spanish treasure worth twice as much as Queen Elizabeth's annual revenue.

After suffering numerous such attacks over a period of two decades, King Philip finally resolved to fight back after Elizabeth's government openly supported the Dutch rebellion against Spain in 1585. In 1588, he dispatched an enormous fleet, confidently called the "Invincible Armada," whose mission was to invade England. But the invasion never occurred. After an indecisive initial encounter between the two fleets, a fierce storm—hailed as a "Protestant wind" by the lucky English—drove the Spanish galleons off course, many of them wrecking off the coast of Ireland. The shattered flotilla eventually limped home after a disastrous circumnavigation of the British isles, with almost half its ships lost. Meanwhile, Elizabeth took credit for her country's miraculous escape. In subsequent years, continued threats from Spain and sporadic skirmishes nurtured a renewed sense of English nationalism and also fueled anti-Catholic sentiment in that realm.

England's Colonial Ambitions

In the early decades of the seventeenth century, the English challenge to Spanish supremacy in the Atlantic began to bear fruit. Unlike New Spain, England's North American colonies had no significant mineral wealth; instead, as we noted above, English colonists sought to profit from the establishment of large-scale agricultural settlements in North America and the Caribbean. The first permanent colony was founded at Jamestown, Virginia, in 1607. Although this settlement was not particularly successful, more than twenty autonomous settlements were planted over the next forty years by a total of about 80,000 English immigrants.

Many of these were motivated by a desire for religious freedom—hence the name we still give to the Pilgrims who landed at Plymouth, Massachusetts, in 1620. These radical Protestants were known as Puritans, and because they were also political dissidents they were almost as unwelcome as Catholics in an England whose church was, after all, an extension of the monarchy. Strikingly, however, English colonists showed little interest in trying to convert Native American peoples to Christianity. Missionizing played a much larger role in Spanish efforts to colonize Central and South America and in French efforts to penetrate the North American hinterlands.

Another difference between Spanish and English colonialism is the fact that these English colonies did not

in England. After Mary's death, her Protestant half sister Elizabeth (r. 1558–1603) came to the throne, and relations with Spain rapidly declined. They declined further when Catholic Ireland—an English colony—rose in rebellion in 1565, with Spain quietly supporting the Irish. Although it took almost thirty bloody years, English forces eventually suppressed the rebellion. Elizabeth then cemented the Irish defeat by encouraging intense colonial settlement in Ireland. Somewhat ironically, she did so in conscious imitation of Spanish policy in the Americas, sending thousands of Protestant English settlers to occupy land in Ireland in the hopes of creating a colonial state with a largely English identity. Instead, these measures created the deep ethnic and religious conflicts that still trouble the island.

England's conflict with Spain, meanwhile, was worsened by the fact that English economic interests were directly opposed to those of Spain. English traders were making steady inroads into Spanish commercial networks in the Atlantic, as English sea captains such as Sir Francis Drake and Sir John Hawkins plundered Spanish vessels

THE DUTCH EAST INDIA COMPANY WAREHOUSE AND TIMBER WHARF AT AMSTERDAM. The substantial warehouse, the stockpiles of lumber, and the company ship under construction in the foreground illustrate the degree to which overseas commerce could stimulate the economy of the mother country.

THE "ARMADA PORTRAIT" OF ELIZABETH. This is one of several portraits that commemorated the defeat of the Spanish Armada in 1588. Through the window on the left (the queen's right hand), an English flotilla sails serenely on sunny seas; on the right, Spanish ships are wrecked by a "Protestant wind." Elizabeth's right hand rests protectively—and commandingly—on the globe. ■ *How would you interpret this image?*

begin as royal enterprises. They were private ventures, farmed either by individual landholders (as in Maryland and Pennsylvania) or managed by joint-stock companies (as in Virginia and the Massachusetts Bay Colony). Building on their experience in Ireland, where colonies had been called "plantations," many English settlers established plantations—planned communities—that attempted to replicate as many features of English life as possible. Geography largely dictated the foundation locations of these English settlements, which were located along the northeast Atlantic coast and on rivers and bays that provided good harbors. Aside from the Hudson, however, there were no great rivers to lead colonists very far inland, so the English colonies clung to the coastline and to each other. The densely populated corridor along the Atlantic seaboard is a direct result of these early settlement patterns.

Since most land in the Old World was owned by royal and aristocratic families, the accumulation of wealth through the control of land was a new and exciting prospect for small-and medium-scale landholders in the new English colonies. This helps to explain their rural, agricultural character—in contrast to the great cities of New Spain. But this focus on agricultural holdings also resulted from the demographic catastrophe that had decimated native populations in this region, as in so many others: by the early seventeenth century, a great deal of rich land had been abandoned simply because there were so few native farmers to till it. As a result, indigenous peoples who had not already succumbed to European diseases were now under threat from colonists who wanted complete and exclusive control over their lands.

To this end, the English soon set out to eliminate, through expulsion and massacre, the former inhabitants of the region. There were a few exceptions; in the Quaker colony of Pennsylvania, colonists and Native Americans maintained friendly relations for more than half a

PLYMOUTH PLANTATION. An English settlement was established at Plymouth in the Massachusetts Bay Colony in 1620. This image shows a reconstruction of the village as it might have looked in 1627. Although speculative, this reconstruction captures something of the plantation's diminutive fragility and isolation.

century. But in the Carolinas, by contrast, there was widespread enslavement of native peoples, either for sale to the West Indies or to work on the rice plantations along the coast. In another contrast to the Spanish and French colonies, intermarriage between English colonists and native populations was rare, creating a nearly unbridgeable racial divide in these North American colonies.

THE THIRTY YEARS' WAR AND THE RISE OF FRANCE

With the promulgation of the French Edict of Nantes in 1598, the end of open hostilities between England and Spain in 1604, and the truce between Spain and the Dutch Republic of 1609, religious warfare in Europe came briefly to an end. In 1618, however, a new series of wars broke out in Central Europe, in some of the German-speaking lands that had felt the first divisive effects of the Reformation and Counter-Reformation (see Chapter 13). Not only was this period of warfare one of the longest in history, it was one of the bloodiest and most widespread, engulfing most of the European continent before it ended thirty years later, in 1648. Although it began as a religious conflict, it quickly became an international struggle for dominance in which these initial provocations were all but forgotten. In the end, some 8 million people died and entire regions were devastated by the rapacity of criss-crossing of armies. The populations of several provinces never recovered and most of the great powers who had fought the war were impoverished

and weakened. The exception was France, which became a preeminent power in Europe for the first time.

The Beginnings of the Thirty Years' War

Like the number and variety of the combatants it involved, the causes of the Thirty Years' War are complicated. On one level, it was an outlet for deeper aggressions and tensions that had been building up since the Peace of Augsburg in 1555 (see above and Chapter 13). On another, it grew out of even longerstanding disputes among rulers and territories (Catholic and Protestant) in the patchwork of provinces that made up the Holy Roman Empire, disputes into which allied powers were drawn. On still another, it was an opportunity for players on the fringes of power to come into prominence.

The catalyst came in 1618, when the Austrian Habsburg (Catholic) prince, Ferdinand, who also ruled Hungary and Poland, was named as heir to the throne of Protestant Bohemia. This prompted a rebellion among the Bohemian aristocracy. A year later, the complex dynastic politics of Central Europe resulted in Ferdinand's election as Holy Roman Emperor. This gave him access to an imperial (Catholic) army, which he now sent in to crush the Protestant revolt. The Bohemians, meanwhile, were bolstered by the support of some Austrian nobility, many of whom were also Protestant and who saw a way to recover power from the Habsburg ruling family.

In 1620, the war escalated further when the Ottomans threw their support behind the Protestants and in so doing touched off a war with the staunchly Catholic kingdom of Poland, whose borders the Muslim army would need to cross in order to get to Prague. The Poles won and the Ottomans retreated. Meanwhile, Ferdinand's Habsburg cousin, the Spanish king and emperor Philip IV, had renewed the war against the Protestant Dutch Republic, which had won its independence from Catholic Spain in 1609; an alliance between the two Habsburg rulers made sense. It led to a major pitched battle between united Protestant forces and a Spanish-led Catholic army (including the young French philosopher, René Descartes) just outside of Prague. The Habsburgs were victorious, and Bohemia was forced to accept Ferdinand's Catholic rule.

The Tangled Politics and Terrible Price of War

The conflict, which had started in Bohemia, should have ended there. But it did not. It metastasized, like a terrible cancer. Unrest between Catholics and Protestants in other

Analyzing Primary Sources

The Devastation of the Thirty Years' War

The author of the following excerpt, Hans Jakob Christoph von Grimmelshausen (1621–1676), barely survived the horrors of the Thirty Years' War. His parents were killed, probably when he was thirteen years old, and he himself was kidnapped the following year and forced into the army. By age fifteen, he was a soldier. His darkly satiric masterpiece, Simplicissimus *("The Simpleton"), drew heavily on these experiences. Although technically a fictional memoir, it portrays with brutal accuracy the terrible realities of this era.*

 lthough it was not my intention to take the peaceloving reader with these troopers to my dad's house and farm, seeing that matters will go ill therein, yet the course of my history demands that I should leave to kind posterity an account of what manner of cruelties were now and again practised in this our German war: yes, and moreover testify by my own example that such evils must often have been sent to us by the goodness of Almighty God for our profit. For, gentle reader, who would ever have taught me that there was a God in Heaven if these soldiers had not destroyed my dad's house, and by such a deed driven me out among folk who gave me all fitting instruction thereupon? . . .

The first thing these troopers did was, that they stabled their horses: thereafter each fell to his appointed task: which task was neither more nor less than ruin and destruction. For though some began to slaughter and to boil and to roast so that it looked as if there should be a merry banquet forward, yet others there were who did but storm through the house above and below stairs. Others stowed together great parcels of cloth and apparel and all manner of household stuff, as if they would set up a frippery market. All that they had no mind to take with them they cut in pieces. Some thrust their swords through the hay and straw as if they had not enough sheep and swine to slaughter: and some shook the feathers out of the beds and in their stead stuffed in bacon and other dried meat and provisions as if such were better and softer to sleep upon. Others broke the stove and the windows as if they had a never-ending summer to promise. Houseware of copper and tin they beat flat, and packed such vessels, all bent and spoiled, in with the rest. Bedsteads, tables, chairs, and benches they burned, though there lay many cords of dry wood in the yard. Pots and pipkins must all go to pieces, either because they would eat none but roast flesh, or because their purpose was to make there but a single meal.

Our maid was so handled in the stable that she could not come out, which is a shame to tell of. Our man they laid bound upon the ground, thrust a gag into his mouth, and poured a pailful of filthy water into his body: and by this, which they called a Swedish draught, they forced him to lead a party of them to another place where they captured men and beasts, and brought them back to our farm, in which company were my dad, my mother, and our Ursula.

And now they began: first to take the flints out of their pistols and in place of them to jam the peasants' thumbs in and so to torture the poor rogues as if they had been about the burning of witches: for one of them they had taken they thrust into the baking oven and there lit a fire under him, although he had as yet confessed no crime: as for another, they put a cord round his head and so twisted it tight with a piece of wood that the blood gushed from his mouth and nose and ears. In a word each had his own device to torture the peasants, and each peasant his several tortures.

Source: Hans Jakob Christoph von Grimmelshausen, *Simplicissimus,* trans. S. Goodrich (New York: 1995), pp. 1–3, 8–10, 32–35.

Questions for Analysis

1. The first-person narrator here recounts the atrocities committed "in this our German war," in which both perpetrators and victims are German. How believable is this description? What lends it credibility?

2. Why might Grimmelshausen have chosen to publish his account as a satirical fiction rather than as a straightforward historical narrative or autobiography? How would this choice affect a reader's response to scenes such as this?

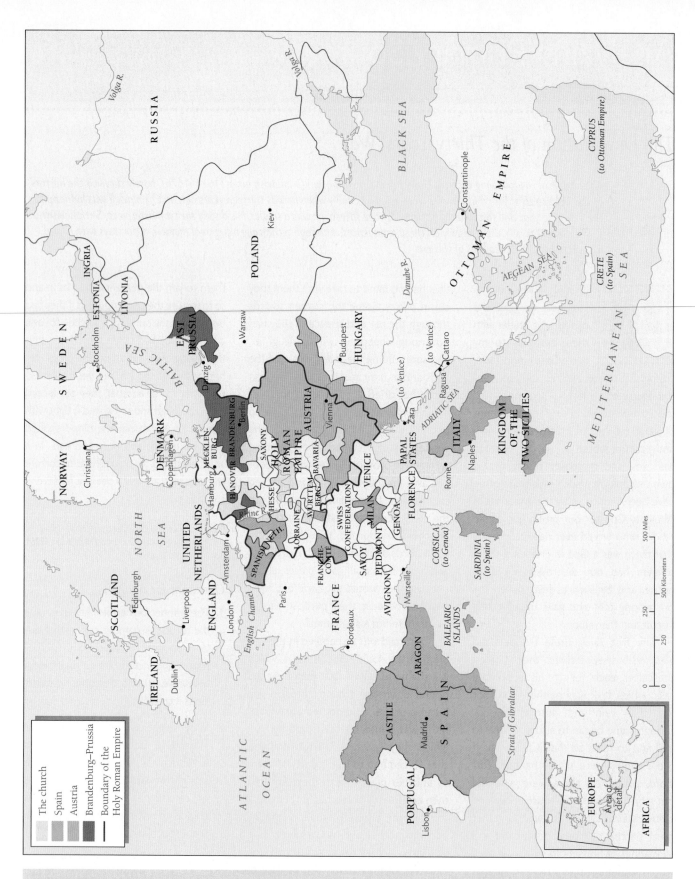

EUROPE AT THE END OF THE THIRTY YEARS' WAR. This map shows the fragile political checkerboard that resulted from the Peace of Westphalia in 1648. ■ *When you compare this map to the map on page 431, what are the most significant territorial changes between 1550 and 1648?* ■ *Which regions would have been weakened or endangered by this arrangement?* ■ *Which would be in a strong position to dominate Europe?*

THE BATTLE OF ROCROI, 1643. Spain's defeat by the French at Rocroi was the first time the Spanish army had lost a land battle since the reign of Ferdinand and Isabella (see Chapter 12) and was yet another contributing factor to the decline of Spanish power during the Thirty Years' War. This painting shows the victorious French general, Duke d'Enghien, surveying the battlefield from afar.

parts of Central Europe erupted into war. French Catholics and Protestants, who had enjoyed relatively peaceful relations since the Edict of Nantes in 1598, came into violent contact once again. Protestant Denmark, fearing that Catholic victories in neighboring parts of the Holy Roman Empire might threaten its sovereignty, was drawn in—losing valuable territories before it was forced to concede defeat.

In this new phase of the conflict, political expediency soon outweighed either religious or dynastic allegiances. When a confederation of Catholic princes seemed close to uprooting Protestantism throughout Germany in 1630, it found its way blocked by other German Catholic princes who were willing to ally with Protestants in order to preserve their own autonomy. Joining them was the (Protestant) king of Sweden, Gustavus Adolphus (r. 1611–32), who championed both the German Lutheran states and his own nation's sovereignty in the wake of Denmark's brush with disaster—but whose Protestant army was secretly subsidized by Catholic France, which would otherwise have been surrounded by a strong Habsburg alliance on its northern, eastern, and southern borders.

One of the great military commanders of all time, Gustavus had become king at age seventeen. Like another young general, Alexander the Great (see Chapter 4), he was not only an expert tactician but a splendid leader. His army became the best-trained and best-equipped fighting force of the era—what some have called the first modern army. When Gustavus died in battle in 1632, a month before his thirty-eighth birthday, Sweden had become one of Europe's great powers, rivaling Spain and Russia in size and prestige.

But in 1635, with Gustavus dead, France was compelled to join Sweden in declaring war on the Spanish and Austrian Habsburgs. In the middle lay the German-speaking lands of Central Europe, already weakened by seventeen years of war and now a helpless battleground. In the next thirteen years, Germany suffered more from warfare than at any time until the twentieth century. Several cities were besieged and sacked nine or ten times over, while soldiers from all nations, who had to sustain themselves by plunder, gave no quarter to defenseless civilians. With plague and disease adding to the toll of outright butchery, some towns and rural areas were nearly eradicated. Most horrifying was the loss of life in the final four years of the war, when the carnage continued even after peace negotiators arrived at broad areas of agreement.

The Peace of Westphalia and the Decline of Spain

The eventual adoption of the Peace of Westphalia in 1648 was a watershed in European history. It marked the emergence of France as the predominant power on the Continent, a position it would hold for the next two centuries. The greatest losers in the conflict (aside from the millions of German victims) were the Austrian Habsburgs, who were forced to surrender all the territory they had gained and to abandon their hopes of using the office of Holy Roman Emperor to dominate Central Europe.

The Spanish Habsburgs were also substantially weakened and were no longer able to fall back on the wealth of their Atlantic empire. Large portions of the Atlantic trade had been infiltrated by merchants from other countries, and the expansion of local economies in Spain's colonies had made them less dependent on trade with Spain itself. In 1600, the Spanish Empire had been the mightiest power in the world. A half century later, this empire had begun to fall apart.

As we've already noted, New Spain's great wealth had begun to turn into a liability when the infusion of silver spiked inflation and slowed economic development at home. Lacking both agricultural and mineral resources of its own, Spain might have developed its own industries and a balanced trading pattern, as some of its Atlantic rivals were doing. Instead, the Spanish used imperial silver to buy manufactured goods from other parts of Europe, offering no incentives to develop exports of their own. When the river of silver began to abate, Spain was plunged into debt.

Meanwhile, the Spanish crown's commitment to supporting the Catholic Church committed it to costly wars, as did attempts to maintain Spain's international dominance. Involvement in the Thirty Years' War was the last straw. The strains of warfare drove the kingdom, with its power base in Castile, to raise more money and soldiers from the other Iberian provinces. First Catalonia and then Portugal (incorporated into Spain in 1580) rose in revolt, followed by the southern Italians who rebelled against their Castilian viceroys in Naples and Sicily. It was only by chance that Spain's greatest external enemies, France and England, could not act in time to take advantage of its plight. This gave the Castilian-based government time to put down the Italian revolts; by 1652, it had also brought Catalonia to heel. But Portugal retained its independence while Spain remained isolated, weakened, and without European allies after the Peace of Westphalia.

The Emergence of French Power in Europe and North America

France emerged from the crisis of the Thirty Years' War with a stronger state, a more dynamic economy, and increased influence abroad. Like Spain, France had grown over the course of the previous centuries by absorbing formerly independent principalities whose inhabitants cherished traditions of local independence and were not always willing to cooperate with the royal government. The fact that France became more powerful as a result of this process, while Spain did not can be attributed in part to France's greater natural resources and the greater prestige of the French monarchy, which can be traced back to the rule of Louis IX (later canonized as Saint Louis; see Chapter 10). Most subjects of the French king, including the Protestants whose welfare had been cultivated by Henry IV, were loyal to the crown. Moreover, France had enormous economic resiliency, owing primarily to its rich and varied agricultural productivity. Unlike Spain, which had to import food, France was able to feed itself. Moreover, Henry IV's ministers had financed the construction of roads, bridges, and canals to facilitate the flow of goods. Royal factories manufactured luxury goods such as crystal, glass, and tapestries, and Henry also supported the production of silk, linen, and wool throughout the kingdom.

Henry's patronage had also allowed the explorer Samuel de Champlain to claim parts of Canada as France's first foothold in the New World. In 1608, Champlain founded the colony of Québec in the Saint Lawrence river valley. Whereas the English initially limited their colonial settlements to regions along the Atlantic coastline, the French set out to dominate the interior of the North American continent. French traders ranged far up and down the few Canadian rivers that led inland, exchanging furs and goods with the Native American groups they encountered, while French missionaries used the same arteries to spread Catholic Christianity from Québec to Louisiana. Eventually, French imperial ventures spread via the Great Lakes and the great river systems along the Mississippi to the prairies of America's Midwest.

These far-flung French colonies were established and administered as royal enterprises like those of Spain, a fact that distinguished them from the private commercial ventures put together by the English and the Dutch. Also like New Spain, the colonies of New France were overwhelmingly populated by men. The elite of French colonial society were military officers and administrators sent from Paris. Below their ranks were fishermen, fur traders, small farmers, and common soldiers who constituted the bulk of French settlers in North America. Because the

ILLINOIS INDIANS TRADING WITH FRENCH SETTLERS. This engraving from Nicholas de Fer's 1705 map of the Western Hemisphere illustrates the economic interdependence that developed between early French colonies and the native peoples of the surrounding region. ▪ *How did this differ from relations between Native Americans and English agricultural communities on the Atlantic coast?*

fishing and fur trades relied on cooperative relationships with native peoples, a mutual economic interdependence grew up between the French colonists and the peoples of surrounding regions. Intermarriage between French traders and native women was common.

Yet in contrast to both Spanish and English colonies, these French colonies remained dependent on the wages and supplies sent to them from the mother country. Only rarely did they become truly self-sustaining economic enterprises. Indeed, their financial rewards were modest. Furs, fish, and tobacco were exported to European markets, but it was not until the late seventeenth century that some French colonies began to realize large profits by building sugar plantations in the Caribbean islands of Hispaniola (the French portion of this large island, now Haiti, was known as Saint-Domingue), Guadeloupe, and Martinique. By 1750, 500,000 slaves on Saint-Domingue were laboring under extraordinarily harsh conditions to produce 40 percent of the world's sugar and 50 percent of its coffee (see Chapter 15).

The Policies of Cardinal Richelieu

This expansion of French power can be credited, in part, to Henry IV's de facto successor, Cardinal Richelieu (*REESH-eh-lyuh*). The real king of France, Henry's son Louis XIII (r. 1610–43), had come to the throne at the age of nine, so Richelieu, as his chief minister of state, dominated his reign. His chief aim was to centralize royal bureaucracy while exploiting opportunities to foster French influence abroad.

Within France, Richelieu amended the Edict of Nantes so that it no longer supported the military and political rights of the Huguenots. He also prohibited these French Protestants from settling in Québec. Yet considering that he owed his political power (in part) to his ecclesiastical position in the Catholic Church, the fact that he allowed the edict to stand speaks to his larger interest in fostering a sense of French national identity that centered on monarchy. In keeping with this policy, he also imposed direct taxation on powerful provinces that had retained their financial autonomy up to that point. Later, to make sure taxes were efficiently collected, Richelieu instituted a new system of local government which empowered royal officials to put down provincial resistance.

These policies made the French royal government more powerful than any in Europe. It also doubled the crown's income, allowing France to engage in the Thirty Years' War that extended its power on the continent. Yet this increased centralization would provoke challenges to royal authority from aristocratic elites in the years after Richelieu's death. Eventually, the extreme centralization of royal authority in France would lead to the French Revolution (see Chapter 18).

The Challenge of the Fronde

One more immediate response to Richelieu's policies was a series of uncoordinated revolts known collectively as the *Fronde* (from the French word for a sling used to hurl stones). In 1643, just after the death of Richelieu, Louis XIII was succeeded by his five-year-old son, Louis XIV. The young king's regents were his mother, Anne of Austria, and her alleged lover, Cardinal Mazarin. Both were foreigners—Anne was a Habsburg and Mazarin was an Italian by birth—and many extremely powerful nobles hated them. They also hated the way that Richelieu's government had curtailed their own authority in their ancestral provinces. Popular resentments were aroused as well, because the costs of the ongoing Thirty Years' War were now combined with several consecutive years of bad harvests. So when cliques of nobles expressed their disgust for Mazarin, they found much popular support. In 1648, the levy of a new tax had protesters on the streets of Paris, armed with slings and projectiles.

However, neither the aristocratic leaders of the Fronde nor the commoners who joined them claimed to be resisting the young king; their targets were the corruption and mismanagement of Mazarin. Some of the rebels, it is true, insisted that part of Mazarin's fault lay in his pursuit of Richelieu's centralizing policy. But most aristocrats wanted to become part of this centralizing process. Years later, when Louis XIV began to rule in his own right in 1651, the memory of these early turbulent years haunted him. He resolved never to let the aristocracy or their provinces get out of hand. Pursuing this aim, he became the most effective absolute monarch in Europe (see Chapter 15).

THE CRISIS OF MONARCHY IN ENGLAND

Of all the crises that shook Europe in this era, the most radical in its consequences was the English Civil War. The causes of this conflict were similar to those that had sparked trouble in other countries: hostilities between the component parts of a composite kingdom; religious animosities between Catholics and Protestants; struggles for power among competing factions of aristocrats at court; and a fiscal system that could not keep pace with the increasing costs of government, much less those of war. But in England, these developments led to the unprecedented criminal trial and execution of a king, an event that sent shock waves throughout Europe and the Atlantic world.

The Origins of the Civil War

The chain of events leading to civil war in England can be traced to the last decades of Queen Elizabeth's reign. The expenses of England's defense against Spain, rebellion in Ireland, widespread crop failures, and the inadequacies of the antiquated English taxation system drove the queen's government deeply into debt. When Elizabeth was succeeded by her cousin, James Stuart—King James VI of Scotland, James I of England—bitter factional disputes at court were complicated by the financial crisis. When the English Parliament rejected James's demands for more taxes, he raised what revenues he could without parliamentary approval, imposing new tolls and selling trading monopolies to favored courtiers. These measures aroused

resentment against the king and made voluntary grants of taxation from Parliament even less likely.

James also struggled with religious divisions among his subjects. His own kingdom of Scotland had been firmly Calvinist since the 1560s. England, too, was Protestant but of a very different kind, since the Church of England retained many of the rituals, hierarchies, and doctrines of the medieval Church (see Chapter 13). Indeed, a significant number of English Protestants, known as Puritans, wanted to bring their church more firmly into line with Calvinist principles; it was a group of Puritan refugees who founded the Massachusetts Bay Colony (above). Although James was largely successful in mediating these conflicts, he stirred up trouble in staunchly Catholic Ireland by encouraging thousands of Scottish Calvinists to settle in the northern Irish province of Ulster. In doing so, he exacerbated a situation that had already become violent under Elizabeth.

Parliament versus the King

English politics became more volatile in 1625, when James was succeeded by his surviving son, Charles. Charles alarmed his Protestant subjects by marrying the (Catholic) sister of France's Louis XIII, and he launched a new war with Spain, straining his already slender financial resources. When Parliament refused to grant him funds, he demanded forced loans from his subjects and punished those who refused by lodging soldiers in their homes. Others were imprisoned without trial. Parliament responded by imposing the Petition of Right in 1628, which declared that taxes not voted by Parliament were illegal, condemned arbitrary imprisonment, and prohibited quartering of soldiers in private houses. Thereafter, Charles tried to rule England without Parliament—something that had not been attempted since the establishment of that body 400 years earlier (see Chapter 9). He also ran into trouble with his Calvinist subjects in Scotland because he began to favor the most Catholic-leaning elements in the English Church. The Scots rebelled in 1640, and a Scottish army marched south into England to demand the withdrawal of Charles's "Catholicizing" measures.

To meet the Scottish threat, Charles was forced to summon Parliament, whose members were determined to impose radical reforms on the king's government before they would even consider granting him funds to raise an army. There was even support for the Scottish Calvinists among Puritans in Parliament. To avoid dealing with this difficult political situation, Charles tried to arrest

Cardinal Richelieu on the Common People of France

Armand Jean du Plessis, Duke of Richelieu and cardinal of the Roman Catholic Church, was the effective ruler of France from 1624 until his death in 1642. His Political Testament *was assembled after his death from historical sketches and memoranda of advice which he prepared for King Louis XIII, the ineffectual monarch whom he ostensibly served. This book was eventually published in 1688, during the reign of Louis XIV.*

ll students of politics agree that when the common people are too well off it is impossible to keep them peaceable. The explanation for this is that they are less well informed than the members of the other orders in the state, who are much more cultivated and enlightened, and so if not preoccupied with the search for the necessities of existence, find it difficult to remain within the limits imposed by both common sense and the law.

It would not be sound to relieve them of all taxation and similar charges, since in such a case they would lose the mark of their subjection and consequently the awareness of their station. Thus being free from paying tribute, they would consider themselves exempted from obedience. One should compare them with mules, which being accustomed to work, suffer more when long idle than when kept busy. But just as this work should be reasonable, with the burdens placed upon these animals proportionate to their strength, so it is likewise with the burdens placed upon the people. If they are not moderate, even when put to good public use, they are certainly unjust. I realize that when a king undertakes a program of public works it is correct to say that what the people gain from it is returned by paying the *taille* [a heavy tax imposed on the peasantry]. In the same fashion it can be maintained that what a king takes from the people returns to them, and that they advance it to him only to draw upon it for the enjoyment of their leisure and their investments, which would be impossible if they did not contribute to the support of the state.

Source: *The Political Testament of Cardinal Richelieu,* trans. Henry Bertram Hill (Madison, WI: 1961), pp. 31–32.

Questions for Analysis

1. According to Cardinal Richelieu, why should the state work to subjugate the common people? What assumptions about the nature and status of "common people" underlie this argument?

2. What theory of the state emerges from this argument? What is the relationship between the king and the state and between the king and the people, according to Richelieu?

Parliament's leaders and force his own agenda. When he failed in this, he withdrew from London to raise his own army. Parliament responded by mustering a seperate military force and voting itself the taxation to pay for it. By the end of 1642, open warfare had erupted between the English king and the English government: something inconceivable in neighboring France, where the king and the government were inseparable.

Arrayed on the king's side were most of England's aristocrats and largest landowners, many of whom owned lands in the Atlantic colonies as well. The parliamentary forces were made up of smaller landholders, tradesmen, and artisans, many of whom were Puritan sympathizers. The king's royalist supporters were commonly known by the aristocratic name of Cavaliers. Their opponents, who cut their hair short in contempt for the fashionable custom of wearing curls, were derisively called Roundheads. After 1644, when the parliamentary army was effectively reorganized, the royalist forces were badly beaten, and in 1646 the king was compelled to surrender. Soon thereafter, the episcopal hierarchy of the Church of England was abolished and a Calvinist-style church was mandated throughout England and Wales.

The struggle might have ended here had not a quarrel developed within the parliamentary party. The majority of its members were ready to restore Charles to the throne as a limited monarch, under an arrangement whereby a uniformly Calvinist faith would be imposed on both Scotland

seized control of the government. In order to ensure that the Puritan agenda would be carried out, he ejected all the moderates from Parliament by force. This "Rump" (remaining) Parliament then proceeded to put the king on trial and eventually to condemn him to death for treason against his own subjects. Charles Stuart was publicly beheaded on January 30, 1649: the first time in history that a reigning king had been legally deposed and executed. Europeans reacted to his death with horror, astonishment, or rejoicing, depending on their own political convictions (see *Interpreting Visual Evidence* on page 480).

After the king's execution, his son (the future King Charles II) joined with the remaining royalist forces in an attempt to restore the monarchy. But he was defeated by Cromwell's army and fled to France. With the heir to the English throne in exile, Cromwell and his supporters abolished Parliament's hereditary House of Lords and declared England a Commonwealth: an English translation of the Latin *res publica*. Technically, the Rump Parliament continued as the legislative body; but Cromwell, with the army at his command, possessed the real power and soon became exasperated by legislators' attempts to enrich themselves by confiscating their opponents' property. In 1653, he

CHARLES I. King Charles of England was a connoisseur of the arts and a patron of artists. He was adept at using portraiture to convey the magnificence of his tastes and the grandeur of his conception of kingship. ■ *How does this portrait by Anthony van Dyck compare to the engravings of the "martyred" king on page 480 in* **Interpreting Visual Evidence?**

and England as the state religion. But a radical minority of Puritans, commonly known as Independents, insisted on religious freedom for themselves and all other Protestants. Their leader was Oliver Cromwell (1599–1658), who had risen to command the Roundhead army, which he had reconstituted as "the New Model Army." Ultimately, he became the new leader of Parliament, too.

The Fall of Charles Stuart and Oliver Cromwell's Commonwealth

Taking advantage of the dissension within the ranks of his opponents, Charles renewed the war in 1648. But he was forced to surrender after a brief campaign, and Cromwell

OLIVER CROMWELL AS PROTECTOR OF THE COMMONWEALTH. This coin, minted in 1658, shows the lord protector wreathed with laurel garlands like a classical hero or a Roman consul, but it also proclaims him to be "by the Grace of God Protector of the Commonwealth." ■ *What mixed messages does this coin convey?*

marched a detachment of troops into the Rump Parliament and disbanded it.

The short-lived Commonwealth was thus replaced by the "Protectorate," a thinly disguised autocracy established under a constitution drafted by officers of the army. Called the *Instrument of Government*, this text is the nearest approximation to a written constitution England has ever had. Extensive powers were given to Cromwell as Lord Protector for life, and his office was made hereditary.

The Restoration of the Monarchy

Many intellectuals noted the similarities between these events and those that had given rise to the Principate of Augustus after the death of Julius Caesar (Chapter 5). And among the people, Cromwell's Puritan military dictatorship was growing unpopular, not least because it prohibited public recreation on Sundays and closed London's theatres. Many became nostalgic for the milder and more tolerant Church of England and began to hope for a restoration of the old royalist regime. The opportunity came with Cromwell's death in 1658. His son Richard had no sooner succeeded to the office of Lord Protector when a faction within the army removed him from power. As groups of royalists plotted an uprising, a new Parliament was organized, and, in April of 1660, it declared that King Charles II had been the ruler of England since his father's execution in 1649. Almost overnight, England became a monarchy again.

Charles II (r. 1660–85) revived the Church of England and was careful not to return to the provocative religious policies of his father. Quipping that he did not wish to "resume his travels," he agreed to respect Parliament and to observe the Petition of Right that had so enraged Charles I. He also accepted all the legislation passed by Parliament immediately before the outbreak of civil war in 1642, including the requirement that Parliament be summoned at least once every three years. England thus emerged from its civil war as a limited monarchy, in which power was exercised by "the king in Parliament." It remains a constitutional monarchy to this day.

The English Civil War and the Atlantic World

These tumultuous events had a significant influence on the development of a new political sensibility within England's Atlantic colonies. The English landed aristocracy had sided with the king during this conflict, but many in the colonies had sympathized with Parliament in its claims to protect the liberties of small landowners, who also bore a dispro-

portionate share of taxation. Even after the Restoration of the monarchy in 1660, many colonial leaders retained an antimonarchist and antiaristocratic bias.

The fact that the royal government had been almost entirely concerned with the business of putting down rebellion at home also meant that England's colonies became used, at an early stage, to a large degree of independence. As a result, once government was restored, all of Parliament's efforts to extend more control over the colonies would result in greater and greater friction (see Chapter 15). Slogans declaring the rights of "free-born Englishmen" would echo among farmers, while "free trade" became a rallying cry against royal interference in colonial commerce. The bitter religious conflicts that had divided the more radical Puritans from the Church of England also forced the colonies to come to grips with the problem of religious diversity. Some, like Massachusetts, took the opportunity to impose their own brand of Puritanism on settlers. Others experimented with forms of religious toleration that sometimes went beyond the forms of religious freedom that existed back in England.

Paradoxically, though, the spread of ideas about the protection of liberties and citizens' rights coincided with a rapid and considerable expansion of unfree labor in the colonies. Prior to the 1640s, the English colonies in North America and the Caribbean had been assured of a steady stream of immigrants, like the Puritan Pilgrims of Massachusetts in 1620. The outbreak of war in 1642 and the subsequent triumph of the Puritans under Cromwell caused a drop in this migration, since many who might have thought of emigrating decided to stay in England. In North America, the decline in the arrival of new settlers was so sudden that it caused a depression in local economies.

Meanwhile, the demand for labor was increasing rapidly owing to the expansion of tobacco plantations in Virginia and sugar plantations in Barbados and Jamaica, which the British captured from the Spanish in 1655. These plantations, with their punishing working conditions and high mortality rates from disease, were insatiable in their demand for workers. Plantation owners thus sought to meet this demand by investing ever more heavily in forms of unfree labor, including indentured servants and African slaves. The social and political crisis unleashed by the English Civil War also led to the forced migration of paupers and political prisoners, especially from Scotland, Wales, and Ireland; and this pattern continued during Cromwell's reign. These exiles, many without resources, swelled the ranks of the unfree and the very poor in England's Atlantic colonies, spurring the formation of new social hierarchies as earlier arrivals sought to distance themselves from newer immigrants they regarded

Competing Viewpoints

Debating the English Civil War

> The English Civil War raised fundamental questions about political rights and responsibilities. Many of these are addressed in the two excerpts below. The first comes from a lengthy debate held within the General Council of Cromwell's army in October of 1647. The second is taken from the speech given by King Charles, moments before his execution in 1649.

The Army Debates, 1647

Colonel Rainsborough: Really, I think that the poorest man that is in England has a life to live as the greatest man, and therefore truly, sir, I think it's clear, that every man that is to live under a government ought first by his own consent to put himself under that government, and I do think that the poorest man in England is not at all bound in a strict sense to that government that he has not had a voice to put himself under . . . insomuch that I should doubt whether I was an Englishman or not, that should doubt of these things.

General Ireton: Give me leave to tell you, that if you make this the rule, I think you must fly for refuge to an absolute natural right, and you must deny all civil right, and I am sure it will come to that in the consequence. . . . For my part, I think it is no right at all. I think that no person has a right to an interest or share in the disposing of the affairs of the kingdom, and in determining or choosing those that shall determine what laws we shall be ruled by here, no person has a right to this that has not a permanent fixed interest in this kingdom, and those persons together are properly the represented of this kingdom who, taken together, and consequently are to make up the representers of this kingdom. . . .

We talk of birthright. Truly, birthright there is. . . . [M]en may justly have by birthright, by their very being born in England, that we should not seclude them out of England. That we should not refuse to give them air and place and ground, and the freedom of the highways and other things, to live amongst us, not any man that is born here, though he in birth or by his birth there come nothing at all that is part of the permanent interest of this kingdom to him. That I think is due to a man by birth. But that by a man's being born here he shall have a share in that power that shall dispose of the lands here, and of all things here, I do not think it is a sufficient ground.

Source: David Wootton, ed., *Divine Right and Democracy: An Anthology of Political Writing in Stuart England* (New York: 1986), pp. 286–87 (language modernized).

---

as inferiors. The crisis of kingship in England thus led to a substantial increase in the African slave trade and a sharpening of social and economic divisions in the English colonies. This is yet another indication of Europe's inseparable relationship with the Atlantic world.

THE PROBLEM OF DOUBT AND THE ART OF BEING HUMAN

On the first day of November in 1611, a new play by William Shakespeare premiered in London, at the royal court. *The Tempest* takes place on a remote island, where an exiled duke from the Italian city-state of Milan has used his magical arts to subjugate the island's inhabitants. This plot drew on widespread reports from the new European colonies of the Atlantic, especially the Caribbean, where slaves were called Caribans and where (it was rumored) cannibalism flourished—hence the name Shakespeare chose for the play's rebellious slave Caliban, who seeks to revenge himself on the magician Prospero, his oppressive master. When reminded that he owes his knowledge of the English language to the civilizing influence of Prospero's daughter, Miranda, Caliban retorts, "You taught me language, and my profit on't / Is, I know how to curse."

According to Caliban, the benefits of a European education could not outweigh the evils of colonization—and

Charles I on the Scaffold, 1649

I think it is my duty, to God first, and to my country, for to clear myself both as an honest man, a good king, and a good Christian.

I shall begin first with my innocence. In truth I think it not very needful for me to insist long upon this, for all the world knows that I never did begin a war with the two Houses of Parliament, and I call God to witness, to whom I must shortly make an account, that I never did intend to incroach upon their privileges. . . .

As for the people—truly I desire their liberty and freedom as much as anybody whatsoever. But I must tell you that their liberty and freedom consists in having of government those laws by which their lives and goods may be most their own. It is not for having share in government. That is nothing pertaining to them. A subject and a sovereign are clean different things, and therefore, until they do

that—I mean that you do put the people in that liberty as I say—certainly they will never enjoy themselves.

Sirs, it was for this that now I am come here. If I would have given way to an arbitrary way, for to have all laws changed according to the power of the sword, I needed not to have come here. And therefore I tell you (and I pray God it be not laid to your charge) that I am the martyr of the people.

Source: Brian Tierney, Donald Kagan, and L. Pearce Williams, eds., *Great Issues in Western Civilization* (New York: 1967), pp. 46–47.

Questions for Analysis

1. What fundamental issues are at stake in both of these excerpts? How do the debaters within the parliamentary army (first excerpt) define "natural" and "civil" rights?

2. How does Charles defend his position? What is his theory of kingship, and how does it compare to that of Cardinal Richelieu's (page 475)? How does it conflict with the ideas expressed in the army's debate?

3. It is interesting that none of the participants in these debates seems to have recognized the implications their arguments might have for the political rights of women. Why would that have been the case?

could, in fact, be used to resist it. Shakespeare's audience was thus confronted with a spectacle of their own colonial ambitions gone awry, as well as with a number of other contemporary problems, including the perils of civil war, the struggle for political legitimacy, the fear of sorcery, and the availability of exotic commodities.

The doubt and uncertainty caused by Europe's extension into the Atlantic world were primary themes and motivators of this era's creative arts, which both documented and critiqued contemporary trends while emphasizing the redemptive qualities of human suffering and compassion. Another example of this artistic response is the novel *Don Quixote*, which its author, Miguel de Cervantes (*sehr-VAHN-tehs*, 1547–1616), composed largely in prison. It recounts the

adventures of an idealistic Spanish gentleman, Don Quixote of La Mancha, who becomes deranged by his constant reading of chivalric romances and sets out to have delusional adventures of his own. His sidekick, Sancho Panza, is his exact opposite: a plain, practical man content with modest bodily pleasures. Together, they represent different facets of human nature. On the one hand, *Don Quixote* is a devastating satire of Spain's decline. On the other, it is a sincere celebration of the human capacity for optimism and goodness.

Throughout the long century between 1550 and 1660, Europeans confronted a world in which all that they had once taken for granted was cast into confusion. Vast continents had been discovered, populated by millions of people whose very existence challenged Western civilizations'

The Execution of a King

his allegorical engraving (image A) accompanied a pamphlet called *Eikon Basilike* ("*The Kingly Image*"), which began to circulate in Britain just weeks after the execution of King Charles I. It purported to be an autobiographical account of the king's last days and a justification of his royal policies. It was intended to arouse widespread sympathy for the king and his exiled heir, Charles II, and it succeeded admirably: the cult of Charles "King and Martyr" became increasingly popular. Here, the Latin inscription on the shaft of light suggests that Charles's piety will beam "brighter through the shadows," while the scrolls at the left proclaim that "virtue grows beneath weight" and "unmoved, triumphant." Charles's earthly crown (on the floor at his side) is "splendid and heavy," while the crown of thorns he grasps is "bitter and light" and the heavenly crown is "blessed and eternal." Even people who could not read these and other Latin mottoes would have known that Charles's last words were: "I shall go from a corruptible to an incorruptible Crown, where no disturbance can be."

At the same time, broadsides showing the moment of execution (image B) circulated in various European countries with explanatory captions. This one was printed in Germany, and there are almost identical versions surviving from the Netherlands. It shows members of the crowd fainting and turning away at the sight of blood spurting from the king's neck while the executioner holds up the severed head.

Questions for Analysis

1. How would you interpret the message of the first image? How might it have been read differently by Catholics and Protestants within Britain and Europe?

2. What would have been the political motives underlying the publication and display of these images? For example, would you expect the depiction of the king's execution to be intended as supportive of monarchy or as antiroyalist? Why?

3. Given what you have learned about political and religious divisions in Europe at the time of the king's execution, where do you think the first image would have found the most sympathetic audiences? Why might it be significant that the second circulated more in Germany and the Netherlands rather than in France or Spain?

A. King Charles I as a martyr.

B. The execution of King Charles I.

former parameters and Europeans' most basic assumptions. Not even religion could be seen as an adequate foundation on which to build new certainties, for European Christians now disagreed about the fundamental truths of their faith. Political allegiances were similarly under threat, as intellectuals and common people alike began to assert a right to resist princes with whom they disagreed. The very notions of morality and custom were beginning to seem arbitrary. Europeans responded to this pervasive climate of doubt in a variety of ways. What united their responses, however, was a sometimes desperate search for new bases on which to construct some measure of certainty in the face of such challenges.

Witchcraft and the Power of the State

Contributing to the anxiety of the age was the widespread conviction that witchcraft was a new and increasing threat to the world. Although the belief that certain individuals could heal or harm through the practice of magic had always been common, it was not until the late fifteenth century that authorities began to insist that such powers could derive only from some kind of satanic bargain. In 1484, Pope Innocent VIII had ordered papal inquisitors to use all means at their disposal to detect and eliminate witchcraft, including torture. Predictably, torture increased the number of accused witches who "confessed" to their alleged crimes. And as more accused witches "confessed," more witches were "discovered," tried, and executed—even in places like England and Scotland, where torture was not legal and where the Catholic Church had no influence. For both Luther and Calvin had also urged that accused witches be tried and sentenced with less leniency than ordinary criminals.

When religious authorities' efforts to detect witchcraft were backed by the coercive powers of secular governments, the fear of witches could escalate into persecution. It was therefore through this fundamental agreement between Catholics and Protestants, and with the complicity of modern secular states, that an early modern "witch craze" claimed tens of thousands of victims in this era. The final death toll will never be known, but the vast majority of the victims were women. In the 1620s, there were, on average, 100 burnings a year in the German cities of Würzburg and Bamberg; around the same time, it was said that the town square of Wolfenbüttel "looked like a little forest, so crowded were the stakes." And when accusations of witchcraft diminished in Europe, they became endemic in some European colonies, as at the English settlement of Salem in the Massachusetts Bay Colony.

This hunt for witches resulted in part from fears that traditional religious remedies (prayer, the sacraments) were no longer adequate to guard against the evils of the world. It also reflects Europeans' growing conviction that only the state had the power to protect them. Even in Catholic countries, where witchcraft prosecutions began in Church courts, these cases would be transferred to the state's courts for final judgment and punishment, because Church courts could not carry out capital penalties. In most Protestant countries, the entire process of detecting, prosecuting, and punishing suspected witches was carried out under state supervision.

The Search for a Source of Authority

The crisis of religious and political authority in Europe also led to more rational approaches to the problem of uncertainty. The French nobleman Michel de Montaigne (*mohn-TEHN-yeh*, 1533–1592), son of a Catholic father and a Huguenot mother of Jewish ancestry, applied a searching skepticism to all traditional ways of knowing the world and adopted instead a practice of profound introspection. His *Essays*, from the French word for "attempts" or "trials," were composed during the French wars of religion and proceed from the same basic question: *Que sais-je?* ("What do I know?").

The *Essays'* first premise is that every human perspective is limited. For example, in a famous essay "On Cannibals," Montaigne argued that what may seem indisputably true and moral to one group of people may seem absolutely false to another because "everyone gives the title of barbarism to everything that is not of his usage." From this follows Montaigne's second main premise: the need for moderation. Because all people think they follow the true religion or have the best form of government, Montaigne concluded that no religion or government is really perfect, and consequently no belief is worth fighting or dying for. Instead, people should accept the teachings of religion on faith and obey the governments constituted to rule over them but without resorting to fanaticism in either sphere.

Another French philosopher, Blaise Pascal (*pahs-KAHL*, 1623–1662), confronted the problem of doubt by embracing an extreme form of puritanical Catholicism known as Jansenism (after its Flemish founder, Cornelius Jansen). Until his death, he worked on a highly ambitious philosophical-religious project meant to establish the truth of Christianity by appealing simultaneously to intellect and emotion. In his posthumous work, *Pensées* (Thoughts), Pascal argued that only faith could resolve the contradictions of the world, because "the heart has its reasons, of which reason itself knows nothing."

Pascal's *Pensées* expressed the author's own anguish and awe in the face of evil and uncertainty but presented that awe as evidence for the existence of God. Pascal's hope was that, on this foundation, some measure of confidence in humanity and its capacity for self-knowledge could be rediscovered.

The Science of Politics

Montaigne's immediate contemporary, the French jurist Jean Bodin (*boh-DAN*, 1530–1596), took a more practical approach to the problem of uncertain authority and found a solution in the power of the state. Like Montaigne, Bodin was troubled by the upheavals of the religious wars. He had witnessed the St. Bartholomew's Day Massacre of 1572 and, in response, developed a theory of absolute sovereignty that would (he surmised) put an end to such catastrophes. His monumental *Six Books of the Commonwealth* (1576) argued that the state has its origins in the needs of family-oriented communities and that its paramount duty is to maintain order. He defined sovereignty as "the most high, absolute, and perpetual power over all subjects," which meant that a sovereign head of state could make and enforce laws without the consent of those governed: precisely what King Charles of England later argued when he tried to dispense with Parliament—and precisely what his subjects ultimately rejected. Even if the ruler proved a tyrant, Bodin insisted that the subject had no right to resist, for any resistance would open the door to anarchy, "which is worse than the harshest tyranny in the world."

In England, experience of the Civil War led Thomas Hobbes (1588–1679) to propose a different theory of state sovereignty in his treatise *Leviathan* (1651). Whereas Bodin assumed that sovereign power should be vested in a monarch, Hobbes argued that any form of government capable of protecting its subjects' lives and property might act as an all-powerful sovereign.

Hobbes' convictions about the need for a strong state arose from his pessimistic view of human nature. The "state of nature" that existed before government, he wrote, was "war of all against all." Because man naturally behaves as "a wolf" toward other men, human life without government is necessarily "solitary, poor, nasty, brutish, and short." To escape such consequences, people must surrender their liberties to a sovereign state, in exchange for the state's obligation to keep the peace. Bodin had seen the ultimate goal of the state as the protection of property; Hobbes saw it as the preservation of people's lives, even at the expense of their liberties.

Hobbes and Bodin developed such theories in response to their direct experience of political and social upheaval caused by the breakdown of traditional authorities. Their different political philosophies thus reflect a practical preoccupation with the observation and analysis of actual occurrences (empirical knowledge) rather than abstract or theological arguments. Because of this, they are seen as early examples of a new kind of discipline, what we now call "political science."

A similar preoccupation with observation and results was also emerging among those who sought to understand the physical universe. Historians have often referred to the rapid developments in the physical sciences in this era as the "scientific revolution," a phenomenon that had its beginnings in the later Middle Ages (see Chapters 12 and 13) and that will be treated at greater length in Chapter 16. This term remains a useful one, even though it belittles the slow accumulation of knowledge in these centuries and ignores the contributions of scientists in earlier eras (as in the Hellenistic world, discussed in Chapter 4).

The World of the Theater

In the late sixteenth century, the construction of public playhouses—enclosed theaters—made drama an especially effective mass medium for the formation of public opinion, the dissemination of ideas, and the articulation of national identities. This was especially so in England during the last two decades of Elizabeth's reign and that of her successor, James. Among the large number of playwrights at work in London during this era, the most noteworthy are Christopher Marlowe (1564–1593), Ben Jonson (c. 1572–1637), and William Shakespeare (1564–1616).

Marlowe, who may have been a spy for Elizabeth's government and who was mysteriously murdered in a tavern brawl, was extremely popular in his own day. In plays such as *Tamburlaine*—about the life of the Mongolian warlord Timur the Lame (see Chapter 12)—and *Doctor Faustus*, Marlowe created vibrant heroes who pursue larger-than-life ambitions only to be felled by their own human limitations. In contrast to the heroic tragedies of Marlowe, Ben Jonson wrote dark comedies that expose human vices and foibles. In the *Alchemist*, he balanced an attack on pseudo-scientific quackery with admiration for resourceful lower-class characters who cleverly take advantage of their supposed betters.

William Shakespeare, who died in the same year as Cervantes, was born into the family of a tradesman in the provincial town of Stratford-upon-Avon, where he attained a modest education before moving to London around the age of twenty. There, he composed or collaborated on an unknown number of plays, of which some forty survive in whole or in part. They owe their longevity to the author's

Montaigne on Skepticism and Faith

The Essays *of Michel de Montaigne (1533–1592) reflect the sincerity of his own attempts to grapple with the contradictions of his time, even if he could not resolve those contradictions. Here, he discusses the relationship between human knowledge and the teachings of religious authorities.*

 Perhaps it is not without reason that we attribute facility in belief and conviction to simplicity and ignorance, for . . . the more a mind is empty and without counterpoise, the more easily it gives beneath the weight of the first persuasive argument. That is why children, common people, women, and sick people are most subject to being led by the ears. But then, on the other hand, it is foolish presumption to go around disdaining and condemning as false whatever does not seem likely to us; which is an ordinary vice in those who think they have more than common ability. I used to do so once. . . . But reason has taught me that to condemn a thing thus, dogmatically, as false and impossible, is to assume the advantage of knowing the bounds and limits of God's will and of the power of our mother Nature, and that there is no more notable folly in the world than to reduce these things to the measure of our capacity and competence. . . .

It is a dangerous and fateful presumption, besides the absurd temerity that it implies, to disdain what we do not comprehend. For after you have established, according to your fine understanding, the limits of truth and falsehood, and it turns out that you must necessarily believe things even stranger than those you deny, you are obliged from then on to abandon these limits. Now what seems to me to bring as much disorder into our consciences as anything, in these religious troubles that we are in, is this partial surrender of their beliefs by Catholics. It seems to them that they are being very moderate and understanding when they yield to their opponents some of the articles in dispute. But, besides the fact that they do not see what an advantage it is to a man charging you for you to begin to give ground and withdraw, and how much that encourages him to pursue his point, those articles which they select as the most trivial are sometimes very important. We must either submit completely to the authority of our ecclesiastical government, or do without it completely. It is not for us to decide what portion of obedience we owe it.

Source: *Montaigne: Selections from the Essays,* ed. and trans. Donald M. Frame (Arlington Heights, IL: 1971), pp. 34–38.

Questions for Analysis

1. Why does Montaigne say that human understanding is limited? How do his assumptions compare to those of Richelieu's (page 475)?

2. What does Montaigne mean by the "partial surrender" of belief? If a Catholic should place his faith in the Church, what then is the purpose of human intellect?

---

unrivaled gifts of verbal expression, humor, and psychological insight. Those written during the playwright's early years reflect the political, religious, and social upheavals of the late sixteenth century. These include many history plays that recount episodes from England's medieval past and the struggles that established the Tudor dynasty of Elizabeth's grandfather, Henry VII. They also include the lyrical tragedy *Romeo and Juliet* and a number of comedies that explore fundamental problems of identity, honor and ambition, love and friendship. The plays from Shakespeare's second period are, like other contemporary artworks, characterized by a troubled searching into the mysteries and meaning of human existence. They showcase the perils of indecisive idealism (*Hamlet*) and the abuse of power (*Macbeth, King Lear*). The plays composed toward the end of his career emphasize the possibilities of reconciliation and peace even after years of misunderstanding and violence: *The Tempest* is one of these.

Past and Present

Shakespeare's Popular Appeal

Although the plays of William Shakespeare are frequently described as elite entertainments, their enduring appeal can hardly be explained in those terms. In fact, Shakespeare wrote for a diverse audience—and a group of actors—who would have been more likely to see the inside of a prison than a royal court. His plays combine high politics, earthy comedy, and deeply human stories that still captivate and motivate audiences at the reconstructed Globe Theatre in London (left). They also lend themselves to inventive adaptations that comment on our own contemporary world, as in the recent film of *Coriolanus*.

 Watch related author interview on StudySpace
wwnorton.com/web/westernciv18

The Artists of Southern Europe

The ironies and tensions inherent in this age were also explored in the visual arts. In Italy and Spain, many painters cultivated a highly dramatic style sometimes known as "Mannerism." The most unusual of these artists was El Greco ("the Greek," c. 1541–1614), a pupil of the Venetian master Tintoretto (1518–1594). Born Domenikos Theotokopoulos on the Greek island of Crete, El Greco absorbed some of the stylized elongation characteristic of Byzantine icon painting (see Chapter 7) before traveling to Italy. He eventually settled in Spain. Many of his paintings were too strange to be greatly appreciated in his own day and even now appear so avant-garde as to be almost surreal. His *View of Toledo*, for example, is a transfigured landscape, mysteriously lit from within. Equally amazing are his swirling biblical scenes and the stunning portraits of gaunt, dignified saints who radiate austerity and spiritual insight.

In the seventeenth century, the dominant artistic style of southern Europe was that of the Baroque, a school whose name has become a synonym for elaborate, highly wrought sculpture and architectural details. This style originated in Rome during the Counter-Reformation and promoted a glorified Catholic worldview. Its most imaginative and influential figure was the architect and sculptor Gianlorenzo Bernini (1598–1680), a frequent employee of the papacy who created a magnificent celebration of papal grandeur in the sweeping colonnades leading up to St. Peter's Basilica. Breaking with the more serene classicism of Renaissance styles (see Chapter 12), Bernini's work drew inspiration from the restless motion and artistic bravado of Hellenistic statuary (see Chapter 4).

Characteristics of this Baroque style can also be found in paintings like those of the great Spanish master Diego Velázquez (*vay-LAH-skwez*, 1599–1660), who served the Spanish Habsburg court in Madrid. Although

VIEW OF TOLEDO BY EL GRECO. This is one of many landscape portraits representing the hilltop city that became the artist's home in later life. Its supple Mannerist style almost defies historical periodization.

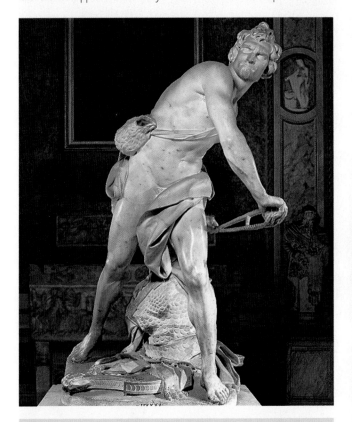

DAVID BY BERNINI (1598–1680). Whereas the earlier conceptions of David by the Renaissance sculptors Donatello and Michelangelo were serene and dignified (see page 000), the Baroque sculptor Bernini chose to portray his young hero at the peak of physical exertion. ▪ *Can you discern the influence of Hellenistic sculpture (see Chapter 4) in this work?* ▪ *What are some shared characteristics?*

many of his canvases display a Baroque attention to motion and drama, those most characteristic of his own style are more conceptually thoughtful and daring. An example is *The Maids of Honor*, completed around 1656 and a masterpiece of self-referentiality. It shows the artist himself at work on a double portrait of the Spanish king and queen, but the scene is dominated by the children and servants of the royal family.

Dutch Painting in the Golden Age

Southern Europe's main rival in the visual arts was the Netherlands, where many exemplary but dissimilar painters explored the theme of man's greatness and wretchedness to the full. Pieter Bruegel the Elder (*BROY-ghul*, c. 1525–1569) exulted in portraying the busy, elemental life of the peasantry. Most famous in this respect are his rollicking *Peasant Wedding* and *Peasant Wedding Dance* and his spacious *Harvesters*, in which field hands are taking a well-deserved break under the noonday sun. Such vistas celebrate the uninterrupted rhythms of life; but late in his career, Bruegel became appalled by the intolerance and bloodshed he witnessed during the Calvinist riots and the Spanish repression of the Netherlands, expressing his criticism in works like *The Massacre of the Innocents*. From a distance, this looks like a snug scene of village

THE MAIDS OF HONOR (LAS MEÑINAS) BY DIEGO VELÁZQUEZ. The artist himself (at left) is shown working at his easel and gazing out at the viewer—or at the subjects of his double portrait, the Spanish king and queen, depicted in a distant mirror. But the real focus of the painting is the delicate, impish princess in the center, flanked by two young ladies-in-waiting, a dwarf, and another royal child. Courtiers in the background look on.

life. In fact, however, soldiers are methodically breaking into homes and slaughtering helpless infants, as Herod's soldiers once did and as warring armies were doing in Bruegel's own day.

Another Dutch painter, Peter Paul Rubens (1577–1640), was inspired by very different politics. A native of Antwerp, still part of the Spanish Netherlands, Rubens was a staunch Catholic who glorified the Roman Church and the local aristocrats who supported the Habsburg regime. Even when his intent was not propagandistic, Rubens reveled in the sumptuous extravagance of the Baroque style; he is most famous today for the pink and rounded flesh of his well-nourished nudes. But Rubens was not lacking in subtlety or depth. Although he celebrated martial valor for most of his career, his late painting of *The Horrors of War* movingly captures what

he called "the grief of unfortunate Europe, which, for so many years now, has suffered plunder, outrage, and misery."

In some ways a blend of Bruegel and Rubens, Rembrandt van Rijn (*vahn-REEN*, 1606–1669) defies all attempts at easy characterization. Living across the border from the Spanish Netherlands in the staunchly Calvinist Dutch Republic, Rembrandt managed to put both realistic and Baroque traits to new uses. In his early career, he gained fame and fortune as a painter of biblical scenes and was also active as a portrait painter who knew how to flatter his subjects—to the great advantage of his purse. But as personal tragedies mounted in his middle and declining years, the painter's art gained in dignity, subtlety, and mystery. His later portraits, including several self-portraits, are highly introspective and suggest

THE MASSACRE OF THE INNOCENTS BY BRUEGEL (c. 1525–1569). This painting shows how effectively art can be used as a means of political and social commentary. Here, Bruegel depicts the suffering of the Netherlands at the hands of the Spanish in his own day, with reference to the biblical story of Herod's slaughter of Jewish children after the birth of Jesus—thereby collapsing these two historical incidents.

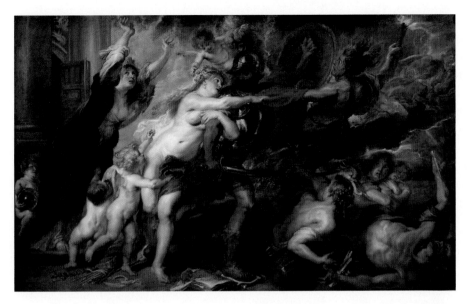

***THE HORRORS OF WAR* BY RUBENS (1577–1640).** In his old age, Rubens took a far more critical view of war than he had done for most of his earlier career. Here, the war-god Mars casts aside his mistress Venus, goddess of love, and threatens humanity with death and destruction.

SELF-PORTRAITS. Self-portraits became common during the sixteenth and seventeenth centuries, reflecting the intense introspection of the period. Left: Rembrandt painted more than sixty self-portraits; this one, dating from around 1660, captures the artist's creativity, theatricality (note the costume), and honesty of self-examination. Right: Judith Leyster was a contemporary of Rembrandt who pursued a successful career during her early twenties, before she married. Respected in her own day, she was all but forgotten for centuries thereafter but is once again the object of much attention.

that only part of the story is being told. Equally fearless is the frank gaze of Rembrandt's slightly younger contemporary, Judith Leyster (1609–1660), who looks out of her own self-portrait with a refreshingly optimistic and good-humored expression.

CONCLUSION

It would take centuries for Europeans to adapt themselves to the changes brought about by their integration into the Atlantic world and to process its implications. Finding new lands and cultures unknown to the ancients and unmentioned in the Bible had exposed the limitations of Western civilizations' accumulated knowledge and called for new ways of knowing and explaining the world. The Columbian exchange of people, plants, livestock, and pathogens that had previously been isolated from one another had a profound and lasting effect on populations and ecosystems throughout the Atlantic zone. The distribution of new agricultural products transformed the lives of the European poor and the rich alike. The transatlantic slave trade, which made all of this possible, brought Africans and their cultures into a world of growing global connections under

After You Read This Chapter

Ⓢ Visit StudySpace for quizzes, additional review materials, and multimedia documents. **wwnorton.com/web/westernciv18**

REVIEWING THE OBJECTIVES

- How were the peoples and ecosystems of the Americas, Africa, and Europe intertwined during this period? What were some consequences of these new linkages?

- Why did the colonies of the Spanish, the English, and the Dutch differ from one another? How did these differences affect the lives and labor of colonists, both free and unfree?

- Which European powers came to dominate the Atlantic world? What factors led to the decline of Spain and to the rise of France?

- What forms did religious and political conflict take in France, the Netherlands, and Germany? What were the causes of the English Civil War, and what impact did this event have on the English colonies?

- How do the arts and political philosophies of this period reflect the turmoil of Europe and the Atlantic world?

the worst possible circumstances for those who were enslaved—yet this did not prevent them from helping to shape this new world. Meanwhile, the influx of silver from New Spain precipitated the great price inflation of the sixteenth and seventeenth centuries, which bewildered contemporary observers and contributed to the atmosphere of crisis in post–Reformation Europe, already riven by religious and civil warfare. The response was a trend toward stronger centralized states, justified by theories of absolute government. Led by the French monarchy of Louis XIV, these absolutist regimes would reach their apogee in the coming century.

PEOPLE, IDEAS, AND EVENTS IN CONTEXT

- What was the **COLUMBIAN EXCHANGE**? How did it affect the relations among the peoples of the Americas, Africa, and Europe during this period?
- What circumstances led to the development of the **TRIANGULAR TRADE**?
- What were the main sources of instability in Europe during the sixteenth century? How did the **PRICE REVOLUTION** exacerbate these?
- How did **HENRY IV** of France and **PHILIP II** of Spain deal with the religious conflict that beset Europe during these years?
- What were the origins of the **THIRTY YEARS' WAR**? Was it primarily a religious conflict?
- How did the policies of **CARDINAL RICHELIEU** strengthen the power of the French monarchy?
- What policies of England's **CHARLES I** were most detested by his subjects? Why was his execution so momentous?
- In what ways did the **WITCH CRAZE** of early modern Europe reveal the religious and social tensions of the sixteenth and seventeenth centuries?
- What were the differences between **JEAN BODIN**'s theory of absolute sovereignty and that of **THOMAS HOBBES**?
- How did philosophers like **MONTAIGNE** and **PASCAL** respond to the uncertainties of the age? How were contemporary trends reflected in the works of **SHAKESPEARE** and in the visual arts?

THINKING ABOUT CONNECTIONS

- The emergence of the Atlantic world can be seen as a *cause* of new developments and as the *result* of historical processes. What long-term political, economic, and demographic circumstances drove the expansion of European influence into the Atlantic? What subsequent historical developments can we attribute to the creation of this interconnected world?
- The political crises of this era reveal the tensions produced by sectarian religious disputes and by a growing rift between powerful centralizing monarchies and landholding elites unwilling to surrender their authority and independence. What other periods in history display similar tensions? How do those periods compare to the one we have studied in this chapter?
- The intellectual currents of this era reveal that a new generation was challenging the assumptions of its predecessors. In what other historical eras do we find a similar phenomena? What social and political circumstances tend to produce consensus, and which tend to produce dissent, skepticism, and doubt?

Before
You
Read
This
Chapter

European Monarchies and Absolutism, 1660–1725

In the mountainous region of south-central France known as the Auvergne in the 1660s, the Marquis of Canillac had a notorious reputation. His noble title gave him the right to collect minor taxes on special occasions, but he insisted that these small privileges be converted into annual tributes. To collect these payments, he housed twelve accomplices in his castle that he called his apostles. Their other nicknames—one was known as Break Everything—gave a more accurate sense of their activities in the local villages. The marquis imprisoned those who resisted and forced their families to buy their freedom. In an earlier age, the marquis might have gotten away with this profitable arrangement. In 1662, however, he ran up against the authority of a king, Louis XIV, who was determined to demonstrate that the power of the central monarch was absolute. The marquis was brought up on charges before a special court of judges from Paris. He was found guilty and forced to pay a large fine. The king confiscated his property and had the marquis's castle destroyed.

Louis XIV's special court in the Auvergne heard nearly a thousand civil cases over four months in 1662. It convicted 692 people, and many of them, like the Marquis of Canillac, were noble. The verdicts were an extraordinary example of Louis XIV's

ability to project his authority into the remote corners of his realm and to do so in a way that diminished the power of other elites. During his long reign (1643–1715), Louis XIV systematically pursued such a policy on many fronts, asserting his power over the nobility, the clergy, and the provincial courts. Increasingly, these elites were forced to look to the crown to guarantee their interests, and their own power became more closely connected with the sacred aura of the monarchy itself. Louis XIV's model of kingship was so successful that it became known as absolute monarchy. In recognition of the success and influence of Louis XIV's political system, the period from around 1660 (when the English monarchy was restored and Louis XIV began his personal rule in France) to 1789 (when the French Revolution erupted) is traditionally known as the age of absolutism. This is a crucial period in the development of modern, centralized, bureaucratic states in Europe.

Absolutism was a political theory that encouraged rulers to claim complete sovereignty within their territories. An absolute monarch could make law, dispense justice, create and direct a bureaucracy, declare war, and levy taxation, without the approval of any other governing body. Assertions of absolute authority were buttressed by claims that rulers governed by divine right, just as fathers ruled over their households. After the chaos and religious wars of the previous century, many Europeans came to believe that it was only by exalting the sovereignty of absolute rulers that order could be restored to European life.

European monarchs also continued to project their power abroad during this period. By 1660, as we have seen, the French, Spanish, Portuguese, English, and Dutch had all established important colonies in the Americas and in Asia. These colonies created trading networks that brought profitable new consumer goods such as sugar, tobacco, and coffee to a wide public in Europe. They also encouraged the colonies' reliance on slavery to produce these goods. Rivalry among colonial powers to control the trade in slaves and consumer goods was intense and often led to wars that were fought both in Europe and in contested colonies. These wars, in turn, increased the motivation of absolutist rulers to extract as much revenue as they could from their subjects and encouraged the development of institutions that enhanced their power: armies, navies, tax systems, tariffs and customs controls.

Absolutism was not universally successful during this period. The English monarchy, restored in 1660 after the turbulent years of the Civil War, attempted to impose absolutist rule but met with resistance from parliamentary leaders who insisted on more inclusive institutions of government. After 1688, England, Scotland, the Dutch Republic, Switzerland, Venice, Sweden, and Poland-Lithuania were all either limited monarchies or republics. In Russia, on the other hand, an extreme autocracy emerged that gave the tsar a degree of control over his subjects' lives and property far beyond anything imagined by western European absolutists. Even in Russia, however, absolutism was never unlimited in practice. Even the most absolute monarchs could rule effectively only with the consent of their subjects (particularly the nobility). When serious opposition erupted, even powerful kings were forced to back down. King George III of Britain discovered this when his North American colonies declared their independence in 1776, creating the United States of America. In 1789, an even more sweeping revolution began in France, and the entire structure of absolutism came crashing to the ground (see Chapter 18).

THE DEFENSE OF CADÍZ AGAINST THE ENGLISH **BY FRANCISCO ZURBARAN.** The rivalry between European powers that played out over the new colonial possessions further proved the decline of Spain, which lost the island of Jamaica and ships in the harbor of Cadíz to the English in the 1650s.

THE APPEAL AND JUSTIFICATION OF ABSOLUTISM

Absolutism's promise of stability and order was an appealing alternative to the disorder of the "iron century" that preceded it. The early theorists of absolutism such as Jean Bodin and Thomas Hobbes looked to strong royal governments as an answer to the violence of religious wars and the crisis of the sixteenth and seventeenth centuries (see Chapter 14). Louis XIV himself was profoundly disturbed by an aristocratic revolt that occurred while he was still a child. When marauding Parisians entered his bedchamber one night in 1651, Louis saw the intrusion as an affront not only to his own person but to the majesty of the French state. Such experiences convinced him that he needed to rule assertively and without limits to his power.

Absolutist monarchs sought control of the state's armed forces and its legal system, and they demanded the right to collect and spend the state's financial resources at will. To achieve these goals, they also needed to create an efficient, centralized bureaucracy that owed its allegiance directly to the monarch. Creating and sustaining such a bureaucracy was expensive but necessary in order to weaken the special interests that hindered the free exercise of royal power. The nobility and the clergy, with their traditional legal privileges; the political authority of semiautonomous regions; and representative assemblies such as parliaments, diets, or estates-general were all obstacles—in the eyes of absolutists—to strong, centralized monarchical government. The history of absolutism is the history of kings who attempted to bring such institutions to heel.

In most Protestant countries, the power of the church had already been subordinated to the state when the age of absolutism began. Even where Roman Catholicism remained the state religion, such as in France, Spain, and Austria, absolutist monarchs now devoted considerable attention to bringing the Church and its clergy under royal control. Louis XIV took an active role in religious matters, appointing his own bishops and encouraging the repression of religious dissidents. Unlike his predecessors, however, he rarely appointed members of the clergy to offices within his administration.

The most important potential opponents of royal absolutism were not churchmen, however, but nobles. Louis XIV deprived the French nobility of political power in the provinces but increased their social prestige by making them live at his lavish court at Versailles. Peter the Great of Russia (1689–1725) forced his nobles into lifelong government service, and successive monarchs in Brandenburg-Prussia managed to co-opt the powerful aristocracy by granting them immunity to taxation and giving them the right to enserf their peasants. In exchange, they ceded administrative control to the increasingly bureaucratized Prussian state. In most European monarchies, including Spain, France, Prussia, and England, the nobility retained their preponderant role within the military.

Struggles between monarchs and nobles frequently affected relations between local and central government. In France, the requirement that nobles live at the king's court undermined the provincial institutions that the nobility used to exercise their political power. In Spain, the monarchy, based in Castile, battled the independent-minded nobles of Aragon and Catalonia. Prussian rulers asserted control over formerly "free" cities by claiming the right to police and tax their inhabitants. The Habsburg emperors tried, unsuccessfully, to suppress the largely autonomous nobility of Hungary. Rarely, however, was the path of confrontation between crown and nobility successful in the long run. The most effective absolutist monarchies of the eighteenth century continued to trade privileges for allegiance, so that nobles came to see their own interests as tied to those of the crown. For this reason, wary cooperation between kings and nobles was more common than open conflict during the eighteenth century.

THE ABSOLUTISM OF LOUIS XIV

In Louis XIV's state portrait, it is almost impossible to discern the human being behind the facade of the absolute monarch dressed in his coronation robes and surrounded by the symbols of his authority. That facade was artfully constructed by Louis, who recognized, more fully than any other early modern ruler, the importance of theater to effective kingship. Louis and his successors deliberately staged spectacular demonstrations of their sovereignty to enhance their position as rulers endowed with godlike powers.

Performing Royalty at Versailles

Louis's most elaborate staging of his authority took place at his palace at Versailles (*vuhr-SY*), outside of Paris. The main facade of the palace was a third of a mile in length. Inside, tapestries and paintings celebrated French military victories and royal triumphs; mirrors reflected shimmering light throughout the building. In the vast gardens outside, statues of the Greek god Apollo, god of the sun, recalled Louis's claim to be the "Sun King" of France. Noblemen vied to attend him when he arose from bed, ate his meals

Interpreting Visual Evidence

The Performance and Display of Absolute Power at the Court of Louis XIV

Historians studying the history of absolutism and the court of Louis XIV in particular have emphasized the Sun King's brilliant use of symbols and display to demonstrate his personal embodiment of sovereignty. Royal portraits, such as that painted by Hyacinthe Rigaud in 1701, vividly illustrate the degree to which Louis's power was based on a studied performance. His pose, with his exposed and shapely calf, was an important indication of power and virility, necessary elements of legitimacy for a hereditary monarch. In the elaborate rituals of court life at Versailles, Louis often placed his own body at the center of attention, performing in one instance as the god Apollo in a ballet before his assembled courtiers. His movements through the countryside, accompanied by a retinue of soldiers, servants, and aristocrats, were another occasion for highly stylized ritual demonstrations of his quasi-divine status. Finally, of course, the construction of his palace at Versailles, with its symmetrical architecture and its sculpted gardens, was a demonstration that his power extended over the natural world as easily as it did over the lives of his subjects.

Questions for Analysis

1. Who was the intended audience for the king's performance of absolute sovereignty?

2. Who were Louis's primary competitors in this contest for eminence through the performance of power?

3. What possible political dangers might lie in wait for a regime that invested so heavily in the sumptuous display of semidivine authority?

A. Hyacinthe Rigaud's 1701 portrait of Louis XIV.

B. Louis XIV as the Sun King.

C. *The Royal Procession of Louis XIV*, 1664, by Adam Franz van der Meulen.

D. Louis XIV arrives at the Palace of Versailles.

Competing Viewpoints

Absolutism and Patriarchy

> These selections show how two political theorists justified royal absolutism by deriving it from the absolute authority of a father over his household. Bishop Jacques-Bénigne Bossuet (1627–1704) was a famous French preacher who served as tutor to the son of King Louis XIV of France before becoming bishop of Meaux. Sir Robert Filmer (1588–1653) was an English political theorist. Filmer's works attracted particular attention in the 1680s, when John Locke directed the first of his Two Treatises of Government to refuting Filmer's views on the patriarchal nature of royal authority.

Bossuet on the Nature of Monarchical Authority

There are four characteristics or qualities essential to royal authority. First, royal authority is sacred; Secondly, it is paternal; Thirdly, it is absolute; Fourthly, it is subject to reason.... All power comes from God.... Thus princes act as ministers of God, and his lieutenants on earth. It is through them that he exercises his empire.... In this way...the royal throne is not the throne of a man, but the throne of God himself....

We have seen that kings hold the place of God, who is the true Father of the human race. We have also seen that the first idea of power that there was among men, is that of paternal power; and that kings were fashioned on the model of fathers. Moreover, all the world agrees that obedience, which is due to public power, is only found ... in the precept which obliges one to honor his parents. From all this it appears that the name "king" is a father's name, and that goodness is the most natural quality in kings....

Royal authority is absolute. In order to make this term odious and insupportable, many pretend to confuse absolute government and arbitrary government. But nothing is more distinct, as we shall make clear when we speak of justice.... The prince need account to no one for what he ordains.... Without this absolute authority, he can neither do good nor suppress evil: his power must be such that no one can hope to escape him.... [T]he sole defense of individuals against the public power must be their innocence....

One must, then, obey princes as if they were justice itself, without which there is neither order nor justice in affairs. They are gods, and share in some way in divine independence.... It follows from this that he who does not want to obey the prince...is condemned irremissibly to death as an enemy of public peace and of human society.... The prince can correct himself when he knows that he has done badly; but against his authority there can be no remedy....

Source: Jacques-Bénigne Bossuet, *Politics Drawn from the Very Words of Holy Scripture*, trans. Patrick Riley (Cambridge: 1990), pp. 46–69 and 81–83.

(usually stone cold after having traveled the distance of several city blocks from kitchen to table), strolled in his gardens (even the way the king walked was choreographed by the royal dancing master), or rode to the hunt. France's leading nobles were required to reside with Louis at Versailles for a portion of the year; the splendor of Louis's court was deliberately calculated to blind them to the possibility of disobedience while raising their prestige by associating them with himself. At the same time, the almost impossibly detailed rules of etiquette at court left these privileged nobles in constant suspense, forever fearful of offending the king by committing some trivial violation of proper manners.

Of course, the nobility did not surrender social and political power entirely. The social order was still hierarchical, and noblemen retained enormous privileges and rights over local peasants within their jurisdiction. The absolutist system forced the nobility to depend on the crown, but it did not seek to undermine their superior place in society. In this sense, the relationship between

Filmer on the Patriarchal Origins of Royal Authority

The first government in the world was monarchical, in the father of all flesh, Adam being commanded to multiply, and people the earth, and to subdue it, and having dominion given him over all creatures, was thereby the monarch of the whole world; none of his posterity had any right to possess anything, but by his grant or permission, or by succession from him. . . . Adam was the father, king and lord over his family: a son, a subject, and a servant or a slave were one and the same thing at first. . . .

I cannot find any one place or text in the Bible where any power . . . is given to a people either to govern themselves, or to choose themselves governors, or to alter the manner of government at their pleasure. The power of government is settled and fixed by the commandment of "honour thy father"; if there were a higher power than the fatherly, then this commandment could not stand and be observed. . . .

All power on earth is either derived or usurped from the fatherly power, there being no other original to be found of any power whatsoever. For if there should be granted two sorts of power without any subordination of one to the other, they would be in perpetual strife which should be the supreme, for two supremes cannot agree. If the fatherly power be supreme, then the power of the people must be subordinate and depend on it. If the power of the people be supreme, then the fatherly power must submit to it, and cannot be exercised without the licence of the people, which must quite destroy the frame and course of nature. Even the power which God himself exercises over mankind is by right of fatherhood: he is both the king and father of us all. As God has exalted the dignity of earthly kings . . . by saying they are gods, so . . . he has been pleased . . . [t]o humble himself by assuming the title of a king to express his power, and not the title of any popular government.

Source: Robert Filmer, "Observations upon Aristotle's Politiques," in *Divine Right and Democracy: An Anthology of Political Writing in Stuart England*, ed. David Wootton (Harmondsworth, UK: 1986), pp. 110–118. First published 1652.

Questions for Analysis

1. Bossuet's definition of *absolutism* connected the sacred power of kings with the paternal authority of fathers within the household. What consequences does he draw from defining the relationship between king and subjects in this way?

2. What does Filmer mean when he says, "All power on earth is either derived or usurped from the fatherly power"? How many examples does he give of paternal or monarchical power?

3. Bossuet and Filmer make obedience the basis for order and justice in the world. What alternative political systems did they most fear?

Louis XIV and the nobility was more of a negotiated settlement than a complete victory of the king over other powerful elites. Louis XIV understood this, and in a memoir that he prepared for his son on the art of ruling he wrote, "The deference and the respect that we receive from our subjects are not a free gift from them but payment for the justice and the protection that they expect from us. Just as they must honor us, we must protect and defend them." In their own way, absolutists depended on the consent of those they ruled.

Administration and Centralization

Louis defined his responsibilities in absolutist terms: to concentrate royal power so as to produce domestic tranquillity. In addition to convincing the nobility to cede political authority, he also recruited the upper bourgeoisie as royal intendants, administrators responsible for running the thirty-six *generalités* into which France was divided. Intendants usually served outside the region where they were born and were thus unconnected with

Past and Present

The Persistence of Monarchies in a Democratic Age

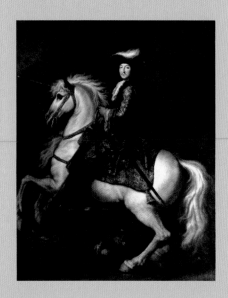

In the past, monarchs such as Louis XIV (left) often ran roughshod over tradition as they sought ways to increase their power. Today, twelve European states still have reigning monarchs, such as Queen Elizabeth II (right), but their popularity would probably be called into question if they sought an active role in government.

 Watch related author interview on StudySpace
wwnorton.com/web/westernciv18

the local elites over whom they exercised authority. They held office at the king's pleasure and were clearly his men. Other administrators, often from families newly ennobled as a reward for their service, assisted in directing affairs of state from Versailles. These men were not actors in the theater of Louis the Sun King; rather, they were the hardworking assistants of Louis the royal custodian of his country's welfare.

Louis's administrators devoted much of their time and energy to collecting the taxes necessary to finance the large standing army on which his aggressive foreign policy depended. Absolutism was fundamentally an approach to government by which ambitious monarchs could increase their own power through conquest and display. As such, it was enormously expensive. In addition to the *taille*, or land tax, which increased throughout the seventeenth century, Louis's government introduced

a *capitation* (a head tax) and pressed successfully for the collection of indirect taxes on salt (the *gabelle*), wine, tobacco, and other goods. Because the nobility was exempt from the taille, its burden fell most heavily on the peasantry, whose local revolts Louis easily crushed.

Regional opposition was curtailed but not eliminated during Louis's reign. By removing the provincial nobility to Versailles, Louis cut them off from their local sources of power and influence. To restrict the powers of regional parlements, Louis decreed that members of any parlement who refused to approve and enforce his laws would be summarily exiled. The Estates-General, the French representative assembly that met at the king's pleasure to act as a consultative body for the state, was last summoned in 1614. It did not meet at all during Louis's reign and, in fact, was not convened again until 1789.

Louis XIV's Religious Policies

Both for reasons of state and of personal conscience, Louis was determined to impose religious unity on France, regardless of the economic and social costs.

Although the vast majority of the French population was Roman Catholic, French Catholics were divided among Quietists, Jansenists, Jesuits, and Gallicans. Quietists preached retreat into personal mysticism, emphasizing a direct relationship between God and the individual human heart. Such doctrine, dispensing as it did with the intermediary services of the Church, was suspect in the eyes of absolutists wedded to the doctrine of *un roi, une loi, une foi* ("one king, one law, one faith"). Jansenism—a movement named for its founder Cornelius Jansen, a seventeenth-century bishop of Ypres—held to an Augustinian doctrine of predestination that could sound and look surprisingly like a kind of Catholic Calvinism. Louis vigorously persecuted Quietists and Jansenists, offering them a choice between recanting and prison or exile. At the same time, he supported the Jesuits in their efforts to create a Counter-Reformation Catholic Church in France. Louis's support for the Jesuits upset the traditional Gallican Catholics of France, however, who desired a French church independent of papal, Jesuit, and Spanish influence. As a result of this dissension among Catholics, the religious aura of Louis's kingship diminished during the course of his reign.

Against the Protestant Huguenots, Louis waged unrelenting war. Protestant churches and schools were destroyed, and Protestants were banned from many professions. In 1685, Louis revoked the Edict of Nantes, the legal foundation of the toleration Huguenots had enjoyed since 1598. Protestant clerics were exiled, laymen were sent to the galleys as slaves, and their children were forcibly baptized as Catholics. Many families converted, but 200,000 Protestant refugees fled to England, Holland, Germany, and America, bringing with them their professional and artisanal skills. Huguenots fleeing Louis XIV's persecution, for example, established the silk industries of Berlin and London. This migration was an enormous loss to France.

Colbert and Royal Finance

Louis's drive to unify France depended on a vast increase in royal revenues engineered by Jean-Baptiste Colbert, the king's finance minister from 1664 until his death in 1683. Colbert tightened the process of tax collection and eliminated wherever possible the practice of tax farming (which permitted collection agents to retain for themselves a percentage of the taxes they gathered for the king). When Colbert assumed office, only about 25 percent of the taxes collected throughout the kingdom reached the treasury. By the time he died, that figure had risen to 80 percent. Under Colbert's direction, the state sold public offices, including judgeships and mayoralties, and guilds purchased the right to enforce trade regulations. Colbert also tried to increase the nation's income by controlling and regulating foreign trade. As a confirmed mercantilist (see **Analyzing Primary Sources** on page 500), Colbert believed that France's wealth would increase if its imports were reduced and its exports increased. He therefore imposed tariffs on foreign goods imported into France while using state money to promote the domestic manufacture of formerly imported goods, such as silk, lace, tapestries, and glass. He was especially anxious to create domestic industries capable of producing the goods France would need for war. To encourage domestic trade, he improved France's roads, bridges, and waterways.

Despite Colbert's efforts to increase crown revenues, his policies ultimately foundered on the insatiable demands of Louis XIV's wars (see pages 505–506). Colbert himself foresaw this result when he lectured the king in 1680: "Trade is the source of public finance and public finance is the vital nerve of war. . . . I beg your Majesty to permit me only to say to him that in war as in peace he has never consulted the amount of money available in determining his expenditures." Louis, however, paid him no heed. By the end of Louis's reign, his aggressive foreign policy lay in ruins and his country's finances had been shattered by the unsustainable costs of war.

French Colonialism under Louis XIV

Finance minister Colbert regarded overseas expansion as an integral part of the French state's economic policy, and with his guidance, Louis IV's absolutist realm emerged as a major colonial power. Realizing the profits to be made in responding to Europe's growing demand for sugar, Colbert encouraged the development of sugar-producing colonies in the West Indies, the largest of which was Saint-Domingue (present-day Haiti). Sugar, virtually unknown in Christian Europe during the Middle Ages, became a popular luxury item in the late fifteenth century (see Chapter 14). It took the slave plantations of the Caribbean to turn sugar into a mass-market product. By 1750, slaves in Saint-Domingue produced 40 percent of the world's sugar and 50 percent of its coffee, exporting more sugar than Jamaica, Cuba, and Brazil combined. By 1700, France also dominated the interior of the North American continent, where French

Mercantilism and War

Jean-Baptiste Colbert (1619–1683) served as Louis XIV's finance minister from 1664 until his death. He worked assiduously to promote commerce, build up French industry, and increase exports. However much Colbert may have seen his economic policies as ends in themselves, to Louis they were always means to the end of waging war. Ultimately, Louis's wars undermined the prosperity that Colbert tried so hard to create. This memorandum, written to Louis in 1670, illustrates clearly the mercantilist presumptions of self-sufficiency on which Colbert operated: every item needed to build up the French navy must ultimately be produced in France, even if it could be acquired at less cost from elsewhere.

 nd since Your Majesty has wanted to work diligently at reestablishing his naval forces, and since afore that it has been necessary to make very great expenditures, since all merchandise, munitions and manufactured items formerly came from Holland and the countries of the North, it has been absolutely necessary to be especially concerned with finding within the realm, or with establishing in it, everything which might be necessary for this great plan.

To this end, the manufacture of tar was established in Médoc, Auvergne, Dauphiné, and Provence; iron cannons, in Burgundy, Nivernois, Saintonge and Périgord; large anchors in Dauphiné, Nivernois, Brittany, and Rochefort; sailcloth for the Levant, in Dauphiné; coarse muslin, in Auvergne; all the implements for pilots and others, at Dieppe and La Rochelle; the cutting of wood suitable for vessels, in Burgundy, Dauphiné, Brittany, Normandy, Poitou, Saintonge, Provence, Guyenne, and the Pyrenees; masts, of a sort once unknown in this realm, have been found in Provence, Languedoc, Auvergne, Dauphiné, and in the Pyrenees. Iron, which was obtained from Sweden and Biscay, is currently manufactured in the realm. Fine hemp for ropes, which came from Prussia and from Piedmont, is currently obtained in Burgundy, Mâconnais, Bresse, Dauphiné; and markets for it have since been established in Berry and in Auvergne, which always provides money in these provinces and keeps it within the realm.

In a word, everything serving for the construction of vessels is currently established in the realm, so that Your Majesty can get along without foreigners for the navy and will even, in a short time, be able to supply them and gain their money in this fashion. And it is with this same objective of having everything necessary to provide abundantly for his navy and that of his subjects that he is working at the general reform of all the forests in his realm, which, being as carefully preserved as they are at present, will abundantly produce all the wood necessary for this.

Source: Charles W. Cole, *Colbert and a Century of French Mercantilism*, 2 vols. (New York: 1939), p. 320.

Questions for Analysis

1. Why would Colbert want to manufacture materials for supplying the navy within France rather than buying them from abroad?

2. From this example, does Colbert see the economy as serving any other interest other than that of the state?

3. Was there a necessary connection between mercantilism and war?

---

traders brought furs to the American Indians and missionaries preached Christianity in a vast territory that stretched from Quebec to Louisiana. The financial returns from North America were never large, however. Furs, fish, and tobacco were exported to European markets but never matched the profits from the Caribbean sugar colonies or from the trading posts that the French maintained in India.

Like the earlier Spanish colonies (see Chapter 14), the French colonies were established and administered as direct crown enterprises. French colonial settlements in North America were conceived mainly as military outposts and trading centers, and they were overwhelmingly populated by men. The elite of French colonial society were military officers and administrators sent from Paris. Below their ranks were fishermen, fur traders, small farmers, and common soldiers who constituted the bulk of French settlers in North America. Because the fishing and the fur trades relied on cooperative relationships with native peoples, a mutual economic interdependence grew up between the French colonies and the peoples of the surrounding region. Intermarriage, especially between French traders and native women, was common. These North American colonies remained dependent on the wages and supplies sent to them from the mother country. Only rarely did they become truly self-sustaining economic enterprises.

The phenomenally successful sugar plantations of the Caribbean had their own social structure, with slaves at the bottom, people of mixed African and European descent forming a middle layer, and wealthy European plantation owners at the top, controlling the lucrative trade with the outside world. Well over half of the sugar and coffee sent to France was resold and sent elsewhere to markets throughout Europe. Because the monarchy controlled the prices that colonial plantation owners could charge French merchants for their goods, traders in Europe who bought the goods for resale abroad could also make vast fortunes. Historians estimate that as many as 1 million of the 25 million inhabitants of France in the eighteenth century lived off the money flowing through this colonial trade, making the slave colonies of the Caribbean a powerful force for economic change in France. The wealth generated from these colonies added to the prestige of France's absolutist system of government.

ALTERNATIVES TO ABSOLUTISM

Although absolutism was the dominant model for seventeenth- and eighteenth-century European monarchs, it was by no means the only system by which Europeans governed themselves. A republican oligarchy continued to rule in Venice. In the Polish-Lithuanian commonwealth, the monarch was elected by the nobility and governed alongside a parliament that met every two years. In the Netherlands, the territories that had won their independence from Spain during the early seventeenth century combined to form the United Provinces, the only truly new country to take shape in Europe during the early modern era. England, which had suffered through a violent civil war between 1642 and 1651, followed by the tumultuous years of Oliver Cromwell's Commonwealth and the Protectorate (see Chapter 14), also took a different path during these years, eventually arriving at a constitutional settlement that gave a larger role to Parliament and admitted a degree of participation by nonnobles in the affairs of state. Arriving at this settlement was not easy, however. The end of the civil wars and the collapse of Cromwell's Protectorate had made it clear that England would be a monarchy and not a republic, but the sort of monarchy England would be remained an open question. Two issues were paramount: the religious question and the relationship between Parliament and the king.

CHARLES II OF ENGLAND (r. 1660–85) IN HIS CORONATION ROBES. This full frontal portrait of the monarch, holding the symbols of his rule, seems to confront the viewer personally with the overwhelming authority of the sovereign's gaze. Compare this classic image of the absolutist monarch with the very different portraits of William and Mary, who ruled after the Glorious Revolution of 1688 (page 503). ■ *What had changed between 1660, when Charles II came to the throne, and 1688, when the more popular William and Mary became the rulers of England?*

The Restoration Monarchy in England

The king who took the throne following the Restoration of the Stuarts in 1660, Charles II (r. 1660–85), was initially welcomed by most English, despite being the son of the beheaded and much-despised Charles I (see Chapter 14). He restored bishops to the Church of England, but he did not initially return to the provocative religious policies of his father. He declared limited religious toleration for Protestant "dissenters" who were not members of the Church of England. He promised to observe the Magna Carta and the Petition of Right, which comforted members of Parliament. He also accepted the legislation passed by Parliament immediately before the outbreak of civil war in 1642, including the requirement that Parliament be summoned at least once every three years. England thus emerged from its civil war as a limited monarchy, in which power was exercised by the "king in Parliament." Meanwhile, the unbuttoned moral atmosphere of Charles II's court, with its risqué plays, dancing, and sexual licentiousness, may have reflected a public desire to forget the restraints of the Puritan past.

During the 1670s, however, Charles began openly to model his kingship on the absolutism of Louis XIV. As a result, the great men of England soon came to be publicly divided between Charles's supporters (known as "Tories," a popular nickname for Irish Catholic bandits) and his opponents (called "Whigs," a nickname for Scottish Presbyterian rebels). In fact, both sides feared absolutism, just as both sides feared a return to the bad old days of the 1640s, when resistance to the crown had led to civil war and ultimately to republicanism. What they could not agree on was which possibility frightened them more.

Charles's known sympathy for Roman Catholicism (he converted on his deathbed in 1685) also generated fodder for the opposition Whigs. During the 1670s, he briefly suspended civil penalties against Catholics and Protestant dissenters by asserting his right as king to ignore parliamentary legislation, and he retreated only in the face of public protest. The Whigs, meanwhile, rallied support by targeting Charles's Catholic brother James, the heir to the throne. The result was a series of Whig electoral victories between 1679 and 1681. A group of radical Whigs tried and failed to exclude James from succeeding his brother by law, and thereafter Charles found that his rising revenues from customs duties, combined with a secret subsidy from Louis XIV, enabled him to govern without relying on Parliament for money. Charles further alarmed Whig politicians by executing several of them on charges of treason and by remodeling local government to make it more amenable to royal control. Charles died in 1685 with his power enhanced, but he left behind a political and religious legacy that was to be the undoing of his less able and adroit successor.

James II was the very opposite of his worldly brother. A zealous Catholic convert, James admired the French monarchy's Gallican Catholicism that sought to further the work of the Church by harnessing it to the power of an absolutist bureaucratic state. His commitment to absolutism also led him to build up the English army and navy, which in turn led him to search for innovative solutions to the problems of taxation and the quartering of troops. To make the tax system more efficient he created new revenue agencies in many English towns. His quest for more accurate intelligence about political opponents led him to take control over the country's new post office, which made domestic surveillance routine, and his government also stepped up its efforts to prosecute seditious speech and writings. For the Whigs, James's policies were all that they had feared.

Meanwhile, James's Catholicism also alienated his Tory supporters, who were close to the established Church of England. Religion was not the only cause of his unpopularity, but resistance to his policies was often mixed with resentment against a perception that he favored Catholics. His decision to appoint Catholics as officers in the army was unpopular, but his decision to maintain a standing army in peacetime was even more so. Towns that were asked to quarter troops resented the expense and the disruptive presence of soldiers in their midst. When, in June 1688, he ordered all Church of England clergymen to read his decree of religious toleration from their pulpits, seven bishops refused and were promptly imprisoned. At their trial, however, they were declared not guilty of sedition, to the enormous satisfaction of the Protestant English populace.

The trial of the bishops was one event that galvanized the growing opposition to James. The other was the unexpected birth of a son in 1688 to James and his second wife, Mary of Modena. This child, who was to be raised a Catholic, replaced James's much older Protestant daughter Mary Stuart as heir to the thrones of Scotland and England. So unexpected was this birth that there were widespread rumors that the child was not in fact James's son at all but had been smuggled into the royal bedchamber in a warming pan.

With the birth of the "warming-pan baby," events moved swiftly toward a climax. A delegation of Whigs and Tories crossed the channel to Holland to invite Mary Stuart and her Protestant husband, William of Orange, to cross to England with an invading army to preserve English Protestantism and English liberties by summoning a new Parliament. As the leader of a continental coalition then at war with France, William also welcomed the opportunity to make England an ally against Louis XIV's expansionist foreign policy.

The Glorious Revolution

Following William and Mary's invasion, James fled the country for exile in France. Parliament declared the throne vacant, clearing the way for William and Mary to succeed him as joint sovereigns. The Bill of Rights, passed by Parliament and accepted by the new king and queen in 1689, reaffirmed English civil liberties, such as trial by jury, habeas corpus (a guarantee that no one could be imprisoned unless charged with a crime), and the right to petition the monarch through Parliament. The Bill of Rights also declared that the monarchy was subject to the law of the land. The Act of Toleration, also passed in 1689, granted Protestant dissenters the right to worship freely, though not to hold political office. And in 1701, the Act of Succession ordained

WILLIAM AND MARY. In 1688, William of Orange and his wife, Mary Stuart, became Protestant joint rulers of England, in a bloodless coup that took power from her father, the Catholic James II. Compare this contemporary print with the portraits of Louis XIV (page 494) and Charles II (page 501). ▪ *What relationship does it seem to depict between the royal couple and their subjects?* ▪ *What is the significance of the gathered crowd in the public square in the background?* ▪ *How is this different from the spectacle of divine authority projected by Louis XIV or the image of Charles II looking straight at the viewer?*

of monarchy into one constitutional document, historians consider the settlement of 1688 as a founding moment in the development of a constitutional monarchy in Britain.

Yet 1688 was not all glory. Contrary to many historical accounts, the revolution of 1688 was not "bloodless." The accession of William and Mary was accompanied by violence in many parts of England, Scotland, and Ireland. There were attacks on royal troops by angry Whigs in York, Hull, Carlisle, Chester, and Portsmouth. James's revenue agencies were also attacked, as were his newly founded Catholic schools. Historians now see this violence as motivated as much by antiabsolutism as by religious bigotry—popular anger against James II focused not so much on his defense of tradition but his innovations, specifically his attempts to strengthen the power of the bureaucratic state. Furthermore, the revolution of 1688 consolidated the position of large property holders, whose control over local government had been threatened by the absolutist policies of Charles II and James II. It thus reinforced the power of a wealthy class of English elites in Parliament who would soon become even wealthier from government patronage and the profits of war. It also brought misery to the Catholic minority in Scotland and to the Catholic majority in Ireland. After 1690, when King William won a decisive victory over James II's forces at the Battle of the Boyne, power in Ireland would lie firmly in the hands of a "Protestant Ascendancy," whose dominance over Irish society would last until modern times.

At the same time, however, England's Glorious Revolution also established a climate that favored the growth and political power of the English commercial classes, especially the growing number of people concentrated in English cities whose livelihood depended on international commerce in the Atlantic world and beyond. In the decades to come, trade became a political issue, and merchant's associations began to lobby parliament for favorable legislation. Whigs in Parliament became the voice of this newly influential pressure group of commercial entrepreneurs, who sought to challenge the monopoly enjoyed by the East India Company (founded with a royal charter in 1600) and open up colonial trade to competitors. They also argued that royal charter companies discouraged English manufacture by importing cheaper goods from abroad. The Whigs also argued for revisions to the tax code that would benefit those engaged in manufacturing and trade, rather than the landed elites who benefited from the tax regime under the Stuarts. In 1694, the Whigs succeeded in establishing the Bank of England, with the explicit goal of facilitating the promotion of English power through the generation of wealth, inaugurating a financial revolution that would make London the center of a vast network of international banking and investment in the eighteenth century.

that every future English monarch must be a member of the Church of England. Queen Mary died childless, and the throne passed from William to Mary's Protestant sister Anne (r. 1702–14) and then to George, elector of the German principality of Hanover and the Protestant great-grandson of James I. In 1707, the formal Act of Union between Scotland and England ensured that the Catholic heirs of King James II would in future have no more right to the throne of Scotland than they did to the throne of England.

The English soon referred to the events of 1688 and 1689 as the "Glorious Revolution," because it firmly established England as a mixed monarchy governed by the "king in Parliament" according to the rule of law. Although William and Mary and their successors continued to exercise a large measure of executive power, after 1688 no English monarch attempted to govern without Parliament, which has met annually from that time on. Parliament, and especially the House of Commons, also strengthened its control over taxation and expenditure. Although Parliament never codified the legal provisions of this form

JOHN LOCKE (1632–1704). Locke was an important foundational thinker in the liberal political tradition, who had a profound influence on the Glorious Revolution of 1688 in England, as well as on the makers of the American Revolution, such as Thomas Jefferson, and French political theorists during the Enlightenment. His debate with Robert Filmer, a defender of absolutism, led him to elaborate a theory of government as a contract between the ruler and the ruled.

John Locke and the Contract Theory of Government

The Glorious Revolution was the product of unique circumstances, but it also reflected antiabsolutist theories of politics that were taking shape in the late seventeenth century in response to the ideas of writers such as Bodin, Hobbes, Robert Filmer, and Bishop Jacques-Bénigne Bossuet. Chief among these opponents of absolutism was the Englishman John Locke (1632–1704), whose *Two Treatises of Government* were written before the Glorious Revolution but published for the first time in 1690.

Locke maintained that humans had originally lived in a state of nature characterized by absolute freedom and equality, with no government of any kind. The only law was the law of nature (which Locke equated with the law of reason), by which individuals enforced for themselves their natural rights to life, liberty, and property. Soon, however, humans perceived that the inconveniences of the state of nature outweighed its advantages. Accordingly, they agreed first to establish a civil society based on absolute equality and then to set up a government to arbitrate the

disputes that might arise within this civil society. But they did not make government's powers absolute. All powers not expressly surrendered to the government were reserved to the people themselves; as a result, governmental authority was both contractual and conditional. If a government exceeded or abused the authority granted to it, society had the right to dissolve it and create another.

Locke condemned absolutism in every form. He denounced absolute monarchy, but he was also critical of claims for the sovereignty of parliaments. Government, he argued, had been instituted to protect life, liberty, and property; no political authority could infringe these natural rights. The law of nature was therefore an automatic and absolute limitation on every branch of government.

In the late eighteenth century, Locke's ideas would resurface as part of the intellectual background of both the American and French Revolutions. Between 1690 and 1720, however, they served a far less radical purpose. The landed gentry who replaced James II with William and Mary read Locke as a defense of their conservative revolution. Rather than protecting their liberty and property, James II had threatened both; hence, the magnates were entitled to overthrow the tyranny he had established and replace it with a government that would defend their interests by preserving these natural rights. English government after 1689 would be dominated by Parliament; Parliament in turn was controlled by a landed aristocracy who were firm in the defense of their common interests, and who perpetuated their control by determining that only men possessed of substantial property could vote or run for office. During the beginning of the eighteenth century, then, both France and Britain had solved the problem of political dissent and social disorder in their own way. The emergence of a limited monarchy in England after 1688 contrasted vividly with the absolutist system developed by Louis XIV, but in fact both systems worked well enough to contain the threats to royal authority posed by powerful landed nobles and religious dissent.

The Dutch Republic

Another exception to absolutist rule in Europe was the Dutch Republic of the United Provinces, which had gained its independence from Spanish rule in 1648, after a long period of struggle (see Chapter 14). The seven provinces of the Dutch Republic (also known as the Netherlands) carefully preserved their autonomy with a federal legislature known as the States General, made up of delegations from each province. Through this flexible structure, the inhabitants of the republic worked hard to prevent the reestablishment of hereditary monarchy in the Dutch Republic. They were all the more jealous of their independence because several Catholic provinces of the southern Low Countries, including present-day Belgium and Luxembourg, remained under Spanish control.

The princes of the House of Orange served the Dutch Republic with a special title, *stadtholder*, or steward. The stadtholder did not technically rule and had no power to make laws, though he did exercise some influence over the appointments of officials and military officers. Instead, powerful merchant families in the United Provinces exercised real authority, through their dominance of the legislature. It was from the Dutch Republic that the stadtholder William of Orange launched his successful bid to become the king of England in the Glorious Revolution of 1688.

The Dutch United Provinces were not, perhaps, the first place that one would choose as a base for a commercial trading empire. Much of the territory of the Dutch Republic was below sea level, and the water was only kept out by an elaborate system of dikes that protected the land from floods. But the Dutch made good use of their proximity to the sea. By 1670, the prosperity of the Dutch Republic was strongly linked to trade: grains and fish from eastern Europe and the Baltic Sea; spices, silks, porcelains and tea from the Indian Ocean and Japan; slaves, silver, coffee, sugar, and tobacco from the Atlantic world. With a population of nearly 2 million and a capital, Amsterdam, that served as an international hub for goods and finance, the Dutch Republic's commercial network was global (see Chapter 14). Trade brought with it an extraordinary diversity of peoples and religions, as Spanish and Portuguese Jews, French Huguenots, English Quakers, and Protestant dissidents from central Europe all sought to take advantage of the relative spirit of toleration that existed in the Netherlands. This toleration did have limits. Jews were not required to live in segregated neighborhoods, as in many other European capitals, but they were prohibited from joining guilds or trade associations. Tensions between Calvinists and Catholics were a perennial issue, with Calvinists living in the western provinces and Catholics concentrated to the east and south.

The last quarter of the seventeenth century witnessed a decline in Dutch power, however, as the Low Countries were increasingly squeezed between the military strength and territorial ambitions of absolutist France to the south and competition from the maritime empire of the British in the Atlantic and Indian Oceans. The turning point came in 1672, when the French king, Louis XIV, put together a coalition that surrounded the United Provinces, threatening an invasion. The English took advantage of this moment of vulnerability to attack a major Dutch convoy returning from the

eastern Mediterranean. Louis XIV invaded and quickly overran all but two of the Dutch provinces. Popular anger at the failures of Dutch leadership turned violent, and in response the panicked assemblies named William of Orange the new stadtholder of Holland, giving him the power to organize the defense of the republic and to quell internal dissent. William opened the dikes that held back the sea, and the French armies were forced to retreat in the face of rising waters. Soon after, the Spanish entered the war on the side of the Dutch, which caused Louis XIV to abandon his plans to conquer the United Provinces. After the Glorious Revolution of 1688 in England, which brought William of Orange to the English throne, the Dutch joined an alliance with the English against the French. This alliance protected the republic against further aggression from France, but it also forced the Dutch into heavy expenditures on fortifications and defense and involved them in a series of costly wars (see below). As a result, the dynamic and flexible political institutions that had been part of the strength of the Dutch Republic became more rigid and inflexible over time. Meanwhile, both the French and the British continued to pressure the Dutch commercial fleet at sea. In the eighteenth century, the Dutch no longer exercised the same influence abroad.

WAR AND THE BALANCE OF POWER, 1661–1715

By the beginning of the eighteenth century, then, Europe was being reshaped by wars whose effects were also felt far beyond Europe's borders. The initial causes of these wars lay in the French monarchy's efforts to challenge his main European rivals, the Habsburg powers in Spain, the Spanish Netherlands, and the Holy Roman Empire. Through his continued campaigns in the Low Countries, Louis XIV expanded his territory, eventually taking Strasbourg (1681), Luxembourg (1684), and Cologne (1688). In response, William of Orange organized the League of Augsburg, which over time included Holland, England, Spain, Sweden, Bavaria, Saxony, the Rhine Palatinate, and the Austrian Habsburgs. The resulting Nine Years' War between France and the League extended from Ireland to India to North America (where it was known as King William's War), demonstrating the broadening imperial reach of European dynastic regimes and the increasing significance of French and English competition in the Atlantic world.

These wars were a sign both of the heightening power of Europe's absolutist regimes and of a growing vulnerability. Financing the increasingly costly wars of the eighteenth century would prove to be one of the central challenges faced by all of Europe's absolutist regimes, and the pressure to raise revenues from royal subjects through taxation would eventually strain European society to a breaking point. By the end of the eighteenth century, popular unrest and political challenges to absolutist and imperial states were widespread, both on the European continent and in the colonies of the Atlantic world.

From the League of Augsburg to the War of the Spanish Succession

The League of Augsburg reflected the emergence of a new diplomatic goal in western and central Europe: the preservation of a balance of power. This goal would animate European diplomacy for the next 200 years, until the balance of power system collapsed with the outbreak of the First World War. The main proponents of balance of power diplomacy were England, the United Provinces (Holland), Prussia, and Austria. By 1697, the League forced Louis XIV to make peace, because France was exhausted by war and famine. Louis gave back much of his recent gains but kept Strasbourg and the surrounding territory of Alsace. In North America, the borders between French and English colonial territory remained the same for the time being (see below). Louis was nevertheless looking at the real prize: a French claim to succeed to the throne of Spain and so control the Spanish Empire in the Americas, Italy, the Netherlands, and the Philippines.

In the 1690s, it became clear that King Charles II of Spain (r. 1665–1700) would soon die without a clear heir, and both Louis XIV of France and Leopold I of Austria (r. 1658–1705) were interested in promoting their own relatives to succeed him. Either solution would have upset the balance of power in Europe, and several schemes to divide the Spanish realm between French and Austrian candidates were discussed. Meanwhile, King Charles II's advisers sought to avoid partition by passing the entire Spanish Empire to a single heir: Louis XIV's grandson, Philip of Anjou. Philip was to renounce any claim to the French throne in becoming king of Spain, but the terms of this were kept secret. When Charles II died, Philip V (r. 1700–46) was proclaimed king of Spain and Louis XIV rushed troops into the Spanish Netherlands while also sending French merchants into the Spanish Americas to break their monopoly on trade from the region. Immediately a war broke out, known as the War of the Spanish Succession, pitting England, the United Provinces, Austria, and Prussia against France, Bavaria, and Spain. Although the English king, William of Orange, died in 1702, just as the war was beginning, his generals led an extraordinary march deep into the European continent, inflicting a devastating defeat on the French and their Bavarian allies at Blenheim (1704). Soon after, the English captured Gibraltar, establishing a commercial foothold in the Mediterranean. The costs of the campaign nevertheless created a chorus of complaints from English and Dutch merchants, who feared the damage that was being done to trade and commerce. Queen Anne of England (Mary's sister and William's successor) gradually grew disillusioned with the war, and her government sent out peace feelers to France.

In 1713, the war finally came to an end with the Treaty of Utrecht. Its terms were reasonably fair to all sides. Philip V, Louis XIV's grandson, remained on the throne of Spain and retained Spain's colonial empire intact. In return, Louis agreed that France and Spain would never be united under the same ruler. Austria gained territories in the Spanish Netherlands and Italy, including Milan and Naples. The Dutch were guaranteed protection of their borders against future invasions by France, but the French retained both Lille and Strasbourg. The most significant consequences of the settlement, however, were played out in the Atlantic world, as the balance of powers among Europe's colonial empires underwent a profound shift.

Imperial Rivalries after the Treaty of Utrecht

The fortunes of Europe's colonial empires changed dramatically owing to the wars of the late seventeenth and early eighteenth centuries. Habsburg Spain proved unable to defend its early monopoly over colonial trade, and by 1700, although Spain still possessed a substantial empire, it lay at the mercy of its more dynamic rivals. Portugal, too, found it impossible to prevent foreign penetration of its colonial empire. In 1703, the English signed a treaty with Portugal allowing English merchants to export woolens duty free into Portugal and allowing Portugal to ship its wines duty free into England. Access to Portugal also led British merchants to trade with the Portuguese colony of Brazil, an important sugar producer and the largest of all the American markets for African slaves.

The 1713 Treaty of Utrecht opened a new era of colonial rivalries. The French retained Quebec and other territories in North America, as well as their small foothold in India. The biggest winner by far was Great Britain, as the combined kingdoms of England and Scotland were known after 1707. The British kept Gibraltar and Minorca in the

1713 Dutch merchants' inability to compete with the British in the slave trade diminished their economic clout. In the Atlantic, Britain and France were now the dominant powers. Although they would duel for another half century for control of North America, the balance of colonial power tilted decisively in Britain's favor after Utrecht. Within Europe, the myth of French military supremacy had been shattered. Britain's navy, not France's army, would rule the new imperial and commercial world of the eighteenth century.

THE REMAKING OF CENTRAL AND EASTERN EUROPE

The decades between 1680 and 1720 were also decisive in reshaping the balance of power in central and eastern Europe. As Ottoman power waned, the Austro-Hungarian Empire of the Habsburgs emerged as the dominant power in central and southeastern Europe. To the north, Brandenburg-Prussia was also a rising power. The most dramatic changes, however, occurred in Russia, which emerged from a long war with Sweden as the dominant power in the Baltic Sea and would soon threaten the combined kingdom of Poland-Lithuania. Within these regimes, the main tension came from ambitious monarchs who sought to increase the power of the centralized state at the expense of other elites, especially aristocrats and the Church. In Brandenburg-Prussia and in Tsarist Russia, these efforts were largely successful, whereas in Habsburg Austria, regional nobilities retained much of their influence.

The Austrian Habsburg Empire

In the second half of the seventeenth century, as Louis XIV of France demonstrated the power of absolutism in western Europe, the Austrian Habsburg Empire, with its capital in Vienna, must have seemed increasingly like a holdover from a previous age. Habsburg Austria was the largest state within what remained of the medieval Holy Roman Empire, a complex federal association of nearly 300 nominally autonomous dynastic kingdoms, principalities, duchies, and archbishoprics that had been created to protect and defend the papacy. Some, such as the kingdom of Bavaria, were large and had their own standing armies. Each Holy Roman emperor was chosen by seven "electors" who were either of noble rank or archbishops—in practice, the emperor was always from the Habsburg family. Through strategic marriages with other royal lines, earlier generations of Habsburg rulers had consolidated their control over a substantial part of Europe, including Austria, Bohemia,

THE TREATY OF UTRECHT, 1713. This illustration from a French royal almanac depicts the treaty that ended the War of Spanish Succession and reshaped the balance of power in western Europe in favor of Britain and France.

Mediterranean and also acquired large chunks of French territory in the New World, including Newfoundland, mainland Nova Scotia, the Hudson Bay, and the Caribbean island of St. Kitts. Even more valuable, however, Britain also extracted from Spain the right to transport and sell African slaves in Spanish America. As a result, the British were now poised to become the principal slave merchants and the dominant colonial and commercial power of the eighteenth-century world.

The Treaty of Utrecht thus reshaped the balance of power in the Atlantic world in fundamental ways. Spain's collapse was already precipitous; by 1713, it was complete. Spain would remain the "sick man of Europe" for the next two centuries. The Dutch decline was more gradual, but by

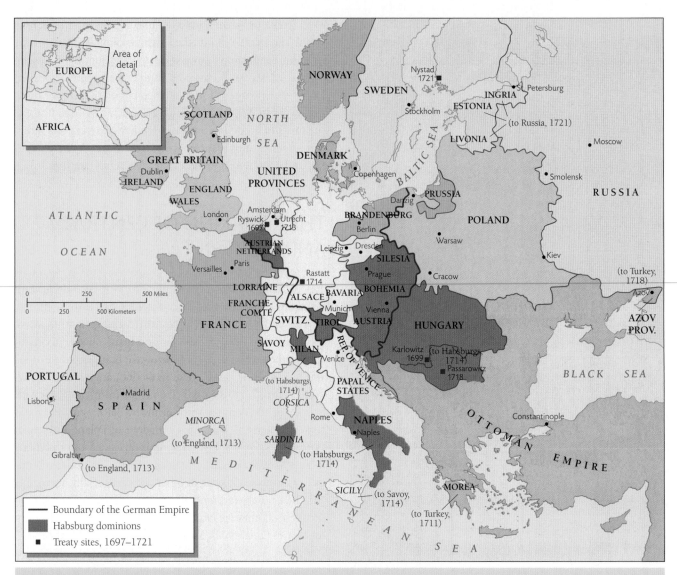

EUROPE AFTER THE TREATY OF UTRECHT (1713). ▪ *What were the major Habsburg dominions?* ▪ *What geographical disadvantage faced the kingdom of Poland as Brandenburg-Prussia grew in influence and ambition?* ▪ *How did the balance of power change in Europe as a result of the Treaty of Utrecht?*

Moravia, and Hungary in central Europe; the Netherlands and Burgundy in the west; and, if one included the Spanish branch of the Habsburg family, Spain and its vast colonial empire as well. After 1648, when the Treaty of Westphalia granted individual member states within the Holy Roman Empire the right to conduct their own foreign policy, the influence of the Austrian Habsburgs waned, at precisely the moment that they faced challenges from France to the west and the Ottoman Empire to the east.

The complicated structure of the Holy Roman Empire limited the extent to which a ruler such as Leopold I of Austria could emulate the absolutist rule of Louis XIV in France. Every constituent state within the empire had its own local political institutions, its own entrenched nobilities, each with a strong interest in resisting any attempt to centralize crucial functions of government, such as taxation, or the raising of armies. Even if direct assertion of absolutist control was impossible, Habsburg rulers found ways of increasing their authority. In Bohemia and Moravia, the Habsburgs encouraged landlords to produce crops for export by forcing peasants to provide three days of unpaid work per week to their lords. In return, the landed elites of these territories permitted the emperors to reduce the political independence of their traditional legislative estates. In Hungary, however, the powerful and independent nobility resisted such compromises. When the Habsburgs began a campaign against Hungarian Protestants, in 1679 an insurrection broke out that forced Leopold to grant concessions to Hungarian nobles in exchange for their assistance in restoring order. When the Ottoman Empire sought to take advantage of this disorder to press an attack against Austria from the east, the Habsburgs survived only by enlisting the help of a Catholic coalition led by the Polish king John Sobieski (r. 1674–96).

In 1683, the Ottomans launched their last assault on Vienna but after their failure to capture the Habsburg capital, Ottoman power in southeastern Europe declined rapidly. By 1699, Austria had reconquered most of Hungary from the Ottomans; by 1718, it controlled all of Hungary and also Transylvania and Serbia. In 1722, Austria acquired the territory of Silesia from Poland. With Hungary now a buffer state between Austria and the Ottomans, Austria became one of the arbiters of the European balance of power. The same obstacles to the development of centralized absolutist rule persisted, however, and Austria was increasingly overshadowed in central Europe by the rise of another German-speaking state: Prussia.

The Rise of Brandenburg-Prussia

After the Ottoman collapse, the main threat to Austria came from the rising power of Brandenburg-Prussia. Like Austria, Prussia was a composite state made up of several geographically divided territories acquired through inheritance by a single royal family, the Hohenzollerns. Their two main holdings were Brandenburg, centered on its capital city, Berlin, and the duchy of East Prussia. Between these two territories lay Pomerania (claimed by Sweden) and an important part of the kingdom of Poland, including the port of Gdansk (Danzig). The Hohenzollerns' aim was to unite their state by acquiring these intervening territories. Over the course of more than a century of steady state building, they finally succeeded in doing so. In the process, Brandenburg-Prussia became a dominant military power and a key player in the balance-of-power diplomacy of the mid-eighteenth century.

The foundations for Prussian expansion were laid by Frederick William, the "Great Elector" (r. 1640–88). He obtained East Prussia from Poland in exchange for help in a war against Sweden. Behind the Elector's diplomatic triumphs lay his success in building an army and mobilizing the resources to pay for it. He gave the powerful nobles of his territories (known as "Junkers" (YUN-kurs)) the right to enserf their peasants and guaranteed them immunity from taxation. In exchange, they staffed the officer corps of his army and supported his highly autocratic taxation system. Secure in their estates and made increasingly wealthy in the grain trade, the Junkers surrendered management of the Prussian state to the Elector's newly reformed bureaucracy, which set about its main task: increasing the size and strength of the Prussian army.

By supporting Austria in the War of the Spanish Succession, the Great Elector's son, Frederick I (r. 1688–1713) earned the right to call himself king of Prussia from the Austrian emperor. He too was a crafty diplomat, but his main attention was devoted to developing the cultural life of his new royal capital, Berlin. His son, Frederick William I (r. 1713–40) focused, like his grandfather, on building the army. During his reign, the Prussian army grew from 30,000 to 83,000 men, becoming the fourth largest army in Europe, after France, Austria, and Russia. To support his army, Frederick William I increased taxes and shunned the luxuries of court life. For him, the theater of absolutism was not the palace but the office, where he personally supervised his army and the growing bureaucracy that sustained it. Frederick William's son, known as Frederick the Great, would take this Prussian army and the bureaucracy that sustained it and transform the

PRUSSIANS SWEARING ALLEGIANCE TO THE GREAT ELECTOR AT KÖNIGSBERG, 1663. The occasion on which the Prussian estates first acknowledged the overlordship of their ruler. This ceremony marked the beginning of the centralization of the Prussian state.

THE CITY OF STETTIN UNDER SIEGE BY THE GREAT ELECTOR FREDERICK WILLIAM IN THE WINTER OF 1677–78 (c. 1680). This painting depicts the growing sophistication and organization of military operations under the Prussian monarchy. Improvements in artillery and siege tactics forced cities to adopt new defensive strategies, especially the zone of battlements and protective walls that became ubiquitous in central Europe during this period. ■ *How might these developments have shaped the layout of Europe's growing towns and cities?* ■ *How might this emphasis on the military and its attendant bureaucracy have affected the relationship between the monarchy and the nobility or between the king and his subjects?*

Europe, however, this increase in state power often came at the expense of an intensification of feudal obligations that the peasantry owed to their local lords.

AUTOCRACY IN RUSSIA

An even more dramatic transformation took place in Russia under Tsar Peter I (r. 1672–1725), Peter's official title was "autocrat of all the Russias" but he was soon known as Peter the Great. His imposing height—he was six feet eight inches tall—and his mercurial personality—jesting one moment, raging the next—added to the outsize impression he made on his contemporaries. Peter was not the first tsar to bring his country into contact with western Europe, but his policies were decisive in making Russia a great European power.

The Early Years of Peter's Reign

Since 1613, Russia had been ruled by members of the Romanov dynasty, who had attempted to restore political stability after the chaotic "time of troubles" that followed the death of the bloodthirsty, half-mad tsar Ivan the Terrible in 1584. The Romanovs faced a severe threat to their rule between 1667 and 1671, when a Cossack leader (the Russian Cossacks were semiautonomous bands of peasant cavalrymen) named Stenka Razin led a rebellion in southeastern Russia. This uprising found widespread support, not only from oppressed serfs but also from non-Russian tribes in the lower Volga region who longed to cast off the domination of Moscow. Ultimately Tsar Alexis I (r. 1654–76) and the Russian nobility were able to defeat Razin's zealous but disorganized bands of rebels, slaughtering more than 100,000 of them in the process.

Like Louis XIV of France, Peter came to the throne as a young boy, and his minority was marked by political dissension and court intrigue. In 1689, however, at the age of

kingdom into a major power in central Europe after 1740 (see Chapter 17).

Thus, in both Prussia and Habsburg Austria, the divided nature of the respective realms and the entrenched strength of local nobilities forced the rulers in each case to grant significant concessions to noble landowners in exchange for incremental increases in the power of the centralized state. Whereas the nobility in France increasingly sought to maximize their power by participating in the system of absolutist rule at the court of Louis XIV, and wealthy landowners in England sought to exercise their influence through Parliament, the nobilities of Prussia and Habsburg Austria had more leverage to demand something in return for their cooperation. Often, what they demanded was the right to enserf or coerce labor from the peasantry in their domains. In both eastern and western Europe, therefore, the state became stronger. In eastern seventeen, he overthrew the regency of his half sister Sophia and assumed personal control of the state. Determined to make Russia into a great military power, the young tsar traveled to Holland and England during the 1690s to study shipbuilding and to recruit skilled foreign workers to help him build a navy. While he was abroad, however, his elite palace guard (the *streltsy*) rebelled, attempting to restore Sophia to the throne. Peter quickly returned home from Vienna and crushed the rebellion with striking savagery. About 1,200 suspected conspirators were summarily executed, many of them gibbeted outside the walls of the Kremlin, where their bodies rotted for months as a graphic reminder of the fate awaiting those who dared challenge the tsar's authority.

The Transformation of the Tsarist State

Peter is most famous as the tsar who attempted to westernize Russia by imposing a series of social and cultural reforms on the traditional Russian nobility: ordering noblemen to cut off their long beards and flowing sleeves; publishing a book of manners that forbade spitting on the floor and eating with one's fingers; encouraging polite conversation between the sexes; and requiring noblewomen to appear, together with men, in Western garb at weddings, banquets, and other public occasions. The children of Russian nobles

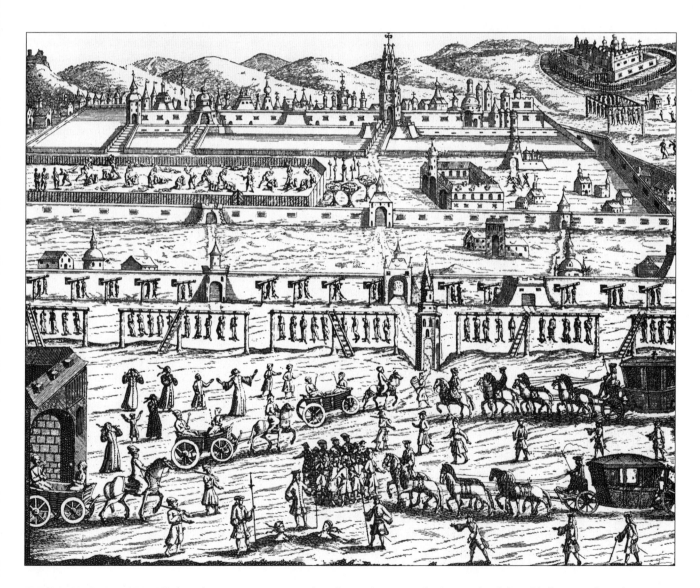

EXECUTION OF THE *STRELTSY* (1698). A contemporary woodcut showing how Peter the Great ordered the public hanging of guard regiments who had rebelled against his authority. How does this display of autocratic power compare with the spectacle of power so carefully orchestrated by Peter's contemporary, Louis XIV of France?

The Revolt of the Streltsy and Peter the Great

The streltsy were four regiments of Moscow guards that became involved in a conspiracy in support of Peter the Great's older sister, Sophia, who had earlier made claim to the throne while Peter was still a child. Approximately 4,000 of the rebels were defeated in June 1698 by troops loyal to Peter. Peter himself was abroad during the fighting, and although his officers had already tortured many of the streltsy to determine the involvement of other nobles, Peter ordered a more far-reaching investigation on his return. Over 1,000 of the streltsy were executed after being tortured again. Afterward, their bodies were placed on display in the capital. Johann Georg Korb, an Austrian diplomat in Moscow, recorded his observations of the power wielded by the Russian autocrat.

 ow sharp was the pain, how great the indignation to which the Czar's Majesty was mightily moved, when he knew of the rebellion of the Strelitz [*streltsy*], betrayed openly a mind panting for vengeance. [SIC] . . . Going immediately to Lefort (the only person almost that he condescended to treat with intimate familiarity), he thus indignantly broke out: "Tell me, Francis, son of James, how I can reach Moscow, by the shortest way, in a brief space, so that I may wreak vengeance on this great perfidy of my people, with punishments worthy of their flagitious crime. Not one of them shall escape with impunity. Around my royal city, of which, with their impious efforts, they meditated the destruction, I will have gibbets and gallows set upon the walls and ramparts, and each and every of them will I put to a direful death." . . .

His first anxiety, after his arrival [in Moscow] was about the rebellion. In what it consisted? What the insurgents meant? Who had dared to instigate such a crime? And as nobody could answer accurately upon all points, and some pleaded their own ignorance, others the obstinacy of the Strelitz, he began to have suspicions of everybody's loyalty, and began to cogitate about a fresh investigation. The rebels that were kept in custody . . . were all brought in by four regiments of the guards, to a fresh investigation and fresh tortures. Prison, tribunal, and rack, for those that were brought in, was in Bebraschentsko. No day, holy, or profane, were the inquisitors idle; every day was deemed fit and lawful for torturing. As many as there were accused there were knouts, and every inquisitor was a butcher. Prince Feodor Jurowicz Romadonowski showed himself by so much more fitted for his inquiry, as he surpassed the rest in cruelty. He put the interrogatories, he examined the criminals, he urged those that were not confessing, he ordered such Strelitz as were more pertinaciously silent, to be subjected to more cruel tortures; those that had already confessed about many things were questioned about more; those who were bereft of strength and reason, and almost of their senses, by excess of torment, were handed over to the skill of the doctors, who were compelled to restore them to strength, in order that they might be broken down by fresh excruciations. The whole month of October was spent in butchering the backs of the culprits with knout and with flames: no day were those that were left alive exempt from scourging or scorching, or else they were broken upon the wheel, or driven to the gibbet, or slain with the axe—the penalties which were inflicted upon them as soon as their confessions had sufficiently revealed the heads of the rebellion.

Source: Johann Georg Korb, *Diary of an Austrian Secretary of Legation at the Court of Czar Peter the Great*, trans. Count MacDonnell (London: 1863), pp. 2:85–87.

Questions for Analysis

1. Why was it important for Korb to begin this description with the monarch's pain?

2. What does this episode reveal about Peter's conception of his own person and of the loyalty that his subjects owed him? Does it show that his power was fragile, immense, or both?

3. What does it mean to describe torture as an "investigation" even while it is also being described as "vengeance?"

PETER THE GREAT CUTS THE BEARD OF AN OLD BELIEVER. This woodcut depicts the Russian emperor's enthusiastic policy of westernization, as he pushed everybody in Russia who was not a peasant to adopt Western styles of clothes and grooming. The Old Believer (a member of a religious sect in Russia) protests that he has paid the beard tax and should therefore be exempt. ▪ *Why would an individual's choices about personal appearance be so politically significant in Peter's Russia?* ▪ *What customs were the target of Peter's reforms?*

were sent to western European courts for their education. Thousands of western European experts were brought to Russia to staff the new schools and academies Peter built; to design the new buildings he constructed; and to serve in the tsar's army, navy, and administration.

These measures were important, but the tsar was not primarily motivated by a desire to modernize or westernize Russia. Peter's policies transformed Russian life in fundamental ways, but his real goal was to make Russia a great military power, not to remake Russian society. His new taxation system (1724), for example, which assessed taxes on individuals rather than on households, rendered many of the traditional divisions of Russian peasant society obsolete. It was created, however, to raise more money for war. His Table of Ranks, imposed in 1722, had a similar impact on the nobility. By insisting that all nobles must work their way up from the (lower) landlord class

to the (higher) administrative class and to the (highest) military class, Peter reversed the traditional hierarchy of Russian noble society, which had valued landlords by birth above administrators and soldiers who had risen by merit. But he also created a powerful new incentive to lure his nobility into administrative and military service to the tsar.

As "autocrat of all the Russias," Peter the Great was the absolute master of his empire to a degree unmatched elsewhere in Europe. After 1649, Russian peasants were legally the property of their landlords; by 1750, half were serfs and the other half were state peasants who lived on lands owned by the tsar himself (by comparison, many peasants in western Europe owned their own land and very few were serfs). State peasants could be conscripted to serve as soldiers in the tsar's army, workers in his factories (whose productive capacity increased enormously during Peter's reign), or as forced laborers in his building projects. Serfs could also be taxed by the tsar and summoned for military service, as could their lords. All Russians, of whatever rank, were expected to serve the tsar, and all Russia was considered in some sense to belong to him. Russia's autocracy thus went even further than the absolutism of Louis XIV.

To further consolidate his power, Peter replaced the Duma—the nation's rudimentary national assembly—with a handpicked senate, a group of nine administrators who supervised military and civilian affairs. In religious matters, he took direct control over the Russian Orthodox Church by appointing an imperial official to manage its affairs. To cope with the demands of war, he also fashioned a new, larger, and more efficient administration, for which he recruited both nobles and non-nobles. But rank in the new bureaucracy did not depend on birth. One of his principal advisers, Alexander Menshikov, began his career as a cook and finished as a prince. This degree of social mobility would have been impossible in any contemporary western European country. In Russia, more so than in western Europe, noble status depended on governmental service, with all nobles expected to participate in Peter's army or administration. Peter was not entirely successful in enforcing this requirement, but the administrative machinery he devised furnished Russia with its ruling class for the next 200 years.

Russian Imperial Expansion

The goal of Peter's foreign policy was to secure year-round ports for Russia on the Black Sea and the Baltic Sea. In the

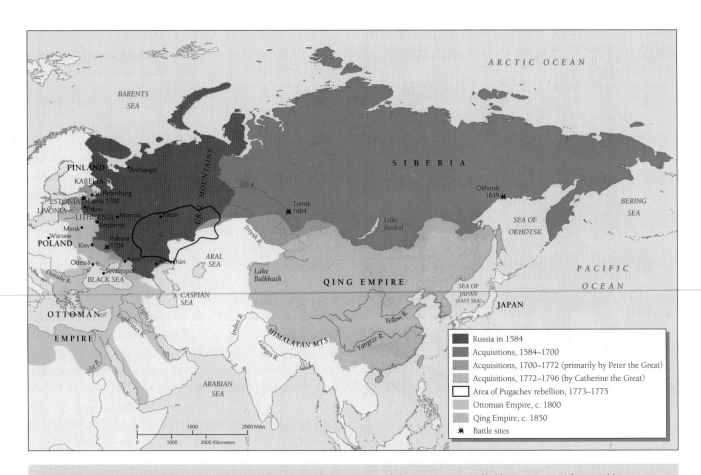

THE GROWTH OF THE RUSSIAN EMPIRE. ▪ *How did Peter the Great expand the territory controlled by Russia?* ▪ *What neighboring dynasties would have been the most affected by Russian expansion?* ▪ *How did the emergence of a bigger, more powerful Russia affect the European balance of power?*

Black Sea, his enemy was the Ottomans. Here, however, he had little success; although he captured the port of Azov in 1696, he was forced to return it in 1711. Russia would not secure its position in the Black Sea until the end of the eighteenth century. Nevertheless, Peter continued to push against the Ottoman Empire in the North Caucasus region throughout his reign. This mountainous area on Russia's southern flank became important sites for Russia's experiments in colonial expansion into central Asia, which began during the sixteenth century and would later mirror the process of colonial conquest undertaken by European powers and the United States in North and South America. Like France and Britain, the Russian state bureaucracy was built during a period of ambitious colonialism; and like Spain, the monarchy's identity was shaped by a long contest with Muslim power on its borders.

Since the late sixteenth century, successive Russian leaders had extended their control over bordering territories of central Asia to the south and east. Although merchants helped fund early expeditions into Siberia, this expansion was primarily motivated by geopolitical concerns; the tsar sought to gain access to the populations of Russia's border areas and bring them into the service of the expanding Russian state. In this sense, Russian colonialism during this period differed from western European expansion into the Atlantic world, which had primarily been motivated by hopes of commercial gain. Nevertheless, tsarist Russia's colonization of central Asia was similar to the process of European colonial expansion elsewhere in some respects. Like European colonizers in the Americas, Russian expansion brought Russian troops into contact with a variety of peoples with different religious beliefs and their own political structures. Some, such as the Muslim Kumyks of northern Dagestan had a highly centralized government. Others, such as the Kabardinians or the Chechens, were more fragmented politically.

In its early stages, as successive Russian emperors moved Russian troops into the region, they relied on a process of indirect rule, often seeking to co-opt local elites. Later in the eighteenth century, they had more success settling

Russians in border regions who ruled over local populations directly. Religion also provided a cover for expansion, and Peter and his successors funded missionary work by Georgian Christians among Muslims in the Caucasus. Efforts to convert Muslim populations to Orthodox Christianity had little effect, and in fact the opposite occurred: the region's commitment to Islam was continuously renewed through contact with different strains of Islamic practice coming from neighboring Ottoman lands and Persia.

Peter could point to more concrete success to the north. In 1700, he began what would become a twenty-one-year war with Sweden, then the dominant power in the Baltic Sea. By 1703, Peter had secured a foothold on the Gulf of Finland and immediately began to build a new capital city there, which he named St. Petersburg. After 1709, when Russian armies, supported by Prussia, decisively defeated the Swedes at the battle of Poltava, work on Peter's new capital city accelerated. An army of serfs was now conscripted to build the new city, whose centerpiece was a royal palace designed to imitate and rival Louis XIV's Versailles.

The Great Northern War with Sweden ended in 1721 with the Peace of Nystad. This treaty marks a realignment of power in eastern Europe comparable to that effected by the Treaty of Utrecht in the West. Sweden lost its North Sea territories to Hanover and its Baltic German territories to Prussia. Its eastern territories, including the entire Gulf of Finland, Livonia, and Estonia, passed to Russia. Sweden was now a second-rank power in the northern European world. Poland-Lithuania survived but it too was a declining power; by the end of the eighteenth century, the kingdom would disappear altogether, its territories swallowed up by its more powerful neighbors (see Chapter 17). The victors at Nystad were the Prussians and the Russians. These two powers secured their position along the Baltic coast, positioning themselves to take advantage of the lucrative eastern European grain trade with western Europe. Peter's accomplishments came at enormous cost. Direct taxation in Russia increased 500 percent during his reign, and his army in the 1720s numbered more than 300,000 men. Peter made Russia a force to be reckoned with on the European scene; but in so doing, he also aroused great resentment, especially among his nobility. Peter's only son and heir, Alexis, became the focus for conspiracies against the tsar, until finally Peter had him arrested and executed in 1718. As a result, when Peter died in 1725, he left no son to succeed him. A series of ineffective tsars followed, mostly creatures of the palace guard, under whom the resentful nobles reversed many of Peter the Great's reforms. In 1762, however, the crown passed to Catherine the Great, a ruler whose ambitions and determination were equal to those of her great predecessor (see Chapter 17).

CONCLUSION

By the time of Peter the Great's death in Russia in 1725, the power of Europe's absolutist realms to reinvigorate European political institutions was visible to all. Government had become more bureaucratic, state service had been more professionalized, administrators loyal to the king had become more numerous, more efficient, and more demanding. Despite the increasing scope of government, however, the structure and principles of government changed relatively little. Apart from Great Britain and the Dutch Republic, the great powers of eighteenth-century Europe were still governed by rulers who styled themselves as absolutist monarchs in the mold of Louis XIV, who claimed an authority that came directly from God and who ruled over a society where social hierarchies based on birth were taken for granted.

These absolutist regimes could not hide the fact, however, that their rule depended on a kind of negotiated settlement with other powerful elites within European society, in particular with landed aristocrats and with religious leaders. Louis XIV used his power to curb the worst excesses of nobles who abused their position, and he defended Catholic orthodoxy against dissident Catholics and Protestants. He could not hide the fact, however, that his power depended on a delicate exchange of favors—French aristocrats would surrender their political authority to the state in exchange for social and legal privileges and immunity from many (but not all) forms of taxation. The Church made a similar bargain. Peter the Great's autocratic rule in Russia worked out a slightly different balance of powers between his state and the Russian aristocracy, one that tied aristocrats more closely to an ideal of state service, a model that also worked well for the rulers of Brandenburg-Prussia. Even in England, the establishment of a limited constitutional monarchy and a king who ruled alongside parliament was not really a radical departure from the European absolutist model. It was merely a different institutional answer to the same problem—what relationship should the monarchical state have with other elites within society?

The demands of state building during this period required that kings raise enormous revenues—for the sumptuous displays of their sovereignty in royal residences like Louis XIV's palace at Versailles, for the sponsorship of royal academies and the patronage of artists, but most of all, for war. Territorial expansion within Europe and holding on to colonial empires in the Atlantic world was costly. Distributing the burden of taxation to pay for these endeavors became an intensely fought political issue for European monarchs during this period, and the financing of royal debt became an increasingly sophisticated art. Colbert's mercantilist policy was an attempt to harness the full power of the economy for the benefit of royal government, and the competition among Spain, Holland, England, and France to control the revenue flows coming from the Atlantic world forced Europe's monarchs to recognize that the "balance of powers" was increasingly being played out on a global stage.

These themes—the expansion of state powers; conflicts between the monarchy and the aristocracy or with religious dissidents; the intensification of the tax burden on the population; and the opening up of Europe to ever more frequent interactions with other peoples in the Atlantic world, the Indian Ocean, and eventually, the Pacific—prompted many in eighteenth-century Europe to reflect on the consequences of these developments. What were the limits to state power, and by what criteria were the actions of rulers to be judged? What was the proper measure of economic prosperity, and who was it for? Could

After You Read This Chapter

Visit StudySpace for quizzes, additional review materials, and multimedia documents. **wwnorton.com/web/westernciv18**

REVIEWING THE OBJECTIVES

- Absolutist rulers claimed a monopoly of power and authority within their realms. Who were the most important absolutist rulers, how did they justify their innovations, and what did they do to achieve their goals?
- Mercantilism was an economic doctrine that guided the policies of absolutist rulers. What did mercantilists believe?
- Between 1660 and 1688, political leaders in England continued to debate the nature of the state, the role of Parliament, and religious divisions. What was the significance of these dates, and what was the outcome of these debates?
- What circumstances led to the decline of the Dutch Republic's power in this period?
- The wars begun by Louis XIV after 1680 drove his opponents to ally with one another to achieve a balance of power. What was the result of these conflicts in Europe and in the Atlantic world?

a well-ordered society tolerate religious diversity? Given Europe's growing awareness of cultures in other parts of the world with different religions, different political systems, and different ways of expressing their moral and ethical values, how might Europeans justify or take the measure of their own beliefs and customs? The intellectuals who looked for answers to these questions were similar to earlier generations of scientific researchers in their respect for reason and rational thought, but they turned their attention beyond problems of natural philosophy and science to the messy world of politics and culture. Their movement—known as the Enlightenment—reached its peak in the middle decades of the eighteenth century, and created the basis for a powerful critique of Europe's absolutist regimes. The Enlightenment itself emerged slowly from a revolution in scientific thinking that had begun earlier in the early modern period, and it is to this history that we now turn.

PEOPLE, IDEAS, AND EVENTS IN CONTEXT

- What did **LOUIS XIV** of France and **PETER THE GREAT** of Russia have in common? How did they deal with those who resisted their attempts to impose absolutist rule?

- Compare the religious policies of **LOUIS XIV** of France with the religious policies of the English Stuart kings **CHARLES II** and **JAMES II**. In what way did religious disagreements limit their ability to rule effectively?

- How did European monarchies use the economic theory known as **MERCANTILISM** to strengthen the power and wealth of their kingdoms, and how did this theory influence **FRENCH COLONIALISM**?

- What was the **CONTRACT THEORY OF GOVERNMENT** according to the English political thinker **JOHN LOCKE**?

- What limits to royal power were recognized in Great Britain as a result of the **GLORIOUS REVOLUTION**?

- What was significant about the new **BALANCE OF POWERS** that developed in Europe as a result of **LOUIS XIV**'s wars?

- What does the **TREATY OF UTRECHT** (1713) tell us about the diminished influence of Spain and the corresponding rise of Britain and France as European and colonial powers?

- What was different about the attempts by rulers in Habsburg Austria and Brandenburg-Prussia to impose **ABSOLUTISM** in central Europe?

- What innovations did **PETER THE GREAT** bring to Russia?

THINKING ABOUT CONNECTIONS

- What makes absolutism different from earlier models of kingship in earlier periods?

- Was the absolutist monarchs' emphasis on sumptuous displays of their authority something new? Is it different from the way that political power is represented today in democratic societies?

STORY LINES

- After c. 1550, new sciences in Europe questioned older beliefs about the physical universe. New methods of inquiry led to the development of astronomy, physics, biology, chemistry, and new institutions that supported scientific research and education.

- The scientific revolution entailed both theoretical breakthroughs in explaining the physical universe as well as advances in the practical knowledge of artisans who built mechanical devices such as telescopes. This combination of scientific inquisitiveness and craft techniques encouraged technological developments that would later be useful in industrialization.

- The new sciences did not mark a clean rupture with older traditions of religious thinking. Most scientists in the 1600s remained essentially religious in their worldview, and in any case, their work was only accessible to a small, literate minority who had access to books.

CHRONOLOGY

1543	Nicolaus Copernicus (1473–1543) publishes *On the Revolutions of the Heavenly Spheres*
1576	Tycho Brahe sets up Uraniborg observatory
1609	Johannes Kepler (1571–1643) publishes *Astronomia Nova*
1610	Galileo (1564–1642) publishes *Starry Messenger*
1620	Francis Bacon (1561–1626) publishes *Novum Organum*
1632	Galileo publishes *Dialogue Concerning the Two Chief World Systems*
1633	Galileo's trial
1637	René Descartes (1596–1650) publishes *Discourse on Method*
1660	Royal Society of London founded
1666	French Academy of Sciences founded
1687	Isaac Newton (1642–1727) publishes *Principia Mathematica*

Before
You
Read
This
Chapter

The New Science of the Seventeenth Century

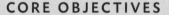

CORE OBJECTIVES

- **DEFINE** *scientific revolution* and explain what is meant by *science* in this historical context.

- **UNDERSTAND** the older philosophical traditions that were important for the development of new methods of scientific investigation in the seventeenth century.

- **IDENTIFY** the sciences that made important advances during this period and understand what technological innovations encouraged a new spirit of investigation.

- **EXPLAIN** the differences between the Ptolemaic view of the universe and the new vision of the universe proposed by Nicolas Copernicus.

- **UNDERSTAND** the different definitions of *scientific method* that emerged from the work of Francis Bacon and René Descartes.

Doubt thou the stars are fire,
Doubt that the sun doth move,
Doubt truth to be a liar,
But never doubt I love.

SHAKESPEARE, *HAMLET*, II.2

"D oubt thou the stars are fire" and "that the sun doth move." Was Shakespeare alluding to controversial ideas about the cosmos that contradicted the teachings of medieval scholars? *Hamlet* (c. 1600) was written more than fifty years after Copernicus had suggested, in his treatise *On the Revolutions of the Heavenly Spheres* (1543), that the sun did not move and that the earth did, revolving around the sun. Shakespeare probably knew of such theories, although they circulated only among small groups of learned Europeans. As Hamlet's love-torn speech to Ophelia makes clear, they were considered conjecture—or strange mathematical hypotheses. These theories were not exactly new—a heliocentric universe had been proposed as early as the second century B.C.E. by ancient Greek astronomers.

519

But they flatly contradicted the consensus that had set in after Ptolemy proposed an earth-centered universe in the second century C.E., and to Shakespeare's contemporaries, they defied common sense and observation. Learned philosophers, young lovers, shepherds, and sailors alike could watch the sun and the stars move from one horizon to the other each day and night, or so they thought.

Still, a small handful of thinkers did doubt. Shakespeare was born in 1564, the same year as Galileo. By the time the English playwright and the Italian natural philosopher were working, the long process of revising knowledge about the universe, and discovering a new set of rules that explained how the universe worked was under way. By the end of the seventeenth century a hundred years later, the building blocks of the new view had been put in place. This intellectual transformation brought sweeping changes to European philosophy and to Western views of the natural world and of humans' place in it.

Science entails at least three things: a body of knowledge, a method or system of inquiry, and a community of practitioners and the institutions that support them and their work. The *scientific revolution* of the seventeenth century (usually understood to have begun in the mid-sixteenth century and culminated in 1687 with Newton's *Principia*) involved each of these three realms. As far as the content of knowledge is concerned, the scientific revolution saw the emergence and confirmation of a heliocentric (sun-centered) view of the planetary system, which displaced the earth—and humans—from the center of the universe. Even more fundamental, it brought a new mathematical physics that described and confirmed such a view. Second, the scientific revolution established a method of inquiry for understanding the natural world: a method that emphasized the role of observation, experiment, and the testing of hypotheses. Third, *science* emerged as a distinctive branch of knowledge. During the period covered in this chapter, people referred to the study of matter, motion, optics, or the circulation of blood as natural philosophy (the more theoretical term), experimental philosophy, medicine, and—increasingly—science. The growth of societies and institutions dedicated to what we now commonly call scientific research was central to the changes at issue here. Science required not only brilliant thinkers but patrons, states, and communities of researchers; the scientific revolution was thus embedded in other social, religious, and cultural transformations.

The scientific revolution was not an organized effort. Brilliant theories sometimes led to dead ends, discoveries were often accidental, and artisans grinding lenses for telescopes played a role in the advance of knowledge just as surely as did great abstract thinkers. Educated women also claimed the right to participate in scientific debate, but their efforts were met with opposition or indifference. Old and new worldviews often overlapped as individual thinkers struggled to reconcile their discoveries with their faith or to make their theories (about the earth's movements, for instance) fit with received wisdom. Science was slow to work its way into popular understanding. It did not necessarily undermine religion, and it certainly did not intend to; figures like Isaac Newton thought their work confirmed and deepened their religious beliefs. In short, change came slowly and fitfully. But as the new scientific method began to produce radical new insights into the workings of nature, it eventually came to be accepted well beyond the small circles of experimenters, theologians, and philosophers with whom it began.

THE INTELLECTUAL ORIGINS OF THE SCIENTIFIC REVOLUTION

The scientific revolution marks one of the decisive breaks between the Middle Ages and the modern world. For all its novelty, however, it was rooted in earlier developments. Medieval artists and intellectuals had been observing and illustrating the natural world with great precision since at least the twelfth century. Medieval sculptors carved plants and vines with extraordinary accuracy, and fifteenth-century painters and sculptors devoted the same careful attention to the human face and form. Nor was the link among observation, experiment, and invention new to the sixteenth century. The magnetic compass had been known in Europe since the thirteenth century; gunpowder since the early fourteenth; printing, which permeated the intellectual life of the period and opened new possibilities—disseminating ideas quickly, collaborating more easily, buying books, and building libraries—since the middle of the fifteenth. "Printing, firearms, and the compass," wrote Francis Bacon, "no empire, sect or star appears to have exercised a greater power and influence on human affairs than these three mechanical discoveries." A fascination with light, which was a powerful symbol of divine illumination for medieval thinkers, encouraged the study of optics and, in turn, new techniques for grinding lenses. Lens grinders laid the groundwork for the seventeenth-century inventions of the telescope and microscope, creating reading glasses along the way. Astrologers were also active in the later Middle Ages, charting the heavens in the firm belief that the stars controlled the fates of human beings.

Behind these efforts to understand the natural world lay a nearly universal conviction that the natural world had been created by God. Religious belief spurred scientific study. One school of thinkers (the Neoplatonists) argued that nature was a book written by its creator to reveal the ways of God to humanity. Convinced that God's perfection must be reflected in nature, Neoplatonists searched for the ideal and perfect structures they believed must lie behind the "shadows" of the everyday world. Mathematics, particularly geometry, were important tools in this quest. The mathematician and astronomer Johannes Kepler, for example, was deeply influenced by Neoplatonism.

Renaissance humanism also helped prepare the grounds for the scientific revolution. The humanists' educational program placed a low value on natural philosophy, directing attention instead toward the recovery and study of classical antiquity. Humanists revered the authority of the ancients. Yet the energies the humanists poured into recovering, translating, and understanding classical texts (the source of conceptions of the natural world) made many of those important works available for the first time, and to a wider audience. Previously, Arabic sources had provided Europeans with the main route to ancient Greek learning; Greek classics were translated into Arabic and then picked up by late medieval scholars in Spain and Sicily. The humanists' return to the texts themselves—and the fact that the new texts could be more easily printed and circulated—encouraged new study and debate. Islamic scholars knew Ptolemy better than did Europeans until the humanist scholar and printer Johannes Regiomontanus recovered and prepared a new summary of Ptolemy's work. The humanist rediscovery of works by Archimedes—the great Greek mathematician who had proposed that the natural world operated on the basis of mechanical forces, like a great machine, and that these forces could be described mathematically—profoundly impressed important late-sixteenth- and seventeenth-century thinkers, including the Italian scientist Galileo, and shaped mechanical philosophy in the 1600s.

The Renaissance also encouraged collaboration between artisans and intellectuals. Twelfth- and thirteenth-century thinkers had observed the natural world, but they rarely tinkered with machines and they had little contact with the artisans who developed expertise in constructing machines for practical use. During the fifteenth century, however, these two worlds began to come together. Renaissance artists such as Leonardo da Vinci were accomplished craftsmen; they investigated the laws of perspective and optics, they worked out geometric methods for supporting the weight of enormous architectural domes, they studied the human body, and they devised new and more effective weapons for war. The Renaissance brought a vogue for alchemy and astrology; wealthy amateurs built observatories and measured the courses of the stars. These social and intellectual developments laid the groundwork for the scientific revolution.

What of the voyages of discovery? Sixteenth-century observers often linked the exploration of the globe to new knowledge of the cosmos. An admirer wrote to Galileo that he had kept the spirit of exploration alive: "The memory of Columbus and Vespucci will be renewed through you, and with even greater nobility, as the sky is more worthy than the earth." The parallel does not work quite so neatly. Columbus had not been driven by an interest in science.

PTOLEMAIC ASTRONOMICAL INSTRUMENTS. Armillary sphere, 1560s, built to facilitate the observation of planetary positions relative to the earth, in support of Ptolemy's theory of an earth-centered universe. In the sphere, seven concentric rings rotated about different axes. When the outermost ring was set to align with a north–south meridian, and the next ring was set to align with the celestial pole (the North Star, or the point around which the stars seem to rotate), one could determine the latitude of the place where the instrument was placed. The inner rings were used to track the angular movements of the planets, key measurements in validating the Ptolemaic system. ▪ *What forms of knowledge were necessary to construct such an instrument?* ▪ *How do they relate to the breakthrough that is known as the scientific revolution?*

Past and Present

Has Science Replaced Religion?

Galileo recanted his claims about the movement of heavenly bodies when challenged by the Church (left); but physicists persisted in their research, leading eventually to the development of modern particle accelerators like the one located in this lab in Grenoble, France (right). Few would say, however, that science has replaced religion in the modern world.

 Watch related author interview on StudySpace
wwnorton.com/web/westernciv18

Moreover, it took centuries for European thinkers to process the New World's implications for different fields of study, and the links between the voyages of discovery and breakthroughs in science were largely indirect. The discoveries made the most immediate impact in the field of natural history, which was vastly enriched by travelers' detailed accounts of the flora and fauna of the Americas. Finding new lands and cultures in Africa and Asia and the revelation of the Americas, a world unknown to the ancients and unmentioned in the Bible, also laid bare gaps in Europeans' inherited body of knowledge. In this sense, the exploration of the New World dealt a blow to the authority of the ancients.

In sum, the late medieval recovery of ancient texts long thought to have been lost, the expansion of print culture and reading, the turmoil in the church and the fierce wars and political maneuvering that followed the Reformation,

and the discovery of a new world across the oceans to explore and exploit all shook the authority of older ways of thinking. What we call the scientific revolution was part of the intellectual excitement that surrounded these challenges, and, in retrospect, the scientific revolution enhanced and confirmed the importance of these other developments.

THE COPERNICAN REVOLUTION

Medieval cosmologists, like their ancient counterparts and their successors during the scientific revolution, wrestled with the contradictions between ancient texts and the evidence of their own observations. Their view of an earth-centered universe was particularly influenced by the teachings of Aristotle (384–322 B.C.E.), especially as they were systematized by Ptolemy of Alexandria (100–178 C.E.). In fact, Ptolemy's vision of an earth-centered universe contradicted an earlier proposal by Aristarchus of Samos (310–230 B.C.E.), who had deduced that the earth and other planets revolve around the sun. Like the ancient Greeks, Ptolemy's medieval followers used astronomical observations to support their theory, but the persuasiveness of the model for medieval scholars also derived from the ways that it fit with their Christian beliefs (see Chapter 4). According to Ptolemy, the heavens orbited the earth in a carefully organized hierarchy of spheres. Earth and the heavens were fundamentally different, made of different matter and subject to different laws of motion. The sun, moon, stars, and planets were formed of an unchanging (and perfect) quintessence or ether. The earth, by contrast, was composed of four elements (earth, water, fire, and air), and each of these elements had its natural place: the heavy elements (earth and water) toward the center and the lighter ones farther out. The heavens—first the planets, then the stars—traced perfect circular paths around the stationary earth. The motion of these celestial bodies was produced by a prime mover, whom Christians identified as God. The view fit Aristotelian physics, according to which objects could move only if acted on by an external force, and it fit with a belief that each fundamental element of the universe had a natural place. Moreover, the view both followed from and confirmed belief in the purposefulness of God's universe.

By the late Middle Ages astronomers knew that this cosmology, called the "Ptolemaic system," did not correspond exactly to what many had observed. Orbits did not conform to the Aristotelian ideal of perfect circles. Planets, Mars in particular, sometimes appeared to loop backward before continuing on their paths. Ptolemy had managed to account for these orbital irregularities, but with complicated mathematics. By the early fifteenth century, the efforts to make the observed motions of the planets fit into the model of perfect circles in a geocentric (earth-centered) cosmos had produced astronomical charts that were mazes of complexity. Finally, the Ptolemaic system proved unable to solve serious difficulties with the calendar. That practical crisis precipitated Nicolaus Copernicus's intellectual leap forward.

By the early sixteenth century, the old Roman calendar was significantly out of alignment with the movement of the heavenly bodies. The major saints' days, Easter, and the other holy days were sometimes weeks off where they should have been according to the stars. Catholic authorities tried to correct this problem, consulting mathematicians and astronomers all over Europe. One of these was a Polish church official and astronomer, Nicolaus Copernicus (1473–1543). Educated in Poland and northern Italy, he was a man of diverse talents. He was trained in astron-

omy, canon law, and medicine. He read Greek. He was well versed in ancient philosophy. He was also a careful mathematician and a devout Catholic, who did not believe that God's universe could be as messy as the one in Ptolemy's model. His proposed solution, based on mathematical calculations, was simple and radical: Ptolemy was mistaken; the earth was neither stationary nor at the center of the planetary system; the earth rotated on its axis and orbited with the other planets around the sun. Reordering the Ptolemaic system simplified the geometry of astronomy and made the orbits of the planets comprehensible.

Copernicus was in many ways a conservative thinker. He did not consider his work to be a break with either the Church or with the authority of ancient texts. He believed, rather, that he had restored a pure understanding

NICOLAUS COPERNICUS. This anonymous portrait of Copernicus characteristically blends his devotion and his scientific achievements. His scholarly work (behind him in the form of an early planetarium) is driven by his faith (as he turns toward the image of Christ triumphant over death). ▪ *What relationship between science and religion is evoked by this image?*

of God's design, one that had been lost over the centuries. Still, the implications of his theory troubled him. His ideas contradicted centuries of astronomical thought, and they were hard to reconcile with the observed behavior of objects on earth. If the earth moved, why was that movement imperceptible? Copernicus calculated the distance from the Earth to the Sun to be at least 6 million miles. Even by Copernicus's very low estimate, the earth was hurtling around the sun at the dizzying rate of many thousands of miles an hour. How did people and objects remain standing? (The earth is actually about 93 million miles from the sun, moving through space at 67,000 miles an hour and spinning on its axis at about 1,000 miles an hour!)

Copernicus was not a physicist. He tried to refine, rather than overturn, traditional Aristotelian physics, but his effort to reconcile that physics with his new model of a sun-centered universe created new problems and inconsistencies that he could not resolve. These frustrations and complications dogged Copernicus's later years, and he hesitated to publish his findings. Just before his death, he consented to the release of his major treatise, *On the Revolutions of the Heavenly Spheres* (*De Revolutionibus*), in 1543. To fend off scandal, the Lutheran scholar who saw his manuscript through the press added an introduction to the book declaring that Copernicus's system should be understood as an abstraction, a set of mathematical tools for doing astronomy and not a dangerous claim about the nature of heaven and earth. For decades after 1543, Copernicus's ideas were taken in just that sense—as useful but not realistic mathematical hypotheses. In the long run, however, as one historian puts it, Copernicanism represented the first "serious and systematic" challenge to the Ptolemaic conception of the universe.

TYCHO'S OBSERVATIONS AND KEPLER'S LAWS

Within fifty years, Copernicus's cosmology was revived and modified by two astronomers also critical of the Ptolemaic model of the universe: Tycho Brahe (*TI-koh BRAH-hee*, 1546–1601) and Johannes Kepler (1571–1630). Each was considered the greatest astronomer of his day. Tycho was born into the Danish nobility, but he abandoned his family's military and political legacy to pursue his passion for astronomy. He was hotheaded as well as talented; at twenty, he lost part of his nose in a duel. Like Copernicus, he sought to correct the contradictions in traditional astronomy.

Unlike Copernicus, who was a theoretician, Tycho championed observation and believed careful study of the heavens would unlock the secrets of the universe. He first made a name for himself by observing a completely new star, a "nova," that flared into sight in 1572. The Danish king Friedrich II, impressed by Tycho's work, granted him the use of a small island, where he built a castle specially designed to house an observatory. For over twenty years, Tycho meticulously charted the movements of each significant object in the night sky, compiling the finest set of astronomical data in Europe.

Tycho was not a Copernican. He suggested that the planets orbited the sun and the whole system then orbited a stationary earth. This picture of cosmic order, though clumsy, seemed to fit the observed evidence better than the Ptolemaic system, and it avoided the upsetting physical and theological implications of the Copernican model. In the late 1590s, Tycho moved his work and his huge collection of data to Prague, where he became court astronomer to the Holy Roman emperor Rudolph II. In Prague, he was assisted by a young mathematician from a troubled family, Johannes Kepler. Kepler was more impressed with the Copernican model than was Tycho, and Kepler combined study of Copernicus's work with his own interest in mysticism, astrology, and the religious power of mathematics.

Kepler believed that everything in creation, from human souls to the orbits of the planets, had been created according to mathematical laws. Understanding those laws would thus allow humans to share God's wisdom and penetrate the inner secrets of the universe. Mathematics was God's language. Kepler's search for the pattern of mathematical perfection took him through musical harmonies, nested geometric shapes inside the planets' orbits, and numerical formulas. After Tycho's death, Kepler inherited Tycho's position in Prague, as well as his trove of observations and calculations. That data demonstrated to Kepler that two of Copernicus's assumptions about planetary motion simply did not match observations. Copernicus, in keeping with Aristotelian notions of perfection, had believed that planetary orbits were circular. Kepler calculated that the planets traveled in elliptical orbits around the sun; this finding became his First Law. Copernicus held that planetary motion was uniform; Kepler's Second Law stated that the speed of the planets varied with their distance from the sun. Kepler also argued that magnetic forces between the sun and the planets kept the planets in orbital motion, an insight that paved the way for Newton's law of universal gravitation formulated nearly eighty years later, at the end of the seventeenth century.

Each of Kepler's works, beginning with *Cosmographic Mystery* in 1596 and continuing with *Astronomia Nova* in 1609 and *The Harmonies of the World* in 1619, revised and augmented Copernicus's theory. His version of Copernicanism fit with remarkable accuracy the best observations of the time (which were Tycho's). Kepler's search for rules of motion that could account for the earth's movements in its new position was also significant. More than Copernicus, Kepler broke down the distinction between the heavens and the earth that had been at the heart of Aristotelian physics.

TYCHO BRAHE, 1662. This seventeenth-century tribute shows the master astronomer in his observatory. ▪ *How much scientific knowledge does one need to understand this image?* ▪ *Is this image, which celebrates science and its accomplishments, itself a scientific statement?* ▪ *What can one learn about seventeenth-century science from such imagery?*

NEW HEAVENS, NEW EARTH, AND WORLDLY POLITICS: GALILEO

Kepler had a friend deliver a copy of *Cosmographic Mystery* to the "mathematician named Galileus Galileus," then teaching mathematics and astronomy at Padua, near Venice. Galileo (1564–1642) thanked Kepler in a letter that nicely illustrates the Italian's views at the time (1597).

> So far I have only perused the preface of your work, but from this I gained some notion of its intent, and I indeed congratulate myself of having an associate in the study of Truth who is a friend of Truth. . . . I adopted the teaching of Copernicus many years ago, and his point of view enables me to explain many phenomena of nature which certainly remain inexplicable according to the more current hypotheses. I have written many arguments in support of him and in refutation of the opposite view—which, however, so far I have not dared to bring into the public light. . . . I would certainly dare to publish my reflections at once if more people like you existed; as they don't, I shall refrain from doing so.

Kepler replied, urging Galileo to "come forward!" Galileo did not answer.

At Padua, Galileo couldn't teach what he believed; Ptolemaic astronomy and Aristotelian cosmology were the established curriculum. By the end of his career, however, Galileo had provided powerful evidence in support of the Copernican model and laid the foundation for a new physics. What was more, he wrote in the vernacular (Italian) as well as in Latin. Kepler may have been a "friend of Truth," but his work was abstruse and bafflingly mathematical. (So was Copernicus's.) By contrast, Galileo's writings were widely translated and widely read, raising awareness of changes in natural philosophy across Europe.

Ultimately, Galileo made the case for a new relationship between religion and science, challenging in the process some of the most powerful churchmen of his day. His discoveries made him the most famous scientific figure of his time, but his work put him on a collision course with Aristotelian philosophy and the authority of the Catholic Church.

Galileo became famous by way of discoveries with the telescope. In 1609, he heard reports from Holland of a lens grinder who had made a spyglass that could magnify very distant objects. Excited, Galileo quickly devised his own telescope; trained it first on earthly objects to demonstrate that it worked; and then, momentously, pointed

Astronomical Observations and the Mapping of the Heavens

One (often-repeated) narrative about the scientific revolution is that it marked a crucial break separating modern science from an earlier period permeated by an atmosphere of superstition and theological speculation. In fact, medieval scholars tried hard to come up with empirical evidence for beliefs that their faith told them must be true, and

without these traditions of observation, scientists like Copernicus would never have been led to propose alternative cosmologies (see "Ptolemaic Astronomical Instruments" on page 521).

The assumption, therefore, that the "new" sciences of the seventeenth century marked an extraordinary rupture with a more ignorant or superstitious past is thus not entirely correct. It would be closer to the truth to suggest

that works such as that of Copernicus or Galileo provided a new context for assessing the relationship between observations and knowledge that came from other sources. Printed materials provided opportunities for early modern scientists to learn as much from each other as from more ancient sources.

The illustrations here are from scientific works on astronomy both before and after the appearance of Coperni-

A. The Ptolemaic universe, as depicted in Peter Apian, *Cosmographia* (1540).

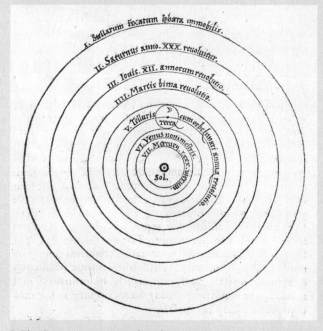

B. The Copernican universe (1543).

it at the night sky. Galileo studied the moon, finding on it mountains, plains, and other features of an earthlike landscape. His observations suggested that celestial bodies resembled the earth, a view at odds with the conception of the heavens as an unchanging sphere of heavenly perfection, inherently and necessarily different from the earth. He saw moons orbiting Jupiter, evidence that earth was not

at the center of all orbits. He saw spots on the sun. Galileo published these results, first in *The Starry Messenger* (1610) and then in *Letters on Sunspots* in 1613. *The Starry Messenger*, with its amazing reports of Jupiter's moons, was short, aimed to be read by many, and bold. It only hinted at Galileo's Copernicanism, however. The *Letters on Sunspots* declared it openly.

cus's work. All of them were based on some form of observation and claimed to be descriptive of the existing universe. Compare the abstract illustrations of the Ptolemaic (image A) and Copernican (image B) universes with Tycho Brahe's (image C) attempt to reconcile heliocentric observations with geocentric assumptions or with Galileo's illustration of sunspots (image D) observed through a telescope.

Questions for Analysis

1. What do these illustrations tell us about the relationship between knowledge and observation in sixteenth- and seventeenth-century science? What kinds of knowledge were necessary to produce these images?

2. Are the illustrations A and B intended to be visually accurate, in the sense that they represent what the eye sees?

Can one say the same of D? What makes Galileo's illustration of the sunspots different from the others?

3. Are the assumptions about observation contained in Galileo's drawing of sunspots (D) applicable to other sciences such as biology or chemistry? How so?

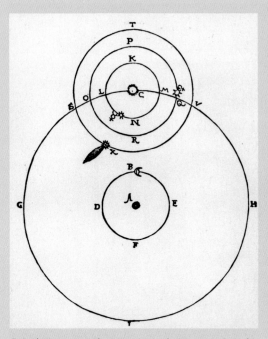

C. Brahe's universe (c. 1572, A, earth; B, moon; C, sun).

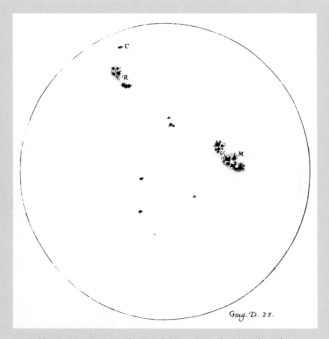

D. Galileo's sunspots, as observed through a telescope (1612).

A seventeenth-century scientist needed powerful and wealthy patrons. As a professor of mathematics, Galileo chafed at the power of university authorities who were subject to church control. Princely courts offered an inviting alternative. The Medici family of Tuscany, like others, burnished its reputation and bolstered its power by surrounding itself with intellectuals as well as artists. Per-

suaded he would be freer at its court than in Padua, Galileo took a position as tutor to the Medicis and flattered and successfully cultivated the family. He addressed *The Starry Messenger* to them. He named the newly discovered moons of Jupiter "the Medicean stars." He was rewarded with the title of chief mathematician and philosopher to Cosimo de' Medici, the grand duke of Tuscany. Now well positioned in Italy's networks of power and patronage, Galileo was able to pursue his goal of demonstrating that Copernicus's heliocentric (sun-centered) model of the planetary system was correct.

This pursuit, however, was a high-wire act, for he could not afford to antagonize the Catholic Church. In 1614, however, an ambitious and outspoken Dominican monk denounced Galileo's ideas as dangerous deviations from biblical teachings. Other philosophers and churchmen began to ask Galileo's patrons, the Medicis, whether their court mathematician was teaching heresy.

Disturbed by the murmurings against Copernicanism, Galileo penned a series of letters to defend himself, by addressing the relationship between natural philosophy and religion, and he argued that one could be a sincere Copernican and a sincere Catholic (see *Analyzing Primary Sources* on page 529). The Church, Galileo said, did

the sacred work of teaching scripture and saving souls. Accounting for the workings of the physical world was a task better left to natural philosophy, grounded in observation and mathematics. For the Church to take a side in controversies over natural science might compromise the Church's spiritual authority and credibility. Galileo envisioned natural philosophers and theologians as partners in a search for truth, but with very different roles. In a brilliant rhetorical moment, he quoted Cardinal Baronius in support of his own argument: the purpose of the Bible was to "teach us how to go to heaven, not how heaven goes."

Nevertheless, in 1616, the Church moved against Galileo. The Inquisition ruled that Copernicanism was "foolish and absurd in philosophy and formally heretical." Copernicus's *De Revolutionibus* was placed on the Index of Prohibited Books, and Galileo was warned not to teach Copernicanism.

GALILEO GALILEI BEFORE THE INQUISITION BY FRANÇOIS FLEURY-RICHARD. This nineteenth-century painting of Galileo before the Holy Office dramatizes the conflict between science and religion and depicts the Italian natural philosopher as defiant. In fact, Galileo submitted but continued his work under house arrest and published, secretly, in the Netherlands. ▪ *Would Galileo himself have subscribed to the message of this much later painting, that religion and science were opposed to one another?*

Galileo on Nature, Scripture, and Truth

One of the clearest statements of Galileo's convictions about religion and science comes from his 1615 letter to the grand duchess Christina, mother of Galileo's patron, Cosimo de' Medici, and a powerful figure in her own right. Galileo knew that others objected to his work. The church had warned him that Copernicanism was inaccurate and impious; it could be disproved scientifically, and it contradicted the authority of those who interpreted the Bible. Thoroughly dependent on the Medicis for support, he wrote to the grand duchess to explain his position. In this section of the letter, Galileo sets out his understanding of the parallel but distinct roles of the Church and natural philosophers. He walks a fine line between acknowledging the authority of the Church and standing firm in his convictions.

ossibly because they are disturbed by the known truth of other propositions of mine which differ from those commonly held, and therefore mistrusting their defense so long as they confine themselves to the field of philosophy, these men have resolved to fabricate a shield for their fallacies out of the mantle of pretended religion and the authority of the Bible. . . .

Copernicus never discusses matters of religion or faith, nor does he use arguments that depend in any way upon the authority of sacred writings which he might have interpreted erroneously. He stands always upon physical conclusions pertaining to the celestial motions, and deals with them by astronomical and geometrical demonstrations, founded primarily upon sense experiences and very exact observations. He did not ignore the Bible, but he knew very well that if his doctrine were proved, then it could not contradict the Scriptures when they were rightly understood. . . .

I think that in discussions of physical problems we ought to begin not from the authority of scriptural passages, but from sense-experiences and necessary demonstrations; for the holy Bible and the phenomena of nature proceed alike from the divine Word, the former as the dictate of the Holy Ghost and the latter as the observant executrix of God's commands. It is necessary for the Bible, in order to be accommodated to the understanding of every man, to speak many things which appear to differ from the absolute truth so far as the bare meaning of the words is concerned. But Nature, on the other hand, is inexorable and immutable; she never transgresses the laws imposed upon her, or cares a whit whether her abstruse reasons and methods of operation are understandable to men. For that reason it appears that nothing physical which sense-experience sets before our eyes, or which necessary demonstrations prove to us, ought to be called in question (much less condemned) upon the testimony of biblical passages which may have some different meaning beneath their words. For the Bible is not chained in every expression to conditions as strict as those which govern all physical effects; nor is God any less excellently revealed in Nature's actions than in the sacred statements of the Bible. . . .

Source: Galileo, "Letter to the Grand Duchess Christina," in *The Discoveries and Opinions of Galileo Galilei*, ed. Stillman Drake (Garden City, NY: 1957), pp. 177–83.

Questions for Analysis

1. How does Galileo deal with the contradictions between the evidence of his senses and biblical teachings?

2. For Galileo, what is the relationship between God, man, and nature?

3. Why did Galileo need to defend his views in a letter to Christina de' Medici?

For a while, he did as he was asked. But when his Florentine friend and admirer Maffeo Barberini was elected pope as Urban VIII in 1623, Galileo believed the door to Copernicanism was (at least half) open. He drafted one of his most famous works, *A Dialogue Concerning the Two Chief World Systems* published in 1632. The *Dialogue* was a hypothetical debate between supporters of the old Ptolemaic system, represented by a character he named Simplicio (simpleton), on the one hand, and proponents of the new astronomy, on the other. Throughout, Galileo gave the best lines to the Copernicans. At the very end, however, to satisfy the letter of the Inquisition's decree, he had them capitulate to Simplicio.

The Inquisition banned the *Dialogue* and ordered Galileo to stand trial in 1633. Pope Urban, provoked by Galileo's scorn and needing support from Church conservatives during a difficult stretch of the Thirty Years' War, refused to protect his former friend. The verdict of the secret trial shocked Europe. The Inquisition forced Galileo to repent his Copernican position, banned him from working on or even discussing Copernican ideas, and placed him under house arrest for life. According to a story that began to circulate shortly afterward, as he left the court for house arrest he stamped his foot and muttered defiantly, looking down at the earth: "Still, it moves."

The Inquisition could not put Galileo off his life's work. He refined the theories of motion he had begun to develop early in his career. He proposed an early version of the theory of inertia, which held that an object's motion stays the same until an outside force changed it. He calculated that objects of different weights fall at almost the same speed and with a uniform acceleration. He argued that the motion of objects follows regular mathematical laws. The same laws that govern the motions of objects on earth (which could be observed in experiments) could also be observed in the heavens—again a direct contradiction of Aristotelian principles and an important step toward a coherent physics based on a sun-centered model of the universe. Compiled under the title *Two New Sciences* (1638), this work was smuggled out of Italy and published in Protestant Holland.

Among Galileo's legacies, however, was exactly the rift between religion and science that he had hoped to avoid. Galileo believed that Copernicanism and natural philosophy in general need not subvert theological truths, religious belief, or the authority of the Church. But his trial seemed to show the contrary, that natural philosophy and Church authority could not coexist. Galileo's trial silenced Copernican voices in southern Europe, and the Church's leadership retreated into conservative reaction. It was therefore in northwest Europe that the new philosophy Galileo had championed would flourish.

METHODS FOR A NEW PHILOSOPHY: BACON AND DESCARTES

As the practice of the new sciences became concentrated in Protestant northwest Europe, new thinkers began to spell out standards of practice and evidence. Sir Francis Bacon and René Descartes (*deh-KAHRT*) loomed especially large

in this development, setting out methods or the rules that should govern modern science. Bacon (1561–1626) lived at roughly the same time as Kepler and Galileo—and Shakespeare; Descartes (1596–1650) was slightly younger. Both Bacon and Descartes came to believe that theirs was an age of profound change, open to the possibility of astonishing discovery. Both were persuaded that knowledge could take the European moderns beyond the ancient authorities. Both set out to formulate a philosophy to encompass the learning of their age.

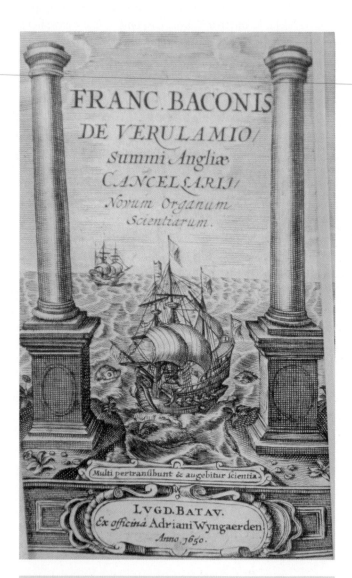

FRONTISPIECE TO BACON'S *NOVUM ORGANUM* (1620). The illustration suggests that scientific work is like a voyage of discovery, similar to a ship setting out through uncharted waters. Is it a voyage of conquest? Compare this image with the fanciful image of Tycho Brahe at work in his observatory (page 525).
- *What metaphors and allegorical imagery did scientists use during this period to characterize the significance of their work?*

"Knowledge is power." The phrase is Bacon's and captures the changing perspective of the seventeenth century and its new confidence in the potential of human thinking. Bacon trained as a lawyer, served in Parliament and, briefly, as lord chancellor to James I of England. His abiding concern was with the assumptions, methods, and practices that he believed should guide natural philosophers and the progress of knowledge. The authority of the ancients should not constrain the ambition of modern thinkers. Deferring to accepted doctrines could block innovation or obstruct understanding. "There is but one course left . . . to try the whole thing anew upon a better plan, and to commence a total reconstruction of sciences, arts, and all human knowledge, raised upon the proper foundations." To pursue knowledge did not mean to think abstractly and leap to conclusions; it meant observing, experimenting, confirming ideas, or demonstrating points. If thinkers will be "content to begin with doubts," Bacon wrote, "they shall end with certainties." We thus associate Bacon with the gradual separation of scientific investigation from philosophical argument.

Bacon advocated an *inductive* approach to knowledge: amassing evidence from specific observations to draw general conclusions. In Bacon's view, many philosophical errors arose from beginning with assumed first principles. The traditional view of the cosmos, for instance, rested on the principles of a prime mover and the perfection of circular motion for planets and stars. The inductive method required accumulating data (as Tycho had done, for example) and then, after careful review and experiment, drawing appropriate conclusions about the motions of heavenly bodies. Bacon argued that scientific knowledge was best tested through the cooperative efforts of researchers performing experiments that could be repeated and verified. The knowledge thus gained would be predictable and useful to philosophers and artisans alike, contributing to a wide range of endeavors from astronomy to shipbuilding.

Bacon's vision of science and progress is vividly illustrated by two images. The first, more familiar, is the title page of Bacon's *Novum Organum* (1620) with its bold ships sailing out beyond the Straits of Gibraltar, formerly the limits of the West, into the open sea, in pursuit of unknown but

FROM RENÉ DESCARTES, *L'HOMME* (1729; ORIGINALLY PUBLISHED AS *DE HOMINI*, 1662). Descartes's interest in the body as a mechanism led him to suppose that physics and mathematics could be used to understand all aspects of human physiology, and his work had an important influence on subsequent generations of medical researchers. In this illustration, Descartes depicts the optical properties of the human eye. ■ *How might such a mechanistic approach to human perception have been received by proponents of Baconian science, who depended so much on the reliability of human observations?*

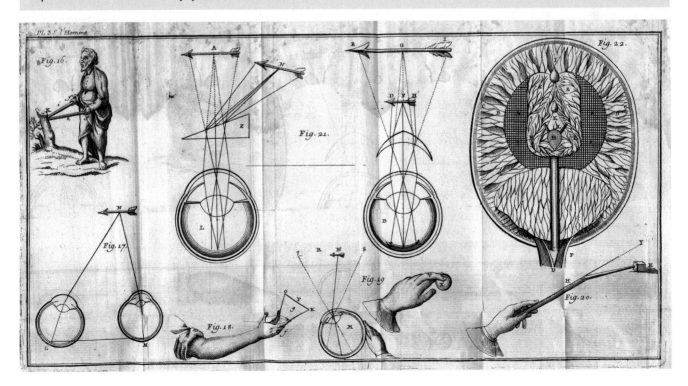

Competing Viewpoints

The New Science and The Foundations of Certainty

Francis Bacon (1561–1626) and René Descartes (1596–1650) were both enthusiastic supporters of science in the seventeenth century, but they differed in their opinions regarding the basis for certainty in scientific argumentation. Bacon's inductive method emphasized the gathering of particular observations about natural phenomena, which he believed could be used as evidence to support more general conclusions about causes, regularity, and order in the natural world. Descartes, on the other hand, defended a deductive method: he believed that certainty could be built only by reasoning from first principles that one knew to be true and was less certain of the value of evidence that came from the senses alone.

Aphorisms from *Novum Organum*

XXXI

It is idle to expect any advancement in science from the super-inducing and engrafting of new things upon old. We must begin anew from the very foundations, unless we would revolve forever in a circle with mean and contemptible progress....

XXXVI

One method of delivery alone remains to us which is simply this: we must lead men to the particulars themselves, and their series and order; while men on their side must force themselves for a while to lay their notions by and begin to familiarize themselves with facts....

XLV

The human understanding of its own nature is prone to suppose the existence of more order and regularity in the world than it finds. And though there be many things in nature which are singular and unmatched, yet it devises for them parallels and conjugates and relatives which do not exist. Hence the fiction that all celestial bodies move in perfect circles.... Hence too the element of fire with its orb is brought in, to make up the square with the other three which the sense perceives.... And so on of other dreams. And these fancies affect not dogmas only, but simple notions also....

XCV

Those who have handled sciences have been either men of experiment or men of dogmas. The men of experiment are like the ant, they only collect and use; the reasoners resemble spiders, who make cobwebs out of their own substance. But the bee takes a middle course: it gathers its material from the flowers of the garden and of the field, but transforms and digests it by a power of its own. Not unlike this is the true business of philosophy; for it neither relies solely or chiefly on the powers of the mind, nor does it take the matter which it gathers from natural history and mechanical experiments and lay it up in the memory whole ... but lays it up in the understanding altered and digested. Therefore, from a closer and purer league between these two faculties, the experimental and the rational (such as has never yet been made), much may be hoped....

Source: Michael R. Matthews, ed., *The Scientific Background to Modern Philosophy: Selected Readings* (Indianapolis, IN: 1989), pp. 47–48, 50–52.

From *A Discourse on Method*

Just as a great number of laws is often a pretext for wrong-doing, with the result that a state is much better governed when, having only a few, they are strictly observed; so also I came to believe that in the place of the great number of precepts that go to make up logic, the following four would be sufficient for my purposes, provided that I took a firm but unshakeable decision never once to depart from them.

The first was never to accept anything as true that I did not *incontrovertibly* know to be so; that is to say, carefully to avoid both *prejudice* and premature conclusions; and to include nothing in my judgments other than that which presented itself to my mind so *clearly* and *distinctly*, that I would have no occasion to doubt it.

The second was to divide all the difficulties under examination into as many parts as possible, and as many as were required to solve them in the best way.

The third was to conduct my thoughts in a given order, beginning with the *simplest* and most easily understood objects, and gradually ascending, as it were step by step, to the knowledge of the most *complex;* and *positing* an order even on those which do not have a natural order of precedence.

The last was to undertake such complete enumerations and such general surveys that I would be sure to have left nothing out.

The long chain of reasonings, every one simple and easy, which geometers habitually employ to reach their most difficult proofs had given me cause to suppose that all those things which fall within the domain of human understanding follow on from each other in the same way, and that as long as one stops oneself taking anything to be true that is not true and sticks to the right order so as to deduce one thing from another, there can be nothing so remote that one cannot eventually reach it, nor so hidden that one cannot discover it. . . .

[B]ecause I wished . . . to concentrate on the pursuit of truth, I came to think that I should . . . reject as completely false everything in which I could

detect the least doubt, in order to see if anything thereafter remained in my belief that was completely indubitable. And so, because our senses sometimes deceive us, I decided to suppose that nothing was such as they lead us to imagine it to be. And because there are men who make mistakes in reasoning, even about the simplest elements of geometry, and commit logical fallacies, I judged that I was as prone to error as anyone else, and I rejected as false all the reasoning I had hitherto accepted as valid proof. Finally, considering that all the same thoughts which we have while awake can come to us while asleep without any one of them then being true, I resolved to pretend that everything that had ever entered my head was no more true than the illusions of my dreams. But immediately afterwards I noted that, while I was trying to think of all things being false in this way, it was necessarily the case that I, who was thinking them, had to be something; and observing this truth: *I am thinking therefore I exist,* was so secure and certain that it could not be shaken by any of the most extravagant suppositions of the sceptics, I judged that I could accept it without scruple,

as the first principle of the philosophy I was seeking.

Source: René Descartes, *A Discourse on the Method,* trans. Ian Maclean (New York: 2006), pp. 17–18, 28.

Questions for Analysis

1. Descartes's idea of certainty depended on a "long chain of reasonings" that departed from certain axioms that could not be doubted and rejected evidence from the senses. What science provided him with the model for this idea of certainty? What was the first thing that he felt he could be certain about? Did he trust his senses?

2. Bacon's idea of certainty pragmatically sought to combine the benefits of sensory knowledge and experience (gathered by "ants") with the understandings arrived at through reason (cobwebs constructed by "spiders"). How would Descartes have responded to Bacon's claims? According to Bacon, was Descartes an ant or a spider?

3. What do these two thinkers have in common?

---

great things to come. The second is Bacon's description of an imagined factory of discovery, "Solomon's house," at end of his utopian *New Atlantis* (1626). Inside the factory, "sifters" would examine and conduct experiments, passing on findings to senior researchers who would draw conclusions and develop practical applications. The work of these scholars would be supplemented by accounts sent in by their emissaries abroad, traveling ambassadors of science who would gather data and information about the natural world and human societies in other places. Bacon's utopian image of

patient researchers and experimenters anticipated the modern university.

René Descartes was French, though he lived all over Europe. He was intellectually restless as well; he worked in geometry, cosmology, optics, and physiology—for a while dissecting cow carcasses daily. He was writing a (Copernican) book on physics when he heard of Galileo's condemnation in 1633, a judgment that impressed on him the dangers of "expressing judgements on this world." Descartes's *Discourse on Method* (1637), for which he is best known, began simply as a preface to three essays on optics, geometry, and meteorology. It is personal, recounting Descartes's dismay at the "strange and unbelievable" theories he encountered in his traditional education. His first response, as he described it, was to systematically doubt everything he had ever known or been taught. Better to clear the slate, he believed, than to build an edifice of knowledge on received assumptions. His first rule was "never to receive anything as a truth which [he] did not clearly know to be such." He took the human ability to think as his point of departure, summed up in his famous and enigmatic *Je pense, donc je suis,* later translated into Latin as *cogito ergo sum* and into English as "I think, therefore I am." As the phrase suggests, Descartes's doubting led (quickly, by our standards) to self-assurance and truth: the thinking individual existed, reason existed, God existed. For Descartes, then, doubt was a ploy, or a piece that he used in an intellectual chess game to defeat skepticism. Certainty, not doubt, was the centerpiece of the philosophy he bequeathed to his followers.

Descartes, like Bacon, sought a "fresh start for knowledge" or the rules for understanding of the world as it was. Unlike Bacon, Descartes emphasized *deductive* reasoning, proceeding logically from one certainty to another. "So long as we avoid accepting as true what is not so," he wrote in *Discourse on Method,* "and always preserve the right order of deduction of one thing from another, there can be nothing too remote to be reached in the end, or too well hidden to be discovered." For Descartes, mathematical thought expressed the highest standards of reason, and his work contributed greatly to the authority of mathematics as a model for scientific reasoning.

Descartes made a particularly forceful statement for *mechanism,* a view of the world shared by Bacon and Galileo and one that came to dominate seventeenth-century scientific thought. As the name suggested, mechanical philosophy proposed to consider nature as a machine. It rejected the traditional Aristotelian distinction between the works of humans and those of nature and the view that nature, as God's creation, necessarily belonged to a different—and higher—order. In the new picture of the universe that was emerging from the discoveries and writings of the early seventeenth century, it seemed that all matter was composed of the same material and all motion obeyed the same laws. Descartes sought to explain everything, including the human body, mechanically. As he put it firmly, "There is no difference between the machines built by artisans and the diverse bodies that nature alone composes." Nature operated according to regular and predictable laws and was thus accessible to human reason. The belief guided, indeed inspired, much of the scientific experiment and argument of the seventeenth century.

The Power of Method and the Force of Curiosity: Seventeenth-Century Experimenters

For nearly a century after Bacon and Descartes, most of England's natural philosophers were Baconian, and most of their colleagues in France, Holland, and elsewhere in northern Europe were Cartesians (followers of Descartes). The English Baconians concentrated on performing experiments in many different fields, producing results that could then be debated and discussed. The Cartesians turned instead toward mathematics and logic. Descartes himself pioneered analytical geometry. Blaise Pascal (1623–1662) worked on probability theory and invented a calculating machine before applying his intellectual skills to theology. The Cartesian thinker Christian Huygens (1629–1695) from Holland combined mathematics with experiments to understand problems of impact and orbital motion. The Dutch Cartesian Baruch Spinoza (1632–1677) applied geometry to ethics and believed he had gone beyond Descartes by proving that the universe was composed of a single substance that was both God and nature.

English experimenters pursued a different course. They began with practical research, putting the alchemist's tool, the laboratory, to new uses. They also sought a different kind of conclusion: empirical laws or provisional generalizations based on evidence rather than absolute statements of deductive truth. Among the many English laboratory scientists of the era were the physician William Harvey (1578–1657), the chemist Robert Boyle (1627–1691), and the inventor and experimenter Robert Hooke (1635–1703).

Harvey's contribution was enormous: he observed and explained that blood circulated through the arteries, heart, and veins. To do this, he was willing to dissect living animals (vivisection) and experiment on himself. Boyle performed experiments and established a law (known as Boyle's law) showing that at a constant temperature the volume of a gas decreases in proportion to the pressure placed on it. Hooke introduced the microscope to the experimenter's tool kit. The compound microscope had been invented in Holland early in the seventeenth century. But it was not until the 1660s that Hooke and others demonstrated its potential by using it to study the cellular structure of plants. Like the telescope before it, the microscope revealed an unexpected dimension of material phenomena. Examining even the most ordinary objects revealed detailed structures of perfectly connected smaller parts and persuaded many that

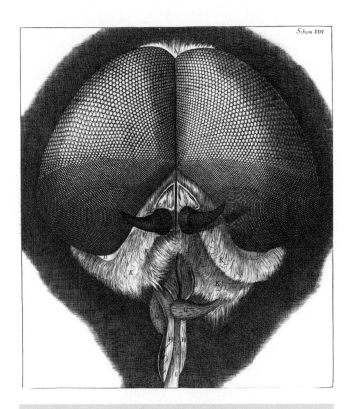

newly crowned King Charles II granted a group of natural philosophers and mathematicians a royal charter (1662) to establish the Royal Society of London, for the "improvement of natural knowledge" and committed to experimentation and collaborative work among natural philosophers. The founders of the Royal Society, in particular Boyle, believed it could serve a political as well as an intellectual purpose. The Royal Society would pursue Bacon's goal of collective research in which members would conduct formal experiments, record the results, and share them with other members. These members would in turn study the methods, reproduce the experiment, and assess the outcome. The enterprise would give England's natural philosophers a common sense of purpose and a system to reach reasoned, gentlemanly agreement on "matters of fact." By separating systematic scientific research from the dangerous language of politics and religion that had marked the civil war, the Royal Society could also help restore a sense of order and consensus to English intellectual life.

with improved instruments they would uncover even more of the world's intricacies.

The microscope also provided what many regarded as new evidence of God's existence. The way each minute structure of a living organism, when viewed under a microscope, corresponded to its purpose testified not only to God's existence but to God's wisdom as well. The mechanical philosophy did not exclude God but in fact could be used to confirm his presence. If the universe was a clock, after all, there must be a clock maker. Hooke himself declared that only imbeciles would believe that what they saw under the microscope was "the production of chance" rather than of God's creation.

The State, Scientific Academies, and Women Scientists

Seventeenth-century state building (see Chapter 14) helped secure the rise of science. In 1660, England's monarchy was restored after two decades of revolution and civil war. The

***OBSERVING THE TRANSIT OF VENUS* (1673).** Elisabetha (1647–1693) and Johannes Hevelius (1611–1687) believed that precise observations about the timing of Venus's passage across the face of the sun when observed from different parts of the earth could be used to calculate the distance from the earth to the sun. This German-speaking husband and wife astronomy team from Gdansk in present-day Poland worked together on many of their projects. After Johannes's death, Elisabetha published their jointly written star catalog.

Gassendi on the Science of Observation and the Human Soul

Pierre Gassendi (1592–1655) was a seventeenth-century French Catholic priest and philosopher. A contemporary of Descartes's, Gassendi was part of a group of intellectuals in France who sought a new philosophy of nature that could replace the traditional teachings of Aristotle that had been so severely criticized by Copernicus and his followers. Gassendi had no doubt that his faith as a Christian was compatible with his enthusiasm for the new sciences of observation, but in order to demonstrate this to his contemporaries he had to show that the mechanical explanations of the universe and the natural world did not necessarily lead to a heretical materialism or atheism. In the following passage, taken from his posthumously published work Syntagma Philosophicum *(1658), Gassendi attempted to demonstrate that one might infer the existence of the human soul, even if it was not accessible to the senses.*

There are many such things for which with the passage of time helpful appliances are being found that will make them visible to the senses. For example, take the little animal the mite, which is born under the skin; the senses perceived it as a certain unitary little point without parts; but since, however, the senses saw that it moved by itself, reason had deduced from this motion as from a perceptible sign that this little body was an animal and because its forward motion was somewhat like a turtle's, reason added that it must get about by the use of certain tiny legs and feet. And although this truth would have been hidden to the senses, which never perceived these limbs, the microscope was recently invented by which sight could perceive that matters were actually as predicted. Likewise, the question had been raised what the galaxy in the sky with the name of the Milky Way was. Democritus, concerning whom it was said that even when he did not know something he was knowing, had deduced from the perceptible sign of its filmy whiteness that it was nothing more than an innumerable multitude of closely packed little stars which could not be seen separately, but produced that effect of spilt milk when many of them were joined together. This truth had become known to him, and yet had remained undisclosed to the senses until our day and age, until the moment that the telescope, recently discovered, made it clear that things were in fact what he had said. But there are many such things which, though they were hidden from the ancients, have now been made manifest for our eyes. And who knows but a great many of those which are concealed in our time, which we perceive only through the intelligence, will one day also be clearly perceived by the senses through the agency of some helpful appliance thought up by our descendants? . . .

Secondly, if someone wonders whether a certain body is endowed with a soul or not, the senses are not at all capable of determining that by taking a look as it were at the soul itself; yet there are operations which when they come to the senses' notice, lead the intellect to deduce as from a sign that there is some soul beneath them. You will say that this sign belongs to the empirical type, but it is not at all of that type, for it is not even one of the indicative signs since it does not inform us of something that the senses have ever perceived in conjunction with the sign, as they have seen fire with smoke, but informs us instead of something that has always been impenetrable to the senses themselves, like our skin's pores or the mite's feet before the microscope.

You will persist with the objection that we should not ask so much whether there is a soul in a body as what its nature is, if it is the cause of such operations, just as there is no question that there is a force attracting iron in a magnet or that there is a tide in the sea, but there are questions over what their nature is or what they are caused by. But let me omit these matters which are to be fully treated elsewhere, and let it be enough if we say that not every truth can be known by the mind, but at least some can concerning something otherwise hidden, or not obvious to the senses themselves. And we bring up the example of the soul both because vital action is proposed by Sextus Empiricus as an example of an indicative sign and because even though it pertains not so much to the nature of the soul as to its existence, still a truth of existence of such magnitude as this, which it is most valuable for us to know, is made indisputable. For when among other questions we hear it asked if God is or exists in the universe, that is a truth of existence which it would be a great service to establish firmly even if it is not proven at the same time what he is or what his nature is. Although God is such that he can no more come under the perusal of the senses than the soul can, still we infer that the soul exists in the body from the actions that occur before the senses and are so peculiarly appropriate to a soul that if one were not present, they would not be either. In the same way we deduce that God exists in the universe from his effects perceived by the senses, which could not be produced by anything but God and which therefore would not be observed unless God were present in the world, such as the great order of the universe, its great beauty, its grandeur, its harmony, which are so great that they can only result from a sovereignly wise, good, powerful, and inexhaustible cause. But these things will be treated elsewhere at greater length.

Source: Craig B. Brush, ed., *The Selected Works of Pierre Gassendi* (New York: 1972), pp. 334–36.

Questions for Analysis

1. What is the relationship between new knowledge and new scientific tools (the microscope and the telescope) in Gassendi's examples of the mite and the Milky Way? Is he a Baconian or a Cartesian?

2. What are the limitations of the senses when it comes to questions of the human soul, according to Gassendi?

3. Given these limitations, does Gassendi conclude that science will never be able to say anything about his religious faith?

The society's journal, *Philosophical Transactions*, reached out to professional scholars and experimenters throughout Europe. Similar societies began to appear elsewhere. The French Academy of Sciences was founded in 1666 and was also tied to seventeenth-century state building, in this case Bourbon absolutism (see Chapter 15). Royal societies, devoted to natural philosophy as a collective enterprise, provided a state (or princely) sponsored framework for science and an alternative to the important but uncertain patronage of smaller nobles or to the religious (and largely conservative, Aristotelian) universities. Scientific societies reached rough agreement about what constituted legitimate research. They established the modern scientific custom of crediting discoveries to those who were first to publish results. They enabled information and theories to be exchanged more easily across national boundaries, although philosophical differences among Cartesians, Baconians, and traditional Aristotelians remained very difficult to bridge. Science began to take shape as a discipline.

The early scientific academies did not have explicit rules barring women, but with few exceptions they contained only male members. This did not mean that women did not practice science, though their participation in scientific research and debate remained controversial. In some cases, the new science could itself become a justification for women's inclusion, as when the Cartesian philosopher François Poullain de la Barre used anatomy to declare in 1673 that "the mind has no sex." Since women possessed the same physical senses as men and the same nervous systems and brains, Poullain asked, why should they not equally occupy the same roles in society? In fact, historians have discovered more than a few women who taught at European universities in the sixteenth and seventeenth centuries, above all in Italy. Elena Cornaro Piscopia received her doctorate of philosophy in Padua in 1678, the first woman to do so. Laura Bassi became a professor of physics at the University of Bologna after receiving her doctorate there in 1733, and based on her exceptional contributions to mathematics she became a member of the Academy of Science in Bologna. Her papers—including titles such as "On the Compression of Air" (1746), "On the Bubbles Observed in Freely Flowing Fluid" (1747), "On Bubbles of Air That Escape from Fluids" (1748)—gained her a stipend from the academy.

Italy appears to have been an exception in allowing women to get formal recognition for their education and research in established institutions. Elsewhere, elite women could educate themselves by associating with learned men. The aristocratic Margaret Cavendish (1623–1673), a natural philosopher in England, gleaned the information necessary to start her career from her family and their friends, a network that included Thomas Hobbes and, while in exile in France in the 1640s, René Descartes. These connections were not enough to overcome the isolation she felt working in a world of letters that was still largely the preserve of men, but this did not prevent her from developing her own speculative natural philosophy and using it to critique those who would exclude her from scientific debate. The "tyrannical government" of men over women, she wrote, "hath so dejected our spirits, that we are become so stupid, that kept on in such capacity, mouths would gape even wider." In spite of this rejection, Winkelmann continued to work as an astronomer, training both her son and two daughters in the discipline.

Like Winkelmann, the entymologist Maria Sibylla Merian (1647–1717) also made a career based on observation. And like Winkelmann, Merian was able to carve out a space for her scientific work by exploiting the precedent of guild women who learned their trade in family workshops. Merian was the daughter of an engraver and illustrator in Frankfurt, and she served as an informal apprentice to her father before beginning her own career as a scientific illustrator, specializing in detailed engravings of insects and plants. Traveling to the Dutch colony of Surinam, Merian supported herself and her two daughters by selling exotic insects and animals she collected and brought back to Europe. She fought the colony's sweltering climate and malaria to publish her most important scientific work, *Metamorphosis of the Insects of Surinam*, which detailed the life cycles of Surinam's insects in sixty ornate illustrations. Merian's *Metamorphosis* was well received in her time; in fact, Peter I of Russia proudly displayed Merian's portrait and books in his study.

FROM MARIA SYBILLA MERIAN, *METAMORPHOSIS OF THE INSECTS OF SURINAM* (1705). Merian, the daughter of a Frankfurt engraver, learned in her father's workshop the skills necessary to become an important early entymologist and scientific illustrator and conducted her research on two continents.

beasts being but a degree below us, men use us but a degree above beasts. Whereas in nature we have as clear an understanding as men, if we are bred in schools to mature our brains."

The construction of observatories in private residences enabled some women living in such homes to work their way into the growing field of astronomy. Between 1650 and 1710, 14 percent of German astronomers were women, the most famous of whom was Maria Winkelmann (1670–1720). Winkelmann had worked with her husband, Gottfried Kirch, in his observatory, and when he died she had already done significant work, discovering a comet and preparing calendars for the Berlin Academy of Sciences. When Kirch died, she petitioned the academy to take her husband's place in the prestigious body but was rejected. Gottfried Leibniz, the academy's president, explained, "Already during her husband's lifetime the society was burdened with ridicule because its calendar was prepared by a woman. If she were now to be

"AND ALL WAS LIGHT": ISAAC NEWTON

Sir Isaac Newton's work marks the culmination of the scientific revolution. Galileo, peering through his telescope in the early 1600s, had come to believe that the earth and the heavens were made of the same material. Galileo's experiments with pendulums aimed to discover the laws of motion, and he proposed theories of inertia. It was Newton who articulated those laws and presented a coherent, unified vision of how the universe worked. All bodies in the universe, Newton said, whether on earth or in the heavens, obeyed the same basic laws. One set of forces and one pattern, which could be expressed mathematically, explained why planets orbited in ellipses and why (and at what speed) apples fell from trees. An Italian mathematician later commented that Newton was the "greatest and most fortunate of mortals"—because there was only one universe, and he had discovered its laws.

Isaac Newton (1642–1727) was born on Christmas Day to a family of small landowners. His father died before his birth, and it fell to a succession of relatives, family friends, and schoolmasters to spot, then encourage, his genius. In

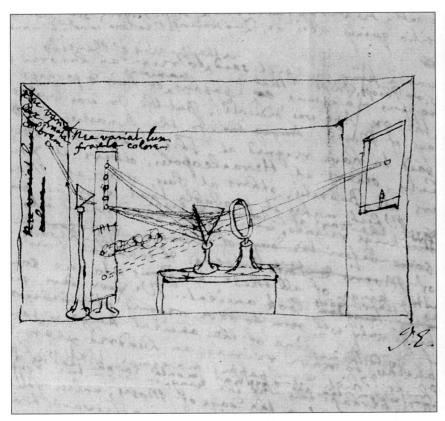

NEWTON'S EXPERIMENTS WITH LIGHT (1672). Newton's own sketch (left) elegantly displays the way he proved that white light was made up of differently colored light rays. Earlier scientists had explained the color spectrum produced by shining sunlight through a prism by insisting that the colors were a by-product of contaminating elements within the prism's glass. Newton disproved this theory by shining the sunlight through two consecutive prisms. The first produced the characteristic division of light into a color spectrum. When one of these colored beams passed through a second prism, however, it emerged on the other side unchanged, demonstrating that the glass itself was not the cause of the dispersal. He was not yet thirty when he published the results of this experiment.

1661, he entered Trinity College in Cambridge University, where he would remain for the next thirty-five years, first as a student, then as the Lucasian Professor of Mathematics. The man who came to represent the personification of modern science was reclusive, secretive about his findings, and obsessive. During his early work with optics, he experimented with his own eyes, pressing them to see how different shapes would change the effects of light and then, intrigued by what he found, inserting a very thick needle "betwixt my eye and the bone as neare to the backside of my eye as I could" to actually curve his eyeball. (Please do not try this at home.)

Newton's first great burst of creativity came at Cambridge in the years from 1664 to 1666, "the prime of my age for invention." During these years, Newton broke new ground in three areas. The first was optics. Descartes believed that color was a secondary quality produced by

the speed of particulate rotation but that light itself was white. Newton, using prisms he had purchased at a local fair, showed that white light was composed of different-colored rays (see image on this page). The second area in which Newton produced innovative work during these years was in mathematics. In a series of brilliant insights, he invented both integral calculus and differential calculus, providing mathematical tools to model motion in space. The third area of his creative genius involved his early works on gravity. Newton later told different versions of the same story: the idea about gravity had come to him when he was in a "contemplative mood" and was "occasioned by the fall of an apple." Why did the apple "not go sideways or upwards, but constantly to the earth's center?...Assuredly the reason is, that the earth draws it. There must be a drawing power in matter." Voltaire, the eighteenth-century French essayist, retold the story to dramatize Newton's simple brilliance. But the theory of gravity rested on mathematical formulations, it was far from simple, and it would not be fully worked out until *Principia,* more than twenty years later.

Newton's work on the composite nature of white light led him to make a reflecting telescope, which used a curved mirror rather than lenses. The telescope earned him election to the Royal Society (in 1672) and drew him out of his sheltered obscurity at Cambridge. Encouraged by the Royal Society's support, he wrote a paper describing his theory of optics and allowed it to be published in *Philosophical Transactions.* Astronomers and scientists across Europe applauded the work. Robert Hooke, the Royal Society's curator of experiments, did not. Hooke was not persuaded by Newton's mode of argument; he found Newton's claims that science had to be mathematical both dogmatic and high-handed; and he objected—in a series of sharp exchanges with the reclusive genius—that Newton had not provided any physical explanation for his results. Stung by the conflict with Hooke and persuaded that few natural philosophers could understand his theories, Newton withdrew to Cambridge and long refused to share his work. Only the patient effort of friends and fellow scientists like the astronomer Edmond Halley (1656–1742), already well known for his astronomical observations in the Southern Hemisphere and the person for whom Halley's Comet is named, convinced Newton to publish again.

Newton's *Principia Mathematica* (Mathematical Principles of Natural Philosophy) was published in 1687. It was prompted by a visit from Halley, in which the astronomer asked Newton for his ideas on a question being discussed at the Royal Society: was there a mathematical basis for the elliptical orbits of the planets? Halley's question inspired Newton to expand calculations he had made earlier into an all-encompassing theory of celestial—and terrestrial—dynamics. Halley not only encouraged Newton's work but supervised and financed its publication (though he had less money than Newton); and on several occasions he had to persuade Newton, enraged again by reports of criticism from Hooke and others, to continue with the project and to commit his findings to print.

Principia was long and difficult—purposefully so, for Newton said he did not want to be "baited by little smatterers in mathematics." Its central proposition was that gravitation was a universal force and one that could be expressed mathematically. Newton built on Galileo's work on inertia, Kepler's findings concerning the elliptical orbits of planets, the work of Boyle and Descartes, and even his rival Hooke's work on gravity. He once said, "If

I have seen further, it is by standing on the shoulders of giants." But Newton's universal theory of gravity, although it drew on work of others before him, formulated something entirely new. His synthesis offered a single, descriptive account of mass and motion. "All bodies whatsoever are endowed with a principle of mutual gravitation." The law of gravitation was stated in a mathematical formula and supported by observation and experience; it was, literally, universal.

The scientific elite of Newton's time was not uniformly persuaded. Many mechanical philosophers, particularly Cartesians, objected to the prominence in Newton's theory of forces acting across empty space. Such attractions smacked of mysticism (or the occult); they seemed to lack any driving mechanism. Newton responded to these criticisms in a note added to the next edition of the *Principia (General Scholium,* 1713). He did not know what *caused* gravity, he said, and he did not "feign hypotheses." "For whatever is not deduced from the phenomena must be called hypothesis," he wrote, and has "no place in the experimental philosophy." For Newton, certainty

NEWTON AND SATIRE. The English artist and satirist William Hogarth mocking both philosophy and "Newton worship" in 1763. The philosophers' heads are being weighed on a scale that runs from "absolute gravity" to "absolute levity" or "stark fool."

Newton on the Purposes of Experimental Philosophy

When Newton added his General Scholium to the second edition of Principia *in 1713, he was seventy-one, president of the Royal Society, and widely revered. Responding to continental critics, he set out his general views on science and its methods, arguing against purely deductive reasoning and reliance on hypotheses about ultimate causes.*

 itherto we have explained the phenomena of the heavens and of our sea by the power of gravity, but have not yet assigned the cause of this power. This is certain, that it must proceed from a cause that penetrates to the very centres of the sun and planets, without suffering the least diminution of its force; that operates not according to the quantity of the surfaces of the particles on which it acts (as mechanical causes used to do), but according to the quantity of the solid matter which they contain, and propagates its virtue on all sides to immense distances, decreasing always as the inverse square of the distances. . . . [H]itherto I have not been able to discover the cause of those properties of gravity from phenomena, and I frame no hypothesis; for whatever is not deduced from the phenomena is to be called an hypothesis and hypotheses, whether metaphysical or physical, whether of occult qualities or mechanical, have no place in experimental philosophy. In this philosophy particular propositions are inferred from the phenomena, and afterwards rendered general by induction. . . . And to us it is enough that gravity does really exist, and acts according to the laws which we have explained, and abundantly serves to account for all the motions of the celestial bodies, and of our sea.

Source: Michael R. Matthews, ed., *The Scientific Background to Modern Philosophy: Selected Readings* (Indianapolis, IN: 1989), p. 152.

Questions for Analysis

1. Why did Isaac Newton declare that "hypotheses, whether metaphysical or physical, whether of occult qualities or mechanical, have no place in experimental philosophy"?

2. Is Newton's thinking similar to Bacon's, or does he argue in ways similar to Descartes's?

---

and objectivity lay in the precise mathematical characterization of phenomena—"the mathematization of the universe," as one historian puts it. Science could not, and need not, always uncover causes. It did describe natural phenomena and accurately predict the behavior of objects as confirmed by experimentation.

Other natural philosophers immediately acclaimed Newton's work for solving long-standing puzzles. Thinkers persuaded that the Copernican version of the universe was right had been unable to piece together the physics of a revolving earth. Newton made it possible to do so. Halley provided a poem to accompany the first edition of *Principia.* "No closer to the gods can any mortal rise," he wrote, of the man with whom he had worked so patiently. Halley did have a financial as well as an intellectual interest in the book, and he also arranged for it to be publicized and reviewed in influential journals. John Locke (whose own *Essay Concerning Human Understanding* was written at virtually the same time, in 1690) read *Principia* twice and summarized it in French for readers across the Channel. By 1713, pirated editions of *Principia* were being published in Amsterdam for distribution throughout Europe. By the time Newton died, in 1727, he had become an English national hero and was given a funeral at Westminster Abbey. The poet Alexander Pope expressed the awe that Newton inspired in some of his contemporaries in a famous couplet:

> Nature and nature's law lay hid in night;
> God said, "Let Newton be!" and all was light.

Voltaire, the French champion of the Enlightenment (discussed in the next chapter), was largely responsible for Newton's reputation in France. In this, he was helped by a woman who was a brilliant mathematician in her own right, Emilie du Châtelet. Du Châtelet coauthored a book with

Voltaire introducing Newton to a French audience; and she translated *Principia*, a daunting scientific and mathematical task and one well beyond Voltaire's mathematical abilities. Newton's French admirers and publicists disseminated Newton's findings. In their eyes, Newton also represented a cultural transformation, a turning point in the history of knowledge.

Science and Cultural Change

From the seventeenth century on, science stood at the heart of what it meant to be "modern." It grew increasingly central to the self-understanding of Western culture, and scientific and technological power became one of the justifications for the expansion of Western empires and the subjugation of other peoples. For all these reasons, the scientific revolution was and often still is presented as a thorough-going break with the past, a moment when Western culture was recast. But, as one historian has written, "no house is ever built of entirely virgin materials, according to a plan bearing no resemblance to old patterns, and no body of culture is able to wholly reject its past. Historical change is not like that, and most 'revolutions' effect less sweeping changes than they advertise or than are advertised for them."

To begin with, the transformation we have canvassed in this chapter involved elite knowledge. Ordinary people inhabited a very different cultural world. Second, natural philosophers' discoveries—Tycho's mathematics and Galileo's observations, for instance—did not undo the authority of the ancients in one blow. They did not seek to do so. Third, science did not subvert religion. Even when traditional concepts collapsed in the face of new discoveries, natural philosophers seldom gave up on the project of restoring a picture of a divinely ordered universe. Mechanists argued that the intricate universe revealed by the discoveries of Copernicus, Kepler, Galileo, Newton, and others was evidence of God's guiding presence. Robert Boyle's will provided the funds for a lecture series on the "confutation of atheism" by scientific means. Isaac Newton was happy to have his work contribute to that project. "Nothing," he wrote to one of the lecturers in 1692, "can rejoice me more than to find [*Principia*] usefull for that purpose." The creation of "the Sun and Fixt stars," "the motion which the Planets now have could not spring from any naturall cause alone but were imprest with a divine Agent." Science was thoroughly compatible with belief in God's providential design, at least through the seventeenth century.

The greatest scientific minds were deeply committed to beliefs that do not fit present-day notions of science. Newton, again, is the most striking case in point. The great twentieth-century economist John Maynard Keynes was one of the first to read through Newton's private manuscripts. On the three hundredth anniversary of Newton's birth (the celebration of which was delayed because of the Second World War), Keynes offered the following reappraisal of the great scientist:

> I believe that Newton was different from the conventional picture of him. . . .
>
> In the eighteenth century and since, Newton came to be thought of as the first and greatest of the modern age of scientists, a rationalist, one who taught us to think on the lines of cold and untinctured reason.
>
> I do not see him in this light. I do not think that any one who has pored over the contents of that box which he packed up when he finally left Cambridge in 1696 and which, though partly dispersed, have come down to us, can see him like that. Newton was not the first of the age of reason. He was the last of the magicians, the last of the Babylonians and Sumerians, the last great mind which looked out on the visible and intellectual world with the same eyes as those who began to build our intellectual inheritance rather less than 10,000 years ago.

Like his predecessors, Newton saw the world as God's message to humanity, a text to be deciphered. Close reading and study would unlock its mysteries. This same impulse led Newton to read accounts of magic, investigate alchemist's claims that base metals could be turned into gold, and to immerse himself in the writings of the Church fathers and in the Bible, which he knew in intimate detail. If these activities sound unscientific from the perspective of the present, it is because the strict distinction between rational inquiry and belief in the occult or religious traditions simply did not exist in his time. Such a distinction is a product of the long history of scientific developments after the eighteenth century. Newton, then, was the last representative of an older tradition, and also, quite unintentionally, the first of a new one.

What, then, did the scientific revolution change? Seventeenth-century natural philosophers had produced new answers to fundamental questions about the physical world. Age-old questions about astronomy and physics had been recast and, to some extent (although it was not

ESTABLISHMENT OF THE ACADEMY OF SCIENCES AND FOUNDATION OF THE OBSERVATORY, 1667. The 1666 founding of the Academy of Sciences was a measure of the new prestige of science and the potential value of research. Louis XIV sits at the center, surrounded by the religious and scholarly figures who offer the fruits of their knowledge to the French state. ▪ *What was the value of science for absolutist rulers like Louis?*

yet clear to what extent), answered. In the process, there had developed a new approach to amassing and integrating information in a systematic way, an approach that helped yield more insights into the workings of nature as time went on. In this period, too, the most innovative scientific work moved out of the restrictive environment of the Church and the universities. Natural philosophers began talking to and working with each other in lay organizations that developed standards of research. England's Royal Society spawned imitators in Florence and Berlin and later in Russia. The French Royal Academy of Sciences had a particularly direct relationship with the monarchy and the French state. France's statesmen exerted control over the academy and sought to share in the rewards of any discoveries its members made.

New, too, were beliefs about the purpose and methods of science. The practice of breaking a complex problem down into parts made it possible to tackle more and different questions in the physical sciences. Mathematics assumed a more central role in the new science. Finally, rather than simply confirming established truths, the new methods were designed to explore the unknown and provide means to discover new truths. As Kepler wrote to Galileo, "How great a difference there is between theoretical speculation and visual experience, between Ptolemy's discussion of the Antipodes and Columbus's discovery of the New World." Knowledge itself was reconceived. In the older model, to learn was to read: to reason logically, to argue, to compare classical texts, and to absorb a finite body of knowledge. In the newer one, to learn was to discover, and what could be discovered was boundless.

CONCLUSION

The pioneering natural philosophers remained circumspect about their abilities. Some sought to lay bare the workings of the universe; others believed humans could only catalog and describe the regularities observed in nature. By unspoken but seemingly mutual agreement, the question of first causes was left aside. The new science did not say *why*, but *how*. Newton, for one, worked toward explanations that would reveal the logic of creation laid out in mathematics. Yet, in the end, he settled for theories explaining motions and relationships that could be observed and tested.

The eighteenth-century heirs to Newton were much more daring. Laboratory science and the work of the

After You Read This Chapter

(S) Visit StudySpace for quizzes, additional review materials, and multimedia documents. **wwnorton.com/web/westernciv18**

REVIEWING THE OBJECTIVES

- The scientific revolution marked a shift toward new forms of explanation in descriptions of the natural world. What made the work of scientists during this period different from earlier forms of knowledge or research?

- The scientific revolution nevertheless depended on earlier traditions of philosophical thought. What earlier traditions proved important in fostering a spirit of scientific investigation?

- Astronomical observations played a central role in the scientific revolution. What technological innovations made new astronomical work possible, and what conclusions did astronomers reach using these new technologies?

- Central to the scientific revolution was the rejection of the Ptolemaic view of the universe and its replacement by the Copernican model. What was this controversy about?

- Francis Bacon and René Descartes had contrasting ideas about scientific method. What approach to science did each of these natural philosophers defend?

scientific societies largely stayed true to the experimenters' rules and limitations. But as we will see in the next chapter, the natural philosophers who began investigating the human sciences cast aside some of their predecessors' caution. Society, technology, government, religion, even the individual human mind seemed to be mechanisms or parts of a larger nature waiting for study. The scientific revolution overturned the natural world as it had been understood for a millennium; it also inspired thinkers more interested in revolutions in society.

PEOPLE, IDEAS, AND EVENTS IN CONTEXT

- How did the traditions of **NEOPLATONISM, RENAISSANCE,** and **HUMANISM** contribute to a vision of the physical world that encouraged scientific investigation and explanation?

- In what way did the work of **NICOLAS COPERNICUS, TYCHO BRAHE, JOHANNES KEPLER,** and **GALILEO GALILEI** serve to undermine the intellectual foundations of the **PTOLEMAIC SYSTEM**? Why did their work largely take place outside of the traditional centers of learning in Europe, such as universities?

- What differences in scientific practice arose from **FRANCIS BACON**'s emphasis on observation and **RENÉ DESCARTES**'s insistence that knowledge could only be derived from unquestionable first principles?

- What were **ISAAC NEWTON**'s major contributions to the scientific revolution? Why have some suggested that Newton's interests and thinking were not all compatible with modern conceptions of scientific understanding?

- What was important about the establishment of institutions such as the British **ROYAL SOCIETY** or the French **ACADEMY OF SCIENCES** for the development of scientific methods and research?

- What prevented women from entering most of Europe's scientific academies? How did educated women such as **LAURA BASSI, MARGARET CAVENDISH, MARIA WINKELMANN,** and **MARIA SYBILLA MERIAN** gain the skills necessary to participate in scientific work?

THINKING ABOUT CONNECTIONS

- How did ideas about the value of ancient scholarship and philosophy change after the development of new sciences of observation in the seventeenth century?

- What possible connections might be made between the intellectual developments in scientific thinking during the seventeenth century and the Reformation of the sixteenth century? Was the new science incompatible with religious faith?

STORY LINES

- In the eighteenth century, intellectuals in Europe sought to answer questions about the nature of good government, morality, and the social order by applying principles of rational argument. They questioned the value of traditional institutions and insisted that "enlightened" reason could solve social problems better than age-old customs.

- Population growth, economic development, and colonial expansion to other continents created new sources of prosperity in western Europe, fostering a new kind of consumer culture and a new awareness of the world's diversity of peoples and customs.

- Absolutist rulers used Enlightenment ideals to justify the centralization of authority and the establishment of rationalized bureaucracies. Enlightenment ideas also helped establish a radical critique of the eighteenth-century social and political order.

CHRONOLOGY

1734	Voltaire (1694–1778), *Philosophical Letters*
1740–80	Maria Theresa of Austria
1740–86	Frederick II of Prussia
1748	Baron Montesquieu (1689–1755), *The Spirit of Laws*
1748	David Hume (1711–1776), *Enquiries Concerning Human Understanding*
1751–72	Denis Diderot (1713–1784), *Encyclopedia*
1756–63	The Seven Years' War
1762–96	Catherine the Great of Russia
1762	Jean-Jacques Rousseau (1712–1778), *The Social Contract*
1776	The American Revolution begins
1776	Adam Smith (1723–1790), *Inquiry into the Nature and Causes of the Wealth of Nations*
1792	Mary Wollstonecraft (1759–1797), *A Vindication of the Rights of Woman*

Before
You
Read
This
Chapter

Europe during the Enlightenment

I n 1762, the *Parlement* (law court) of Toulouse, in France, convicted Jean Calas of murdering his son. Calas was Protestant in a region where Catholic–Protestant tensions ran high. Witnesses claimed that the young Calas had wanted to convert to Catholicism, and the father had killed him to prevent this conversion. Following French law, Jean Calas was tortured twice: first to force a confession and, next, to identify his alleged accomplices. His arms and legs were slowly pulled apart, gallons of water were poured down his throat, and his body was publicly broken on the wheel, each of his limbs smashed with an iron bar. Then the executioner cut off his head. Throughout the trial, torture, and execution, Calas maintained his innocence. Two years later, the Parlement reversed its verdict, declared Calas not guilty, and offered the family a payment in compensation.

François Marie Arouet, also known as Voltaire, was appalled by the verdict and punishment. At the time of the case, Voltaire was the most famous personality in the European intellectual movement known as the Enlightenment. Prolific and well connected, Voltaire took up his pen to clear Calas's name. He hired

547

THE CRUEL DEATH OF CALAS. This print, reproduced in a pamphlet that circulated in Britain in the late eighteenth century, portrayed the French Protestant Jean Calas as a martyr to his beliefs and directly implicated the Roman Catholic Church in the cruelty of his execution by placing an enthusiastic priest prominently at the scene. The pamphlet may also have sought to reinforce anti-French sentiments among an increasingly nationalistic British population. ▪ *How might Enlightenment authors have used such a scene to promote their message of toleration?* ▪ *How might Church officials have responded to such attacks?*

and from the Italian writer Cesare Beccaria, whose *On Crimes and Punishments* appeared in 1764. Voltaire's reputation did not rest on his originality as a philosopher. It came from his effectiveness as a writer and advocate, his desire and ability to reach a wide audience in print.

The emergence of this wide audience for Voltaire's writings was just as significant as the arguments that he made. The growth of European cities, the spread of literacy and new forms of social interaction at all levels of society helped fuel the Enlightenment's atmosphere of critical reflection about religion, law, the power of the state, and the dignity of the individual. The fact that a writer such as Voltaire could become a celebrity showed that a new kind of literate reading public had developed in Europe. Enough people who read and had income to spare on printed material created a market for newspapers and novels, which in turn showed the emergence of a new kind of consumer society. The works of writers like Voltaire and his peers were discussed over sweetened caffeinated drinks in coffeehouses and cafes where ordinary people gathered to smoke and debate the issues of the day. (Coffee, sugar, and tobacco all came from the Atlantic colonial trade.) Similar scenes took place in the homes of aristocrats. The Enlightenment was thus not only an intellectual movement—it was a cultural phenomenon, which exposed an increasingly broad part of the population to new forms of consumption, of goods as well as ideas.

PROSPERITY, COMMERCE, AND CONSUMPTION

The Enlightenment's audience consisted of urban readers and consumers who were receptive to new cultural forms: the essay, the political tract, the satirical engraving, the novel, the newspaper, theatrical spectacles, and even musical performances. Clearly, such developments could only occur in a society where significant numbers of people had achieved a level of wealth that freed them from the immediate cares of daily sustenance. By the beginning of the eighteenth century, this level of wealth had been achieved in the cities of northwestern Europe. The North Atlantic economies of France and

lawyers for the family and wrote briefs, letters, and essays to bring the case to the public eye. These essays circulated widely among an increasingly literate middle-class audience. For Voltaire, Calas's case exemplified nearly everything he found backward in European culture. Intolerance, ignorance, and religious "fanaticism" had made a travesty of justice. "Shout everywhere, I beg you, for Calas and against fanaticism, for it is this infamy that has caused their misery." Torture demonstrated the power of the courts but could not uncover the truth. Secret interrogations, trials behind closed doors, summary judgment (Calas was executed the day after being convicted, with no review by a higher court), and barbaric punishments defied reason, morality, and human dignity. Any criminal, however wretched, "is a man," wrote Voltaire, "and you are accountable for his blood."

Voltaire's writings on the Calas case illustrate the classic concerns of the Enlightenment: the dangers of arbitrary and unchecked authority, the value of religious toleration, and the overriding importance of law, reason, and human dignity in all affairs. He borrowed most of his arguments from others—from his predecessor the Baron de Montesquieu

Britain, in particular, made these two countries the preponderant powers both in Europe and the wider world.

Economic Growth in Eighteenth-Century Europe

Rapid economic and demographic growth in northwestern Europe was made possible by cheaper food and declines in mortality from infectious disease. In Britain and Holland, new intensive agricultural systems produced more food per acre. Improved transportation and new farming methods resulted in fewer famines and a better-nourished population. New crops, especially maize and potatoes from the Americas, also increased the supply of food. Infectious disease continued to kill half of all Europeans before the age of twenty, but plague was ceasing to be a major killer, as a degree of immunity (perhaps the result of a genetic mutation) began to emerge within the European population. Better diet and improved sanitation may also have

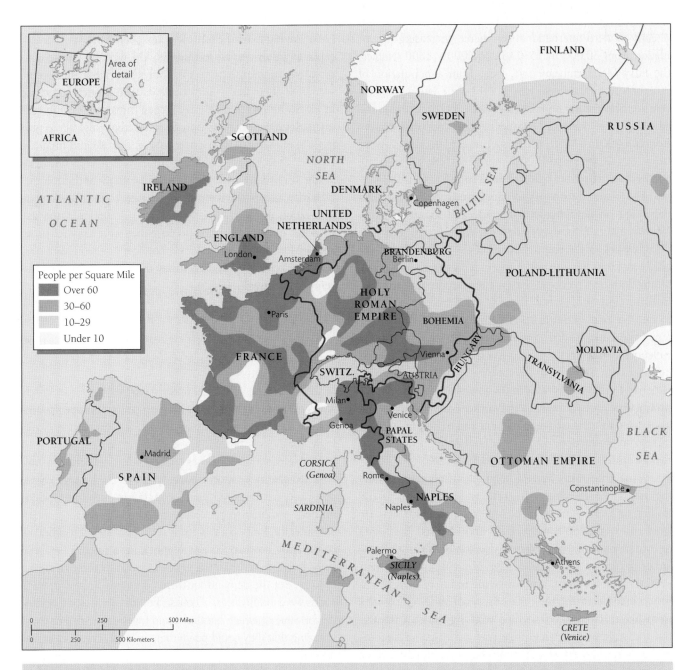

POPULATION GROWTH C. 1600. ▪ *Where did the population grow more rapidly?* ▪ *Why were the largest gains in population on the coasts?* ▪ *How did urbanization affect patterns of life and trade?*

reduced infection rates from typhoid, cholera, smallpox, and measles.

Northwestern Europe was also increasingly urbanized. The total number of urban dwellers in Europe did not change much between 1600 and 1800. At both dates, approximately 200 cities in Europe had a population of over 10,000. These cities were increasingly concentrated in northern and western Europe, however, and the largest experienced extraordinary growth, especially those connected with Atlantic trade. Cities such as Hamburg in Germany, Liverpool in England, Toulon in France, and Cádiz in Spain grew by about 250 percent between 1600 and 1750. Amsterdam, the hub of early modern international commerce, increased in population from 30,000 in 1530 to 200,000 by 1800. Naples, the busy Mediterranean port, went from a population of 300,000 in 1600 to nearly 500,000 by the late eighteenth century. Spectacular population growth also occurred in the administrative capitals of Europe: London's population grew from 674,000 in 1700 to 860,000 a century later; Paris's went from 180,000 people in 1600 to more than 500,000 in 1800; and Berlin's grew from 6,500 in 1661 to 140,000 in 1783.

The rising prosperity of northwestern Europe also depended on developments in trade and manufacturing. Improvements in transportation led entrepreneurs to produce textiles in the countryside. They distributed, or "put out," wool and flax to rural workers who spun it and wove it into cloth on a piece-rate basis. The entrepreneur sold the finished cloth in a market that extended from local towns to international exporters. For country dwellers, this system (sometimes called "protoindustrialization") provided welcome employment during slack seasons of the agricultural year. The system also allowed merchants to avoid expensive guild restrictions in the towns and reduced their production costs. Urban cloth workers suffered, but the system led to increased employment and to higher levels of industrial production, not only for textiles but also for iron, metalworking, and even toy and clock making.

Some cities also became manufacturing centers during the eighteenth century. In northern France, many of the million or so men and women employed in the textile trade lived and worked in Amiens, Lille, and Rheims. The rulers of Prussia made it their policy to develop Berlin as a manufacturing center, taking advantage of an influx of French Protestants to establish a silk-weaving industry there. Most urban manufacturing took place in small shops employing from five to twenty journeymen working under a master. But the scale of such enterprise was growing and becoming more specialized, as workshops began to group together to form a single manufacturing district in which several thousand workers might be employed to produce the same product.

Techniques in some crafts remained much as they had been for centuries. In others, however, inventions changed the pattern of work as well as the nature of the product. Knitting frames, simple devices to speed the manufacture of textile goods, made their appearance in Britain and Holland. Wire-drawing machines and slitting mills, which allowed nail makers to convert iron bars into rods, spread from Germany into Britain. Techniques for printing colored designs directly on calico cloth were imported from Asia. New and more efficient printing presses appeared, first in Holland and then elsewhere.

Workers did not readily accept innovations of this kind. Labor-saving machines threw people out of work. Artisans, especially those organized into guilds, were by nature conservative, anxious to protect not only their rights but also the secrets of their trade. Governments would often intervene to block the use of machines if they threatened to increase unemployment or create unrest. States might also act to protect the interests of their powerful commercial and financial backers. Both Britain and France outlawed calico printing for a time, to protect local textile manufacturers and importers of Indian goods. Mercantilist doctrines could also impede innovation. In both Paris and Lyons, for example, the use of indigo dyes was banned because they were manufactured abroad. But the pressures for economic innovation were irresistible, because behind them lay an insatiable eighteenth-century appetite for goods.

A World of Goods

In the eighteenth century, a mass market for consumer goods emerged, concentrated at first in northwestern Europe. Houses became larger, particularly in towns; but even more strikingly, the houses of middling ranks were now stocked with hitherto uncommon luxuries such as sugar, tobacco, tea, coffee, chocolate, newspapers, books, pictures, clocks, toys, china, glassware, pewter, silver plate, soap, razors, furniture (including beds with mattresses, chairs, and chests of drawers), shoes, cotton cloth, and spare clothing. Demand for such products consistently outstripped the supply, causing prices for these items to rise faster than the price of foodstuffs throughout the century. But the demand for them continued unabated. Such goods were indulgences, of course, but they were also repositories of value in which families could invest their surplus cash, knowing that they could pawn them in hard times if cash was needed.

The exploding consumer economy of the eighteenth century also encouraged the provision of services. In eighteenth-century Britain, the service sector was the

TOPSY-TURVY WORLD BY JAN STEEN. This Dutch painting depicts a household in the throes of the exploding consumer economy that hit Europe in the eighteenth century. Consumer goods ranging from silver and china to clothing and furniture cluttered the houses of ordinary people as never before.

fastest-growing part of the economy, outstripping both agriculture and manufacturing. Almost everywhere in urban Europe, the eighteenth century was the golden age of the small shopkeeper. People bought more prepared foods and more ready-made (as opposed to personally tailored) clothing. Advertising became an important part of doing business, helping create demand for new products and shaping popular taste for changing fashions. Even political allegiances could be expressed through consumption when people purchased plates and glasses commemorating favorite rulers or causes.

The result of all these developments was a European economy vastly more complex, more specialized, more integrated, more commercialized, and more productive than anything the world had seen before. These developments necessarily affected the way people thought of the world and their place in it—above all, people in the Enlightenment shared a sense of living in a time marked by change. Many Enlightenment thinkers defended such changes as "progress." Others were more critical, fearing that valued traditions were being lost. Such debates lay at the heart of Enlightenment thought.

The Foundations of the Enlightenment

Enlightenment thinkers did not agree on everything, but most shared a sense that they lived in an exciting moment in history in which human reason would prevail over the accumulated superstitions and traditions of the past. Enlightenment authors believed themselves to be the defenders of a new ideal, "the party of humanity."

The confidence that Enlightenment thinkers placed in the powers of human reason stemmed from the accomplishments of the scientific revolution. Even when the details of Newton's physics were poorly understood, his methods provided a model for scientific inquiry into other phenomena. Nature operated according to laws that could be grasped by study, observation, and thought. The work of the Scottish writer David Hume (*A Treatise of Human Nature,* 1739–40, and the *Enquiries Concerning Human Understanding,* 1748) provided the most direct bridge from science to the Enlightenment. Newton had refused speculation about ultimate causes, arguing instead for a precise description of natural phenomena (see Chapter 16). Hume took this same rigor and skepticism to the study of morality, the mind, and government, often drawing analogies to scientific laws. Hume criticized the "passion for hypotheses and systems" that dominated earlier philosophical thinking. Experience and careful observation, he argued, usually did not support the premises on which those systems rested.

Embracing human reason also required confronting the power of Europe's traditional monarchies and the religious institutions that supported them. "Dare to know!" the German philosopher Immanuel Kant challenged his contemporaries in his classic 1784 essay "What Is Enlightenment?" For Kant, the Enlightenment represented a declaration of intellectual independence. (He also called it an awakening and credited Hume with rousing him from his "dogmatic slumber.") Kant likened the intellectual history of humanity to the growth of a child. Enlightenment, in this view, was an escape from humanity's "self-imposed immaturity" and a long overdue break with humanity's self-imposed parental figure, the Catholic Church. Coming of age meant the "determination and courage to think without the guidance of someone else" as an individual. Reason required autonomy, and freedom from tradition.

Enlightenment thinkers nevertheless recognized a great debt to their predecessors, especially John Locke, Francis Bacon, and Isaac Newton. Enlightenment thinkers drew heavily on Locke's studies of human knowledge, especially his *Essay concerning Human Understanding* (1690).

DIVINE LIGHT. The frontispiece for Voltaire's book on the science of Isaac Newton portrays Newton as the source of a divine light that is reflected onto Voltaire's desk through a mirror held by Émilie du Châtelet, the French translator of Newton who also was Voltaire's lover. Newton's clouded throne and the adoring angels holding du Châtelet aloft were familiar motifs from earlier generations of religious paintings, but the significance of the carefully portrayed ray of light is recast by the books, inkwell, and precise scientific measuring tools surrounding Voltaire. ▪ *What does this image say about the relationship between religious thought and Enlightenment science?*

which became a central premise for those who followed, was the goodness and perfectibility of humanity. Building on Locke, eighteenth-century thinkers made education central to their project, because education promised that social progress could be achieved through individual moral improvement. Locke's theories had potentially radical implications for eighteenth-century society: if all humans were capable of reason, education might also level hierarchies of status, sex, or race. As we will see, only a few Enlightenment thinkers made such egalitarian arguments. Still, optimism and a belief in universal human progress constituted a second defining feature of nearly all Enlightenment thinking.

Enlightenment thinkers sought nothing less than the organization of all knowledge. The *scientific method,* by which they meant the empirical observation of particular phenomena to arrive at general laws, offered a way to pursue research in all areas—to study human affairs as well as natural ones. Thus they collected evidence to learn the laws governing the rise and fall of nations, and they compared governmental constitutions to arrive at an ideal and universally applicable political system. As the English poet Alexander Pope stated in his *Essay on Man* (1733), "The science of human nature [may be] like all other sciences reduced to a few clear points," and Enlightenment thinkers became determined to learn exactly what those few clear points were. They took up a strikingly wide array of subjects in this systematic manner: knowledge and the mind, natural history, economics, government, religious beliefs, customs of indigenous peoples in the New World, human nature, and sexual (or what we would call gender) and racial differences.

As one can see from these examples, the culture of the *philosophes*, or Enlightenment thinkers, was international. French became the lingua franca of much Enlightenment discussion, but "French" books were often published in Switzerland, Germany, and Russia. Enlightenment thinkers admired British institutions and British scholarship, and Great Britain produced important Enlightenment thinkers: the historian Edward Gibbon and the Scottish philosophers David Hume and Adam Smith. The philosophes considered the Americans Thomas Jefferson and Benjamin Franklin to be a part of their group. Despite stiffer resistance from religious authorities, stricter state censors, and smaller networks of educated elites, the Enlightenment also flourished across central and southern Europe. Frederick II of Prussia housed Voltaire during one of his exiles from France, and he also patronized a small but unusually productive group of Enlightenment thinkers. Northern Italy was also an important center of Enlightenment thought.

Locke's theories of how humans acquire knowledge gave education and environment a critical role in shaping human character. All knowledge, he argued, originates from sense perception. The human mind at birth is a "blank tablet" (in Latin, *tabula rasa*). Only when an infant begins to perceive the external world with its senses, does anything register in its mind. Education, then, was essential to the creation of a good and moral individual. Locke's starting point,

THE WORLD OF THE PHILOSOPHES

Although Enlightenment thought was European in a broad sense, France provided the stage for some of the most widely followed Enlightenment projects. For this reason, Enlightenment thinkers, regardless of where they lived, are often called by the French word *philosophes*. Hardly any of the philosophes, with the exceptions of David Hume and Immanuel Kant, were true philosophers, in the sense of being highly original abstract thinkers. Most Enlightenment thinkers shunned forms of expression that might seem incomprehensible, priding themselves instead on their clarity. *Philosophe*, in French, simply meant "a free thinker," a person whose reflections were unhampered by the constraints of religion or dogma in any form.

Voltaire

The best known of the philosophes was Voltaire, born François Marie Arouet (1694–1778). As Erasmus two centuries earlier had embodied Christian humanism, Voltaire virtually personified the Enlightenment, commenting on an enormous range of subjects in a wide variety of literary forms. Educated by the Jesuits, he became a gifted and sharp-tongued writer. His gusto for provocation landed him in the Bastille (a notorious prison in Paris) for libel and soon afterward in temporary exile in England. In his three years there, Voltaire became an admirer of British political institutions, British culture, and British science; above all, he became an extremely persuasive convert to the ideas of Newton, Bacon, and Locke. His single greatest accomplishment may have been popularizing Newton's work in France and more generally championing the cause of British empiricism and the scientific method against the more Cartesian French.

Voltaire's *Philosophical Letters* ("*Letters on the English Nation*"), published after his return in 1734, made an immediate sensation. Voltaire's themes were religious and political liberty, and his weapons were comparisons. His admiration for British culture and politics became a stinging critique of France—and other absolutist countries on the Continent. He praised British open-mindedness and empiricism: the country's respect for scientists and its support for research. He considered the relative weakness of the British aristocracy a sign of Britain's political health. Unlike the French, the British respected commerce and people who engage in it, Voltaire wrote. The British tax system was rational, free of the complicated exemptions for the privileged that were ruining French finances. The British House of Commons represented

VOLTAIRE'S *CANDIDE*. Voltaire's best-selling novel gently mocked the optimism of some Enlightenment thinkers. The young Candide's tutor, Pangloss, insisted on repeating that "this is the best of all possible worlds," even as he, Candide, and Candide's love, the beautiful Cunegonde, suffered terrible accidents and misfortune. In the scene shown here Candide is thrown out of the castle by Cunegonde's father, with "great kicks in the rear" after they have been caught kissing behind a screen. This mix of serious message and humorous delivery was quite common in Enlightenment literature. ▪ *How might this combination of humor and philosophic meditation have been received by the educated middle-class audience that made up the readership of works such as* **Candide**?

the middle classes and, in contrast with French absolutism, brought balance to British government and checked arbitrary power. In one of the book's more incendiary passages, he argued that in Britain, violent revolution had actually produced political moderation and stability: "The idol of arbitrary power was drowned in seas of blood. . . . The English nation is the only nation in the world that has succeeded in moderating the power of its kings by resisting them."

Of all Britain's reputed virtues, religious toleration loomed largest of all. Britain, Voltaire argued, brought together citizens of different religions in a harmonious and productive culture. In this and other instances, Voltaire oversimplified: British Catholics, Dissenters, and Jews did not have equal civil rights. Yet the British policy of "toleration" did contrast with Louis XIV's intolerance of Protestants.

Revoking the Edict of Nantes (1685) had stripped French Protestants of civil rights and had helped create the atmosphere in which Jean Calas—and others—were persecuted.

Of all forms of intolerance, Voltaire opposed religious bigotry most, and with real passion he denounced religious fraud, faith in miracles, and superstition. His most famous battle cry was "*Écrasez l'infâme!*" ("Crush this infamous thing"), by which he meant all forms of repression, fanaticism, and bigotry. "The less superstition, the less fanaticism; and the less fanaticism, the less misery." He did not oppose religion per se; rather, he sought to rescue morality, which he believed to come from God, from dogma—elaborate ritual, dietary laws, formulaic prayers—and from a powerful Church bureaucracy. He argued for common sense and simplicity, persuaded that these would bring out the goodness in humanity and establish stable authority. "The simpler the laws are, the more the magistrates are respected; the simpler the religion will be, the more one will revere its ministers. Religion can be simple. When enlightened people will announce a single God, rewarder and avenger, no one will laugh, everyone will obey."

Voltaire relished his position as a critic, and he was regularly exiled from France and other countries, his books banned and burned. As long as his plays attracted large audiences, however, the French king felt he had to tolerate their author. Voltaire had an attentive international public, including Frederick of Prussia, who invited him to his court at Berlin, and Catherine of Russia, with whom he corresponded about reforms she might introduce in Russia. When he died in 1778, a few months after a triumphant return to Paris, he was possibly the best-known writer in Europe.

Montesquieu

The Baron de Montesquieu (*mahn-tuhs-KYOO,* 1689–1755) was a very different kind of Enlightenment figure. Montesquieu was born to a noble family. He inherited both an estate and, since state offices were property that passed from father to son, a position as magistrate in the Parlement of Bordeaux. He was not a stylist or a provocateur like Voltaire but a relatively cautious jurist, though he did write a satirical novel, *The Persian Letters* (1721), as a young man. The novel, which he published anonymously in Amsterdam, was composed as letters from two Persian visitors to France. The visitors detailed the odd religious superstitions they witnessed, compared manners at the French court with those in Turkish harems, and likened French absolutism to their own brands of *despotism,* or the abuse of government authority. *The Persian Letters* was an immediate best seller, which inspired many imitators,

MONTESQUIEU. The French baron's *Spirit of Laws* (1748) was probably the most influential single text of the Enlightenment. Montesquieu's suggestion that liberty could best be preserved in a government whose powers were divided among executive, legislative, and judicial functions had a notable influence on the authors of the U.S. Constitution.

as other authors used the formula of a foreign observer to criticize contemporary French society.

Montesquieu's treatise, *The Spirit of Laws* (1748), may have been the most influential work of the Enlightenment. It was a groundbreaking study in what we would call comparative historical sociology and very Newtonian in its careful, empirical approach. Montesquieu asked about the structures that shaped law. How had different environments, histories, and religious traditions combined to create such a variety of governmental institutions? What were the different forms of government: what spirit characterized each, and what were their respective virtues and shortcomings?

Montesquieu suggested that there were three forms of government: republics, monarchies, and despotisms. A republic was governed by many individuals—either an elite aristocracy of citizens or the people as a whole. The soul of a republic was virtue, which allowed individual citizens to transcend their particular interests and rule in accordance with the common good. In a monarchy, on the other hand, one person ruled in accordance with the law. The soul of a monarchy, wrote Montesquieu, was honor, which gave individuals an incentive to behave with loyalty toward their sovereign. The third form of government, despotism, was rule by a single person unchecked by law or other powers. The soul of despotism was fear, since no citizen could feel secure and punishment took the place of education. Lest this seem abstract, Montesquieu devoted two chapters to the French monarchy, in which he spelled out what he saw as a dangerous drift toward despotism in his own land. Like other Enlightenment thinkers, Montesquieu admired the British system and its separation of the executive, legislative, and judicial functions of government. Such a balance of powers preserved liberty by avoiding a concentration of authority in a single individual or group. His idealization of "checks and balances" had a formative influence on Enlightenment political theorists and helped to guide the authors of the U.S. Constitution in 1787.

Diderot and the Encyclopedia

The most remarkable and ambitious Enlightenment project was a collective one: the *Encyclopedia*. The *Encyclopedia* claimed to summarize all the most advanced contemporary philosophical, scientific, and technical knowledge, making it available to any reader. It demonstrated how scientific analysis could be applied in nearly all realms of thought, and it further aimed to encourage critical reflection of an enormous range of traditions and institutions. The guiding spirit behind the venture was Denis Diderot (1713–1784). Diderot was helped by the mathematician Jean Le Rond d'Alembert (1717–1783) and other leading men of letters, including Voltaire and Montesquieu. Published in installments between 1751 and 1772, the *Encyclopedia* ran to seventeen large volumes of text and eleven more of illustrations, with over 71,000 articles.

Diderot commissioned articles on science and technology, showing how machines worked and illustrating new industrial processes. The point was to demonstrate how science could promote progress and alleviate human misery. Diderot turned the same methods to politics and the social order, including articles on economics, taxes, and the slave trade. Censorship made it difficult to write openly antireligious articles. Diderot thumbed his nose at religion in oblique ways; at the entry on the Eucharist, the reader found a terse cross-reference: "See *cannibalism*." At one point, the French government revoked the publishing permit for the *Encyclopedia*, declaring in 1759 that the encyclopedists were trying to "propagate materialism" (by which they meant atheism) "to destroy Religion, to inspire a spirit of independence, and to nourish the corruption of morals." The volumes sold remarkably well despite such bans and their hefty price. Purchasers belonged to the elite: aristocrats, government officials, prosperous merchants, and a scattering of

TECHNOLOGY AND INDUSTRY. This engraving, from the mining section, is characteristic of Diderot's *Encyclopedia*. The project aimed to detail technological changes, manufacturing processes, and forms of labor—all in the name of advancing human knowledge.

members of the higher clergy. That elite stretched across Europe, including its overseas colonies.

Although the French philosophes sparred with the state and the church, they sought political stability and reform. Montesquieu hoped that an enlightened aristocracy would press for reforms and defend liberty against a despotic king. Voltaire, persuaded that aristocrats would represent only their particular narrow interests, looked to an enlightened monarch for leadership. Neither was a democrat, and neither conceived of reform from below. Still, their widely read critiques of arbitrary power stung. By the 1760s, the French critique of despotism provided the language in which many people across Europe articulated their opposition to existing regimes.

MAJOR THEMES OF ENLIGHTENMENT THOUGHT

Enlightenment thinkers across Europe raised similar themes: humanitarianism, or the dignity and worth of all individuals; religious toleration; and liberty. These ideals inspired important debates about three issues in particular: law and punishment, the place of religious minorities, and the state's relationship to society and the economy.

Law and Punishment

The Enlightenment beliefs about education and the perfectibility of human society led many thinkers to question the harsh treatment of criminals by European courts. An influential work by the Italian jurist Cesare Beccaria (1738–1794), *On Crimes and Punishments* (1764), provided Voltaire with most of his arguments in the Calas case. Beccaria criticized the use of arbitrary power and attacked the prevalent view that punishments should represent society's vengeance on the criminal. The only legitimate rationale for punishment was to maintain social order and to prevent other crimes. Beccaria argued for the greatest possible leniency compatible with deterrence; respect for individual dignity dictated that humans should punish other humans no more than is absolutely necessary.

Above all, Beccaria's book eloquently opposed torture and the death penalty. Public execution, he argued, was intended to dramatize the power of the state and the horrors of hell, but it dehumanized the victim, judge, and spectators. In 1766, a few years after the Calas case, another French trial provided an example of what horrified Beccaria and the philosophes. A nineteen-year-old French nobleman, convicted of blasphemy, had his tongue cut out and his hand cut off before he was burned at the stake. The court discovered the blasphemer had read Voltaire, and it ordered his *Philosophical Dictionary* burned along with the body. Sensational cases such as this helped publicize Beccaria's work. *On Crimes and Punishments* was quickly translated into a dozen languages. Owing primarily to its influence, most European countries by around 1800 abolished torture, branding, whipping, and mutilation and reserved the death penalty for capital crimes.

Humanitarianism and Religious Toleration

Humanitarianism and reason also counseled religious toleration. Enlightenment thinkers spoke almost as one on the need to end religious warfare and the persecution of heretics and religious minorities. Most Enlightenment authors distinguished between religious belief, which they accepted, and the Church as an institution and as dogma, which they rebelled against. It was in this sense that Voltaire opposed the Church's influence over society. Few Enlightenment authors were atheists—a notable exception was Paul-Henri d'Holbach (1723–1789)—and only a few more were agnostics. Many, including Voltaire, were deists, believing in a God that acted as a "divine watchmaker" who at the beginning of time constructed a perfect universe and left it to run with predictable regularity. Enlightenment inquiry proved compatible with very different stances on religion.

Nevertheless, Enlightenment support for toleration was sometimes limited. Most Christians saw Jews as heretics and Christ killers. Although Enlightenment thinkers deplored persecution, they commonly viewed Judaism and Islam as backward, superstitious religions. One of the few Enlightenment figures to treat Jews sympathetically was the German philosophe Gotthold Lessing (1729–1781). Lessing's play *Nathan the Wise* (1779) takes place in Jerusalem during the Fourth Crusade and begins with a pogrom—or violent,

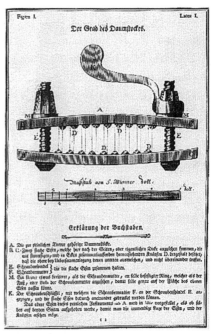

INSTRUMENTS OF TORTURE. A man being stretched on the rack (left) and a thumbscrew (right), both from an official Austrian government handbook. By 1800, Beccaria's influence had helped phase out the use of such instruments.

orchestrated attack—in which the wife and children of Nathan, a Jewish merchant, are murdered. Nathan survives to become a sympathetic and wise father figure. He adopts a Christian-born daughter and raises her with three religions: Christianity, Islam, and Judaism. At several points, authorities ask him to choose the single true religion. Nathan shows none exists. The three great monotheistic religions are three versions of the truth. Religion is authentic, or true, only insofar as it makes the believer virtuous.

Lessing modeled his hero on his friend Moses Mendelssohn (1729–1786), a self-educated rabbi and bookkeeper (and the grandfather of the composer Felix Mendelssohn). Moses Mendelssohn moved—though with some difficulty—between the Enlightenment circles of Frederick II and the Jewish community of Berlin. Repeatedly attacked and invited to convert to Christianity, he defended Jewish communities against anti-Semitic policies and Judaism against Enlightenment criticism. At the same time, he also promoted reform within the Jewish community, arguing that his community had special reason to embrace the broad Enlightenment project: religious faith should be voluntary, states should promote tolerance, humanitarianism would bring progress to all.

Government, Administration, and the Economy

Enlightenment ideas had a very real influence over affairs of state. The philosophes defended reason and knowledge for humanitarian reasons. But they also promised to make nations stronger, more efficient, and more prosperous. Beccaria's proposed legal reforms were a good case in point; he sought to make laws not simply more just but also more effective. In other words, the Enlightenment spoke to individuals but also to states. The philosophes addressed issues of liberty and rights but also took up matters of administration, tax collection, and economic policy.

The rising fiscal demands of eighteenth-century states and empires made these issues newly urgent. Which economic resources were most valuable to states? In the seventeenth century, mercantilists had argued that regulation of trade was necessary to maximize government revenues (see Chapter 15). In the eighteenth century, Enlightenment economic thinkers known as the physiocrats argued that real wealth came from the land and agricultural production, which prospered with less government interference. They advocated simplifying the tax system and following a policy of laissez-faire, which comes from the French expression *laissez faire la nature* ("let nature take its course"), letting wealth and goods circulate without government interference.

LESSING AND MENDELSSOHN. This painting of a meeting between the philosophe Gotthold Lessing (standing) and his friend Moses Mendelssohn (seated right) emphasizes the personal nature of their intellectual relationship, which transcended their religious backgrounds (Christian and Jewish, respectively). The Enlightenment's atmosphere of earnest discussion is invoked both by the open book before them and the shelf of reading material behind Lessing. Compare this image of masculine discussion (note the role of the one woman in the painting) with the image of the aristocratic salon on page 570 and the coffeehouse on page 571. ■ *What similarities and differences might one point to in these various illustrations of the Enlightenment public sphere?*

The classic expression of laissez-faire economics, however, came from the Scottish economist Adam Smith (1723–1790) and his landmark treatise, *Inquiry into the Nature and Causes of the Wealth of Nations* (1776). Smith disagreed with the physiocrats on the value of agriculture, but he shared their opposition to mercantilism. For Smith, the central issues were the productivity of labor and how labor was used in different sectors of the economy. Mercantile restrictions—such as high taxes on imported goods, one of the grievances of the colonists throughout the American empires—did not encourage the productive deployment of labor and thus did not create real economic health. For Smith, general prosperity could be obtained by allowing the famous "invisible hand" of competition to guide economic activity. Individuals, in other words, should pursue their own interests by buying and selling goods and labor freely on the open market without interference from state-chartered monopolies or legal restraints. As Smith wrote in his earlier *Theory of Moral Sentiments* (1759), self-interested individuals could be "led by an invisible hand . . . without knowing it, without intending it, [to] advance the interest of the society."

The Wealth of Nations spelled out, in more technical and historical detail, the different stages of economic development, how the invisible hand actually worked, and the beneficial aspects of competition. Its perspective owed much to Newton and to the Enlightenment's idealization of both nature and human nature. Smith thought of himself as the champion of liberty against state-sponsored economic privilege and monopolies. And he became the most influential of the new eighteenth-century economic thinkers. In the following century, his work and his followers became the target of reformers and critics who had less faith in the power of markets to generate wealth and prosperity for all.

EMPIRE AND ENLIGHTENMENT

The colonial world loomed large in Enlightenment thinking. Enlightenment thinkers saw the Americas as an uncorrupted territory where humanity's natural simplicity was expressed in the lives of native peoples. In comparison, Europe and Europeans appeared decadent or corrupt. European colonial activities—especially the slave trade—raised pressing issues about humanitarianism, individual rights, and natural law. The effects of colonialism on Europe were a central Enlightenment theme.

Smith wrote in *The Wealth of Nations* that the "discovery of America, and that of a passage to the East Indies by the cape of Good Hope are the two greatest and most important events recorded in the history of mankind. What benefits, or what misfortunes to mankind may hereafter result from those great events," he continued, "no human wisdom can foresee." Smith's language was nearly identical to that of a Frenchman, the abbé Guillaume Thomas François Raynal. Raynal's massive *Philosophical and Political History of European Settlements and Trade in the Two Indies* (1770), a coauthored work like the *Encyclopedia,* was one of the most widely read works of the Enlightenment, going through twenty printings and at least forty pirated editions. Raynal drew his inspiration from the *Encyclopedia* and aimed at nothing less than a total history of colonization: customs and civilizations of indigenous peoples, natural history, exploration, and commerce in the Atlantic world and India.

Raynal also asked whether colonization had made humanity happier, more peaceful, or better. The question was fully in the spirit of the Enlightenment. So was the answer: Raynal believed that industry and trade brought improvement and progress. Like other Enlightenment writers, however, he and his coauthors considered natural simplicity an antidote to the corruptions of their culture. They sought out and idealized what they considered examples of "natural" humanity, many of them in the New World. What Europeans considered savage life might be "a hundred times preferable to that of societies corrupted by despotism," and they lamented the loss of humanity's "natural liberty." They condemned the tactics of the Spanish in Mexico and Peru, of the Portuguese in Brazil, and of the British in North America. They echoed Montesquieu's theme that good government required checks and balances against arbitrary authority. In the New World, they argued, Europeans found themselves with virtually unlimited power, which encouraged them to be arrogant, cruel, and despotic. In a later edition, after the outbreak of the American Revolution, the book went even further, drawing parallels between exploitation in the colonial world and inequality at home: "We are mad in the way we act with our colonies, and inhuman and mad in our conduct toward our peasants," asserted one author. Eighteenth-century radicals repeatedly warned that overextended empires sowed seeds of decadence and corruption at home.

Such critiques did little, however, to check the growing importance of colonial commerce in the eighteenth century. The wealth generated by colonial trade tied the interests of governments and transoceanic merchants in an increasingly tight embrace. Merchants engaged in the colonial trade depended on their governments to protect and defend their overseas investments; but governments in turn depended on merchants and their financial backers to build the ships and sustain the trade on which national power depended. As this colonial trade grew in importance, no issue challenged Enlightenment thinkers as much as the institution of slavery, which was central to the Atlantic trade.

Slavery and the Atlantic World

The Atlantic slave trade (see Chapter 14) reached its peak in the eighteenth century. European slave traders sent at least 1 million Africans into New World slavery in the late seventeenth century, and at least 6 million in the eighteenth century. Control of the slave trade became fundamental to great power politics in Europe during this period, as the British used their dominance of the trade to their advantage in their long-running competition with France.

Analyzing Primary Sources

The Impact of the New World on Enlightenment Thinkers

The abbé Guillaume Thomas François Raynal (1713–1796) was a clergyman and intellectual who moved in the inner circles of the Enlightenment. As a senior cleric, he had access to the royal court; as a writer and intellectual, he worked with the encyclopedists and other authors who criticized France's institutions, including the Catholic Church of which Raynal himself was a part. Here, he tries to offer a perspective on the profound effects of discovering the Americas and ends by asking whether particular historical developments and institutions lead to the betterment of society.

here has never been any event which has had more impact on the human race in general and for Europeans in particular, as that of the discovery of the New World, and the passage to the Indies around the Cape of Good Hope. It was then that a commercial revolution began, a revolution in the balance of power, and in the customs, the industries and the government of every nation. It was through this event that men in the most distant lands were linked by new relationships and new needs. The produce of equatorial regions were consumed in polar climes. The industrial products of the north were transported to the south; the textiles of the Orient became the luxuries of Westerners; and everywhere men mutually exchanged their opinions, their laws, their customs, their illnesses, and their medicines, their virtues and their vices. Everything changed, and will go on changing. But will the changes of the past and those that are to come be useful to humanity? Will they give man one day more peace, more happiness, or more pleasure? Will his condition be better, or will it be simply one of constant change?

Source: Abbé Guillaume Thomas François Raynal, *Philosophical and Political History of European Settlements and Trade in the Two Indies* (1770), as cited in Dorinda Outram, *The Enlightenment* (Cambridge: 1995), p. 73.

Questions for Analysis

1. Why does Raynal attribute such significance to the voyages of exploration that connected Europe to the Americas and to Africa and Asia? Which peoples were changed by these voyages?

2. Why is Raynal concerned with people's conduct and happiness rather than, say, the wealth of states?

3. Is Raynal clear about whether the changes he enumerates are a gain or a loss for humanity?

Even thinkers as radical as Raynal and Diderot hesitated to criticize the slave trade, however, and their hesitations are revealing about the tensions in Enlightenment thought. Enlightenment thinking began with the premise that individuals could reason for and govern themselves. Individual moral freedom lay at the heart of what the Enlightenment considered to be a just, stable, and harmonious society. Slavery defied natural law and natural freedom. Montesquieu, for instance, wrote that civil law created chains, but natural law would always break them. Nearly all Enlightenment thinkers condemned slavery in the metaphorical sense. That the "mind should break free of its chains" and that "despotism enslaved the king's subjects" were phrases that echoed through much eighteenth-century writing. It was common for the central characters of eighteenth-century fiction, such as Voltaire's hero Candide, to meet enslaved people, learning compassion as part of their moral education. Writers dealt more gingerly, however, with the actual enslavement and slave labor of Africans.

Some Enlightenment thinkers skirted the issue of slavery. Others reconciled principle and practice in different ways. Smith condemned slavery as uneconomical. Voltaire, quick to expose his contemporaries' hypocrisy, wondered whether Europeans would look away if Europeans—rather than Africans—were enslaved. Voltaire, however, did not question his belief that Africans were inferior peoples. Montesquieu (who came from Bordeaux, one of the central ports for the Atlantic trade) believed that slavery debased master and slave alike. But he also argued that all societies balanced their systems of labor in accordance with their different needs, and slave labor was one such system.

Slavery and the Enlightenment

The encyclopedists made an exhaustive and deliberate effort to comment on every institution, trade, and custom in Western culture. The project was conceived as an effort to catalog, analyze, and improve each facet of society. Writing in an age of burgeoning maritime trade and expanding overseas empires, they could not, and did not wish to, avoid the subject of slavery. These were their thoughts on plantation slavery, the African slaves who bore its brunt, and broader questions of law and liberty posed by the whole system.

Thus there is not a single one of these hapless souls—who, we maintain, are but slaves—who does not have the right to be declared free, since he has never lost his freedom; since it was impossible for him to lose it; and since neither his ruler nor his father nor anyone else had the right to dispose of his freedom; consequently, the sale of his person is null and void in and of itself: this Negro does not divest himself, indeed cannot under any condition divest himself of his natural rights; he carries them everywhere with him, and he has the right to demand that others allow him to enjoy those rights. Therefore, it is a clear case of inhumanity on the part of the judges in those free countries to which the slave is shipped, not to free the slave instantly by legal declaration, since he is their brother, having a soul like theirs.

Source: From *Encyclopédie*, vol. 16 (1765), as cited in David Brion Davis, *The Problem of Slavery in Western Culture* (Ithaca, NY: 1966), p. 416.

Questions for Analysis

1. What arguments against slavery does this *Encyclopedia* article present? What "natural rights" were violated by the practice, according to this view?

2. The enslavement of conquered peoples was historically an ancient and well-established custom, approved by civil and religious authorities. Even some Enlightenment figures, such as Thomas Jefferson, were slave owners. How did some Enlightenment philosophes use universal ideas of freedom to argue against custom in regard to slavery and other questions?

Finally, like many Enlightenment thinkers, Montesquieu defended property rights, including those of slaveholders.

The *Encyclopedia*'s article on the slave trade did condemn the slave trade in the clearest possible terms as a violation of self-government. Humanitarian antislavery movements, which emerged in the 1760s, advanced similar arguments. From deploring slavery to imagining freedom for slaves, however, proved a very long step, and one that few were willing to take. In the end, the Enlightenment's environmental determinism—the belief that environment shaped character—provided a common way of postponing the entire issue. Slavery corrupted its victims, destroyed their natural virtue, and crushed their natural love of liberty. Enslaved people, by this logic, were not ready for freedom. It was characteristic for Warville de Brissot's Society of the Friends of Blacks to call for abolition of the slave trade and to invite Thomas Jefferson, a slaveholder, to join the organization. Only a very few advocated abolishing slavery, and they insisted that emancipation be gradual. The debate about slavery demonstrated that different currents in Enlightenment thought could lead to very different conclusions.

Exploration and the Pacific World

The Pacific world also figured prominently in Enlightenment thinking. Systematically mapping new sections of the Pacific was among the crucial developments of the age and had tremendous impact on the public imagination. These explorations were also scientific missions, sponsored as part of the Enlightenment project of expanding scientific knowledge. In 1767, the French government sent Louis-Antoine de Bougainville (1729–1811) to the South Pacific in search of a new route to China, new lands suitable for colonization, and new spices for the ever lucrative trade. Bougainville found none of what he sought, but his travel accounts—above all his fabulously lush descriptions of the earthly paradise of Nouvelle-Cythère, or Tahiti—captured the imaginations of many at home. The British captain James Cook (1728–1779), who followed Bougainville, made two trips into the South Pacific (1768–1771 and 1772–1775), with impressive results. He charted the coasts of New Zealand and New Holland and added the New Hebrides and Hawaii to European maps. He explored the outer limits of the Antarctic continent, the shores of the Bering Sea, and the Arctic Ocean.

The artists and scientists who accompanied Cook and Bougainville vastly expanded the boundaries of European botany, zoology, and geology. Their drawings—such as Sydney Parkinson's extraordinary portraits of the Maori and William Hodge's portraits of Tahitians—appealed to a wide public. So did the accounts of dangers overcome and peoples encountered. A misguided attempt to communicate with South Pacific islanders, perhaps with the intention of conveying them to Europe, ended in the grisly deaths of Cook and four royal marines on Hawaii in late January 1779. Large numbers of people in Europe avidly read travel accounts of these voyages. When Cook and Bougainville brought Pacific islanders to the metropolis, they attracted large crowds.

The Impact of the Scientific Missions

Back in Europe, Enlightenment thinkers drew freely on reports of scientific missions. Since they were already committed to understanding human nature and the origins of society and to studying the effects of the environment on character and culture, stories of new peoples and cultures were immediately fascinating. In 1772, Diderot, one of many eager readers of Bougainville's accounts, published his own reflections on the cultural significance of those accounts, the *Supplément au Voyage de Bougainville*. For Diderot, the Tahitians were the original human beings and, unlike the inhabitants of the New World, were virtually free of European influence. They represented humanity in its natural state, Diderot believed, uninhibited about sexuality and free of religious dogma. Their simplicity exposed the hypocrisy and rigidity of overcivilized Europeans. Others considered the indigenous peoples of the Pacific akin to the classical civiliza-

tions of Greeks and Romans, associating Tahitian women, for instance, with Venus, the Roman goddess of love.

All these views said more about Europe and European utopias than about indigenous cultures in the Pacific. Enlightenment thinkers found it impossible to see other peoples as anything other than primitive versions of Europeans. Even these views, however, marked a change from former times. In earlier periods, Europeans had understood the world as divided between Christendom and heathen others. Now all peoples were seen to be part of a shared humanity, with cultures and beliefs that reflected their own experiences. In sum, during the eighteenth century a religious understanding of Western identity was giving way to more secular and historical explanations for human diversity.

One of the most important scientific explorers of the period was the German scientist Alexander von Humboldt. Humboldt spent five years in Spanish America, aiming to do nothing less than assess the civilization and natural resources of the continent. He went equipped with the most advanced scientific instruments Europe could provide. Humboldt, in good Enlightenment fashion, attempted to demonstrate that climate and physical environment determined which forms of life would survive in any given region. These investigations inspired nineteenth-century discussions of evolutionary change. Charles Darwin referred to Humboldt as "the greatest scientific traveler who ever lived,"

MAORIS IN A WAR CANOE NEAR LOOKOUT POINT. This copy of an illustration by Sydney Parkinson, who accompanied James Cook's explorations, is typical of the images of the South Pacific that may have circulated in Europe in the late eighteenth century.

▪ *What questions might have been prompted among Enlightenment thinkers by an increased awareness of different cultures throughout the globe?*

Interpreting Visual Evidence

The Europeans Encounter the Peoples of the Pacific in the Eighteenth Century

When European explorers set out to map the Pacific, they brought with them artists to paint the landscapes and peoples they encountered. Later, other artists produced engravings of the original paintings and these engravings were made available to a wider public. In this way, even people of modest means or only limited literacy could learn something about the different cultures and peoples that were now in more regular contact with European commerce elsewhere in the world.

These artists documented what they saw, but their vision was also shaped by the ideas that they brought with them and by the classical European styles of portraiture and landscape painting that they had been trained to produce. On the one hand, their images sometimes emphasized the exotic or essentially different quality of life in the Pacific. At the same time, the use of conventional poses in the portraiture or in the depiction of human forms suggested hints of a developing understanding of the extent to which Europeans and people elsewhere in the world shared essential human characteristics. This ambiguity was

A. *Portrait of Omai* by Joshua Reynolds (c. 1774).

B. "Omiah [*sic*] the Indian from Otaheite, presented to their Majesties at Kew," 1774.

and the German scientist's writing inspired Darwin's voyage to the Galápagos Islands off the coast of Ecuador.

Thus Europeans who looked outward did so for a variety of reasons and reached very different conclusions. For some Enlightenment thinkers and rulers, scientific reports from overseas fitted into a broad inquiry about civilization and human nature. That inquiry at times encouraged self-criticism and at others simply shored up Europeans' sense of their superiority. These themes reemerged during the nineteenth century, when new empires were built and the West's place in the world was reassessed.

THE RADICAL ENLIGHTENMENT

How revolutionary was the Enlightenment? Enlightenment thought did undermine central tenets of eighteenth-century culture and politics. It had wide resonance, well beyond a small group of intellectuals. Yet Enlightenment thinkers did not hold to any single political position. Even the most radical among them disagreed on the implications of their thought. Jean-Jacques Rousseau and Mary Wollstonecraft provide good examples of such radical thinkers.

C. *View of the Inside of a House in the Island of Ulietea, with the Representation of a Dance to the Music of the Country,* engraving after Sydney Parkinson, 1773.

The two artists had never visited the South Pacific, and their image is note-worthy for the way that the bodies of the islanders were rendered according to the classical styles of European art.

Questions for Analysis

1. Does the Reynolds portrait, in its choice of posture and expression, imply that Europeans and the peoples of the Pacific might share essential traits? What uses might Enlightenment thinkers have made of such a universalist implication?

2. How might a contemporary person in Britain have reacted to the portrait of Omai kneeling before the king?

3. Do you think image C is an accurate representation of life in the South Pacific? What purpose did such imaginary and idyllic scenes serve for their audience in Europe?

typical of Enlightenment political and social thought, which sought to uncover universal human truths, while at the same time remaining deeply interested and invested in exploring the differences they observed in peoples from various parts of the globe.

The first two images depict a Tahitian named Omai, who came to Britain as a crew member on a naval vessel in July 1774. Taken three days later to meet King George III and Queen Charlotte at Kew (image B), he became a celebrity in England and had his portrait drawn by Joshua Reynolds, a famous painter of the period (image A). The third image is an engraving by two Florentine artists after a drawing by Sydney Parkinson, who was with James Cook on his first voyage to the Pacific in 1768 (image C).

The World of Rousseau

Jean-Jacques Rousseau (*roo-SOH,* 1712–1778) was an "outsider" who quarreled with the other philosophes. He shared the philosophes' search for intellectual and political freedom, and he attacked inherited privilege, yet he introduced other strains into Enlightenment thought, especially what was then called "sensibility," or the cult of feeling. Rousseau's interest in emotions led him to develop a more complicated portrait of human psychology than that of Enlightenment writers, who emphasized reason as the most important attribute of human beings.

He was also considerably more radical than his counterparts, one of the first to talk about popular sovereignty and democracy.

Rousseau's milestone and difficult treatise on politics, *The Social Contract,* began with a now famous paradox: "Man was born free, and everywhere he is in chains." How had humans freely forged these chains? What were the origins of government? Was government's authority legitimate? If not, Rousseau asked, how could it become so?

Rousseau argued that in the state of nature all men had been equal. (On women, men, and nature, see **Competing Viewpoints** on pages 566–67) Social inequality, anchored

Rousseau's Social Contract (1762)

Jean-Jacques Rousseau (1712–1778) was one of the most radical Enlightenment thinkers. In his works, he suggested that humans needed not only a clearer understanding of natural laws but also a much closer relationship with nature itself and a thorough reorganization of society. He believed that a sovereign society, formed by free association of equal citizens without patrons or factions, was the clearest expression of natural law. This society would make laws and order itself by the genuinely collective wisdom of its citizens. Rousseau sets out the definition of his sovereign society and its authority in the passages reprinted here.

Book I, Chapter 6

"To find a form of association that defends and protects the person and possessions of each associate with all the common strength, and by means of which each person, joining forces with all, nevertheless obeys only himself, and remains as free as before." Such is the fundamental problem to which the social contract furnishes the solution.

Book II, Chapter 4

What in fact is an act of sovereignty? It is not an agreement between a superior and an inferior, but an agreement between the body and each of its members, a legitimate agreement, because it is based upon the social contract; equitable, because it is common to all; useful, because it can have no other purpose than the general good; and reliable, because it is guaranteed by the public force and the supreme power. As long as the subjects are only bound by agreements of this sort, they obey no one but their own will, and to ask how far the respective rights of the sovereign and citizens extend is to ask to what point the latter can commit themselves to each other, one towards all and all towards one.

Source: Jean-Jacques Rousseau, *Rousseau's Political Writings*, trans. Julia Conaway Bondanella, ed. Allan Ritter and Julia Conaway Bondanella (New York: 1988), pp. 92–103.

Questions for Analysis

1. What was the goal of political association, according to Rousseau?

2. How did Rousseau claim to overcome the tension between the need for some form of social constraint and the desire to preserve liberty?

3. What is more important for Rousseau: equality or liberty?

---

in private property, profoundly corrupted "the social contract," or the formation of government. Under conditions of inequality, governments and laws represented only the rich and privileged. They became instruments of repression and enslavement. Legitimate governments could be formed, Rousseau argued. "The problem is to find a form of association . . . in which each, while uniting himself with all, may still obey himself alone, and remain as free as before." Freedom did not mean the absence of restraint, it meant that equal citizens obeyed laws they had made themselves. Rousseau hardly imagined any social leveling, and by *equality* he meant only that no one would be "rich enough to buy another, nor poor enough to have to sell oneself."

Rousseau's argument about legitimate authority has three parts. First, sovereignty belonged to the people alone. This meant sovereignty should not be divided among different branches of government (as suggested by Montesquieu), and it could not be usurped by a king. Second, exercising sovereignty transformed the nation. Rousseau argued that when individual citizens formed a "body politic," that body became more than just the sum of its parts. He offered what was to many an appealing image of a regenerated and more powerful nation, in which citizens were bound by mutual obligation rather than coercive laws and united in equality rather than divided and weakened by privilege. Third, the national community would be united by what Rousseau called the "general will." This term is notoriously difficult. Rousseau proposed it as a way to understand the common interest, which rose above particular individual demands. The general will favored equality; that made it general, and in principle at least equality guaranteed that citizens' common interests would be represented in the whole.

Rousseau's lack of concern for balancing private interests against the general will leads some political theorists to

ENLIGHTENMENT EDUCATION AS ILLUSTRATED IN *EMILE*. These colored engravings from Rousseau's influential novel depict Emile's studies in the great outdoors as opposed to the classroom.

consider him authoritarian, coercive, or moralistic. Others interpret the general will as one expression of his utopianism. In the eighteenth century, *The Social Contract* was the least understood of Rousseau's works. Yet it provided influential radical arguments and, more important, extraordinarily powerful images and phrases, which were widely cited during the French Revolution.

Rousseau was also well known for his writing on education and moral virtue. His widely read novel *Emile* (1762) tells the story of a young man who learns virtue and moral autonomy in the school of nature rather than in the academy. Rousseau disagreed with other *philosophes'* emphasis on reason, insisting instead that "the first impulses of nature are always right." Children should not be forced to reason early in life. Books, which "teach us only to talk about things we do not know," should not be central to learning until adolescence. Emile's tutor thus walked him through the woods, studying nature and its simple precepts, cultivating his conscience, and above all, his sense of independence. "Nourished in the most absolute liberty, the greatest evil he can imagine is servitude."

Such an education aimed to give men moral autonomy and make them good citizens. Rousseau argued that women should have very different educations. "All education of women must be relative to men, pleasing them, being useful to them, raising them when they are young and caring for them when they are old, advising them, consoling

them, making their lives pleasant and agreeable, these have been the duties of women since time began." Women were to be useful socially as mothers and wives. In *Emile,* Rousseau laid out just such an education for Emile's wife-to-be, Sophie. At times, Rousseau seemed convinced that women "naturally" sought out such a role: "Dependence is a natural state for women, girls feel themselves made to obey." At other moments he insisted that girls needed to be disciplined and weaned from their "natural" vices.

Rousseau's conflicting views on female nature provide a good example of the shifting meaning of nature, a concept central to Enlightenment thought. Enlightenment thinkers used nature as a yardstick against which to measure society's shortcomings. "Natural" was better, simpler, uncorrupted. What, though, was nature? It could refer to the physical world. It could refer to allegedly primitive societies. Often, it was a useful invention.

Rousseau's novels sold exceptionally well, especially among women. *Julie* (subtitled *La nouvelle Héloïse*), published just after *Emile*, went through seventy editions in three decades. *Julie* tells the story of a young woman who falls in love with one man but dutifully obeys her father's order to marry another. At the end, she dies of exposure after rescuing her children from a cold lake—a perfect example of domestic and maternal virtue. The tragic love story and Rousseau's conviction that the heart was as important as the mind and that passion was more important than reason appealed to his audience. Rousseau's novels became part of a larger cult of *sensibilité* ("feeling") in middle-class and aristocratic circles, an emphasis on spontaneous expressions of feeling, and a belief that sentiment was an expression of authentic humanity. Thematically, this aspect of Rousseau's work contradicted much of the Enlightenment's cult of reason. It is more closely related to the concerns of nineteenth-century romanticism.

The World of Wollstonecraft

Rousseau's sharpest critic was the British writer Mary Wollstonecraft (1759–1797). Wollstonecraft published her best known work, *A Vindication of the Rights of Woman,* in 1792, during the French Revolution. Her argument, however, was anchored in Enlightenment debates and needs to be

Rousseau and His Readers

> *Jean-Jacques Rousseau's writings provoked very different responses from eighteenth-century readers—women as well as men. Many women readers loved his fiction and found his views about women's character and prescriptions for their education inspiring. Other women disagreed vehemently with his conclusions. In the first excerpt here, from Rousseau's novel* Emile *(1762), the author sets out his views on a woman's education. He argues that her education should fit with what he considers her intellectual capacity and her social role. It should also complement the education and role of a man. The second selection is an admiring response to* Emile *from Anne-Louise-Germaine Necker, or Madame de Staël (1766–1817), a well-known French writer and literary critic. While she acknowledged that Rousseau sought to keep women from participating in political discussion, she also thought that he had granted women a new role in matters of emotion and domesticity. The third excerpt is from Mary Wollstonecraft, who shared many of Rousseau's philosophical principles but sharply disagreed with his assertion that women and men should have different virtues and values. She believed that women like Madame de Staël were misguided in embracing Rousseau's ideas.*

Rousseau's *Emile*

Researches into abstract and speculative truths, the principles and axioms of sciences—in short, everything which tends to generalize our ideas—is not the proper province of women; their studies should be relative to points of practice; it belongs to them to apply those principles which men have discovered.... All the ideas of women, which have not the immediate tendency to points of duty, should be directed to the study of men, and to the attainment of those agreeable accomplishments which have taste for their object; for as to works of genius, they are beyond their capacity; neither have they sufficient precision or power of attention to succeed in sciences which require accuracy; and as to physical knowledge, it belongs to those only who are most active, most inquisitive, who comprehend the greatest variety of objects....

She must have the skill to incline us to do everything which her sex will not enable her to do herself, and which is necessary or agreeable to her; therefore she ought to study the mind of man thoroughly, not the mind of man in general, abstractedly, but the dispositions of those men to whom she is subject either by the laws of her country or by the force of opinion. She should learn to penetrate into the real sentiments from their conversation, their actions, their looks and gestures. She should also have the art, by her own conversation, actions, looks, and gestures, to communicate those sentiments which are agreeable to them without seeming to intend it. Men will argue more philosophically about the human heart; but women will read the heart of men better than they.... Women have most wit, men have most genius; women observe, men reason. From the concurrence of both we derive the clearest light and the most perfect knowledge which the human mind is of itself capable of attaining.

Source: Jean-Jacques Rousseau, *Emile* (1762), as cited in Mary Wollstonecraft, *A Vindication of the Rights of Woman* (New York: 1992), pp. 124–25.

understood here. Wollstonecraft shared Rousseau's political views and admired his writing and influence. Like Rousseau and her countryman Thomas Paine, a writer who supported the American and French Revolutions, Wollstonecraft was a republican. She called monarchy "the pestiferous purple which renders the progress of civilization a curse, and warps the understanding." She spoke even more forcefully than Rousseau against inequality and the artificial distinctions of rank, birth, or wealth. Believing that equality laid the basis for virtue, she contended, in classic Enlightenment language, that the society should seek "the perfection of our nature and capability of happiness." She argued more forcefully than any other Enlightenment thinker that (1) women had the same innate capacity for reason and self-government as men, (2) *virtue* should mean the same thing for men and women, and (3) relations between the sexes should be based on equality.

Madame De Staël

Though Rousseau has endeavoured to prevent women from interfering in public affairs, and acting a brilliant part in the theatre of politics; yet in speaking of them, how much has he done it to their satisfaction! If he wished to deprive them of some rights foreign to their sex, how has he for ever restored to them all those to which it has a claim! And in attempting to diminish their influence over the deliberations of men, how sacredly has he established the empire they have over their happiness! In aiding them to descend from an usurped throne, he has firmly seated them upon that to which they were destined by nature; and though he be full of indignation against them when they endeavour to resemble men, yet when they come before him with all the *charms, weaknesses, virtues,* and *errors* of their sex, his respect for their *persons* amounts almost to adoration.

Source: Cited in Mary Wollstonecraft, *A Vindication of the Rights of Woman* (New York: 1992), pp. 203–4.

Mary Wollstonecraft

Rousseau declares that a woman should never, for a moment, feel herself independent, that she should be governed by fear to exercise her *natural* cunning, and made a coquettish slave in order to render her a more alluring object of desire, a *sweeter* companion to man, whenever he chooses to relax himself. He carries the arguments, which he pretends to draw from the indications of nature, still further, and insinuates that truth and fortitude, the corner stones of all human virtue, should be cultivated with certain restrictions, because, with respect to the female character, obedience is the grand lesson which ought to be impressed with unrelenting rigour.

What nonsense! When will a great man arise with sufficient strength of mind to puff away the fumes which pride and sensuality have thus spread over the subject! If women are by nature inferior to men, their virtues must be the same in quality, if not in degree, or virtue is a relative idea; consequently, their conduct should be founded on the same principles, and have the same aim.

Source: Cited in Susan Bell and Karen Offen, eds., *Women, the Family, and Freedom: The Debate in Documents*, vol. 1, 1750–1880 (Stanford, CA: 1983), p. 58.

Questions for Analysis

1. Why did Rousseau seek to limit the sphere of activities open to women in society? What capacities did he feel they lacked? What areas of social life did he feel women were most suited for?

2. Did Madame de Staël agree with Rousseau that women's social roles were essentially different from men's roles in society?

3. What is the basis for Mary Wollstonecraft's disagreement with Rousseau?

4. Why did gender matter to Enlightenment figures such as Rousseau, De Staël, and Wollstonecraft?

Wollstonecraft did what few of her contemporaries even imagined. She applied the radical Enlightenment critique of monarchy and inequality to the family. The legal inequalities of marriage law, which among other things deprived married women of property rights, gave husbands "despotic" power over their wives. Just as kings cultivated their subjects' deference, so culture, she argued, cultivated women's weakness. "Civilized women are . . . so weakened by false refinement, that, respecting morals, their condition is much below what it would be were they left in a state nearer to nature." Middle-class girls learned manners, grace, and seductiveness to win a husband; they were trained to be dependent creatures. "My own sex, I hope, will excuse me, if I treat them like rational creatures instead of flattering their *fascinating* graces, and viewing them as if they were in a state of perpetual childhood, unable to stand

MARY WOLLSTONECRAFT. The British writer and radical suggested that Enlightenment critiques of monarchy could also be applied to the power of fathers within the family.

THE ENLIGHTENMENT AND EIGHTEENTH-CENTURY CULTURE

The Book Trade

What about the social structures that produced these debates and received these ideas? To begin with, the Enlightenment was bound up in a much larger expansion of printing and print culture. From the early eighteenth century on, book publishing and selling flourished, especially in Britain, France, the Netherlands, and Switzerland. National borders, though, mattered very little. Much of the book trade was both international and clandestine. Readers bought books from stores, by subscription, and by special mail order from book distributors abroad. Cheaper printing and better distribution also helped multiply the numbers of journals, some specializing in literary or scientific topics and others quite general. They helped bring daily newspapers, which first appeared in London in 1702, to Moscow, Rome, and cities and towns throughout Europe. By 1780, Britons could read 150 different magazines, and thirty-seven English towns had local newspapers. These changes have been called a "revolution in communication," and they form a crucial part of the larger picture of the Enlightenment.

Governments did little to check this revolutionary transformation. In Britain, the press encountered few restrictions, although the government did use a stamp tax on printed goods to raise the price of newspapers or books and discourage buyers. Elsewhere, laws required publishers to apply in advance for the license or privilege (in the sense of "private right") to print and sell any given work. In practice, publishers frequently printed books without advance permission, hoping that the regime would not notice. Russian, Prussian, and Austrian censors tolerated much less dissent, but those governments also sought to stimulate publishing and, to a certain degree, permitted public discussion. In the smaller states of Germany and Italy, governed by many local princes, it was easier to find progressive local patrons, and English and French works also circulated widely through those regions. That governments were patrons as well as censors of new scholarship illustrates the complex relationship between the age of absolutism and the Enlightenment.

As one historian puts it, censorship only made banned books expensive, keeping them out of the hands of the poor. Clandestine booksellers, most near the French border in Switzerland and the Rhineland, smuggled

alone. I earnestly wish to point out in what true dignity and human happiness consists—I wish to persuade women to endeavor to acquire strength, both of mind and body." A culture that encouraged feminine weakness produced women who were childish, cunning, cruel—and vulnerable. To Rousseau's specific prescriptions for female education, which included teaching women timidity, chasteness, and modesty, Wollstonecraft replied that Rousseau wanted women to use their reason to "burnish their chains rather than to snap them." Instead, education for women had to promote liberty and self-reliance. She was considered scandalously radical for merely hinting that women might have political rights.

The Enlightenment as a whole left a mixed legacy on gender, one that closely paralleled that on slavery. Enlightenment writers developed and popularized arguments about natural rights. They also elevated natural differences to a higher plane by suggesting that nature should dictate different, and quite possibly unequal, social roles. Mary Wollstonecraft and Jean-Jacques Rousseau shared a radical opposition to despotism and slavery, a moralist's vision of a corrupt society, and a concern with virtue and community. Their divergence on gender is characteristic of Enlightenment disagreements about nature and its imperatives and a good example of different directions in which the logic of Enlightenment thinking could lead.

thousands of books across the border to bookstores, distributors, and private customers. What did readers want, and what does this tell us about the reception of the Enlightenment? Many clandestine dealers specialized in what they called "philosophical books," which meant subversive literature of all kinds: stories of languishing in prison, gossipy memoirs of life at the court, pornographic fantasies (often about religious and political figures), and tales of crime and criminals. Much of this flourishing eighteenth-century "literary underground" echoed the radical Enlightenment's themes, especially the corruption of the aristocracy and the monarchy's degeneration into despotism.

High Culture, New Elites, and the Public Sphere

The Enlightenment was not simply embodied in books; it was produced in networks of readers and new forms of sociability and discussion. These networks included people of diverse backgrounds. Eighteenth-century elite, or "high," culture was small in scale but cosmopolitan and very literate, and it took literary and scientific discussion seriously. Middle-class men and women also became consumers of literature. Meanwhile, popular discussions of Enlightenment themes developed in the coffeehouses and taverns of European cities, where printed material might be read aloud, allowing even illiterate people to have access to the news and debates of the day. Together, this permissive atmosphere of frequent discussion among people of different social position led to the development of a new idea: "public opinion."

Among the institutions that produced a new elite were learned societies: the American Philosophical Society of Philadelphia, British literary and philosophical societies, and the Select Society of Edinburgh. Such groups organized intellectual life outside of the universities, and they provided libraries, meeting places for discussion, and journals that published members' papers or organized debates on issues from literature and history to economics and ethics. Elites also met in "academies," financed by governments to advance knowledge, whether through research into the natural sciences (the Royal Society of London, and the French Academy of Science, both founded in 1660, and the Berlin Royal Academy in 1701), promoting the national language (the Académie Française, or French Academy of Literature), or safeguarding traditions in the arts (the various academies of painting). In smaller cities in the countryside, provincial academies played much the same role,

providing a way for Enlightenment discussions to spread beyond European capitals.

Salons provided an alternative venue for discussion but operated informally. Usually they were organized by well-connected and learned aristocratic women who invited local personalities to their homes to meet with authors and discuss their latest works. The prominent role of women distinguished the salons from the academies and universities. Salons brought together men and women of letters with members of the aristocracy for conversation, debate, drink, and food. Rousseau loathed this kind of ritual and viewed salons as a sign of superficiality and vacuity in a privileged and overcivilized world. Thomas Jefferson thought the influence of women in salons had put France in a "desperate state." Some of the salons reveled in parlor games. Others, such as the one organized in Paris by Madame Necker, wife of the future French reform minister, lay quite close to the halls of power and served as testing ground for new policy ideas. Madame Marie-Thérèse Geoffrin, another celebrated French *salonière,* became an important patron of the *Encyclopedia* and exercised influence in placing scholars in academies. Moses Mendelssohn held an open house for intellectuals in Berlin. Salons in London, Vienna, Rome, and Berlin worked the same way, and like academies, they promoted among their participants a sense of belonging to an active, learned elite.

Scores of similar societies emerged in the eighteenth century, eventually breaking the hold of elites over public debate and literate discussion. Masonic lodges, organizations with elaborate secret rituals whose members pledged themselves to the regeneration of society, attracted a remarkable array of aristocrats and middle-class men. The composer Wolfgang Amadeus Mozart, Emperor Frederick II, and Montesquieu were Masons. Behind their closed doors, the lodges were egalitarian. They pledged themselves to a common project of rational thought and benevolent action and to banishing religion and social distinction—at least from their ranks. Other networks of sociability were even less exclusive. Coffeehouses multiplied with the colonial trade in sugar, coffee, and tea, and they occupied a central spot in the circulation of ideas. A group of merchants gathering to discuss trade, for instance, could turn to politics; and the many newspapers lying about the cafe tables provided a ready-to-hand link between their smaller discussions and news and debates elsewhere.

Eighteenth-century cultural changes—the expanding networks of sociability, the flourishing book trade, the new genres of literature, and the circulation of Enlightenment ideas—widened the circles of reading and discussion, expanding what some historians and political theorists call the "public sphere." That, in turn, began to change politics. Informal deliberations, debates about how to regenerate

A READING IN THE SALON OF MADAME GEOFFRIN, 1755. Enlightenment salons encouraged a spirit of intellectual inquiry and civil debate, at least among educated elites. Such salon discussions were notable for the extent to which women helped organize and participate in the conversations. This fact led Rousseau to attack the salons for encouraging unseemly posturing and promiscuity between the sexes, which he believed were the antithesis of rational pursuits. In this painting, Madame Geoffrin, a famed hostess (at left in gray), presides over a discussion of a learned work. Note the bust of Voltaire in the background, the patron saint of rationalist discourse. ▪ *What developments were required for this notion of free public discussion among elites to become more general in society?* ▪ *Would Enlightenment thinkers favor such developments? (Compare with images on pages 557 and 571).*

the nation, discussions of civic virtue, and efforts to forge a consensus played a crucial role in moving politics beyond the confines of the court.

A French observer described the changes this way: "In the last thirty years alone, a great and important revolution has occurred in our ideas. Today, public opinion has a preponderant force in Europe that cannot be resisted." Few thought the "public" involved more than the elite. Yet, by the late eighteenth century, European governments recognized the existence of a civic-minded group that stretched from salons to coffeehouses, academies, and circles of government and to which they needed, in some measure, to respond.

Middle-Class Culture and Reading

Enlightenment fare constituted only part of the new cultural interests of the eighteenth-century middle classes. Lower on the social scale, shopkeepers, small merchants, lawyers, and professionals read more and more different kinds of books. Instead of owning one well-thumbed Bible to read aloud, a middle-class family would buy and borrow books to read casually, pass on, and discuss. This literature consisted of science, history, biography, travel literature, and fiction. A great deal of it was aimed at middle-class women, among the fastest-growing groups of readers in the eighteenth century. Etiquette books sold very well; so did how-to manuals for the household. Scores of books about the manners, morals, and education of daughters, popular versions of Enlightenment treatises on education and the mind, illustrate close parallels between the intellectual life of the high Enlightenment and everyday middle-class reading matter.

The rise of a middle-class reading public, much of it female, helps account for the soaring popularity and production of novels, especially in Britain. Novels were the single most popular new form of literature in the eighteenth century. A survey of library borrowing in late-eighteenth-century Britain, Germany, and North America showed that 70 percent of books taken out were novels. For centuries,

Europeans had read romances such as tales of the Knights of the Round Table. The setting of popular novels was closer to home. The novel's more recognizable, nonaristocratic characters seemed more relevant to common middle-class experience. Moreover, examining emotion and inner feeling also linked novel writing with a larger eighteenth-century concern with personhood and humanity. As we have seen, classic Enlightenment writers like Voltaire, Goethe, and Rousseau wrote very successful novels; and those should be understood alongside the *Pamela* or *Clarissa* of Samuel Richardson (1689–1761), the *Moll Flanders* or *Robinson Crusoe* of Daniel Defoe (1660–1731), and the *Tom Jones* of Henry Fielding (1707–1754).

Many historians have noted that women figured prominently among fiction writers. The works of Jane Austen (1775–1817), especially *Pride and Prejudice* and *Emma,* are to many readers the height of a novelist's craft. Women writers, however, were not the only ones to write novels, nor were they alone in paying close attention to the domestic or private sphere. Their work took up central eighteenth-century themes of human nature, morality, virtue, and reputation. Their novels, like much of the non-fiction of the period, explored those themes in domestic as in public settings.

Popular Culture: Urban and Rural

How much did books and print culture touch the lives of the common people? Literacy rates varied dramatically by gender, social class, and region, but were generally higher in northern than in southern and eastern Europe. It is not surprising that literacy ran highest in cities and towns—higher, in fact, than we might expect. In early eighteenth-century Paris, 85 percent of men and 60 percent of women could read. Well over half the residents of poorer Parisian neighborhoods, especially small shopkeepers, domestic servants and valets, and artisans, could read and sign their names. Even the illiterate lived in a culture of print, though they had few books on their own shelves. They saw one-page newspapers and broadsides or fly sheets posted on streets and tavern walls and regularly heard them read aloud. Moreover, visual material—inexpensive woodcuts, especially, but also prints, drawings, satirical cartoons—figured as prominently as text in much popular reading material. By many measures, then, the circles of reading and discussion were even larger than literacy rates might suggest, especially in cities.

Neither England nor France required any primary schooling, leaving education to haphazard local initiatives. In central Europe, some regimes made efforts to develop state-sponsored education. Catherine of Russia summoned an Austrian consultant to set up a system of primary schools, but by the end of the eighteenth century only 22,000 of a population of 40 million had attended any kind of school. In the absence of primary schooling, most Europeans were self-taught. The varied texts in the peddler's cart—whether religious, political propaganda, or entertainment—attest to a widespread and rapidly growing popular interest in books and reading.

Like its middle-class counterpart, popular culture rested on networks of sociability. Guild organizations offered discussion and companionship. Street theater and singers mocking local political figures offered culture to

A COFFEEHOUSE IN LONDON, 1798. Coffeehouses served as centers of social networks and hubs of opinion contributing to a public consciousness that was new to the Enlightenment. This coffeehouse scene illustrates a mixing of classes, lively debate, and a burgeoning culture of reading. Compare this image with that of the aristocratic salon on page 570 and the meeting of Lessing and Mendelssohn on page 557. ▪ *How were coffeehouses different from aristocratic salons or the middle-class drawing room discussion between the two German thinkers?* ▪ *Can they all be seen as expressions of a new kind of "public sphere" in eighteenth-century Europe?*

The Internet and the Enlightenment Public Sphere

In many ways, today's Internet is simply a technologically sophisticated version of the public sphere of literate readers that was created and celebrated by the philosophes of the Enlightenment. It contains the same confusing mix of the educational, the commercial, the pleasurable . . . and the perverse.

 Watch related author interview on StudySpace
wwnorton.com/web/westernciv18

people from different social classes. The difficulties of deciphering popular culture are considerable. Most testimony comes to us from outsiders who regarded the common people as hopelessly superstitious and ignorant. Still, historical research has begun to reveal new insights. It has shown, first, that popular culture did not exist in isolation. Particularly in the countryside, market days and village festivals brought social classes together, and popular entertainments reached a wide social audience. Folktales and traditional songs resist pigeonholing as elite, middle-class, or popular culture, for they passed from one cultural world to another, being revised and reinterpreted in the process. Second, oral and literate culture overlapped. In other words, even people who could not read often had a great deal of "book knowledge": they argued seriously about points from books and believed that books conferred authority. A group of villagers, for

instance, wrote this eulogy to a deceased friend: "He read his life long, and died without ever knowing how to read." The logic and worldview of popular culture needs to be understood on its own terms.

It remains true that the countryside, especially in less economically developed regions, was desperately poor. Life there was far more isolated than in towns. A yawning chasm separated peasants from the world of the high Enlightenment. The philosophes, well established in the summits of European society, looked at popular culture with distrust and ignorance. They saw the common people of Europe much as they did indigenous peoples of other continents. They were humanitarians, critical thinkers, and reformers; they were not democrats. The Enlightenment, while well entrenched in eighteenth-century elite culture, nonetheless involved changes that reached well beyond elite society.

WAR AND POLITICS IN ENLIGHTENMENT EUROPE

War and Empire in the Eighteenth-Century World

After 1713, western Europe remained largely at peace for a generation. In 1740, however, that peace was shattered when Frederick the Great of Prussia seized the Austrian province of Silesia (see below). In the resulting War of the Austrian Succession, France and Spain fought on the side of Prussia, hoping to reverse some of the losses they had suffered in the Treaty of Utrecht. As they had done since the 1690s, Britain and the Dutch Republic sided with Austria. Like those earlier wars, this war quickly spread beyond the frontiers of Europe. In India, the British East India Company lost control over the coastal area of Madras to its French rival; but in North America, British colonists from New England captured the important French fortress of Louisbourg on Cape Breton Island, hoping to put a stop to French interference with their fishing and shipping. When the war finally ended in 1748, Britain recovered Madras and returned Louisbourg to France.

Eight years later, these colonial conflicts reignited when Prussia once again attacked Austria. This time, however, Prussia allied itself with Great Britain. Austria found support from both France and Russia. In Europe, the Seven Years' War (1756–63) ended in stalemate. In India and North America, however, the war had decisive consequences. In India, mercenary troops employed by the British East India Company joined with native allies to eliminate their French competitors. In North America (where the conflict was known as the French and Indian War), British troops captured both Louisbourg and Québec and also drove French forces from the Ohio River Valley and the Great Lakes. By the Treaty of Paris in 1763, which brought the Seven Years' War to an end, France formally surrendered both Canada and India to the British. Six years later, the French East India Company was dissolved.

Enlightened Absolutism in Eastern Europe

The rulers of Prussia, Austria, and Russia who initiated these wars on the continent were among the pioneers of a new style of "enlightened absolutism" within their realms. They demonstrated their commitment to absolutist rule by centralizing their administrations, increasing taxation, creating a professional army, and tightening their control of the Church. They justified this expansion of powers, however, in the name of the enlightenment ideal of reason—as rational solutions to the problems of government.

Rulers influenced by the spirit of enlightened absolutism included Empress Maria Theresa (r. 1740–80) of Austria and her son Joseph II (r. 1765–90; from 1765 until 1780 the two were co-rulers). The two rulers created statewide systems of primary education, relaxed censorship, and instituted a more liberal criminal code for the Habsburg Empire. Joseph II was particularly energetic in challenging the power of the Church: he closed hundreds of monasteries, drastically limited the number of monks and nuns permitted to live in contemplative orders, and ordered that the education of priests be placed under government supervision (see Chapter 15).

The most emblematic enlightened absolutist, however, was Frederick II (1740-1786) of Prussia. As a young man, Frederick devoted himself to the flute and admired French culture, exasperating his military-minded father, Frederick William I. When Frederick rebelled by running away from court with a friend, his father had them apprehended and the friend was executed before Frederick's eyes. The grisly lesson took. Although Frederick never gave up his love of music and literature, he applied himself energetically to his royal duties, earning himself the title of Frederick the Great.

Frederick raised Prussia to the status of a major power. In 1740, as soon as he became king, he mobilized his army and occupied the Austrian province of Silesia, with French support. Empress Maria Theresa, also new to the throne, counterattacked; but, despite support of Britain and Hungary, she could not recover Silesia. Eventually Frederick consolidated his gains over all the Polish territories that lay between East Prussia and Brandenburg, transforming Prussia by 1786 into a powerful, contiguous kingdom. Frederick was careful to cultivate support from the Prussian nobility, known as the Junkers. His father had recruited civil servants according to merit rather than birth, but Frederick relied on the Junkers to staff the army and his expanding administration. Frederick's strategy worked. His nobility remained loyal, and he fashioned the most professional and efficient bureaucracy in Europe.

Frederick supervised a series of "enlightened" social reforms: he prohibited the judicial torture of accused criminals, abolished the bribing of judges, and established a system of elementary schools. Although strongly anti-Semitic,

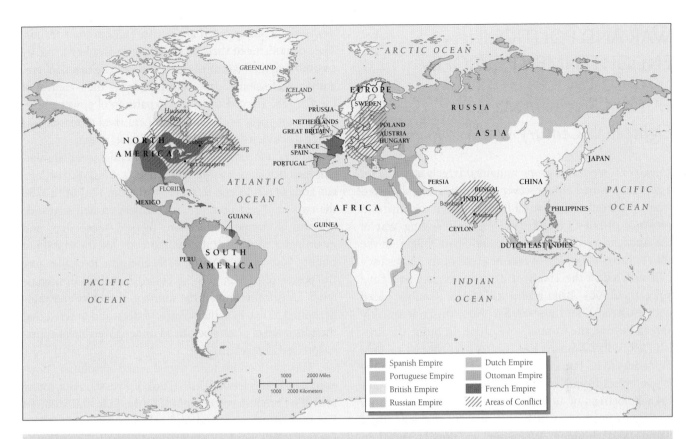

THE SEVEN YEARS' WAR, 1756–1763. ▪ *What continents were involved in the Seven Years' War?* ▪ *What was the impact of naval power on the outcome of the war?* ▪ *What were the consequences for the colonies involved in the conflict?*

he encouraged religious toleration toward Jews and declared that he would happily build a mosque in Berlin if he could find enough Muslims to fill it. On his own royal estates, he abolished capital punishment, curtailed the forced labor services of his peasantry, and granted these peasants long leases on the land they worked. He encouraged scientific forestry and the cultivation of new crops. He cleared new lands in Silesia and brought in thousands of immigrants to cultivate them. When wars ruined their farms, he supplied his peasants with new livestock and tools. But he never attempted to extend these reforms to the estates of the Prussian nobility. To have done so would have alienated the very group on whom Frederick's rule depended.

Like Frederick, Catherine the Great of Russia (r. 1762–96) thought of herself as an enlightened ruler and she corresponded with French philosophers. Also like Frederick, she could not afford to lose the support of the Russian nobility, who had placed her on the throne after executing her husband, the weak and possibly mad Peter III. Catherine's efforts at enlightened reform were limited: she founded hospitals and orphanages, created an elementary school system for the children of the provincial nobility, and called a commission to examine the possi-

bility of codifying Russian law. The commission's radical proposals—abolition of capital punishment and judicial torture, prohibitions on the selling of serfs—were set aside, however, after a massive peasant revolt in 1773–75 led by a Cossack named Emelyan Pugachev briefly threatened Moscow itself. Catherine's greatest achievements were gained through war and diplomacy. In 1774, she won control over the northern coast of the Black Sea after a war with the Ottoman Empire, and she also took several Ottoman provinces along the Danube River. Russia thus obtained a long-sought goal: a warm-water port for the Russian navy. In addition, Catherine succeeded in expanding Russian territory in the west, at the expense of the weaker kingdom of Poland.

The plan for Russia, Austria, and Prussia to divide Poland among them was originally proposed by Frederick the Great: Russia would abandon its Danubian provinces and receive in exchange the grain fields of eastern Poland (and between 1 and 2 million Poles); Austria would take Galicia (population 2.5 million) while Prussia would consolidate the divided lands of its kingdom by taking Poland's coastal regions on the Baltic coast. When the agreement was finalized in 1772, Poland had lost 30 percent of its

MARIA THERESA OF AUSTRIA AND HER FAMILY. A formidable and capable ruler who fought to maintain Austria's dominance in central Europe against the claims of Frederick the Great of Prussia, Maria Theresa had sixteen children, including Marie Antoinette, later queen of France as wife of Louis XVI. ▪ *Why did she emphasize her role as mother in a royal portrait such as this one rather than her other undeniable political skills?* ▪ *How does this compare to the portraits of Louis XIV or of William and Mary in Chapter 15, pages 494 and 503?*

CATHERINE THE GREAT. Rumored to have ordered the assassination of Peter III, Catherine oversaw an era of expansion in what was to become the longest female reign in Russian history.

territory and half of its population. After a second war between Russia and the Ottomans in 1788, Poland tried to reassert itself, but it was no match for the three major powers—Russia, Austria, and Prussia—and by 1795 Poland had disappeared from the map altogether.

As a political program, enlightened absolutism clearly had its limits. On the one hand, Catherine the Great, Frederick the Great, and Joseph II in Austria were clearly personally inspired by the literary culture of the philosophes, and their political programs reflected Enlightenment ideas about the rational organization of state institutions. On the other hand, they were ready to abandon the humanitarian impulse of Enlightenment thought and the ideal of self-government when it came to preserving their own power and the social hierarchies that sustained it.

The American Revolution

The American Revolution of 1776 provided a more fruitful opportunity for putting Enlightenment ideals into practice. Along the Atlantic seaboard, the rapidly growing Brit-

ish colonies chafed at rule from London. To recover some of the costs of the Seven Years' War and to pay for the continuing costs of protecting its colonial subjects, the British Parliament imposed a series of new taxes on its American colonies. These taxes were immediately unpopular. Colonists complained that because they had no representatives in Parliament, they were being taxed without their consent—a fundamental violation of their rights as British subjects. They also complained that British restrictions on colonial trade, particularly the requirement that certain goods pass first through British ports before being shipped to the Continent, were strangling American livelihoods and making it impossible to pay even the king's legitimate taxes.

The British government, led since 1760 by the young and inexperienced King George III, responded to these complaints with a badly calculated mixture of vacillation and force. Various taxes were imposed and then withdrawn in the face of colonial resistance. In 1773, however, when East India Company tea was dumped in Boston Harbor by rebellious colonials objecting to the customs duties that had been imposed on it, the British government closed the port of Boston and curtailed the colony's representative institutions. These "Coercive Acts" galvanized the support of the other American colonies for Massachusetts. In 1774, representatives from all the American colonies

The American Declaration of Independence

The Declaration of Independence, issued from Philadelphia on July 4, 1776, is perhaps the most famous single document of American history. But its familiarity does not lessen its interest as a piece of political philosophy. The indebtedness of the document's authors to the ideas of John Locke will be obvious from the selections here. But Locke, in turn, drew many of his ideas about the contractual and conditional nature of human government from the conciliarist thinkers of the fifteenth and early sixteenth centuries. The appeal of absolutism notwithstanding, the Declaration shows how vigorous the medieval tradition of contractual, limited government remained at the end of the eighteenth century.

When in the course of human events, it becomes necessary for one people to dissolve the political bonds which have connected them with another, and to assume among the powers of the earth the separate and equal station to which the Laws of Nature and of Nature's God entitle them, a decent respect to the opinions of mankind requires that they should declare the causes which impel them to the separation.... We hold these truths to be self-evident, that all men are created equal, that they are endowed by their Creator with certain unalienable rights, that among these are Life, Liberty and the pursuit of Happiness.... That to secure these rights, Governments are instituted among men, deriving their just powers from the consent of the governed.... That whenever any form of Government becomes destructive of these ends, it is the Right of the People to alter or to abolish it, and to institute new Government, laying its foundation upon such principles and organizing its power in such form, as to them shall seem most likely to effect their Safety and Happiness. Prudence, indeed, will dictate that Governments long established should not be changed for light and transient causes; and accordingly all experience has shown, that mankind are more disposed to suffer, while evils are sufferable, than to right themselves by abolishing the forms to which they are accustomed. But when a long train of abuses and usurpations, pursuing invariably the same Object, evinces a design to reduce them under absolute despotism, it is their right, it is their duty, to throw off such Government, and to provide new Guards for their future security.... Such has been the patient sufferance of these Colonies; and such is now the necessity which constrains them to alter their former Systems of Government....

Questions for Analysis

1. Who are "the people" mentioned in the first sentence of this selection? Are the rights of "the people" the same as individual rights? How did the authors of this document come to think of themselves as the representatives of such a body?

2. What is the purpose of government, according to this document? Who gets to decide if the government is doing its job?

3. How does this document's use of the term *political bonds* compare with Rousseau's "form of association" in the *Social Contract*? What is similar about these two texts? What is different?

met at Philadelphia to form the Continental Congress to negotiate with the Crown over their grievances. In April 1775, however, local militiamen at Lexington and Concord clashed with regular British troops sent to disarm them. Soon thereafter, the Continental Congress began raising an army, and an outright rebellion erupted against the British government.

On July 4, 1776, the thirteen colonies formally declared their independence from Great Britain, in language that showed their debt to Enlightenment writers (see **Analyzing Primary Sources** above). During the first two years of the war, it seemed unlikely that such independence would ever become a reality. In 1778, however, France, anxious to undermine the colonial hegemony Great Britain had established since 1713, joined the war on the side of the Americans. Spain entered the war in support of France, hoping to recover Gibraltar and Florida (the latter lost in 1763 to Britain). In 1780, Britain also declared war on the Dutch

gained its independence; its western border was fixed on the Mississippi River, and it secured valuable fishing rights off the eastern coast of Canada. France gained only the satisfaction of defeating its colonial rival, but even that satisfaction was short lived. Six years later, the massive debts France had incurred in supporting the American Revolution helped bring about another, very different kind of revolution in France that would permanently alter the history of Europe.

CONCLUSION

The Enlightenment arose from the scientific revolution, from the new sense of power and possibility that rational thinking made possible, and from the rush of enthusiasm for new forms of inquiry. Enlightenment thinkers scrutinized a remarkably wide range of topics: human nature, reason, understanding, religion, belief, law, the origins of government, economics, new forms of technology, and social practices—such as marriage, child rearing, and education. Enlightenment ideas about social improvement and progress could and did occasionally serve the interests of European rulers, who saw in them a means to both rationalize their administrations and to challenge social groups or institutions that resisted the centralization of authority. Maria Theresa in Austria, Frederick the Great in Prussia and Catherine the Great in Russia all found ways to harness aspects of Enlightenment thought to their strategies of government.

At the same time, however, the radical implications of the Enlightenment critique of tradition made many people uncomfortable. Ideas with subversive implications circulated in popular forms from pamphlets and journalism

DIVIDING THE ROYAL SPOILS. A contemporary cartoon showing the monarchs of Europe at work carving up a hapless Poland. Note there is little reference here to the people who lived in the Polish territories that were being divided up among Russia, Prussia, and the Habsburg Empire. All three of these realms already contained people who spoke different languages and practiced different religions. The result of such expansion was to increase the linguistic and cultural diversity of these kingdoms.

■ *How might this have complicated the internal politics of these monarchies?* ■ *What long-term consequences might one expect from such multiethnic or multireligious societies?*

Republic for continuing to trade with the rebellious colonies. Now facing a coalition of its colonial rivals, Great Britain saw the war turn against it. In 1781, combined land and sea operations by French and American troops forced the surrender of the main British army at Yorktown in Virginia. As the defeated British soldiers surrendered their weapons, their band played a song titled "The World Turned Upside Down."

Negotiations for peace began soon after the defeat at Yorktown but were not concluded until September 1783. The Treaty of Paris left Great Britain in control of Canada and Gibraltar. Spain retained its possessions west of the Mississippi River and recovered Florida. The United States

SEVENTEENTH- AND EIGHTEENTH-CENTURY WARS	
Glorious Revolution	1688–1689
War of the League of Augsburg	1689–1697
War of the Spanish Succession	1702–1713
Seven Years' War	1756–1763
American Revolution	1775–1783
The Russo-Turkish War	1787–1792

to plays and operas. The intellectual movement that lay behind the Enlightenment thus had broad consequences for the creation of a new kind of elite based not on birth but on the acquisition of knowledge and the encouragement of open expression and debate. A new sphere of public opinion had come into existence, one which was difficult for the state to monitor and to control, and one which would have profound consequences in the nineteenth and twentieth centuries.

The prosperity that had made the Enlightenment possible remained very unevenly distributed in late eighteenth-century Europe. In the cities, rich and poor lived separate lives in separate neighborhoods. In the countryside, regions bypassed by the developing commercial economy of the period continued to suffer from hunger and famine, just as they had done in the sixteenth and seventeenth centuries. In eastern Europe, the contrasts between rich and poor were even more extreme, as many peasants fell into a new style of serfdom that would last until the end of the nineteenth century. War, too, remained a fact of European life, bringing death and destruction to hundreds of thousands of people across the Continent and around the world—yet

After You Read This Chapter

(S) Visit StudySpace for quizzes, additional review materials, and multimedia documents. **wwnorton.com/web/westernciv18**

REVIEWING THE OBJECTIVES

- Many eighteenth-century thinkers used the term *Enlightenment* to describe what their work offered to European society. Who were they, and what did they mean by the term?

- Enlightenment ideas spread rapidly throughout Europe and in European colonies. How did this expanded arena for public discussion shape the development of Enlightenment thought?

- Enlightenment debates were shaped by the availability of new information about peoples and cultures in different parts of the globe. How did Enlightenment thinkers incorporate this new information into their thought?

- Enlightenment thinkers were often critical of widely held cultural and political beliefs. What was radical about the Enlightenment?

another consequence of the worldwide reach of these European colonial empires.

Finally, the Atlantic revolutions (the American Revolution of 1776, the French Revolution of 1789, and the Latin American upheavals of the 1830s) were steeped in the language of the Enlightenment. The constitutions of the new nations formed by these revolutions made reference to the fundamental assumptions of Enlightenment liberalism: on the liberty of the individual conscience and the freedom from the constraints imposed by religious or government institutions. Government authority could not be arbitrary; equality and freedom were natural; and humans sought happiness, prosperity, and the expansion of their potential. These arguments had been made earlier, though tentatively, and even after the Atlantic revolutions, their aspirations were only partially realized. But when the North American colonists declared their independence from Britain in 1776, they called such ideas "self-evident truths." That bold declaration marked both the distance traveled since the late seventeenth century and the self-confidence that was the Enlightenment's hallmark.

PEOPLE, IDEAS, AND EVENTS IN CONTEXT

- How did the **COMMERCIAL REVOLUTION** change social life in Europe?

- Who were the **PHILOSOPHES**? What gave them such confidence in **REASON**?

- What did **DAVID HUME** owe to **ISAAC NEWTON**? What made his work different from that of the famous physicist?

- What did **VOLTAIRE** admire about the work of **FRANCIS BACON AND JOHN LOCKE**? What irritated Voltaire about French society?

- What was **MONTESQUIEU**'s contribution to theories of government?

- What made **DENIS DIDEROT'S** *ENCYCLOPEDIA* such a definitive statement of the Enlightenment's goals?

- What influence did **CESARE BECCARIA** have over legal practices in Europe?

- What contributions did **ADAM SMITH** make to economic theory?

- What was radical about **JEAN-JACQUES ROUSSEAU**'s views on education and politics?

- What does the expansion of the **PUBLIC SPHERE** in the eighteenth century tell us about the effects of the Enlightenment?

THINKING ABOUT CONNECTIONS

- Compare the Enlightenment as an intellectual movement to the Reformation of the sixteenth century. What is similar about the two movements? What is distinctive?

- Did increases in literacy; the rise of print culture; and the emergence of new forms of intellectual sociability such as salons, reading societies, and coffeehouses really make public opinion more rational? How has our understanding of public opinion changed since the eighteenth century?

Before You Read This Chapter

The French Revolution

CORE OBJECTIVES

- **UNDERSTAND** the origins of the French Revolution in 1789.

- **EXPLAIN** the goals of French revolutionaries and the reactions of people elsewhere in Europe and the Atlantic world.

- **DESCRIBE** the events that made the Revolution more radical in 1792–1794.

- **IDENTIFY** the connections between the Revolution and Napoleon's regime after 1799, and the effects of Napoleon's conquests on Europe.

- **CONSIDER** the links between the French Revolution and the Atlantic world, which also saw revolutions in the Americas and in the Caribbean during these decades.

When a crowd of Parisians attacked the antiquated and nearly empty royal prison known as the Bastille on July 14, 1789, they were doing several things all at once. On the one hand, the revolt was a popular expression of support for the newly created National Assembly. This representative body had only weeks earlier declared an intention to put an end to absolutism in France by writing a constitution that made the nation, rather than the king, the sovereign authority in the land. But the Parisians in the street on July 14 did not express themselves like members of the National Assembly, who spoke the language of the Enlightenment. The actions of the revolutionary crowd were an expression of violent anger at the king's soldiers, who they feared might turn their guns on the city in a royal attempt to restore order by force. When the governor of the Bastille prison opened fire on the attackers, killing as many as a hundred, they responded with redoubled fury. By the end of the day, the prison had fallen, and the governor's battered body was dragged to the square before the city hall, where he was beheaded. Among the first to meet such an end as a consequence of revolution in France, he would not be the last.

This tension between noble political aspirations and cruel violence lies at the heart of the French Revolution. The significance of this contradiction was not lost on the millions of people throughout Europe who watched in astonishment as France was engulfed in turmoil in the 1790s. In 1789, one European out of every five lived in France, a kingdom that many considered to be the center of European culture. Other kingdoms were not immune to the same social and political tensions that divided the French. Aristocrats across Europe and the colonies resented monarchical inroads on their ancient freedoms. Members of the middle classes chafed under a system of official privilege that they increasingly saw as unjust and outmoded. Peasants fiercely resented the endless demands of central government on their limited resources. Nor were resentments focused exclusively on absolutist monarchs. Bitter resentments and tensions existed between country and city dwellers, between rich and poor, overprivileged and underprivileged, slave and free. The French Revolution was the most dramatic and tumultuous expression of all of these conflicts.

This age of revolution opened on the other side of the Atlantic Ocean. The American Revolution of 1776 was a crisis of the British Empire, linked to a long series of conflicts between England and France over colonial control of North America. It led to a major crisis of the old regime in France. Among "enlightened" Europeans, the success with which citizens of the United States had thrown off British rule and formed a republic based on Enlightenment principles was a source of tremendous optimism. Change would come, many believed. Reform was possible. The costs would be modest.

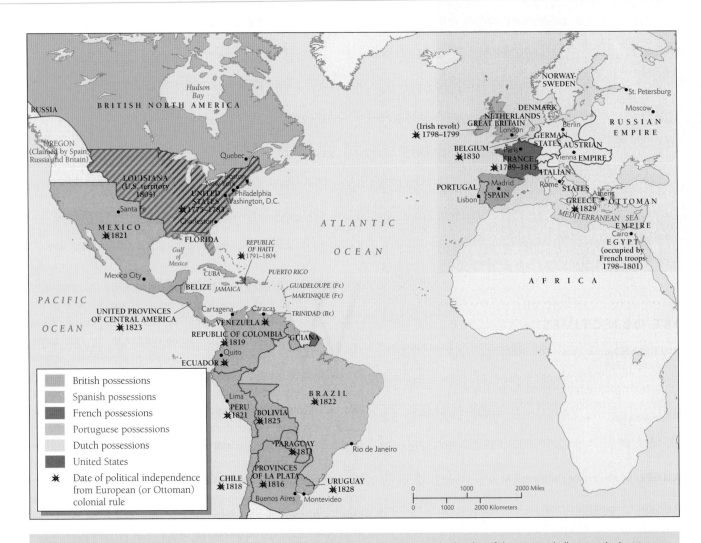

THE ATLANTIC REVOLUTIONS. The Atlantic revolutions shook nations and empires on both sides of the ocean, challenging the legitimacy of Europe's dynastic realms, lending further support to notions of popular sovereignty and forcing contemporaries to rethink the meanings of citizenship in a context of intense political and economic struggle. ▪ *How many of these struggles took place within Europe?* ▪ *How many appear to have taken place on the periphery of the Atlantic world?* ▪ *What circumstances may have made it more difficult for such revolutionary movements to develop within Europe itself?*

The French Revolution did not live up to these expectations, though change certainly did come. By any measure, the accomplishments of the revolutionary decade were extraordinary: it successfully proved that the residents of an old monarchy in the heart of Europe could come together to constitute themselves as citizens of a new political idea, the nation. Freed from the shackles of tradition, revolutionaries in France posed new questions about the role of women in public life, about the separation of church and state, about the rights of Jews and other minorities. A slave revolt in the French colonies convinced the revolutionaries that the new liberties they defended so ardently also belonged to African slaves, though few had suggested such a thing at the outset. Meanwhile, the European wars precipitated by the revolution marked the first time that entire populations were mobilized as part of a new kind of devastating international conflict, the first "total wars." In other words, in spite of the optimism of those who began the revolution in 1789, it quickly became something much more costly, complex, and violent. Its effects were to resonate throughout Europe for the next half century.

THE FRENCH REVOLUTION: AN OVERVIEW

The term *French Revolution* is a shorthand for a complex series of events between 1789 and 1799. (Napoleon ruled from 1799 to 1814–1815.) To simplify, those events can be divided into four stages. In the first stage, running from 1788 to 1792, the struggle was constitutional and relatively peaceful. An increasingly bold elite articulated its grievances against the king. Like the American revolutionaries, French elites refused taxation without representation; attacked despotism, or arbitrary authority; and offered an Enlightenment-inspired program to rejuvenate the nation. Reforms, many of them breathtakingly wide ranging, were instituted—some accepted or even offered by the king, and others passed over his objections. The peaceful, constitutional phase did not last. Unlike the American Revolution, the French Revolution did not stabilize around one constitution or one set of political leaders, for many reasons.

Reforms met with resistance, dividing the country. The threat of dramatic change within one of the most powerful countries in Europe created international tensions. In 1792, these tensions exploded into war, and the crises of war, in turn, spelled the end of the Bourbon monarchy and the beginning of the republic. This second stage of the revolution, which lasted from 1792 to 1794, was one of acute crisis, consolidation, and repression. A ruthlessly central-ized government mobilized all the country's resources to fight the foreign enemy as well as counterrevolutionaries at home, to destroy traitors and the vestiges of the Old Regime.

The Terror, as this policy was called, did save the republic, but it exhausted itself in factions and recriminations and collapsed in 1794. In the third phase, from 1794 to 1799, the government drifted. France remained a republic. It continued to fight with Europe. Undermined by corruption and division, the state fell prey to the ambitions of a military leader, Napoleon Bonaparte. Napoleon's rule, punctuated by astonishing victories and catastrophes, stretched from 1799 to 1815. It began as a republic, became an empire, and ended—after a last hurrah—in the muddy fields outside the Belgian village of Waterloo. After Napoleon's final defeat, the other European monarchs restored the Bourbons to the throne. That restoration, however, would be short lived, and the cycle of revolution and reaction continued into the nineteenth century.

THE COMING OF THE REVOLUTION

What were the long-term causes of the revolution in France? Historians long ago argued that the causes and outcomes should be understood in terms of class conflict. According to this interpretation, a rising bourgeoisie, or middle class, inspired by Enlightenment ideas and by its own self-interest, overthrew what was left of the aristocratic order. This interpretation drew on the writings of the nineteenth-century philosopher Karl Marx and on much twentieth-century sociology.

Historians have substantially modified this bold thesis. To be sure, the origins of the revolution lie in eighteenth-century French society. Yet that society was not simply divided between a bourgeois class and the aristocracy. Instead, it was increasingly dominated by a new elite or social group that brought together aristocrats, officeholders, professionals, and—to a lesser degree—merchants and businessmen. To understand the revolution, we need to understand this new social group and its conflicts with the government of Louis XVI.

French society was legally divided into Three Estates. (An individual's *estate* marked his standing, or status, and it determined legal rights, taxes, and so on.) The First Estate comprised all the clergy; the Second Estate, the nobility. The Third Estate, by far the largest, included everyone else, from wealthy lawyers and businessmen to urban laborers and poor peasants. Within the political and social elite of the country, a small but powerful group, these legal distinctions often seemed artificial. To begin with, in the upper reaches of society, the social boundaries between nobles and wealthy commoners were ill defined. Noble title was accessible to those who could afford to buy an ennobling office. For example, close to 50,000 new nobles were created between 1700 and 1789. The nobility depended on a constant infusion of talent and economic power from the wealthy social groups of the Third Estate.

To preserve their elite status, aristocrats spoke of a distinction between the nobility of the sword and of the robe, the former supposedly of a more ancient and distinguished lineage derived from military service, the latter aristocrats because they had purchased administrative or judicial office (hence the robe).

Nevertheless, wealth did not take predictable forms. Most noble wealth was proprietary—that is, tied to land, urban properties, purchased offices, and the like. Yet noble families did not disdain trade or commerce, as historians long thought. In fact, noblemen financed most industry, and they also invested heavily in banking and such enterprises as ship owning, the slave trade, mining, and metallurgy. Moreover, the very wealthy members of the Third Estate also preferred to invest in secure, proprietary holdings. Thus, throughout the century, much middle-class wealth was transformed into noble wealth, and a significant num-

ber of rich bourgeois became noblemen. Wealthy members of the bourgeoisie did not see themselves as a separate class. They thought of themselves as different from—and often opposed to—the common people, who worked with their hands, and they identified with the values of a nobility to which they frequently aspired.

There were, nonetheless, important social tensions. Less prosperous lawyers—and there were an increasing number of them—were jealous of the privileged position of a favored few in their profession. Over the course of the century, the price of offices rose, making it more difficult to buy one's way into the nobility, and creating tensions between middling members of the Third Estate and the very rich in trade and commerce who, by and large, were the only group able to afford to climb the social ladder. Less wealthy nobles resented the success of rich, upstart commoners whose income allowed them to live in luxury. In sum, several fault lines ran through the elite and the middle classes. All these social groups could nonetheless join in attacking a government and an economy that were not serving their interests.

The Enlightenment had changed public debate (see Chapter 17). Although ideas did not cause the revolution, they played a critical role in articulating grievances. The political theories of Locke, Voltaire, and Montesquieu could appeal to both discontented nobles and members of the

PREREVOLUTIONARY PROPAGANDA. Political cartoons in late-eighteenth-century France commonly portrayed the Third Estate as bearing the burden of taxation while performing the bulk of the nation's productive work. On the left, a peasant bears the burden of his tools and his harvest, as a cleric and a nobleman look on; on the right, the commoner is literally carrying his social superiors. ▪ *What visual cues indicate the status of individuals in these images?* ▪ *Would one expect the nobility or the clergy to defend their status on the basis of their usefulness to society?* ▪ *Can one detect the power of certain Enlightenment ideas behind these forms of social critique?* ▪ *Which ones?* ▪ *How might an opponent of Enlightenment thought have confronted such arguments?*

middle class. Voltaire was popular because of his attacks on noble privileges; Locke and Montesquieu gained widespread followings because of their defense of private property and limited sovereignty. Montesquieu's ideas appealed to the noble lawyers and officeholders who dominated France's powerful law courts, the *parlements*. They read his doctrine of checks and balances as support for their argument that parlements could provide a check to the despotism of the king's government. When conflicts arose, noble leaders presented themselves as defenders of the nation threatened by the king and his ministers.

The campaign for change was also fueled by economic reformers. The "physiocrats" urged the government to simplify the tax system and free the economy from mercantilist regulations. They advocated an end to price controls in the grain trade, which had been imposed to keep the cost of bread low. Such interventions, they argued, interfered with the market's ability to find an equilibrium between supply and demand.

In the countryside, peasants did not think in terms of markets. They were caught in a web of obligations to landlords, church, and state: a tithe, or levy, on farm produce owed to the church; fees for the use of a landlord's mill or wine press; fees to the landlord; and fees when land changed hands. In addition, peasants paid a disproportionate share of both direct and indirect taxes—the most onerous of which was the salt tax—levied by the government. (For some time, the production of salt had been a state monopoly; every individual was required to buy at least seven pounds a year from the government works. The result was a commodity whose cost was often as much as fifty or sixty times its actual value.) Further grievances stemmed from the requirement to maintain public roads (the corvée) and from the hunting privileges that nobles for centuries had regarded as the distinctive badge of their order.

Social and economic conditions deteriorated on the eve of the revolution. A general price increase during much of the eighteenth century, which permitted the French economy to expand by providing capital for investment, created hardship for the peasantry and for urban tradesmen and laborers. Their plight deteriorated further at the end of the 1780s, when poor harvests sent bread prices sharply higher. In 1788, families found themselves spending more than 50 percent of their income on bread, which made up the bulk of their diet. The following year the figure rose to as much as 80 percent. Poor harvests reduced demand for manufactured goods, and contracting markets in turn created unemployment. Many peasants left the countryside for the cities, hoping to find work there—only to discover that urban unemployment was far worse than that in rural areas. Evidence indicates that between 1787 and 1789 the unemployment rate in many parts of urban France was as high as 50 percent.

Failure and Reform

An inefficient tax system further weakened the country's financial position. Taxation differed according to social standings and varied from region to region—some areas were subject to a much higher rate than others. Special exemptions made the task of collectors more difficult. The financial system, already burdened by debts incurred under Louis XIV, all but broke down completely under the increased expenses brought on by French participation in the American Revolution. The cost of servicing the national debt in the 1780s consumed 50 percent of the nation's budget.

Problems with the economy reflected weaknesses in France's administrative structure, ultimately the responsibility of the country's absolutist monarch, Louis XVI (1774–1792).

LOUIS XVI. The last prerevolutionary French king, who was to lose his life in the Terror, combined in his person a strong attachment to the monarchy's absolutist doctrine with an inability to find workable solutions to the financial crisis facing his government. His royal portrait mimicked the forms of spectacular display that proved so useful to Louis XIV in shoring up the power of the monarchy. ▪ *What made this display so much less potent in the late eighteenth century?* ▪ *What caused the monarchy to lose its aura?*

What is the Third Estate? (1789)

The Abbé Emmanuel-Joseph Sieyès (1748–1836) was, by virtue of his office in the Church, a member of the First Estate of the Estates General. Nevertheless, his political savvy led him to be elected as a representative of the Third Estate from the district of Chartres. Sieyès was a formidable politician as well as a writer. His career during the revolution, which he ended by assisting Napoleon's seizure of power, began with one of the most important radical pamphlets of 1789. In What Is the Third Estate?, *Sieyès posed fundamental questions about the rights of the estate, which represented the great majority of the population and helped provoke its secession from the Estates General.*

he plan of this book is fairly simple. We must ask ourselves three questions.

1. What is the Third Estate? *Everything.*

2. What has it been until now in the political order? *Nothing.*

3. What does it want to be? *Something.*

It suffices to have made the point that the so-called usefulness of a privileged order to the public service is a fallacy; that without help from this order, all the arduous tasks in the service are performed by the Third Estate; that without this order the higher posts could be infinitely better filled; that they ought to be the natural prize and reward of recognized ability and service; and that if the privileged have succeeded in usurping all well-paid and honorific posts, this is both a hateful iniquity towards the generality of citizens and an act of treason to the commonwealth.

Who is bold enough to maintain that the Third Estate does not contain within itself everything needful to constitute a complete nation? It is like a strong and robust man with one arm still in chains. If the privileged order were removed, the nation would not be something less but something more. What then is the Third Estate? All; but an "all" that is fettered and oppressed. What would it be without the privileged order? It would be all; but free and flourishing. Nothing will go well without the Third Estate; everything would go considerably better without the two others.

Source: Emmanuel-Joseph Sieyès, *What Is the Third Estate?*, ed. S. E. Finer, trans. M. Blondel, (London: 1964), pp. 53–63.

Questions for Analysis

1. How might contemporaries have viewed Sieyès's argument that the Three Estates should be evaluated according to their usefulness to the "commonwealth"?

2. Was Sieyès's language—accusing the privileged orders of "treason" and arguing for their "removal"—an incitement to violence?

3. What did Sieyès mean by the term *nation*? Could one speak of France as a nation in these terms before 1789?

Louis wished to improve the lot of the poor, abolish torture, and shift the burden of taxation onto the richer classes, but he lacked the ability to accomplish these tasks. He appointed reformers like Anne-Robert-Jacques Turgot, a physiocrat, and Jacques Necker, a Swiss Protestant banker, as finance ministers, only to arouse the opposition of traditionalists at court. When he pressed for new taxes to be paid by the nobility, he was defeated by the provincial parlements, who defended the aristocracy's immunity from taxation. He allowed his wife, the young but strong-willed Marie Antoinette—daughter of Austria's Maria Theresa—a free hand to dispense patronage among her friends. The result was constant intrigue and frequently reshuffled alliances at Versailles. By 1788, a weak monarch, together with a chaotic financial situation and severe social tensions, brought absolutist France to the edge of political disaster.

THE DESTRUCTION OF THE OLD REGIME

The fiscal crisis precipitated the revolution. In 1787 and 1788, the king's principal ministers, Charles de Calonne and Loménie de Brienne, proposed new taxes to meet the growing deficit, notably a stamp duty and a direct tax on the annual produce of the land.

Hoping to persuade the nobility to agree to these reforms, the king summoned an Assembly of Notables from among the aristocracy. This group insisted that any new tax scheme must be approved by the Estates General, the representative body of the Three Estates of the realm, and that the king had no legal authority to arrest and imprison arbitrarily. These proposed constitutional changes echoed the English aristocrats of 1688 and the American revolutionaries of 1776.

Faced with economic crisis and financial chaos, Louis XVI summoned the Estates General (which had not met since 1614) to meet in 1789. His action appeared to many as the only solution to France's deepening problems. Long-term grievances and short-term hardships produced bread riots across the country in the spring of 1789. Fear that the forces of law and order were collapsing and that the common people might take matters into their own hands

spurred the Estates General. Each of the three orders elected its own deputies—the Third Estate indirectly through local assemblies. These assemblies were charged as well with the responsibility of drawing up lists of grievances (*cahiers des doléances*), further heightening expectations for fundamental reform.

The delegates of the Third Estate, though elected by assemblies chosen in turn by artisans and peasants, represented the outlook of an elite. Only 13 percent were men of business. About 25 percent were lawyers; 43 percent were government officeholders of some sort.

By tradition, each estate met and voted as a body. In the past, this had generally meant that the First Estate (the clergy) had combined with the Second (the nobility) to defeat the Third. Now the Third Estate made it clear it would not tolerate such an arrangement. The Third's interests were articulated most memorably by the Abbé Emmanuel Sieyès, a radical member of the clergy. "What is the Third Estate?" asked Sieyès, in his famous pamphlet

THE TENNIS COURT OATH BY JACQUES LOUIS DAVID (1748–1825). In June 1789, the members of the Third Estate, now calling themselves the National Assembly, swear an oath not to disband until France has a constitution. In the center stands Jean Bailly, president of the new assembly. The Abbé Sieyès is seated at the table. In the foreground, a clergyman, an aristocrat, and a member of the Third Estate embrace in a symbol of national unity. The single deputy who refused to take the oath sits at far right, his hands clasped against his chest. ▪ *What is the significance of this near unanimity expressed in defiance of the king?* ▪ *What options were available to those who did not support this move?*

of January 1789. Everything, he answered, and pointed to eighteenth-century social changes to bolster his point. In early 1789, Sieyès's views were still unusually radical. But the leaders of the Third Estate agreed that the three orders should sit together and vote as individuals. More important, they insisted that the Third Estate should have twice as many members as the First and Second.

The king first opposed "doubling the Third" and then changed his position. His unwillingness to take a strong stand on voting procedures cost him support he might otherwise have obtained from the Third Estate. Shortly after the Estates General opened at Versailles in May 1789, the Third Estate, angered by the king's attitude, took the revolutionary step of leaving the body and declaring itself the National Assembly. Locked out of the Estates General meeting hall on June 20, the Third Estate and a handful of sympathetic nobles and clergymen moved to a nearby indoor tennis court.

Here, under the leadership of the volatile, maverick aristocrat Mirabeau and the radical clergyman Sieyès, they bound themselves by a solemn oath not to separate until they had drafted a constitution for France. This Tennis Court Oath, sworn on June 20, 1789, can be seen as the beginning of the French Revolution. By claiming the authority to remake the government in the name of the people, the National Assembly was asserting its right to act as the highest sovereign power in the nation. On June 27, the king virtually conceded this right by ordering all the delegates to join the National Assembly.

First Stages of the French Revolution

The first stage of the French Revolution extended from June 1789 to August 1792. In the main, this stage was moderate, its actions dominated by the leadership of liberal nobles and men of the Third Estate. Yet three events in the summer and fall of 1789 furnished evidence that their leadership would be challenged.

POPULAR REVOLTS

From the beginning of the political crisis, public attention was high. It was roused not merely by interest in political reform but also by the economic crisis that, as we have seen, brought the price of bread to astronomical heights. Many believed that the aristocracy and the king were conspiring to punish the Third Estate by encouraging scarcity and high prices. Rumors circulated in Paris during the latter days of June 1789 that the king's troops were mobilizing to march on the city. The electors of Paris (those who had voted for the Third Estate—workshop masters, artisans, and shopkeepers) feared not only the king but also the Parisian poor, who had been parading through the streets and threatening violence. The common people would soon be referred to as sans-culottes (sahn koo-LAWTS). The term, which translates to "without breeches," was an antiaristocratic badge of pride: a man of the people wore full-length trousers rather than aristocratic breeches with stockings and gold-buckled shoes. Led by the electors, the people formed a provisional municipal government and organized a militia of volunteers to maintain order. Determined to obtain arms, they made their way on July 14 to the Bastille, an ancient fortress where guns and ammunition were stored. Built in the Middle Ages, the Bastille had served as a prison for many years but was no longer much used. Nevertheless, it symbolized hated royal authority. When crowds demanded arms from its governor, he procrastinated and then, fearing a frontal assault, opened fire, killing ninety-eight of the attackers. The crowd took revenge, capturing the fortress (which held only seven prisoners—five common criminals and two people confined for mental incapacity) and decapitating the governor. Similar groups took control in other cities across France. The fall of the Bastille was the first instance of the people's role in revolutionary change.

The second popular revolt occurred in the countryside. Peasants, too, expected and feared a monarchical and aristocratic counterrevolution. Rumors flew that the king's armies were on their way, that Austrians, Prussians, or "brigands" were invading. Frightened and uncertain, peasants and villagers organized militias; others attacked and burned manor houses, sometimes to look for grain but usually to find and destroy records of manorial dues. This "Great Fear," as historians have labeled it, compounded the confusion in rural areas. The news, when it reached Paris, convinced deputies at Versailles that the administration of rural France had simply collapsed.

The third instance of popular uprising, the "October Days of 1789," was brought on by economic crisis. This time, Parisian women from the market district, angered by the soaring price of bread and fired by rumors of the king's continuing unwillingness to cooperate with the assembly, marched to Versailles on October 5 and demanded to be heard. Not satisfied with its reception by the assembly, the crowd broke through the gates to the palace, calling for the king to return to Paris from Versailles. On the afternoon of the following day the king yielded and returned to Paris, accompanied by the crowd and the National Guard.

Each of these popular uprisings shaped the political events unfolding at Versailles. The storming of the Bastille persuaded the king and nobles to agree to the creation of the National Assembly. The Great Fear compelled the most

WOMEN OF PARIS LEAVING FOR VERSAILLES, OCTOBER 1789. A crowd of women, accompanied by Lafayette and the National Guard, marched to Versailles to confront the king about shortages and rising prices in Paris. ■ *Did the existence of the National Assembly change the meaning of such popular protests?*

sweeping changes of the entire revolutionary period. In an effort to quell rural disorder, on the night of August 4 the assembly took a giant step toward abolishing all forms of privilege. It eliminated the Church tithe (tax on the harvest), the labor requirement known as the corvée, the nobility's hunting privileges, and a wide variety of tax exemptions and monopolies. In effect, these reforms obliterated the remnants of feudalism. One week later, the assembly abolished the sale of offices, thereby sweeping away one of the fundamental institutions of the Old Regime. The king's return to Paris during the October Days of 1789 undercut his ability to resist further changes.

THE NATIONAL ASSEMBLY AND THE RIGHTS OF MAN

The assembly issued its charter of liberties, the Declaration of the Rights of Man and of the Citizen, in September 1789. It declared property to be a natural right, along with liberty, security, and "resistance to oppression." It declared freedom of speech, religious toleration, and liberty of the press inviolable. All citizens were to be treated equally before the law. No one was to be imprisoned or punished without due process of law. Sovereignty resided in the people,

who could depose officers of the government if they abused their powers. These were not new ideas; they represented the outcome of Enlightenment discussions and revolutionary debates and deliberations. The Declaration became the preamble to the new constitution, which the assembly finished in 1791.

Whom did the Declaration mean by "man and the citizen"? The constitution distinguished between "passive" citizens, guaranteed rights under law, and "active" citizens, who paid a certain amount in taxes and could thus vote and hold office. About half the adult males in France qualified as active citizens. Even their power was curtailed, because they could vote only for "electors," men whose property ownership qualified them to hold office. Later in the revolution, the more radical republic abolished the distinction between active and passive, and the conservative regimes reinstated it. Which men could be trusted to participate in politics and on what terms was a hotly contested issue.

Also controversial were the rights of religious minorities. The revolution gave full civil rights to Protestants, though in areas long divided by religious conflict those rights were challenged by Catholics. The revolution did, hesitantly, give civil rights to Jews, a measure that sparked protest in areas of eastern France. Religious toleration, a central theme of the Enlightenment, meant ending persecution; it did not mean that the regime was prepared to accommodate religious difference. The assembly abolished serfdom and banned slavery in continental France. It remained silent on colonial slavery, and although delegations pressed the assembly on political rights for free people of color, the assembly exempted the colonies from the constitution's provisions. Events in the Caribbean, as we will see, later forced the issue.

The rights and roles of women became the focus of sharp debate, as revolutionaries confronted demands that working women participate in guilds or trade organizations, and laws on marriage, divorce, poor relief, and education were reconsidered. The Englishwoman Mary Wollstonecraft's milestone book *A Vindication of the Rights of Woman* (see Chapter 17) was penned during the revolutionary debate over national education. Should girls be educated? To what end? Wollstonecraft, as we have seen, argued strongly that reforming education required forging a new concept of independent and equal womanhood. Even Wollstonecraft, however, only hinted at political representation, aware that such an idea would "excite laughter."

Only a handful of thinkers broached the subject of women in politics: the aristocratic Enlightenment thinker the Marquis de Condorcet and, from another shore, Marie Gouze, the self-educated daughter of a butcher. Gouze became an intellectual and playwright and renamed herself Olympe de Gouges. Like many "ordinary" people, she found in the explosion of revolutionary activity the opportunity to address the public by writing speeches, pamphlets, or newspapers. She composed her own manifesto, the *Declaration of the Rights of Woman and the Citizen* (1791). Beginning with the proposition that "social distinctions can only be based on the common utility," she declared that women had the same rights as men, including resistance to authority, participation in government, and naming the fathers of illegitimate children. This last demand offers a glimpse of the shame, isolation, and hardship faced by an unmarried woman.

De Gouges's demand for equal rights was unusual, but many women nevertheless participated in the everyday activities of the revolution, joining clubs, demonstrations, and debates and making their presence known, sometimes forcefully. Women artisans' organizations had a well-established role in municipal life, and they used the revolution as an opportunity to assert their rights to produce and sell goods. Market women were familiar public figures, often central to the circulation of news and spontaneous popular demonstrations (the October Days are a good example). Initially, the regime celebrated the support of women "citizens," and female figures were favorite symbols for liberty, prudence, and the bounty of nature in

DECLARATION OF THE RIGHTS OF MAN (1789). Presented as principles of natural law inscribed on stone, this print gives a good indication of how the authors of the Declaration wished it to be perceived by the French people. Over the tablets is a beneficent and all-seeing deity accompanied by two female allegorical figures representing strength and virtue on one side and the French nation on the other. Two armed soldiers wear the uniform of the newly created National Guard. The image's symbols refer to Masonic lore (the triangle or pyramid with an eye at the center, the snake grasping its tail), and a set of historical references from the Roman Republic: a Phrygian cap, used by Romans as a symbol of liberty, is mounted on a spear emerging from a bundle of sticks. This bundle was known as a *faisceau* and was carried in ancient Rome by magistrates as symbols of their authority. ■ *Given the absence of any monarchical symbolism or references to the Catholic Church, why was it important for the authors to come up with an alternative set of historical references?*

revolutionary iconography. When the revolution became more radical, however, some revolutionaries saw autonomous political activity by women's organizations as a threat to public order, and in 1793 the revolutionaries shut down the women's political clubs. Even so, many ordinary women were able to make use of the revolution's new legislation on marriage (divorce was legalized in 1792) and inheritance to support claims for relief from abusive husbands or absent

Declaration of the Rights of Man and of the Citizen

One of the first important pronouncements of the National Assembly after the Tennis Court Oath was the Declaration of the Rights of Man and of the Citizen. *The authors drew inspiration from the American Declaration of Independence, but the language is even more heavily influenced by the ideals of French Enlightenment philosophers, particularly Rousseau. Following are the* Declaration's *preamble and some of its most important principles.*

he representatives of the French people, constituted as the National Assembly, considering that ignorance, disregard, or contempt for the rights of man are the sole causes of public misfortunes and the corruption of governments, have resolved to set forth, in a solemn declaration, the natural, inalienable, and sacred rights of man, so that the constant presence of this declaration may ceaselessly remind all members of the social body of their rights and duties; so that the acts of legislative power and those of the executive power may be more respected . . . and so that the demands of the citizens, grounded henceforth on simple and incontestable principles, may always be directed to the maintenance of the constitution and to the welfare of all. . . .

Article 1. Men are born and remain free and equal in rights. Social distinctions can be based only on public utility.

Article 2. The aim of every political association is the preservation of the natural and imprescriptible rights of man. These rights are liberty, property, security, and resistance to oppression.

Article 3. The source of all sovereignty resides essentially in the nation. No body, no individual can exercise authority that does not explicitly proceed from it.

Article 4. Liberty consists in being able to do anything that does not injure another; thus the only limits upon each man's exercise of his natural laws are those that guarantee enjoyment of these same rights to the other members of society.

Article 5. The law has the right to forbid only actions harmful to society. No action may be prevented that is not forbidden by law, and no one may be constrained to do what the law does not order.

Article 6. The law is the expression of the general will. All citizens have the right to participate personally, or through representatives, in its formation. It must be the same for all, whether it protects or punishes. All citizens, being equal in its eyes, are equally admissable to all public dignities, positions, and employments, according to their ability, and on the basis of no other distinction than that of their virtues and talents. . . .

Article 16. A society in which the guarantee of rights is not secured, or the separation of powers is not clearly established, has no constitution.

Source: Declaration of the Rights of Man and of the Citizen, as cited in K. M. Baker, ed., *The Old Regime and the French Revolution* (Chicago: 1987), pp. 238–239.

Questions for Analysis

1. Who is the Declaration addressed to? Is it just about the rights of the French, or do these ideas apply to all people?

2. What gave a group of deputies elected to advise Louis XVI on constitutional reforms the right to proclaim themselves a National Assembly? What was revolutionary about this claim to represent the French nation?

3. Article 6, which states that "law is the expression of general will," is adapted from Rousseau's *Social Contract*. Does the Declaration give any indication of how the "general will" can be known?

---

fathers, claims that would have been impossible under the prerevolutionary legislation.

THE NATIONAL ASSEMBLY AND THE CHURCH

In November 1789 the National Assembly decided to confiscate all Church lands to use them as collateral for issuing interest-bearing notes known as *assignats*. The assembly hoped that this action would resolve the economy's inflationary crisis, and eventually these notes circulated widely as paper money. In July 1789, the assembly enacted the Civil Constitution of the Clergy, bringing the Church under state authority. The new law forced all bishops and priests to swear allegiance to the state, which henceforth paid their salaries. The aim was to make the Catholic Church of France a national institution, free from interference from Rome.

These reforms were bitterly divisive. Many people resented the privileged status of the Church, and its vast monastic land holdings. On the other hand, for centuries the parish church had been a central institution in small towns and villages, providing poor relief and other services, in addition to baptisms and marriages. The Civil Constitution of the Clergy sparked fierce resistance in some parts of rural France. When the pope threatened to excommunicate priests who signed the Civil Constitution, he raised the stakes: allegiance to the new French state meant damnation. Many people, especially peasants in the deeply Catholic areas of western France, were driven into open revolt.

The National Assembly made a series of economic and governmental changes with lasting effects. To raise money, it sold off Church lands, although few of the genuinely needy could afford to buy them. To encourage the growth of economic enterprise, it abolished guilds. To rid the country of local aristocratic power, it reorganized local governments, dividing France into eighty-three equal departments. These measures aimed to defend individual liberty and freedom from customary privilege. Their principal beneficiaries were, for the most part, members of the elite, people on their way up under the previous regime who were able to take advantage of the opportunities, such as buying land or being elected to office, that the new one offered. In this realm as elsewhere, the social changes of the revolution endorsed changes already under way in the eighteenth century.

A NEW STAGE: POPULAR REVOLUTION

In the summer of 1792, the revolution's moderate leaders were toppled and replaced by republicans, who repudiated the monarchy and claimed to rule on behalf of a sovereign people. Why this abrupt and drastic change? Was the revolution blown off course? These are among the most difficult questions about the French Revolution. Historians have focused on three factors to explain the revolution's radical turn: changes in popular politics, a crisis of leadership, and international polarization.

First, the revolution politicized the common people, especially in cities. Newspapers filled with political and social commentary multiplied, freed from censorship. From 1789 forward, a wide variety of political clubs became part of daily political life. Some were formal, almost like political parties, gathering members of the elite to debate issues facing the country and influence decisions in the assembly. Other clubs opened their doors to those excluded from formal politics, and they read aloud from newspapers and discussed the options facing the country, from the provisions of the constitution to the trustworthiness of the king and his ministers.

This political awareness was heightened by nearly constant shortages and fluctuating prices. Prices particularly exasperated the working people of Paris who had eagerly awaited change since their street demonstrations of 1789. Urban demonstrations, often led by women, demanded cheaper bread; political leaders in clubs and newspapers called for the government to control rising inflation. Club leaders spoke for men and women who felt cheated by the constitution.

A second major reason for the change of course was a lack of effective national leadership. Louis XVI remained a weak monarch. He was forced to support measures personally distasteful to him, in particular the Civil Constitution of the Clergy. He was sympathetic to the plottings of the queen, who was in contact with her brother Leopold II of Austria. Urged on by Marie Antoinette, Louis agreed to attempt an escape from France in June 1791, hoping to rally foreign support for counterrevolution. The members of the royal family managed to slip past their palace guards in Paris, but they were apprehended near the border at Varennes and brought back to the capital. The constitution of 1791 declared France a monarchy, but after the escape to Varennes, Louis was little more than a prisoner of the assembly.

The Counterrevolution

The third major reason for the dramatic turn of affairs was war. From the outset of the revolution, men and women across Europe had been compelled, by the very intensity of events in France, to take sides in the conflict. In the years immediately after 1789, the revolution in France won the enthusiastic support of a wide range of thinkers. The British poet William Wordsworth, who later became disillusioned, recalled his initial mood: "Bliss was it in that dawn to be alive." His sentiments were echoed across the Continent by poets and philosophers, including the German Johann Gottfried von Herder, who declared the revolution the most important historical moment since the Reformation. In Britain, the Low Countries, western Germany, and Italy, "patriots" proclaimed their allegiance to the new revolution.

Others opposed the revolution from the start. Exiled nobles, who fled France for sympathetic royal courts in Germany and elsewhere, did all they could to stir up counterrevolutionary sentiment. In Britain, the conservative cause was strengthened by the publication in 1790 of Edmund Burke's *Reflections on the Revolution in France*. A Whig politician who had sympathized with the American revolutionaries, Burke deemed the revolution in France a monstrous crime against the social order (see **Competing Viewpoints** on pages 594–95).

Social Grievances on the Eve of the Revolution (1789)

During the elections to the Estates General, communities drew up "notebooks of grievances" to be presented to the government. The following comes from a rural community, Lignère la Doucelle.

For a long time now, the inhabitants have been crushed beneath the excessive burden of the multiplicity of taxes that they have been obliged to pay. Their parish is large and spread out, but it is a hard land with many uncultivated areas, almost all of it divided into small parcels. There is not one single farm of appreciable size, and these small properties are occupied either by the poor or by people who are doing so poorly that they go without bread every other day. They buy bread or grain nine months of the year. No industries operate in this parish, and from the time they began complaining, no one has ever listened. The cry of anguish echoed all to the way to the ministry after having fruitlessly worn out their intendants. They have always seen their legitimate claims being continuously denied, so may the fortunate moment of equality revive them.

* * *

That all lords, country gentlemen, and others of the privileged class who, either directly or through their proxies, desire to make a profit on their wealth, regardless of the nature of that wealth, pay the same taxes as the common people.

* * *

That the seigneur's mills not be obligatory, allowing everyone to choose where he would like to mill his grain.

* * *

That the children of common people living on a par with nobles be admitted for military service, as the nobility is.

That the king not bestow noble titles upon someone and their family line, but that titles be bestowed only upon those deserving it.

That nobility not be available for purchase or by any fashion other than by the bearing of arms or other service rendered to the State.

* * *

That church members be only able to take advantage of one position. That those who are enjoying more than one be made to choose within a fixed time period.

That future abbeys all be placed into the hands of the king, that His Majesty benefit from their revenue as the head abbots have been able to.

That in towns where there are several convents belonging to the same order, there be only one, and the goods and revenue of those that are to be abolished go to the profit of the crown.

That the convents where there are not normally twelve residents be abolished.

That no tenth of black wheat be paid to parish priests, priors or other beneficiaries, since this grain is only used to prepare the soil for the sowing of rye.

That they also not be paid any tenths of hemp, wool, or lamb. That in the countryside they be required to conduct burials and funerals free of charge. That the ten sous for audit books, insinuations, and the 100 [sous] collected for the parish be abolished.

* * *

That grain be taxed in the realm at a fixed price, or rather that its exportation abroad be forbidden except in the case where it would be sold at a low price.

Source: Armand Bellée, ed., *Cahiers de plaintes & doléances des paroisses de la province du Maine pour les Etats-généraux de 1789*, vol. 2 (Le Mans: 1881–1892), pp. 578–582.

Questions for Analysis

1. Do these grievances reflect the interests of only one social group, or can one hear demands being made from different groups within this rural community?

2. What do you think were the main problems faced by this community?

3. How did the revolutionaries receive these grievances?

Competing Viewpoints

Debating the French Revolution: Edmund Burke and Thomas Paine

The best-known debate on the French Revolution set the Irish-born conservative Edmund Burke against the British radical Thomas Paine. Burke opposed the French Revolution from the beginning. His Reflections on the Revolution in France *was published early, in 1790, when the French king was still securely on the throne. Burke disagreed with the premises of the revolution. Rights, he argued, were not abstract and "natural" but the results of specific historical traditions. Remodeling the French government without reference to the past and failing to pay proper respect to tradition and custom had, in his eyes, destroyed the fabric of French civilization.*

Thomas Paine was one of many to respond to Burke. The Rights of Man *(1791–1792) defended the revolution and, more generally, conceptions of human rights. In the polarized atmosphere of the revolutionary wars, simply possessing Paine's pamphlet was cause for imprisonment in Britain.*

Edmund Burke

You will observe, that from the Magna Carta to the Declaration of Rights, it has been the uniform policy of our constitution to claim and assert our liberties, as an entailed inheritance derived to us from our forefathers. . . . We have an inheritable crown; an inheritable peerage; and a house of commons and a people inheriting privileges, franchises, and liberties, from a long line of ancestors. . . .

You had all these advantages in your ancient states, but you chose to act as if you had never been moulded into civil society, and had every thing to begin anew. You began ill, because you began by despising every thing that belonged to you. . . . If the last generations of your

country appeared without much luster in your eyes, you might have passed them by, and derived your claims from a more early race of ancestors. . . . Respecting your forefathers, you would have been taught to respect yourselves. You would not have chosen to consider the French as a people of yesterday, as a nation of low-born servile wretches until the emancipating year of 1789. . . . [Y]ou would not have been content to be represented as a gang of Maroon slaves, suddenly broke loose from the house of bondage, and therefore to be pardoned for your abuse of liberty to which you were not accustomed and ill fitted. . . .

. . . The fresh ruins of France, which shock our feelings wherever we can

turn our eyes, are not the devastation of civil war; they are the sad but instructive monuments of rash and ignorant council in time of profound peace. They are the display of inconsiderate and presumptuous, because unresisted and irresistible authority. . . .

Nothing is more certain, than that of our manners, our civilization, and all the good things which are connected with manners, and with civilization, have, in this European world of ours, depended upon two principles; and were indeed the result of both combined; I mean the spirit of a gentleman, and the spirit of religion. The nobility and the clergy, the one by profession, the other by patronage, kept learning in existance, even

Burke's famous book aroused some sympathy for the counterrevolutionary cause, but active opposition came slowly. The first European states to express public concern about events in revolutionary France were Austria and Prussia, declaring in 1791 that order and the rights of the monarch of France were matters of "common interest to all sovereigns of Europe." The leaders of the French assembly

pronounced the declaration an affront to national sovereignty. Nobles who had fled France played into their hands with plots and pronouncements against the government. Oddly, perhaps, both supporters and opponents of the revolution in France believed war would serve their cause. The National Assembly's leaders expected an aggressive policy to shore up the people's loyalty and bring freedom to the rest

in the midst of arms and confusions.... Learning paid back what it received to nobility and priesthood.... Happy if they had all continued to know their indissoluble union, and their proper place.

Happy if learning, not debauched by ambition, had been satisified to continue the instructor, and not aspired to be the master! Along with its natural protectors and guardians, learning will be cast into the mire, and trodden down under the hoofs of a swinish multitude.

Source: Edmund Burke, *Reflections on the Revolution in France (1790)* (New York: 1973), pp. 45, 48, 49, 52, 92.

Thomas Paine

Mr. Burke, with his usual outrage, abuses the *Declaration of the Rights of Man*.... Does Mr. Burke mean to deny that man has any rights? If he does, then he must mean that there are no such things as rights any where, and that he has none himself; for who is there in the world but man? But if Mr. Burke means to admit that man has rights, the question will then be, what are those rights, and how came man by them originally?

The error of those who reason by precedents drawn from antiquity, respecting the rights of man, is that they do not go far enough into antiquity. They stop in some of the intermediate stages of an hundred or a thousand years, and produce what was then a rule for the present day. This is no authority at all....

To possess ourselves of a clear idea of what government is, or ought to be, we must trace its origin. In doing this, we shall easily discover that governments must have arisen either *out* of the people, or *over* the people. Mr. Burke has made no distinction....

What were formerly called revolutions, were little more than a change of persons, or an alteration of local circumstances. They rose and fell like things of course, and had nothing in their existance or their fate that could influence beyond the spot that produced them. But what we now see in the world, from the revolutions of America and France, is a renovation of the natural order of things, a system of principles as universal as truth and the existence of man, and combining moral with political happiness and national prosperity.

Source: Thomas Paine, *The Rights of Man (1791)* (New York: 1973), pp. 302, 308, 383.

Questions for Analysis

1. How does Burke define *liberty*? Why does he criticize the revolutionaries for representing themselves as slaves freed from bondage?

2. What does Paine criticize about Burke's emphasis on history? According to Paine, what makes the French Revolution different from previous changes of regime in Europe?

3. How do these two authors' attitudes about the origins of human freedoms shape their understandings of the revolution?

of Europe. Counterrevolutionaries hoped the intervention of Austria and Prussia would undo all that had happened since 1789. Radicals, suspicious of aristocratic leaders and the king, believed that war would expose traitors with misgivings about the revolution and flush out those who sympathized with the king and European tyrants. On April 20, 1792, the assembly declared war against Austria and Prus-

sia. Thus began the war that would keep the Continent in arms for a generation.

As the radicals expected, the French forces met serious reverses. By August 1792, the allied armies of Austria and Prussia had crossed the frontier and were threatening to capture Paris. Many, including soldiers, believed that the military disasters were evidence of the king's treason.

On August 10, Parisian crowds, organized by their radical leaders, attacked the royal palace. The king was imprisoned and a second and far more radical revolution began.

The French Republic

From this point, the country's leadership passed into the hands of the more egalitarian leaders of the Third Estate. These new leaders were known as Jacobins, the name of a political club to which many of them belonged. Although their headquarters were in Paris, their membership extended throughout France. Their members included large numbers of professionals, government officeholders, and lawyers; but they proclaimed themselves spokesmen for the people and the nation. An increasing number of artisans joined Jacobin clubs as the movement grew, and other, more democratic clubs expanded as well.

The National Convention, elected by free white men, became the effective governing body of the country for the next three years. It was elected in September 1792, at a time when enemy troops were advancing, spreading panic. Rumors flew that prisoners in Paris were plotting to aid the enemy. They were hauled from their cells, dragged before hastily convened tribunals, and killed. The "September Massacres" killed more than a thousand "enemies of the Revolution" in less than a week. Similar riots engulfed Lyons, Orléans, and other French cities.

The newly elected convention was far more radical than its predecessor, and its leadership was determined to end the monarchy. On September 21, the convention declared France a republic. In December, it placed the king on trial, and in January 1793 he was condemned to death by a narrow margin. The heir to the grand tradition of French absolutism met his end bravely as "citizen Louis Capet," beheaded by the guillotine. Introduced as a swifter

THE EXECUTION OF LOUIS XVI. The execution of Louis XVI shocked Europe. Even committed revolutionaries in France debated the necessity of such a dramatic act. The entire National Convention (over 700 members) acted as jury, and although the assembly was nearly unanimous in finding the king guilty of treason, a majority of only one approved the final death sentence. Those who voted for Louis XVI's execution were known forever after as "regicides." ▪ *What made this act necessary from the point of view of the most radical of revolutionaries?* ▪ *What made it repugnant from the point of view of the revolution's most heated enemies?*

and more humane form of execution, the frightful mechanical headsman came to symbolize revolutionary fervor.

The convention took other radical measures. It confiscated the property of enemies of the revolution, breaking up some large estates and selling them on easier terms to less-wealthy citizens. It abruptly canceled the policy of compensating nobles for their lost privileges. It repealed primogeniture, so that property would not be inherited exclusively by the oldest son but would be divided in substantially equal portions among all immediate heirs. It abolished slavery in French colonies (see below). It set maximum prices for grain and other necessities. In an astonishing effort to root out Christianity from everyday life, the convention adopted a new calendar. The calendar year began with the birth of the republic (September 22, 1792) and divided months in such a way as to eliminate the Catholic Sunday.

Most of this program was a hastily improvised response to crisis and political pressure from the common people in the cities and their leaders. In the three years after 1790, prices had risen staggeringly: wheat by 27 percent, beef by 136 percent, potatoes by 700 percent. While the government imposed its maximums in Paris, small vigilante militias, representing the sans-culottes, attacked those they considered hoarders and profiteers.

The convention also reorganized its armies, with astonishing success. By February 1793, Britain, Holland, Spain, and Austria were in the field against the French. Britain came into the war for strategic and economic reasons: it feared a French threat to Britain's growing global power. The allied coalition, though united only in its desire to contain France, was nevertheless a formidable force. To counter it, the revolutionary government mustered all men capable of bearing arms. The revolution flung fourteen hastily drafted armies into battle under the leadership of newly promoted, young, and inexperienced officers. What they lacked in training and discipline they made up for in organization, mobility, flexibility, courage, and morale. In 1793–1794, the French armies preserved their homeland. In 1794–1795, they occupied the Low Countries; the Rhineland; and parts of Spain, Switzerland, and Savoy. In 1796, they invaded and occupied key parts of Italy and broke the coalition that had arrayed itself against them.

The Reign of Terror

In 1793, however, those victories lay in a hard-to-imagine future. France was in crisis. In 1793, the convention drafted a new democratic constitution based on male suffrage. That constitution never took effect—suspended indefinitely by wartime emergency. Instead, the convention prolonged its own life year after year and increasingly delegated its responsibilities to a group of twelve leaders, the Committee of Public Safety. The committee's ruthlessness had two purposes: to seize control of the revolution and to prosecute all the revolution's enemies—"to make terror the order of the day." The Terror lasted less than two years but left a bloody and authoritarian legacy.

Perhaps the three best-known leaders of the radical revolution were Jean Paul Marat, Georges Jacques Danton, and Maximilien Robespierre, the latter two members of the Committee of Public Safety. Marat was educated as a physician and by 1789 had already earned enough distinction in that profession to be awarded an honorary degree by St. Andrews University in Scotland. Marat opposed nearly all of his moderate colleagues' assumptions, including their admiration for Great Britain, which Marat considered corrupt and despotic. Persecuted by powerful factions in the constituent assembly who feared his radicalism, he was forced to take refuge in unsanitary sewers and dungeons.

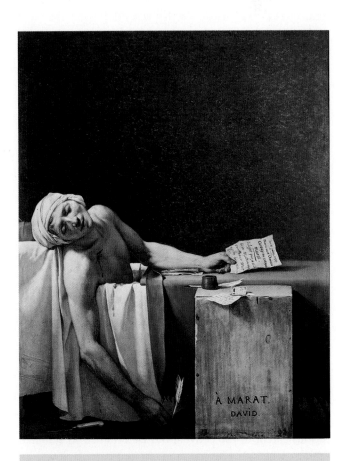

THE DEATH OF MARAT. This painting by the French artist Jacques-Louis David in 1793 immortalized Marat. The note in the slain leader's hand is from Charlotte Corday, his assassin. ▪ *Why was it important to represent Marat as a martyr?*

He persevered as the editor of the popular news sheet *The Friend of the People*. Exposure to infection left him with a chronic and painful skin disease, from which baths provided the only relief. In the summer of 1793, at the height of the crisis of the revolution, he was stabbed in his bath by Charlotte Corday, a young royalist, and thus became a revolutionary martyr.

Danton, like Marat, was a popular political leader, well known in the more plebian clubs of Paris. Elected a member of the Committee of Public Safety in 1793, he had much to do with organizing the Terror. As time went on, however, he wearied of ruthlessness and displayed a tendency to compromise, which gave his opponents in the convention their opportunity. In April 1794, Danton was sent to the guillotine. On mounting the scaffold, he is reported to have said, "Show my head to the people; they do not see the like every day."

The most famous of the radical leaders was Maximilien Robespierre. Born of a family reputed to be of Irish descent, Robespierre trained in law and quickly became a modestly successful lawyer. His eloquence and his consistent, or ruthless, insistence that leaders respect the "will of the people" eventually won him a following in the Jacobin club. Later, he became president of the National Convention and a member of the Committee of Public Safety. Though he had little to do with starting the Terror, he was nevertheless responsible for enlarging its scope. Known as "the Incorruptible," he came to represent ruthlessness justified as virtue and necessary to revolutionary progress.

The two years of the radical republic (August 1792–July 1794) brought dictatorship, centralization, suspension of any liberties, and war. The committee faced foreign enemies and opposition from both the political right and left at home. In June 1793, responding to an escalating crisis, leaders of the "Mountain," a party of radicals allied with Parisian artisans, purged moderates from the convention. Rebellions broke out in the provincial cities of Lyons, Bordeaux, and Marseilles, mercilessly repressed by the committee and its local representatives. The government also faced counterrevolution in the western region known as the Vendée, where movements enlisted peasants and artisans, who believed their local areas were being invaded and who fought for their local priest or against the summons from the revolutionaries' conscription boards. By the summer, the forces in the Vendée posed a serious threat to the convention. Determined to stabilize France, whatever the cost, the committee redeployed its forces, defeated the counterrevolutionaries, and launched murderous campaigns of pacification—torching villages, farms, and fields and killing all who dared oppose them and many who did not.

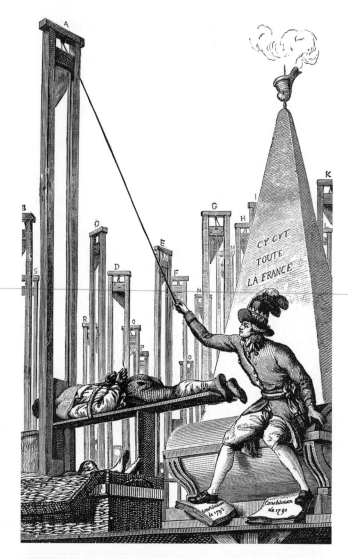

ROBESPIERRE GUILLOTINING THE EXECUTIONER. The original caption for this 1793 engraving read "Robespierre guillotines the executioner after having had all the French guillotined." In fact, Robespierre himself was guillotined after his fall from power in July 1794. ■ *What made the struggle for power and authority among revolutionaries so merciless and uncompromising?*

During the period of the Terror, from September 1793 to July 1794, the most reliable estimates place the number of deaths at close to 40,000 to about 16,500 from actual death sentences, with the rest resulting from extra-judicial killings and deaths in prison. Approximately 300,000 were incarcerated between March 1793 and August 1794. These numbers, however, do not include the pacification of the Vendée and rebellious cities in the Rhone Valley, which took more than 100,000 lives. Few victims of the Terror were aristocrats. Many more were peasants or laborers accused of hoarding, treason, or counterrevolutionary activity. Anyone who appeared to threaten the republic, no matter what his or her social or economic position, was at risk. When some time later the Abbé Sieyès was asked what he had done to distinguish himself during the Terror, he responded dryly, "I lived."

The Legacy of the Second French Revolution

The "second" French Revolution affected the everyday life of French men, women, and children in a remarkably direct way. Workers' trousers replaced the breeches that had been a sartorial badge of the middle classes and the nobility. A red cap, said to symbolize freedom from slavery, became popular headgear, and wigs vanished. Men and women addressed each other as "citizen" or "citizeness." Public life was marked by ceremonies designed to dramatize the break with the Old Regime and celebrate new forms of fraternity. In the early stages of the revolution, these festivals seem to have captured genuine popular enthusiasm for new ways of living and thinking. Under the Committee of Public Safety, they became didactic and hollow.

The radical revolution of 1792–1793 also dramatically reversed the trend toward decentralization and democracy. The assembly replaced local officials, some of them still royalist in sympathy, with "deputies on mission," whose task was to conscript troops and generate patriotic fervor. When these deputies appeared too eager to act independently, they were replaced by "national agents," with instructions to report directly to the committee. In another effort to stabilize authority, the assembly closed down all the women's political clubs, decreeing them a political and social danger. Ironically, those who claimed to govern in the name of the people found the popular movement threatening.

Finally, the revolution eroded the strength of those traditional institutions—church, guild, parish—that had for centuries given people a common bond. In their place now stood patriotic organizations and a culture that insisted on loyalty to one national cause. Those organizations had first emerged with the election campaigns, meetings, and pamphlet wars of 1788 and the interest they heightened. They included the political clubs and local assemblies, which at the height of the revolution (1792–1793) met every day of the week and offered an apprenticeship in politics. The army of the republic became the premier national institution.

On the one hand, the revolution divided France, mobilizing counterrevolutionaries as well as revolutionaries. At the same time, the revolution, war, and culture of sacrifice forged new bonds. The sense that the rest of Europe, carrying what the verses of the "Marseillaise," the most famous anthem of the revolution, called the "blood-stained flag of tyranny," sought to crush the new nation and its citizens unquestionably strengthened French national identity.

FROM THE TERROR TO BONAPARTE: THE DIRECTORY

The Committee of Public Safety might have saved France from enemy armies, but it could not save itself. Inflation became catastrophic. The long string of military victories convinced growing numbers that the committee's demands for continuing self-sacrifice and Terror were no longer justified. By July 1794, the committee was virtually without allies. On July 27 (9 Thermidor, according to the new calendar), Robespierre was shouted down while attempting to speak on the floor of the convention. The following day, along with twenty-one other conspirators, he met his death by guillotine.

Ending the Terror did not immediately bring moderation. Vigilante groups of royalists hunted down Jacobins. The repeal of price controls, combined with the worst winter in a century, caused widespread misery. Other measures that had constituted the Terror were gradually repealed. In 1795, the National Convention adopted a new and more conservative constitution. It granted suffrage to all adult male citizens who could read and write. Yet it set up indirect elections: citizens voted for electors, who in turn chose the legislative body. Wealthy citizens thus held authority. Eager

PATRIOTIC WOMEN'S CLUB. The members of this patriotic club wear constitutional bonnets to show their support for the revolution and the reforms of the convention. ▪ *What can one conclude about the atmosphere in Paris during the revolution from the existence of such associations?*

to avoid personal dictatorship, it vested executive authority in a board of five men known as the Directory, chosen by the legislative body. The new constitution included not only a bill of rights but also a declaration of the duties of the citizen.

The Directory lasted longer than its revolutionary predecessors. It still faced discontent on both the radical left and the conservative right. On the left, the Directory repressed radical movements to abolish private property and parliamentary-style government, including one led by the radical "Gracchus Babeuf." Dispatching threats from the right proved more challenging. In 1797, the first free elections held in France as a republic returned a large number of

monarchists to the councils of government, alarming politicians who had voted to execute Louis XVI. Backed by the army, the Directory annulled most of the election results. After two years of more uprisings and purges, and with the country still plagued by severe inflation, the Directors grew desperate. This time they called for help from a brilliant young general named Napoleon Bonaparte.

Bonaparte's first military victory had come in 1793, with the recapture of Toulon from royalist and British forces, and had earned him promotion from captain to brigadier general at the age of twenty-four. After the Terror, he was briefly arrested for his Jacobin associations. But he proved his usefulness to the Directory in October 1795 when he put down an uprising with "a whiff of grapeshot," saving the new regime from its opponents. Promoted, he won a string of victories in Italy, forcing Austria to withdraw (temporarily) from the war. He attempted to defeat Britain by attacking British forces in Egypt and the Near East, a campaign that went well on land but ran into trouble at sea, where the French fleet was defeated by Admiral Horatio Nelson (Abukir Bay, 1798). Bonaparte found himself trapped in Egypt by the British and unable to win a decisive victory.

It was at this point that the call came from the Directory. Bonaparte slipped away from Egypt and appeared in Paris, already having agreed to participate in a coup d'état with the leading Director, that former revolutionary champion of the Third Estate, the Abbé Sieyès. On November 9, 1799 (18 Brumaire), Bonaparte was declared a "temporary consul." He was the answer to the Directory's prayers: a strong, popular leader who was not a king. Sieyès declared that Bonaparte would provide "[c]onfidence from below, authority from above." With those words Sieyès pronounced the end of the revolutionary period.

NAPOLEON AND IMPERIAL FRANCE

Few figures in Western history have compelled the attention of the world as Napoleon Bonaparte did during the fifteen years of his rule in France. Few men lived on with such persistence as myth, not just in their own countries, but across the West. Why? For the great majority of ordinary Europeans, memories of the French Revolution were dominated by those of the Napoleonic Wars, which devastated Europe, convulsed its politics, and traumatized its peoples for a generation.

Yet Bonaparte's relationship to the revolution was not simple. His regime consolidated some of the revolution's

FRANCE AND ITS SISTER REPUBLICS. ▪ *The French revolutionaries, fighting against the conservative monarchs of Europe, conquered and annexed large sections of what three countries?* ▪ *Who were potential supporters of the French Revolution in areas outside France during the Napoleonic era?* ▪ *Who was most likely to oppose it in these areas?*

political and social changes but sharply repudiated others. He presented himself as the son of the revolution, but he also borrowed freely from very different regimes, fashioning himself as the heir to Charlemagne or to the Roman Empire. His regime remade revolutionary politics and the French state; offered stunning examples of the new kinds of warfare; and left a legacy of conflict and legends of French glory that lingered in the dreams, or nightmares, of Europe's statesmen and citizens for more than a century.

Consolidating Authority: 1799–1804

Bonaparte's early career reinforced the claim that the revolution rewarded the efforts of able men. The son of a provincial Corsican nobleman, he attended the École Militaire in Paris. In prerevolutionary France he would have been unable to rise beyond the rank of major, which required buying a regimental command. The revolution, however, abolished the purchase of military office, and Bonaparte quickly became a general. Here, then, was a man who had risen from obscurity because of his own gifts, which he lent happily to the service of France's revolution.

Once in power, however, Bonaparte showed less respect for revolutionary principles. After the coup of 1799, he assumed the title of "first consul." A new constitution established universal white male suffrage and set up two legislative bodies. Elections, however, were indirect, and the power of the legislative bodies sharply curbed. "The government?" said one observer. "There is Bonaparte." Bonaparte instituted what has since become a common authoritarian device, the plebiscite, which put a question directly to popular vote. This allows the head of state to bypass politicians or legislative bodies who might disagree with him—as well as permitting local officials to tamper with ballot boxes. In 1802, flush with victory abroad, he asked the legislature to proclaim him consul for life. When the Senate refused to do so, Bonaparte's Council of State stepped in, offered him the title, and had it ratified by plebiscite. Throughout, his regime retained the appearance of consulting with the people, but its most important feature was the centralization of authority.

That authority came from reorganizing the state, and on this score Bonaparte's accomplishments were extraordinary and lasting. Bonaparte's regime confirmed the abolition of privilege, thereby promising "careers open to talent." Centralizing administrative departments, he accomplished what no recent French regime had yet achieved: an orderly and generally fair system of taxation. More efficient tax collection and fiscal management also helped halt the inflationary spiral that had crippled the revolutionary governments,

although Bonaparte's regime relied heavily on resources from areas he had conquered to fund his military ventures. As we have seen, earlier revolutionary regimes began to reorganize France's administration—abolishing the ancient fiefdoms with their separate governments, legal codes, privileges, and customs—setting up a uniform system of departments. Bonaparte continued that work, pressing it further and putting an accent on centralization. He replaced elected officials and local self-government with centrally appointed prefects and subprefects, who answered directly to the Council of State in Paris. The prefects wielded considerable power, much more than any elected representative: they were in charge of everything from collecting statistics and reporting on the economy and the population to education, roads, and public works. With more integrated administration, in which the different branches were coordinated (and supervised from above), a more professional bureaucracy, and more rational and efficient taxation (though the demands of war strained the system), Napoleon's state marked the transition from Bourbon absolutism to the modern state.

Law, Education, and a New Elite

Napoleon's most significant contribution to modern state building was the promulgation of a new legal code in 1804. Each revolutionary regime had taken up the daunting task of modernizing the laws; each had run out of time. Napoleon tolerated no delays, and threw himself into the project, pressing his own ideas and supervising half the meetings. The Napoleonic Code, as the civil code came to be called, pivoted on two principles that had remained significant through all the constitutional changes since 1789: uniformity and individualism. It cleared through the thicket of contradictory legal traditions that governed the ancient provinces of France, creating one uniform law. It confirmed the abolition of feudal privileges of all kinds: not only noble and clerical privileges but the special rights of craft guilds, municipalities, and so on. It set the conditions for exercising property rights: the drafting of contracts, leases, and stock companies. The code's provisions on the family, which Napoleon developed personally, insisted on the importance of paternal authority and the subordination of women and children. In 1793, during the most radical period of the revolution, men and women had been declared "equal in marriage"; now Napoleon's code affirmed the "natural supremacy" of the husband. Married women could not sell property, run a business, or have a profession without their husbands' permission. Fathers had the sole right to control their children's financial affairs, consent to their marriages, and (under the ancient right to correction) to imprison

Interpreting Visual Evidence

Representing the People during the French Revolution

From the moment the population of Paris came to the assistance of the beleaguered National Assembly in July 1789, representations of "the people" in the French Revolution took on an overwhelming significance. Building a new government that was committed to an idea of popular sovereignty meant that both the revolution's supporters and its opponents were deeply invested in shaping perceptions of the people. And of course, Article III of the Declaration of the Rights of Man ("The principle of sovereignty resides essentially in the

nation") meant that any individual, group, or institution that could successfully claim to represent the will of the people could wield tremendous power, as long as others accepted that claim.

Of course, revolutionary crowds did not always conform to the images of them that circulated so widely in prints and paintings during the period 1789–1799. Some were spontaneous, and others were organized; some were made up of recognizable social and professional groups with clear political goals, and others were a hodgepodge of conflicting and even inarticulate aspirations. Many were nonviolent; some were exceedingly

threatening and murderous. All politicians sought to use them to support their political programs, and many learned to fear their unpredictable behavior.

These four images give a sense of the competing visions of the people that appeared in the public realm during the French Revolution. The first (image A) shows the killing of Foulon, a royal official who was lynched and beheaded by an enthusiastic crowd barely a week after the fall of the Bastille because he was suspected of conspiring to starve the Parisian population as punishment for their rebellion against the king. The second (image B) shows a more care-

A. The punishment of Foulon (anonymous print, 1789).

B. *The Festival of Federation* by Charles Thévenin, 1790.

fully choreographed representation of the people during the Festival of Federation, organized in July 1790 by the revolutionary government to commemorate the first anniversary of the fall of the Bastille. Finally, the last two documents show contrasting images of the revolutionary sans-culottes, the working-class revolutionaries who supported the government during the Terror in 1792–1794. The first (image C), a sympathetic portrait of a sans-culottes as a virtuous and self-sacrificing working man, standing with an eye to the future, seems completely incongruous when paired with the British satirist James Gilray's portrait of a cannibalistic sans-culottes family (image D), drawn literally "without pants," feasting on the bodies of their victims after a hard day's work.

Questions for Analysis

1. Image A depicts an event from July 1789—that is, before the August publication of the Declaration of the Rights of Man. How does this image portray the crowd's vengeance on Foulon? What possible political messages are contained in this image?

2. Image B, on the other hand, chooses to display the people celebrating their own birth as a political body, by convening on the anniversary of the fall of the Bastille. What emotions is this painting designed to invoke, and how is it related to more disturbing images such as image A?

3. How are the positive and negative portrayals of sans-culottes as political actors (images C and D) constructed? Can one imagine a painting of a worker like image C being produced before 1789? What does image D tell us about how the revolution was viewed from Britain?

C. A typical sans-culotte, painting by Louis-Léopold Boilly, 1792.

D. A family of sans-culottes [sic] refreshing after the fatigues of the day. (British satirical cartoon by James Gilray, 1793).

them for up to six months without showing cause. Divorce remained legal, but under unequal conditions; a man could sue for divorce on the grounds of adultery, but a woman could do so only if her husband moved his "concubine" into the family's house. Most important to the common people, the code prohibited paternity suits for illegitimate children.

In all, Napoleon developed seven legal codes covering commercial law, civil law and procedures, crime, and punishment. Like the civil code, the new criminal code consolidated some of the gains of the revolution, treating citizens as equals before the law and outlawing arbitrary arrest and imprisonment. Yet it, too, reinstated brutal measures that the revolutionaries had abolished, such as branding and cutting off the hands of parricides. The Napoleonic legal regime was more egalitarian than law under the Old Regime but no less concerned with authority.

Napoleon also rationalized the educational system. He ordered the establishment of *lycées* (high schools) in every major town to train civil servants and army officers and a school in Paris to train teachers. To supplement these changes, Napoleon brought the military and technical schools under state control and founded a national university to supervise the entire system. It is not surprising that he built up a new military academy. He reorganized and established solid financing for the premier schools of higher education: the polytechnic (for engineers) and the normal (for teachers), to which students would be admitted based on examinations and from which would issue the technical, educational, and political elites of the country. Like almost all his reforms, this one reinforced reforms introduced during the revolution, and it intended to abolish privilege and create "careers open to talent." Napoleon also embraced the burgeoning social and physical sciences of the Enlightenment. He sponsored the Institute of France, divided into four sections, or academies: fine arts, sciences, humanities, and language (the famous Académie française). These academies dated back to the age of absolutism—now they were coordinated and put on a new footing. They acquired under Napoleon the character that they have preserved to this day: centralized, meritocratic, and geared to serving the state.

Who benefited from these changes? Like Bonaparte's other new institutions, the new schools helped confirm the power of a new elite. The new elite included businessmen, bankers, and merchants but was still composed primarily of powerful landowners. What was more, at least half of the fellowships to the high schools went to the sons of military officers and high civil servants. Finally, like most of Bonaparte's reforms, changes in education aimed to strengthen the empire: "My object in establishing a teaching corps is to have a means of directing political and moral opinion," Napoleon said bluntly.

Bonaparte's early measures were ambitious. To win support for them, he made allies without regard for their past political affiliations. He admitted back into the country exiles of all political stripes. His two fellow consuls were a regicide of the Terror and a bureaucrat of the Old Regime. His minister of police had been an extreme radical republican; his minister of foreign affairs was the aristocrat and opportunist Charles Talleyrand. The most remarkable act of political reconciliation came in 1801, with Bonaparte's concordat with the pope, an agreement that put an end to more than a decade of hostility between the French state and the Catholic Church. Although it shocked anticlerical revolutionaries, Napoleon, ever the pragmatist, believed that reconciliation would create domestic harmony and international solidarity. The agreement gave the pope the right to depose French bishops and to discipline the French clergy. In return, the Vatican agreed to forgo any claims to Church lands expropriated by the revolution. That property would remain in the hands of its new middle-class rural and urban proprietors. The concordat did not revoke the principle of religious freedom established by the revolution, but it did win Napoleon the support of conservatives who had feared for France's future as a godless state.

Such political balancing acts increased Bonaparte's general popularity. Combined with early military successes (peace with Austria in 1801 and with Britain in 1802), they muffled any opposition to his personal ambitions. He had married Josephine de Beauharnais, a Creole from Martinique and an influential mistress of the revolutionary period. Josephine had given the Corsican soldier-politician legitimacy and access among the revolutionary elite early in his career. Neither Bonaparte nor his ambitious wife were content to be first among equals, however; and in December of 1804, he finally cast aside any traces of republicanism. In a ceremony that evoked the splendor of medieval kingship and Bourbon absolutism, he crowned himself Emperor Napoleon I in the Cathedral of Notre Dame in Paris. Napoleon did much to create the modern state, but he did not hesitate to proclaim his links to the past.

In Europe as in France: Napoleon's Empire

The nations of Europe had looked on—some in admiration, others in horror, all in astonishment—at the phenomenon that was Napoleon. Austria, Prussia, and Britain led two coalitions against revolutionary France in 1792–1795 and in 1798, and both were defeated. After Napoleon came to power in 1799, the alliance split. Russia and Austria withdrew from the fray in 1801, and even the intransigent British were forced to make peace the following year.

By 1805, the Russians, Prussians, Austrians, and Swedes had joined the British in an attempt to contain France. Their efforts were to no avail. Napoleon's military superiority led to defeats, in turn, of all the continental allies. Napoleon was a master of well-timed, well-directed shock attacks on the battlefield: movement, regrouping, and pressing his advantage. He led an army that had transformed European warfare; first raised as a revolutionary militia, it was now a trained conscript army, loyal, well supplied by a nation whose economy was committed to serving the war effort, and led by generals promoted largely on the basis of talent. This new kind of army inflicted crushing defeats on his enemies. The battle of Austerlitz, in December 1805, was a triumph for the French against the combined forces of Austria and Russia and became a symbol of the emperor's apparent invincibility. His subsequent victory against the Russians at Friedland in 1807 only added to his reputation.

Out of these victories, Napoleon created his new empire and affiliated states. To the southeast, the empire included Rome and the pope's dominions, Tuscany, and the Dalmatian territories of Austria (now the coastline of Croatia). To the east, Napoleon's rule extended over a federation of German states known as the Confederation of the Rhine and a section of Poland. These new states were presented as France's gift of independence to patriots elsewhere in Europe, but in practice they served as a military buffer against renewed expansion by Austria. The empire itself was ringed by the allied kingdoms of Italy, Naples, Spain, and Holland, whose thrones were occupied by Napoleon's brothers, brothers-in-law, and trusted generals.

The empire brought the French Revolution's practical consequences—a powerful, centralizing state and an end to old systems of privilege—to Europe's doorstep, applying to the empire principles that had already transformed France. Administrative modernization, which meant overhauling the procedures, codes, and practices of the state, was the most powerful feature of changes introduced. The empire changed the terms of government service (careers open to talent), handing out new titles and recruiting new men for the civil service and the judiciary. It ended the nobility's monopoly on the officer corps. The new branches of government hired engineers, mapmakers, surveyors, and legal consultants. Public works and education were reorganized. Prefects in the outer reaches of the empire, as in France, built roads, bridges, dikes (in Holland), hospitals, and prisons; they reorganized universities and built observatories. In the empire and some of the satellite kingdoms, tariffs were eliminated, feudal dues abolished, new tax districts formed, and plentiful new taxes collected to support the new state.

In the realm of liberty and law, Napoleon's rule eliminated feudal and church courts and created a single legal system. The Napoleonic Code was often introduced, but not always or entirely. (In southern Italy measures against the Catholic Church were deemed too controversial.) Reforms eliminated many inequalities and legal privileges. The Duchy of Warsaw in Poland ended serfdom but offered no land reform, so former serfs became impoverished tenants. In most areas, the empire gave civil rights to Protestants and Jews. In Rome, the conquering French opened the gates of the Jewish ghetto—and made Jews subject to conscription. In some areas, Catholic monasteries, convents, and other landholdings were broken up and sold, almost always to wealthy buyers. In the empire as in France, and under Napoleon as during the revolution, many who benefited were the elite: people and groups already on their way up and with the resources to take advantage of opportunities.

In government, the regime sought a combination of legal equality (for men) and stronger state authority. The French and local authorities created new electoral districts, expanded the suffrage, and wrote constitutions, but newly elected representative bodies were dismissed if they failed to cooperate, few constitutions were ever fully applied, and political freedoms were often fleeting. Napoleon's regime referred to revolutionary principles to anchor its legitimacy, but authority remained its guiding light. All governmental direction emanated from Paris and therefore from Napoleon.

Finally, in the empire as in France, Napoleon displayed his signature passions. The first of these was an Enlightenment zeal for accumulating useful knowledge. The empire gathered statistics as never before, for it was important to know the resources—including population—that a state had at its disposal. That spirit had been evident already in Bonaparte's extraordinary 1798 excursion into Egypt. He took hundreds of scholars and artists along with the army, founded the Egyptian institute in Cairo, and sent researchers off to make a systematic inventory of the country (its geology, rivers, minerals, antiquities, animal life) and to conduct archaeological expeditions to Upper Egypt, where they sketched the pyramids and excavated what would turn out to be the Rosetta Stone (see Chapter 20). Napoleon's second passion was cultivating his relationship to imperial glories of the past. He poured time and energy into (literally) cementing his image for posterity. The Arc de Triomphe in Paris, designed to imitate the Arc of Constantine in Rome, is the best example; but Napoleon also ordered work to be undertaken to restore ruins in Rome, to make the Prado Palace in Madrid a museum, and to renovate and preserve the Alhambra in Granada.

Such were Napoleon's visions of his legacy and himself. How did others see him? Europe offered no single

reaction. Some countries and social groups collaborated enthusiastically, some negotiated, some resisted. Napoleon's image as a military hero genuinely inspired young men from the elite, raised in a culture that prized military honor. By contrast, Catholic peasants in Spain fought him from the beginning. In many small principalities previously ruled by princes—the patchwork states of Germany, for example, and the repressive kingdom of Naples—reforms that provided for more efficient, less corrupt administration, a workable tax structure, and an end to customary privilege were welcomed by most of the local population. Yet the Napoleonic presence proved a mixed blessing. Vassal states contributed heavily to the maintenance of the emperor's military power. The French levied taxes, drafted men, and required states to support occupying armies. In Italy, the policy was called "liberty and requisitions"; and the Italians, Germans, and Dutch paid an especially high price for reforms—in terms of economic cost and numbers of men recruited. From the point of view of the common people, the local lord and priest had been replaced by the French tax collector and army recruiting board.

It is telling that even Napoleon's enemies came to believe that the upstart emperor represented the wave of the future,

NAPOLEON'S EUROPEAN EMPIRE AT ITS HEIGHT. At the height of his power in 1812, Napoleon controlled most of Europe, ruling either directly or through dependent states and allies. ▪ *Compared to the map on page 600, by what means had Napoleon expanded French control on continental Europe?* ▪ *Which major countries remained outside of French control?* ▪ *Which areas felt the most long-lasting impact of Napoleon's reign?*

NAPOLEON ON HORSEBACK AT THE ST. BERNARD PASS BY JACQUES-LOUIS DAVID, 1801, AND *LITTLE BONEY GONE TO POT* BY GEORGE CRUIKSHANK, 1814. The depth of Napoleon's celebrity in Europe can be measured in the equal shares of adulation and hatred that he stirred up within Europe among his supporters and his enemies. David's portrait, painted before he became emperor of France, captures the ardent hopes that many attached to his person. The painting explicitly compared Napoleon to two previous European conquerors, Charlemagne and the ancient Roman emperor Hannibal, by evoking their names in the stones at the base of the painting. In George Cruikshanks's bitter caricature, published after Napoleon's exile to Elba, the devil offers him a pistol to commit suicide, and the former emperor, seated on a chamber pot, says he might, but only if the firing mechanism is disabled. Both images use assumptions about virility and masculine authority to make their point. ▪ *Who are the intended audiences for these images, and how do they convey their respective arguments?*

particularly in regard to the reorganization of the state. Though they fought Napoleon, Prussian and Austrian administrators set about instituting reforms that resembled his: changing rules of promotion and recruitment, remodeling bureaucracies, redrawing districts, eliminating some privileges, and so on. Many who came of age under Napoleon's empire believed that, for better or worse, his empire was modern.

THE RETURN TO WAR AND NAPOLEON'S DEFEAT: 1806–1815

Napoleon's boldest attempt at consolidation, a policy banning British goods from the Continent, was a dangerous failure. Britain had bitterly opposed each of France's revolutionary regimes since the death of Louis XVI; now it tried to rally Europe against Napoleon with promises of generous financial loans and trade. Napoleon's Continental System, established in 1806, sought to starve Britain's trade and force its surrender. The system failed for several reasons. Throughout the war, Britain retained control of the seas. The British naval blockade of the Continent, begun in 1807, effectively countered Napoleon's system. While the French Empire strained to transport goods and raw materials overland to avoid the British blockade, the British successfully developed a lively trade with South America. A second reason for the failure of the system was its internal tariffs. Europe divided into economic camps, at odds with each other as they tried to subsist on what the Continent alone could produce and manufacture. Finally, the system hurt the Continent more than Britain. Stagnant trade in Europe's ports and unemployment in its manufacturing centers eroded public faith in Napoleon's dream of a working European empire.

The Continental System was Napoleon's first serious mistake. His ambition to create a European empire, modeled on Rome and ruled from Paris, was to become a second cause of his decline. The symbols of his empire—reflected in painting, architecture, and the design of furniture and clothing—were deliberately Roman in origin. Where early revolutionaries referred to the Roman Republic for their imagery, Napoleon looked to the more ostentatious style of the Roman emperors. In 1809, he divorced the empress Josephine and ensured himself a successor of royal blood by marrying a Habsburg princess, Marie Louise—the great-niece of Marie Antoinette. Such actions lost Napoleon the support of revolutionaries, former Enlightenment thinkers, and liberals across the Continent.

Over time, the bitter tonic of defeat began to have an effect on Napoleon's enemies, who changed their own approach to waging war. After the Prussian army was humiliated at Jena in 1806 and forced out of the war, a whole generation of younger Prussian officers reformed their military and their state by demanding rigorous practical training for commanders and a genuinely national army made up of patriotic Prussian citizens rather than well-drilled mercenaries.

The myth of Napoleon's invincibility worked against him as well, as he took ever greater risks with France's military and national fortunes. Russian numbers and Austrian artillery inflicted horrendous losses on the French at Wagram in 1809, although these difficulties were forgotten in the glow of victory. Napoleon's allies and supporters shrugged off the British admiral Horatio Nelson's victory at Trafalgar in 1805 as no more than a temporary check to the emperor's ambitions. But Trafalgar broke French naval power in the Mediterranean and led to a rift with Spain, which had been France's equal partner in the battle and suffered equally in the defeat. In the Caribbean, too, Napoleon was forced to cut growing losses (see below).

A crucial moment in Napoleon's undoing came with his invasion of Spain in 1808. Napoleon overthrew the Spanish king, installed his own brother on the throne, and then imposed a series of reforms similar to those he had instituted elsewhere in Europe. Napoleon's blow against the Spanish monarchy weakened its hold on its colonies across the Atlantic, and the Spanish crown never fully regained its grip (see Chapter 20). But in Spain itself,

NAPOLEON ON THE BATTLEFIELD OF EYLAU. Amid bitter cold and snow, Napoleon engaged with the Russian army in February 1807. Although technically a victory for the French, it was only barely that, with the French losing at least 10,000 men and the Russians twice as many. This painting, characteristic of Bonaparte propaganda, emphasizes not the losses but the emperor's saintlike clemency—even enemy soldiers reach up toward him.

Napoleon reckoned without two factors that led to the ultimate failure of his mission: the presence of British forces and the determined resistance of the Spanish people, who detested Napoleon's interference in the affairs of the church. The Peninsular Wars, as the Spanish conflicts were called, were long and bitter. The smaller British force learned how to concentrate a devastating volume of gunfire on the French pinpoint attacks on the open battlefield and laid siege to French garrison towns. The Spanish quickly began to wear down the French invaders through guerrilla warfare. Terrible atrocities were committed by both sides; the French military's torture and execution of Spanish guerrillas and civilians was immortalized by the Spanish artist Francisco Goya (1746–1828) with sickening accuracy in his prints and paintings. Though at one point Napoleon himself took charge of his army, he could not achieve anything more than temporary victory. The Spanish campaign was the first indication that Napoleon could be beaten, and it encouraged resistance elsewhere.

The second, and most dramatic, stage in Napoleon's downfall began with the disruption of his alliance with Russia. As an agricultural country, Russia had suffered a severe economic crisis when it was no longer able to trade its surplus grain for British manufactures. The consequence was that Tsar Alexander I began to wink at trade with Britain and to ignore or evade the protests from Paris. By 1811, Napoleon decided that he could no longer endure this flouting of their agreement. He collected an

army of 600,000 and set out for Russia in the spring of 1812. Only a third of the soldiers in this "Grande Armée" were French; nearly as many were Polish or German, joined by soldiers and adventurers from the rest of France's client states. It was the grandest of Napoleon's imperial expeditions, an army raised from across Europe and sent to punish the autocratic tsar. The invasion ended in disaster. The Russians refused to make a stand, drawing the French farther and farther into the heart of their country. Just before Napoleon reached the ancient Russian capital of Moscow, the Russian army drew the French forces into a bloody, seemingly pointless battle in the narrow streets of a town called Borodino, where both sides suffered terrible losses of men and supplies, harder on the French who were now so far from home. After the battle, the Russians permitted Napoleon to occupy Moscow. But on the night of his entry, Russian partisans put the city to the torch, leaving little but the blackened walls of the Kremlin palaces to shelter the French troops.

Hoping that the tsar would eventually surrender, Napoleon lingered amid the ruins for more than a month. On October 19, he finally ordered the homeward march. The delay was a fatal blunder. Long before he had reached the border, the terrible Russian winter was on his troops. Frozen streams, mountainous drifts of snow, and bottomless mud slowed the retreat almost to a halt. To add to the miseries of frostbite, disease, and starvation, mounted Cossacks rode out of the blizzard to harry the exhausted army. Each morning the miserable remnant that pushed on left behind circles of corpses around the campfires of the night before. Temperatures dropped to −27°F. On December 13, a few thousand broken soldiers crossed the frontier into Germany—a fragment of the once proud Grande Armée. Nearly 300,000 of its soldiers and untold thousands of Russians lost their lives in Napoleon's Russian adventure.

After the retreat from Russia, the anti-Napoleonic forces took renewed hope. United by a belief that they might finally succeed in defeating the emperor, Prussia, Russia, Austria, Sweden, and Britain renewed their attack. Citizens of many German states in particular saw this as a war of liberation, and indeed most of the fighting took

THE DISASTERS OF WAR* BY FRANCISCO GOYA (1746–1828).** Goya was a Spanish painter and political liberal who had initially supported the French revolution. After Napoleon invaded Spain in 1807, Spaniards rose up in revolt, leading to the Peninsular War of 1808–1814. Between 1810 and 1820, Goya documented the war's violence in a series of black-and-white prints containing stark images of atrocity, rape, and the aftermath of famine. Note the absence of political imagery and the pointed and bitter irony of Goya's caption: "A great heroic feat! With dead people!" ▪ ***Who or what is the target of Goya's sarcasm here?

place in Germany. The climax of the campaign occurred in October 1813 when, at what was thereafter known as the Battle of the Nations, fought near Leipzig, the allies dealt the French a resounding defeat. Meanwhile, allied armies won significant victories in the Low Countries and Spain. By the beginning of 1814, they had crossed the Rhine into France. Left with an army of inexperienced youths, Napoleon retreated to Paris, urging the French people to resist despite constant setbacks at the hands of the larger invading armies. On March 31, Tsar Alexander I of Russia and King Frederick William III of Prussia made their triumphant entry into Paris. Napoleon was forced to abdicate unconditionally and was sent into exile on the island of Elba, off the Italian coast.

Napoleon was back on French soil in less than a year. In the interim, the allies had restored the Bourbon dynasty to the throne, in the person of Louis XVIII, brother of Louis XVI. Despite his administrative abilities, Louis could not fill the void left by Napoleon's abdication. It was no surprise that when the former emperor staged his escape from Elba, his fellow countrymen once more rallied to his

Analyzing Primary Sources

Napoleon the "Liberator"?

Did Napoleon continue the work of the French Revolution? These two documents, from early and late moments in Napoleon's career, allow one to judge the extent to which Napoleon's regime shared the goals of revolutionaries who preceded him.

The first document concerns Napoleon's decision to reestablish slavery in French colonies. The slaves of Saint-Domingue had freed themselves by insurrection in 1791, and the French revolutionary government made this freedom official by abolishing slavery on French territory in 1794. In 1802, Napoleon launched an expeditionary force to reimpose French control over the colony, and in the course of this conflict it became clear that his goal was reenslavement. The former slaves of Saint-Domingue defeated Napoleon's troops and established Haiti as an independent nation, but in the nearby French colonies of Tobago, Martinique, and Guadeloupe, as well as in French holdings in the Indian Ocean, Napoleon reinstituted slavery. The first excerpt below is from a preliminary draft for the law on reenslavement that Napoleon drew up himself.

The second selection is excerpted from a proclamation that Napoleon addressed to the sovereigns of Europe on his return to France in March 1815, after escaping from his exile on the island of Elba. It is an excellent illustration of Napoleon's self-image at the end of his career, his rhetoric, and his belief that he represented the force of history itself.

Letter to Consul Cambacérès, April 27, 1802

The consuls of the Republic and informed council of State decree:

Article One: According to the reports made to the captain-general of the colony of _____ by those individuals who will commit to this result, a list will be composed comprising first the names of black people who enjoyed freedom before 26 Pluviôse, Year II, and second, the names of blacks who have united to defend the territory of the Republic from its enemies, or who, in any other matter, have served the state.

Article Two: All the individuals named on this list will be declared free.

Article Three: Those among them who do not own property, and who have not trade or skill which can assure their subsistence, will be subjected to the regulations of the police who will assign them to property owners who will support them in agricultural work, determine their pay, and will stipulate above all arrangements for preventing vagabondage and insubordination.

Article Four: Insubordinates and outspoken vagabonds will be, in cases determined by the regulations, struck from the list and deprived of the advantages which result from it. One can substitute for this arrangement deportation to colonies where the emancipation laws have not been enacted.

Article Five: All blacks not included on the aforementioned list in article one will be subjected to the laws which in 1789 comprised the Black Code in the colonies [the Black Code was the law regulating the practice of slavery].

Article Six: It will be permitted to import blacks in the colony of _____ in accordance with the laws and regulations of the trade which were in place in 1789. The minister of the marine is charged with the execution of the present order.

Source: Laura Mason and Tracey Rizzo, *The French Revolution: A Document Collection* (Boston: 1999), pp. 349–50.

side. By the time Napoleon reached Paris, he had generated enough support to cause Louis to flee the country. The allies, meeting in Vienna to conclude peace treaties with the French, were stunned by the news of Napoleon's return. They dispatched a hastily organized army to meet the emperor's typically bold offensive push into the Low Countries. At the battle of Waterloo, fought over three bloody days from June 15 to 18, 1815, Napoleon was stopped by the forces of his two most persistent enemies, Britain and Prussia, and suffered his final defeat. This time, the allies took no chances and shipped their prisoner off to the bleak island of St. Helena in the South Atlantic. The once-mighty emperor, now the exile Bonaparte, lived out a dreary existence writing self-serving memoirs until his death in 1821.

Circular Letter to the Sovereigns of Europe, April 4, 1815

onsieur, My Brother,

You will have learnt, during the course of last month, of my landing again in France, of my entry into Paris, and of the departure of the Bourbon family. Your Majesty must by now be aware of the real nature of these events. They are the work of an irresistible power, of the unanimous will of a great nation conscious of its duties and of its rights. A dynasty forcibly reimposed upon the French people was no longer suitable for it: the Bourbons refused to associate themselves with the natural feelings or the national customs; and France was forced to abandon them. The popular voice called for a liberator. The expectation which had decided me to make the supreme sacrifice was in vain. I returned; and from the place where my foot first touched the shore I was carried by the affection of my subjects into the bosom of my capital.

My first and heartfelt anxiety is to repay so much affection by the maintenance of an honourable peace. The re-establishment of the Imperial throne was necessary for the happiness of Frenchmen: my dearest hope is that it may also secure repose for the whole of Europe. Each national flag in turn has had its gleam of glory: often enough, by some turn of fortune, great victories have been followed by great defeats. . . . I have provided the world in the past with a programme of great contests; it will please me better in future to acknowledge no rivalry but that of the advocates of peace, and no combat but a crusade for the felicity of mankind. It is France's pleasure to make a frank avowal of this noble ideal. Jealous of her independence, she will always base her policy upon an unqualified respect for the independence of other peoples. . . .

Monsieur my Brother,
Your good Brother,
Napoleon

Source: K. M. Baker, ed., *The Old Regime and the French Revolution* (Chicago: 1987), pp. 419–420, 426–427.

Questions for Analysis

1. Who in the Caribbean colonies did Napoleon intend to send back into slavery in 1802? Who was to remain free? What did Napoleon hope to accomplish by returning to the prerevolutionary legislation that authorized slavery?

2. In his 1815 address to the monarchs of Europe, can one still detect certain aspects of revolutionary rhetoric in Napoleon's words, even as he harnessed this rhetoric to his project of reestablishing the empire after his 1814 defeat?

3. Looking back on his career of ambitious conquests, what can Napoleon have hoped to accomplish in 1815 by boasting that France's "jealous" protection of her own independence gave her an "unqualified respect for the independence of other peoples"? Do his statements reveal a contradiction between the French revolution's commitment to the "universal" rights of man and the pursuit of national self-interests?

Liberty, Politics, and Slavery: The Haitian Revolution

In the French colonies across the Atlantic, the revolution took a different course, with wide-ranging ramifications. The Caribbean islands of Guadeloupe, Martinique, and Saint-Domingue occupied a central role in the eighteenth-century French economy because of the sugar trade. Their planter elites had powerful influence in Paris.

The French National Assembly (like its American counterpart) declined to discuss the matter of slavery in the colonies, unwilling to encroach on the property rights of slave owners and fearful of losing the lucrative sugar islands to their British or Spanish rivals should discontented slave owners talk of independence from France. (Competition between the European powers for the islands of the Caribbean was intense; that islands would change hands was a real possibility.) French men in the National Assembly also had to consider the question of

The Atlantic Revolutions and Human Rights

The eighteenth-century revolutions in the Atlantic world, such as the slave revolt in Saint Domingue (left), were based on the idea that individual rights were universal—they applied to everybody. Since the world is divided into autonomous nation-states, however, it has been challenging for defenders of universal human rights, like the organization Amnesty International (right), to ensure their enforcement globally.

 Watch related author interview on StudySpace
wwnorton.com/web/westernciv18

rights for free men of color, a group that included a significant number of wealthy owners of property (and slaves).

Saint-Domingue had about 40,000 whites of different social classes, 30,000 free people of color, and 500,000 slaves, most of them recently enslaved in West Africa. In 1790, free people of color from Saint-Domingue sent a delegation to Paris, asking to be seated by the assembly, underscoring that they were men of property and, in many cases, of European ancestry. The assembly refused. Their refusal sparked a rebellion among free people of color in Saint-Domingue. The French colonial authorities repressed the movement quickly—and brutally. They captured Vincent Ogé, a member of the delegation to Paris and one of the leaders of the rebellion, and publicly executed him and his allies by breaking on the wheel and decapitation. Radical deputies in Paris, including Robespierre, expressed outrage but could do little to change the assembly's policy.

In August 1791, the largest slave rebellion in history broke out in Saint-Domingue. How much that rebellion owed to revolutionary propaganda is unclear; like many rebellions during the period, it had its own roots. The British and the Spanish invaded, confident they could crush the rebellion and take the island. In the spring of 1792, the French government, on the verge of collapse and war with Europe, scrambled to win allies in Saint-Domingue by making free men of color citizens. A few months later (after the revolution of August 1792), the new French Republic dispatched commissioners to Saint-Domingue with troops and instructions to hold the island. There they faced a combination of different forces: Spanish and British troops, defiant Saint-Domingue planters, and slaves in rebellion. In this context, the local French commissioners reconsidered their commitment to slavery; in 1793, they promised freedom to slaves who would join the French. A year later, the assembly in Paris extended to slaves in all the colonies a liberty that had already been accomplished in Saint-Domingue, by the slave rebellion.

Emancipation and war brought new leaders to the fore, chief among them a former slave, Toussaint Bréda, later Toussaint L'Ouverture (*too-SAN LOO-vehr-tur*), meaning "the one who opened the way." Over the course of the next five years, Toussaint and his soldiers, now allied with the French army, emerged victorious over the French planters, the British (in 1798), and the Spanish (in 1801). Toussaint also broke the power of his rival generals in both the mulatto and former slave armies, becoming the statesman of the revolution. In 1801, Toussaint set up a constitution, swearing allegiance to France but denying France any right to interfere in Saint-Domingue affairs. The constitution abolished slavery, reorganized the military, established Christianity as the state religion (this entailed a rejection of vodoun, a blend of Christian and various West and Central African traditions), and made Toussaint governor for life. It was an extraordinary moment in the revolutionary period: the formation of an authoritarian society but also an utterly unexpected symbol of the universal potential of revolutionary ideas.

TOUSSAINT L'OUVERTURE. A portrait of L'Ouverture, leader of what would become the Haitian Revolution, as a general.

Toussaint's accomplishments, however, put him on a collision course with the other French general he admired and whose career was remarkably like his own: Napoleon Bonaparte. Saint-Domingue stood at the center of Bonaparte's vision of an expanded empire in the New World, an empire that would recoup North American territories France had lost under the Old Regime and pivot around the lucrative combination of the Mississippi, French Louisiana, and the sugar and slave colonies of the Caribbean. In January 1802, Bonaparte dispatched 20,000 troops to bring the island under control. Toussaint, captured when he arrived for discussions with the French, was shipped under heavy guard to a prison in the mountains of eastern France, where he died in 1803. Fighting continued in Saint-Domingue, however, with fires now fueled by Bonaparte's decree reestablishing slavery where the convention had abolished it. The war turned into a nightmare for the French. Yellow fever killed thousands of French troops, including one of Napoleon's best generals and brother-in-law. Armies on both sides committed atrocities. By December 1803, the French army had collapsed. Napoleon scaled back his vision of an American empire and sold the Louisiana territories to Thomas Jefferson. "I know the value of what I abandon . . . I renounce it with the greatest regret," he told an aide. In Saint-Domingue, a general in the army of former slaves, Jean-Jacques Dessalines, declared the independent state of Haiti in 1804.

The Haitian Revolution remained, in significant ways, an anomaly. It was the only successful slave revolution in history and by far the most radical of the revolutions that occurred in this age. It suggested that the emancipatory ideas of the revolution and Enlightenment might apply to non-Europeans and enslaved peoples—a suggestion that residents of Europe attempted to ignore but one that struck home with planter elites in North and South America. Combined with later rebellions in the British colonies, it contributed to the British decision to end slavery in 1838. And it cast a long shadow over nineteenth-century slave societies from the southern United States to Brazil. The Napoleonic episode, then, had wide-ranging effects across the Atlantic: in North America, the Louisiana purchase; in the Caribbean, the Haitian Revolution; in Latin America, the weakening of Spain and Portugal's colonial empires.

CONCLUSION

The tumultuous events in France formed part of a broad pattern of late-eighteenth-century democratic upheaval. The French Revolution was the most violent, protracted, and contentious of the revolutions of the era; but the dynamics of revolution were much the same everywhere. One of the most important developments of the French Revolution was the emergence of a popular movement, which included political clubs representing people previously excluded from politics, newspapers read by and to the common people, and political leaders who spoke for the sans-culottes. In the French Revolution, as in other revolutions, the popular movement challenged the early and moderate revolutionary leadership, pressing for more radical and democratic measures. And, as in other revolutions, the popular movement in France was defeated, and authority was reestablished by a quasi-military figure. Likewise, the revolutionary ideas of liberty, equality, and fraternity were not specifically French; their roots lay in the social structures of the eighteenth century and in the ideas and culture of the Enlightenment. Yet French armies brought them, literally, to the doorsteps of many Europeans.

What was the larger impact of the revolution and the Napoleonic era? Its legacy is partly summed up in three key concepts: liberty, equality, and nation. Liberty meant individual rights and responsibilities and, more

After You Read This Chapter

Visit StudySpace for quizzes, additional review materials, and multi-media documents. **wwnorton.com/web/westernciv18**

REVIEWING THE OBJECTIVES

- The French Revolution resulted both from an immediate political crisis and long-term social tensions. What was this crisis, and how did it lead to popular revolt against the monarchy?
- The revolutionaries in the National Assembly in 1789 set out to produce a constitution for France. What were their political goals, and what was the reaction of monarchs and peoples elsewhere in Europe?
- After 1792, a more radical group of revolutionaries seized control of the French state. How did they come to power, and how were their political goals different from their predecessors?
- Napoleon's career began during the revolution. What did he owe to the revolution, and what was different about his regime?
- Three major revolutions took place in the Atlantic world at the end of the eighteenth century: the American Revolution, the French Revolution, and the Haitian Revolution. What was similar about these revolutions? What was different?

specifically, freedom from arbitrary authority. By equality, as we have seen, the revolutionaries meant the abolition of legal distinctions of rank among European men. Though their concept of equality was limited, it became a powerful mobilizing force in the nineteenth century. The most important legacy of the revolution may have been the new term *nation*. Nationhood was a political concept. A nation was formed of citizens, not a king's subjects; it was ruled by law and treated citizens as equal before the law; sovereignty did not lie in dynasties or historic fiefdoms but in the nation of citizens. This new form of nation gained legitimacy when citizen armies repelled attacks against their newly won freedoms; the victories of "citizens in arms" lived on in myth and history and provided the most powerful images of the period. As the war continued, military nationhood began to overshadow its political cousin. By the Napoleonic period, this shift became decisive; a new political body of freely associated citizens was most powerfully embodied in a centralized state, its army and a kind of citizenship defined by individual commitment to the needs of the nation at war. This understanding of national identity spread throughout Europe in the coming decades.

PEOPLE, IDEAS, AND EVENTS IN CONTEXT

- Why was **LOUIS XVI** forced to convene the **ESTATES GENERAL** in 1789?

- What argument did **ABBÉ SIEYÈS** make about the role of the **THIRD ESTATE**?

- What made the **TENNIS COURT OATH** a revolutionary act?

- What was the role of popular revolt (the attack on the **BASTILLE**, the **GREAT FEAR**, the **OCTOBER DAYS**) in the revolutionary movements of 1789?

- What was the connection between the French Revolution with the **SLAVE REVOLT IN SAINT-DOMINGUE** that began in 1791?

- What was the **DECLARATION OF THE RIGHTS OF MAN AND OF THE CITIZEN**?

- What was the **CIVIL CONSTITUTION OF THE CLERGY**?

- What circumstances led to the abolition of the monarchy in 1792?

- Why did the **JACOBINS** in the **NATIONAL CONVENTION** support a policy of the **TERROR**?

- What were **NAPOLEON**'s most significant domestic accomplishments in France? What significance did Napoleon's military campaigns have for other parts of Europe and for the French Empire?

- What was the significance of the **HAITIAN REVOLUTION** of 1804?

THINKING ABOUT CONNECTIONS

- Popular movements in favor of democracy, social justice, or national self-determination in the more than two centuries since 1789 have often used the French Revolution as a point of reference or comparison. Obvious comparisons are those movements that saw themselves as "revolutionary," such as the Russian Revolution of 1917 or the Chinese Revolution of 1949. More recent comparisons might be the popular movements for democratic change in eastern Europe that resulted in the end of the Cold War in 1989 or the Arab Spring of 2011.

- Make a list of factors or circumstances that one might want to compare in considering the outcome of such movements. You might consider the degree to which elites support the current regime, the degree of consensus, and the goals of those who are protesting the status quo, economic circumstances, or international support for either the regime or for revolutionaries. What other factors might determine the outcome of revolutionary situations?

STORY LINES

- Industrialization put Europe on the path to a new form of economic development, based on the concentration of labor and production in areas with easy access to new sources of energy. This led to rapid growth of new industrial cities and to the development of new transportation to connect industrial centers to growing markets.

- Industrialization created new social groups in society, defined less by their status at birth than by their place in the new economy. Workers faced new kinds of discipline in the workplace, and women and children entered the new industrial workforce in large numbers. A new elite, made up of businessmen, entrepreneurs, bankers, engineers, and merchants, emerged as the primary beneficiaries of industrialization.

- Population growth in rural areas spurred migration to cities where laborers and the middle classes did not mix socially. They adopted different dress, speech, and leisure activities and had significantly different opportunities when it came to marriage, sex, and children.

CHRONOLOGY

1780s	Industrialization begins in Britain
1825	First railroad in Britain
1830s	Industrialization begins in France and Belgium
1845–1849	Irish potato famine
1850s	Industrialization begins in Prussia and German states of central Europe
1861	Russian tsar emancipates the serfs

Before
You
Read
This
Chapter

Rulers of Principal States

THE CAROLINGIAN DYNASTY

Pepin of Heristal, Mayor of the Palace, 687–714
Charles Martel, Mayor of the Palace, 715–741
Pepin III, Mayor of the Palace, 741–751; King, 751–768
Charlemagne, King, 768–814; Emperor, 800–814
Louis the Pious, Emperor, 814–840

West Francia

Charles the Bald, King, 840–877; Emperor, 875–877
Louis II, King, 877–879
Louis III, King, 879–882
Carloman, King, 879–884

Middle Kingdoms

Lothair, Emperor, 840–855
Louis (Italy), Emperor, 855–875
Charles (Provence), King, 855–863
Lothair II (Lorraine), King, 855–869

East Francia

Ludwig, King, 840–876
Carloman, King, 876–880
Ludwig, King, 876–882
Charles the Fat, Emperor, 876–887

HOLY ROMAN EMPERORS

Saxon Dynasty

Otto I, 962–973
Otto II, 973–983
Otto III, 983–1002
Henry II, 1002–1024

Franconian Dynasty

Conrad II, 1024–1039
Henry III, 1039–1056
Henry IV, 1056–1106
Henry V, 1106–1125
Lothair II (Saxony), 1125–1137

Hohenstaufen Dynasty

Conrad III, 1138–1152
Frederick I (Barbarossa), 1152–1190
Henry VI, 1190–1197
Philip of Swabia, 1198–1208 } Rivals
Otto IV (Welf), 1198–1215

Frederick II, 1220–1250
Conrad IV, 1250–1254

Interregnum, 1254–1273

Emperors from Various Dynasties

Rudolf I (Habsburg), 1273–1291
Adolf (Nassau), 1292–1298
Albert I (Habsburg), 1298–1308
Henry VII (Luxemburg), 1308–1313
Ludwig IV (Wittelsbach), 1314–1347
Charles IV (Luxemburg), 1347–1378
Wenceslas (Luxemburg), 1378–1400
Rupert (Wittelsbach), 1400–1410
Sigismund (Luxemburg), 1410–1437

Habsburg Dynasty

Albert II, 1438–1439
Frederick III, 1440–1493

Maximilian I, 1493–1519
Charles V, 1519–1556
Ferdinand I, 1556–1564
Maximilian II, 1564–1576
Rudolf II, 1576–1612
Matthias, 1612–1619
Ferdinand II, 1619–1637
Ferdinand III, 1637–1657

Leopold I, 1658–1705
Joseph I, 1705–1711
Charles VI, 1711–1740
Charles VII (not a Habsburg), 1742–1745
Francis I, 1745–1765
Joseph II, 1765–1790
Leopold II, 1790–1792
Francis II, 1792–1806

RULERS OF FRANCE FROM HUGH CAPET

Capetian Dynasty

Hugh Capet, 987–996
Robert II, 996–1031
Henry I, 1031–1060
Philip I, 1060–1108
Louis VI, 1108–1137
Louis VII, 1137–1180
Philip II (Augustus), 1180–1223
Louis VIII, 1223–1226
Louis IX (St. Louis), 1226–1270
Philip III, 1270–1285
Philip IV, 1285–1314
Louis X, 1314–1316
Philip V, 1316–1322
Charles IV, 1322–1328

Valois Dynasty

Philip VI, 1328–1350
John, 1350–1364
Charles V, 1364–1380
Charles VI, 1380–1422
Charles VII, 1422–1461
Louis XI, 1461–1483
Charles VIII, 1483–1498
Louis XII, 1498–1515
Francis I, 1515–1547

Henry II, 1547–1559
Francis II, 1559–1560
Charles IX, 1560–1574
Henry III, 1574–1589

Bourbon Dynasty

Henry IV, 1589–1610
Louis XIII, 1610–1643
Louis XIV, 1643–1715
Louis XV, 1715–1774
Louis XVI, 1774–1792

After 1792

First Republic, 1792–1799
Napoleon Bonaparte, First Consul, 1799–1804
Napoleon I, Emperor, 1804–1814
Louis XVIII (Bourbon dynasty), 1814–1824
Charles X (Bourbon dynasty), 1824–1830
Louis Philippe, 1830–1848
Second Republic, 1848–1852
Napoleon III, Emperor, 1852–1870
Third Republic, 1870–1940
Pétain regime, 1940–1944
Provisional government, 1944–1946
Fourth Republic, 1946–1958
Fifth Republic, 1958–

RULERS OF ENGLAND

Anglo-Saxon Dynasty

Alfred the Great, 871–899
Edward the Elder, 899–924
Ethelstan, 924–939
Edmund I, 939–946
Edred, 946–955
Edwy, 955–959
Edgar, 959–975

Edward the Martyr, 975–978
Ethelred the Unready, 978–1016
Canute, 1016–1035 (Danish Nationality)
Harold I, 1035–1040
Hardicanute, 1040–1042
Edward the Confessor, 1042–1066
Harold II, 1066

House of Normandy

William I (the Conqueror), 1066–1087
William II, 1087–1100
Henry I, 1100–1135
Stephen, 1135–1154

House of Plantagenet

Henry II, 1154–1189
Richard I, 1189–1199
John, 1199–1216
Henry III, 1216–1272
Edward I, 1272–1307
Edward II, 1307–1327
Edward III, 1327–1377
Richard II, 1377–1399

House of Lancaster

Henry IV, 1399–1413
Henry V, 1413–1422
Henry VI, 1422–1461

House of York

Edward IV, 1461–1483
Edward V, 1483
Richard III, 1483–1485

House of Tudor

Henry VII, 1485–1509
Henry VIII, 1509–1547
Edward VI, 1547–1553
Mary, 1553–1558
Elizabeth I, 1558–1603

House of Stuart

James I, 1603–1625
Charles I, 1625–1649

Commonwealth and Protectorate, 1649–1659

House of Stuart Restored

Charles II, 1660–1685
James II, 1685–1688
William III and Mary II, 1689–1694
William III alone, 1694–1702
Anne, 1702–1714

House of Hanover

George I, 1714–1727
George II, 1727–1760
George III, 1760–1820
George IV, 1820–1830
William IV, 1830–1837
Victoria, 1837–1901

House of Saxe-Coburg-Gotha

Edward VII, 1901–1910
George V, 1910–1917

House of Windsor

George V, 1917–1936
Edward VIII, 1936
George VI, 1936–1952
Elizabeth II, 1952–

RULERS OF AUSTRIA AND AUSTRIA-HUNGARY

*Maximilian I (Archduke), 1493–1519
*Charles V, 1519–1556
*Ferdinand I, 1556–1564
*Maximilian II, 1564–1576
*Rudolf II, 1576–1612
*Matthias, 1612–1619
*Ferdinand II, 1619–1637
*Ferdinand III, 1637–1657
*Leopold I, 1658–1705
*Joseph I, 1705–1711
*Charles VI, 1711–1740
Maria Theresa, 1740–1780

*Joseph II, 1780–1790
*Leopold II, 1790–1792
*Francis II, 1792–1835 (Emperor of Austria as Francis I after 1804)
Ferdinand I, 1835–1848
Francis Joseph, 1848–1916 (after 1867 Emperor of Austria and King of Hungary)
Charles I, 1916–1918 (Emperor of Austria and King of Hungary)
Republic of Austria, 1918–1938 (dictatorship after 1934)
Republic restored, under Allied occupation, 1945–1956
Free Republic, 1956–

*Also bore title of Holy Roman Emperor

RULERS OF PRUSSIA AND GERMANY

*Frederick I, 1701–1713
*Frederick William I, 1713–1740
*Frederick II (the Great), 1740–1786
*Frederick William II, 1786–1797
*Frederick William III,1797–1840
*Frederick William IV, 1840–1861
*William I, 1861–1888 (German Emperor after 1871)
Frederick III, 1888

*Kings of Prussia

*William II, 1888–1918
Weimar Republic, 1918–1933
Third Reich (Nazi Dictatorship), 1933–1945
Allied occupation, 1945–1952
Division into Federal Republic of Germany in west and German Democratic Republic in east, 1949–1991
Federal Republic of Germany (united), 1991–

RULERS OF RUSSIA

Ivan III, 1462–1505
Vasily III, 1505–1533
Ivan IV, 1533–1584
Theodore I, 1534–1598
Boris Godunov, 1598–1605
Theodore II,1605
Vasily IV, 1606–1610
Michael, 1613–1645
Alexius, 1645–1676
Theodore III, 1676–1682
Ivan V and Peter I, 1682–1689
Peter I (the Great), 1689–1725
Catherine I, 1725–1727
Peter II, 1727–1730

Anna, 1730–1740
Ivan VI, 1740–1741
Elizabeth, 1741–1762
Peter III, 1762
Catherine II (the Great), 1762–1796
Paul, 1796–1801
Alexander I,1801–1825
Nicholas I, 1825–1855
Alexander II,1855–1881
Alexander III, 1881–1894
Nicholas II, 1894–1917
Soviet Republic, 1917–1991
Russian Federation, 1991–

RULERS OF UNIFIED SPAIN

Ferdinand { and Isabella, 1479–1504
and Philip I, 1504–1506
and Charles I, 1506–1516
Charles I (Holy Roman Emperor Charles V), 1516–1556
Philip II, 1556–1598
Philip III, 1598–1621
Philip IV, 1621–1665
Charles II, 1665–1700
Philip V, 1700–1746
Ferdinand VI, 1746–1759
Charles III, 1759–1788
Charles IV, 1788–1808

Ferdinand VII, 1808
Joseph Bonaparte, 1808–1813
Ferdinand VII (restored), 1814–1833
Isabella II, 1833–1868
Republic, 1868–1870
Amadeo, 1870–1873
Republic, 1873–1874
Alfonso XII, 1874–1885
Alfonso XIII, 1886–1931
Republic, 1931–1939
Fascist Dictatorship, 1939–1975
Juan Carlos I, 1975–

RULERS OF ITALY

Victor Emmanuel II, 1861–1878
Humbert I, 1878–1900
Victor Emmanuel III, 1900–1946

Fascist Dictatorship, 1922-1943 (maintained in northern Italy until 1945)
Humbert II, May 9–June 13, 1946
Republic, 1946–

PROMINENT POPES

Silvester I, 314–335
Leo I, 440–461
Gelasius I, 492–496
Gregory I, 590–604
Nicholas I, 858–867
Silvester II, 999–1003
Leo IX, 1049–1054
Nicholas II, 1058–1061
Gregory VII, 1073–1085
Urban II, 1088–1099
Paschal II, 1099–1118
Alexander III, 1159–1181
Innocent III, 1198–1216
Gregory IX, 1227–1241
Innocent IV, 1243–1254
Boniface VIII, 1294–1303
John XXII, 1316–1334
Nicholas V, 1447–1455
Pius II, 1458–1464

Alexander VI, 1492–1503
Julius II, 1503–1513
Leo X, 1513–1521
Paul III, 1534–1549
Paul IV, 1555–1559
Sixtus V, 1585–1590
Urban VIII, 1623–1644
Gregory XVI, 1831–1846
Pius IX, 1846–1878
Leo XIII, 1878–1903
Pius X, 1903–1914
Benedict XV, 1914–1922
Pius XI, 1922–1939
Pius XII, 1939–1958
John XXIII, 1958–1963
Paul VI, 1963–1978
John Paul I, 1978
John Paul II, 1978–2005
Benedict XVI, 2005–2013
Francis, 2013–

Further Readings

CHAPTER 10

Abu-Lughod, Janet L. *Before European Hegemony: The World System A.D. 1250–1350*. Oxford and New York, 1989. A study of the trading links among Europe, the Middle East, India, and China, with special attention to the role of the Mongol Empire; extensive bibliography.

Allsen, Thomas T. *Culture and Conquest in Mongol Eurasia*. Cambridge and New York, 2001. A synthesis of the author's earlier studies, emphasizing Mongol involvement in the cultural and commercial exchanges that linked China, Central Asia, and Europe.

Christian, David. *A History of Russia, Central Asia and Mongolia*. Vol. 1, *Inner Eurasia from Prehistory to the Mongol Empire*. Oxford, 1998. The authoritative English-language work on the subject.

Cole, Bruce. *Giotto and Florentine Painting, 1280–1375*. New York, 1976. A clear and stimulating introduction.

Crummey, Robert O. *The Formation of Muscovy, 1304–1613*. New York, 1987. The standard account.

Dante Alighieri. *The Divine Comedy*. Trans. Mark Musa. 3 vols. Baltimore, MD, 1984–86.

Dunn, Ross E. *The Adventures of Ibn Battuta: A Muslim Traveler of the Fourteenth Century*. Berkeley, rev. ed. 2005. Places the writings and experiences of this far-reaching Muslim traveler in their historical and geographical contexts.

Dyer, Christopher. *Standards of Living in the Later Middle Ages: Social Change in England, c. 1200–1520*. Cambridge and New York, 1989. Detailed but highly rewarding.

Foltz, Richard. *Religions of the Silk Road: Premodern Patterns of Globalization*. New York, 2nd ed. 2010. A compelling and thought-provoking study of the varieties of religious experience and cross-cultural interaction in medieval Eurasia.

The History and the Life of Chinggis Khan: The Secret History of the Mongols. Trans. Urgunge Onon. Leiden, 1997. A newer version of *The Secret History*, now the standard English version of this important Mongol source.

Horrox, Rosemary, ed. *The Black Death*. New York, 1994. A fine collection of documents reflecting the impact of the Black Death, especially in England.

Jackson, Peter. *The Mongols and the West, 1221–1410*. Harlow, UK, 2005. A well-written survey that emphasizes the interactions among the Mongol, Latin Christian, and Muslim worlds.

Jordan, William Chester. *The Great Famine: Northern Europe in the Early Fourteenth Century*. Princeton, NJ, 1996. An outstanding social and economic study.

Keen, Maurice, ed. *Medieval Warfare: A History*. Oxford and New York, 1999. The most attractive introduction to this important subject. Lively and well illustrated.

Kitsikopoulos, Harry, ed. *Agrarian Change and Crisis in Europe, 1200–1500*. London, 2011. An up-to-date collection of scholarly essays that addresses a classic and complicated set of historical questions.

Komaroff, Linda and Stefano Carboni, eds. *The Legacy of Ghenghis Khan: Courtly Art and Culture in Western Asia, 1256–1353*. New York, 2002. An informative and lavishly illustrated catalog of an acclaimed exhibition.

Larner, John. *Marco Polo and the Discovery of the World*. New Haven, CT, 1999. A study of the influence of Marco Polo's *Travels* on Europeans.

Mandeville's Travels. Ed. M. C. Seymour. Oxford, 1968. An edition of the *Book of Marvels* based on the Middle English version popular in the fifteenth century.

Memoirs of a Renaissance Pope: The Commentaries of Pius II. Abridged ed. Trans. F. A. Gragg, New York, 1959. Remarkable insights into the mind of a particularly well-educated mid-fifteenth-century pope.

Nicholas, David. *The Transformation of Europe, 1300–1600*. Oxford and New York, 1999. The best textbook presently available.

Rossabi, M. *Khubilai Khan: His Life and Times*. Berkeley, CA, 1988. The standard English biography.

Swanson, R. N. *Religion and Devotion in Europe, c. 1215–c. 1515*. Cambridge and New York, 1995. An excellent study of late-medieval popular piety; an excellent complement to Oakley.

The Travels of Marco Polo. Ed. Peter Harris. London, 2008 repr. A new edition of a classic translation.

Vaughan, Richard. *Valois Burgundy*. London, 1975. A summation of the author's four-volume study of the Burgundian dukes.

CHAPTER 11

Alberti, Leon Battista. *The Family in Renaissance Florence (Della Famiglia)*. Trans. Renée Neu Watkins. Columbia, SC, 1969.

Allmand, Christopher T., ed. *Society at War: The Experience of England and France During the Hundred Years' War*. Edinburgh, 1973. An outstanding collection of documents.

———. *The Hundred Years' War: England and France at War, c. 1300–c. 1450*. Cambridge and New York, 1988. Still the best analytic account of the war; after a short narrative, the book is organized topically.

Boccaccio, Giovanni. *The Decameron*. Trans. Mark Musa and P. E. Bondanella. New York, 1977.

Brucker, Gene. *Florence, the Golden Age, 1138–1737*. Berkeley and Los Angeles, CA, 1998. The standard account.

Bruni, Leonardo. *The Humanism of Leonardo Bruni: Selected Texts*. Trans. Gordon Griffiths, James Hankins, and David Thompson. Binghamton, NY, 1987. Excellent translations, with introductions, to the Latin works of a key Renaissance humanist.

Burke, Peter. *The Renaissance*. New York, 1997. A brief introduction by an influential modern historian.

Burkhardt, Jacob. *The Civilization of the Renaissance in Italy*. Many editions. The nineteenth-century work that first crystallized an image of the Italian Renaissance, and with which scholars have been wrestling ever since.

Canning, Joseph. *Ideas of Power in the Late Middle Ages, 1296–1417*. Cambridge, 2011. An old fashioned but nonetheless original synthesis.

Cassirer, Ernst, et al., eds. *The Renaissance Philosophy of Man*. Chicago, 1948. Important original works by Petrarch, Ficino, and Pico della Mirandola, among others.

Chaucer, Geoffrey. *The Canterbury Tales*. Trans. Nevill Coghill. New York, 1951. A modern English verse translation, lightly annotated.

Cohn, Samuel K., Jr. *Lust for Liberty: The Politics of Social Revolt in Medieval Europe, 1200–1425. Italy, France, and Flanders*. Cambridge, MA, 2006. An important new study.

Coles, Paul. *The Ottoman Impact on Europe*. London, 1968. An excellent introductory text, still valuable despite its age.

Dobson, R. Barrie. *The Peasants' Revolt of 1381*, 2d ed. London, 1983. A comprehensive source collection, with excellent introductions to the documents.

Fernández-Armesto, Felipe. *Before Columbus: Exploration and Colonisation from the Mediterranean to the Atlantic, 1229–1492*. London, 1987. An indispensible study of the medieval background to the sixteenth-century European colonial empires.

Froissart, Jean. *Chronicles*. Trans. Geoffrey Brereton. Baltimore, MD, 1968. A selection from the most famous contemporary account of the Hundred Years' War to about 1400.

Goffman, Daniel. *The Ottoman Empire and Early Modern Europe*. Cambridge and New York, 2002. A revisionist account that presents the Ottoman Empire as a European state.

Hankins, James. *Plato in the Italian Renaissance*. Leiden and New York, 1990. A definitive study of the reception and influence of Plato on Renaissance intellectuals.

————, ed. *Renaissance Civic Humanism: Reappraisals and Reflections*. Cambridge and New York, 2000. An excellent collection of scholarly essays reassessing republicanism in the Renaissance.

Hobbins, Daniel, ed. and trans. *The Trial of Joan of Arc*. Cambridge, MA, 2007. A new and excellent translation of the transcripts of Joan's trial.

Inalcik, Halil. *The Ottoman Empire: The Classical Age, 1300–1600*. London, 1973. The standard history by the dean of Turkish historians.

————, ed. *An Economic and Social History of the Ottoman Empire, 1300–1914*. Cambridge, 1994. An important collection of essays, spanning the full range of Ottoman history.

John Hus at the Council of Constance. Trans. M. Spinka, New York, 1965. The translation of a Czech chronicle with an expert introduction and appended documents.

Kafadar, Cemal. *Between Two Worlds: The Construction of the Ottoman State*. Berkeley and Los Angeles, 1995. An important study of Ottoman origins in the border regions between Byzantium, the Seljuk Turks, and the Mongols.

Kempe, Margery. *The Book of Margery Kempe*. Trans. Barry Windeatt. New York, 1985. A fascinating personal narrative by an early-fifteenth-century Englishwoman who hoped she might be a saint.

Lane, Frederic C. *Venice: A Maritime Republic*. Baltimore, MD, 1973. An authoritative account.

Morgan, David. *The Mongols*. 2d ed. Oxford, 2007. An accessible introduction to Mongol history and its sources, written by a noted expert on medieval Persia.

Ormrod, W. Mark. *Edward III*. New Haven, 2012. A new biography of this English monarch by a leading social historian.

Saunders, J. J. *The History of the Mongol Conquests*. London, 1971. Still the standard English-language introduction; somewhat more positive about the Mongols' accomplishments than is Morgan.

Shirley, Janet, trans. *A Parisian Journal, 1405–1449*. Oxford, 1968. A marvelous panorama of Parisian life recorded by an eyewitness.

Sumption, Jonathan. *The Hundred Years' War*. Vol. 1: *Trial by Battle*. Vol. 2: *Trial by Fire*. Philadelphia, 1999. The first two volumes of a massive narrative history of the war, carrying the story up to 1369.

The Four Voyages: Christopher Columbus. Trans. J. M. Cohen. New York, 1992. Columbus's own self-serving account of his four voyages to the Indies.

CHAPTER 12

Baxandall, Michael. *Painting and Experience in Fifteenth-Century Italy*. Oxford, 1972. A classic study of the perceptual world of the Renaissance.

Castiglione, Baldassare. *The Book of the Courtier*. Many editions. The translations by C. S. Singleton (New York, 1959) and by George Bull (New York, 1967) are both excellent.

Cellini, Benvenuto. *Autobiography*. Trans. George Bull. Baltimore, MD, 1956. This Florentine goldsmith (1500–1571) is the source for many of the most famous stories about the artists of the Florentine Renaissance.

Erasmus, Desiderius. *The Praise of Folly*. Trans. J. Wilson. Ann Arbor, MI, 1958.

Fernández-Armesto, Felipe. *1492: The Year the World Began*. London, 2010. A panoramic view of the world in a pivotal year, putting the voyage of Columbus in a broad historical perspective.

Flint, Valerie I. J. *The Imaginative Landscape of Christopher Columbus*. Princeton, NJ, 1992. A short, suggestive analysis of the intellectual influences that shaped Columbus's geographical ideas.

Fox, Alistair. *Thomas More: History and Providence*. Oxford, 1982. A balanced account of a man too easily idealized.

Grafton, Anthony, and Lisa Jardine. *From Humanism to the Humanities: Education and the Liberal Arts in Fifteenth- and Sixteenth-Century Europe*. London, 1986. An account that presents Renaissance humanism as the elitist cultural program of a self-interested group of pedagogues.

Grendler, Paul, ed. *Encyclopedia of the Renaissance*. New York, 1999. A valuable reference work.

Jardine, Lisa. *Worldly Goods*. London, 1996. A revisionist account that emphasizes the acquisitive materialism of Italian Renaissance society and culture.

Kanter, Laurence, Hilliard T. Goldfarb, and James Hankins. *Botticelli's Witness: Changing Style in a Changing Florence*. Boston, 1997. This catalog for an exhibition of Botticelli's works, at the Gardner Museum in Boston, offers an excellent introduction to the painter and his world.

King, Margaret L. *Women of the Renaissance*. Chicago, 1991. Deals with women in all walks of life and in a variety of roles.

Kristeller, Paul O. *Renaissance Thought: The Classic, Scholastic, and Humanistic Strains*. New York, 1961. Very helpful in defining the main trends of Renaissance thought.

Machiavelli, Niccolò. *The Discourses* and *The Prince*. Many editions. These two books must be read together if one is to understand Machiavelli's political ideas properly.

Mallett, Michael and Christine Shaw. *The Italian Wars, 1494–1559: War, State, and Society in Early Modern Europe*. Boston, 2012. Argues that the endemic warfare of this period within Italy revolutionized European military tactics and technologies.

Mann, Charles. C. *1491: New Revelations of the Americas Before Columbus*. New York, 2006.

———. *1493: Uncovering the New World Columbus Created*. New York, 2012. Written for a popular audience, these are also engaging and well-informed syntheses of historical research.

Martines, Lauro. *Power and Imagination: City-States in Renaissance Italy*. New York, 1979. Insightful account of the connections among politics, society, culture, and art.

More, Thomas. *Utopia*. Many editions.

Olson, Roberta, *Italian Renaissance Sculpture*. New York, 1992. The most accessible introduction to the subject.

Parker, Geoffrey. *The Military Revolution: Military Innovation and the Rise of the West (1500–1800)*. 2d ed. Cambridge and New York, 1996. A work of fundamental importance for understanding the global dominance achieved by early modern Europeans.

Perkins, Leeman L. *Music in the Age of the Renaissance*. New York, 1999. A massive new study that needs to be read in conjunction with Reese.

Phillips, J. R. S. *The Medieval Expansion of Europe*. 2d ed. Oxford, 1998. An outstanding study of the thirteenth- and fourteenth-century background to the fifteenth-century expansion of Europe. Important synthetic treatment of European relations with the Mongols, China, Africa, and North America. The second edition includes a new introduction and a bibliographical essay; the text is the same as in the first edition (1988).

Phillips, William D., Jr., and Carla R. Phillips. *The Worlds of Christopher Columbus*. Cambridge and New York, 1991. The first book to read on Columbus: accessible, engaging, and scholarly. Then read Fernández-Armesto's biography.

Rabelais, François. *Gargantua and Pantagruel*. Trans. J. M. Cohen. Baltimore, MD, 1955. A robust modern translation.

Reese, Gustave. *Music in the Renaissance,* rev. ed. New York, 1959. A great book; still authoritative, despite the more recent work by Perkins, which supplements but does not replace it.

Rice, Eugene F., Jr., and Anthony Grafton. *The Foundations of Early Modern Europe, 1460–1559,* 2d ed. New York, 1994. The best textbook account of its period.

Rowland, Ingrid D. *The Culture of the High Renaissance: Ancients and Moderns in Sixteenth-Century Rome*. Cambridge and New York, 2000. Beautifully written examination of the social, intellectual, and economic foundations of the Renaissance in Rome.

Russell, Peter. *Prince Henry "The Navigator": A Life*. New Haven, CT, 2000. A masterly biography by a great historian who has spent a lifetime on the subject. The only book one now needs to read on Prince Henry.

Scammell, Geoffrey V. *The First Imperial Age: European Overseas Expansion, 1400–1715*. London, 1989. A useful introductory survey, with a particular focus on English and French colonization.

CHAPTER 13

Bainton, Roland. *Erasmus of Christendom*. New York, 1969. Still the best biography in English of the Dutch reformer and intellectual.

Benedict, Philip. *Christ's Churches Purely Reformed: A Social History of Calvinism*. New Haven, CT, 2002. A wide-ranging recent survey of Calvinism in both western and eastern Europe.

Bossy, John. *Christianity in the West, 1400–1700*. Oxford and New York, 1985. A brilliant, challenging picture of the changes that took place in Christian piety and practice as a result of the sixteenth-century reformations.

Bouwsma, William J. *John Calvin: A Sixteenth-Century Portrait*. Oxford and New York, 1988. The best biography of the magisterial reformer.

Dixon, C. Scott, ed. *The German Reformation: The Essential Readings*. Oxford, 1999. A collection of important recent articles.

Duffy, Eamon. *The Stripping of the Altars: Traditional Religion in England, c. 1400–c. 1550*. A brilliant study of religious exchange at the parish level.

———. *The Voices of Morebath: Reformation and Rebellion in an English Village*. New Haven, 2003. How the crises of this period affected and are reflected in the history of a single parish.

Hart, D. G. *Calvinism: A History*. New Haven, 2013. A new survey of this leading Protestant movement from its beginnings to the present day.

John Calvin: Selections from His Writings, ed. John Dillenberger. Garden City, NY, 1971. A judicious selection, drawn mainly from Calvin's *Institutes*.

Koslofsky, Craig. *The Reformation of the Dead: Death and Ritual in Early Modern Germany*. Basingstoke, 2000. How essential rituals and responses to death were reshaped in this period.

Loyola, Ignatius. *Personal Writings*. Trans. by Joseph A. Munitiz and Philip Endean. London and New York, 1996. An excellent collection that includes Loyola's autobiography, his spiritual diary, and some of his letters, as well as his *Spiritual Exercises*.

Luebke, David, ed. *The Counter-Reformation: The Essential Readings*. Oxford, 1999. A collection of nine important recent essays.

MacCulloch, Diarmaid. *Reformation: Europe's House Divided, 1490–1700*. London and New York, 2003. A definitive new survey; the best single-volume history of its subject in a generation.

Martin Luther: Selections from His Writings, ed. John Dillenberger. Garden City, NY, 1961. The standard selection, especially good on Luther's theological ideas.

McGrath, Alister E. *Reformation Thought: An Introduction*. Oxford, 1993. A useful explanation, accessible to non-Christians, of the theological ideas of the major Protestant reformers.

Mullett, Michael A. *The Catholic Reformation*. London, 2000. A sympathetic survey of Catholicism from the mid-sixteenth to the eighteenth century that presents the mid-sixteenth-century Council of Trent as a continuation of earlier reform efforts.

Murray, Linda. *High Renaissance and Mannerism*. London, 1985. The place to begin a study of fifteenth- and sixteenth-century Italian art.

Oberman, Heiko A. *Luther: Man between God and the Devil*. Trans. by Eileen Walliser-Schwarzbart. New Haven, CT, 1989. A biography stressing Luther's preoccupations with sin, death, and the devil.

O'Malley, John W. *The First Jesuits*. Cambridge, MA, 1993. A scholarly account of the origins and early years of the Society of Jesus.

———. *Trent and All That: Renaming Catholicism in the Early Modern Era*. Cambridge, MA, 2000. Short, lively, and with a full bibliography.

———. *Trent: What Happened at the Council*. Cambridge, MA, 2012. A clear and comprehensive narrative of the Church council that gave birth to the modern Catholic Church.

Pettegree, Andrew, ed. *The Reformation World*. New York, 2000. An exhaustive multi-author work representing the most recent thinking about the Reformation.

Pelikan, Jaroslav. *Reformation of Church and Dogma, 1300–1700*. Vol. 4 of *A History of Christian Dogma*. Chicago, 1984. A masterful synthesis of Reformation theology in its late-medieval context.

Roper, Lyndal. *The Holy Household: Women and Morals in Reformation Augsburg*. Oxford, 1989. A pathbreaking study of Protestantism's effects on a single town, with special attention to its impact on attitudes toward women, the family, and marriage.

Shagan, Ethan H. *Popular Politics and the English Reformation*. Cambridge, 2002. Argues that the English Reformation reflects an ongoing process of negotiation, resistance, and response.

Tracy, James D. *Europe's Reformations, 1450–1650*. 2d ed. Lanham, MD, 2006. An outstanding survey, especially strong on Dutch and Swiss developments, but excellent throughout.

Williams, George H. *The Radical Reformation*. 3d ed. Kirksville, MO, 1992. Originally published in 1962, this is still the best book on Anabaptism and its offshoots.

CHAPTER 14

Bonney, Richard. *The European Dynastic States, 1494–1660*. Oxford and New York, 1991. An excellent survey of continental Europe during the "long" sixteenth century.

Briggs, Robin. *Early Modern France, 1560–1715*, 2d ed. Oxford and New York, 1997. Updated and authoritative, with new bibliographies.

———. *Witches and Neighbors: The Social and Cultural Context of European Witchcraft*. New York, 1996. An influential recent account of Continental witchcraft.

Cervantes, Miguel de. *Don Quixote*. Trans. Edith Grossman. New York, 2003. A splendid new translation.

Clarke, Stuart. *Thinking with Demons: The Idea of Witchcraft in Early Modern Europe*. Oxford and New York, 1999. By placing demonology into the context of sixteenth- and seventeenth-century intellectual history, Clarke makes sense of it in new and exciting ways.

Cochrane, Eric, Charles M. Gray, and Mark A. Kishlansky. *Early Modern Europe: Crisis of Authority*. Chicago, 1987. An outstanding source collection from the University of Chicago Readings in Western Civilization series.

Elliot, J. H. *The Old World and the New, 1492–1650*. Cambridge, 1992 repr. A brilliant and brief set of essays on the ways that the discovery of the Americas challenged European perspectives on the world and themselves.

———. *Empires of the Atlantic World: Britain and Spain in America, 1492–1830*. An illuminating comparative study. New Haven, 2007.

Hibbard, Howard. *Bernini*. Baltimore, MD, 1965. The basic study in English of this central figure of Baroque artistic activity.

Hirst, Derek. *England in Conflict, 1603–1660: Kingdom, Community, Commonwealth*. Oxford and New York, 1999. A complete revision of the author's *Authority and Conflict* (1986), this is an up-to-date and balanced account of a period that has been a historical battleground over the past twenty years.

Hobbes, Thomas. *Leviathan*. Ed. Richard Tuck. 2d ed. Cambridge and New York, 1996. The most recent edition, containing the entirety of *Leviathan*, not just the first two parts.

Holt, Mack P. *The French Wars of Religion, 1562–1629*. Cambridge and New York, 1995. A clear account of a confusing time.

Kors, Alan Charles, and Edward Peters. *Witchcraft in Europe, 400–1700: A Documentary History*, 2d ed. Philadelphia, 2000. A superb collection of documents, significantly expanded in the second edition, with up-to-date commentary.

Kingdon, Robert. *Myths about the St. Bartholomew's Day Massacres, 1572–1576*. Cambridge, MA, 1988. A detailed account of this pivotal moment in the history of France.

Levack, Brian P. *The Witch-Hunt in Early Modern Europe*, 2d ed. London and New York, 1995. The best account of the persecution of suspected witches; coverage extends from Europe in 1450 to America in 1750.

Levin, Carole. *The Heart and Stomach of a King: Elizabeth I and the Politics of Sex and Power*. Philadelphia, PA, 1994. A provocative argument for the importance of Elizabeth's gender for understanding her reign.

Limm, Peter, ed. *The Thirty Years' War*. London, 1984. An outstanding short survey, followed by a selection of primary-source documents.

Lynch, John. *Spain, 1516–1598: From Nation-State to World Empire*. Oxford and Cambridge, MA, 1991. The best book in English on Spain at the pinnacle of its sixteenth-century power.

MacCaffrey, Wallace. *Elizabeth I*. New York, 1993. An outstanding traditional biography by an excellent scholar.

Martin, Colin, and Geoffrey Parker. *The Spanish Armada*. London, 1988. Incorporates recent discoveries from undersea archaeology with more traditional historical sources.

Mattingly, Garrett. *The Armada*. Boston, 1959. A great narrative history that reads like a novel; for more recent work, however, see Martin and Parker.

McGregor, Neil. *Shakespeare's Restless World*. London, 2013. Based on an acclaimed BBC Radio program, this book illuminates Shakespeare's life, times, and plays with reference to specific objects in the British Museum.

Newson, Linda A. and Susie Minchin. *From Capture to Sale: The Portuguese Slave Trade to Spanish South America in the Early Seventeenth Century*. London, 2007. Makes use of slave traders' own rich archives to track the process of human trafficking.

Parker, Geoffrey. *The Dutch Revolt*, 2d ed. Ithaca, NY, 1989. The standard survey in English on the revolt of the Netherlands.

———. *Philip II*. Boston, 1978. A fine biography by an expert in both the Spanish and the Dutch sources.

———, ed. *The Thirty Years' War*, rev. ed. London and New York, 1987. A wide-ranging collection of essays by scholarly experts.

Pascal, Blaise. *Pensées* (French-English edition). Ed. H. F. Stewart. London, 1950.

Pestana, Carla. *Protestant Empire: Religion and the Making of the British Atlantic World*. Philadelphia, 2010. How the Reformation helped to drive British imperial expansion.

Roberts, Michael. *Gustavus Adolphus and the Rise of Sweden*. London, 1973. Still the authoritative English-language account.

Russell, Conrad. *The Causes of the English Civil War*. Oxford, 1990. A penetrating and provocative analysis by one of the leading "revisionist" historians of the period.

Schmidt, Benjamin. *Innocence Abroad: The Dutch Imagination and the New World, 1570–1670*. Cambridge, 2006. A cultural history of Europeans' encounter with the Americas that highlights the perspective and experience of Dutch merchants, colonists, and artists.

Tracy, James D. *Holland under Habsburg Rule, 1506–1566: The Formation of a Body Politic*. Berkeley and Los Angeles, CA, 1990. A political history and analysis of the formative years of the Dutch state.

CHAPTER 15

Beik, William. *A Social and Cultural History of Early Modern France*. Cambridge, UK, 2009. A broad synthesis of French history from the end of the Middle Ages to the French Revolution, by one of the world's foremost authorities on absolutism.

Clark, Christopher, *Iron Kingdom: The Rise and Downfall of Prussia, 1600–1947*. Cambridge, MA, 2009. A definitive account of Prussian history over nearly four centuries.

Jones, Colin. *The Great Nation: France From Louis XV to Napoleon*. New York, 2002. An excellent and readable scholarly account that argues that the France of Louis XV in the eighteenth century was even more dominant than the kingdom of Louis XIV in the preceding century.

Kishlansky, Mark A. *A Monarchy Transformed: Britain, 1603–1714*. London, 1996. An excellent survey that takes seriously its claims to be a "British" rather than merely an "English" history.

Klein, Herbert S. *The Atlantic Slave Trade*. Cambridge and New York, 1999. An accessible survey by a leading quantitative historian.

Lewis, William Roger, gen. ed. *The Oxford History of the British Empire*. Vol. I: *The Origins of Empire: British Overseas Enterprise to the Close of the Seventeenth Century*, ed. Nicholas Canny. Vol. II: *The Eighteenth Century*, ed. Peter J. Marshall. Oxford and New York, 1998. A definitive, multiauthor account.

Locke, John. *Two Treatises of Government*. Ed. Peter Laslett. Rev. ed. Cambridge and New York, 1963. Laslett has revolutionized our understanding of the historical and ideological context of Locke's political writings.

Massie, Robert. *Peter the Great, His Life and World*. New York, 1980. Prize-winning and readable narrative account of the Russian tsar's life.

Monod, Paul K. *The Power of Kings: Monarchy and Religion in Europe, 1589–1715*. New Haven, CT, 1999. A study of the seventeenth century's declining confidence in the divinity of kings.

Quataert, Donald. *The Ottoman Empire, 1700–1822*. Cambridge and New York, 2000. Well balanced and intended to be read by students.

Riasanovsky, Nicholas V., and Steinberg, Mark D. *A History of Russia*. 7th ed. Oxford and New York, 2005. Far and away the best single-volume textbook on Russian history: balanced, comprehensive, intelligent, and with full bibliographies.

Saint-Simon, Louis. *Historical Memoirs*. Many editions. The classic source for life at Louis XIV's Versailles.

Snyder, Timothy, *The Reconstruction of Nations: Poland, Ukraine, Lithuania, Belarus, 1569–1999*. New Haven, CT, 2004. Essential account of nation-building and state-collapse in Eastern Europe with significant relevance to the region's contemporary situation.

Thomas, Hugh. *The Slave Trade: The History of the Atlantic Slave Trade, 1440–1870*. London and New York, 1997. A survey notable for its breadth and depth of coverage and for its attractive prose style.

Tracy, James D. *The Rise of Merchant Empires: Long-Distance Trade in the Early Modern World, 1350–1750*. Cambridge and New York, 1990. Important collection of essays by leading authorities.

White, Richard. *The Middle Ground: Indians, Empires and Republics in the Great Lakes Region, 1650–1815*. Cambridge, UK, 1991. A path-breaking account of interactions between Europeans and Native Americans during the colonial period.

CHAPTER 16

Biagioli, Mario. *Galileo, Courtier*. Chicago, 1993. Emphasizes the importance of patronage and court politics in Galileo's science and career.

Cohen, I. B. *The Birth of a New Physics.* New York, 1985. Emphasizes the mathematical nature of the revolution; unmatched at making the mathematics understandable.

Daston, Lorraine, and Elizabeth Lunbeck, eds. *Histories of Scientific Observation.* Chicago, IL, 2011. Field-defining collection of essays on the history of scientific observation from the seventeenth to the twentieth centuries.

Daston, Lorraine. *Wonders and the Order of Nature, 1150–1750.* Cambridge, MA, 2001. Erudite sweeping account of the history of science in the early modern period, emphasizing the natural philosopher's awe and wonder at the marvelous, the unfamiliar, and the counter-intuitive.

Dear, Peter. *Revolutionizing the Sciences: European Knowledge and Its Ambitions, 1500–1700.* Princeton, NJ, 2001. Among the best short histories.

Drake, Stillman. *Discoveries and Opinions of Galileo.* Garden City, NY, 1957. The classic translation of Galileo's most important papers by his most admiring modern biographer.

Feingold, Mardechai, *The Newtonian Moment: Isaac Newton and the Making of Modern Culture.* New York, 2004. An engaging essay on the dissemination of Newton's thought, with excellent visual material.

Gaukroger, Stephen. *Descartes: An Intellectual Biography.* Oxford, 1995. Detailed and sympathetic study of the philosopher.

Gleick, James. *Isaac Newton.* New York, 2003. A vivid and well-documented brief biography.

Grafton, Anthony. *New Worlds, Ancient Texts: The Power of Tradition and the Shock of Discovery.* Cambridge, MA, 1992. Accessible essay by one of the leading scholars of early modern European thought.

Jacob, Margaret. *Scientific Culture and the Making of the Industrial West.* Oxford, 1997. A concise examination of the connections between developments in science and the Industrial Revolution.

Kuhn, Thomas. *The Structure of Scientific Revolutions.* Chicago, 1962. A classic and much-debated study of how scientific thought changes.

Pagden, Anthony, *European Encounters with the New World.* New Haven, CT, and London, 1993. Subtle and detailed on how European intellectuals thought about the lands they saw for the first time.

Scheibinger, Londa. *The Mind Has No Sex? Women in the Origins of Modern Science.* Cambridge, MA, 1989. A lively and important recovery of the lost role played by women mathematicians and experimenters.

Shapin, Steven. *The Scientific Revolution.* Chicago, 1996. Engaging, accessible, and brief—organized thematically.

Shapin, Steven, and Simon Schaffer. *Leviathan and the Air Pump.* Princeton, NJ, 1985. A modern classic, on one of the most famous philosophical conflicts in seventeenth-century science.

Stephenson, Bruce. *The Music of the Heavens: Kepler's Harmonic Astronomy.* Princeton, NJ, 1994. An engaging and important explanation of Kepler's otherworldly perspective.

Thoren, Victor. *The Lord of Uranibourg: A Biography of Tycho Brahe.* Cambridge, 1990. A vivid reconstruction of the scientific revolution's most flamboyant astronomer.

Westfall, Richard. *The Construction of Modern Science.* Cambridge, 1977.

———. *Never at Rest: A Biography of Isaac Newton.* Cambridge, 1980. The standard work.

Wilson, Catherine. *The Invisible World: Early Modern Philosophy and the Invention of the Microscope.* Princeton, NJ, 1995. An important study of how the "microcosmic" world revealed by technology reshaped scientific philosophy and practice.

Zinsser, Judith P. *La Dame d'Esprit: A Biography of the Marquise Du Châtelet.* New York, 2006. An excellent cultural history. To be issued in paper as *Emilie du Châtelet: Daring Genius of the Enlightenment* (2007).

CHAPTER 17

Baker, Keith. *Condorcet: From Natural Philosophy to Social Mathematics.* Chicago, 1975. An important reinterpretation of Condorcet as a social scientist.

Blum, Carol. *Rousseau and the Republic of Virtue: The Language of Politics in the French Revolution.* Ithaca and London, 1986. Fascinating account of how eighteenth-century readers interpreted Rousseau.

Buchan, James. *The Authentic Adam Smith: His Life and Ideas.* New York, 2006.

Calhoun, Craig, ed. *Habermas and the Public Sphere.* Cambridge, MA, 1992. Calhoun's introduction is a good starting point for Habermas's argument.

Cassirer, E. *The Philosophy of the Enlightenment.* Princeton, NJ, 1951.

Chartier, Roger. *The Cultural Origins of the French Revolution.* Durham, NC, 1991. Looks at topics from religion to violence in everyday life and culture.

Darnton, Robert. *The Business of Enlightenment: A Publishing History of the* Encyclopédie, *1775–1800.* Cambridge, MA, 1979. Darnton's work on the Enlightenment offers a fascinating blend of intellectual, social, and economic history. See his other books as well: *The Literary Underground of the Old Regime* (Cambridge, MA, 1982); *The Great Cat Massacre and Other Episodes in French Cultural History* (New York, 1984); and *The Forbidden Best Sellers of Revolutionary France* (New York and London, 1996).

Davis, David Brion. *The Problem of Slavery in Western Culture.* New York, 1988. A Pulitzer Prize–winning examination of a central issue as well as a brilliant analysis of different strands of Enlightenment thought.

Gay, Peter. *The Enlightenment: An Interpretation.* Vol. 1, *The Rise of Modern Paganism.* Vol. 2, *The Science of Freedom.* New York, 1966–1969. Combines an overview with an interpretation. Emphasizes the *philosophes'* sense of identification with the classical world and takes a generally positive view of their accomplishments. Includes extensive annotated bibliographies.

Gray, Peter. *Mozart.* New York, 1999. Brilliant short study.

Goodman, Dena. *The Republic of Letters: A Cultural History of the French Enlightenment.* Ithaca, NY, 1994. Important in its attention to the role of literary women.

Hazard, Paul. *The European Mind: The Critical Years (1680–1715).* New Haven, CT, 1953. A basic and indispensable account of the changing climate of opinion that preceded the Enlightenment.

Hunt, Lynn, Margaret C. Jacob, and Wijnand Mijnhardt. *The Book That Changed Europe: Picart and Bernard's Religious Ceremonies of the World*. Cambridge, MA, 2010. Lively study of a book on global religions that came out of the fertile world of the Dutch Enlightenment in the eighteenth century.

Israel, Jonathan Irvine. *Radical Enlightenment: Philosophy and the Making of Modernity, 1650–1750*. New York, 2001. Massive and erudite, a fresh look at the international movement of ideas.

———. *Enlightenment Contested: Philosophy, Modernity, and the Emancipation of Man, 1670–1752*. New York, 2006. Massive and erudite, a fresh look at the international movement of ideas.

Munck, Thomas. *The Enlightenment: A Comparative Social History 1721–1794*. London, 2000. An excellent recent survey, especially good on social history.

Outram, Dorinda. *The Enlightenment*. Cambridge, 1995. An excellent short introduction and a good example of new historical approaches.

Pagden, Anthony. *The Enlightenment: And Why It Still Matters*. New York, 2013. Spirited history of the Enlightenment and a defense of its continued relevance.

Porter, Roy. *The Creation of the Modern World: The Untold Story of the British Enlightenment*. New York, 2000.

Sapiro, Virginia. *A Vindication of Political Virtue: The Political Theory of Mary Wollstonecraft*. Chicago, 1992. A subtle and intelligent analysis for more advanced readers.

Shklar, Judith. *Men and Citizens: A Study of Rousseau's Social Theory*. London, 1969.

———. *Montesquieu*. Oxford, 1987. Shklar's studies are brilliant and accessible.

Taylor, Barbara. *Mary Wollstonecraft and the Feminist Imagination*. Cambridge and New York, 2003. Fascinating study that sets Wollstonecraft in the radical circles of eighteenth-century England.

Taylor, Barbara and Sarah Knott, eds. *Women, Gender, and Enlightenment*. New York, 2007. Multi-author collection examining the significance of sex, gender, and politics across a wide swath of the Enlightenment world, from Europe to the American colonies.

Venturi, Franco. *The End of the Old Regime in Europe, 1768–1776: The First Crisis*. Trans. R. Burr Litchfield. Princeton, NJ, 1989.

———. *The End of the Old Regime in Europe, 1776–1789*. Princeton, NJ, 1991. Both detailed and wide-ranging, particularly important on international developments.

Watt, Ian P. *The Rise of the Novel*. London, 1957. The basic work on the innovative qualities of the novel in eighteenth-century England.

Wolff, Larry. *Inventing Eastern Europe: The Map of Civilization on the Mind of the Enlightenment*. Stanford, CA, 1994. The place of Eastern Europe in the imagination of Enlightenment thinkers interested in the origins and destiny of the civilizing process.

CHAPTER 18

Applewhite, Harriet B., and Darline G. Levy, eds. *Women and Politics in the Age of the Democratic Revolution*. Ann Arbor, MI, 1990. Essays on France, Britain, the Netherlands, and the United States.

Bell, David A. *The First Total War: Napoleon's Europe and the Birth of Warfare as We Know It*. Boston and New York, 2007. Lively and concise study of the "cataclysmic intensification" of warfare.

Blackburn, Robin. *The Overthrow of Colonial Slavery*. London and New York, 1988. A longer view of slavery and its abolition.

Blanning, T. C. W. *The French Revolutionary Wars, 1787–1802*. Oxford, 1996. On the revolution and war.

Blum, Carol. *Rousseau and the Republic of Virtue: The Language of Politics in the French Revolution*. Ithaca, NY, 1986. Excellent on how Rousseau was read by the revolutionaries.

Cobb, Richard. *The People's Armies*. New Haven, CT, 1987. Brilliant and detailed analysis of the popular militias.

Cole, Juan. *Napoleon's Egypt: Invading the Middle East*. New York, 2007. Readable history by a scholar familiar with sources in Arabic as well as European languages.

Connelly, Owen. *The French Revolution and Napoleonic Era*. 3rd ed. New York, 2000. Accessible, lively, one-volume survey.

Darnton, Robert, *The Forbidden Best-Sellers of Pre-Revolutionary France*. New York, 1995. One of Darnton's many imaginative studies of subversive opinion and books on the eve of the revolution.

Desan, Suzanne. *The Family on Trial in Revolutionary France*. Berkeley, CA, 2006. Persuasive study of the ways that women in France were able to take advantage of the revolution and defend their interests in debates about marriage, divorce, parenthood, and the care of children.

Desan, Suzanne, Lynn Hunt, and William Max Nelson, eds. *The French Revolution in Global Perspective*. Ithaca, NY, 2013. Multi-author exploration of the French Revolution's global resonance.

Doyle, William. *Origins of the French Revolution*. New York, 1988. A revisionist historian surveys recent research on the political and social origins of the revolution and identifies a new consensus.

———. *Oxford History of the French Revolution*. New York, 1989.

Dubois, Laurent. *Avengers of the New World. The Story of the Haitian Revolution*. Cambridge, MA, 2004. Now the best and most accessible study.

———, and John D. Garrigus. *Slave Revolution in the Caribbean, 1789–1804: A Brief History with Documents*. New York, 2006. A particularly good collection.

Englund, Steven. *Napoleon, A Political Life*. Cambridge, MA, 2004. Prize-winning biography, both dramatic and insightful.

Forrest, Alan. *The French Revolution and the Poor*. New York, 1981. A moving and detailed social history of the poor, who fared little better under revolutionary governments than under the Old Regime.

Furet, Francois. *Revolutionary France, 1770–1880*. Trans. Antonia Nerill. Cambridge, MA, 1992. Overview by the leading revisionist.

Hunt, Lynn. *The French Revolution and Human Rights*. Boston, 1996. A collection of documents.

———. *Politics, Culture, and Class in the French Revolution*. Berkeley, CA, 1984. An analysis of the new culture of democracy and republicanism.

Hunt, Lynn, and Jack R. Censer. *Liberty, Equality, Fraternity: Exploring the French Revolution*. University Park, PA, 2001. Two leading historians of the revolution have written a lively, accessible study, with excellent documents and visual material.

Landes, Joan B. *Women and the Public Sphere in the Age of the French Revolution*. Ithaca, NY, 1988. On gender and politics.

Lefebvre, Georges. *The Coming of the French Revolution*. Princeton, NJ, 1947. The classic Marxist analysis.

Lewis, G., and C. Lucas. *Beyond the Terror: Essays in French Regional and Social History, 1794–1815.* New York, 1983. Shifts focus to the understudied period after the Terror.

O'Brien, Connor Cruise. *The Great Melody: A Thematic Biography of Edmund Burke.* Chicago, 1992. Passionate, partisan, and brilliant study of Burke's thoughts about Ireland, India, America, and France.

Palmer, R. R. *The Age of the Democratic Revolution: A Political History of Europe and America, 1760–1800.* 2 vols. Princeton, NJ, 1964. Impressive for its scope; places the French Revolution in the larger context of a worldwide revolutionary movement.

————, and Isser Woloch. *Twelve Who Ruled: The Year of the Terror in the French Revolution.* Princeton, NJ, 2005. The terrific collective biography of the Committee of Public Safety, now updated.

Schama, Simon. *Citizens: A Chronicle of the French Revolution.* New York, 1989. Particularly good on art, culture, and politics.

Scott, Joan. *Only Paradoxes to Offer: French Feminists and the Rights of Man.* Cambridge, MA, 1997. A history of feminist engagement with a revolutionary ideology that promised universal liberties while simultaneously excluding women from citizenship.

Soboul, Albert. *The Sans-Culottes: The Popular Movement and Revolutionary Government, 1793–1794.* Garden City, NY, 1972. Dated, but a classic.

Sutherland, D. M. G. *France, 1789–1815: Revolution and Counterrevolution.* Oxford, 1986. An important synthesis of work on the revolution, especially in social history.

Tocqueville, Alexis de. *The Old Regime and the French Revolution.* Garden City, NY, 1955. Originally written in 1856, this remains a provocative analysis of the revolution's legacy.

Trouillot, Michel Rolph. *Silencing the Past.* Boston, 1995. Essays on the Haitian revolution.

Woloch, Isser. *The New Regime: Transformations of the French Civic Order, 1789–1820.* New York, 1994. The fate of revolutionary civic reform.

Woolf, Stuart. *Napoleon's Integration of Europe.* New York, 1991. Technical but very thorough.

Glossary

1973 OPEC oil embargo Some leaders in the Arab-dominated Organization of the Petroleum Exporting Countries (OPEC) wanted to use oil as a weapon against the West in the Arab-Israeli conflict. After the 1972 Arab-Israeli war, OPEC instituted an oil embargo against Western powers. The embargo increased the price of oil and sparked spiraling inflation and economic troubles in Western nations, triggering in turn a cycle of dangerous recession that lasted nearly a decade. In response, Western governments began viewing the Middle Eastern oil regions as areas of strategic importance.

Abbasid Caliphate (750–930) The Abbasid family claimed to be descendants of Muhammad, and in 750 they successfully led a rebellion against the Umayyads, seizing control of Muslim territories in Arabia, Persia, North Africa, and the Near East. The Abbasids modeled their behavior and administration on that of the Persian princes and their rule on that of the Persian Empire, establishing a new capital at Baghdad.

Peter Abelard (1079–1142) Highly influential philosopher, theologian, and teacher, often considered the founder of the University of Paris.

absolutism Form of government in which one body, usually the monarch, controls the right to make war, tax, judge, and coin money. The term was often used to refer to the state monarchies in seventeenth- and eighteenth-century Europe. In other countries the end of feudalism is often associated with the legal abolition of serfdom, as in Russia in 1861.

abstract expressionism The mid-twentieth-century school of art based in New York that included Jackson Pollock, Willem de Kooning, and Franz Kline. It emphasized form, color, gesture, and feeling instead of figurative subjects.

Academy of Sciences This French institute of scientific inquiry was founded in 1666 by Louis XIV. France's statesmen exerted control over the academy and sought to share in the rewards of any discoveries its members made.

Aeneas Mythical founder of Rome, Aeneas was a refugee from the city of Troy whose adventures were described by the poet Virgil in the *Aeneid,* which mimicked the oral epics of Homer.

Aetolian and Achaean Leagues These two alliances among Greek poleis formed during the Hellenistic period in opposition to the Antigonids of Macedonia. Unlike the earlier defensive alliances of the classic period, each league represented a real attempt to form a political federation.

African National Congress (ANC) Multiracial organization founded in 1912 whose goal was to end racial discrimination in South Africa.

Afrikaners Descendants of the original Dutch settlers of South Africa; formerly referred to as Boers.

agricultural revolution Numerous agricultural revolutions have occurred in the history of Western civilizations. One of the most significant began in the tenth century C.E., and increased the amount of land under cultivation as well as the productivity of the land. This revolution was made possible through the use of new technology, an increase in global temperatures, and more efficient methods of cultivation.

AIDS Acquired Immunodeficiency Syndrome. AIDS first appeared in the 1970s and has developed into a global health catastrophe; it is spreading most quickly in developing nations in Africa and Asia.

Akhenaten (r. 1352–1336 B.C.E.) Pharaoh whose attempt to promote the worship of the sun god, Aten, ultimately weakened his dynasty's position in Egypt.

Alexander the Great (356–323 B.C.E.) The Macedonian king whose conquests of the Persian Empire and Egypt created a new Hellenistic world.

Tsar Alexander II (1818–1881) After the Crimean War, Tsar Alexander embarked on a program of reform and modernization, which included the emancipation of the serfs. A radical assassin killed him in 1881.

Alexius Comnenus (1057–1118) This Byzantine emperor requested Pope Urban II's help in raising an army to recapture Anatolia from the Seljuk Turks. Instead, Pope Urban II called for knights to go to the Holy Land and liberate it from its Muslim captors, which launched the First Crusade.

Algerian War (1954–1962) The war between France and Algerians seeking independence. Led by the National Liberation Front (FLN), guerrillas fought the French army in the mountains and desert of Algeria. The FLN also initiated a campaign of bombing and terrorism in Algerian cities that led French soldiers to torture many Algerians, attracting world attention and international scandal.

Dante Alighieri (c. 1265–1321) Florentine poet and intellectual whose *Divine Comedy* was a pioneering work in the Italian vernacular and a vehicle for political and religious critique.

Allied Powers The First World War coalition of Great Britain, Ireland, Belgium, France, Italy, Russia, Portugal, Greece, Serbia, Montenegro, Albania, and Romania.

al Qaeda The radical Islamic organization founded in the late 1980s by former mujahidin who had fought against the Soviet Union in Afghanistan. Al Qaeda carried out the 9/11 terrorist attacks and is responsible as well for attacks in Africa, Southeast Asia, Europe, and the Middle East.

Ambrose (c. 340–397) One of the early "fathers" of the Church, he helped to define the relationship between the sacred authority of bishops and other Church leaders and the secular authority of worldly rulers. He believed that secular rulers were a part of the Church and therefore subject to it.

Americanization The fear of many Europeans, since the 1920s, that U.S. cultural products, such as film, television, and music, exerted too much influence. Many of the criticisms centered on America's emphasis on mass production and organization. The fears about Americanization were not limited to culture. They extended to corporations, business techniques, global trade, and marketing.

Americas The name given to the two great landmasses of the New World, derived from the name of the Italian geographer Amerigo Vespucci. In 1492, Christopher Columbus reached the Bahamas and the island of Hispaniola, which began an era of Spanish conquest in North and South America. Originally, the Spanish sought a route to Asia. Instead they discovered two continents whose wealth they decided to exploit. They were especially interested in gold and silver, which they either stole from indigenous peoples or mined using indigenous peoples as labor. Silver became Spain's most lucrative export from the New World.

Amnesty International Nongovernmental organization formed in 1961 to defend "prisoners of conscience"—those detained for their beliefs, color, sex, ethnic origin, language, or religion.

Anabaptists Protestant movement that emerged in Switzerland in 1521; its adherents insisted that only adults could be baptized Christians.

anarchists In the nineteenth century, they were a political movement with the aim of establishing small-scale, localized, and self-sufficient democratic communities that could guarantee a maximum of individual sovereignty. Renouncing parties, unions and any form of modern mass organization, the anarchists fell back on the tradition of conspiratorial violence.

Anti–Corn Law League This organization successfully lobbied Parliament to repeal Britain's Corn Laws in 1846. The Corn Laws of 1815 had protected British landowners and farmers from foreign competition by establishing high tariffs, which kept bread prices artificially high for British consumers. The league saw these laws as unfair protection of the aristocracy and pushed for their repeal in the name of free trade.

anti-Semitism Anti-Semitism refers to hostility toward Jewish people. Religious forms of anti-Semitism have a long history in Europe, but in the nineteenth century anti-Semitism emerged as a potent ideology for mobilizing new constituencies in the era of mass politics. Playing on popular conspiracy theories about alleged Jewish influence in society, anti-Semites effectively rallied large bodies of supporters in France during the Dreyfus Affair, and then again during the rise of National Socialism in Germany after the First World War. The Holocaust would not have been possible without the acquiescence or cooperation of many thousands of people who shared anti-Semitic views.

apartheid The racial segregation policy of the Afrikaner-dominated South African government. Legislated in 1948 by the Afrikaner National Party, it existed in South Africa for many decades.

appeasement The policy pursued by Western governments in the face of German, Italian, and Japanese aggression leading up to the Second World War. The policy, which attempted to accommodate and negotiate peace with the aggressive nations, was based on the belief that another global war like the First World War was unimaginable, a belief that Germany and its allies had been mistreated by the terms of the Treaty of Versailles, and a fear that fascist Germany and its allies protected the West from the spread of Soviet communism.

Thomas Aquinas (1225–1274) Dominican friar and theologian whose systematic approach to Christian doctrine was influenced by Aristotle.

Arab-Israeli conflict Between the founding of the state of Israel in 1948 and the present, a series of wars has been fought between Israel and neighboring Arab nations: the war of 1948 when Israel defeated attempts by Egypt, Jordon, Iraq, Syria, and Lebanon to prevent the creation of the new state; the 1956 war between Israel and Egypt over the Sinai peninsula; the 1967 war, when Israel gained control of additional land in the Golan Heights, the West Bank, the Gaza strip, and in the Sinai; and the Yom Kippur War of 1973, when Israel once again fought with forces from Egypt and Syria. A particularly difficult issue in all of these conflicts has been the situation of the 950,000 Palestinian refugees made homeless by the first war in 1948 and the movement of Israeli settlers into the occupied territories (outside of Israel's original borders). In the late 1970s, peace talks between Israel and Egypt inspired some hope of peace, but an ongoing cycle of violence between Palestinians and the Israeli military have made a final settlement elusive.

Arab nationalism During the period of decolonization, secular forms of Arab nationalism, or pan-Arabism, found a wide following in many countries of the Middle East, especially in Egypt, Syria, and Iraq.

Arianism A variety of Christianity condemned as a heresy by the Roman Church, it derives from the teaching of a fourth-century priest called Arius, who rejected the idea that Jesus could be the divine equal of God.

aristocracy From the Greek word meaning "rule of the best." By 1000 B.C.E., the accumulated wealth of successful traders in Greece had created a new type of social class, which was based on wealth rather than warfare or birth. These men saw their wealth as a reflection of their superior qualities and aspired to emulate the heroes of old.

Aristotle (384–322 B.C.E.) A student of Plato, his philosophy was based on the rational analysis of the material world. In contrast to his teacher, he stressed the rigorous investigation of real phenomena, rather than the development of universal ethics. He was, in turn, the teacher of Alexander the Great.

Asiatic Society A cultural organization founded in 1784 by British Orientalists who lauded native culture but believed in colonial rule.

Assyrians A Semitic-speaking people that moved into northern Mesopotamia around 2400 B.C.E.

Athens Athens emerged as the Greek polis with the most markedly democratic form of government through a series of political struggles during the sixth century B.C.E. After its key role in the defeat of two invading Persian forces, Athens became the preeminent naval power of ancient Greece and the exemplar of Greek culture. But it antagonized many other poleis, and became embroiled in a war with Sparta and her allies in 431 B.C.E. Called the Peloponnesian War, this bloody conflict lasted until Athens was defeated in 404 B.C.E.

atomic bomb In 1945, the United States dropped atomic bombs on Hiroshima and Nagasaki in Japan, ending the Second World War. In 1949, the Soviet Union tested its first atomic bomb, and in 1953 both superpowers demonstrated their new hydrogen bombs. Strategically, the nuclearization of warfare polarized the world. Countries without nuclear weapons found it difficult to avoid joining either the Soviet or American military pacts. Over time, countries split into two groups: the superpowers with enormous military budgets and those countries that relied on agreements and international law. The nuclearization of warfare also encouraged "proxy wars" between clients of superpowers. Culturally, the hydrogen bomb came to symbolize the age and both humanity's power and vulnerability.

Augustine (c. 354–397) One of the most influential theologians of all time, Augustine described his conversion to Christianity in his autobiographical *Confessions* and articulated a new Christian worldview in *The City of God*, among other works.

Augustus (63 B.C.E.–14 C.E.) Born Gaius Octavius, this grandnephew and adopted son of Julius Caesar came to power in 27 B.C.E. His reign signals the end of the Roman Republic and the beginning of the Principate, the period when Rome was dominated by autocratic emperors.

Auschwitz-Birkenau The Nazi concentration camp in Poland that was designed to systematically murder Jews and Gypsies. Between 1942 and 1944 over 1 million people were killed in Auschwitz-Birkenau.

Austro-Hungarian Empire The dual monarchy established by the Habsburg family in 1867; it collapsed at the end of the First World War.

authoritarianism A centralized and dictatorial form of government, proclaimed by its adherents to be superior to parliamentary democracy. Authoritarian governments claim to be above the law, do not respect individual rights, and do not tolerate political opposition. Authoritarian regimes that have developed a central ideology such as fascism or communism are sometimes termed "totalitarian."

Avignon A city in southeastern France that became the seat of the papacy between 1305 and 1377, a period known as the "Babylonian Captivity" of the Roman Church.

Aztecs An indigenous people of central Mexico; their empire was conquered by Spanish conquistadors in the sixteenth century.

baby boom (1950s) The post–Second World War upswing in U.S. birth rates; it reversed a century of decline.

Babylon An ancient city between the Tigris and Euphrates Rivers, which became the capital of Hammurabi's empire in the eighteenth century B.C.E. and continued to be an important administrative and commercial capital under many subsequent imperial powers, including the Neo-Assyrians, Chaldeans, Persians, and Romans. It was here that Alexander the Great died in 323 B.C.E.

Babylonian captivity Refers both to the Jews' exile in Babylon during the sixth century B.C.E. and the period from 1309 to 1378, when papal authority was subjugated to the French crown and the papal court was moved from Rome to the French city of Avignon.

Francis Bacon (1561–1626) British philosopher and scientist who pioneered the scientific method and inductive reasoning. In other words, he argued that thinkers should amass many observations and then draw general conclusions or propose theories on the basis of these data.

balance of powers The principle that no country should be powerful enough to destabilize international relations. Starting in the seventeenth century, this goal of maintaining balance influenced diplomacy in western and central Europe for two centuries until the system collapsed with the onset of the First World War.

Balfour Declaration A letter dated November 2, 1917, by Lord Arthur J. Balfour, British foreign secretary, that promised a homeland for the Jews in Palestine.

Laura Bassi (1711–1778) She was accepted into the Academy of Science in Bologna for her work in mathematics, which made her one of the few women to be accepted into a scientific academy in the seventeenth century.

Bastille The Bastille was a royal fortress and prison in Paris. In June 1789, a revolutionary crowd attacked the Bastille to show support for the newly created National Assembly. The fall of the Bastille was the first instance of the people's role in revolutionary change in France.

Bay of Pigs (1961) The unsuccessful invasion of Cuba by Cuban exiles, supported by the U.S. government. The rebels intended to incite an insurrection in Cuba and overthrow the communist regime of Fidel Castro.

Cesare Beccaria (1738–1794) An influential writer during the Enlightenment who advocated for legal reforms. He believed that the only legitimate rationale for punishments was to maintain social order and to prevent other crimes. He argued for the greatest possible leniency compatible with deterrence and opposed torture and the death penalty.

Beer Hall Putsch (1923) An early attempt by the Nazi party to seize power in Munich; Adolf Hitler was imprisoned for a year after the incident.

Benedict of Nursia (c. 480–c. 547) Benedict's rule for monks formed the basis of western monasticism and is still observed in monasteries all over the world.

Benedictine Monasticism This form of monasticism was developed by Benedict of Nursia. Its followers adhere to a defined cycle of daily prayers, lessons, communal worship, and manual labor.

Berlin airlift (1948) The transport of vital supplies to West Berlin by air, primarily under U.S. auspices, in response to a blockade of the city that had been instituted by the Soviet Union to force the Allies to abandon West Berlin.

Berlin Conference (1884) At this conference, the leading colonial powers met and established ground rules for the partition of Africa by European nations. By 1914, 90 percent of African territory was under European control. The Berlin Conference ceded control of the Congo region to a private company run by King Leopold II of Belgium. They agreed to make the Congo valleys open to free trade and commerce, to end the slave trade in the region, and to establish a Congo Free State. In reality, King Leopold II's company established a regime that was so brutal in its treatment of local populations that an international scandal forced the Belgian state to take over the colony in 1908.

Berlin Wall The wall built in 1961 by East German Communists to prevent citizens of East Germany from fleeing to West Germany; it was torn down in 1989.

birth control pill This oral contraceptive became widely available in the mid-1960s. For the first time, women had a simple method of birth control that they could take themselves.

Otto von Bismarck (1815–1898) The prime minister of Prussia and later the first chancellor of a unified Germany, Bismarck was the architect of German unification and helped to consolidate the new nation's economic and military power.

Black Death The epidemic of bubonic plague that ravaged Europe, Asia, and North Africa in the fourteenth century, killing one third to one half of the population.

Black Jacobins A nickname for the rebels in Saint-Domingue, including Toussaint L'Ouverture, a former slave who in 1791 led the slaves of this French colony in the largest and most successful slave insurrection.

Blackshirts The troops of Mussolini's fascist regime; the squads received money from Italian landowners to attack socialist leaders.

Black Tuesday (October 29, 1929) The day on which the U.S. stock market crashed, plunging U.S. and international trading systems into crisis and leading the world into the "Great Depression."

William Blake (1757–1827) Romantic writer who criticized industrial society and factories. He championed the imagination and poetic vision, seeing both as transcending the limits of the material world.

Blitzkrieg The German "lightning war" strategy used during the Second World War; the Germans invaded Poland, France, Russia, and other countries with fast-moving and well-coordinated attacks using aircraft, tanks and other armored vehicles, followed by infantry.

Bloody Sunday On January 22, 1905, the Russian tsar's guards killed 130 demonstrators who were protesting the tsar's mistreatment of workers and the middle class.

Giovanni Boccaccio (1313–1375) Florentine author best known for his *Decameron*, a collection of prose tales about sex, adventure, and trickery written in the Italian vernacular after the Black Death.

Jean Bodin (1530–1596) A French political philosopher whose *Six Books of the Commonwealth* advanced a theory of absolute sovereignty, on the grounds that the state's paramount duty is to maintain order and that monarchs should therefore exercise unlimited power.

Boer War (1898–1902) Conflict between British and ethnically European Afrikaners in South Africa, with terrible casualties on both sides.

Boethius (c. 480–524) Member of a prominent Roman family, he sought to preserve aspects of ancient learning by compiling a series of handbooks and anthologies appropriate for Christian readers. His translations of Greek philosophy provided a crucial link between classical Greek thought and the early intellectual culture of Christianity.

Bolsheviks Former members of the Russian Social Democratic Party who advocated the destruction of capitalist political and economic institutions and started the Russian Revolution. In 1918, the Bolsheviks changed their name to the Russian Communist Party. Prominent Bolsheviks included Vladimir Lenin and Josef Stalin. Leon Trotsky joined the Bolsheviks late but became a prominent leader in the early years of the Russian Revolution.

Napoleon Bonaparte (1769–1821) Corsican-born French general who seized power and ruled as dictator from 1799 to 1814. After the successful conquest of much of Europe, he was defeated by Russian and Prussian forces and died in exile.

Boniface VIII During his pontificate (1294–1303), repeated claims to papal authority were challenged by King Philip IV of France. When Boniface died in 1309 (at the hands of Philip's thugs), the French king moved the papal court from Rome to the French city of Avignon, where it remained until 1378.

Sandro Botticelli (1445–1510) An Italian painter devoted to the blending of classical and Christian motifs by using ideas associated with the pagan past to illuminate sacred stories.

bourgeoisie Term for the middle class, derived from the French word for a town-dweller, *bourgeois*.

Boxer Rebellion (1899–1900) Chinese peasant movement that opposed foreign influence, especially that of Christian missionaries; it was finally put down after the Boxers were defeated by a foreign army composed mostly of Japanese, Russian, British, French, and American soldiers.

Tycho Brahe (1546–1601) Danish astronomer who believed that the careful study of the heavens would unlock the secrets of the universe. For over twenty years, he charted the movements of significant objects in the night sky, compiling the finest set of astronomical data in Europe.

British Commonwealth of Nations Formed in 1926, the Commonwealth conferred "dominion status" on Britain's white settler colonies in Canada, Australia, and New Zealand.

Bronze Age (3200–1200 B.C.E.) The name given to the era characterized by the discovery of techniques for smelting bronze (an alloy of copper and tin), which was then the strongest known metal.

Brownshirts Troops of young German men who dedicated themselves to the Nazi cause in the early 1930s by holding street marches, mass rallies, and confrontations. They engaged in beatings of Jews and anyone who opposed the Nazis.

Lord Byron (1788–1824) Writer and poet whose life helped give the Romantics their reputation as rebels against conformity. He was known for his love affairs, his defense of working-class movements, and his passionate engagement in politics, which led to his death in the war for Greek independence.

Byzantium The name of a small settlement located at the mouth of the Black Sea and at the crossroads between Europe and Asia, it was chosen by Constantine as the site for his new imperial capital of Constantinople in 324. Modern historians use this name to refer to the eastern Roman Empire that persisted in this region until 1453, but the inhabitants of that empire referred to themselves as Romans.

Julius Caesar (100–44 B.C.E.) The Roman general who conquered the Gauls, invaded Britain, and expanded Rome's territory in Asia Minor. He became the dictator of Rome in 46 B.C.E. His assassination led to the rise of his grandnephew and adopted son, Gaius Octavius Caesar, who ruled the Roman Empire as Caesar Augustus.

caliphs Islamic rulers who claim descent from the prophet Muhammad.

John Calvin (1509–1564) French-born theologian and reformer whose radical form of Protestantism was adopted in many Swiss cities, notably Geneva.

Canary Islands Islands off the western coast of Africa that were colonized by Portugal and Spain in the mid-fifteenth century, after which they became bases for further expeditions around the African coast and across the Atlantic.

Carbonari An underground organization that opposed the Concert of Europe's restoration of monarchies. They held influence in southern Europe during the 1820s, especially in Italy.

Carolingian Derived from the Latin name Carolus (Charles), this term refers to the Frankish dynasty that began with the rise to power of Charlemagne's grandfather, Charles Martel (688–741). At its height under Charlemagne (Charles the Great), the dynasty controlled what is now France, Germany, northern Italy, Catalonia, and portions of central Europe. The Carolingian Empire collapsed under the combined weight of Viking raids, economic disintegration, and the growing power of local lords.

Carolingian Renaissance A cultural and intellectual flowering that took place around the court of Charlemagne in the late eighth and early ninth centuries.

Carthage The great maritime empire that grew out of Phoenician trading colonies in North Africa and rivaled the power of Rome. Its wars with Rome, collectively known as the Punic Wars, ended in its destruction in 146 B.C.E.

Cassidorus (c. 490–c. 583) Member of an old senatorial family, he was largely responsible for introducing classical learning into the monastic curriculum and for turning monasteries into centers for the collection, preservation, and transmission of knowledge. His *Institutes*, an influential handbook of classical literature for Christian readers, was intended as a preface to more intensive study of theology and the Bible.

Catholic Church The "universal" (catholic) church based in Rome, which was redefined in the sixteenth century, when the Counter-Reformation resulted in the rebirth of the Catholic faith at the Council of Trent.

Margaret Cavendish (1623–1673) English natural philosopher who developed her own speculative natural philosophy. She used this philosophy to critique those who excluded her from scientific debate.

Camillo Benso di Cavour (1810–1861) Prime minister of Piedmont-Sardinia and founder of the Italian Liberal party; he played a key role in the movement for Italian unification under the Piedmontese king, Victor Emmanuel II.

Central Powers The First World War alliance between Germany, Austria-Hungary, Bulgaria, and Turkey.

Charlemagne (742–814) As king of the Franks (767–813), Charles "the Great" consolidated much of western Europe under his rule. In 800, he was crowned emperor by the pope in Rome, establishing a problematic precedent that would have wide-ranging consequences for western Europe's relationship with the eastern Roman Empire in Byzantium and for the relationship between the papacy and secular rulers.

Charles I (1625–1649) The second Stuart king of England, Charles attempted to rule without the support of Parliament, sparking a controversy that erupted into civil war in 1642. The king's forces were ultimately defeated and Charles himself was executed by act of Parliament, the first time in history that a reigning king was legally deposed and executed by his own government.

Charles II of England Nominally King of England, Ireland, and Scotland after his father Charles I's execution in 1649, Charles II lived in exile until he was restored to the throne in 1660. Influenced by his cousin, King Louis XIV of France, he presided over an opulent royal court until his death in 1685.

Chartists A working-class movement in Britain that called for reform of the British political system during the 1840s. They were supporters of the "People's Charter," which had six demands: universal white male suffrage, secret ballots, an end to property qualifications as a condition of public office, annual parliamentary elections, salaries for members of the House of Commons, and equal electoral districts.

Geoffrey Chaucer (1340–1400) English poet whose collection of versified stories, *The Canterbury Tales*, features characters from a variety of different classes.

Christine de Pisan (c. 1364–c. 1431) Born in Italy, Christine spent her adult life attached to the French court and, after her husband's death, became the first laywoman to earn her living by writing. She is the author of treatises in warfare and chivalry as well as of books and pamphlets that challenge long-standing misogynistic claims.

Church of England Founded by Henry VIII in the 1530s, as a consequence of his break with the authority of the Roman pope.

Winston Churchill (1874–1965) British prime minister who led the country during the Second World War. He also coined the phrase "Iron Curtain" in a speech at Westminster College in 1946.

Cicero (106–43 B.C.E.) Influential Roman senator, orator, Stoic philosopher, and prose stylist. His published writings still form the basis of the instruction in classical Latin grammar and usage.

Cincinnatus (519–c. 430 B.C.E.) A legendary citizen-farmer of Rome who reluctantly accepted an appointment as dictator. After defeating Rome's enemies, he allegedly left his political office and returned to his farm.

Civil Constitution of the Clergy Issued by the French National Assembly in 1790, the Civil Constitution of the Clergy decreed that all bishops and priests should be subject to the authority of the state. Their salaries were to be paid out of the public treasury, and they were required to swear allegiance to the new state, making it clear they served France rather than Rome. The Assembly's aim was to make the Catholic Church of France a truly national and civil institution.

civilizing mission An argument made by Europeans to justify colonial expansion in the nineteenth century. Supporters of this idea believed that Europeans had a duty to impose western ideas of economic and political progress on the indigenous peoples they ruled over in their colonies. In practice, the colonial powers often found that ambitious plans to impose European practices on colonial subjects led to unrest that threatened the stability of colonial rule, and by the early twentieth century most colonial powers were more cautious in their plans for political or cultural transformation.

Civil Rights Movement The Second World War increased African American migration from the American South to northern cities, intensifying a drive for rights, dignity, and independence. By 1960, civil rights groups had started organizing boycotts and demonstrations directed at discrimination against blacks in the South. During the 1960s, civil rights laws passed under President Lyndon B. Johnson did bring African Americans some equality with regard to voting rights and, to a much lesser degree, school desegregation. However, racism continued in areas such as housing, job opportunities, and the economic development of African American communities.

Civil War (1861–1865) Conflict between the northern and southern states of America that cost over 600,000 lives; this struggle led to the abolition of slavery in the United States.

classical learning The study of ancient Greek and Latin texts. After Christianity became the only legal religion of the Roman Empire, scholars needed to find a way to make classical learning applicable to a Christian way of life. Christian monks played a significant role in resolving this problem by reinterpreting the classics for a Christian audience.

Cluny A powerful Benedictine monastery founded in 910 whose enormous wealth and prestige would derive from its independence from secular authorities as well as from its wide network of daughter houses (priories).

Cold War (1945–1991) Ideological, political, and economic conflict in which the USSR and Eastern Europe opposed the United States and Western Europe in the decades after the Second World War. The Cold War's origins lay in the breakup of the wartime alliance between the United States and the Soviet Union in 1945 and resulted in a division of Europe into two spheres: the West, committed to market capitalism, and the East, which sought to build Socialist republics in areas under Soviet Control. The Cold War ended with the collapse of the Soviet Union in 1991.

collectivization Stalin's plan for nationalizing agricultural production, begun in 1929. Twenty-five million peasants were forced to give up their land and join 250,000 large collective farms. Many who resisted were deported to labor camps in the Far East, and Stalin's government cut off food rations to those areas most marked by resistance to collectivization. In the ensuing man-made famines, millions of people starved to death.

Columbian Exchange The widespread exchange of peoples, plants, animals, diseases, goods, and culture between the African and Eurasian landmass (on the one hand) and the region that encompasses the Americas, Australia, and the Pacific Islands (on the other); precipitated by voyage of Columbus in 1492.

Christopher Columbus (1451–1506) A Genoese sailor who persuaded King Ferdinand and Queen Isabella of Spain to fund his expedition across the Atlantic, with the purpose of discovering a new trade route to Asia. His miscalculations landed him in the Bahamas and the island of Hispaniola in 1492.

Commercial Revolution A period of economic development in Europe lasting from c. 1500–c.1800. Advances in agriculture and handicraft production, combined with the expansion of trade networks in the Atlantic world, brought new wealth and new kinds of commercial activity to Europe. The commercial revolution prepared the way for the industrial revolution of the 1800s.

Committee of Public Safety Political body during the French Revolution that was controlled by the Jacobins, who defended the revolution by executing thousands during the Reign of Terror (September 1793–July 1794).

commune A community of individuals who have banded together in a sworn association, with the aim of establishing their independence and setting up their own form of representative government. Many medieval towns originally founded by lords or monasteries gained their independence through such methods.

The Communist Manifesto Radical pamphlet by Karl Marx (1818–1883) that predicted the downfall of the capitalist system and its replacement by a classless egalitarian society. Marx believed that this revolution would be accomplished by workers (the proletariat).

Compromise of 1867 Agreement between the Habsburgs and the peoples living in Hungarian parts of the empire that the Habsburg state would be officially known as the Austro-Hungarian Empire.

Concert of Europe (1814–1815) The body of diplomatic agreements designed primarily by Austrian minister Klemens von Metternich between 1814 and 1848 and supported by other European powers until 1914. Its goal was to maintain a balance of power on the Continent and to prevent destabilizing social and political change in Europe.

conciliarism A doctrine developed in the thirteenth and fourteenth centuries to counter the growing power of the papacy, conciliarism holds that papal authority should be subject to a council of the Church at large. Conciliarists emerged as a dominant force after the Council of Constance (1414–1418) but were eventually outmatched by a rejuvenated papacy.

Congress of Vienna (1814–1815) International conference to reorganize Europe after the downfall of Napoleon and the French Revolution. European monarchies restored the Bourbon family to the French throne, agreed to respect each other's borders and to cooperate in guarding against future revolutions and war.

conquistador Spanish term for "conqueror," applied to the mercenaries and adventurers who campaigned against indigenous peoples in central and southern America.

Conservatives In the nineteenth century, conservatives aimed to legitimize and solidify the monarchy's authority and the hierarchical social order. They believed that change had to be slow, incremental, and managed so that the structures of authority were strengthened and not weakened.

Constantine (275–337) The first emperor of Rome to convert to Christianity, Constantine came to power in 312. In 324, he founded a new imperial capital, Constantinople, on the site of a maritime settlement known as Byzantium.

Constantinople Founded by the emperor Constantine on the site of a village called Byzantium, Constantinople became the new capital of the Roman Empire in 324 and continued to be the seat of imperial power after its capture by the Ottoman Turks in 1453. It is now known as Istanbul.

contract theory of government A theory of government written by Englishman John Locke (1632–1704) which posits that government authority was both contractual and conditional; therefore, if a government has abused its given authority, society had the right to dissolve it and create another.

Nicholas Copernicus (1473–1543) Polish astronomer who advanced the idea that the earth moved around the sun.

cosmopolitanism Stemming from the Greek word meaning "universal city," the culture characteristic of the Hellenistic world challenged and transformed the more narrow worldview of the Greek polis.

cotton gin Invented by Eli Whitney in 1793, this device mechanized the process of separating cotton seeds from the cotton fiber, which sped up the production of cotton and reduced its price. This change made slavery profitable in the United States.

Council of Constance (1417–1420) A meeting of clergy and theologians in an effort to resolve the Great Schism within the Roman Church. The council deposed all rival papal candidates and elected a new pope, Martin V, but it also adopted the doctrine of conciliarism, which holds that the supreme authority within the Church rests with a representative general council and not with the pope. However, Martin V himself was an opponent of this doctrine and refused to be bound by it.

Council of Trent The name given to a series of meetings held in the Italian city of Trent (Trento) between 1545 and 1563, when leaders of the Roman Church reaffirmed Catholic doctrine and instituted internal reforms.

Counter-Reformation The movement to counter the Protestant Reformation, initiated by the Catholic Church at the Council of Trent in 1545.

coup d'état French term for the overthrow of an established government by a group of conspirators, usually with military support.

Crimean War (1854–1856) War waged by Russia against Great Britain and France. Spurred by Russia's encroachment on Ottoman territories, the conflict revealed Russia's military weakness when Russian forces fell to British and French troops.

Cuban missile crisis (1962) Diplomatic standoff between the United States and the Soviet Union that was provoked by the Soviet Union's attempt to base nuclear missiles in Cuba; it brought the world closer to nuclear war than ever before or since.

Cuius regio, eius religio A Latin phrase meaning "as the ruler, so the religion." Adopted as a part of the settlement of the Peace of Augsburg in 1555, it meant that those principalities ruled by Lutherans would have Lutheranism as their official religion and those ruled by Catholics must practice Catholicism.

cult of domesticity Concept associated with Victorian England that idealized women as nurturing wives and mothers.

cult of the Virgin The beliefs and practices associated with the veneration of Mary, the mother of Jesus, which became increasingly popular in the twelfth century.

cuneiform An early writing system that began to develop in Mesopotamia in the fourth millennium B.C.E. By 3100 B.C.E., its distinctive markings were impressed on clay tablets using a wedge-shaped stylus.

Cyrus the Great (c. 585–529 B.C.E.) As architect of the Persian Empire, Cyrus extended his dominion over a vast territory stretching from the Persian Gulf to the Mediterranean and incorporating the ancient civilizations of Mesopotamia. His successors ruled this Persian Empire as "Great Kings."

Darius (521–486 B.C.E.) The Persian emperor whose conflict with Aristagoras, the Greek ruler of Miletus, ignited the Persian Wars. In 490 B.C.E., Darius sent a large army to punish the Athenians for their intervention in Persian imperial affairs, but this force was defeated by Athenian hoplites on the plain of Marathon.

Charles Darwin (1809–1882) British naturalist who wrote *On the Origin of Species* and developed the theory of natural selection to explain the evolution of organisms.

D-Day (June 6, 1944) Date of the Allied invasion of Normandy, under General Dwight Eisenhower, to liberate Western Europe from German occupation.

Decembrists Russian army officers who were influenced by events in France and formed secret societies that espoused liberal governance. They were put down by Nicholas I in December 1825.

Declaration of Independence (1776) Historic document stating the principles of government on which the United States was founded.

Declaration of the Rights of Man and of the Citizen (1789) French charter of liberties formulated by the National Assembly during the French Revolution. The seventeen articles later became the preamble to the new constitution, which the assembly finished in 1791.

democracy In ancient Greece, this form of government allowed a class of propertied male citizens to participate in the governance of their polis; but excluded women, slaves, and citizens without property from the political process. As a result, the ruling class amounted to only a small percentage of the entire population.

René Descartes (1596–1650) French philosopher and mathematician who emphasized the use of deductive reasoning.

Denis Diderot (1713–1784) French philosophe and author who was the guiding force behind the publication of the first encyclopedia. His *Encyclopedia* showed how reason could be applied to nearly all realms of thought and aimed to be a compendium of all human knowledge.

Dien Bien Phu (1954) Defining battle in the war between French colonialists and the Viet Minh that secured North Vietnam for Ho Chi Minh and his army and left the south to form its own government, to be supported by France and the United States.

Diet of Worms The select council of the Church that convened in the German city of Worms and condemned Martin Luther on a charge of heresy in 1521.

Diocletian (245–316) As emperor of Rome from 284 to 305, Diocletian recognized that the empire could not be governed by one man in one place. His solution was to divide the empire into four parts, each with its own imperial ruler, but he himself remained the dominant ruler of the resulting tetrarchy (rule of four). He also initiated the Great Persecution, a time when many Christians became martyrs to their faith.

Directory (1795–1799) Executive committee that governed after the fall of Robespierre and held control until the coup of Napoleon Bonaparte.

Discourse on Method Philosophical treatise by René Descartes (1596–1650) proposing that the path to knowledge was through logical deduction, beginning with one's own self: "I think, therefore I am."

Dominican Order Also called the Order of Preachers, it was founded by Dominic of Osma (1170–1221), a Castilian preacher and theologian, and approved by Innocent III in 1216. The order was dedicated to the rooting out of heresy and the conversion of Jews and Muslims. Many of its members held teaching positions in European universities and contributed to the development of medieval philosophy and theology. Others became the leading administrators of the Inquisition.

Dominion in the British Commonwealth Canadian promise to maintain their fealty to the British crown, even after their independence in 1867; later applied to Australia and New Zealand.

Dreyfus Affair The 1894 French scandal surrounding accusations that a Jewish captain, Alfred Dreyfus, sold military secrets to the Germans. Convicted, Dreyfus was sentenced to solitary confinement for life. However, after public outcry, it was revealed that the trial documents were forgeries, and Dreyfus was pardoned after a second trial in 1899. In 1906, he was fully exonerated and reinstated in the army. The affair revealed the depths of popular anti-Semitism in France.

Alexander Dubček (1921–1992) Communist leader of the Czechoslovakian government who advocated for "socialism with a human face." He encouraged debate within the party, academic and artistic freedom, and less censorship, which led to the "Prague spring" of 1968. People in other parts of Eastern Europe began to demonstrate in support of Dubček and demand their own reforms. When Dubček tried to democratize the Communist party and did not attend a meeting of the Warsaw Pact, the Soviets sent tanks and troops into Prague and ousted Dubček and his allies.

Duma The Russian parliament, created in response to the revolution of 1905.

Dunkirk The French port on the English Channel where the British and French forces retreated after sustaining heavy losses against the German military. Between May 27 and June 4, 1940, the Royal Navy evacuated over 300,000 troops using commercial and pleasure boats.

Eastern Front Battlefront between Berlin and Moscow during the First and Second World Wars..

East India Company (1600–1858) British charter company created to outperform Portuguese and Spanish traders in the Far East; in the eighteenth century the company became, in effect, the ruler of a large part of India. There was also a Dutch East India Company.

Edict of Nantes (1598) Issued by Henry IV of France in an effort to end religious violence. The edict declared France to be a Catholic country but tolerated some forms of Protestant worship.

Edward I of England King of England from 1272 to his death in 1307, Edward presided over the creation of new legal and bureaucratic institutions in his realm, violently subjugated the Welsh, and attempted to colonize Scotland. He expelled English Jews from his domain in 1290.

Eleanor of Aquitaine (1122–1204) Ruler of the wealthy province of Aquitaine and wife of Louis VII of France, Eleanor had her marriage annulled in order to marry the young count of Anjou, Henry Plantagenet, who became King Henry of England a year later. Mother of two future kings of England, she was an important patron of the arts.

Elizabeth I (1533–1603) Protestant daughter of Henry VIII and his second wife, Anne Boleyn, Elizabeth succeeded her sister Mary as the second queen regnant of England (1558–1603).

emancipation of the serfs (1861) The abolition of serfdom was central to Tsar Alexander II's program of modernization and reform, but it produced a limited amount of change. Former serfs now had legal rights. However, farm land was granted to the village communes instead of to individuals. The land was of poor quality and the former serfs had to pay for it in installments to the village commune.

emperor Originally the term for any conquering commander of the Roman army whose victories merited celebration in an official triumph. After Augustus seized power in 27 B.C.E., it was the title born by the sole ruler of the Roman Empire.

empire A centralized political entity consolidated through the conquest and colonization of other nations or peoples in order to benefit the ruler and/or his homeland.

Enabling Act (1933) Emergency act passed by the Reichstag (German parliament) that helped transform Hitler from Germany's chancellor, or prime minister, into a dictator, following the suspicious burning of the Reichstag building and a suspension of civil liberties.

enclosure Long process of privatizing what had been public agricultural land in eighteenth-century Britain; it helped to stimulate the development of commercial agriculture and forced many people in rural areas to seek work in cities during the early stages of industrialization.

The Encyclopedia Joint venture of French philosophe writers, led by Denis Diderot (1713–1784), which proposed to summarize all modern knowledge in a multivolume illustrated work with over 70,000 articles.

Friedrich Engels (1820–1895) German social and political philosopher who collaborated with Karl Marx on many publications.

English Civil War (1642–1649) Conflicts between the English Parliament and King Charles I erupted into civil war, which ended in the defeat of the royalists and the execution of Charles on charges of treason against the crown. A short time later, Parliament's hereditary House of Lords was abolished and England was declared a Commonwealth.

English Navigation Act of 1651 Act stipulating that only English ships could carry goods between the mother country and its colonies.

Enlightenment Intellectual movement in eighteenth-century Europe, that believed in human betterment through the application of reason to solve social, economic, and political problems.

Epicureanism A philosophical position articulated by Epicurus of Athens (c. 342–270 B.C.E.), who rejected the idea of an ordered universe governed by divine forces; instead, he emphasized individual agency and proposed that the highest good is the pursuit of pleasure.

Desiderius Erasmus (c. 1469–1536) Dutch-born scholar, social commentator, and Catholic humanist whose new translation of the Bible influenced the theology of Martin Luther.

Estates-General The representative body of the three estates in France. In 1789, King Louis XVI summoned the Estates-General to meet for the first time since 1614 because it seemed to be the only solution to France's worsening economic crisis and financial chaos.

Etruscans Settlers of the Italian peninsula who dominated the region from the late Bronze Age until the rise of the Roman Republic in the sixth century B.C.E.

Euclid Hellenistic mathematician whose *Elements of Geometry* forms the basis of modern geometry.

eugenics A Greek term, meaning "good birth," referring to the project of "breeding" a superior human race. It was popularly championed by scientists, politicians, and social critics in the late nineteenth and early twentieth centuries.

European Common Market (1957) The Treaty of Rome created the European Economic Community (EEC), or Common Market. The original members were France, West Germany, Italy, Belgium, Holland, and Luxembourg. The EEC sought to abolish trade barriers between its members and it pledged itself to common external tariffs, the free movement of labor and capital among the member nations, and uniform wage structures and social security systems to create similar working conditions in all member countries.

European Union (EU) Successor organization to the European Economic Community or European Common Market, formed by the Maastricht Treaty, which took effect in 1993. Currently twenty-eight member states compose the EU, which has a governing council, an international court, and a parliament. Over time, member states of the EU have relinquished some of their sovereignty, and cooperation has evolved into a community with a single currency, the euro.

Exclusion Act of 1882 U.S. congressional act prohibiting nearly all immigration from China to the United States; fueled by animosity toward Chinese workers in the American West.

existentialism Philosophical movement that arose out of the Second World War and emphasized the absurdity of human condition. Led by Jean-Paul Sartre and Albert Camus, existentialists encouraged humans to take responsibility for their own decisions and dilemmas.

expulsion of the Jews European rulers began to expel their Jewish subjects from their kingdoms beginning in the 1280s, mostly due to their inability to repay the money they had extorted from Jewish money-lenders but also as a result of escalating anti-Semitism in the wake of the Crusades, Jews were also expelled from the Rhineland in the fourteenth century and from Spain in 1492.

fascism The doctrine founded by Benito Mussolini, which emphasized three main ideas: statism ("nothing above the state, nothing outside the state, nothing against the state"), nationalism, and militarism. Its name derives from the Latin *fasces*, a symbol of Roman imperial power adopted by Mussolini.

Fashoda Incident (1898) Disagreements between the French and the British over land claims in North Africa led to a standoff between armies of the two nations at the Sudanese town of Fashoda. The crisis was solved diplomatically. France ceded southern Sudan to Britain in exchange for a stop to further expansion by the British.

The Feminine Mystique Groundbreaking book by feminist Betty Friedan (b. 1921), which tried to define *femininity* and explored how women internalized those definitions.

Franz Ferdinand (1863–1914) Archduke of Austria and heir to the Austro-Hungarian Empire; his assassination led to the beginning of the First World War.

Ferdinand (1452–1516) **and Isabella** (1451–1504) In 1469, Ferdinand of Aragon married the heiress to Castile, Isabella. Their union allowed them to pursue several ambitious policies, including the conquest of Granada, the last Muslim principality in Spain, and the expulsion of Spain's large Jewish community. In 1492, Isabella granted three ships to Christopher Columbus of Genoa (Italy), who went on to claim portions of the New World for Spain.

Fertile Crescent An area of fertile land in what is now Syria, Israel, Turkey, eastern Iraq, and western Iran that was able to sustain settlements due to its wetter climate and abundant natural food resources. Some of the earliest known civilizations emerged there between 9000 and 4500 B.C.E.

feudalism A problematic modern term that attempts to explain the diffusion of power in medieval Europe, and the many different kinds of political, social, and economic relationships that were forged through the giving and receiving of fiefs (*feoda*). But because it is anachronistic and inadequate, this term has been rejected by most historians of the medieval period.

First Crusade (1095–1099) Launched by Pope Urban II in response to a request from the Byzantine emperor Alexius Comnenus, who had asked for a small contingent of knights to assist him in fighting Turkish forces in Anatolia; Urban instead directed the crusaders' energies toward the Holy Land and the recapture of Jerusalem, promising those who took the cross (*crux*) that they would merit eternal salvation if they died in the attempt. This crusade prompted attacks against

Jews throughout Europe and resulted in six subsequent—and unsuccessful—military campaigns.

First World War A total war from August 1914 to November 1918, involving the armies of Britain, France, and Russia (the Allies) against Germany, Austria-Hungary, and the Ottoman Empire (the Central Powers). Italy joined the Allies in 1915, and the United States joined them in 1917, helping to tip the balance in favor of the Allies, who also drew upon the populations and raw materials of their colonial possessions. Also known as the Great War.

Five Pillars of Islam The Muslim teaching that salvation is only assured through observance of five basic precepts: submission to God's will as described in the teachings of Muhammad, frequent prayer, ritual fasting, the giving of alms, and an annual pilgrimage to Mecca (the Hajj).

Five-Year Plan Soviet effort launched under Stalin in 1928 to replace the market with a state-owned and state-managed economy in order to promote rapid economic development over a five-year period and thereby "catch and overtake" the leading capitalist countries. The First Five-Year Plan was followed by the Second Five-Year Plan (1933–1937) and so on, until the collapse of the Soviet Union in 1991.

fly shuttle Invented by John Kay in 1733, this device sped up the process of weaving.

Fourteen Points President Woodrow Wilson proposed these points as the foundation on which to build peace in the world after the First World War. They called for an end to secret treaties, "open covenants, openly arrived at," freedom of the seas, the removal of international tariffs, the reduction of arms, the "self-determination of peoples," and the establishment of a League of Nations to settle international conflicts.

Franciscan Order Also known as the Order of the Friars Minor. The earliest Franciscans were followers of Francis of Assisi (1182–1226) and strove, like him, to imitate the life and example of Jesus. The order was formally established by Pope Innocent III in 1209. Its special mission was the care and instruction of the urban poor.

Frankfurt Parliament (1848–1849) Failed attempt to create a unified Germany under constitutional principles. In 1849, the assembly offered the crown of the new German nation to Frederick William IV of Prussia, but he refused the offer and suppressed a brief protest. The delegates went home disillusioned.

Frederick the Great (1712–1786) Prussian ruler (1740–1786) who engaged the nobility in maintaining a strong military and bureaucracy and led Prussian armies to notable military victories. He also encouraged Enlightenment rationalism and artistic endeavors.

French Revolution of 1789 In 1788, a severe financial crisis forced the French monarchy to convene an assembly known as the Estates General, representing the three estates of the realm: the clergy, the nobility, and the commons (known as the Third Estate). When the Estates General met in 1789, representatives of the Third Estate demanded major constitutional changes, and when the king and his government proved uncooperative, the Third Estate broke with the other two estates and renamed themselves the National Assembly, demanding

a written constitution. The position of the National Assembly was confirmed by a popular uprising in Paris and the king was forced to accept the transformation of France into a constitutional monarchy. This constitutional phase of the revolution lasted until 1972, when the pressures of foreign invasion and the emergence of a more radical revolutionary movement caused the collapse of the monarchy and the establishment of a Republic in France.

French Revolution of 1830 The French popular revolt against Charles X's July Ordinances of 1830, which dissolved the French Chamber of Deputies and restricted suffrage to exclude almost everyone except the nobility. After several days of violence, Charles abdicated the throne and was replaced by a constitutional monarch, Louis Philippe.

French Revolution of 1848 Revolution overthrowing Louis-Philippe in February, 1848, leading to the formation of the Second Republic (1848–1852). Initially enjoying broad support from both the middle classes and laborers in Paris, the new government became more conservative after elections in which the French peasantry participated for the first time. A workers' revolt was violently repressed in June, 1848, and in December 1848, Napoleon Bonaparte's nephew, Louis-Napoleon Bonaparte, was elected president. In 1852, Louis-Napoleon declared himself emperor and abolished the republic.

Sigmund Freud (1856–1939) The Austrian physician who founded the discipline of psychoanalysis and suggested that human behavior was largely motivated by unconscious and irrational forces.

Galileo Galilei (1564–1642) Italian physicist and inventor; the implications of his ideas raised the ire of the Catholic Church, and he was forced to retract most of his findings.

Gallipoli (1915) In the First World War, a combined force of French, British, Australian and New Zealand troops tried to invade the Gallipoli Peninsula, in the first large-scale amphibious attack in history, and seize it from the Turks. After seven months of fighting, the Allies had lost 200,000 soldiers. Defeated, they withdrew.

Mohandas K. (Mahatma) Gandhi (1869–1948) The Indian leader who advocated nonviolent noncooperation to protest colonial rule and helped win home rule for India in 1947.

Giuseppe Garibaldi (1807–1882) Italian revolutionary leader who led the fight to free Sicily and Naples from the Habsburg Empire; the lands were then peaceably annexed by Sardinia to produce a unified Italy.

Gaul The region of the Roman Empire that was home to the Celtic people of that name, comprising modern France, Belgium, and western Germany.

Geneva Peace Conference (1954) International conference to restore peace in Korea and Indochina. The chief participants were the United States, the Soviet Union, Great Britain, France, the People's Republic of China, North Korea, South Korea, Vietnam, the Viet Minh party, Laos, and Cambodia. The conference resulted in the division of North and South Vietnam.

Genoa Maritime city on Italy's northwestern coast, the Genoese were active in trading ventures along the Silk Road and in the establishment of trading colonies in the Mediterranean. They were also involved in the world of finance and backed the commercial ventures of other powers, especially Spain's.

German Democratic Republic Nation founded from the Soviet zone of occupation of Germany after the Second World War; also known as East Germany.

German Social Democratic party Founded in 1875, it was the most powerful socialist party in Europe before 1917.

Gilgamesh Sumerian ruler of the city of Uruk around 2700 B.C.E., Gilgamesh became the hero of one of the world's oldest epics, which circulated orally for nearly a millennium before being written down.

Giotto (c. 1266–1337) Florentine painter and architect who is often considered a forerunner of the Renaissance.

glasnost Introduced by Soviet leader Mikhail Gorbachev in June 1987, *glasnost* was one of the five major policies that constituted *perestroika*. Often translated into English as "openness," it called for transparency in Soviet government and institutional activities by reducing censorship in mass media and lifting significant bans on the political, intellectual, and cultural lives of Soviet civilians.

globalization The term used to describe political, social, and economic networks that span the globe. These global exchanges are not limited by nation-states and in recent decades are associated with new technologies, such as the Internet. Globalization is not new, however, as human cultures and economies have been in contact with one another for centuries.

Glorious Revolution The overthrow of King James II of England and the installation of his Protestant daughter, Mary Stuart, and her husband, William of Orange, to the throne in 1688 and 1689. It is widely regarded as the founding moment in the development of a constitutional monarchy in Britain, while also establishing a more favorable climate for the economic and political growth of the English commercial classes.

Gold Coast Name that European mariners and merchants gave to that part of West Equatorial Africa from which gold and slaves were exported. Originally controlled by the Portuguese, this area later became the British colony of the Gold Coast.

Mikhail Gorbachev (1931–) Soviet leader who attempted to reform the Soviet Union through his programs of glasnost and perestroika in the late 1980s. He encouraged open discussions in other countries in the Soviet bloc, which helped inspire the velvet revolutions throughout Eastern Europe. Eventually the political, social, and economic upheaval he had unleashed would lead to the breakup of the Soviet Union.

Gothic style A type of graceful architecture emerging in twelfth- and thirteenth-century England and France. The style is characterized by pointed arches, delicate decoration, and large windows.

Olympe de Gouges (1748–1793) French political radical and feminist whose *Declaration of the Rights of Woman* demanded an equal place for women in France.

Great Depression Global economic crisis following the U.S. stock market crash on October 29, 1929, and ending with the onset of the Second World War.

Great Famine A period of terrible hunger and deprivation in Europe that peaked between 1315 and 1317, caused by a cooling of the climate and by the exhaustion of over-farming. It is estimated to have reduced the population of Europe by 10 to 15 percent.

Great Fear (1789) Following the outbreak of revolution in Paris, fear spread throughout the French countryside, as rumors circulated that armies of brigands or royal troops were coming. The peasants and villagers organized into militias, while others attacked and burned the manor houses in order to destroy the records of manorial dues.

Great Schism (1378–1417) Also known as the Great Western Schism, to distinguish it from the longstanding rupture between the Greek East and Latin West. During the schism, the Roman Church was divided between two (and, ultimately, three) competing popes. Each pope claimed to be legitimate and each denounced the heresy of the others.

Great Terror (1936–1938) The systematic murder of nearly a million people and the deportation of another million and a half to labor camps by Stalin's regime in an attempt to consolidate power and remove perceived enemies.

Greek East After the founding of Constantinople, the eastern Greek-speaking half of the Roman Empire grew more populous, prosperous and central to imperial policy. Its inhabitants considered themselves to be the true heirs of Rome, and their own Orthodox Church to be the true manifestation of Jesus's ministry.

Greek independence Nationalists in Greece revolted against the Ottoman Empire and fought a war that ended in Greek independence in 1827. They received crucial help from British, French, and Russian troops as well as widespread sympathy throughout Europe.

Pope Gregory I (r. 590–604) Also known as Gregory the Great, he was the first bishop of Rome to successfully negotiate a more universal role for the papacy. His political and theological agenda widened the rift between the western Latin (Catholic) Church and the eastern Greek (Orthodox) Church in Byzantium. He also articulated the Church's official position on the status of Jews, promoted affective approaches to religious worship, encouraged the Benedictine monastic movement, and sponsored missionary expeditions.

Guernica The Basque town bombed by German planes in April 1937 during the Spanish Civil War. It is also the subject of Pablo Picasso's famous painting from the same year.

guilds Professional organizations in commercial towns that regulated business and safeguarded the privileges of those practicing a particular craft. Often identical to confraternities ("brotherhoods").

Gulag The vast system of forced labor camps under the Soviet regime; it originated in 1919 in a small monastery near the Arctic Circle and spread throughout the Soviet Union. Penal labor was required of both ordinary criminals and those accused of political crimes. Tens of millions of people were sent to the camps between 1928 and 1953; the exact figure is unknown.

Gulf War (1991) Armed conflict between Iraq and a coalition of thirty-two nations, including the United States, Britain, Egypt, France, and Saudi Arabia. The seeds of the war were planted with Iraq's invasion of Kuwait on August 2, 1990.

Johannes Gutenberg European inventor of the printing press, his shop in Mainz produced the first printed book—a Bible—between the years 1453 and 1455.

Habsburg Dynasty A powerful European dynasty which came to power in the eleventh century in a region now part of Switzerland. Early generations of Habsburgs consolidated their control over neighboring German-speaking lands; through strategic marriages with other royal lines, later rulers eventually controlled a substantial part of Europe—including much of central Europe, the Netherlands, and even Spain and all its colonies for a time. In practice, the Holy Roman Emperor chosen from a member of the Habsburg lineage. By the latter half of the seventeenth century, the Austrian Habsburg Empire was made of up nearly 300 nominally autonomous dynastic kingdoms, principalities, duchies, and archbishoprics.

Hagia Sophia The enormous church dedicated to "Holy Wisdom," built in Constantinople at the behest of the emperor Justinian in the sixth century C.E. When Constantinople fell to Ottoman forces in 1453, it became an important mosque.

Haitian Revolution (1802–1804) In 1802, Napoleon sought to reassert French control of Saint-Domingue, but stiff resistance and yellow fever crushed the French army. In 1804, Jean-Jacques Dessalines, a general in the army of former slaves, declared the independent state of Haiti. (See **slave revolt in Saint-Domingue**.)

Hajj The annual pilgrimage to Mecca; an obligation for Muslims.

Hammurabi Ruler of Babylon from 1792 to 1750 B.C.E., Hammurabi issued a collection of laws that were greatly influential in the Near East and which constitute the world's oldest surviving law code.

Harlem Renaissance Cultural movement in the 1920s that was based in Harlem, a part of New York City with a large African American population. The movement gave voice to black novelists, poets, painters, and musicians, many of whom used their art to protest racial subordination.

Hatshepsut (1479–1458 C.E.) As a pharaoh during the New Kingdom, she launched several successful military campaigns and extended trade and diplomacy. She was an ambitious builder who probably constructed the first tomb in the Valley of the Kings. Though she never pretended to be a man, she was routinely portrayed with a masculine figure and a ceremonial beard.

Hebrews Originally a pastoral people divided among several tribes, they were briefly united under the rule of David and his son, Solomon, who promoted the worship of a single god, Yahweh, and constructed the first temple at the new capital city of Jerusalem. After Solomon's death, the Hebrew tribes were divided between the two kingdoms of Israel and Judah, which were eventually conquered by the Neo-Assyrian and Chaldean empires. It was in captivity that the Hebrews came to define themselves through worship of Yahweh and to develop a religion, Judaism, that could exist outside of Judea. They were liberated by the Persian king Cyrus the Great in 539 B.C.E.

Hellenistic art The art of the Hellenistic period bridged the tastes, ideals, and customs of classical Greece and those that would be more characteristic of Rome. The Romans strove to emulate Hellenistic city planning and civic culture and thereby exported Hellenistic culture to their own far-flung colonies in western Europe.

Hellenistic culture The "Greek-like" culture that dominated the ancient world in the wake of Alexander's conquests.

Hellenistic kingdoms Following the death of Alexander the Great, his vast empire was divided into three separate states: Ptolemaic Egypt (under the rule of the general Ptolemy and his successors), Seleucid Asia (ruled by the general Seleucus and his heirs) and Antigonid Greece (governed by Antigonus of Macedonia). Each state maintained its independence, but the shared characteristics of Greco-Macedonian rule and a shared Greek culture and heritage bound them together in a united cosmopolitan world.

Hellenistic world The various Western civilizations of antiquity that were loosely united by shared Greek language and culture, especially around the eastern Mediterranean.

Heloise (c. 1090–1164) One of the foremost scholars of her time, she became the pupil and the wife of the philosopher and teacher Peter Abelard. In later life, she was the founder of a new religious order for women.

Henry IV of Germany King of Germany and Holy Roman Emperor from 1056—when he ascended the throne at the age of six years old—until his death in 1106. Henry's reign was first weakened by conflict with the Saxon nobility and later marked by the Investiture Controversy with Pope Gregory VII.

Henry VIII (1491–1547) King of England from 1509 until his death, Henry rejected the authority of the Roman Church in 1534 when the pope refused to annul his marriage to his queen, Catherine of Aragon; he became the founder of the Church of England.

Henry of Navarre (1553–1610) Crowned King Henry IV of France, he renounced his Protestantism but granted limited toleration for Huguenots (French Protestants) by the Edict of Nantes in 1598.

Prince Henry the Navigator (1394–1460) A member of the Portuguese royal family, Henry encouraged the exploration and conquest of western Africa and the trade in gold and slaves.

hieroglyphs The writing system of ancient Egypt, based on a complicated series of pictorial symbols. It fell out of use when Egypt was absorbed into the Roman Empire and was only deciphered after the discovery of the Rosetta Stone in the early nineteenth century.

Hildegard of Bingen (1098–1179) A powerful abbess, theologian, scientist, musician, and visionary who claimed to receive regular revelations from God. Although highly influential in her own day, she was never officially canonized by the Church, in part because her strong personality no longer matched the changing ideal of female piety.

Hiroshima Japanese port devastated by an atomic bomb on August 6, 1945.

Adolf Hitler (1889–1945) The author of *Mein Kampf* and leader of the Nazis who became chancellor of Germany in 1933. Hitler and his Nazi regime started the Second World War and orchestrated the systematic murder of over 5 million Jews.

Hitler-Stalin Pact (1939) Treaty between Stalin and Hitler, which promised Stalin a share of Poland, Finland, the Baltic States, and Bessarabia in the event of a German invasion of Poland, which began shortly thereafter, on September 1, 1939.

HIV epidemic The first cases of HIV-AIDS appeared in the late 1970s. As HIV-AIDS became a global crisis, international organizations recognized the need for an early, swift, and comprehensive response to future outbreaks of disease.

Thomas Hobbes (1588–1679) English political philosopher whose *Leviathan* argued that any form of government capable of protecting its subjects' lives and property might act as an all-powerful sovereign. This government should be allowed to trample over both liberty and property for the sake of its own survival and that of his subjects. For in his natural state, Hobbes argued, man was like "a wolf" toward other men.

Holy Roman Empire The loosely allied collection of lands in central and western Europe ruled by the kings of Germany (and later Austria) from the twelfth century until 1806. Its origins are usually identified with the empire of Charlemagne, the Frankish king who was crowned emperor of Rome by the pope in 800.

homage A ceremony in which an individual becomes the "man" (French: *homme*) of a lord.

Homer (fl. eighth century B.C.E.) A Greek rhapsode ("weaver" of stories) credited with merging centuries of poetic tradition in the epics known as the *Iliad* and the *Odyssey*.

hoplite A Greek foot-soldier armed with a spear or short sword and protected by a large round shield (*hoplon*). In battle, hoplites stood shoulder to shoulder in a close formation called a phalanx.

Huguenots French Protestants who endured severe persecution in the sixteenth and seventeenth centuries.

humanism A program of study associated with the movement known as the Renaissance, humanism aimed to replace the scholastic emphasis on logic and philosophy with the study of ancient languages, literature, history, and ethics.

human rights The belief that all people have the right to legal equality, freedom of religion and speech, and the right to participate in government. Human rights laws prohibit torture, cruel punishment, and slavery.

David Hume (1711–1776) Scottish writer who applied Newton's method of scientific inquiry and skepticism to the study of morality, the mind, and government.

Hundred Years' War (1337–1453) A series of wars between England and France, fought mostly on French soil and prompted by the territorial and political claims of English monarchs.

Jan Hus (c. 1373–1415) A Czech reformer who adopted many of the teachings of the English theologian John Wycliffe, and who also demanded that the laity be allowed to receive both the consecrated bread and wine of the Eucharist. The Council of Constance burned him at the stake for heresy. In response, his supporters, the Hussites, revolted against the Church.

Saddam Hussein (1937–2006) The former dictator of Iraq who invaded Iran in 1980 and started the eight-year-long Iran-Iraq War; invaded Kuwait in 1990, which led to the Gulf War of 1991; and was overthrown when the United States invaded Iraq in 2003. Involved in Iraqi politics since the mid-1960s, Hussein became the official head of state in 1979.

Iconoclast Controversy (717–787) A serious and often violent theological debate that raged in Byzantium after Emperor Leo III ordered the destruction of religious art on the grounds that any image representing a divine or holy personage is prone to promote idol worship and blasphemy. Iconoclast means "breaker of icons." Those who supported the veneration of icons were called iconodules, "adherents of icons."

Il-khanate Mongol-founded dynasty in thirteenth-century Persia.

Indian National Congress Formed in 1885, this Indian political party worked to achieve Indian independence from British colonial control. The Congress was led by Ghandi in the 1920s and 1930s.

Indian Rebellion of 1857 The uprising began near Delhi, when the military disciplined a regiment of Indian soldiers employed by the British for refusing to use rifle cartridges greased with pork fat—unacceptable to either Hindus or Muslims. Rebels attacked law courts and burned tax rolls, protesting debt and corruption. The mutiny spread through large areas of northwest India before being violently suppressed by British troops.

Indo-Europeans A group of people speaking variations of the same language who moved into the Near East and Mediterranean region shortly after 2000 B.C.E.

indulgences Grants exempting Catholic Christians from the performance of penance, either in life or after death. The abusive trade in indulgences was a major catalyst of the Protestant Reformation.

Incas The highly centralized South American empire that was toppled by the Spanish conquistador Francisco Pizarro in 1533.

Innocent III (1160/61–1216) As pope, he wanted to unify all of Christendom under papal hegemony. He furthered this goal at the Fourth Lateran Council of 1215, which defined one of the Church's dogmas as the acknowledgment of papal supremacy. The council also took an unprecedented interest in the religious education and habits of every Christian.

Inquisition Tribunal of the Roman Church that aims to enforce religious orthodoxy and conformity.

International Monetary Fund (IMF) Established in 1945 to ensure international cooperation regarding currency exchange and monetary policy, the IMF is a specialized agency of the United Nations.

Investiture Conflict The name given to a series of debates over the limitations of spiritual and secular power in Europe during the eleventh and early twelfth century, it came to a head when Pope Gregory VII and Emperor Henry IV of Germany both claimed the right to appoint and invest bishops with the regalia of office. After years of diplomatic and military hostility, it was partially settled by the Concordat of Worms in 1122.

Irish potato famine Period of agricultural blight from 1845 to 1849 whose devastating results produced widespread starvation and led to mass immigration to America.

Iron Curtain Term coined by Winston Churchill in 1946 to refer to the borders of Eastern European nations that lay within the zone of Soviet control.

Italian invasion of Ethiopia (1896) Italy invaded Ethiopia, which was the last major independent African kingdom. Menelik II, the Ethiopian emperor, soundly defeated them.

Ivan the Great (1440–1505) Russian ruler who annexed neighboring territories and consolidated his empire's position as a European power.

Jacobins Radical French political group during the French Revolution that took power after 1792, executed the French king, and sought to remake French culture.

Jacquerie Violent 1358 peasant uprising in northern France, incited by disease, war, and taxes.

James I (1566–1625) Monarch who ruled Scotland as James VI, and who succeeded Elizabeth I as king of England in 1603. He oversaw the English vernacular translation of the Bible known by his name.

James II of England King of England, Ireland, and Scotland from 1685–88 whose commitment to absolutism and Catholic zealotry led to his exile to France in the Glorious Revolution of 1688.

Janissaries Corps of enslaved soldiers recruited as children from the Christian provinces of the Ottoman Empire and brought up to display intense personal loyalty to the Ottoman sultan, who used these forces to curb local autonomy and as his personal bodyguards.

Jerome (c. 340–420) One of the early "fathers" of the Church, he translated the Bible from Hebrew and Greek into a popular form of Latin—hence the name by which this translation is known: the Vulgate, or "vulgar" (popular), Bible.

Jesuits The religious order formally known as the Society of Jesus, founded in 1540 by Ignatius Loyola to combat the spread of Protestantism. The Jesuits would become active in politics, education, and missionary work.

Jesus (c. 4 B.C.E.–c. 30 C.E.) A Jewish preacher and teacher in the rural areas of Galilee and Judea who was arrested for seditious political activity, tried, and crucified by the Romans. After his execution, his followers claimed that he had been resurrected from the dead and taken up into heaven. They began to teach that Jesus had been the divine representative of God, the Messiah foretold by ancient Hebrew prophets, and that he had suffered for the sins of humanity and would return to judge all the world's inhabitants at the end of time.

Joan of Arc (c. 1412–1431) A peasant girl from the province of Lorraine who claimed to have been commanded by God to lead French forces against the English occupying army during the Hundred Years' War. Successful in her efforts, she was betrayed by the French king and handed over to the English, who condemned her to death for heresy. Her reputation underwent a process of rehabilitation, but she was not officially canonized as a saint until 1920.

Judaism The religion of the Hebrews as it developed in the centuries after the establishment of the Hebrew kingdoms under David and Solomon, especially during the period of Babylonian Captivity.

Justinian (527–565) Emperor of Rome who unsuccessfully attempted to reunite the eastern and western portions of the empire. Also known for his important codification of Roman law, in the *Corpus Juris Civilis.*

Justinian's Code of Roman Law Formally known as the *Corpus Juris Civilis* or "body of civil law," this compendium consisted of a systematic compilation of imperial statutes, the writings of Rome's great legal authorities, a textbook of legal principles, and the legislation of Justinian and his immediate successors. As the most authoritative collection of Roman law, it formed the basis of canon law (the legal system of the Roman Church) and became essential to the developing legal traditions of every European state as well as of many countries around the world.

Das Kapital (Capital) The 1867 book by Karl Marx that outlined the theory behind historical materialism and attacked the socioeconomic inequities of capitalism.

Johannes Kepler (1571–1630) Mathematician and astronomer who elaborated on and corrected Copernicus's theory and is chiefly remembered for his discovery of the three laws of planetary motion that bear his name.

Keynesian Revolution Postdepression economic ideas developed by the British economist John Maynard Keynes, wherein the state took a greater role in managing the economy, stimulating it by increasing the money supply and creating jobs.

KGB Soviet political police and spy agency, first formed as the Cheka not long after the Bolshevik coup in October 1917. It grew to more than 750,000 operatives with military rank by the 1980s.

Genghis Khan (c. 1167–1227) "Oceanic Ruler," the title adopted by the Mongol chieftain Temujin, founder of a dynasty that conquered much of southern Asia.

Khanate The major political unit of the vast Mongol Empire. There were four Khanates, including the Yuan Empire in China, forged by Chingiz Khan's grandson Kubilai in the thirteenth century.

Ruhollah Khomeini (1902–1989) Iranian Shi'ite religious leader who led the revolution in Iran after the abdication of the shah in 1979. His government allowed some limited economic and political populism combined with strict constructions of Islamic law, restrictions on women's public life, and the prohibition of ideas or activities linked to Western influence.

Nikita Khrushchev (1894–1971) Leader of the Soviet Union during the Cuban missile crisis, Khrushchev came to power after Stalin's death in 1953. His reforms and criticisms of the excesses of the Stalin regime led to his fall from power in 1964.

Kremlin Once synonymous with the Soviet government, it refers to Moscow's walled city center and the palace originally built by Ivan the Great.

Kristallnacht Organized attack by Nazis and their supporters on the Jews of Germany following the assassination of a German embassy official by a Jewish man in Paris. Throughout Germany, thousands of stores, schools, cemeteries and synagogues were attacked on November 9, 1938. Dozens of people were killed, and tens of thousands of Jews were arrested and held in camps, where many were tortured and killed in the ensuing months.

Labour party Founded in Britain in 1900, this party represented workers and was based on socialist principles.

Latin West After the founding of Constantinople, the western Latin-speaking half of the Roman Empire became poorer and more peripheral, but it also fostered the emergence of new barbarian kingdoms. At the same time, the Roman pope claimed to have inherited both the authority of Jesus and the essential elements of Roman imperial authority.

League of Nations International organization founded after the First World War to solve international disputes through arbitration; it was dissolved in 1946 and its assets were transferred to the United Nations.

Leonardo da Vinci (1452–1519) Florentine inventor, sculptor, architect, and painter whose breadth of interests typifies the ideal of "the Renaissance man."

Vladimir Lenin (1870–1924) Leader of the Bolshevik Revolution in Russia (1917) and the first leader of the Soviet Union.

Leviathan A book by Thomas Hobbes (1588–1679) that recommended a ruler have unrestricted power.

liberalism Political and social theory that judges the effectiveness of a government in terms of its ability to protect individual rights. Liberals support representative forms of government, free trade, and freedom of speech and religion. In the economic realm, liberals believe that individuals should be free to engage in commercial or business activities without interference from the state or their community.

lithograph Art form that involves putting writing or design on stone and producing printed impressions.

John Locke (1632–1704) English philosopher and political theorist known for his contributions to liberalism. Locke had great faith in human reason and believed that just societies were those that infringed the least on the natural rights and freedoms of individuals. This led him to assert that a government's legitimacy depended on the consent of the governed, a view that had a profound effect on the authors of the United States' Declaration of Independence.

Louis IX of France King of France from 1226 to his death on Crusade in 1270, Louis was famous for his piety and for his close attention to the administration of law and justice in his realm. He was officially canonized as Saint Louis in 1297.

Louis XIV (1638–1715) Called the "Sun King," he was known for his success at strengthening the institutions of the French absolutist state.

Louis XVI (1754–1793) Well-meaning but ineffectual king of France, finally deposed and executed during the French Revolution.

Ignatius Loyola (1491–1556) Founder of the Society of Jesus (commonly known as the Jesuits), whose members vowed to serve God through poverty, chastity, and missionary work. He abandoned his first career as a mercenary after reading an account of Christ's life written in his native Spanish.

Lucretia According to Roman legend, Lucretia was a virtuous Roman wife who was raped by the son of Rome's last king and who virtuously committed suicide in order to avoid bringing shame on her family.

Luftwaffe Literally "air weapon," this is the name of the German air force, which was founded during the First World War, disbanded in 1945, and reestablished when West Germany joined NATO in 1950.

Lusitania The British passenger liner that was sunk by a German U-boat (submarine) on May 7, 1915. Public outrage over the sinking contibuted to the U.S. decision to enter the First World War.

Martin Luther (1483–1546) A German monk and professor of theology whose critique of the papacy launched the Protestant Reformation.

ma'at The Egyptian term for the serene order of the universe, with which the individual soul (*ka*) must remain in harmony. The power of the pharaoh was linked to *ma'at*, insofar as it ensured the prosperity of the kingdom. After the upheavals of the First Intermediate Period, the perception of the pharaoh's relationship with ma'at was revealed to be conditional, something that had to be earned.

Niccolò Machiavelli (1469–1527) As the author of *The Prince* and the *Discourses on Livy*, he looked to the Roman past for paradigms of greatness while at the same time hoping to win the patronage of contemporary rulers who would restore Italy's political independence.

Magna Carta The "Great Charter" of 1215, enacted during the reign of King John of England and designed to limit his powers. Regarded now as a landmark in the development of constitutional government. In its own time, its purpose was to restore the power of great lords.

Magyar nationalism Lajos Kossuth led this national movement in the Hungarian region of the Habsburg Empire, calling for national independence for Hungary in 1848. With the support of Russia, the Habsburg army crushed the movement and all other revolutionary activities in the empire. Kossuth fled into exile.

Moses Maimonides (c. 1137–1204) Jewish scholar, physician, and scriptural commentator whose *Mishneh Torah* is a fundamental exposition of Jewish law.

Thomas Malthus (1766–1834) British political economist who believed that populations inevitably grew faster than the available food supply. Societies that could not control their population growth would be checked only by famine, disease, poverty, and infant malnutrition. He argued that governments could not alleviate poverty. Instead, the poor had to exercise "moral restraint," postpone marriage, and have fewer children.

Nelson Mandela (b. 1918) The South African opponent of apartheid who led the African National Congress and was imprisoned from 1962 until 1990. After his release from prison, he worked with Prime Minister Frederik Willem De Klerk to establish majority rule. Mandela became the first black president of South Africa in 1994.

Manhattan Project The secret U.S. government research project to develop the first nuclear bomb. The vast project involved dozens of sites across the United States, including New Mexico, Tennessee, Illinois, California, Utah, and Washington. The first test of a nuclear bomb was near Alamogordo, New Mexico on July 16, 1945.

manors Common farmland worked collectively by the inhabitants of entire villages, sometimes on their own initiative, sometimes at the behest of a lord.

Mao Zedong (1893–1976) The leader of the Chinese Revolution who defeated the Nationalists in 1949 and established the Communist regime in China.

Marne A major battle of the First World War in September 1914, which halted the German invasion of France and led to protracted trench warfare on the Western Front.

Marshall Plan Economic aid package given to Europe by the United States after the Second World War to promote reconstruction and economic development and to secure the countries from a feared communist takeover.

Karl Marx (1818–1883) German philosopher and economist who believed that a revolution of the working classes would overthrow the capitalist order and create a classless society. Author of *Das Kapital* and *The Communist Manifesto.*

Marxists Followers of the socialist political economist Karl Marx who called for workers everywhere to unite and create an independent political force. Marxists believed that industrialization produced an inevitable struggle between laborers and the class of capitalist property owners, and that this struggle would culminate in a revolution that would abolish private property and establish a society committed to social equality.

Mary See **cult of the Virgin**.

Mary I (1516–1558) Catholic daughter of Henry VIII and his first wife, Catherine of Aragon, Mary Tudor was the first queen regnant of England. Her attempts to reinstitute Catholicism in England met with limited success, and after her early death she was labeled "Bloody Mary" by the Protestant supporters of her half sister and successor, Elizabeth I.

mass culture The spread of literacy and public education in the nineteenth century created a new audience for print entertainment and a new class of entrepreneurs in the media to cater to this audience. The invention of radio, film, and television in the twentieth century carried this development to another level, as millions of consumers were now accessible to the producers of news, information, and entertainment. The rise of this "mass culture" has been celebrated as an expression of popular tastes but also criticized as a vehicle for the manipulation of populations through clever and seductive propaganda.

Mayans Native American peoples whose culturally and politically sophisticated empire encompassed lands in present-day Mexico and Guatemala.

Giuseppe Mazzini (1805–1872) Founder of Young Italy and an ideological leader of the Italian nationalist movement.

Mecca Center of an important commercial network of the Arabian Peninsula and birthplace of the prophet Muhammad. It is now considered the holiest site in the Islamic world.

Medici A powerful dynasty of Florentine bankers and politicians whose ancestors were originally apothecaries ("medics").

Meiji Empire Empire created under the leadership of Mutsuhito, emperor of Japan from 1868 until 1912. During the Meiji period Japan became a world industrial and naval power.

Mensheviks Within the Russian Social Democratic Party, the Mensheviks advocated slow changes and a gradual move toward socialism, in contrast with the Bolsheviks, who wanted to push for a proletarian revolution. Mensheviks believed that a proletarian revolution in Russia was premature and that the country needed to complete its capitalist development first.

mercantilism A theory and policy for directing the economy of monarchical states between 1600 and 1800 based on the assumption that wealth and power depended on a favorable balance of trade (more exports and fewer imports) and the accumulation of precious metals. Mercantilists advocated forms of economic protectionism to promote domestic production.

Maria Sybilla Merian (1647–1717) A scientific illustrator and an important early entomologist. She conducted research on two continents and published the well-received *Metamorphosis of the Insects of Surinam.*

Merovingian A Frankish dynasty that claimed descent from a legendary ancestor called Merovic, the Merovingians were the only powerful family to establish a lasting kingdom in western Europe during the fifth and sixth centuries.

Mesopotamia The "land between the Tigris and the Euphrates rivers," Tigris and Euphrates where the civilization of Sumer, the first urban society, flourished.

Klemens von Metternich (1773–1859) Austrian foreign minister whose primary goals were to bolster the legitimacy of monarchies and, after the defeat of Napoleon, to prevent another large-scale war in Europe. At the Congress of Vienna, he opposed social and political change and wanted to check Russian and French expansion.

Michelangelo Buonarroti (1475–1564) A virtuoso Florentine sculptor, painter, and poet who spent much of his career in the service of the papacy. He is best known for the decoration of the Sistine Chapel and for his monumental sculptures.

Middle Kingdom of Egypt (2055–1650 B.C.E.) The period following the First Intermediate Period of dynastic warfare, which ended with the reassertion of pharonic rule under Mentuhotep II.

Miletus A Greek polis and Persian colony on the Ionian coast of Asia Minor. Influenced by the cultures of Mesopotamia, Egypt, and Lydia, it produced several of the ancient world's first scientists and sophists. Thereafter, a political conflict between the ruler of Miletus, Aristagoras, and the Persian Emperor, Darius, sparked the Persian Wars with Greece.

John Stuart Mill (1806–1873) English liberal philosopher whose faith in human reason led him to support a broad variety of civic and political freedoms for men and women, including the right to vote and the right to free speech.

Slobodan Milosevic (1941–2006) The Serbian nationalist politician who became president of Serbia and whose policies during the Balkan wars of the early 1990s led to the deaths of thousands of Croatians, Bosnian Muslims, Albanians, and Kosovars. After leaving office in 2000, he was arrested and tried for war crimes at the International Court in The Hague. The trial ended before a verdict with his death in 2006.

Minoan Crete A sea empire based at Knossos on the Greek island of Crete and named for the legendary King Minos. The Minoans dominated the Aegean for much of the second millennium B.C.E.

Modernism There were several different modernist movements in art and literature, but they shared three key characteristics. First, they had a sense that the world had radically changed and that this change should be embraced. Second, they believed that traditional aesthetic values and assumptions about creativity were ill-suited to the present. Third, they developed a new conception of what art could do that emphasized expression over representation and insisted on the value of novelty, experimentation, and creative freedom.

Mongols A nomadic people from the steppes of Central Asia who were united under the ruler Genghis Khan. His conquest of China was continued by his grandson Kubilai and his great-grandson son Ogedei, whose army also seized southern Russia and then moved through Hungary and through Poland toward eastern Germany. The Mongol armies withdrew from eastern Europe after the death of Ogedei, but his descendants continued to rule his vast empire for another half century.

Michel de Montaigne (1533–1592) French philosopher and social commentator, best known for his *Essays*.

Montesquieu (1689–1755) An Enlightenment philosophe whose most influential work was *The Spirit of Laws*. In this work, he analyzed the structures that shaped law and categorized governments into three types: republics, monarchies, and despotisms. His ideas about the separation of powers among the executive, the legislative, and the judicial branches of government influenced the authors of the U.S. Constitution.

Thomas More (1478–1535) Christian humanist, English statesman, and author of *Utopia*. In 1529, he was appointed lord chancellor of England but resigned because he opposed King Henry VIII's plans to establish a national church under royal control. He was eventually executed for refusing to take an oath acknowledging Henry to be the head of the Church of England and has since been canonized by the Catholic Church.

mos maiorum Literally translated as "the code of the elders" or "the custom of ancestors." This unwritten code governed the lives of Romans under the Republic and stressed the importance of showing reverence to ancestral tradition. It was sacrosanct and essential to Roman identity, and an important influence on Roman culture, law, and religion.

Wolfgang Amadeus Mozart (1756–1791) Austrian composer, famous at a young age as a concert musician and later celebrated as a prolific composer of instrumental music and operas that are seen as the apogee of the Classical style in music.

Muhammad (570–632 C.E.) The founder of Islam, regarded as God's last and greatest prophet by his followers.

Munich Conference (1938) Hitler met with the leaders of Britain, France, and Italy and negotiated an agreement that gave Germany a major slice of Czechoslovakia. British prime minister Chamberlain believed that the agreement would bring peace to Europe. Instead, Germany invaded and seized the rest of Czechoslovakia.

Muscovy The duchy centered on Moscow whose dukes saw themselves as heirs to the Roman Empire. In the early fourteenth century, Moscow was under the control of the Mongol Khanate. After the collapse of the Khanate, the Muscovite grand duke, Ivan III, conquered all the Russian principalities between Moscow and the border of Poland-Lithuania, and then Lithuania itself. By the time of his death, Ivan had established Muscovy as a dominant power.

Muslim learning and culture The Crusades brought the Latin West in contact with the Islamic world, which impacted European culture in myriad ways. Europeans adapted Arabic numerals and mathematical concepts as well as Arabic and Persian words. Through Arabic translations, Western scholars gained access to Greek learning, which had a profound influence on Christian theology. European scholars also learned from the Islamic world's accomplishments in medicine and science.

Benito Mussolini (1883–1945) The Italian founder of the Fascist party who came to power in Italy in 1922 and allied himself with Hitler and the Nazis during the Second World War.

Mycenaean Greece (1600–1200 B.C.E.) The term used to describe the civilization of Greece in the late Bronze Age, when territorial kingdoms like Mycenae formed around a king, a warrior caste, and a palace bureaucracy.

Nagasaki Second Japanese city on which the United States dropped an atomic bomb. The attack took place on August 9, 1945; the Japanese surrendered shortly thereafter, ending the Second World War.

Napoleon III (1808–1873) Nephew of Napoleon Bonaparte, Napoleon III was elected president of the French Second Republic in 1848 and made himself emperor of France in 1852. During his reign (1852–70), he rebuilt the French capital of Paris. Defeated in the France-Prussian War of 1870, he went into exile.

Napoleonic Code Legal code drafted by Napoleon in 1804 and based on Justinian's *Corpus Iuris Civilis*. It distilled different legal traditions to create one uniform law. The code confirmed the abolition of feudal privileges of all kinds and set the conditions for exercising property rights.

Napoleon's military campaigns In 1805, the Russians, Prussians, Austrians, Swedes, and British attempted to contain Napoleon, but he defeated them. Out of his victories, Napoleon created a new empire and affiliated states. In 1808, he invaded Spain, but fierce resistance prevented Napoleon from achieving a complete victory. In 1812, Napoleon invaded Russia, and his army was decimated as it retreated from Moscow during the winter. After the Russian campaign, the united European powers defeated Napoleon and forced him into exile. He escaped and reassumed command of his army, but the European powers defeated him for the final time at the Battle of Waterloo.

Gamal Abdel Nasser (1918–1970) Former president of Egypt and the most prominent spokesman for secular pan-Arabism. He became a target for Islamist critics, such as Sayyid Qutb and the Muslim Brotherhood, angered by the Western-influenced policies of his regime.

National Assembly of France Governing body of France that succeeded the Estates General in 1789 during the French Revolution. It was composed of, and defined by, the delegates of the Third Estate.

National Association for the Advancement of Colored People (NAACP) Founded in 1910, this U.S. civil rights organization was dedicated to ending inequality and segregation for black Americans.

National Convention The governing body of France from September 1792 to October 1795. It declared France a republic and then tried and executed the French king. The Convention also confiscated the property of the enemies of the revolution, instituted a policy of de-Christianization, changed marriage and inheritance laws, abolished slavery in its colonies, placed a cap on the price of necessities, and ended the compensation of nobles for their lost privileges.

nationalism Movement to unify a country under one government based on perceptions of the population's common history, customs, and social traditions.

nationalism in Yugoslavia In the 1990s, Slobodan Milosevic and his allies reignited Serbian nationalism in the former Yugoslavia, which led non-Serb republics in Croatia and Slovenia to seek independence. The country erupted into war, with the worst violence taking place in Bosnia, a multi-ethnic region with Serb, Croatian and Bosnian Muslim populations. European diplomats proved powerless to stop attempts by Croatian and Serbian military and paramilitary forces to claim territory through ethnic cleansing and violent intimidation. Atrocities were committed on all sides, but pro-Serb forces were responsible for the most deaths.

NATO The North Atlantic Treaty Organization, a 1949 military agreement among the United States, Canada, Great Britain, and eight Western European nations, which declared that an armed attack against any one of the members would be regarded as an attack against all. Created during the Cold War in the face of the Soviet Union's control of Eastern Europe, NATO continues to exist today and the membership of twenty-eight states includes former members of the Warsaw Pact as well as Albania and Turkey.

Nazi party Founded in the early 1920s, the National Socialist German Workers' Party (NSDAP) gained control over Germany under the leadership of Adolf Hitler in 1933 and continued in power until Germany was defeated in 1945.

Nazism The political movement in Germany led by Adolf Hitler, which advocated a violent anti-Semitic, anti-Marxist, pan-German ideology.

Neo-Assyrian Empire (883–859 B.C.E.–612–605 B.C.E.) Assurnasirpal II laid the foundations of the Neo-Assyrian Empire through military campaigns against neighboring peoples. Eventually, the empire stretched from the Mediterranean Sea to western Iran. A military dictatorship governed the empire through its army, which it used to frighten and oppress both its subjects and its enemies. The empire's ideology was based on waging holy war in the name of its principal god, Assur, and the exaction of tribute through terror.

Neoliberalism Neoliberals believe that free markets, profit incentives, and restraints on both budget deficits and social welfare programs are the best guarantee of individual liberties. Beginning in the 1980s, neoliberal theory was used to structure the policy of financial institutions like the International Monetary Fund and the World Bank, which turned away from interventionist policies in favor of market-driven models of economic development.

Neolithic Revolution The "New" Stone Age, which began around 11,000 B.C.E., saw new technological and social developments, including managed food production, the beginnings of permanent settlements, and the rapid intensification of trade.

Neoplatonism A school of thought based on the teachings of Plato and prevalent in the Roman Empire, which had a profound effect on the formation of Christian theology. Neoplatonists argued that nature is a book written by its creator to reveal the ways of God to humanity. Convinced that God's perfection must be reflected in nature, neoplatonists searched for the ideal and perfect structures that they believed must lie behind the "shadows" of the everyday world.

New Deal President Franklin Delano Roosevelt's package of government reforms that were enacted during the depression of the 1930s to provide jobs for the unemployed, social welfare programs for the poor, and security to the financial markets.

New Economic Policy In 1921, the Bolsheviks abandoned war communism in favor of the New Economic Policy (NEP). Under NEP, the state still controlled all major industry and financial concerns, while individuals could own private property, trade freely within limits, and farm their own land for their own benefit. Fixed taxes replaced grain requisition. The policy successfully helped Soviet agriculture recover from the civil war but was later abandoned in favor of collectivization.

Isaac Newton (1642–1727) One of the foremost scientists of all time, Newton was an English mathematician and physicist; he is noted for his development of calculus, work on the properties of light, and theory of gravitation.

Tsar Nicholas II (1868–1918) The last Russian tsar, who abdicated the throne in 1917. He and his family were executed by the Bolsheviks on July 17, 1918.

Friedrich Nietzsche (1844–1900) The German philosopher who denied the possibility of knowing absolute "truth" or "reality," since all knowledge comes filtered through linguistic, scientific, or artistic systems of representation. He also criticized Judeo-Christian morality for instilling a repressive conformity that drained civilization of its vitality.

nongovernmental organizations (NGOs) Private organizations like the Red Cross that play a large role in international affairs.

Novum Organum Work by English statesman and scientist Francis Bacon (1561–1626) that advanced a philosophy of study through observation.

October Days (1789) The high price of bread and the rumor that the king was unwilling to cooperate with the assembly caused the women who worked in Paris's large central market to march to Versailles along with their supporters to address the king. Not satisfied with their initial reception, they broke through the palace gates and called for the king to return to Paris from Versailles, which he did the following day.

Old Kingdom of Egypt (c. 2686–2160 B.C.E.) During this time, the pharaohs controlled a powerful and centralized bureaucratic state whose vast human and material resources are exemplified by the pyramids of Giza. This period came to an end as the pharaoh's authority collapsed, leading to a period of dynastic warfare and localized rule.

OPEC (Organization of the Petroleum Exporting Countries) Organization created in 1960 by oil-producing countries in the Middle East, South America, and Africa to regulate the production and pricing of crude oil.

Operation Barbarossa The codename for Hitler's invasion of the Soviet Union in 1941.

Opium Wars (1839–1842) War fought between the British and Qing China to protect British trade in opium; resulted in the ceding of Hong Kong to the British.

Oracle at Delphi The most important shrine in ancient Greece. The priestess of Apollo who attended the shrine was believed to have the power to predict the future.

Ottoman Empire (c.1300–1923) During the thirteenth century, the Ottoman dynasty established itself as leader of the Turks. From the fourteenth to sixteenth centuries, they conquered Anatolia, Armenia, Syria, and North Africa as well as parts of southeastern Europe, the Crimea, and areas along the Red Sea. Portions of the Ottoman Empire persisted up to the time of the First World War, but it was dismantled in the years following it.

Reza Pahlavi (1919–1980) The Western-friendly shah of Iran who was installed during a 1953 coup supported by Britain and the United States. After a lengthy economic downturn, public unrest, and personal illness, he retired from public life under popular pressure in 1979.

Pan-African Conference 1900 assembly in London that sought to draw attention to the sovereignty of African people and their mistreatment by colonial powers.

Panhellenism The "all Greek" culture that allowed ancient Greek colonies to maintain a connection to their homeland and to each other through their shared language and heritage. These colonies also exported their culture into new areas and created new Greek-speaking enclaves, which permanently changed the cultural geography of the Mediterranean world.

pan-Slavism Cultural movement that sought to unite native Slavic peoples within the Russian and Habsburg Empires under Russian leadership.

Partition of India (1947) At independence, British India was partitioned into the nations of India and Pakistan. The majority of the population in India was Hindu and the majority of the population in Pakistan was Muslim. The process of partition brought brutal religious and ethnic warfare. More than 1 million Hindus and Muslims died and 12 million became refugees.

Blaise Pascal (1623–1662) A Catholic philosopher who wanted to establish the truth of Christianity by appealing simultaneously to intellect and emotion. In his *Pensées*, he argued that faith alone can resolve the world's contradictions and that his own awe in the face of evil and uncertainty must be evidence of God's existence.

Paul of Tarsus Originally known as Saul, Paul was a Greek-speaking Jew and Roman citizen who underwent a miraculous conversion experience and became the most important proponent of Christianity in the 50s and 60s C.E.

Pax Romana (27 B.C.E.–180 C.E.) Literally translated as "the Roman Peace." During this time, the Roman world enjoyed an unprecedented period of peace and political stability.

Peace of Augsburg A settlement negotiated in 1555 among factions within the Holy Roman Empire, it formulated the principle *cuius regio, eius religio,* "he who rules, his religion": meaning that the inhabitants of any given territory should follow the religion of its ruler, whether Catholic or Protestant.

Peace of Paris The 1919 Paris Peace Conference established the terms to end the First World War. Great Britain, France, Italy, and the United States signed five treaties with each of the defeated nations: Germany, Austria, Hungary, Turkey, and Bulgaria. The settlement is notable for the territory that Germany had to give up, including large parts of Prussia to the new state of Poland, and Alsace and Lorraine to France; the disarming of

Germany; and the "war guilt" provision, which required Germany and its allies to pay massive reparations to the victors.

Peace of Westphalia (1648) An agreement reached at the end of the Thirty Years' War that altered the political map of Europe. France emerged as the predominant power on the Continent, while the Austrian Habsburgs had to surrender all the territories they had gained and could no longer use the office of the Holy Roman Emperor to dominate central Europe. Spain was marginalized and Germany became a volatile combination of Protestant and Catholic principalities.

Pearl Harbor The American naval base in Hawaii that was bombed by the Japanese on December 7, 1941, bringing the United States into the Second World War.

peasantry Term used in continental Europe to refer to rural populations that lived from agriculture. Some peasants were free and could own land. Serfs were peasants who were legally bound to the land and subject to the authority of the local lord.

Peloponnesian War The name given to the series of wars fought between Sparta (on the Greek Peloponnesus) and Athens from 431 B.C.E. to 404 B.C.E., and which ended in the defeat of Athens and the loss of her imperial power.

perestroika Introduced by Soviet leader Mikhail Gorbachev in June 1987, *perestroika* was the name given to economic and political reforms begun earlier in his tenure. It restructured the state bureaucracy, reduced the privileges of the political elite, and instituted a shift from the centrally planned economy to a mixed economy, combining planning with the operation of market forces.

Periclean Athens Following his election as *strategos* in 461 B.C.E., Pericles pushed through political reforms in Athens, which gave poorer citizens greater influence in politics. He promoted Athenians' sense of superiority through ambitious public works projects and lavish festivals to honor the gods, thus ensuring his continual reelection. But eventually, Athens' growing arrogance and aggression alienated it from the rest of the Greek world.

Pericles (c. 495–429) Athenian politician who occupied the office of strategos for thirty years and who presided over a series of civic reforms, building campaigns, and imperialist initiatives.

Persian Empire Consolidated by Cyrus the Great in 559, this empire eventually stretched from the Persian Gulf to the Mediterranean and also encompassed Egypt. Persian rulers were able to hold this empire together through a policy of tolerance and a mixture of local and centralized governance. This imperial model of government would be adopted by many future empires.

Persian Wars (490–479 B.C.E.) In 501 B.C.E., a political conflict between the Greek ruler of Miletus, Aristagoras, and the Persian Emperor, Darius, sparked the first of the Persian Wars when Darius sent an army to punish Athens for its intervention on the side of the Greeks. Despite being heavily outnumbered, Athenian hoplites defeated the Persian army at the plain of Marathon. In 480 B.C.E., Darius's son Xerxes invaded Greece but was defeated at sea and on land by combined Greek forces under the leadership of Athens and Sparta.

Peter the Great (1672–1725) Energetic tsar who transformed Russia into a leading European country by centralizing government, modernizing the army, creating a navy, and reforming education and the economy.

Francesco Petrarca (Petrarch) (1304–1374) Italian scholar who revived interest in classical writing styles and was famed for his vernacular love sonnets.

pharaoh A term meaning "household" which became the title borne by the rulers of ancient Egypt. The pharaoh was regarded as the divine representative of the gods and the embodiment of Egypt itself. The powerful and centralized bureaucratic state ruled by the pharaohs was more stable and longlived than any another civilization in world history, lasting (with few interruptions) for approximately 3,000 years.

Pharisees A group of Jewish teachers and preachers who emerged in the third century B.C.E. They insisted that all of Yahweh's (God's) commandments were binding on all Jews.

Philip II (382–336 B.C.E.) King of Macedonia and father of Alexander, he consolidated the southern Balkans and the Greek city-states under Macedonian domination.

Philip II of Spain King of Spain from 1556–98 and briefly King of England and Ireland during his marriage to Queen Mary I of England. As a staunch Catholic, Philip responded with military might to the desecration of Catholic churches in the Spanish Netherlands in the 1560s. When commercial conflict with England escalated, Philip sent the Spanish Armada to conquer England in 1588, but it was largely destroyed by stormy weather.

Philip II Augustus (1165–1223) The first French ruler to use the title "king of France" rather than "king of the French." After he captured Normandy and its adjacent territories from the English, he built an effective system of local administration, which recognized regional diversity while promoting centralized royal control. This administrative pattern would characterize French government until the French Revolution.

Philip IV of France King of France from 1285 until his death, Philip's conflict with Pope Boniface VIII led to the transfer of the papal court to Avignon from 1309 to 1378.

Philistines Descendants of the Sea Peoples who fled to the region that now bears their name, Palestine, after their defeat at the hands of the pharaoh Ramses III. They dominated their neighbors, the Hebrews, who used writing as an effective means of discrediting them (the Philistines themselves did not leave a written record to contest the Hebrews' views).

philosophe During the Enlightenment, this word referred to a person whose reflections were unhampered by the constraints of religion or dogma.

Phoenicians A Semitic people known for their trade in exotic purple dyes and other luxury goods, they originally settled in present-day Lebanon around 1200 B.C.E. and from there established commercial colonies throughout the Mediterranean, notably Carthage.

Plato (429–349 B.C.E.) A student of Socrates, Plato dedicated his life to transmitting his teacher's legacy through the writing of dialogues on philosophical subjects, in which Socrates himself plays the major role. The longest and most famous of these, known as the *Republic*, describes an idealized polis governed by a superior group of individuals chosen for their natural attributes of intelligence and character, who rule as "philosopher-kings."

Plotinus (204–270 C.E.) A Neoplatonist philosopher who taught that everything in existence has its ultimate source in the divine, and that the highest goal of life should be the mystic reunion of the soul with this divine source, something that can be achieved through contemplation and asceticism. This outlook blended with that of early Christianity and was instrumental in the spread of that religion within the Roman Empire.

poleis One of the major political innovations of the ancient Greeks was the *polis*, or city-state (plural *poleis*). These independent social and political entities began to emerge in the ninth century B.C.E., organized around an urban center and fostering markets, meeting places, and religious worship; frequently, poleis also controlled some surrounding territory.

Marco Polo (1254–1324) Venetian merchant who traveled through Asia for twenty years and published his observations in a widely read memoir.

population growth In the nineteenth century, Europe experienced a dramatic population growth. During this period, the spread of rural manufacturing allowed men and women to begin marrying younger and raising families earlier, which increased the size of the average family. As the population grew, the portion of young and fertile people also increased, which reinforced the population growth. By 1900, population growth was strongest in Britain and Germany, and slower in France.

portolan charts Also known as *portolani*, these special charts were invented by medieval mariners during the fourteenth century and were used to map locations of ports and sea routes, while also taking note of prevailing winds and other conditions at sea.

Potsdam (1945) At this conference, Truman, Churchill and Stalin met to discuss their options at the conclusion of the Second World War, including making territorial changes to Germany and its allies and the question of war reparations.

Prague spring A period of political liberalization in Czechoslovakia between January and August 1968 that was initiated by Alexander Dubček, the Czech leader. This period of expanding freedom and openness in this Eastern bloc nation ended on August 20, when the USSR and Warsaw Pact countries invaded with 200,000 troops and 5,000 tanks.

pre-Socratics A group of philosophers in the Greek city of Miletus, who raised questions about humans' relationship with the natural world and the gods and who formulated rational theories to explain the physical universe they observed. Their name reflects the fact that they flourished prior to the lifetime of Socrates.

price revolution An unprecedented inflation in prices in the latter half of the sixteenth century, resulting in part from the enormous influx of silver bullion from Spanish America.

principate Modern term for the centuries of autocratic rule by the successors of Augustus, who seized power in 27 B.C.E. and styled himself *princeps* or Rome's "first man." See **Roman Republic**.

printing press Introduced in Europe by Johannes Gutenberg of Mainz in 1453–55, this new technology quickly revolutionized communication and played a significant role in political, religious, and intellectual revolutions.

Protestantism The name given to the many dissenting varieties of Christianity that emerged during the Reformation in sixteenth-century western Europe. While Protestant beliefs and practices differed widely, all were united in their rejection of papal authority and the dogmas of the Roman Catholic Church.

provisional government After the collapse of the Russian monarchy, leaders in the Duma organized this government and hoped to establish a democratic system under constitutional rule. They also refused to concede military defeat, and it was impossible to institute domestic reforms and fight a war at the same time. As conditions worsened, the Bolsheviks gained support. In October 1917, they attacked the provisional government and seized control.

Claudius Ptolomeus, called Ptolemy (c. 85–165 C.E.) A Greek-speaking geographer and astronomer active in Roman Alexandria, he rejected the findings of previous Hellenistic scientists in favor of the erroneous theories of Aristotle, publishing highly influential treatises that promulgated these errors and suppressed (for example) the accurate findings of Aristarchus (who had discovered the Heliocentric universe) and Erathosthenes (who had calculated the circumference of the earth).

Ptolemaic system Ptolemy of Alexandria promoted Aristotle's understanding of cosmology. In this system, the heavens orbit the earth in an organized hierarchy of spheres, and the earth and the heavens are made of different matter and subject to different laws of motion. A prime mover produces the motion of the celestial bodies.

Ptolemy (c. 367–c. 284 B.C.E.) One of Alexander the Great's trusted generals (and possibly his half brother), he became pharaoh of Egypt and founded a new dynasty that lasted until that kingdom's absorption into the Roman Empire in 30 B.C.E.

public sphere Between the official realm of state activities and the private realm of the household and individual, lies the "public sphere." The public sphere has a political dimension—it is the space of debate, discussion, and expressions of popular opinion. It also has an economic dimension—it is where business is conducted, where commercial transactions take place, where people enter into contracts, search for work, or hire employees.

Punic Wars (264–146 B.C.E.) Three periods of warfare between Rome and Carthage, two maritime empires who struggled for dominance of the Mediterranean. Rome emerged as the victor, destroyed the city of Carthage and took control of Sicily, North Africa and Hispania (Spain).

pyramid Constructed during the third millennium B.C.E., these structures were monuments to the power and divinity of the pharaohs entombed inside them.

Qur'an (often Koran) Islam's holy scriptures, comprised of the prophecies revealed to Muhammad and redacted during and after his death.

Raphael (Raffaelo Sanzio) (1483–1520) Italian painter active in Rome, his works include *The School of Athens*.

realism Artistic and literary style which sought to portray common situations as they would appear in reality.

Realpolitik Political strategy based on advancing power for its own sake.

reason The human capacity to solve problems and discover truth in ways that can be verified intellectually. Philosophers distinguish the knowledge gained from reason from the teachings of instinct, imagination, and faith, which are verified according to different criteria.

Reformation Religious and political movement in sixteenth-century Europe that led to a break between dissenting forms of Christianity and the Roman Catholic Church; notable figures include Martin Luther and John Calvin.

Reich A term for the German state. The First Reich corresponded to the Holy Roman Empire (9th c.–1806), the Second Reich was from 1871 to 1919, and the Third Reich lasted from 1933 through May 1945.

Renaissance From the French word meaning "rebirth," this term came to be used in the nineteenth century to describe the artistic, intellectual, and cultural movement that emerged in Italy after 1300 and that sought to recover and emulate the heritage of the classical past.

Restoration period (1815–1848) European movement after the defeat of Napoleon to restore Europe to its pre–French Revolution status and to prevent the spread of revolutionary or liberal political movements.

Cardinal Richelieu (1585–1642) First minister to King Louis XIII, he is considered by many to have ruled France in all but name, centralizing political power and suppressing dissent.

Roman army Under the Republic, the Roman army was made up of citizen-soldiers who were required to serve in wartime. As Rome's empire grew, the need for more fighting men led to the extension of citizenship rights and, eventually, to the development of a vast, professional, standing army that numbered as many as 300,000 by the middle of the third century B.C.E. By that time, however, citizens were not themselves required to serve, and many legions were made up of paid conscripts and foreign mercenaries.

Roman citizenship The rights and responsibilities of Rome's citizens were gradually extended to the free (male) inhabitants of other Italian provinces and later to most provinces in the Roman world. In contrast to slaves and non-Romans, Romans had the right to be tried in an imperial court and could not be legally subjected to torture.

Roman Republic The Romans traced the founding of their republic to the overthrow of their last king and the establishment of a unique form of constitutional government, in which the power of the aristocracy (embodied by the Senate) was checked by the executive rule of two elected consuls and the collective will of the people. For hundreds of years, this balance of power provided the Republic with a measure of political stability and prevented any single individual or clique from gaining too much power.

Romanticism Beginning in Germany and England in the late eighteenth century and continuing up to the end of the nineteenth century, Romanticism was a movement in art, music, and literature that countered the rationalism of the Enlightenment by placing greater value on human emotions and the power of nature to stimulate creativity.

Jean-Jacques Rousseau (1712–1778) Philosopher and radical political theorist whose *Social Contract* attacked privilege and inequality. One of the primary principles of Rousseau's political philosophy is that politics and morality should not be separated.

Royal Society This British society's goal was to pursue collective research. Members would conduct experiments, record the results, and share them with their peers, who would study the methods, reproduce the experiment, and assess the results. The arrangement gave English scientists a sense of common purpose as well as a system to reach a consensus on facts.

Russian Revolution of 1905 After Russia's defeat in the Russo-Japanese War, Russians began clamoring for political reforms. Protests grew over the course of 1905, and the autocracy lost control of entire towns and regions as workers went on strike, soldiers mutinied, and peasants revolted. Forced to yield, Tsar Nicholas II issued the October Manifesto, which pledged individual liberties and provided for the election of a parliament (called the Duma). The most radical of the revolutionary groups were put down with force, and the pace of political change remained very slow in the aftermath of the revolution.

Russo-Japanese War (1904–1905) Japanese and Russian expansion collided in Mongolia and Manchuria. Russia was humiliated after the Japanese navy sunk its fleet, which helped provoke a revolt in Russia and led to an American-brokered peace treaty.

sacrament A sacred rite. In the Catholic tradition, the administration of the sacraments is considered necessary for salvation.

Saint Bartholomew's Day Massacre The mass murder of French Protestants (Huguenots) instigated by Queen Catherine de' Medici of France and carried out by Catholics. It began in Paris on 24 August 1572 and spread to other parts of France, continuing into October of that year. More than 70,000 people were killed.

salons Informal gatherings of intellectuals and aristocrats that allowed discourse about Enlightenment ideas.

Sappho (c. 620–c. 550 B.C.E.) One of the most celebrated Greek poets, she was revered as "the Tenth Muse" and emulated by many male poets. Ironically, though, only two of her poems survive intact, and the rest must be pieced together from fragments quoted by later poets.

Sargon the Great (r. 2334–2279 B.C.E.) The Akkadian ruler who consolidated power in Mesopotamia.

SARS epidemic (2003) The successful containment of severe acute respiratory syndrome (SARS) is an example of how international health organizations can effectively work together to recognize and respond to a disease outbreak. The disease itself, however, is a reminder of the dangers that exist in a globalized economy with a high degree of mobility in both populations and goods.

Schlieffen Plan Devised by German general Alfred von Schlieffen in 1905 to avoid the dilemma of a two-front war against France and Russia. The Schlieffen Plan required that Germany attack France first through Belgium and secure a quick victory before wheeling to the east to meet the slower armies of the Russians on the Eastern Front. The Schlieffen Plan was put into operation on August 2, 1914, at the outset of the First World War.

scientific revolution of antiquity The Hellenistic period was the most brilliant age in the history of science before the seventeenth century C.E. Aristarchus of Samos posited the existence of a heliocentric universe. Eratosthenes of Alexandria accurately calculated the circumference of the earth. Archimedes turned physics into its own branch of experimental science. Hellenistic anatomists became the first to practice human dissection, which improved their understanding of human physiology. Ironically, most of these discoveries were suppressed by pseudo-scientists who flourished under the Roman Empire during the second century C.E., notably Claudus Ptolomeus Ptolemy) and Aelius Galenus (Galen).

second industrial revolution The technological developments in the last third of the nineteenth century, which included new techniques for refining and producing steel; increased availability of electricity for industrial, commercial, and domestic use; advances in chemical manufacturing; and the creation of the internal combustion engine.

Second World War Worldwide war that began in September 1939 in Europe, and even earlier in Asia (the Japanese invasion of Manchuria began in 1931), pitting Britain, the United States, and the Soviet Union (the Allies) against Nazi Germany, Italy, and Japan (the Axis). The war ended in 1945 with Germany and Japan's defeat.

Seleucus (d. 280 B.C.E.) The Macedonian general who ruled the Persian heartland of Alexander the Great's empire.

Semitic The Semitic language family has the longest recorded history of any linguistic group and is the root for most languages of the Middle and Near East. Ancient Semitic languages include those of the ancient Babylonians and Assyrians, Phoenician, the classical form of Hebrew, early dialects of Aramaic, and the classical Arabic of the Qu'ran.

Sepoy Mutiny of 1857 See **Indian Rebellion of 1857**.

serfdom Peasant labor. Unlike slaves, serfs are "attached" to the land they work, and are not supposed to be sold apart from that land.

William Shakespeare (1564–1616) An English playwright who flourished during the reigns of Elizabeth I and James I, Shakespeare received a basic education in his hometown of Stratford-upon-Avon and worked in London as an actor before achieving success as a dramatist and poet.

Shi'ites An often-persecuted minority within Islam, Shi'ites believe that only descendants of Muhammad's successor Ali and his wife Fatimah (Muhammad's daughter) can have any authority over the Muslim community. Today, Shi'ites constitute the ruling party in Iran and are numerous in Iraq but otherwise comprise only 10 percent of Muslims worldwide.

Abbé Sieyès (1748–1836) In 1789, he wrote the pamphlet "What is the Third Estate?" in which he posed fundamental questions about the rights of the Third Estate and helped provoke its secession from the Estates-General. He was a leader at the Tennis Court Oath, but he later helped Napoleon seize power.

Sinn Féin The Irish revolutionary organization that formed in 1900 to fight for Irish independence.

Sino-Japanese War (1894–1895) Conflict over the control of Korea in which China was forced to cede the province of Taiwan to Japan.

slave revolt in Saint-Domingue (1791–1804) In September of 1791, the largest slave rebellion in history broke out in Saint-

Domingue, an important French colony in the Caribbean. In 1794, the revolutionary government in France abolished slavery in the colonies, though this act was essentially only recognizing the liberty that the slaves had seized by their own actions. Napoleon reestablished slavery in the French Caribbean in 1802, but failed in his attempt to reconquer Saint-Domingue. Armies commanded by former slaves succeeded in winning independence for a new nation, Haiti, in 1804, making the revolt in Saint-Domingue the first successful slave revolt in history.

slavery The practice of subjugating people to a life of bondage, and of selling or trading these unfree people. For most of human history, slavery had no racial or ethnic basis, and was widely practiced by all cultures and civilizations. Anyone could become a slave, for example, by being captured in war or by being sold for the payment of a debt. It was only in the fifteenth century, with the growth of the African slave trade, that slavery came to be associated with particular races and peoples.

Adam Smith (1723–1790) Scottish economist and liberal philosopher who proposed that competition between self-interested individuals led naturally to a healthy economy. He became famous for his influential book, *The Wealth of Nations* (1776).

Social Darwinism Belief that Charles Darwin's theory of natural selection (evolution) was applicable to human societies and justified the right of the ruling classes or countries to dominate the weak.

social democracy The belief that democracy and social welfare go hand in hand and that diminishing the sharp inequalities of class society is crucial to fortifying democratic culture.

socialism Political ideology that calls for a classless society with collective ownership of all property.

Society of Jesus See **Jesuits.**

Socrates (469–399 B.C.E.) The Athenian philosopher and teacher who promoted the careful examination of all inherited opinions and assumptions on the grounds that "the unexamined life is not worth living." A veteran of the Peloponnesian War, he was tried and condemned by his fellow citizens for engaging in allegedly seditious activities and was executed in 399 B.C.E. His most influential pupils were the philosopher Plato and the historian and social commentator Xenophon.

Solon (d. 559 B.C.E.) Elected archon in 594 B.C.E., this Athenian aristocrat enacted a series of political and economic reforms that formed the basis of Athenian democracy.

Somme (1916) During this battle of the First World War, Allied forces attempted to take entrenched German positions from July to mid-November of 1916. Neither side was able to make any real gains despite massive casualties: 500,000 Germans, 400,000 British, and 200,000 French.

Soviet bloc International alliance that included the East European countries of the Warsaw Pact as well as the Soviet Union; it also came to include Cuba.

soviets Local councils elected by workers and soldiers in Russia. Socialists started organizing these councils in 1905, and the Petrograd soviet in the capital emerged as one of the centers of power after the Russian monarchy collapsed in 1917 in the midst of World War I. The soviets became increasingly powerful and pressed for social reform, the redistribution of land, and called for Russian withdrawal from the war effort.

Spanish-American War (1898) War between the United States and Spain in Cuba, Puerto Rico, and the Philippines. It ended with a treaty in which the United States took over the Philippines, Guam, and Puerto Rico; Cuba won partial independence.

Spanish Armada Supposedly invincible fleet of warships sent against England by Philip II of Spain in 1588 but vanquished by the English fleet and bad weather in the English Channel.

Sparta Around 650 B.C.E., after the suppression of a slave revolt, Spartan rulers militarized their society in order to prevent future rebellions and to protect Sparta's superior position in Greece, orienting their society toward the maintenance of their army. Sparta briefly joined forces with Athens and other poleis in the second war with Persia in 480–479 B.C.E., but these two rivals ultimately fell out again in 431 B.C.E. when Sparta and her Peloponnesian allies went to war against Athens and her allies. This bloody conflict lasted until Athens was defeated in 404 B.C.E., after Sparta received military aid from the Persians.

Spartiate A full citizen of Sparta, hence a professional soldier of the hoplite phalanx.

spinning jenny Invention of James Hargreaves (c. 1720–1774) that revolutionized the British textile industry by allowing a worker to spin much more thread than was possible on a hand spinner.

SS (Schutzstaffel) Formed in 1925 to serve as Hitler's personal security force and to guard Nazi party (NSDAP) meetings, the SS grew into a large militarized organization that became notorious for their participation in carrying out Nazi policies.

Joseph Stalin (1879–1953) The Bolshevik leader who succeeded Lenin as the leader of the Soviet Union and ruled until his death in 1953.

Stalingrad (1942–1943) The turning point on the Eastern Front during the Second World War came when the German army tried to take the city of Stalingrad in an effort to break the back of Soviet industry. The German and Soviet armies fought a bitter battle, in which more than a half million German, Italian, and Romanian soldiers were killed and the Soviets suffered over a million casualties. The German army surrendered after over five months of fighting. After Stalingrad, the Soviet army launched a series of attacks that pushed the Germans back.

Stoicism An ancient philosophy derived from the teachings of Zeno of Athens (fl. c. 300) and widely influential within the Roman Empire; it also impacted the development of Christianity. Stoics believe in the essential orderliness of the cosmos, and that everything that occurs happens for the best. Since everything is determined in accordance with rational purpose, no individual is master of his or her fate, and the only agency that human beings have consists in their responses to good fortune or adversity.

Sumerians The ancient inhabitants of southern Mesopotamia (modern Iraq and Kuwait) whose sophisticated civilization emerged around 4000 B.C.E.

Sunnis Proponents of Islam's customary religious practices (*sunna*) as they developed under the first two caliphs to succeed Muhammad, his father-in-law Abu-Bakr and his disciple Umar. Sunni orthodoxy is dominant within Islam but is opposed by the Shi'ites (from the Arabic word *shi'a*, "faction").

syndicalists A nineteenth-century political movement that embraced a strategy of strikes and sabotage by workers. Their hope was that a general strike of all workers would bring down the capitalist state and replace it with workers' syndicates or trade associations. Their refusal to participate in politics limited their ability to command a wide influence.

tabula rasa Term used by John Locke (1632–1704) to describe man's mind before he acquired ideas as a result of experience; Latin for "clean slate."

Tennis Court Oath (1789) Oath taken by representatives of the Third Estate in June 1789, in which they pledged to form a National Assembly and write a constitution limiting the powers of the king.

Reign of Terror (1793–1794) Campaign at the height of the French Revolution in which violence, including systematic executions of opponents of the revolution, was used to purge France of its "enemies" and to extend the revolution beyond its borders; radicals executed as many as 40,000 persons who were judged enemies of the state.

Tetrarchy The result of Diocletian's political reforms of the late third century C.E., which divided the Roman Empire into four quadrants.

Theban Hegemony The term describing the period when the polis of Thebes dominated the Greek mainland, which reached its height after 371 B.C.E., under leadership of the Theban general Epaminondas. It was in Thebes that the future King Philip II of Macedon spent his youth, and it was the defeat of Thebes and Athens at the hands of Philip and Alexander—at the Battle of Chaeronea in 338—that Macedonian hegemony was forcefully asserted.

theory of evolution Darwin's theory that linked biology to history. Darwin believed that competition between different organisms and struggle with the environment were fundamental and unavoidable facts of life. In this struggle, those individuals who were better adapted to their environment survived, whereas the weak perished. This produced a "natural selection," or favoring of certain adaptive traits over time, leading to a gradual evolution of different species.

Third Estate The population of France under the Old Regime was divided into three estates, corporate bodies that determined an individual's rights or obligations under royal law. The nobility constituted the First Estate, the clergy the Second, and the commoners (the vast bulk of the population) made up the Third Estate.

Third Reich The German state from 1933 to 1945 under Adolf Hitler and the Nazi party.

Third World nations—mostly in Asia, Latin America, and Africa—that are not highly industrialized.

Thirty Years' War (1618–1648) Beginning as a conflict between Protestants and Catholics in Germany, this series of skirmishes escalated into a general European war fought on German soil by armies from Sweden, France, and the Holy Roman Empire.

Timur the Lame (1336–1405) Also known as Tamerlane, he was the last ruler of the Mongol Khans' Asian empire.

Marshal Tito (1892–1980) The Yugoslavian communist and resistance leader who became the leader of Yugoslavia and fought to keep his government independent of the Soviet Union. In response, the Soviet Union expelled Yugoslavia from the communist countries' economic and military pacts.

towns Centers for markets and administration. Towns existed in a symbiotic relationship with the countryside. They provided markets for surplus food from outlying farms as well as producing manufactured goods. In the Middle Ages, towns tended to grow up around a castle or monastery which afforded protection.

transatlantic triangle The trading of African slaves by European colonists to address labor shortages in the Americas and the Caribbean. Slaves were treated like cargo, loaded onto ships and sold in exchange for molasses, tobacco, rum, and other precious commodities.

Treaty of Brest-Litovsk (1918) Separate peace between imperial Germany and the new Bolshevik regime in Russia. The treaty acknowledged the German victory on the Eastern Front and withdrew Russia from the war.

Treaty of Utrecht (1713) Resolution to the War of Spanish Succession that reestablished a balance of power in Europe, to the benefit of Britain and in ways that disadvantaged Spain, Holland, and France.

Treaty of Versailles Signed on June 28, 1919, this peace settlement ended the First World War and required Germany to surrender a large part of its most valuable territories and to pay huge reparations to the Allies.

trench warfare Weapons such as barbed wire and the machine gun gave tremendous advantage to defensive positions in World War I, leading to prolonged battles between entrenched armies in fixed positions. The trenches eventually consisted of 25,000 miles of holes and ditches that stretched across the Western Front in northern France, from the Atlantic coast to the Swiss border during the First World War. On the eastern front, the large expanse of territories made trench warfare less significant.

triangular trade The eighteenth-century commercial Atlantic shipping pattern that took rum from New England to Africa, traded it for slaves taken to the West Indies, and brought sugar back to New England to be processed into rum.

Triple Entente Alliance developed before the First World War that eventually included Britain, France, and Russia.

Truman Doctrine (1947) Declaration promising U.S. economic and military intervention to counter any attempt by the Soviet Union to expand its influence. Often cited as a key moment in the origins of the Cold War.

tsar Russian word for "emperor," derived from the Latin *caesar* and similar to the German *kaiser,* it was the title claimed by the rulers of medieval Muscovy and of the later Russian Empire.

Ubaid culture An early civilization that flourished in Mesopotamia between 5500 and 4000 B.C.E., it was characterized by large village settlements and temple complexes: a precursor to the more urban civilization of the Sumerians.

Umayyad Caliphate (661–930) The Umayyad family resisted the authority of the first two caliphs who succeeded Muhammad but eventually placed a member of their own family in that position of power. The Umayyad Caliphate ruled the Islamic world from 661 to 750, modeling their administration on that of the Roman Empire. But after a rebellion led by the rival Abbasid family, the power of the Umayyad Caliphate was confined to their territories in al-Andalus (Spain).

Universal Declaration of Human Rights (1948) United Nations declaration that laid out the rights to which all human beings were entitled.

University of Paris The reputation of Peter Abelard and his students attracted many intellectuals to Paris in the twelfth century, some of whom began offering instruction to aspiring scholars. By 1200, this loose association of teachers had formed themselves into a *universitas,* or corporation. They began collaborating in the higher academic study of the liberal arts with a special emphasis on theology.

Pope Urban II (1042?–1099) Instigator of the First Crusade (1096–1099), who promised that anyone who fought or died in the service of the Church would receive absolution from sin.

urban populations During the nineteenth century, urban populations in Europe increased sixfold. For the most part, urban areas had medieval infrastructures, which new populations and industries overwhelmed. As a result, many European cities became overcrowded and unhealthy.

Utopia Title of a semi-satirical social critique by the English statesman Sir Thomas More (1478–1535); the word derives from the Greek "best place" or "no place."

Lorenzo Valla (1407–1457) One of the first practitioners of scientific philology (the historical study of language), Valla's analysis of the so-called Donation of Constantine showed that the document could not possibly have been written in the fourth century C.E., but must have been forged centuries later.

vassal A person who pledges to be loyal and subservient to a lord in exchange for land, income, or protection.

velvet revolutions The peaceful political revolutions throughout Eastern Europe in 1989.

Verdun (1916) This battle between German and French forces lasted for ten months during the First World War. The Germans saw the battle as a chance to break French morale through a war of attrition, and the French believed the battle to be a symbol of France's strength. In the end, over 400,000 lives were lost and the German offensive failed.

Versailles Conference (1919) Peace conference between the victors of the First World War; resulted in the Treaty of Versailles, which forced Germany to pay reparations and to give up its colonies to the victors.

Queen Victoria (1819–1901) Influential monarch who reigned from 1837 until her death; she presided over the expansion of the British Empire as well as the evolution of English politics and social and economic reforms.

Viet Cong Vietnamese communist group formed in 1954; committed to overthrowing the government of South Vietnam and reunifying North and South Vietnam.

Vikings (800–1000) The collapse of the Abbasid Caliphate disrupted Scandinavian commercial networks and turned traders into raiders (the word *viking* describes the activity of raiding). These raids often escalated into invasions that contributed to the collapse of the Carolingian Empire, resulted in the devastation of settled territories, and ended with the establishment of Viking colonies. By the tenth century, Vikings controlled areas of eastern England, Scotland, the islands of Ireland, Iceland, Greenland, and parts of northern France. They had also established the beginnings of the kingdom that became Russia and made exploratory voyages to North America, founding a settlement at Newfoundland (Canada).

A Vindication of the Rights of Woman Noted work of Mary Wollstonecraft (1759–1797), English republican who applied Enlightenment political ideas to issues of gender.

Virgil (70–19 B.C.E.) An influential Roman poet who wrote under the patronage of the emperor Augustus. His *Aeneid* mimicked the ancient Greek epics of Homer and told the mythical tale of Rome's founding by the Trojan refugee Aeneas.

Visigoths The tribes of "west" Goths who sacked Rome in 410 C.E. and later established a kingdom in the Roman province of Hispania (Spain).

Voltaire Pseudonym of French philosopher and satirist François Marie Arouet (1694–1778), who championed the cause of human dignity against state and Church oppression. Noted deist and author of *Candide.*

Lech Wałęsa (1943–) Leader of the Polish labor movement Solidarity, which organized a series of strikes across Poland in 1980. They protested working conditions, shortages, and high prices. Above all, they demanded an independent labor union. Solidarity's leaders were imprisoned and the union banned, but they launched a new series of strikes in 1988, which led to the legalization of Solidarity and open elections.

war communism The Russian civil war forced the Bolsheviks to take a more radical economic stance. They requisitioned grain from the peasantry and outlawed private trade in consumer goods as "speculation." They also militarized production facilities and abolished money.

Wars of the Roses Fifteenth-century civil conflict between the English dynastic houses of Lancaster and York, each of which was symbolized by the heraldic device of a rose (red and white, respectively). It was ultimately resolved by the accession of the Lancastrian king Henry VII, who married Elizabeth of York.

Warsaw Pact (1955–1991) Military alliance between the USSR and other communist states that was established as a response to the creation of the NATO alliance.

The Wealth of Nations 1776 treatise by Adam Smith, whose laissez-faire ideas predicted the economic boom of the Industrial Revolution.

Weimar Republic The government of Germany between 1919 and the rise of Hitler and the Nazi party.

Western Front Military front that stretched from the English Channel through Belgium and France to the Alps during the First World War.

Whites Refers to the "counterrevolutionaries" of the Bolshevik Revolution (1918–1921) who fought the Bolsheviks (the "Reds"); included former supporters of the tsar, Social Democrats, and large independent peasant armies.

William the Conqueror (1027–1087) Duke of Normandy who laid claim to the throne of England in 1066, defeating the Anglo-Saxon King Harold at the Battle of Hastings. He and his

Norman followers imposed imperial rule in England through a brutal campaign of military conquest, surveillance, and the suppression of the indigenous Anglo-Saxon language.

William of Ockham (d. 1349) An English philosopher and Franciscan friar, he denied that human reason could prove fundamental theological truths, such as the existence of God: he argued that there is no necessary connection between the observable laws of nature and the unknowable essence of divinity. His theories, derived from the work of earlier scholastics, form the basis of the scientific method.

Woodrow Wilson (1856–1924) U.S. president who requested and received a declaration of war from Congress so that America could enter the First World War. After the war, his prominent role in the Paris Peace Conference signaled the rise of the United States as a world power. He also proposed the Fourteen Points, which influenced the peace negotiations.

Maria Winkelmann (1670–1720) German astronomer who worked with her husband in his observatory. Despite discovering a comet and preparing calendars for the Berlin Academy of Sciences, the academy would not let her take her husband's place within the body after he died.

witch craze The rash of persecutions that took place in both Catholic and Protestant countries of early modern Europe and their colonies, facilitated by secular governments and religious authorities.

women's associations Because European women were excluded from the workings of parliamentary and mass politics, some women formed organizations to press for political and civil rights. Some groups focused on establishing educational opportunities for women while others campaigned energetically for the vote.

William Wordsworth (1770–1850) Romantic writer whose central themes were nature, simplicity, and feeling. He considered nature to be man's most trustworthy teacher and source of sublime power that nourished the human soul.

World Bank International agency established in 1944 to provide economic assistance to war-torn nations and countries in need of economic development.

John Wycliffe (c. 1330–1384) A professor of theology at the University of Oxford, Wycliffe urged the English king to confiscate ecclesiastical wealth and to replace corrupt priests and bishops with men who would live according to the apostolic standards of poverty and piety. He advocated direct access to the scriptures and promoted an English translation of the Bible. His teachings played an important role in the Peasants' Revolt of 1381 and inspired the still more radical initiatives of a group known as Lollards.

Xerxes (519?–465 B.C.E.) Xerxes succeeded his father, Darius, as Great King of Persia. Seeking to avenge his father's shame and eradicate any future threats to Persian hegemony, he launched his own invasion of Greece in 480 B.C.E. An allied Greek army defeated his forces in 479 B.C.E.

Yalta Accords Meeting among President Franklin D. Roosevelt, Prime Minister Winston Churchill, and Premier Joseph Stalin that occurred in the Crimea in 1945 shortly before the end of the Second World War to plan for the postwar order.

Young Turks The 1908 Turkish reformist movement that aimed to modernize the Ottoman Empire, restore parliamentary rule, and depose Sultan Abdul Hamid II.

ziggurats Temples constructed under the Dynasty of Ur in what is now Iraq, beginning around 2100 B.C.E.

Zionism A political movement dating to the end of the nineteenth century holding that the Jewish people constitute a nation and are entitled to a national homeland. Zionists rejected a policy of Jewish assimilation and advocated the reestablishment of a Jewish homeland in Palestine.

Zollverein In 1834, Prussia started a customs union, which established free trade among the German states and a uniform tariff against the rest of the world. By the 1840s, the union included almost all of the German states except German Austria. It is considered an important precedent for the political unification of Germany, which was completed in 1870 under Prussian leadership.

Zoroastrianism One of the three major universal faiths of the ancient world, alongside Judaism and Christianity, it was derived from the teachings of the Persian Zoroaster around 600 B.C.E. Zoroaster redefined religion as an ethical practice common to all, rather than as a set of rituals and superstitions that cause divisions among people. Zoroastrianism teaches that there is one supreme god in the universe, Ahura-Mazda (Wise Lord) but that his goodness will be constantly assailed by the forces of evil until the arrival of a final "judgment day." Proponents of this faith should therefore help good to triumph over evil by leading a good life, and by performing acts of compassion and charity. Zoroastrianism exercised a profound influence over many early Christians, including Augustine.

Ulrich Zwingli (1484–1531) A former priest from the Swiss city of Zurich, Zwingli joined Luther and Calvin in attacking the authority of the Roman Catholic Church.

Text Credits

Leon B. Alberti: "On the Family" from *The Family in Renaissance Florence*, trans./ed. by Renée Neu Watkins (University of South Carolina Press, 1969), pp. 208–213. Reprinted by permission of the translator.

Aristophanes: 300 words from *Lysistrata and Other Plays* by Aristophanes, translated with an introduction by Alan H. Sommerstein (Penguin Classics, 1973). Copyright © Alan H. Sommerstein, 1973. Reproduced by permission of Penguin Books Ltd.

Arrian: 300 words from *The Campaigns of Alexander* by Arrian, translated by Aubrey de Sélincourt, revised with an introduction and notes by J.R. Hamilton (Penguin Classics 1958, Revised edition 1971). Copyright © the Estate of Aubrey de Sélincourt, 1958. Introduction and Notes copyright © J.R. Hamilton, 1971. Reproduced by permission of Penguin Books Ltd.

Nels Bailkey (ed.): From Bailkey, *Readings in Ancient History*, 5th Edition. © 1996 Wadsworth, a part of Cengage Learning, Inc. Reproduced by permission. www.cengage.com/permissions.

Armand Bellee (ed.): *Cahiers de plaintes & doleances des paroisses de la province du Maine pour les Etats-generaux de 1789*, 4 vols. (Le Mans: Monnoyer, 1881-92), 2: 578–82. Translated by the American Social History Project, "Liberty, Equality, Fraternity: Exploring the French Revolution" by Jack R. Censer and Lynn Hunt. Reprinted by permission.

Bernard of Angers: "Miracles of Saint Foy" from *Readings in Medieval History*, 2nd Edition, edited by Patrick J. Geary (Toronto, Ont: University of Toronto Press, 2003). Copyright © 2003. Reprinted by permission of the publisher.

Henry Bettenson (ed.): "Obedience as a Jesuit Hallmark" from *Documents of the Christian Church*, 2nd Edition. Copyright © 1967, Oxford University Press. Reprinted by permission of Oxford University Press.

Gabriel Biel: "Execrabilis." Reprinted by permission of the publisher from *Defensorium Obedientiae Apostolicae Et Alia Documenta* by Gabriel Biel, edited and translated by Heiko A. Oberman, Daniel E. Zerfoss and William J. Courtenay, pp. 224–227, Cambridge, Mass.: The Belknap Press of Harvard University Press, Copyright © 1968 by the President and Fellows of Harvard College.

Jose Bove: *The World Is Not for Sale: Farmers Against Junk Food*, pp. 3–13, © Verso, 2001. Reprinted by permission of the publisher.

Walter Bower: "A Declaration of Scottish Independence," from *Scotichronicon*, Volume 7, by Walter Bower. Edited by B. Scott and D. E. R. Watt. Copyright © 1996 Aberdeen University Press. Reprinted with permission.

Boyer, Baker & Kirshner (eds): "Declaration of the Rights of Man and of the Citizen", "Napoleon's Letter to Prince Eugene" and "Circular Letter to Sovereigns" from *University of Chicago Readings in Western Civilization, Vol. 7*, pp. 238–239; 419–420; 426–427, Copyright © 1987 by The University of Chicago. Reprinted by permission of The University of Chicago Press.

Anna Comnena: 340 words from *The Alexiad of Anna Comnena*, translated by E.R.A. Sewter (Penguin Classics, 1969). Copyright © E.R.A. Sewter, 1969. Reproduced by permission of Penguin Books Ltd.

James Cracraft: "Alexander II's Decree Emancipating the Serfs, 1861," *Major Problems in the History of Imperial Russia*. Copyright © 1994 by D.C. Heath and Company.

David Brion Davis: From *Encyclopédie*, Vol. 16, Neuchâtel, 1765, p. 532 as cited in David Brion Davis, *The Problem of Slavery in Western Culture*. (Ithaca, N.Y.: Cornell University Press, 1966), p. 416. Copyright © 1966 by David Brion Davis. Reprinted by permission.

Simone de Beauvoir: From *The Second Sex* by Simone de Beauvoir, translated by Constance Borde & Sheila Malovany-Chevalier, published by Jonathan Cape, translation copyright © 2009 by Constance Borde and Sheila Malovany-Chevalier, Introduction copyright © 2010 by Judith Thurman. Reprinted by permission of Alfred A. Knopf, a division of Random House, Inc. and The Random House Group Ltd.

Geoffrey de Charny: From *The Book of Chivalry of Geoffrey de Charny: Text, Context, and Translation*, translated by Richard W. Kaeuper and Elspeth Kennedy, pp. 99. Copyright © 1996 University of Pennsylvania Press. Reprinted with permission.

Marie de France: "Equitan" in The Lais of Marie de France, translated by Gllyn S. Burgess and Kieth Burgess. Pp. 56–57. Copyright © 1985. Reproduced by permission of Penguin Books Ltd.

Bartolome de las Casas: 500 words from *A Short Account of the Destruction of the Indies* by Bartolome de las Casas, edited and translated by Nigel Griffin, introduction by Anthony Pagden (Penguin Classics, 1992). Translation and Notes copyright © Nigel Griffin, 1992. Introduction copyright © Anthony Pagden 1992. Reproduced by permission of Penguin Books Ltd.

Michel de Montaigne: From *Montaigne: Selections from the Essays*, translated and edited by Donald M. Frame (Harlan Davidson, Inc., 1973), pp. 34–38. Reprinted by permission of Harlan Davidson, Inc.

Alexis de Tocqueville: From *Recollections: The French Revolution of 1848*; trans. George Lawrence, ed. J.P. Mayer, pp. 436–437. Copyright © 1987 by Transaction Publishers. Reprinted by permission of the publisher.

Rene Descartes: From *A Discourse on the Method of Correctly Conducting One's Reason*, trans. Ian Maclean. Copyright © Ian Maclean 2006. Reprinted by permission of Oxford University Press.

Armand J. du Plessis: "Cardinal Richelieu on the Common People of France," pp. 31–32 from Hill, Henry Bertram, *The Political Testament of Cardinal Richelieu*. © 1961 by the Board of Regents of the University of Wisconsin System. Reprinted by permission of The University of Wisconsin Press.

Ecumenical Councils: "Epitome of the Definition of the Iconoclastic Conciliabulum" from *A Select Library of Nicene and Post-Nicene Fathers of the Christian Church, Vol. XIV*, eds. Schaff & Wace (Grand Rapids, MI: Wm. B. Eerdmans Publishing Company, 1955), pp. 543–544.

Frantz Fanon: Excerpt from *The Wretched of the Earth* by Frantz Fanon, copyright © 1963 by *Présence Africaine*. Used by permission of Grove/Atlantic, Inc.

Robert Filmer: "Observations upon Aristotle's Politiques" (1652), in *Divine Right and Democracy: An Anthology of Political Writing in Stuart England*, edited by David Wootton. Pp 110–18. Copyright © 1986. Reproduced by permission of Penguin Books Ltd.

Gregory L. Freeze (ed.): From *From Supplication to Revolution: A Documentary Social History of Imperial Russia*. Copyright © 1988, Oxford University Press, Inc. Reprinted by permission of Oxford University Press.

Betty Friedan: From *The Feminine Mystique* by Betty Friedan. Copyright © 1983, 1974, 1973, 1963 by Betty Friedan. Used by permission of Victor Gollancz, an imprint of The Orion Publishing Group, London and W.W. Norton & Company, Inc.

Galileo Galilei: From *Discoveries and Opinions of Galileo* by Galileo Galilei, translated by Stillman Drake, copyright © 1957 by Stillman Drake. Used by permission of Doubleday, a division of Random House, Inc.

Mohandas K. Gandhi: From *Hind Swaraj* or *Indian Home Rule* by M.K. Gandhi, p. 56, Ahmedabad: Navajivan Trust, 1946. Reprinted by permission of the publisher.

Pierre Gassendi: From *The Selected Works of Pierre Gassendi*, Edited by Craig B. Brush. (New York: Johnson Reprint Corporation, 1972) pp. 334–336. Reprinted with permission.

Joseph Goebbels: "Why are we enemies of the Jews?" from Snyder, Louis, *Documents of German History*. Copyright © 1958 by Rutgers, the State University. Reprinted by permission of Rutgers University Press.

Homer: *Iliad*, translated by Stanley Lombardo, selections from pp. 115–118. Copyright © 1997 by Hackett Publishing Company, Inc. Reprinted by permission of Hackett Publishing Company, Inc. All rights reserved.

Rosemary Horrox (ed.): From *The Black Death*, by Horrox (Trans., Ed.), 1994, Manchester University Press, Manchester, UK. Reprinted with permission.

Juvenal: 224 words from *The Sixteen Satires* by Juvenal, translated by Peter Green (Penguin Classics 1967, Revised edition 1974). Copyright © Peter Green 1967, 1974. Reproduced by permission of Penguin Books Ltd.

Nikita Khrushchev: "Report to the Communist Party Congress (1961)" from *Current Soviet Policies IV*, eds. Charlotte Saikowski and Leo Gruliow, from the translations of the Current Digest of the Soviet Press. Joint Committee on Slavic Studies, 1962, pp. 42–45. Reprinted by permission of the Current Digest of the Soviet Press.

Maureen Gallery Kovacs (trans.): Excerpts from *The Epic of Gilgamesh*, with an Introduction and Notes by Kovacs, Maureen Gallery, translator. Copyright © 1985, 1989 by the Board of Trustees of the Leland Stanford Junior University. All rights reserved. Used with the permission of Stanford University Press, www.sup.org.

Heda Margolius Kovály: *Under a Cruel Star: A Life in Prague 1941–1968*. Translated from the Czech by Franci Epstein and Helen Epstein with the author. (Cambridge, Mass.: Plunkett Lake Press, 1986), pp. 45–46.

Fritz Lang: "The Future of the Feature Film in Germany" from *The Weimar Republic Sourcebook*, edited by Anton Kaes, Martin Jay, and Edward Dimendberg (Berkeley: University of California Press, 1959), pp. 622–623. © 1994 by the Regents of the University of California. Reprinted by permission of the University of California Press.

Carolyne Larrington: "The Condemnation of Joan of Arc by the University of Paris" from *Women and Writing in Medieval Europe*, Carolyne Larrington, Copyright © 1995 Routledge. Reproduced by permission of Taylor & Francis Books UK.

Chapter 10: p. 322: Bibliotheque Nationale, Paris, France/ The Bridgeman Art Library; p. 326: Wikimedia Commons; Christie's Images/Bridgeman Art Library; p. 327: Wikimedia Commons; p. 330: Bibliotheque Nationale, Paris, France/ The Bridgeman Art Library; p. 334: Danita Delimont/Getty; Bibliothèque Royale Albert I, Brussels, ms. 11209, fol. 3 recto; p. 335: Wikimedia Commons; p. 338 (left): The Granger Collection, NYC; p. 338 (right): Wikimedia Commons; p. 339: Wikimedia Commons; p. 340: Camera-photo Arte, Venice / Art Resource, NY; p. 341: Chris Hellier/Corbis; p. 343: Simone Martini/Wikimedia Commons; p. 345 (left): Didier B./Wikimedia Commons; p. 345 (right): Graham Bell/Getty Images; p. 349 (left): akg-images/British Library; p. 349 (right): Associated Press.

Chapter 11: p. 356: Réunion des Musées Nationaux / Art Resource, NY; p. 358: HIP / Art Resource, NY; p. 360: Réunion des Musées Nationaux / Art Resource, NY; p. 361: Réunion des Musées Nationaux / Art Resource, NY; p. 363: akg-images / British Library; p. 365 (left): Bildarchiv Preussischer Kulturbesitz / Art Resource, NY; p. 365 (right): Scala / Art Resource, NY; p. 366: Wikimedia Commons; p. 371: John Massey Stewart Picture Library; p. 373: Werner Forman Archive/Topkapi Palace Library, Istanbul/Art Resource, NY; p. 375: Bibliothèque Royale Albert I, Brussels; p. 376: Réunion des Musées Nationaux / Art Resource, NY; p. 381 (left): The Bridgeman Art Library; p. 381 (right): Associated Press; p. 385 (left): Wikimedia Commons; p. 385 (right): The Art Archive / British Library.

Chapter 12: p. 388: The Art Archive / Topkapi Museum Istanbul / Gianni Dagli Orti; p. 396: Erich Lessing/Art Resource, NY; p. 397 (top): Erich Lessing/Art Resource, NY; p. 397 (bottom): Réunion des Musées Nationaux / Art Resource, NY; p. 399 (top): Scala/Art Resource, NY; p. 399 (bottom): Ted Spiegel/Corbis; p. 400 (top): Scala/Art Resource, NY; p. 400 (left): Nimatallah/ Art Resource, NY; p. 400 (center): Scala/Art Resource, NY; p. 400 (right): Erich Lessing / Art Resource, NY; p. 401: Bildarchiv Preussischer Kulturbesitz / Art Resource, NY; p. 402: Louvre, Paris, France / Giraudon / The Bridgeman Art Library; p. 403 (left): DEA PICTURE LIBRARY/Getty Images; p. 403 (right): © University of Leicester/Corbis; p. 404: National Portrait Gallery, London, UK / The Bridgeman Art Library; p. 406: Bildarchiv Preussischer Kulturbesitz / Art Resource, NY; p. 408: Vova Pomortzeff / Alamy; p. 409: Museo del Prado, Madrid/ Art Archive; p. 413: Myriam Thyes / Wikimedia Commons; p. 416: Bibliotheque Nationale, Paris, France/ Giraudon/ The Bridgeman Art Library; p. 417: AKG-images; p. 418: The Art Archive / Biblioteca Nacional de Madrid / Dagli Orti.

Chapter 13: p. 422: The Art Archive / Nationalmuseet Copenhagen Denmark / Alfredo Dagli Orti; p. 424: Erich Lessing/Art Resource, NY; p. 425: Bildarchiv Preussischer Kulturbesitz / Art Resource, NY; p. 426: Sandro Vannini/Corbis; p. 427: Erich Lessing/Art Resource, NY; p. 428 (left): Staatsbibliothek, Bern; p. 428 (right): Staatsbibliothek, Bern; p. 429 (left): Staatliche Museen zu Berlin-Preußischer Kulturbesitz, Kupferstichkabinett; p. 429 (right): By permission of the British Library/Art Resource, NY; p. 432: Bayerische Staatsgemäldesammlungen/Alte Pinakothek, Munich; © Dietrich Rose/ Corbis; p. 434 (left): akg-images; p. 434 (right): Erich Lessing/ Art Resource; p. 436 (left): Erich Lessing/Art Resource, NY; p. 436 (right): Wikimedia Commons; p. 441: Alfredo Dagli Orti/The Art Archive at Art Resource, NY; p. 443 (left): Scala/Art Resource, NY; p. 443 (right): Scala/Art Resource, NY; p. 445 (left): Erich Lessing/ Art Resource, NY; p. 445 (right): Michael Cizek/AFP/Getty Images/ Newscom; p. 446 (left): Scala/Art Resource, NY; p. 446 (right): Kunsthistorisches Museum, Vienna; p. 449: Corbis.

Chapter 14: p. 452: Wikimedia Commons; p. 454: James Reeves/ Wikimedia Commons; p. 460: Peter Newark American Pictures/The Bridgeman Art Library; p. 461: Bettmann/Corbis; p. 464: Archivo Iconografico, S.A./Corbis; p. 465: British Museum/Wikimedia Commons, p. 467 (top): John R. Freeman & Co.; p. 467 (bottom): Wikimedia Commons; p. 468: Wikimedia Commons; p. 471: Giraudon/The Bridgeman Art Library; p. 473: The Granger Collection, NYC ; p. 476 (top): The National Trust Photolibrary / Alamy; p. 476 (bottom): Wikimedia Commons; p. 480 (left): Wikimedia Commons; p. 480 (right): Interfoto / Alamy; p. 484 (left): © Franz-Marc Frei/Corbis; p. 484 (right): Icon Entertainment International / The Kobal Collection; p. 485 (top): Image copyright © The Metropolitan Museum of Art / Art Resource, NY; p. 485 (left): Scala/Art Resource, NY; p. 485 (right): Wikimedia Commons; p. 486: Erich Lessing/Art Resource, NY; p. 487 (top): Wikimedia Commons; p. 487 (left): © English Heritage Photo Library; p. 487 (right): Gift of Mr. and Mrs. Robert Woods Bliss, © 1997 Board of Trustees, National Gallery of Art, Washington, D.C.

Chapter 15: p. 490: The Royal Collection © 2010 Her Majesty Queen Elizabeth II; p. 492: Gianni Dagli Orti/Corbis; p. 494 (left): The Granger Collection, New York; p. 494 (right): Wikimedia Commons; p. 495 (top): With kind permission of the University of Edinburgh / The Bridgeman Art Library International p. 495 (bottom): Erich Lessing / Art Resource, NY; p. 498 (left): The Granger Collection, New York; p. 498 (right): Getty Images; p. 501: The Royal Collection © 2010 Her Majesty Queen Elizabeth II; p. 503: Snark /

Art Resource, NY; **p. 504**: Photo © Philip Mould Ltd, London / The Bridgeman Art Library; **p. 507**: The Art Archive/Musee du Chateau de Versailles/Dagli Orti; **p. 509**: Interfoto / Alamy; **p. 510**: Bildarchiv Preussischer Kulturbesitz / Art Resource, NY; **p. 511**: Lebrecht Authors; **p. 513**: Courtesy Dr. Alexander Boguslawski, Professor of Russian Studies, Rollins College.

Chapter 16: p. 518: Cellarius, Andreas/The Bridgeman Art Library; **p. 521**: Jeffrey Coolidge/Getty Images; **p. 522 (left)**: Private Collection/The Bridgeman Art Library; **p. 522 (right)**: © Peter Ginter/ Science Faction/Corbis; **p. 523**: Erich Lessing/Art Resource, NY; **p. 525**: Stapleton Collection/Corbis; **p. 526 (left)**: The Granger Collection, NY; **p. 526 (right)**: Wikimedia Commons; **p. 528**: Erich Lessing/Art Resource, NY; **p. 530**: John P. McCaskey cropped by Smartse/Wikimedia Commons; **p. 531**: Rene Descartes, L'homme de René Descartes, et la formation du foetus . . . Paris: Compagnie des Libraires, 1729/"Courtesy of Historical Collections & Services, Claude Moore Health Sciences Library, University of Virginia;" **p. 535**: Wikimedia Commons; **p. 538**: Plate 20 from Metamorphosis Insectorum (1705) by Maria Sybilla Merian (1647–1717). ©The Natural History Museum, London / The Image Works; **p. 539 (right)**: Bettmann/Corbis; **p. 539 (left)**: Newton, Sir Isaac (1642-1727) / © Courtesy of the Warden and Scholars of New College, Oxford / The Bridgeman Art Library; **p. 540**: Bodleian Library; **p. 543**: Giraudon/Art Resource, NY.

Chapter 17: p. 546: Bridgeman Art Library; **p. 548**: Elizabeth Nesbitt Room Chapbook Collection/Information Sciences Library/ University of Pittsburgh; **p. 551**: © Ali Meyer/CORBIS; **p. 552**: The New York Public Library / Art Resource, NY; **p. 553**: Bibliotheque Nationale, Paris, France/ Lauros / Giraudon/ The Bridgeman Art Library; **p. 554**: Erich Lessing / Art Resource, NY; **p. 555**: Giraudon / Bridgeman; **p. 556**: Historisches Museum der Stadt Wien; **p. 557**: Moritz Daniel Oppenheim, "Lavater and Lessing Visit Moses Mendelssohn." In the permanent collections, Judah L. Magnes Museum.

Photo: Ben Ailes; **p. 561**: Stapletib Collection/Corbis **p. 562 (left)**: Sir Joshua Reynolds/Omai of the Friendly Isles/ nla.pic-an5600097/ National Library of Australia; **p. 562 (right)**: William Hodges/ King of Otaheite//National Library of Australia; **p. 563**: Francesco Bartolozzi/A view of the inside of a house in the island of Ulietea, with the representation of a dance to the music of the country/nla. pic-an9184905/National Library of Australia; **p. 565 (top)**: Bibliotheque Nationale, Paris, France / Bridgeman Art Library, Flammarion; **p. 565 (bottom)**: © Tate Gallery, London/Art Resource, NY; **p. 570**: Bridgeman Art Library; **p. 571**: Bettmann/Corbis; **p. 573 (left)**: The Granger Collection, New York; **p. 573 (right)**: Bluberries/iStock Photo; **p. 575 (left)**: Scala / Art Resource, NY; **p. 575: (right)**: akg-images; **p. 577**: The Granger Collection, New York.

Chapter 18: p. 580: Erich Lessing / Art Resource, NY; **p. 584 (left)**: AKG-Images; **p. 584 (right)**: The Art Archive / Musée Carnavalet Paris / Marc Charmet; **p. 585**: Giraudon / The Bridgeman Art Library; **p. 587**: Chateau de Versailles, France / The Bridgeman Art Library; **p. 589**: Musee de la Ville de Paris, Musee Carnavalet, Paris, France / Giraudon / The Bridgeman Art Library; **p. 590**: Musee de la Revolution Francaise, Vizille, France / The Bridgeman Art Library; **p. 596**: Bibliotheque Nationale, Paris, France / The Bridgeman Art Library; **p. 597**: Erich Lessing / Art Resource, NY; **p. 598**: Bettmann/Corbis; **p. 599**: Scala/White Images / Art Resource, NY; **p. 602 (left)**: Risma Archivo / Alamy; **p. 602 (right)**: The Art Archive; **p. 603 (left)**: Musee de la Ville de Paris, Musee Carnavalet, Paris, France/ Lauros / Giraudon/ The Bridgeman Art Library; **p. 603 (right)**: Courtesy of the Warden and Scholars of New College, Oxford / The Bridgeman Art Library; **p. 607 (left)**: The Gallery Collection/Corbis; **p. 607 (right)**: Wikimedia Commons; **p. 608**: Erich Lessing/Art Resource, NY; **p. 609**: © The Trustees of the British Museum / Art Resource, NY; **p. 612 (left)**: The Granger Collection, New York; **p. 612 (right)**: © Thorsten Strasas/Demotix/Corbis; **p. 613**: © Gianni Dagli Orti/ CORBIS.

Index

Page numbers in *italics* refer to illustrations, maps, and tables.